AF269458

IMMINENT COMMONS: THE EXPANDED CITY

EDITED BY ALEJANDRO ZAERA-POLO
AND JEFFREY S. ANDERSON

SEOUL BIENNALE OF ARCHITECTURE
AND URBANISM 2017

Welcome to the Seoul Biennale of Architecture and Urbanism!

**Won-Soon Park
(Mayor of Seoul)**

The Seoul Biennale of Architecture and Urbanism is taking its first step. Long dormant in the heart of our city, the Seoul Biennale, after two years of preparation, has emerged as a new cultural event for Seoul. Throughout the dizzying growth of the past half-century, architecture has served as the primary instrument of the city's development. Now, our citizens stand at the center of Seoul's urbanity. Architecture's contribution in creating a just and sustainable city is not a dream of the distant future but a reality that stands alongside our citizens. Since my inauguration as the Mayor of Seoul, I have implemented a robust range of policies such as regeneration-centered urban renovation, moving Seoul towards a pedestrian friendly city, promotion of urban manufacturing and urban farming, revitalization of local communities, and youth start-up support projects. These initiatives have brought about a new architectural paradigm, one that had long been cultivated in everyday life of the city. The Seoul Biennale provides a milestone in the formation of architecture's new role for Seoul.

In 2013, the Seoul Metropolitan Government announced the Seoul Architecture Manifesto. It begins with the following resolution: "All architecture in Seoul is fundamentally a public asset for all of its citizens. We will work toward an architecture and urbanism of the commons that provides joy and a sense of civic pride." Based on the conviction that this consistent civic policy is the philosophical and methodological basis for addressing the impending issues of cities worldwide, Imminent Commons has been presented as the inaugural theme for the Seoul Biennale of Architecture and Urbanism. The Seoul Biennale presents the essentials of the urban commons, expanding beyond city policies to the what and how of the commons.

Along with Dongdaemun Design Plaza and Donuimun Museum Village, the main exhibition venues of the biennale, the historical downtown of Seoul will serve as a laboratory for discovery and experiments in policy initiatives as well as social and technological innovation. To be able to share is a blessing and a source of joy. The Seoul Biennale offers an open setting to enjoy exhibitions, participate in various projects, and engage in in-depth discussions on the future of the city. The Seoul Biennale will continue to provide a forum for cities to come together to learn, and in turn, Seoul will learn from this amazing gathering of the cities of the world.

Seoul and the Biennale of Architecture and Urbanism:

Imminent Commons

Young Joon Kim
(City Architect of Seoul)

Since its very beginning, Seoul has maintained an urban structure that embraced its natural gifts of mountains and rivers, which have been carefully integrated into the city's fabric. But as a result of the fast development that took place in the post-war period, some of its original harmony has been endangered by brutal development. A powerful urban governance has been established during this age of phenomenal expansion and provided a stable legal and administrative framework which has served the city well during this era of massive development. However, the stability provided by this planning system has sometimes become technocratic, detached from its citizens, and sometimes too slow to respond to the challenges and opportunities raised by new global developments. We must now consider how to tweak this system we have created to adjust it to the realities of a new era.

Like many other global metropolises, Seoul has suffered important changes with the rapid increase of tourism, immigration, the aging of the population, and the reorganization of the economy and workforce. The City should now adjust to these changes with innovations in transportation, communication, production, energy, reuse, and many other urban technologies available now.

The situation of Seoul today is twofold: internally, it must refine parts of the urban system that were neglected in the past in favor of a ensuring stable economic development; externally, it must deal with conditions that are undermining the very foundations of urban life.

These are the points that the Seoul Biennale of Architecture and Urbanism aims to address in the future. Seoul has now reached a point where it can no longer simply follow the precedents of other cities. The challenges we face today need Seoul-specific solutions which cannot be found in any manual, and therefore should be discussed in an open arena. Beyond preparing fragmentary solutions to individual cases, we must now set a goal to seek a way out through collective debate which will put Seoul citizens in touch with experts from all over the world.

This inaugural Seoul Biennale, titled "Imminent Commons" addresses these issues as a collective question, not just a diligent application of technocratic recipes. "Imminent Commons" emphasizes the need to review the basic elements of architecture and the city, such as air, water, energy, and the biosphere, and to tap into the potential of our cities and buildings through new developments in sensing, communicating, moving, making, and recycling. The biennale reminds us that there is a great gap between our new urban realities—microdust, climate change, floods, nuclear power, urban agriculture, big data, the Internet of Things, internet shopping, urban manufacturing, etc.—and the existing protocols and readymade solutions in architecture and urbanism.

The basic elements and variables covered in the Thematic Exhibition are often overlooked because they are so basic and are likely to be deferred by the more obvious tasks of making buildings and urban infrastructures. Yet, the "Imminent Commons" pose critical and imminent urban questions of our time, and therefore must be incorporated into urban and architectural solutions. These fundamental questions are crucial for both experts and citizens alike, as we amend our past and prepare for the future.

May the Seoul Biennale provide a fruitful platform for exploring new approaches to architecture and urbanism.

Imminent Commons: The Expanded City

Alejandro Zaera-Polo and Jeffrey S. Anderson

AIR
WATER
FIRE
EARTH
SENSING
COMMUNICATING
MOVING
MAKING
RECYCLING

The inaugural edition of the Seoul Biennale of Architecture and Urbanism takes place at a historic moment. The process of rampant globalization which has been at play since the 1970s has produced important effects on contemporary geopolitics which are crucial to understand when trying to discuss the current status and the near future of cities. The most remarkable effect has become brutally visible in the last few years: the re-emergence of city states and their walls—in a new form— after centuries of their dissolution. In many countries of the developed world, the urban/rural and urban/national divide has recently become an even more significant political opposition than the customary left/right divide of the past.

In light of the increasing disengagement between urban and rural areas, we believe that a contemporary discourse on urbanism must not sink into a formal, programmatic, or historical study of the city itself, but must address the interdependency of cities with ecological and technological processes outside the purview of traditional urban planning. The most important topics that cities must address today are issues such as their connection with global data networks, natural cycles, and flows of resources which supersede the traditional boundaries of urbanism. For this reason, we have framed our investigation of contemporary urbanism on nine *Imminent Commons* which engage collective ecological and technological resources relevant to all cities and even extra-urban territories.

Grouping the urban commons into resources and technologies led us to the arcane classification of natural resources: *air, water, fire, and earth,* the four elements of ancient cosmologies, and five basic technological commons based on expanded human capacities: *sensing, communicating, moving, making, and recycling.* We believe that, following decades of increasing detachment between cities and their associated territories, it is now crucial to find areas of continuity between them to avoid worsening the contemporary polarization of geopolitics. With our curatorial strategy, we are seeking not just a discussion on contemporary urban technologies and ecologies, but to find alternatives to the return of the city walls and the dangerous politics associated with them. The commons we investigate here attempt to construct an expanded urbanism which is able to integrate greater milieus rather than reinforce urban/rural polarization. This is a deliberate stance vis-à-vis the emerging global geopolitics of nationalism and isolationism.

While cities have become the primary engines—and beneficiaries—of globalization, rural and industrial territories have been mostly left out of this process, to the point that in many cases they have become entirely alienated. Cities and extra-urban areas followed entirely divergent fortunes during globalization, and the resulting tensions have now begun to surface violently many different geographies. We can see the outcome of this in the massive inequalities between newly wealthy Chinese cities and the miserable poverty in China's rural populations, the closed down–factories in the rust belt of the United States, and the forgotten working class of the rural and industrial provinces in the United Kingdom and France. This is not to say that cities do not have their own problems, pockets of marginalization, scars of inequality, and decreasing environmental quality; these problems have in fact expanded during the so-called neoliberal phase of hyper-globalization. However, regardless of the successes and failures of any one city, it seems that the more economically successful, populated, and international a city is, the taller its walls have become, while small–scale cities and suburbs have suddenly become "swing territories" where their engagement with the global economy will tilt their political leanings in or out of their "city wall."

In the United States, Donald Trump's victory relied heavily on the rural and industrial vote, opening a newly Jeffersonian view of the country after decades of prevalent urban regeneration. In the United Kingdom, Brexit was equally traceable back to the rural vote and the constituencies in decaying former industrial populations. Populist movements in France, Germany, Greece, and Spain, both on the left and the right, have resorted to an extra-urban, anti-globalization, nationalist, protectionist, and isolationist discourse which has crashed quite literally into the globalizing nature of the relevant urban areas. The resurgence of

the city wall has become evident in the "sanctuary cities" stance
vis-a-vis Trump's national immigration policies and the signature
of adherence to the Paris Climate Agreement by sixty-one major
US cities in response to the president's decision to exit the
agreement. The confrontation over Brexit between Sadiq Khan,
mayor of London, the British Prime Minister Theresa May,
and Jeremy Corbyn, the head of the Labor Party, is another
important index of the same phenomena.

The current return of a hard division between cities and the
nation state is one of the most important geopolitical processes
occurring today, and is having a definitive effect on cities and the
world at large. However, our stance is that these hard divisionsare
entirely fictional. We know that cities have a powerful effect
on global natural cycles, metabolize resources from vast extra-
urban areas, and greatly impact local and regional economies.
The notion of the carbon footprint, for example, is evidence of
the impossibility of drawing these hard edges. Rural populations
could legitimately accuse the inhabitants of cities of causing the
global environmental crisis, as a disproportionate amount of
energy—with the associated emission of greenhouse gases—is
consumed in cities. Therefore, cities may be seen as largely
responsible for globally rising water levels, air pollution, and
global warming, even if these processes do not take place within
their boundaries.

The nine *Imminent Commons* which we have defined in the
first volume of this catalog are deliberately placed in respect
to this contrived urban/rural opposition and the re-emergence
of nationalism, isolationism, and protectionism. At the onus
of this debate, there is a growing interest in a "United Cities"
organization, modeled on historical trans-urban organizations
such as the Silk Road, the Phoenicia, or the Hanseatic League
of trading cities,which were able to co-defend themselves from
the siege of the nation state. There may be legitimate reasons for
the rebirth of city walls and urban leagues in the aftermath of
Friedman-style neoliberalism, butwe believe that cities cannot
retreat into new isolationist forms of governance, even as they
are besieged by failing states loaded with nationally—rather

than globally—sized industries, health and security services, and national armies. If we pursue the League of the Cities model, we believe this will likely form a league of the wealthy, the educated, and the polluting versus the general populace, only serving to further inequality and marginalization. This will propel new nationalisms and perpetuate the disenfranchisement of non-urban populations. To avoid this further polarization, we believe it is necessary to outline an expanded theory of the city as the new nature, an ecology of humans, machines, materials, and networks which permeate the borders of the city itself into a vast territory of common resources and technologies.

Our curatorial position for the *Imminent Commons* is that cities—as the primary engines of irreversible globalization—have the power and the duty to overcome the ongoing fracture with rural and industrial milieus, their expanded territories, and nature in general. This convolutes the notion of the city as the site of "the artificial" and the rural as the domain of the "natural." Artificial and natural processes intertwine them both: in the most general sense, most of the oxygen we breathe in cities, the energy we consume, and the food we eat comes from the country side. A political ecology of cities that understands them as interdependent with natural cycles, rural areas, industrial estates, global infrastructural networks, and with the whole earth itself requires a formulation of an *expanded urbanity*, to avoid a retreat into the fractured world of the Middle Ages and the nation state. Ours is not a politically innocent or neutral position; it is openly against the creeping Trump world, the Brexit world, the Putin world, the worldsof Le Pen and AFD, all of which are the same nostalgic attempt to claim national identities and cultures when the reasons for these to exist, the nations, are long gone. We live in a world of digital technologies where—as Mario Carpo has correctly pointed out in his contribution to book 1—the economies of scale which legitimated nation building are no longer prevalent, and markets are no longer bound to the national states; a worldwith increasing evidence that urban carbon footprints and pollution are invading rural territories, and nation states are systematically trespassing the borders of neighboring nations.

We know that a retreat into the "nation" is suicidal, but we are
not convinced that the League of Cities is much more productive.
This is because the League of Cities continues to understand
cities as discrete entities where local identities and cultures take
precedence over greater natural and artificial ecologies such as
forests, oceans, sustainable energy, animals, sensors, algorithms,
and wireless local area or Bluetooth networks. Likewise, the
Imminent Commons are also a rejection of the neoliberal city,
which is entirely driven by stock-market speculation and the
securitization of urban space, oblivious to natural cycles and
industrial processes. Our central curatorial structure for the
inaugural Seoul Biennale proposes to set up a structure to engage
effectively with this global, posthuman world, laying out a
conceptual infrastructure able to connect between cities, but also
to draw bridges between the urbanand its affected territories.

The original notion of the commons, first stated by political
economist William Foster Lloyd in 1833 in his *Two Lectures
on the Checks to Population,* gave us an opportunity to generate
a discourse on urbanism by analyzing the very formation of
human collectives which shared certain types of natural resources
such as pastures, herds, water, and forests. We referenced these
collectives and their shared resources and technologies in order
to connect the collective life of cities with nature, the territory,
and the countryside. The commons are the curatorial argument
which enables us to overcome the presentation of urban projects
as independent events (as we have stated, claiming cultural
uniqueness and identity for cities may be even more politically
dangerous than reverseto the nation). Instead, the commons are
global, existing across cities and across human and non-human
communities. They enable us to connect across cities but also
between the city and the territory, generating a true political
ecology, a regime where the distinction between urban facts—the
object of urban sciences—and urban values—the object of urban
politics—tends to disappear.

The process of identifying the relevant urban commons took
us to the Neolithic Age, where cities began to appear through
the domestication of plants and animalsand the development of

agricultural technologies. The first human commons were the
natural resources around populated areas and the technologies
that allowed humans to use them to sustain increasingly
large population densities. The four resource-based commons
represent the most fundamental sources of ecological capital:
the air we breathe, the water we drink, the energy we consume,
and the earth we harvest. The five technology-based commons
deal with the most basic urban technologies across history: the
devices we use to identify environmental patterns and sense the
world around us, the enhanced capacity to share information
and knowledge, the capacity to move in space beyond the range
of the human body, the capacity to produce goods which do not
exist in nature, and the ability to process and dispose of waste.

In light of these urban commons, we believe that, even if
fortuitous, the selection of the Donuimun Museum Village as the
venue for stagingthis debate is an important one. The Donuimun
Museum Village is a recently renovated area of Seoul located
near the historical West Gate and comprising a complex fabric
of small *hanok* houses and 1960s jerry-built residential fabric.
Importantly, the concept of recycling urban capital became a
source of friction in the planning of this renovation, as this fabric
was originally destined to make way for a new park to serveas an
amenity for neighboring development. The decision to preserve
the Donuimun Museum Village as a culture and leisure-driven
complex poses a strong stance on urban regeneration which we
hope to expand upon with our exhibition.

Based on the brief for the Seoul Biennale, we have collected
40 exhibitions to address the nine imminent commons with
roughly four to five examples per common. The two distinct
territories of ecology-based commons and technology-based
commons guide the distribution of spaces in the Donuimun
Museum Village. At the northeast end of the site we have
installed a collection of ecology-based commons exhibitions
including air, water, energy, and earth exhibitions. Across
the southern half of the site are distributed technology-
based commons including sensing, communicating, moving,
recycling, and making exhibitions. From the beginning, the

brief for every one of these exhibitions did not stop at the exhibition itself: the installations were to become a prototypical deployment of a deeper research, which is presented in this document. The co-relations between these different proposals are left to the visitor to build, embedded within an existing urban fabric which acts as the medium between them. Though we have used the commons as a general organizational structure, there are no hard boundaries between them, as multiple imbrications between topics blur their edges. Locally, the exhibitions are arranged according to tangencies and overlaps between the commons: air has to do with sensing, moving has to do with communicating, the urban metabolisms of recycling and making are intimately tied; and earth, energy, and recycling demonstrate multiple overlaps and correlations. The relevance of the experiment is the co-location of all these installations within a pre-existing urban setting.

Many of the exhibits have sought to relate specifically to Seoul, as we tried to engage the local public as a relevant audience which will be exposed to the potential outcomes of these installations. We have deliberately sought to avoid architectural representations, which have traditionally been the vehicle to present and debate architecture. Instead, the authors have been asked to present 1:1 prototypes of their research and observations of the imminent commons or to present didactic explorations about them. If architecture as a medium is difficult to showcase—as opposed to other arts where the object is easily transportable—the installations are always partial prototypes of processes, rather than architectural projects, mostly operating on a pre-architectural level. We are well aware of the limitations of this scope in respect to the architectural public and we believe that this level of discussion is necessary at a time when we are facing a wholesale re-foundation of the discipline, and that it should engage a much wider constituency than the one that architectural biennales usually have. Moreover, we have a hunch that the new relevant scale of architecture is the detail, where the flows of air, energy, and water are controlled, and where technologies are embedded. So, architecture can be discussed pretty much at 1:1.

These days, a large number of emerging architectural practices claim their engagement with the history of the discipline, which is being posed as a resistance to the techno-corporate forms of neo-liberal architecture. The retreat into a historicist approach is becoming a serious obstacle for architects to engage with in a world where the tenets of the architectural discipline no longer seem to matter to anyone except architects. For example, the association of everything technical to techno-corporate liberalism and the "end of history" has recently prompted a contemporary retreat into the inner landscape of the discipline, returning to architectural language games, often mixed with the old anarcho-syndicalist rhetoric. This is certainly a smokescreen, a temporary foil to the very real and rampant neo-liberal and techno-corporate empires of the Late Anthropocene.

Historically constructed disciplines face major limitations in effectively addressing the commons. In light of very recent technological advancements—so recent that they have no relevant historical content—and their tremendous impact on cities, we wonder if the retrospective eye, gazing at the past life of cities, has any relevance in providing guidelines for their contemporary development. The most important factors impacting cities and cultures today have only appeared in the last few decades: the mass consciousness of global warming, real-time data collection and distribution, "social media," "going viral," artificial intelligence algorithms, facial tracking, smartphones, fifth-generation mobile networks, GPS, etc. Rather than national triumphs or disasters, our collective memory has begun to gravitate around record temperatures, meme calendars, iOS updates, and incrementally increasing download speeds. Rather than a historical survey, we believe a co-relational analysis may be more effective at understanding the consequences of technological developments on different commons (for example, the relation between developments in sensing technologies and environmental policies).

If we have something to learn from the history of architecture, it is that progressive practices rarely emerge out of a review of tradition. We live in an age which is historically similar to the early twentieth century when a number of technical developments had exceeded the formal and performative possibilities of historical forms of the discipline and could no longer be expressed by them. A number of architects—many of whom had a non-academic upbringing, such as Le Corbusier and Mies van der Rohe—tried to engage with these technical developments and move away from architectural traditions. The result was one of the most fruitful periods of architectural invention. There was no more distance between historicist architecture at the end of the nineteenth century and the paquebots, airplanes, cars, and silos that modern architects were looking at in the 1920s than there is today between the neo-postmodern repertoires being broadcast as we speak by the architectural media and the bio-technologies, robots, and social media that we are trying to engage here.

What is at stake with this exhibition is the question of where architects get our intelligence from. We believe that the history of architecture is no longer a very relevant repository of architectural knowledge and that, more so than ever, architects must look to the greater ecologies and technologies outside the traditional scope of the discipline in order to remain relevant. In the same way that the historical forms of architecture were not the locus of design intelligence for Le Corbusier, Mies van der Rohe, and many other early modern architects, we know that we must look outwards from the discipline, not inwards, to move forward. Who wants to be the new Garnier, Lutyens, or Richardson, when one can aspire to be the new Le Corbusier? Is an analysis of the history of architecture or mastery of the discipline culturally relevant vis-à-vis global warming, big data, or the automation of work? We do not think so. History has always been unforgiving to those who did not look forward.

VISITORS GALLERY

The Building Where We Keep the World

<u>Liam Young</u>

In an anonymous town in the middle of Oregon, at the confluence of cool air, cheap hydro power, and tax incentives is the largest cultural landscape in human history. These forgotten streets and their sprawling periphery contain everything about who we are. All of our dreams and fears, histories and futures are here, just behind the Thriftway, drenched in the stench of diner pancakes and simulated syrup. This is where the internet lives.

Terms like "cloud," "wifi," and "web" are suggestive of something omnipresent, ephemeral, everywhere, and nowhere; yet this network is organised around an extraordinary, planetary-scaled physical infrastructure. We are following the fibre optic tendrils that connect the world to explore the internet as a landscape and chronicle the strange architectures of the network. If you were to yank your cable from the wall and follow this loose thread, you might eventually find yourself standing beside me in this unremarkable part of the world surrounded by the server stacks of Facebook, Google, and Apple. All the world's data is setting

up a home here, and the chilly breeze that brushes my face and muffles our interview microphone has set in motion a storm of infrastructure.

In front of us is the white powder-coated grill of the perimeter fence that wraps Google's data centre. We force our camera through the bars, focusing through a layer of heat vent steam that hangs heavy in the air. Out of the data mist an SUV painted with a colourful Google logo on its side approaches and a security guard tells us we have to leave. This is as close as we get to the racks and racks of search histories, Gmails, scanned books, and encyclopaedia of everything that sits behind the tank-proof fence. Just a handful of photos of the interior of this building exist online; it is simultaneously a space we all occupy but can never enter. Images of the site present a forest of playfully coloured ductwork suggesting a disarming and accessible public face, but this is a daycare architecture that has been militarised and fortified into one of the most secure sites on the planet.

As we head to the town of Prineville, just a couple of hours up the road, we see, looming on the horizon, a long and low black monolith that sits in the landscape like a stranded Richard Serra sculpture. We are told that this is Apple's secret data centre, but there is no glowing Apple logo here; instead, there is just another fence line, a proxy company name, and unbroken, windowless walls.

A few minutes further and we reach the 30,000-square-metre field of flickering servers that constitutes Facebook's own data centre (see image below). Every like, love letter, embarrassing photo, and ironic update is stored in the purring machines contained in this vast concrete box. The buildings of the internet are difficult to grasp; they hide behind a type of disappearance formed through radical banality, and their designers seem to confuse anonymity with a sense of security. At a time when our collective history is digital, however, these blank forms are our generation's great library, our cathedral, our cultural legacy.

At first glance, there appears to be little architecture here, no grand monumental gesture, but instead, this network of spaces so fundamental to our modern experience of the world seems to be conceived of as little more than air-conditioning infrastructure.

in a million LEDs of Facebook blue. He swipes a security card, pushes a door against a rush of air, and the deafening whir of a million cooling fans fills the room. This is the soundscape of the internet, a digital springtime, humming endlessly, across a landscape without seasons.

We are in Prineville to meet Neil Sheehan, designer of the Facebook facility and one of just four or five architects who are responsible for building every data centre in the world. "We do data centres," Neil says when we meet in Facebook's lobby, "we don't have time to do anything else." Neil is largely responsible for this new history of the network and he has agreed to take us on a rare tour inside, a pilgrimage of sorts, to meet our digital selves, to gaze across server racks, and watch ourselves winking back,

Facebook, like all data centres, is essentially just row upon row of identical floor to ceiling server stacks, spinning and writing the lives of 1.9 billion global users. Each of the four thousand servers in this hall has a blue LED that illuminates when it is accessed and a yellow flashing light that flickers with the writing of data. The server floor trembles like a forest of fireflies, a map of social media territory, a spatialized internet, a field of flickering Facebookers all waving hello.

Ancient craftsmen once measured the world using parts of the human body: the cubit is based on the length of a forearm; the inch, the length of a thumb. Le Corbusier designed his buildings based around the Modulor, a scale he derived from the proportions of the human body. We once understood our world through systems founded on human size, vision, and patterns of occupation. In the sites of the internet, however, the body is no longer the dominant measure of space; it is the nineteen-inch industry standard server rack that has become the new modular. The entire architecture of the internet is structured around this universal building block even to the extent that the European Facebook centres are feet and inches in plan but metric in section just to accommodate it. "You have to start somewhere," Neil says.

As we wander through the data halls we see a space that entirely defers to the logic of these machines. "There is no design here," Neil quips. He still finds it difficult to understand why we have come. In his mind he is not taking us on a tour through a critical site of contemporary culture, but rather a building that is optimised as a membrane to filter air. He relishes the innovations made to maximise flows, reduce energy draws, and eke out unimagined efficiencies. We follow the path of the Oregon air through the building as it is cooled, funnelled into areas of higher temperature, and then exhausted back into the world, in a steam cloud of Superbowl posts, fake news, and birthday well-wishers. "We designed the facility to move air very slowly, from outside to inside, through the servers and back out again with the most

minimal amount of power," Neil says. A typical server cabinet at Facebook uses 24000 kilowatt hours a year—twice the load of an average family house. Sitting beside a nearby river dam and hydro plant, energy is cheap here in Prineville, however, about half the cost of elsewhere in the States and that's why they have all come. "Data centres are like mushrooms, once one pops up the rest follow," laughs Neil.

Prineville is a town that turns electricity into bits, and Facebook's data centre is a giant machine for organising our culture and archiving our lives based on clicks and views. When we first post something on Facebook, it is stored on the cache servers that are blinking in front of us. Our data sits here for anywhere from two hours to two days depending on how frequently it is shared and accessed. Only 2% of Facebook is visible at any moment so as data ages and interest wanes, it is transferred from flash drive to flash drive to flash drive and ultimately, when the world has become bored with it, to long-term storage drives. These hard drives are where you data lives indefinitely— in a way, where we all will live indefinitely.

"Do you see those little white buildings over there? They are for cold storage," Neil says as he takes us behind the general server hall to see a row of galvanised sheds, each about the size of a two-car garage. In every one of these little sheds is room for an exabyte of data, and currently they are being filled entirely with the one petabyte of photos users upload every month. "Now we are all putting our baby pictures on Facebook and are expecting them to

be kept forever. When a photo gets old and is no longer liked or looked at, then this is where we store them," explains Neil. In these modest pavilions are every photograph that ever has been taken and every photograph that ever will be taken. This visual portrait of human history is sitting somewhere outside of Prineville, along a two-lane road, near a parking lot, beside a tree, baking in the afternoon sun. We ask Neil how he feels to be designing the containers for all our treasured memories. We are fishing for some degree of sentiment, a sense of what it means to be responsible for one of the biggest archive projects in existence. "If I were to pull a drive out of the rack, then what I would hold in my hand is just a minute portion of any one photo. The system writes a piece of data across multiple drives so it would be just a fragment of an image at such a scale that it is almost atomic in relation to the whole. It just isn't tangible to me, when we can lose up to fourteen server racks without corrupting any data, it is like losing a skin cell rather than an entire body." In this way our digital selves have been blown apart, spreading their molecules across the entire building and, in actuality, across the entirety of the earth. Somehow, despite Neil's argument for the logic of software it still feels like somewhere important, a place that deserves to be regarded differently. We continue our stroll through the hot aisles, breathing the air that was warmed by our photos.

In Neil's mind we have no business being here. The data centre is a site for machines, for efficiency and optimisation, not cultural meaning. It isn't a site of pilgrimage, it's not a picturesque forest through which we might hike or a space of congregation we could inhabit like a church on Sundays. As we exit each room

on our tour, my job is to switch off the lights. There is no one left behind in the dark, it is a building of empty rooms, quietly humming away without us. Just one Facebook engineer is able to maintain 25,000 servers each day. We are surplus to the practical needs of the data centre. It is a landscape filled with our digital avatars but strangely absent of people. Just a few wandering techs stalk the aisles, babysitting the servers, watching the lights, waiting for something to do. It is a new typology of the post-human, a building of extraordinary meaning that sits at the core of what it means to exist today but at the same time turns its back on any expression of that significance. "The people that ask us to do these buildings couldn't care less what they look like," Neil explains, but is that enough for such sites at the centre of our mediated world?

The data centre is a typology without history. The contemporary aesthetic language of the server farm is derived from the expectations of what an IT worker thinks one should look like after watching a lifetime of science fiction films. In the wake of the dotcom boom, a company called Exodus played on these assumptions and built their brand around the marketing of secretive, ultra-secure data centres. It was through Exodus that the design totems of fortification, optical scanners and finger-print IDs were introduced, and they gave rise to the guarded Fight Club mentality that no one talks about data centres. If we are to make a claim for something more, then what are the alternative traditions on which we should draw? If we no longer consider the internet as a concern of corporate security but as one of cultural identity, then should we look to the library, the museum, the archive, the monument or the public forum? Is the internet a landscape, in the traditions of the technological sublime, where incalculable awe is cast no longer across an untamed nature but across intricately platted cables of turquoise and purple plastic, white noise, and the concrete geologies of vast data complexes? Will we soon write soliloquies for the server aisles as we once did for rolling hills? Will couples steam up car windows, parked in the artificial moonlight of power plant security lights? Will we picnic under the fluorescent glow of a grid of synthetic suns and ceiling tiles. Our new spaces of culture glitch and buffer? the electromagnetics hum and they smell of hard drives and fibre optics and Red Bull.

Prineville is the territory behind the screen and beyond the fog of the cloud. The data centres of the networked world are the extraordinary material consequences of our ever digital selves. In a world where the terms "virtual" and "real" no longer apply, these flickering architectures are more than just computational infrastructures; they are becoming the defining cultural constructions of our age and whether he likes it or not, Neil Sheehan is the star architect of a new generation. Architecture has always been defined by the prevailing means of production. Stonemasons once carved column capitals and modern architects harnessed the prefabricated components made possible by industrialization. Every era has its own iconic architectural typology. The dream commission was once the church, modernism had the factory and then the house; in the past decade we celebrated the decadent museum and the gallery. Now we have the data centre.

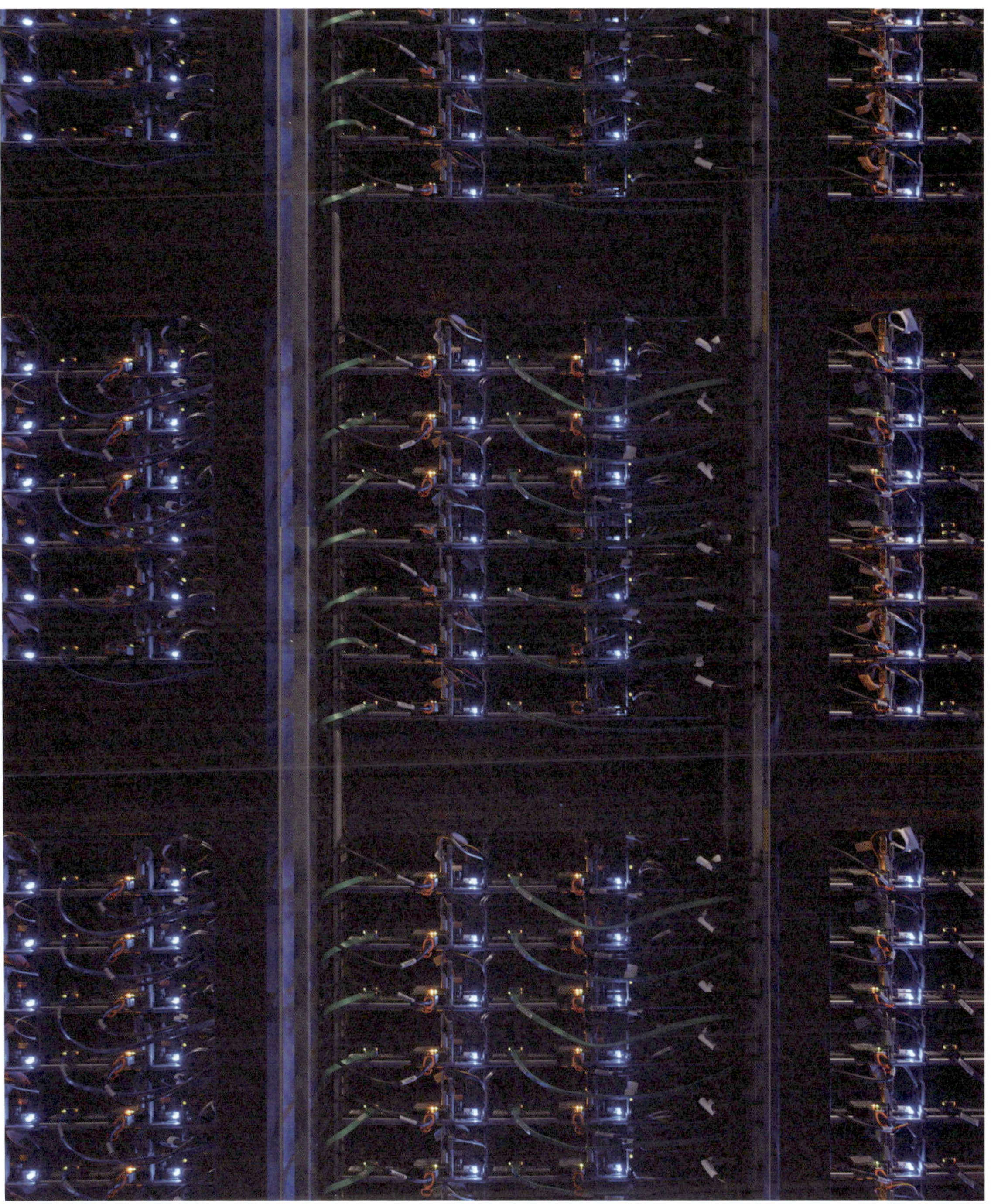

The Aerocene— Sensing Air

Tomás Saraceno

The Aerocene is an open-source, multi-disciplinary project that foregrounds the artistic and scientific exploration of environmental issues. In the wake of the Anthropocene, the project promotes common links between social, mental, and environmental ecologies in the way of shaping a new epoch—the Aerocene.

To be aware of the air is to be sensitive to one's environment, to be aware of an element which sustains you, transmits, carries. If you leave a room, vacate a building, climb a mountain, float on the seas, you are still contained within air. Air, in this sense, *is* the environment. Naturally, air evades the senses, occasionally being felt as a breeze against the skin, and only rarely made visible as vapour or smog. Yet, this element no longer escapes empirical perception; its natural invisibility has been compromised as humans have increasingly industrialised. Waters have become filled with rubbish, the earth has been covered with concrete, energy is the object of political conflict, and the air absorbs pollutants from every source. This is what is found in the Anthropocene—a geological epoch that, it is argued, commenced when human action became the dominant force in transforming the environment.

Air has now moved out of metaphorical obscurity. In highly polluted areas you can feel the air congested with soot, you can smell and taste it as petrol fumes, and visibility is compromised by smog. True blue skies, now miraculous in some urban environments, end up marked by streaks of vapour trails. Airspace is something to be owned and fought over. As heavy industry continues to emit toxic gases into the atmosphere, the air will become ever thicker with pollution. All of this has transformed the way human senses react to air. To achieve long-lasting

change, people must relearn their relationship with this element and understand how to live in tandem with it, rather than control it.

How can we succeed? The planet needs a new era, a new way of living, independent from the destructive nature of the Anthropocene. This shall be called the Aerocene. The Aerocene, imagined by artist Tomás Saraceno, is an open-source project that aims to found a more-than-geological epoch, which places its focus on the atmosphere. The Aerocene encourages air travel, but not via fossil-fueled means. The difference between the two eras can be understood through the following example: Anthropogenic journeys consist of travelling from point A to point B in the fastest possible way, regardless of concerns over harmful emissions or consumption of fuel. Conversely, journeys in the Aerocene will move with the air. To move in this way is to float following winding trajectories, guided by the wind and propelled by thermal air currents.

In fact, specially designed lighter-than-air sculptures that are capable of travelling in this way have been developed by Tomás Saraceno, in collaboration with engineers, technologists, balloonists, and scientists.

Eclipse of the Aerocene Explorer, 2016
Performance in Salar de Uyuni, Bolivia, January 2016, during Tomás Saraceno's artistic expedition. Salar de Uyuni salt flat is estimated to be the biggest lithium depository on earth. Lithium is an alkali metal used widely in the electronic industry for mobile batteries, and is becoming increasingly scarce. Saraceno's Aerocene sculptures floated above the Uyuni salt crust, proposing that natural resources be kept in the ground and that humans relate to energy cycles differently, by harnessing the sun and the earth as the sole batteries.

The Aerocene project thus manifests as a series of air-fueled sculptures that aim to achieve the longest emission-free journey around the world. The sculptures become buoyant only with the heat of the sun and infrared radiation from the surface of the earth. Their speed is dependent on the winds, their flight duration is at the whim of the sun, and their uplift force is determined by the difference between the temperature inside and the temperature of the air outside. The sculptures float without burning fossil fuels, without using solar panels or batteries, and without helium, hydrogen, or other rare gases—utilising only the kinetic energy of running with the sculpture in order to fill it with air. Once full, it is only a matter of time until the air inside a sculpture is gradually heated by the sun, slowly expanding until the sculpture becomes lighter than air.

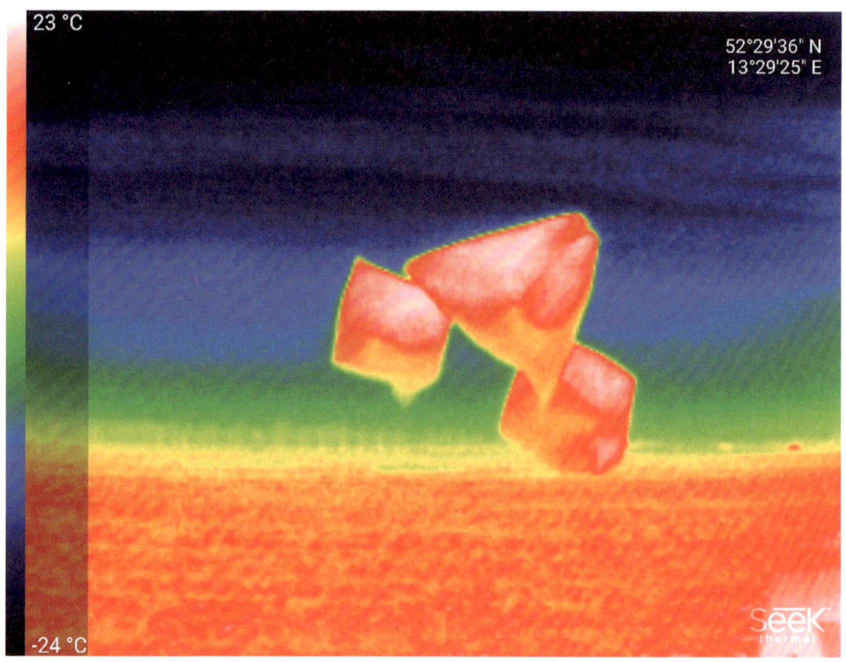

Aerocene: 51 Pegasi B Flight, 2017
On Saturday, 4 March 2017, the Aerocene sculpture 51 Pegasi B was launched as a part of Tomás Saraceno's solo exhibition "Aerosolar Journeys" at Wilhelm Hack Museum, Ludwigshafen. The flight was achieved without any carbon, fossil fuels, helium, hydrogen, burners, or engines—using only air currents and the heat of the sun. During the journey, geo-fencing and cut-down mechanisms were implemented and tested.

"What if there was a way of working with, as well as railing against, the heat and turbulence we have added to the earth's atmosphere; a way of turning around and reaching upwards, outwards in the direction of our energy-emitting star? Becoming Aerosolar, in this sense, would mean lightening up, loosening the hold of heavy modernity, easing off from accumulation without end." (Clark 2015)

Given the power of the forces at play here—the sun and wind—the window of opportunity for this mode of transport is wide open. The Aerocene project currently holds the world record for the longest, and most sustainable, certified, manned flight (without fossil fuels, solar panels, helium, or batteries). This took place on 8 November 2015 in the White Sands Desert, New Mexico, USA. The area was chosen for its links to the Anthropocene, having been the test-site for the first nuclear bomb, detonated on 16 July 1945. In the shadow of this historic event, an emblem for climate-change action rose into the sky, floating for three hours without fuel, and allowing seven people to fly. The movement of the balloon relied only on the heating of its black fabric by the sun and the infrared radiation reflected back by the white landscape. Since this was an occasion to test the potential of manned balloon flight, and given the restrictions of international aviation law, the balloon remained connected to the ground by a tether rope. The event provided a glimpse into what alternate travel methods the Aerocene can offer.

Aerocene, launches in White Sands, New Mexico (United States), 2015
The launches in White Sands and the symposium "Space without Rockets," initiated by Tomás Saraceno, were organized together with curators Rob La Frenais and Kerry Doyle for the exhibition "Territory of the Imagination" at the Rubin Center for the Visual Arts. The sculpture D-O AEC Aerocene is made possible due to the generous support of Christian Just Linde. The artistic experiment achieved two world records as the first and the longest solely solar flight by a lighter-than-air vehicle. It took place close to the missile range where the first test of a nuclear bomb, Trinity, happened a half-century ago, marking the beginning of the Anthropocene geological epoch.

"Inhabiting the air and opening up to the elements would also involve us recognising contingency and hazard as a necessary part of creaturely existence, rather than something that can ever be eradicated. As Tim Ingold puts it, life (anima) is not something carried by the wind; it is being carried by the wind (anemos): 'life is not in things; rather, things are in life, caught up in a current of continual generation' (13). 'We need new forms of solidarity and security, predicated not on closure and independence but on the recognition of mutual vulnerability and interdependence' (914). The Aerocene provides a framework for that vision, a metaphorical—and maybe literal—lifting and opening up into the constant becoming of airy being." (Szerszynski 2015)

The possibility of losing the tether and achieving free flight is being explored by taking steps to change aviation laws. The Aerocene Foundation is working on a petition that will hopefully see fossil-fueled vehicles give way to fully aerosolar models in airspace. The petition has been signed by many and has even reached Christina Figueres, Executive Secretary of the United Nations Framework Convention on Climate Change, and Jennifer Morgan, International Executive Director of Greenpeace. This support is crucial in helping the Aerocene Foundation evolve a post–fossil fuel future. Under the current legal restrictions however, it has still been possible to test what the future of aerosolar free-flight will look like. On 27 August 2016, the Aerocene Gemini, a set of conjoined, twin aerosolar sculptures, were launched into the air from Schönfeld, Germany.

Aerocene Gemini, Free Flight, 2016
Saturday, 27 August 2016: Aerocene Gemini travels 605 km distance, floats for more than 12 hours, and reaches 16.283 m altitude. All without any carbon, fossil fuels, helium, hydrogen, burners, or engines—using only air currents and the heat of the sun.

"Like a cloud, a balloon is not simply a massive entity that floats in the air. Both balloons and clouds are defined by the dynamics of atmospheric variations, even if they take shape through different processes and logics. … Their mode of being and becoming is the shape of change, taking form and becoming manifest through condensation or envelopment, in a process of rising and falling. In that sense, they are related in a profound way in terms of their mode of being and coming-into-being. They are both localized, circumstance-specific stabilizations of wider fields of fluctuations and variations. And both clouds and balloons share something else: left to their own devices, they drift. They lack dirigibility; they are absolutely responsive, submissive even, to their elemental circumstances." (Engelmann, McCormack, and Szerszynski 2015)

The sculptures were laid out on white tarps on the ground to increase the albedo of the launch surface. Doing so reflects the intensity of the sun's rays on the sculptures, resulting in greater buoyancy. Once inflated, the sculptures gained height quickly, disappearing into the blue sky, floating in the air as humans do on water. The sculptures carried an array of devices: a GoPro camera, lightweight sensors recording air temperature, humidity, and pressure, and a DustDuino air-quality and particulate-matter sensor, which was provided by Public Lab—an open community that develops open-source, do-it-yourself technologies for investigating local environmental concerns. The sculptures both aesthetically inspire the imagination and root themselves in practical data collection.

Along their journey, the sculptures constantly transmitted information and images from their aerial perspective, allowing those on the ground to livestream their course. This offers viewers an extension to their senses, the opportunity to experience life in the air by proxy, without the hum of engines or the mark of vapour trails. Floating and becoming one with the wind, the aerostatic sculptures danced in the sky for over twelve hours. They travelled 605 km and reached a maximum altitude of 16283 m, landing in northern Poland by nightfall.

Aerocene Gemini, Free Flight, 2016
Saturday, 27 August 2016: Aerocene Gemini travels 605 km distance, floats for more than 12 hours, reaches 16.283 m altitude. All without any carbon, fossil fuels, helium, hydrogen, burners, or engines—using only air currents and the heat of the sun.

Travelling like this will allow the air to start to clear. It will return to invisibility, but remain tangible as humans learn how to harness its natural currents and rhythms. This is a vision of symbiosis between the planet, its species, and the elements. Indeed, the Aerocene sculptures are weather-dependent; this phenomenon is rarely found in the post-industrial world, given that humans have managed to create machines which can ignore natural forces. A dam can stop a river flowing and a car can drive in a hurricane. But, at what cost? Dams devastate ecosystems by blocking fish migrations and cars emit carbon dioxide, contributing to the greenhouse effect. In contrast, the sculptures of the Aerocene do not fight against the elements and the weather, but float with them. The Aerocene conveys a message of simplicity, creativity, and cooperation for a world of tumultuous geopolitical relations and an uncertain ecological future.

Relationships are what will grow the Aerocene. The project gathers people—students of design, arts, engineering, and other disciplines, scholars, thinkers, researchers, and scientists of different fields—to think together about different ways to access this new epoch. Currently being developed is the Aerocene Explorer. It enables anyone to launch his or her own personal aerosolar sculpture and explore the atmosphere. The Aerocene Explorer is fully open-source, having been developed by Studio Saraceno and a community of collaborators. Each Aerocene Explorer starter kit comes with a small camera, a livestreaming appliance, and sensing devices to record air temperature, humidity, and air pressure. The Explorer allows participants to take aerial photographs and videos, and to collect meteorological data using nonintrusive, emission-free scientific exploration tools. All the kit's contents are secured in a backpack to ensure portability and comfort when out in the field. The Explorer focuses on community, offering a platform for explorers to share their findings online and thereby form an Aerocene network. The results of this experience will be turned into a film, a story of the Aerocene from the perspective of participants from around the world. Explorers can use the footage gathered by their sculptures, as well as film taken during the event of the flight, to bring together a snapshot of real life in the Aerocene. This capability serves as a reminder of the do-it-together (DIT) ethos of the Aerocene as it continues to subvert the divisive Anthropocene.

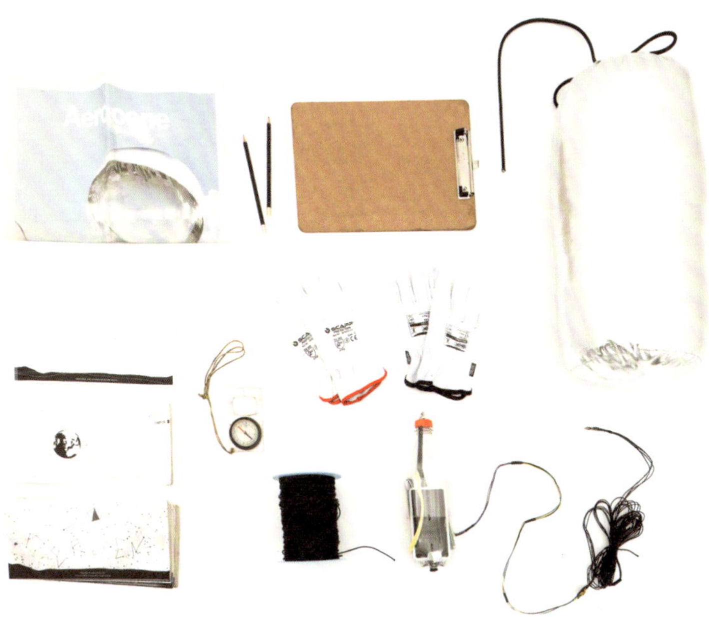

resists this flow in just the manner that is specific to it. When prehended together these variables form an ocean of particularities rife with harvestable action and energy."
(Kwinter 2015)

The Aerocene harnesses collective spirit and knowledge which builds the project up horizontally, on a strong base of community and wide cooperation that becomes a crossroad of diverse skills and experiences. This has inspired the project to expand by learning to hack its own systems. To hack is to creatively overcome the limitations of a system, to improve or subvert the intentions of its original form in a spirit of playfulness and exploration. Which geopolitical, social, legal, and philosophical "hacks" do we need in order to enter the Aerocene? With this central question, the Aerocene Foundation has set up Campuses that call upon researchers,

scientists, students, and activists to address three key Aerocene challenges: Free Flight, Life in the Air, and Sounding. The Sounding hacking session that took place at Exhibition Road, London, in November 2016 identified applications of sensing, sounding, and aerial communication capacities for Aerocene flights and research practices. "Sounding" is the measurement of the physical properties of the atmosphere using surface, airborne, or orbiting instruments. The earliest scientific balloon campaigns such as GHOST (although they used helium-filled balloons) were experiments in "sounding" the atmosphere of the Southern Hemisphere through the transmission and reception of signals from unmanned, long-distance stratospheric balloon flights. While the origin of the term "sounding" has no direct relationship to the sounds of the atmosphere, massive atmospheric events (weather systems,

Aerocene Explorer, 2016
Developed by the Aerocene Foundation and collaborators.
www.aerocene.org

meteorite entry) can be detected or heard at great distances through the propagation of low-frequency infrasound. This leads to speculation on how sonification might provide new insights or a different sensory experience of atmospheric data. Understanding what the stratosphere sounds like and how these sounds might be interpreted, in a meteorological or acoustic sense, would greatly enrich human understanding of air. The key inspirations for various sounding experiments with Aerocene Explorer sculptures might be located in atmospheric science and fluid dynamics, as well as musicality, choreography, and composition. In addition to modifications to Aerocene Explorer flights, what would need to happen "on the ground" to shift cultural imaginaries of atmosphere as a more-than-visual space and medium? The Aerocene Sounding hacking session invited atmospheric scientists, musicians, music technologists, engineers, and social scientists to hack sensory and sonic exploration of the atmosphere.

"Becoming aerosolar, lifting our dwelling to the cloud level, would allow us to pacify cultural conflicts, to abolish national borders, and to solve geopolitical issues. In return it would bring socially distributed equality, thus freeing this aerosolar society from its common contingencies, and leave its further shape and structure for atmospheric elements." (Chabard, 2015)

The Aerocene sculptures participate in collective sensing. Floating freely in the air, but always connected to the earth, via either tether or data transmission, they breathe energy into the imaginative capacities of humans to consider different modes of being and dreaming different futures. The Aerocene therefore rises as a way of resolving the Anthropocene by awakening perspectives that have the power to initiate a new epoch. The Aerocene proposes new forms of observation that are ethical in their sensitivity to the air and the other elements. This new attention can gather communities and nations,

Aerocene Explorer, launches in San Francisco, California (USA), 2016

regardless of borders and politics, to ultimately tell a story of the future—a future beyond the Anthropocene, with clear skies and symbiosis between all forms of life and elements; a way of taking back the air.

"More than any other model for living and formation today, Saraceno challenges our current modes of imagination and reasoning and, in a gush of goodwill and optimism, offers a beguiling and ponderous alternative model for how we might best live today." (Moe 2015)

References

Chabard, Pierre (2015). "Air Crafted Architecture." Published by Studio Tomás Saraceno during UN COP21 Climate Summit, Paris, 2015. © Studio Tomás Saraceno, Berlin.

Clark, Nigel (2015). "Atmospheres of Invention, Passages of Light." Published by Studio Tomás Saraceno during UN COP21 Climate Summit, Paris, 2015. © Studio Tomás Saraceno, Berlin.

Engelmann, Sasha, Dereck McCormack, and Bronislaw Szerszynski (2015). "Becoming Aerosolar and the Politics of Elemental Association." In Tomás Saraceno, *Becoming Aerosolar*. Belvedere, Vienna: 21er Haus.

Kwinter, Sanford (2015). "High Altitude, Low Opening (H.A.L.O)." Published by Studio Tomás Saraceno during UN COP21 Climate Summit, Paris, 2015. © Studio Tomás Saraceno, Berlin.

Michelon, Olivier (2015). "I Bind the Sun's Throne with a Burning Zone." Published by Studio Tomás Saraceno during UN COP21 Climate Summit, Paris, 2015. © Studio Tomás Saraceno, Berlin.

Moe, Kiel (2015). "Saraceno's Model of Models: The Magnificence of Aerocene." Published by Studio Tomás Saraceno during UN COP21 Climate Summit, Paris, 2015. © Studio Tomás Saraceno, Berlin.

Szerszynski, Bronislaw (2015). "Up." Published by Studio Tomás Saraceno during UN COP21 Climate Summit, Paris, 2015. © Studio Tomás Saraceno, Berlin.

Aerocene, 2015
An oceanographic expedition to the Solomon Islands upon the invitation of Thyssen-Bornemisza Art 21 (TBA21) Academy

SEOUL ON-AIR Augmented Environments for Urban Activism

Maider Llaguno-Munitxa,
Biayna Bogosian, Elie Bou-Zeid,
Abdulghafar Al Tair, David Radcliff,
Scott Fischer, and Youngryel Ryu

While the study of urban sensing tools has been a consistent focus of research within the environmental, earth, and citizen science communities, little attention has been paid on the development of on-site visualization techniques and methods for an interactive exploration of urban environmental data. Environmental data are generally visualized as tabular data or two-dimensional plots, which fails to enable an experiential visualization of the microclimate and thus prevents citizens from gaining a detailed understanding of the site-specific variability of pollutant concentrations and thermal comfort in their cities. This research explores three-dimensional immersive environmental visualization techniques to enable a user-friendly interactive analysis of the urban air quality data. The research focuses on the implementation of low-cost mobile urban-sensing technologies and immersive environmental data exploration mechanisms with the ambition to enable citizens to reframe their role in the politics of urban air quality.

1. Introduction

Big data is changing urban science. Digitalization of information and ubiquitous sensing in cities are enabling the collection of data at unprecedentedly high temporal and spatial resolutions. This is most true in regard to urban environmental data. Sensor networks, remote sensing, thermal imaging, and crowd-sourced environmental monitoring are rapidly increasing the availability of urban environmental data.

While high-spatiotemporal-resolution urban microclimate data are continuously becoming easier to collect, these data often fail to reach public audiences. Citizens are generally only aware of city scale mean pollutant concentration values, and fail to understand the variable environmental quality

"

Urban environmental
fashion in Korea

conditions present in the urban fabric. One of the reasons for the persistence of this challenge is that while the study of urban sensing tools and strategies has been a consistent focus of research within the environmental and earth science communities, little attention has been paid on the development of data compilation and visualization techniques and methods for interactive exploration of environmental data for urban analysis.

Environmental data are generally visualized as tabular data or two-dimensional plots that generally fail to enable an experiential visualization of the microclimatic data. Three-dimensional immersive environmental visualization techniques, on the other hand,

could potentially facilitate a user-centered interactive analysis and rationalization of the available urban environmental data.

With this ambition, the proposal *Seoul On-Air* for the 2017 Seoul Biennale focuses on the development of Augmented Reality (AR) visualizations of urban air quality data. The urban air quality data is analyzed in conjunction with urban data gathered from Geographic Information Systems (GIS) and real time video processing and object-analysis techniques. The combination of these technologies aims to enable an on-site and off-site visualization of urban air quality against city characteristics. The proposed AR environmental visualization techniques will enable citizens to become active participants in the mediation of this common.

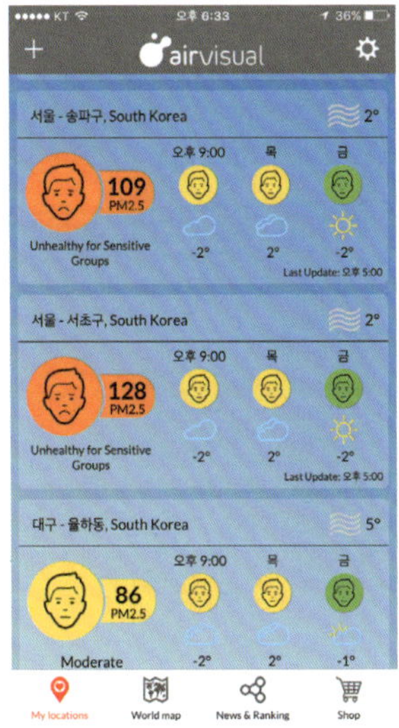

Air quality applications.
(a) Plume labs
(b) Airvisual

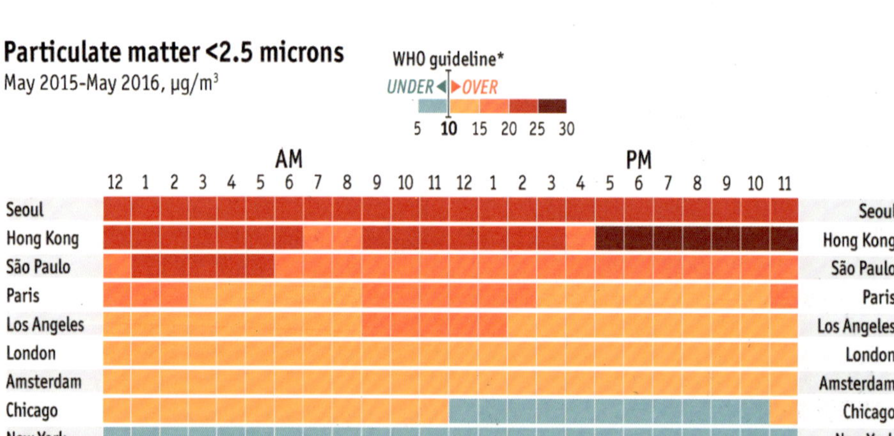

Comparison of PM 2.5 in cities around the world. (The Economist, Source: Plume labs. Url: https://www.economist.com/news/science-and-technology/21702743-air-quality-indices-make-pollution-seem-less-bad-it-breathtaking

2. Seoul air quality

The context of the 2017 Seoul Biennale is a particularly interesting forum for research on air quality, as Seoul citizens suffer from some of the most polluted air in the planet. Today the Namsan Tower alerts them on the mean concentration of ultrafine particles, PM10 in the air. If the lights projected over the tower are blue, it means Seoul is experiencing "good" air quality. The concentration levels can also be monitored by following the hourly tweets by *@yellowdust*. As per the national standards, concentrations below 45 µg m⁻³ are considered safe for performing outdoor activities. However, this limit is often exceeded, and the local standard more than doubles the maximum guidelines defined by the World Health Organization for fine and ultrafine particle concentrations. This is the case also with ozone concentrations which given the high temperatures and radiation present primarily in summer time, often exceed the recommended limits reaching alarming concentrations. Furthermore, the broadcasted mean concentration values are acquired from weather stations located in idealized conditions (sometimes elevated roofs or green space) that fail to reflect the real concentration values present in the city streets. Therefore, it is not surprising that Seoul citizens have a growing concern about the serious health risks associated with their exposure to poor air quality. In this context, the Seoul city government is exploring alternative urban sensing and air quality remediation strategies and has set out various policies to meet a 20% reduction target of ultrafine particle concentrations by 2018 (SMG 2016). Moreover, given the possibility that some of the pollution affecting Seoul is actually advected from China, the air quality of Seoul also takes a regional political dimension.

The Namsan Tower in Seoul

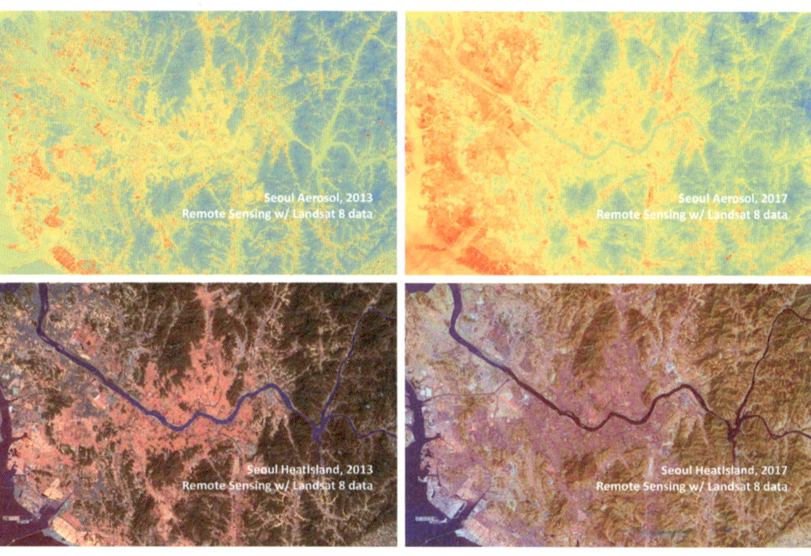

Seoul Aerosol and Heat Island Imagery. Comparison of data from 2013 and 2017. Source: GSAPP AC 2017

In this context, the Seoul On-Air research aims to communicate high spatiotemporal air quality data to its citizens using more user-friendly and accessible means. The research has been organized into three sections: The first section focuses on the acquisition of high-spatiotemporal-resolution urban air quality data through Mobile Urban Sensing Technologies (MUST).

The second section focuses on the introduction of on-site immersive environmental visualization strategies. The third section focuses on the setting up of an off-site interactive citizen participation interface to actively engage Seoul citizens in the analysis and rationalization of the acquired data.

Mobile Urban Sensing Technologies (MUST). a) Sensing kit over private vehicle in Princeton University campus. b) Sensing kit circuit.

3. Acquisition of high-spatiotemporal-resolution urban air quality data

In order to understand the local variability of the air quality across the different neighborhoods in the city, data with higher spatiotemporal resolutions are to be collected. For this purpose, we have developed novel mobile urban sensing technologies through the coupling of sensing kits to mobile platforms such as private vehicles or public transportation networks.

The main advantage of the proposed sensing methodology lies in its flexibility that allows mounting the kit on any type of mobile vehicle. Furthermore, readily available and cheap sensors are used to enable the scalability of the project. Through these two strategies, a high-spatial-resolution air quality collection is sought.

The proposed sensing kit contains sensors for Carbon Monoxide, Ozone, Particulate Matter, Carbon Dioxide, Temperature, and Humidity. The sensing kits are also equipped with a GPS shield that enables them to be geolocalized in real time. Furthermore, the kit also comprises a cellular antenna that enables the acquired data to be transmitted in near real time to an online database. The kit is powered by a Photovoltaic cell which is connected to a rechargeable Lithium-ion battery to enhance its flexibility to be coupled to diverse mobile platforms. Some of the sensing kits are also equipped with video cameras which, depending on the collected environmental values, are triggered, and snapshots of the context are saved in the online database.

4. Augmented environmental visualizations

Aiming for a qualitative display of the acquired air quality data, we sought a three-dimensional visualization strategy. With this ambition, the research focuses on the implementation of environmental representation platforms designed to visualize air quality data. Video processing techniques, Geographic Information Systems (GIS), and Augmented Reality (AR) technologies are combined to provide photorealistic live-streaming of the recorded air quality data over the local urban setting. This approach aims for an intuitive and informational understanding of local environmental conditions in relation to further urban parameters.

While the use of AR technologies for immersive representational purposes is becoming more wide-spread, their use for environmental visualization has not yet been explored. In this context, this re-search argues that the use of AR for environmental visualization may prove powerful for engaging citizens in the discussion of urban environmental quality. With this ambition, two AR environmental visualization strategies have been developed:

1. An AR mobile app has been designed for on-site air quality visualization. Its information visualization corresponds to real-time data acquired from urban GIS, sensing networks, and real-time video processing techniques.
2. An off-site AR immersive environmental visualization is also currently under development to display data also acquired from GIS and sensing networks.

Both approaches will enable the visualization of urban parameters such as streets and buildings, as well as their surface characteristics against urban environmental and microclimatic data to inform citizens by uncovering relationships between air quality and further urban metrics.

4.1 AR app for environmental visualization on smartphones

We have been developing a mobile app that combines mobile GIS technologies with computer vision and video processing techniques to correlate urban and environmental parameters as compre-hensible visualizations.

The goal is to create a user-centered app that enables a direct engagement with the surround-ing environment.

Two AR environmental visualization modes will be enabled: the first-person view and the map view. In the first-person view, locational services

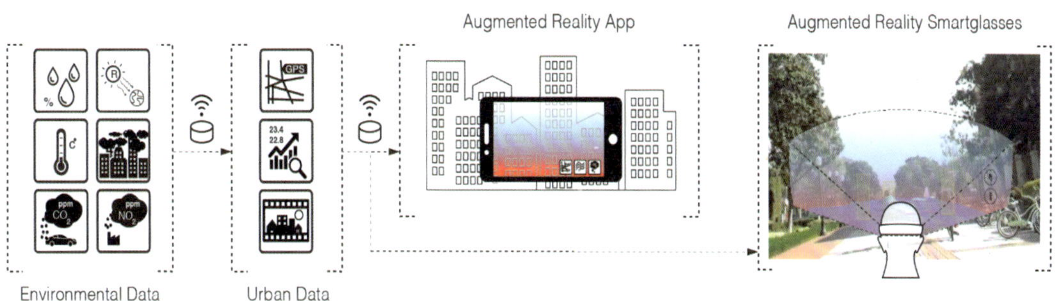

(a) The Collected Environmental Data is coupled with (b) Urban Data which is visual-ized through (c) An App interface (The example shows a temperature gradient visualiza-tion) as well as through d) Spatial environmental visualization over urban intersections

App interface design. Left, temperature gradient visualization.
Right, humidity gradient visualization

of the user's mobile device are accessed, and by referencing the mobile GIS platform, geotagged environmental data is overlaid on the camera view as graphic filters. The app also enables a map view of the environmental data by accessing geolocation and using Google Map API services over which environmental gradients are overlaid.

The local weather data for the app visualization are acquired from the sensing kit described in section 3 and through queries to online web services such as OpenWeatherMap and AQICN. Through these combined sources, data on temperature, humidity, and air quality are collected. Furthermore, through GeoNames geocoding, the location for the different urban intersections is stored. Intersection are then identified with markers and their spatially-distributed air quality values displayed. That is, when a user points the smartphone towards a nearby intersection, the app draws a marker over the intersection to show the street names as well as the relevant environmental data for that given intersection. Thus, the app allows the user to associate certain temperatures or AQI values with the urban fabric. Finally, the collected

environmental data are stored in an online database, and these data can be queried by each user through the app based on their geolocation.

4.2 Augmented Reality exhibition space Seoul 2017 Biennale

The exhibition space for the Seoul 2017 Architecture and Urbanism Biennale is being designed as an off-site space for data analysis and rationalization. A narrative on the research methodology will be included along with the interactive data visualizations. AR interface handsets will be made available to the visitors so they can experience the collected air quality data as well as the historical air quality data available in the Seoul city archives.

The air quality data displayed at the city-scale visualization will be gathered through queries to online web services such as OpenWeatherMap and AQICN as well as Seoul city weather station databases. These data will be visualized alongside the air quality data gathered from MUST. The combination of weather station with pedestrian level recordings aims to offer a holistic description of the local air quality characteristics.

Exhibition AR work in progress

Through the AR interface, the visitor will be able to select environmental parameters and compare them against urban parameters such as building structures or urban surface characteristics. Through an immersive visualization, the user will be able to zoom in on the desired areas, look into the environmental parameters of interest, or establish correlations with other urban parameters. The interaction of Biennale visitors with the deployed visualization interface will be tracked in order to study user behavior. This backend survey will be exhibited along with the projections.

Acknowledgements

The authors thank the SEAS Princeton University Innovation grant and the USC Media Arts and Practice school for their financial support, and would like to extend their gratitude to Arman Atoyan, Arman Zakaryan, Jongmin Kim, Jeehwan Bae and Zhan Chen for their contribibution to the research.

Yellow Dust

Nerea Calvillo

Since the Industrial Revolution, the air has been
an artificial environment that has become an
indicator of the Anthropocene. Peter Sloterdijk
claims that it was not until the twentieth century
that the air was designed, when the Germans
used toxic gas as a weapon during World War I
(2005; 2009). However, as the architect historian
Reyner Banham pointed out, the air—and, even
more, air pollution—has been mostly absent
from debates about architecture and urbanism.
What do we need to know about it in order to
operate in/with it? How can we, as architects,
start dealing with it? Can we think of doing
what Sloterdijk termed "air design" (2009), and
if so, which tools do we have to develop it?

To respond to these questions, and inspired
by Science and Technology Studies (STS) and
feminist technoscience, we have been thinking
about urban air as a complex sociotechnical
assemblage (Farías and Bender 2010), in order to
acknowledge its materiality, its effects, its bodies,
and its politics. If, as a heuristic, we considered
this aerial sociotechnical assemblage as a city,
what would its urbanisms be?

Commons and infrastructures

The atmosphere is the (sometimes) invisible
dump of capitalist practices, but it is also a
fundamental component of human and more
than human life, that which makes us breathers.
We inhale and exhale thousands of times a day,
and still we take the air for granted. However,
the more polluted the air is becoming globally,
the more its image is shifting from an infinite
resilient space with never-ending waste-
absorption capacities, to a limited resource that
needs to be taken care for. For this reason it
has been conceptualised as one of the global

commons (see Helfrich 2008; Klein 2014). And, as this book's introduction also suggests, we need infrastructures to deal with them, as part of the "imminent urban commons."

This proposal is a speculation about infrastructures for the air. However, there are some practical difficulties when thinking about how to deal with air. The air is a relational entity, with components that react among themselves, with the weather, or any material that gets suspended in it. This implies that the air is different at neighbourhood, national, or global scales. The air is not apprehensible, controllable, or limitable, which poses difficulties for its management. It also travels with the wind, very far away, carrying seeds, ashes, microbes, dust, or radiation to places where they may not be expected or wanted. Very often, in our times, the air is polluted, which makes palpable its pharmakon condition of being a cure and a danger according to its concentrations. One immediate response to this fact would be to claim that it needs to be cleaned. But how does one clean a global circulating entity when the economic system that has set up this situation does not seem to be changing soon? Deep structural changes are needed to transition from an approach of merely cleaning the air towards not polluting it, no doubt about it. But as Laurent Berlant (2016) has argued, we need forms to deal with the transition which involve, among other things, inhabiting polluted sites.

However, there is also a conceptual difficulty when thinking about the infrastructures needed to engage with the commons. What kind of infrastructures are we talking about, and what do we mean exactly by "commons"? Infrastructures are not only technological devices, but as STS

have well demonstrated, they are socio-technical assemblages composed by hard, soft, human, and nonhuman entities, situated and networked in different ways (Graham and Marvin 2009; Leigh and Bowker 2006; Schick and Winthereik 2016; Star 1999). Thus, we are interested here in the infrastructures that allow us to manage the "terms of transition that alter the harder and softer, tighter and looser infrastructures of sociality itself" (Berlant 2016: 394). And in the infrastructures able to engage with the different materialities of air, but which also take into consideration and engage openly with their social implications, inspired by Berlant's question: "what kind of life is an infrastructure" (2016: 394)?

The commons is an unruly concept, as it takes various forms and approaches depending on the context and author. It tends to bring together resources, property rights, and regulations. But one of the problems of relating the concept of the commons to limited resource management is that the discussion ends up being about economy and costs. Frequently, the infrastructures designed to deal with toxic air are framed from this perspective, mostly as infrastructures to clean the polluted air. These may partially contribute to remediating particles' concentrations, but are clearly not addressing the causes, the emission of pollutants. So, in which other ways can an infrastructure of a common (the air) also be an infrastructure for an expanded idea of the common, one that addresses other forms of being together? With this question comes another problem, because as Berlant (2016) argues, the desired common often reinforces an idea of the collective based on agreement and belonging (to a community, a state). Considering the challenges that these idealistic approaches imply in terms of who belongs to that common and how—inspired in nonsovereign critiques, for instance—we follow Berlant in her proposal of focusing instead on proximity and detection, as "the experience of affect, of being receptive, in real time" (2016: 402). How do we start thinking about infrastructures to deal with the air that enable these other forms of co-habitation in our context of industrial toxicity, financial insecurity, and permanent war?

Philosopher Marina Garcés (2013) argues that due to the complexity of this context, thinking "what to do" can be paralysing. Therefore, she suggests thinking instead about how to change our modes of dealing with things, with each other, and the world. If before these modes have been focused on representation and action, she proposes to shift towards "attention and treatment." Following Garcés, Yellow Dust is conceived as an infrastructure to deal with the toxic air in a common world; instead of asking what to do with the polluted air, this infrastructure aims to test whether there are other modes of paying attention to it that involve forms of treatment other than cleaning. But again as Berlant (2016) argues, these infrastructures for the commons acknowledge a broken world, but they also trigger new ways of living in it. I take this as an invitation (and responsibility, from Berlant) to speculate, which is the only possible way of dealing with our troubled times, as Haraway claims (2016); this means not only observing the state of reality, but intervening in it (Guggenheim et al., forthcoming). So overall, Yellow Dust is a speculation on what air design can do to engage with the urbanisms of the air, what can it mean to care for the environment, and more specifically, to deal with air pollution . In other words, it asks: what can "air design" do for dealing with the Anthropocene? What can other forms of sensing do in our relation with the air?

Yellow Dust

Yellow Dust is a three-dimensional water vapour canopy that provides information about air pollution and, more specifically, about particulate matter (PM 2.5). Drawing on architectural references like Diller and Scofidio's Blur Building (2002), it is made of fog and is reactive to meteorological changes. It is also an inhabitable and media infrastructure, with a fundamental difference from the Blur Building: the media is not meant to be a display of art or information, but to reveal its own constitution and experience data. In this sense it relates to Philippe Rahm Architecte's Jade Eco Park in Taiwan (2005-) in its intention to condition the public space, as well as to Living Light, The Living's pavilion in Seoul (2009), relying not only on vision, but also exploring less representational and more experiential modes of dealing with knowledge and information.

Yellow Dust's canopy generates a floating misty environment that changes density (and therefore the conditions of visibility, humidity, etc.) in relation to the concentrations of particulate matter in the air. It performs counter-intuitively, almost paired with the visual conditions of the dust: the more dust, the thicker the cloud, embracing and intensifying the blurriness of our contemporary cities, where the transparency of the modern movement cannot be achieved anymore.

The data is collected by two self-made DIY sensors, which provide alternative data to the Seoul Metropolitan Government. The reason for using DIY sensors, instead of getting the data from the closest official monitoring station, is to test the remediation capacity of the cloud, because as water sediments dust, it may reduce

Yellow Dust, prototype

Yellow Dust, detail

the concentrations of aerial particles. Thus, one sensor is above the cloud and the other below it, at ground level. The main objective is to explore forms of engagement with the toxic air alternative to existing monitoring practices, by paying attention to and speculating about other conditions of the air.

But, what do we need to know about air pollution in the city, as passers-by, neighbours, and architects? Yellow Dust suggests other aspects of the air that deserve attention. It moves from numbers to intensities of water vapour, showing the changes of particle concentrations by other means. The decoding of the information is therefore not immediate, and it may take time for passers-by to be able to compare the conditions of the mist with those of previous hours or days. It requires time to get to know it, detaching from speed of information tropes.

The intensities do not relate to the Air Quality Index, either. The Air Quality Index (AQI) is a colour gradient that correlates the concentration of particles with their effect in human health. There are two reasons for avoiding this relation. First, the project is part of wider research that aims to find other modes of attending to the air beyond human health. This is not to say that human health does not matter. It takes into consideration that every body— human or not—reacts to pollution differently. So, from a cosmopolitical approach, to account for all bodies and their diverse sensitivities to particles, it does not specifically address any of them. Each body might get used to or attuned to the infrastructure, or learn to be affected by it. Second, it is not clear what role human health plays when informing citizens in real-time at a specific location. As AQI advises when to stay indoors, if displayed at a specific location it could reduce the quantity of passers-by, for instance, and put local commerce at risk and therefore threaten other aspects of human life, affecting the less privileged people.

It is relevant to note at this point that the project is not focused on prediction. It reacts to positivist understandings of information, where knowledge produces immediate behavioural change. This is because studies of the impact of air pollution data on citizens have demonstrated that information does not necessarily produce behavioural change. Therefore, the project aims to find alternative modes of engaging with the environment beyond the cognitive, by being attuned to toxicity, recognizing, or detecting it.

The colour of the fog also plays a role in paying attention differently; in this case, it helps to identify and locate oneself within conditions that are simultaneously local and planetary. It is coloured yellow in reference to the Yellow Dust (*Hwangsa* in Korean), transboundary fine soil particles carried by the wind from Mongolia and Northern China, mostly during the spring, which bring with them other types of industrial pollutants. Although there are frequently high levels of particles created by local sources, Yellow Dust creates a sense of invasion, of matter out of place, which reinforces the distinction between local and foreign air, and triggers legal and political international battles. Which forms of intervention could be opened up that may not get trapped in colonial bias and forms of dealing with the other? Our installation unsettles the idea of the yellow dust as a foreign and unwanted entity, and reveals, in the months when Hwangsa is not blowing, whether there is pollution of local particles in Seoul's atmosphere.

Other forms of knowing

Yellow Dust proposes an alternative form of getting to know the air. Currently, to get information about air pollution we need to look at digital devices, from mobile phones, to computers or even urban screens. Yellow Dust instead surpasses this mediation and displays air quality information right *in* the air, exactly where it has been measured. The project also expands other forms of sensing or experiencing environmental data that differ from those used by institutional monitoring systems based on vision. The water vapour creates a soft mist of humidity that can be experienced by breath and contact with the skin, which aims to democratise the perception of air pollution and to pay attention to the unevenness of its effects. Only sensitive bodies sense pollution, but it is likely that more bodies sense humidity. In days of high particle concentrations (Hwangsa or not), there are several modes of sensory overlap: visual (the colour of pollution, the colour of the mist), skin-based (through humidity and the temperature of the mist), and the nose, eyes, or lungs (for particle-sensitive bodies). Water vapour sometimes alleviates asthma symptoms, so the infrastructure may also serve as a relief. Overall, it produces an overlapping—or even excessive—sensorial experience.

Transforming environments

The fog not only alters human forms of sensing data, but conditions the urban space, changing its temperature and humidity conditions. This conditioning may also have other effects such as remediating particulate matter. As water deposits particles, water vapour may contribute to this process, reducing its concentrations. The installation is therefore an experiment in remediation that tests the decrease in particles from above and below the mist. This hypothesis is inspired by the old practice in many countries of watering the streets to reduce dust storms. Should we water parts of our cities? Could this be a coping strategy for highly polluted areas?

Urban infrastructures

Yellow Dust is also a speculation on urban infrastructures. As a monitoring infrastructure, it measures and makes visible in the same place, right where the measured object is. It reveals its own infrastructure, the steel that sustains the water vaporisers, the sensors, the cables that channel the water, the lights, and so on, as opposed to scientific and policy-making versions of air monitoring devices, which are invisible and black-boxed. Yellow Dust has a visible infrastructure because one of the problems of ubiquitous systems is that their invisibility reduces our possibility of understanding their performance, and therefore our possibility of intervention. From an eco-systemic perspective, it also makes visible what it takes to monitor and display air pollution information, through water- and energy-consumption meters.

However, the main components of the installation are water vapour and data, distributed across space and time in an untraceable way. They create some sort of atmospheric media, bringing together technologies and urban conditions below the threshold of sensing. Media and the air become the same thing, elemental conditions that perform as a chemical interaction, as a milieu, and as an environment. From here we ask whether in this specific type of infrastructure, it is possible to distinguish between the technology and the matter that acts upon it, since the infrastructure and what is sensed cannot be disentangled, or indeed differentiated. The water vapour dissolves in the air, becoming one. So not only does the infrastructure become atmospheric, but it makes the air infrastructural too, by being the support of its own data, literally making itself visible.

References

Berlant, L. (2016) "The Commons: Infrastructures for Troubling Times." *Environment and Planning D: Society and Space* 34 (3): 393–419.

Farías, I., and Benders, T. (eds.) (2010) *Urban Assemblages*. London, New York: Routledge.

Garcés, M. (2013) *Un mundo común*. Barcelona: Ediciones Bellaterra.

Graham, S., and Marvin, S. (2009) *Splintering Urbanism: Networked Infrastructures, Technological Mobilities and the Urban Condition*. London, New York: Routledge.

Guggenheim, M., Kräftner, B., and Kröll, J. (forthcoming) "Creating Idiotic Speculators: Disaster Cosmopolitics in the Sandbox." In Rosengarten, M., Savransky, M., and Wilkie, A. (eds.), *Speculative Research: The Lure of the Possible*. London: Routledge.

Haraway, D. (2016) *Staying with the Trouble: Making Kin in the Chthulucene*. Durham, NC: Duke University Press.

Helfrich, S. (ed.) (2008) *Genes, Bytes y Emisiones: Bienes Comunes y Ciudadanía*. Mexico: Fundación Heinrich Böll.

Klein, N. (2014) *This Changes Everything: Capitalism vs. the Climate*. New York: Simon & Shuster.

Leigh, S., and Bowker, G. C. (2006) "How to Infrastructure." In Lievrouw, L. A., and Livingstone, S. (eds.), *The Handbook of New Media*, 230–245. London: Sage.

Schick, L., and Winthereik, B. R. (2016) "Making Energy Infrastructure: Tactical Oscillations and Cosmopolitics." *Science as Culture* 25 (1): 44–68.

Sloterdijk, P. (2005) *Esferas III*. Barcelona: Siruela.

Sloterdijk, P. (2009) *Terror from the Air*. Cambridge, London: The MIT Press.

Star, S. L. (1999) "The Ethnography of Infrastructure." *American Behavioral Scientist* 43 (3): 377–391.

Floating Lives, Eastern Clouds, a Seaweed Archipelago

MAP Office
(Laurent Gutierrez and Valérie Portefaix)

"The biomass of seaweed and algae in the ocean is enormous. Algae are responsible for 80% of the organic production on our planet and almost 90% of the oxygen production."
Ole Mouritsen

The ocean is a research domain ripe with possibilities, which can aid in the future development of the planet. With many zones yet to be fully explored, maritime study is critical at this moment in history when the oceans are so endangered by human activities. One of the potential ways to preserve the ocean's assets for future generations is to exploit the economic value of its ecosystems (estimated at US$25,000 billion). Another is to consider the complex organisms that inhabit oceans, such as marine algae and sea grasses, which together produce more oxygen than coral reefs and rainforests combined. This is a starting point for exploring a new territory that offers an irreplaceable archive for recognizing and sustaining the future.[1]

One of the primary goals of MAP Office's research is to reveal the relationships which exist between the lives of Pacific coastline communities and the abundance of seaweed found in those areas. Learning from the history of the algae in these regions, we aim to forge a new perspective on how humans have sustained themselves through dynamic exchanges between nature and culture, sea and soil, survival and production. An important medical and dietary product, seaweed has long been feeding and protecting a majority of sea life, fish, and shellfish—as well as their surrounding human communities. Considered prehistorically as an essential "brain food," these "vegetables of the

---

1. In March 2016, MAP Office organized the first Ocean Archive discussion as part of AAA Open Platform Art Basel HK. Inviting several art historians, an art critic, a sociologist, artists, and designers to participate in a roundtable discussion, we questioned the mapping of Asia through a compilation of islands, archipelagoes, and what is left in between.

sea," along with other maritime products, have been a primary source of omega-3 fatty acids in the human diet—encouraging the brain to grow bigger and therefore aiding in the development of human intelligence. In China, Korea, Japan, and India, the early use of seaweed followed a parallel history to the use of tea. Herbal medicines from the land, as well as from the sea, have been used for centuries to relieve muscle tensions, constipation, and chronic bronchitis. These associations can be observed in various writings and poetry promoting marine algae as a precious source of wellness. According to Ole Mouritsen,[2] in the oldest Japanese-Chinese dictionary, dated to 934 CE, twenty-one different species of edible seaweeds are described, and instructions are given for their preparation. This knowledge has been transferred along the coastline and across time. Sometimes considered a noble product, seaweed was also associated with wealth, used as a means to produce salt and to pay taxes to local authorities. More recently, its use was extended onto land as a fertilizer for plants or as food for domestic animals, including cattle and mutton, when grass was unattainable.

The starting point of our research is Asia, where the specific geography of the coastline has led to the development of various unique and extensive examples of floating communities. Located at the periphery of the land, most of the floating villages and clusters are found on rivers, lakes, or nearby coastlines, small bays protected from storms and other difficult climatic conditions. Generally, life on the periphery presents a strategic position with specific characteristics that define the condition of the floating village itself. For example, the coastal areas of Japan, Korea, China, the Philippines, and Hawaii have been greatly influenced by the collection and/

or cultivation of seaweed, which is celebrated in festivals and food culture. The Pacific Ocean, older and less affected by ice formation than the Atlantic, contains the largest variety of seaweed of all the oceans. Growing at the interface between land and sea, most of the marine flora is natural and reaches human beings as a gift from the sea. Since prehistory, the Pacific Islands population migrated along the coastlines and harvested various shellfish and seaweed, which provided them with their daily nutrients. For thousands of years in the Polynesian Islands, seaweed was cultivated in special sea gardens designed to host no less than seventy different species. Meeting the early morning tide along the coastline of Okinawa, Jeju Island, or in the Philippines, it is still quite common to observe inhabitants (often elderly) collecting seaweed for their own daily consumption or to pickle in jars.

In Hong Kong, communities which live on the water are still very active, protected by little bays around Sai Kung or Lantau Island. They appear as single entities, disconnected from the others, even when located in the vicinity of small urban settlements. Their floating infrastructures are made with simple materials—a mix of bamboo, fabrics, and plastic containers. They appear as a fragile group of platforms ready to be swept away by the next typhoon, especially when compared to the enormous weight of the city nearby. Yet, it is their diversity, flexibility, and fluidity that have allowed these structures to last for hundreds of years—surviving climatic pressures, political movements, border lines, wars, and economic crises.

In contrast to the (unstable) land, water has often played the role of a peaceful shelter where poor and endangered communities can take refuge.

2. Ole Mouritsen, *Seaweeds: Edible, Available, and Sustainable* (Chicago: University of Chicago Press, 2013).

Little bays, called *agea* in Greek according to Aristotle,[3] are an archetype of comfort geography, providing sustainable protection for a population. As a result, their principal relation with the land has mainly been trade, creating a positive ecological complement to their land-dwelling neighbors—for example, trading fish or salt for rice or fabrics.

In the northeast of Hong Kong, on High Island, we have been mapping an enduring model of a floating village, one which survives by cultivating seafood directly underneath their little houses. With about sixty inhabitants whose average age is seventy, the village is a model that could soon disappear. As the next generation long ago chose to live on land, this three-dimensional live/work economy and ecology represents a mode of living which could soon be replaced by new modes of leisure and tourist industry. As a paradigmatic case study, this floating village is the site for "The Island of Sea," one of the eight fictional island scenarios we developed for "Uneven Growth,"[4] an exhibition speculating on the future of cities that we shifted into the future of the sea.

In Asia, the network of floating settlements cannot constitute a distinctive region, even if many of them are inhabited by the same tribes: Hakka, Tonka, Mergui, etc. The coastlines are extremely complicated due to the extensive number of islands, and include thousands of bays, each with specific, unique characteristics. Nonetheless, several typologies of life on the water are shared by China's Fujian Province, Ha Long Bay in Vietnam, and Bobojong in Indonesia. They have each set up an industrial economy rather than just producing enough to feed themselves. They also share the same types of problems today, including an aging population, pollution, climate change, and exhaustion of resources.

China's Fujian Province contains the world's largest seafood and seaweed farming community. The region of Ningde accommodates the famous floating village Sandu'dao, which is made up of five islets and one peninsula. Recognized as the world's largest floating community, with about 12,000 inhabitants, it has developed in complete autonomy from the land; in fact, until the 1950s its inhabitants were not allowed to enter China. Sandu'dao is a complete floating settlement, with a gas station, post office, police station, medical center, and a few restaurants and convenience stores. Completely dependent on seafood production originally, and on aquaculture tourism more recently, it is a self-contained community that has managed to develop a unique complex economy combining seaweed with abalone farming. Yet, since the late 1980s, the introduction of artificial breeding and the increasing prices of abalone have transformed Sandu'dao into a powerful floating industrial infrastructure, employing hundreds of migrant workers in the management of the sea farms.

In North Asia, seaweed still represents a major food source in the everyday diet. To meet the demand, seaweed aquaculture has recently been scaled up. In Japan, the method of mass producing nori dates from the 1950s when systems of nets suspended above water could adjust to the various depths needed to grow the Porphyra algae in its complex germination stage. Specific depths, currents, temperatures, and levels of sun perforation are all essential to the development of specific types of seaweeds and help to explain their rich variety.

3. Aristotle, *Historia Animalium* IX, 622a: 2–10. About 400 BC.

4. "Uneven Growth," curated by Pedro Gadanho, Museum of Modern Art, New York, 2014.

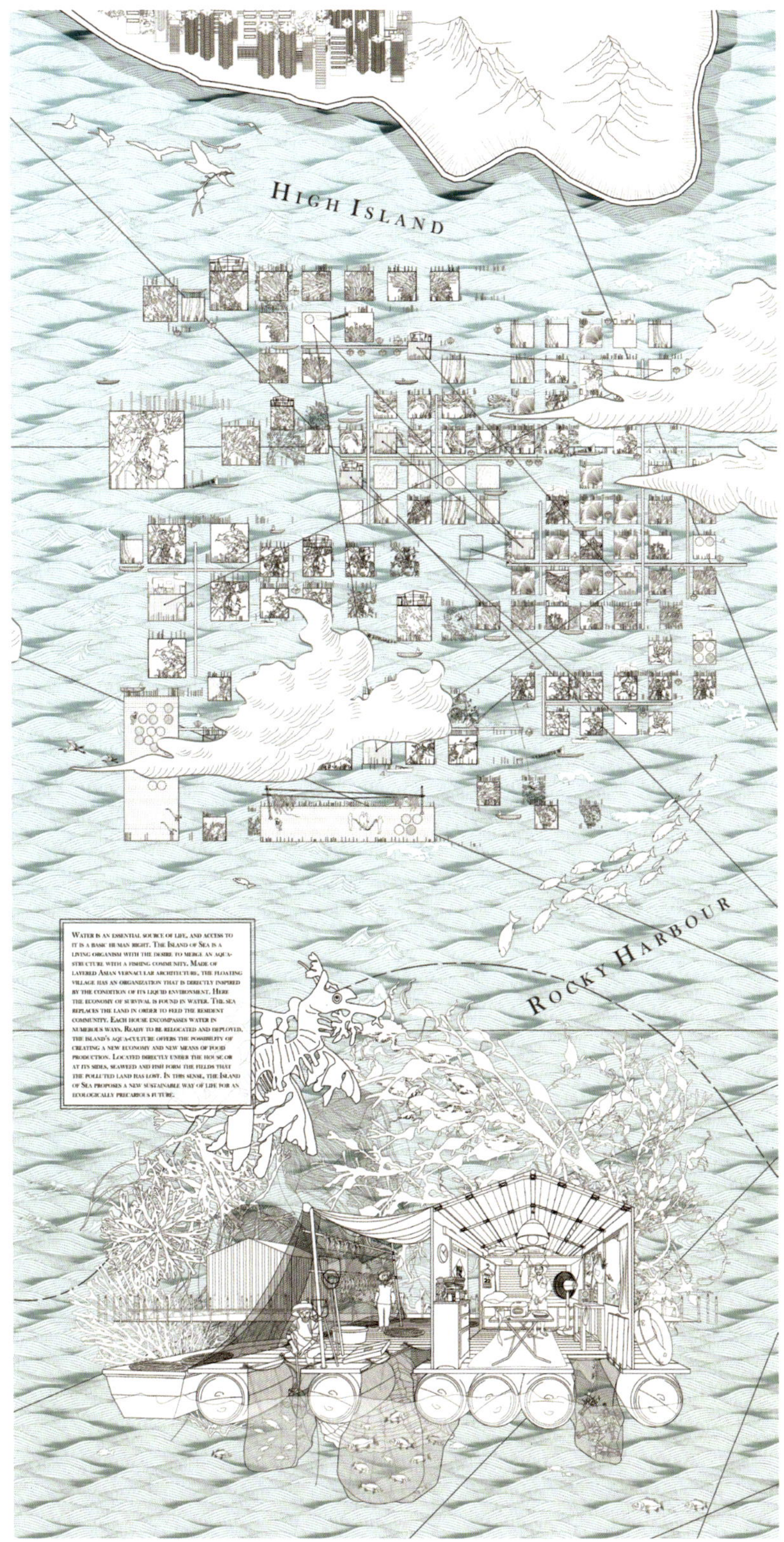

HIGH ISLAND
ROCKY HARBOUR
WATER IS AN ESSENTIAL SOURCE OF LIFE, AND ACCESS TO IT IS A BASIC HUMAN RIGHT. THE ISLAND OF SEA IS A LIVING ORGANISM WITH THE DESIRE TO MERGE AN AQUA-STRUCTURE WITH A FISHING COMMUNITY. MADE OF LAYERED ASIAN VERNACULAR ARCHITECTURE, THE FLOATING VILLAGE HAS AN ORGANIZATION THAT IS DIRECTLY INSPIRED BY THE CONDITION OF ITS LIQUID ENVIRONMENT. HERE THE ECONOMY OF SURVIVAL IS FOUND IN WATER. THE SEA REPLACES THE LAND IN ORDER TO FEED THE RESIDENT COMMUNITY. EACH HOUSE ENCOMPASSES WATER IN NUMEROUS WAYS. READY TO BE RELOCATED AND DEPLOYED, THE ISLAND'S AQUA-CULTURE OFFERS THE POSSIBILITY OF CREATING A NEW ECONOMY AND NEW MEANS OF FOOD PRODUCTION. LOCATED DIRECTLY UNDER THE HOUSE OR AT ITS SIDES, SEAWEED AND FISH FORM THE FIELDS THAT THE POLLUTED LAND HAS LOST. IN THIS SENSE, THE ISLAND OF SEA PROPOSES A NEW SUSTAINABLE WAY OF LIFE FOR AN ECOLOGICALLY PRECARIOUS FUTURE.

And it is specifically their diversity that offers an opportunity for exploration in the art of gastronomy. For example, traditional Japanese cuisine and new Nordic cuisine both use seaweeds for their special umami flavor. In Hong Kong, we organized with Chef Christina Keung the first Seaweed Gala Dinner at the Genuine Lamma Hilton Fishing Village Restaurant. Keung prepared an eleven-course dinner which combined seaweeds that she had collected at the restaurant's pier with shrimp, razor clams, crabs, and rabbit fish. As she joked: "The enemy of the seaweed is the rabbit fish since they eat seaweed. If you see a lot of rabbit fish, it means it is seaweed season! Then, a few local fishermen will use a sampan armed with a bamboo stick to harvest the seaweed. They will dry them, and beyond their own consumption, they sell them to the herbal shop or to tourists… On our side we eat them together with the rabbit fish; it's yummy…"[5]

While taking the opportunity to participate in the Seoul Biennale of Architecture and Urbanism, this research will find new locations of seaweed in Seoul and will develop specific local knowledge, learning from the Korean culture of seaweeds and its 5,000-year history. An exhibition will develop the six principles of seaweed (as marine organisms, benthic organisms, filters, motile, colonies, and productive machines); a film will retrace the history of the Korean birthday soup and its mythologies; and a special two-day seaweed food event with Hong Kong–based Korean Chef Sook[6] (Mina Park) will experiment with seaweeds in contemporary cuisine.
In Korea, marine algae have been considered with reverence, as they constitute about 10% of the population's total nutritional intake.

Cultivation of seaweed, especially the green and red algae, has been mastered over a period of centuries. Growing in the wild along the shallow waters of the Korean Peninsula, there is also a brown algae (Hijiki) used for its blades, which are sun-dried, boiled, and sun-dried again until they are black. The practice of eating seaweed is common; seaweed can be found in every kitchen and in a great diversity of regional cuisines. Today, it is also consumed as pressed, roasted, and dried seaweed, which is now recognized as a healthy snack, packaged in ten rectangular pieces, and sold for a cheap price in any type of food store. Organic, iodine-rich, abundant in minerals and vitamins, seaweeds are now seasoned with a multiplicity of flavors to respond to the multiplicity in the demand of the market.

Capitalizing on the food chain, the eco/nomy/logy of the seaweed appears to us today as one of the biggest opportunities for the planet in the age of the Anthropocene. Beyond offering a simple and picturesque conception of a sustainable environment, we want to suggest that seaweed can offer a bright future where we are able to live in symbiosis with our eco-system.

* We would like to express our gratitude to Ingrid Chu, Christina Keung, and Pelin Tan.

5. Christina Keung, interviewed by MAP Office and Pelin Tan, Hong Kong, 23 April 2016.

6. Sook produces a series of private kitchen and pop-up dining events in Hong Kong and internationally; see her website, www.sook.hk

The Six Principles of Seaweed

SCALE 1 – GLOBAL Atmosphere
Can we still behave as if the human species is
the most essential organism on the planet? An
affirmative answer to this question echoes the
Anthropocene epoch, complete with its set of
emerging problems. Today, there is no doubt that
human production and consumption have had
and continue to have a tremendous impact on the
earth's atmospheric cycle. Yet, it is also true that
we humans as organisms contribute only a small
amount to the production of the atmosphere.
In fact, it is the small, almost invisible micro
and macro algae, phytoplankton, and seaweeds
that produce an average of 70% to 80% of the
air (and oxygen) in the atmosphere through the
process of photosynthesis. If one of the oldest
living organisms on the planet is essential to
the production of the atmosphere, they must
have also contributed to human development in
various ways so as to support human life.

SCALE 2 – LOCAL coastlines
With around 12,000 species currently known,
the biodiversity of seaweed offers a complex
family structure from which we can extract six
principles to establish the relationship between
coastline settlements and their immediate
environment. Together, they propose a lexical
construction of the macro algae and their
possible contribution to life around them.
In that sense, the six sequences represent the
majority of the characteristics with which most
of the species can be identified.

First seaweed principle: The majority of
seaweeds are **marine** organisms, or live in
an aquatic environment. They inhabit a very
large portion of the ocean and therefore of the

planet. Attached to the seabed or floating across
currents, they are an essential source of life for
many species, including human beings.

Second seaweed principle: Seaweeds are
benthic organisms, along with crabs, clams,
sponges, and other tiny organisms living in
bottom sediments. They live attached to the sea
floor along the littoral zone, cleaning up the sea
floors and scavenging on dead organisms.

Third seaweed principle: Seaweeds are natural
filters. As they filter the water for food, they
remove sediments and organic substances,
cleaning the water. They have proven to be useful
tools in improving water quality in endangered
areas such as the Great Barrier Reef.

Fourth seaweed principle: Seaweeds are **motile**.
Motility allows their constant adaptation to the
host environment, with an ability to reproduce
itself. This biological faculty is the key to their
survival and their proliferation in extreme
contexts. They are considered to have been the
first organism in history with self-sexual ability.

Fifth seaweed principle: Seaweeds aggregate to
live in **colonies**. They coexist with other species
through integration and sometimes through
collaboration. They can source the basis for their
growth and development from their immediate
living environment.

Sixth seaweed principle: Seaweeds are
productive machines; they convert sunlight
energy into chemical components—vitamins,
minerals, iodine, and omega-3. The
photosynthesis process visible through their
pigmentation (red, brown, and green) is the basis
of 70% of the world's oxygen production.

The Seoul Biome

Carlo Ratti and Newsha Ghaeli

A vast reservoir of information on human health and behavior lives in our sewage, yet this resource is untapped. We envision a future in which sewage is mined for real-time information that can inform policy makers, health practitioners, and researchers alike. An innovative and cross-disciplinary research endeavor for monitoring urban health patterns, this work aims to shape more inclusive public health strategies and push the boundaries of urban epidemiology. Spearheaded by the Senseable City Lab and Alm Lab at the Massachusetts Institute of Technology, a team of architects and biologists travelled to Seoul to investigate the Korean capital's microbiome. This real-time human-health monitoring project, named Underworlds and explained herein, consists of a physical infrastructure, biological and chemical measurement technologies, and downstream computational tools and analytics to interpret and act on the findings.

Why Sewage?

From Dr. Jon Snow to the 21st century city

The Underworlds project aims to draw conclusions about the health of our communities. This is often a challenging task: we rely on unreliable surveys and individual doctor's visits for invasive, time-consuming, and costly procedures. But collectively we're parting with health data daily and flushing it down the toilet. As this information aggregates in our sewers, a vast reservoir of information on human health and behavior is born. By tapping into this information highway beneath our feet, Underworlds promises to fundamentally change the way that large-scale public health studies are carried out, and usher in the era of real-time epidemiology.

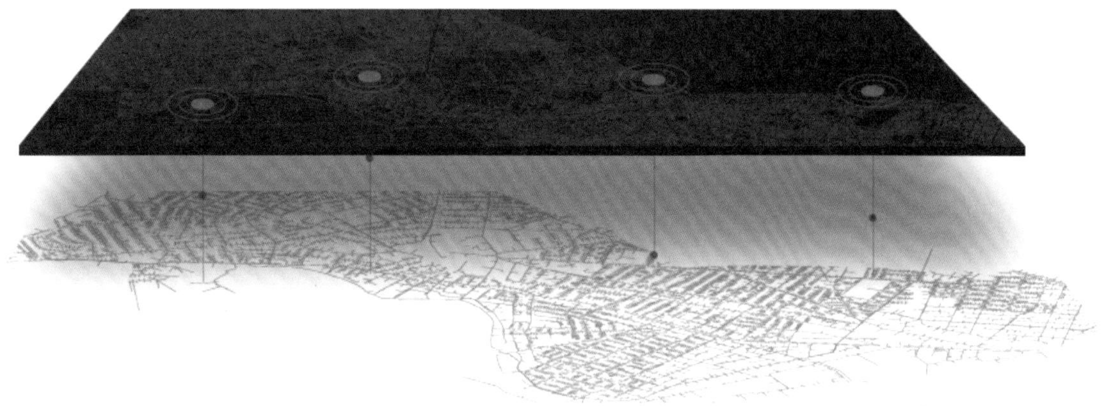

The concept of mapping health data at the neighborhood scale isn't a new one. It was first attempted by Dr. Jon Snow in a very analogue way with his map of London showing the clusters of cholera cases in the 1854 epidemic. The dominant theory held by doctors at the time was that cholera was caused by pollution and was an airborne disease. Snow was skeptical, so he began an elaborate investigation correlating instances of the disease to water quality. Using residents as his data points, he mapped clusters of cholera cases and was able to convincingly trace the source of the outbreak to a single public water pump. With this, Snow gave birth to the modern science of epidemiology and prompted a transformation in wastewater management in London. Today, the combination of rapidly evolving technology and data analytics strategies provide us with an opportunity to bring Jon Snow's approach into the twenty-first century and digitally monitor a population's biological signature.

City science and public health

Underworlds combines novel concepts in smart city design and urban informatics with advancements in biological engineering and bioinformatics. Today's real-time smart city infrastructure is made possible by the combination of rapidly evolving sensor technology, data analytics strategies, and advancements in information communication technologies. Underworlds adds an entirely new dimension to our current ability to capture the behavior and needs of urban populations. Its real-time geo-located monitoring of a population's aggregate biological signature as present in the sewers offers new possibilities for the study of urban health and hygiene patterns. As it contributes to addressing immediate urban health challenges, this new infrastructure will be feeding into the larger picture of a growing urban information economy in ways that expand far beyond the project's currently imaginable applications.

From a public health perspective, the Underworlds project is the first of its kind, and a proof of concept that cities can make use of their wastewater system to do near real-time urban epidemiology and understand human health and behavior with a fine spatio-temporal resolution. Probably the most obvious first application of this smart sewage technology is contagious-disease surveillance and the prediction of outbreaks of infectious disease before symptoms arise. Early warnings in relation to the presence of new flu strains in urban centers could significantly reduce a community's medical costs, save lives, and help prevent epidemics. In addition, smart sewage could change the way noncommunicable diseases are studied, because biomarkers for diseases such as obesity and diabetes can be measured at unprecedented scale and temporal resolution. Beyond refining our present ability to detect and respond to population health, the technologies developed here will give life to a data platform that aims to guide public health policy, municipal strategy, urban planning, and epidemiological science in a larger sense. The system offers the possibility to build rich databases that document, integrate, and analyze fluctuations in urban health parameters over time. Furthermore, it aims to provide a fine spatial and temporal contextualization of health-related data by correlating biometrics with static variables such as wealth distribution, urban density coefficients, and other demographics.

A visionary research project

The Underworlds project has two main goals. First, the project will develop and deploy a novel cyber-physical platform for environmental sensing and sampling from sewage and wastewater networks. This will be coupled with

Underworlds team. The Underworlds team in Cambridge, MA, consisting of architects, biologists, engineers, and visualization specialists.

computational biology tools to characterize biological signatures including metagenomics and metabolomics. The platform will be equipped with data visualization, analytics, and processing tools.

Next, we are focusing on the investigation of several specialized aims using the developed infrastructure. In one aim, they are screening sewage for the prevalence and distribution of infectious pathogens. In another, they are tracking the emergence of antibiotic-resistance genes in the urban microbiome. A third aim focuses on toxicology and monitoring of substances known as phthalates and the use of sewage as a real-time data source to gauge the efficacy of public health policy. An additional aim is to develop bioprospecting strategies in sewage to establish phage therapy as an alternative to antibiotics in combating infectious agents.

A visionary research project spearheaded by the Senseable City Lab and the Alm Lab at the Massachusetts Institute of Technology, the Underworlds group has expanded to include researchers from the Kuwait Institute for Scientific Research, Kuwait University, and MIT researchers from the Department of Biological Engineering, the Department of Civil and Environmental Engineering, and the Computer Science and Artificial Intelligence Laboratory (CSAIL).

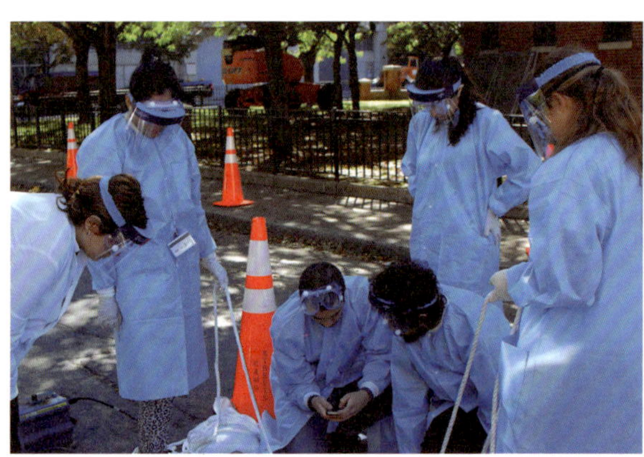

Seoul Underground

In May 2017, MIT researchers from the Underworlds project traveled to the South Korean capital. Armed with their sewage-scavenging robot, Luigi, we sampled three locations: the upscale residential towers of Gangnam, the hilly timeworn homes in Songbuk, and student housing around Hongik University. Presented here is a glimpse into the diverse bacterial and chemical communities that live below these neighborhoods. Leveraging the power of data visualization techniques, we're able to render visible the invisible wealth of information underground.

Sampling methodology

The collection of biological signatures from sewage requires a physical understanding of the wastewater network as well as chemical and biological understanding of the signals themselves. The sampling strategy is in part determined by both of these aspects.

To determine the optimal sampling locations, we studied the network map, urban topology, and demographic distribution in conjunction with wastewater loads over time. With this, we proposed three varying sampling locations. Moreover, we have developed a computational tool which packs this data together into an automated system capable of outputting access points for sampling catchment areas determined by optimizing for population sample size, area, wastewater travel time, and demographic parameters of age, ethnicity, and income.

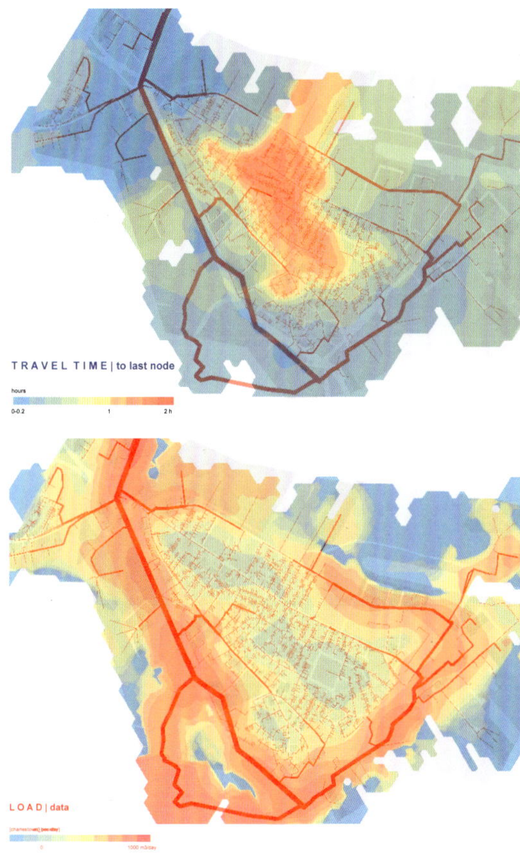

Travel time in sewage system of Charlestown, Boston. (Top) Travel time of waste-water by path length, with the longest path delineated. (Bottom) Waste-water load by population and built area modeling.

Population health census

Our experiments are designed to look for human-derived viruses, bacteria, and chemicals. Viruses for the tracking of disease, as current disease monitoring, is symptomatic. So only when people get sick, and if they choose to go to the hospital, are we able to map outbreaks. With this platform, we can identify the emergence of disease during the incubation period before people become symptomatic, so that hospitals can prepare at the local level. As our understanding of the microbiome continues to grow, this will provide the first expansive database of gut microbiome information at the city-scale. Chemical compounds allow us to measure non-communicable diseases such as obesity and diabetes and we can begin to measure the downstream effects of public health policy. For example, when former former New York Mayor Bloomberg attempted to ban soft drinks, would we have been able to measure the downstream effects of this ban?

Furthermore, the Underworlds platform will be the first proof of concept for estimating human population size based on an endogenous human biomarker. In order to gauge measurements of risk (i.e. viral load and chemical exposures), real-time knowledge of population sizes will be imperative. We will build on published ideas by EPA Research Physical Scientist in the Environmental Chemistry Branch Christian Daughton, who has made an extensive literature review on the subject and has suggested various biomarkers that may correlate with human population sizes. These various human-produced biomarkers (such as creatinine, coprostanol, cortisol, and andro-

stenedione) will be tested, as well as chemicals present in commonly consumed products (such as caffeine, ibuprofen, and paracetamol).

Sampling device

In order to build the rich population health census described above, a tool was required to facilitate sampling over a dozen locations at the scale of the city. This prompted the design priority for a minimum viable tool that could automate the sampling process while at the same time maintaining the integrity of the sample for downstream lab analysis. We developed multiple prototypes (called Mario and Luigi) with varying capabilities and levels of automation. The device used in Seoul—Luigi—allowed for a composite sample to be collected over twenty minutes in an efficient, clean, and easy way. The results are visualized here in a truly holistic representation of their respective communities.

Beyond the Seoul Biennale, the data generated here will be used to compare and contrast against data collected in communities in Cambridge and Boston, Massachusetts, as well as Kuwait City in Kuwait. Together, this will be the first step towards building a comprehensive global database of urban health trends and parameters.

Sampling devices. (Left) Mario, with six discrete sampling containers, was made mostly with custom-made components. (Right) Luigi is a lot smaller, built with mostly off-the-shelf components.

Invasive
Regeneration

RAAD Studio

Invasive Regeneration seeks to explore the complex relationship between nature and the built environment. Nature represents both decay and renewal, and the continual struggle to gain mastery over the natural world can be inverted to foster growth and rebirth.

Natural sunlight is funneled into the installation site via an advanced solar technology, appearing to create plant growth below where the light is delivered. The plant growth then can be observed in the process of rending apart the concrete building. Our technical abilities give us the power to seemingly accelerate time, raising questions of relative scales of time.

1. Introduction

If applying systems of control to the natural world is the hallmark of civilization, as V. Gordon Childe once said, the iconography of the loss of that control is immediately recognizable in the public mind.

When the first images of Hiram Bingham's expedition to Machu Picchu in 1922 or Henri Mouhot's famous images from the discovery of Angkor Wat were published, the imagery of human ambition, loss, and the nearly unmatchable power of nature was crystalized in the public's imagination. People marveled and wondered: how could the mighty have been brought so low? What catastrophe might possibly have toppled a culture with such mastery of the built environment?

Years later, some startling and disturbing realizations about the disappearance of several ancient civilizations invited inevitable comparisons to our own. The Angkor peoples, for example, relentlessly extended their reach

across the surrounding countryside, irrigating,
forming, taming, and controlling nature in
order to fulfill the needs of their complex cities.
But for all their mastery over their environment
and all their cleverness, their resources were
ultimately exhausted. Starvation, conflict, and
collapse followed, and the stone Angkor cities
were in time consumed by the inexorable creep
of the natural world. This is a story mirrored in
those of the fabled Mayan cities, the people of
Pohnpei, and the people of Easter Island.

In our own age, existential questions about the
reach of our built world swiftly come into focus.
What if technological prowess, the progress of
civilization, and the taming of our planet are
actually the agents of our own undoing? What if
the very tools that grew our society put us along
the path to ultimate demise?

The cultural zeitgeist around these sorts of
disturbing thoughts has proven to be fertile
ground for works of art and fiction. The film
Silent Running (1972) envisioned a ruined earth,
one in which all plant life has been preserved
technologically in orbiting pods and cared for by
small robots. In *Twelve Monkeys* (1995), human
life has fled belowground, and we are confronted
by images of a ruined Philadelphia that has been
completely overrun by plants and wildlife.

Taken together, we have a vision in which
technology has become our undoing, with nature
pitifully and completely dependent on us; and
on the other hand, a vision in which humanity
has been vanquished and devoured by nature.

Examining these perspectives on the relationship
of civilization to nature, we have other points
of reference in the creative world as well. *Host

Analog* (1991), a work by Buster Simpson, looks
at human intervention as a means of fostering
both decay and regeneration. A simple bamboo
irrigation tube diverts resources to a fallen tree,
but in doing so creates a planting medium for
new saplings.

My own piece, *Lowline LAB* (2015), draws heavily
upon *The World Without Us* (2007), a "semi-
fictional" book by Alan Weisman, but interpreted
through the lens of technological intervention.
In Weisman's book, several case study sites are
explored in a sort of thought experiment, in
which he envisions what would happen to these
locations if humanity were suddenly gone.

In *Lowline LAB*, we introduced a technology
that harvested natural sunlight and channeled
it into a dark warehouse space. In crafting our
installation, we examined the notion of the built
environment, but on a huge timeline, creating a
planted landscape installation in an abandoned

building that embodied our vision of what might occur if we ran our solar technologies into the distant future, past the time of human civilization. Our past, embodied by the abandoned warehouse, was united, via a vision of the distant future, with visitors of the present day.

Against these examinations of history, scales of timelines, and the relationship of the built environment to nature, our piece for the Seoul Biennale, *Invasive Regeneration*, is set.

2. Context and Content

Each generation strives to build an environment useful to themselves and their children. What we build can live beyond us, but ultimately even what we intend to be permanent wears away with time. Where the life of a human is but the blink of an eye to a solid building, the lifespan of that building in turn is fleeting in the face of natural forces.

The site for our installation piece is the basement of the concrete skeleton of a multistory building that once anchored a traditional-scale neighborhood. That neighborhood is currently being reinvented, repurposed to accommodate the changing needs of the community.

Our installation seeks to impose a new historical layer, a bright and positive one representing the rise of present-day Korea at the global forefront of technology and green initiatives. We can use our advanced Korean daylighting systems as a means of fostering nature and regrowth. By encouraging natural forces, we can acknowledge Seoul's history while also using nature as a way to heal old wounds.

The design will introduce natural light into a buried space that exists in complete darkness. Technology will suddenly connect the defunct foundations of this building to the rhythms and natural forces of the outside world.

In this instance, however, the natural cycle of a day is put into fast-forward, something enabled

by our technological mastery of the elements of nature. The rhythms of day and night appear to happen in quick succession. The processes of nature and life are accelerated, and the slow process of decay is quickened.

Simply, a fissure in the ceiling glows with relocated sunlight, while a reciprocal fissure in the floor filled with plants illustrates how nature ultimately consumes the manmade.

3. Technological Control

Within the context of *Invasive Regeneration*, nature is systematized into component elements. Though "nature" embodies countless forces, our installation seeks to supply two reductive components: water and light.

The basement space is effectively isolated from the outside world, so the challenge of supplying sun deep into its core is met by the application of technology.

Outside the site, a heliostat is positioned to reflect light deep into the ground. Light is reflected and passed through relays, to be delivered to the core of the installation.

That light is then sent to a crevasse in the ceiling and distributed to the components below. Our ability to precisely control the behavior of the light allows us to determine when and how the light is delivered.

To communicate our perverse mastery over the elements, as well as to create the perspective of a distortion of time, we are sending the diurnal cycle into a sort of "fast-forward." In the installation space, the "sun" will rise and set every few minutes, creating the sense of different timescales. Our everyday perception of the passage of time is compressed, so that the visitor is able to see in geological timescales.

The corresponding growth of invasive nature, which (in our thought experiment) will someday reduce the whole city to dust, is thus hastened, and we are able to visually break down the building well in advance of when its ruin might actually occur.

4. Coda

Our relationship to nature is complex. Nature is at times an adversary, something to be tamed, whose return can herald our demise.

The forward march of our civilization has the potential to either subdue nature completely or to eradicate humans, ceding ultimate dominion back to nature. Or perhaps we might look to generate balance, by working alongside nature's chaos. We hope to foster an examination of this choice.

By altering our perception and perspective of the movement of time, we can see the impermanence of the things we build, and intuit the forces of nature that are ultimately stronger than us.

Towards the End of Air Conditioning

Andrew Cruse

Comfort is the energetic and symbolic nexus between citizens and cities. It simultaneously describes the thermal relationship between a body and its environment, and the social one between the individual and larger groups. Architects are professionally predisposed see buildings as the primary context for comfort. Yet, shifting focus from the building to the body highlights how clothing responds to and shapes contemporary notions of comfort in ways that buildings cannot. The dominant concept of thermal comfort that developed during the twentieth century relies almost exclusively on conditioned air within sealed building envelopes. This air is kept at "ideal" steady-state conditions so that an average body maintains homeostasis with the interior climate without the occupant's conscious attention. Yet, comfort is not the result of a simple interplay between the body and an enclosed volume of air; instead, it results from the dynamic energetic exchanges at the narrow boundary layer around the skin. Clothing, not air conditioning, is a principal mediator of such comfort. Exploring this energetic boundary focuses attention on the beginning of a new approach to comfort and the end of air conditioning.

Driven in part by global climatic instability and a focus on energy use, attention to comfort is increasing. Architects typically bracket comfort within normative practice, focusing on improving the efficiency of materials and systems we already use.[1]

1. That is not to say that architects pay no attention to clothing and fashion. See, for example, Mark Wigley, *White Walls, Designer Dresses: Fashioning Modern Architecture* (Cambridge, MA: MIT Press, 2001). Several design exhibitions have also dealt with the substance and material of clothing, including Bernard Rudofsky's exhibition "Are Clothes Modern?" (1944) at New York's Museum of Modern Art. The museum will revisit the topic of this show in the upcoming exhibition "Items: Is Fashion Modern?" (2017). MoMA's "Mutant Materials in Contemporary Design" (1995) and the National Design Museum's "Extreme Textiles" (2005), also in New York, highlighted many material advances including fabric for clothing. The protective role of clothing and the effect it has on comfort is less well studied.

We are trapped in what we have typically done.[2] Shifting focus from air to clothing as a principal means of providing comfort opens new lines of inquiry, and presents new opportunities for rethinking the relationship between design and energy at personal, architectural, and urban scales. Clothing is a visible register of our expectations about what types of climates we expect to find ourselves in, and what kinds of comfort we hope to achieve there. It embodies fine-grain modes of expressing and shaping our relationship to buildings, cities, and the changing environment. It is nimble in ways that buildings are not. Unlike buildings, clothing is a dynamic element in the overall environment. It doesn't distinguish between inside and outside climates. It can easily be changed based on external factors like location and season, or internal ones like age, gender, activity level, or personal preference. Clothing can address climate variability in real and visible ways that link physiology and fashion, individual and collective, inside and outside. It can help to turn the idea of climate from an abstract, statistical index to a lived experience, giving it agency to connect social habits with meteorological phenomena through design.

Skin Is a Thermally Active Surface

Skin is the body's original thermally active surface. Compared to skin, clothing and buildings are relatively recent inventions used to mediate the relationship between the body and its environment. While clothing and buildings emerged over the last 40,000 years, the body's thermoregulatory mechanisms developed beginning with the emergence of the genus Homo around 2 million years ago.[3] Since then, the body's thermoregulatory system has developed into its current state through the slow process of biological evolution. Much of its control is involuntary. The thermoregulatory process begins as information about temperature at the body's surface is transmitted from thermal receptors in the skin through the nervous system to the brain's hypothalamus. If this temperature is outside of the desired range, the body involuntarily responds by regulating heat production and distribution. In the case of excess heat, this happens through vasodilation, where blood vessels in the skin expand, allowing heat, carried by the blood, to be moved from the body's core to its surface where it can easily be moved out of the body and into the environment through the different modes of heat transfer. In the case of excess cold, the opposite happens: the process of vasoconstriction reduces blood flow through the skin, thus conserving heat in the body's core. The body can also shiver to produce additional heat through metabolic combustion in the muscles. The goal of this thermoregulation is homeostasis. Homeostasis is the ability of an organism to maintain a stable internal environment despite external influences. On a functional level, all adaptive responses of an organism—involuntary or voluntary, internal or external—are made to restore internal homeostasis.

Mythical paradise settings often assume a harmony between the body's internal environment and the external one. In the Garden of Eden, Adam and Eve needed neither clothing nor

2. The architect and engineer Michelle Addington has written regularly about this topic. See, for example, her "Energy, Body, Building: Rethinking Sustainable Design Solutions," *Harvard Design Magazine* 18 (Spring/Summer 2003): 18–21.

3. Artifacts such as awls and needles—indirect evidence of clothing, as they could have been used to sew animal skins into simple garments—are confined to the last 40,000 years of human history and are found primarily outside the tropics. See Nina G. Jablonski, *Skin: A Natural History* (Berkeley: University of California Press, 2006), 42.

Adam and Eve in the Garden of Eden, where the climate was in perfect harmony with the body's surface temperature of 32°C. [Based on Albrecht Dürer's *Adam and Eve* (1504)]

Although it builds on the biological evolution of the body's thermoregulatory mechanisms, the modern history of comfort is more determined by the cultural evolution of clothing and buildings. Unlike the slow process of biological evolution that passes through genes from parents to offspring, cultural evolution can be passed among multiple sources. As such, it's a faster, more potent form of change. In the case of clothing and buildings, cultural evolution ameliorates or negates the effects of the environment on the body, thus buffering the body from the effects of natural selection that might otherwise occur.[4]

Clothing is used outside of the skin to extend the body's range of thermoregulatory control, and to reduce the metabolic cost of this control. Although buildings are used largely for the same purpose, there are some important distinctions between them. While clothing's interaction with the body's physiology happens at the surface of the skin, buildings typically rely on large volumes of conditioned air, only a small part of which is needed to provide thermal comfort. As buildings become larger, smaller percentages of this air is used to meet the body's needs. Clothing can provide thermal comfort regardless of climate or enclosure. It can be used inside, outside, and anywhere in between. Buildings, on the other hand, rely on a clear separation between inside and outside in order to effectively condition the air that they contain. In fact, the very idea of modern thermal comfort in buildings is based on this separation. In privileging the building-based comfort model, architecture reduces the potential for clothing-based comfort.

architecture as the outdoor climate was ideally suited to the comfort provided by their exposed skin. Only after their Original Sin, when they were cast from the Garden, did such external means of controlling comfort become necessary for protection against original climate change.

4. Differences between biological and cultural evolution, and other insights of deep history are discussed in many sources. My source has been Daniel Lieberman, *The Story of the Human Body* (New York: Penguin, 2013), 126–153.

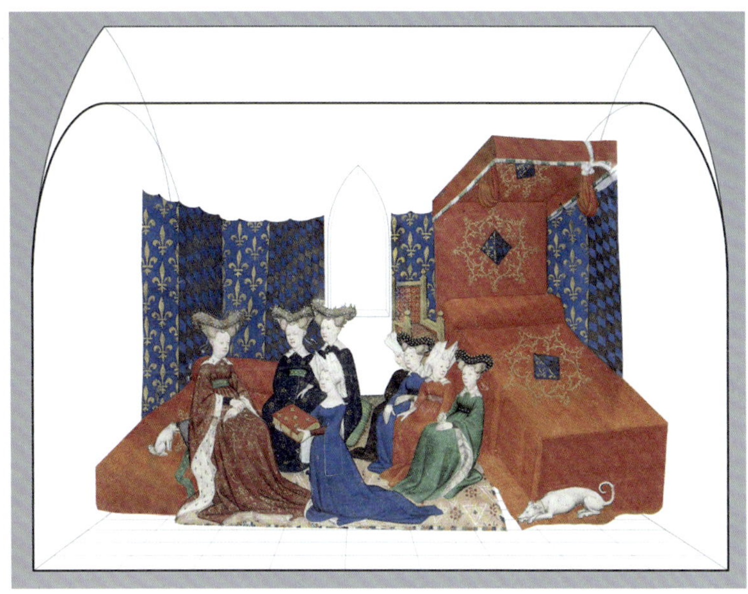

Medieval comforts relied largely on clothing and textiles, rather than architecture, to provide comfort. [Based on a close-up of the miniature painting from *The Book of the Queen* showing Christine de Pizan presenting her manuscript to Isabel of Bavaria]

Building Standards and Dress Codes

The environmental buffering role of clothing and buildings has not always been so clearly established in favor of buildings. Medieval design for comfort gave priority to mobility.[5]

This is most evident in furniture design and can also be seen in different applications for textiles. Buildings, heated with inefficient open-hearth fireplaces, were drafty, and uninsulated stone construction held in the cold. In this context, wall hangings, bedding, and most importantly clothing were used to provide essential environmental protection against the exterior climate, as well as to convey status through their material and decoration.

Historian John Crowley locates the emergence of physical comfort—the self-conscious satisfaction with the relationship between one's body and its immediate environment—in the first half of the eighteenth century as an innovation of Anglo-American culture.[6] While previously, "comfort" had referred to psychological and spiritual circumstances, theories of political economy that developed at the time used comfort as a legitimizing motive for popular consumption patterns. As value of physical comfort became more explicit and more desirable, the technology of its improvement gained intellectual prestige. This can be seen in the development of different enclosed combustion technologies such as the Franklin stove and the Rumford fireplace, which burned fuel more efficiently than open fireplaces.

5. Siegfried Giedion, *Mechanization Takes Command* (New York: Oxford UP, 1955), 258–304.

6. John E. Crowley, *The Invention of Comfort: Sensibilities and Design in Early Modern Britain and Early America* (Baltimore: Johns Hopkins UP, 2001), 141–170.

From this followed the well-known progression of building system technologies that led to increasingly greater degrees of control over the interior environment. Beginning in the nineteenth century, heating grew in scale from the individual control of single rooms to the centralized control of entire buildings. Building ventilation systems developed to circulate this centralized heat, as well as to separate interior air from the poorer-quality outside air often found in urban settings. And cooling technology was invented to remove humidity from the air, thus lowering its temperature. Collectively, the ability to control the temperature, cleanliness, and humidity of air within a building was called "air conditioning." At the beginning of the twentieth century, building engineers proposed an explicit connection between air conditioning and thermal comfort in order to settle a professional dispute between themselves and the medical community about how best to ventilate public school classrooms. While engineers favored artificial ventilation using mechanical equipment, physicians favored natural ventilation through open windows. Engineers saw the development of scientifically based quantitative thermal comfort standards as the best way to establish the superiority of mechanical systems and to gain public confidence in their professional authority.[7]

Working under the auspices of the American Society of Heating and Ventilating Engineers (ASHVE), researchers began to study thermal comfort in the laboratory. To do this they used a psychrometric chamber—a sealed, insulated, windowless room in which temperature and humidity could be precisely set and independently controlled.

Early comfort testing in psychrometric chambers established an "ideal" temperature of about 26°C, and represented the origin of architecture's interior climate as artificially created and separate from the exterior one. [Based on allegorical engraving of the Vitruvian primitive hut from Laugier's *Essay on Architecture* (1755) and an undated photograph from the Kansas State University Institute of Environmental Research

Psychrometric chamber testing was based on the idea that comfort resulted when the body reached homeostasis with the air in the chamber. That is, when the heat produced by metabolism was balanced with the air temperature and humidity of the surrounding environment, people felt comfortable. Test subjects would spend a fixed period of time in the chamber at

7. For a description of this debate, see Gail Cooper, *Air-Conditioning America: Engineers and the Controlled Environment, 1900–1960* (Baltimore: Johns Hopkins UP 1998), 51–79.

specific temperature and humidity levels. On leaving, they were asked if they found those conditions comfortable, and, if not, if it was too warm or too cool. ASHVE researchers recorded this data and, in 1924, published the first thermal comfort chart showing the temperature and humidity conditions under which people felt most comfortable.

Researchers recognized that there were limits to their concept of ideal thermal comfort based only on temperature and humidity. These limits included environmental factors such as air movement and radiant heat sources, and personal ones such as activity level and clothing. Continued research over the following decades worked to address these factors as the comfort chart evolved to become a comfort equation. Expressing comfort in an equation, rather than on a chart, allowed for the different factors affecting thermal comfort to be treated individually. By 1970 the Danish researcher Ole Fanger proposed the Predicted Mean Vote (PMV) comfort model which relied on a multivariable equation (solved using early computer technology) to predict different combinations that would be comfortable. The PMV model underlies two of today's most widely used engineering comfort standards, the ASHRAE 55—Thermal Environmental Conditions for Human Occupancy, and ISO 7730—Moderate Thermal Environments.

Within the comfort equation, clothing was expressed by the unit CLO. In 1941 researchers at Yale University's John B. Pierce Laboratory proposed the CLO to quantify the thermal resistance value of clothing. CLO represented the insulation value for clothing much as R and U-values represented the insulation value for building materials.

The 1.0 CLO business suit was thermally tailored to the air-conditioner based office environment. Just as Fredrick Taylor's *Principles of Scientific Management* (1911) had been used to improve the efficiency of blue-collar factory workers, thermal comfort standards were used to improve the productivity of white-collar office workers.

However, the protective role of clothing inside of buildings (as expressed in the comfort equation) was different from the protective role of building insulation. Clothing was to connect the building occupant's skin with the building's static interior climate to achieve homeostasis, while building insulation was to thermally separate inside and outside climates to provide shelter.

For the purposes of indoor thermal comfort, one CLO unit was set based on a man's "everyday clothing" worn in an office environment. As such, it represented a dress code thermally tailored to the office environment.

These thermal dress codes (which are now recognized as having a gender bias)[8] and the building standards that supported them became part of the white-collar work environment, along with fluorescent lighting, open office plans, and curtain wall construction. Such homeostatic, air-conditioned thermal environments were valued in part because they were thought to make workers more productive. In 1959, the General Services Administration of the US government conducted a five-month study of the effects of air conditioning in office environments. They found that air-conditioned office workers were 7% to 14% more productive than non-air-conditioned workers, and had lower absentee rates.[9] Like Frederick Taylor's *Principles of Scientific Management* (1911), which had been used to improve the efficiency of blue-collar factory workers, thermal comfort standards were used to improve the productivity of white-collar office workers. These comfort standards were maintained at the building level, using air conditioning, while clothing played a passive supporting role..

Civic Clothing

On February 2, 1977, only two weeks into his presidency, Jimmy Carter delivered a fireside chat where he encouraged fellow Americans to save energy by putting on a warm sweater and turning down their thermostats. He recommended 18°C (65°F) during the day, 13°C (55°F) at night. The television broadcast showed President Carter informally dressed in a beige wool cardigan that became the most memorable symbol of his administration. In making his appeal, Carter both directly related air-based comfort models to excessive energy use, and recognized the role clothing could play in providing a less energy-intensive approach to comfort. Carter's sweater made an important point: that buildings' energy use was, in part, a cultural construct. Although it relied on human physiology and building technology, thermal comfort also reflected the expectations of a larger society. While mechanical engineers responded to the energy crisis of the 1970s largely by advocating increased equipment efficiency, Carter's sweater showed another way: it offered a reorientation of comfort towards clothing as a way citizens could help to address the important national priority of energy conservation.[10] In the eyes of the public, however, this puritanical approach advocating self-sacrifice effectively linked energy savings with discomfort.

8. See Boris Kingma and Wouter van Marken Lichtenbelt, "Energy Consumption in Buildings and Female Thermal Demand," *Nature Climate Change* 5 (2015), http://www.nature.com/nclimate/journal/v5/n12/full/nclimate2741.html. Last accessed March 10, 2017.

9. Neville S. Billington and Brian M. Roberts, *Building Services Engineering: A Review of Its Development* (New York: Pergamon Press, 1982), 21.

10. Indeed, the American Society of Heating, Refrigerating, and Air-Conditioning Engineers (ASHRAE) had stopped their scientific research of thermal research in the 1970s, focusing instead on the political task of turning their building standards into building codes. See W. Stephen Comstock, ed., *Proclaiming the Truth: An Illustrated History of the American Society of Heating, Refrigerating and Air-Conditioning Engineers, Inc.* (Atlanta: ASHRAE, 1995).

In response to the 1970s oil crisis, President Jimmy Carter encouraged fellow Americans to turn their thermostats down to 18°C and put on a sweater. While architects and engineers responded to the crisis by advocating increased equipment efficiency, Carter's appeal showed how citizens could address energy conservation with their wardrobes.

As the energy crisis eased, people packed away their sweaters and turned the winter thermostats back up. It would be nearly thirty years until another world leader made the political connection between clothing, comfort, and energy.

Although office fashion typically cycles within a limited bandwidth, it has recently experienced larger disruptions due to evolving ideas of comfort and energy use as they relate to global warming. During the summer of 2005, the Japanese Ministry of the Environment introduced the Cool Biz program as a way to reduce electricity consumption by limiting the use of air conditioning and promoting more liberal office dress codes. Employees were encouraged to wear lightweight pants and short-sleeved shirts, while business owners were asked to set office thermostats to 28°C (82°F) during the cooling season. Although many workers initially felt self-conscious about coming to work dressed in this lighter, less conventional style of clothing, when then Prime Minister Koizumi appeared on television in shirt sleeves, participation increased.

The Cool Biz program has since expanded to include a winter Warm Biz program that encourages employees to dress warmly while office thermostats are set to 20°C (68°F). After the 2011 Tōhoku earthquake and tsunami shut down many of the country's nuclear power plants, the Japanese government launched the Super Cool Biz program to encourage workers to wear polo shirts and sandals to the office in appropriate circumstances. These programs have had significant energy and economic savings, and have been influential elsewhere in Asia. There are now Cool Biz fashion shows in Japan and Korea highlighting the expanded range of choice workers have when it comes to acceptable office clothing.

Unlike Jimmy Carter's cardigan sweater, Cool Biz and related programs have been successful in linking clothing comfort to positive attitudes towards personal expression. This recognition of the importance of clothing in providing comfort begins to shift responsibility from the building to the individual in providing for his or her own thermal comfort. Employees and employers are recognizing increased productivity through worker satisfaction, and savings through lower energy use, by allowing for greater fashion freedom.

From the oil embargo of the 1970s to the growing impact of global warming today, the connection between comfort standards and energy use is now explicit. This connection offers a clear picture of how energy use is a social construction.[11] Modern thermal comfort standards rely almost exclusively on buildings to produce thermal comfort, while taking a passive approach towards clothing. These examples show how clothing can be used as an active agent in shaping the relationship between comfort and energy, as well as between the body and climate.

The word "climate" has traditionally referred to outdoor conditions. It is defined as weather averaged over a long period of time. Yet, thermal comfort standards rely on the idea of a separate indoor climate, representing ideal thermal conditions for human homeostasis. Given that today people in the industrialized world spend about 90% of their time inside, the indoor climate contained in buildings has a larger impact on the thermal comfort of this population than do outdoor climates.[12]

In advocating for moving thermostat set points away from established thermal comfort standards, Carter and Koizumi were promoting indoor climate change. Much as there are positive and negative sides to the greenhouse effect—it both warms the earth's atmosphere to make it livable and, when accelerated by excess greenhouse gas emissions, is the process behind global warming—so too can climate change act in positive and negative ways. Interior climate change is a choice. It can be made at the level of a building, a company, a city, or a nation. While outdoor climate change is also a choice (based on increased carbon emissions), it exists on a global scale and on a longer time horizon that is not easily or directly affected by individual and collective actions. Voluntary indoor climate change foregrounds the relationship between individual choice and the larger environment. It establishes a relationship between interior and exterior climates and the potential of clothing to provide thermal comfort. Clothing becomes a register of the relationship of indoors and outdoors, individual and collective, physiology and fashion.

An Ethos of Exposure

While off-the-rack fashion, such as that worn for the Cool Biz program, is having a real impact on building energy use, runway fashion is becoming the site of climatic imaginaries in which bodies, buildings, and cities directly confront the changing climate in both real and speculative ways.[13] These fashion mash-ups—drawing on thermally and symbolically established fashion tropes such as rain coats, sun hats, camouflage, long underwear, formal wear, ties, etc.—serve as both vehicles of self-expression and climatic engagement. The fashion cycle absorbs technical developments and clothing styles from specialized domains. Technology transfer from battle fields and job sites, ski slopes and athletic fields become part of the larger fashion landscape. A former US Secretary of Defense said the textile industry

11. For a broad discussion of the social construction of energy use, see Elizabeth Shove, *Comfort, Cleanliness and Convenience: The Social Organization of Normality* (New York: Berg, 2003), 21–42.

12. Neil E. Klepeis et al, "The National Human Activity Pattern Survey (NHAPS): A Resource for Assessing Exposure to Environmental Pollutants," *Journal of Exposure Analysis and Environmental Epidemiology* 11 (2001): 231–252.

13. Dehlia Hannah and Cynthia Selin, "Unseasonable Fashion: A Manifesto," in James Graham, ed., *Climates: Architecture and the Planetary Imaginary* (Zurich: Lars Müller Publishers, 2016), 222–231.

Initiated by Prime Minister Koizumi, the Japanese Cool Biz program encourages building owners to set thermostats to 28°C during the summer while promoting more liberal office dress. By highlighting the connections between clothing and comfort, Cool Biz demonstrates that energy use is a social construct as well as a technological one

and climate? How could dress codes inform building codes? How can clothing comfort be a catalyst for design? In a 1960 article "Stocktaking," Reyner Banham recognized the disruptive potential of clothing as a challenge to architectural traditions and normative practice.[14] There, Banham contrasted traditional approaches to architecture with technological ones. After expressing his frustration with the continued influence of architecture's "institutional lore," he had a more positive assessment of technology. He wrote: "Architecture, as a service to human societies, can only be defined by the provision of fit environments for human activities. It shows a narrowly professional frame of mind to refer to beginnings solely to the cave or primitive hut." He would develop this interest in "fit environments" nine years later in *The Architecture of the Well-Tempered Environment*. In these and other writings, Banham's attention to technology in architecture shifted from the priority of style and structure to focus on satisfying human environmental needs. But his focus was on the technology needed for comfort rather than on the idea of comfort itself. In "Stocktaking," Banham included a plan image of the human body cut through the chest and showing its "personal architecture" of clothing from undershirt to overcoat. Although there is no reference to this image in the text, it suggests an ethos of exposure that recalls the shared cultural evolution of clothing and building that link human physiology with meteorological patterns in the creation of thermal comfort. Seen from this perspective, the concept of thermal comfort links issues of energy and social priority, technology and shelter. The ethos of exposure embodied in clothing comfort challenges the goal of homeostasis embodied in an air-conditioned approach to architectural comfort, and suggest a consideration of comfort as the energetic and symbolic nexus between citizens and cities.

is "second only to steel in importance to the armed forces." Technologies such as Aerogel, passive cooling fabrics, phase change materials, and microfluidics are making their way into the commercial sphere as ways to locally control comfort through clothing. Far from the one CLO dress code and the sealed, homogeneous interior climate that contained it, such clothing provokes us to imagine new types of spaces that bridge between the body and the larger environment in active and compelling ways.

These anticipatory aesthetics beg the question of what the architectural and urban environments would be for such attitudes toward comfort

14. Reyner Banham, "Stocktaking," *Architectural Review* 756 (February 1960): 93–100.

Energy is Everywhere and nowhere

Forrest Meggers, Dorit Aviv,
Andrew Cruse, Kiel Moe, Kipp Bradford,
Salmaan Craig, and Marcel Brülisauer

Energy is an elusive concept. While universally recognized, it is rarely understood. We continually misinterpret our thermal interactions with our surroundings. We have curated interfaces that elucidate often-overlooked aspects of energy—from the potentials of low-exergy buildings to the misperceived heat transfer from surfaces around us—contextualized within a framework of energy opportunities that are literally everywhere, but nowhere to be seen. This exhibition reveals the manifestations of energy by unexpected means at three radically different scales: the human body, the building, and the city. The various projects displayed explore the transfer of thermal energy which connects all three into an interdependent network of exchange.

Energy and the Human Body

The human body utilizes energy for you to move, think, and operate. It does so in constant thermodynamic exchange with its surroundings. As with any engine, your body cannot use energy at 100% efficiency; this is dictated by the second law of thermodynamics. The inefficiencies are manifested in the heat your body must dissipate to operate. Your body is therefore generally warmer than its surroundings, as can be viewed on a thermal camera.

Your comfort is the sensation of how easily your body is rejecting heat. Although it is always operating at the same temperature, your body must adjust to many thermal inputs. Air temperature is what we consider first in terms of comfort, but it is one of several factors that all have significant impacts. Along with air temperature, humidity, air speed, and radiation all play major roles in defining how easily your body can operate at its requisite temperature. Additionally, varying clothing layers and metabolic rates can dramatically shift your perception of comfort and your desire for warmth or coolness. Managing that desire has now become a central component of architecture and its heating and cooling infrastructures. However, current techniques still only consider air temperature, and neglect the many other factors that can be influenced by design.

Energy & Buildings
The vast majority of energy demand in buildings is used for maintaining thermal comfort. Thermal comfort is what determines the heat transfers driven by modern heating and cooling systems. But most will agree that thermal comfort is not readily achieved, even when nearly every building has automated heating and cooling systems.

Buildings are the largest single sector of energy demand. In the United States, 40% of primary energy is generated for use in buildings. Energy in buildings now has an importance rivalling that of the occupants' needs and the architectural design process. As a result, architects often sidestep away from energy rather than engaging with it. But we argue and demonstrate in this exhibition that energy is not an independent concept to be dealt with only through technical engineered solutions. Energy is full of potential, both physically and literally. Understanding both the physically measurable potential and the architectural and human interactions that influence potential is necessary to successfully address the energy challenge in buildings.

The enormous primary energy demand of buildings results in their also being a significant source of greenhouse gas emissions. Both in operation and construction there is a vast amount of latent potential found in overlooked forms of energy, which can help mitigate negative environmental impacts. Whether the form of energy is thermal or electrical, it may present a similar absolute energy quantity, but its usability is dramatically different. Transforming high-quality electricity into the tempering of room air is a huge loss of potential. Heating and cooling are in fact relatively benign forms of energy, but when they are produced with electricity or high-temperature boilers and furnaces, a lot of energy is wasted. This is recognized in the difference in temperatures needed to create these forms of energy, and is quantified by the concept of *exergy* that recognizes the added value of energy forms created from high temperatures or high-potential generation techniques.

Energy & the Urban Environment
Energy is everywhere; its complex range of potentials is present at the urban, regional, and global scales. District energy systems can leverage common potentials to reduce the demand placed on high-quality energy resources. District heating and cooling systems have evolved over the past decades to match the waste sources of heat at the community scale with the demand for low temperature heating in buildings. For cooling, using the latent energy of evaporation to access moderate temperatures with much better cooling capacity has long been a way to improve performance in large systems, but has rarely been considered for its application to smaller and residential systems, which would experience the same performance gains. Across cities, there are numerous sites where latent thermal energy from industry has the potential to be used for urban district heating and cooling. Even at the scale of entire countries, places like Iceland and Denmark deliver heating and cooling to

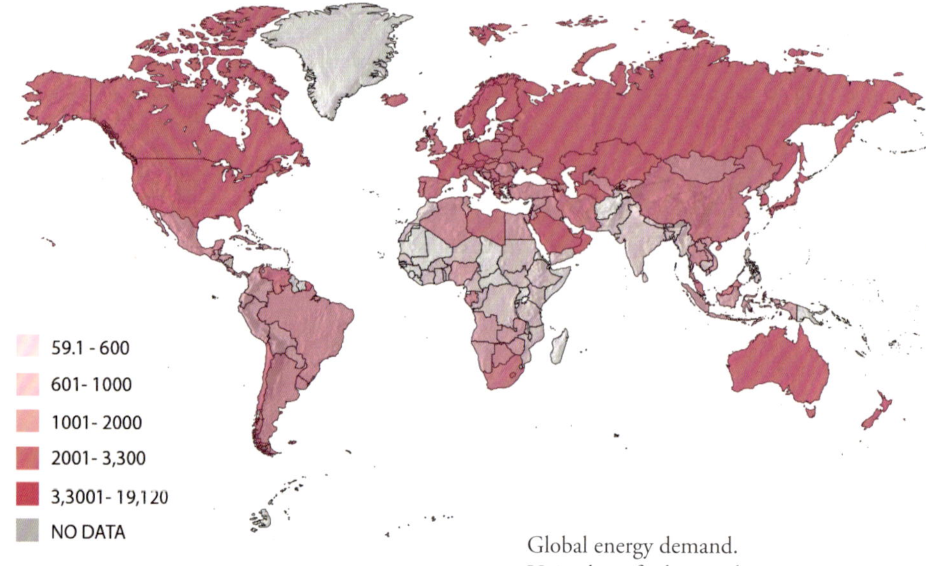

Global energy demand.
Units: kgs of oil equivalent per annum

hundreds of kilometers. Planners and designers can engage in those systems to align thermal resource supply and demand across regions.

Understanding the inherent changes in system capacity and the ability of thermal energy to be stored at large regional scales can also have huge benefits to managing the inherent intermittency of renewable electricity sources like wind and solar. Understanding how the occupant's need for thermal energy can be delivered through a system that acts as an intermediate thermal sink matched both to the heat transfer most relevant to the user and to locally available temperatures, while at the same time requiring electrical inputs only when available on the grid, is a way that energy's role can truly be considered everywhere while remaining nowhere to be seen.

CURATORS

Forrest Meggers and Dorit Aviv, Princeton University

PARTICIPANTS

Andrew Cruse, Ohio State University
Kipp Bradford, MIT Media Lab
Marcel Brülisauer, ETH Zürich
Kiel Moe, Harvard University
Salmaan Craig, Harvard University

TEAM

Eric Teitelbaum, Tyler Kvochick,
François Sabourin, Sean Rucewicz,
Hongshan Guo, Melanie Daguin,
Yshai Yudekovitz

EXHIBITION DESIGN

Georgina Baronian

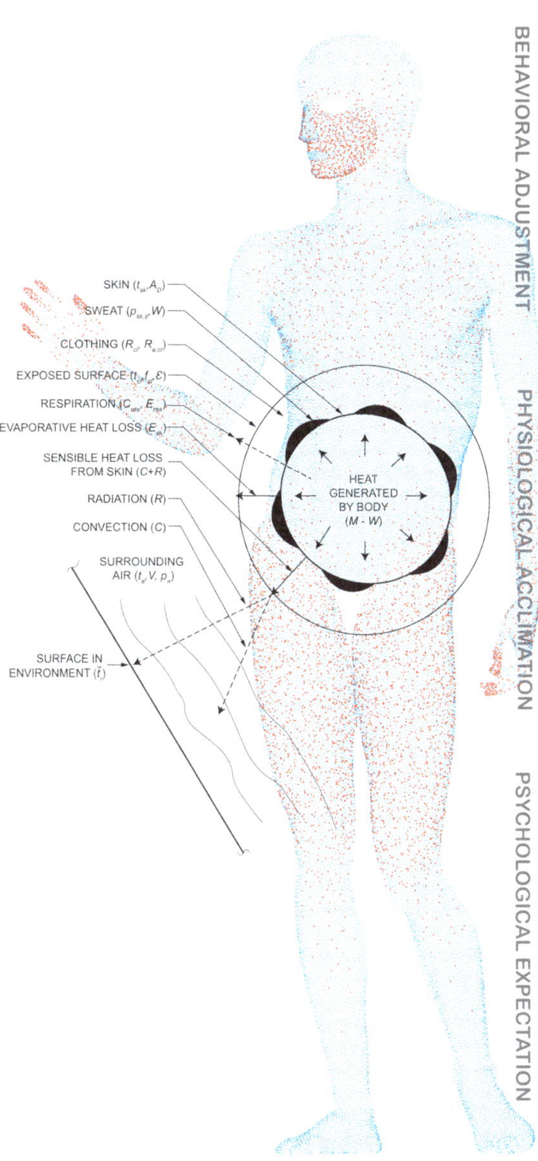

BODY BUILDING
Andrew Cruse

Comfort is an energetic and symbolic nexus between citizens and cities. Its definition simultaneously contains the thermal relationship between a body and its environment, and our individual identities as part of larger societies. Architects are professionally predisposed to see architecture as the primary context for comfort. However, shifting focus from the building to the body highlights how clothing—our personal architecture—shapes contemporary notions of comfort in ways that buildings cannot. The exhibition "Personal Architecture" examines how the comfort of clothing presents design opportunities for rethinking the relationships between the body, energy, and architecture from the scale of the individual to the scale of the city.

The body's skin is a thermally active surface. Clothing mediates the microclimate between the skin and the surrounding environment to provide comfort. While building comfort standards typically consider only the insulation value of clothing (using the CLO unit), this exhibition examines a range of textile technologies and the different conditions they create for the skin in terms of their breathability, absorption, heat release, layering, and stretchiness. Such features allow clothing to satisfy individual comfort preferences and to adapt to varying climatic conditions. Instead of the fixed collective comfort conditions maintained within a building's envelope, clothing allows for varied personal comfort at the scale of the body. Such improved comfort can also result in improved energy efficiency, as less demands are made of building HVAC systems. "Personal Architecture" links physiology and fashion, the individual and the collective, and indoors and outdoors as the introductory exhibition in the Energy Pavilion.

THERMAL EFFUSIVITY
Kiel Moe

Even if they are the same temperature, a block of wood "feels" warmer than a block of steel or concrete. While seemingly a subjective experience, there is a quantifiable material property that explains this difference in sensation: thermal effusivity. Thermal effusivity is a measure of a material's ready ability to exchange heat with its milieu. When touching steel, we transiently transfer more heat than when we touch wood. This is the basis of our sensations of warmth and coolness. Because the sensation of heat transfer plays such an important role in the perception of human comfort, so does this material property.

But the implications of this property are much larger than our localized, individual experience of a material. Even if two rooms are at the same operative temperature, a wooden room will physically feel quite different from a concrete one. Or, to state it another way, the wooden room could maintain the same level of comfort with less input exergy. Thermal effusivity could, in fact, be the basis of a very different approach to human comfort, one deeply connected to the physiology of our bodies and to the materials we use to build.

Rather than sensing temperature, our hands and other sensory organs sense relative rates of thermal exchange or flow across our body-boundary. So, when we touch architecture, the transient behavior of our skin and adjacent materials becomes very important. For example, in the handrail leading to the upper level of the exhibition, a series of high- and low-effusivity materials are designed to trigger varying sensations of warmth and coolness as your hand moves up and down the handrail. The specification of materials according to thermal effusivity yields not only a range of thermal experiences even at the same temperature, but can also make a much cooler space feel warmer and vice versa. Thermal effusivity is a way to quantitatively incorporate our qualitative sensations of materials and our thermal milieu.

THERMALLY ALIVE SPACE
Forrest Meggers & Dorit Aviv

Our goal is to reconsider heat transfer as a fundamental part of space creation, by making visible the constant hidden exchange between our body and the architectural elements surrounding it. The human body is a complex thermal engine, with multiple sophisticated mechanisms for exchanging energy with its environment. Air temperature is just one of many factors that have significant physical impact on perceived comfort, yet thermostats measuring only air temperature control how buildings deliver thermal amenities, completely disengaging the architect's opportunity to influence that interaction. It has been left to the engineering consultant to deliver a fixed solution to control the temperature of a room within a set of artificial criteria for temperature. These solutions aim at conditioning the space, not the occupant. They are also delivered as independent solutions that do not appreciate the many ways they impact the actual space of the room.

Here we exploit heat transfer by radiation, whereby surfaces of higher or lower temperatures exchange heat through blackbody radiation of electromagnetic waves. This exchange is independent of any interaction with the air temperature or movement. Like the sun, people

Thermal map of installation space

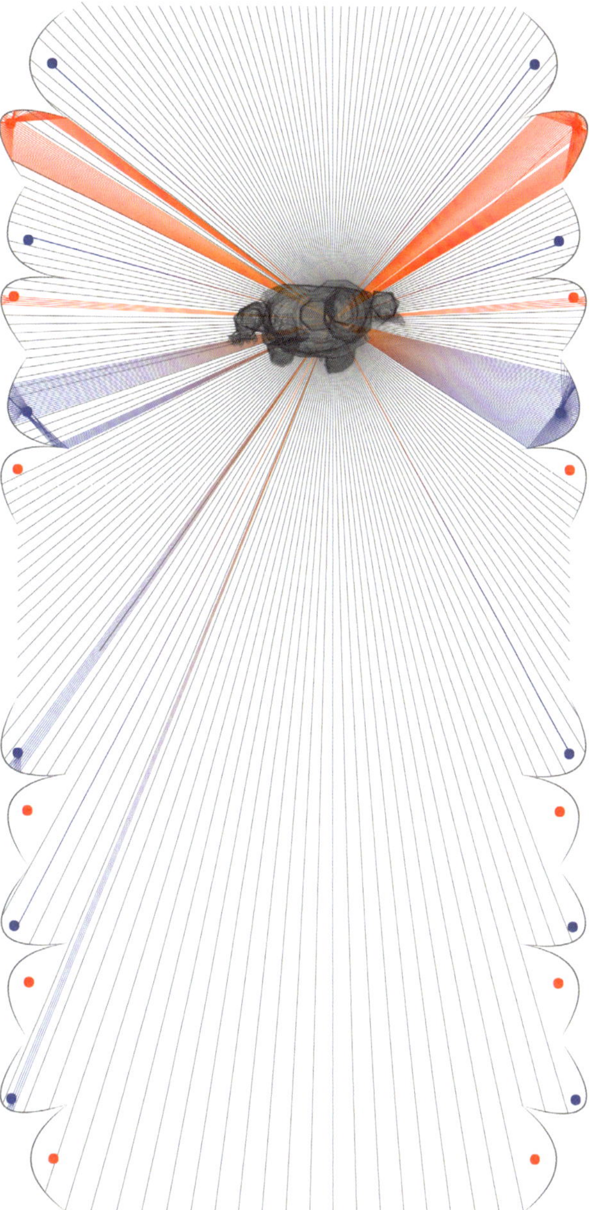

Body mean radiant temperature at a specific point in space based on the reflections of infrared radiation from the reflective surfaces.

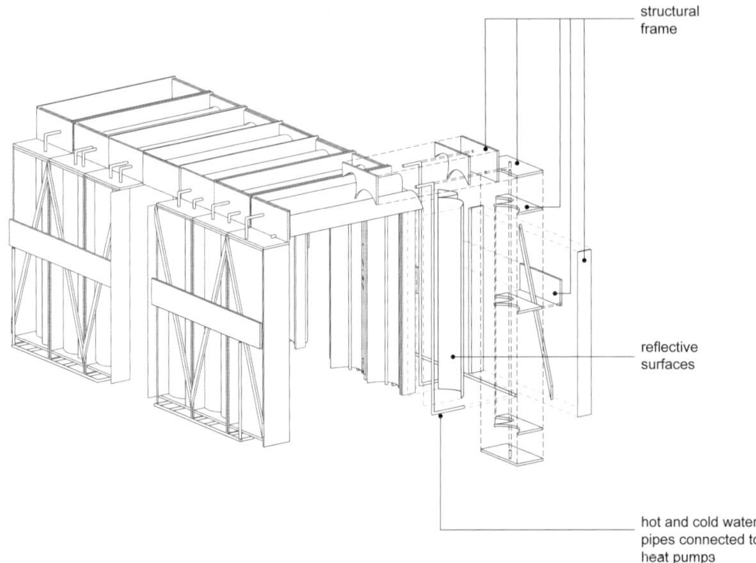

are glowing masses emitting electromagnetic radiation; we just don't see in that wavelength. The radiation emitted from a warm person has more energy than the surrounding lower-temperature surfaces, causing a net heat exchange independent of the exchange with the air in immediate contact. By placing someone in view of a surface that is ten degrees cooler than the air temperature, they will have the sensation that the space is cooler. If all surfaces around an occupant were dropped by ten degrees, research has shown they will predict the temperature of the room to be five degrees cooler than the actual air temperature. The same goes for warming the surfaces.

This means that the "undifferentiated" space becomes activated by walls, ceilings, and other surfaces around it. The shape of the void determines the thermal interaction between its defining surfaces and the human beings occupying it. If the contemporary convention is that the walls, floors, and roof are the domain of the architect, and thermal control by manipulating air temperature is the domain of the mechanical engineer, we divert here the ability and responsibility for thermal control back to the domain of the architect. The walls, floors, roofs, and windows all store heat or reflect it, emit it to people through radiation, or convect it into the moving air. Architecture is anything but silent in this game of energy exchange, and surfaces are not real limits, but a layer of interface between themselves and their surroundings. The architectural elements that bound the void also constantly fill it and transform it.

To make this invisible fullness visible, we create a darkened space where the sense which always overwhelms all others in architecture—vision— is subdued. Instead, we heighten the thermal senses of the occupants by constructing the space out of hot and cold surfaces. To achieve this, we install a highly discretized and controllable series of radiant heating and cooling surfaces. Asymmetric radiant fluxes guide people around the room. Thermal sensations become the differentiating element in a space that visually looks quite repetitive. In this space, humans are not disinterested observers as they move through the room; rather, the movement and proximity of bodies and surfaces become triggers for action. As soon as a hot body comes near a cold surface, they both must engage with one another in an exchange of energy.

Meanwhile, infrared thermal cameras record the thermal interactions as they take place. As people move through the room, the cameras record the bodies' and surfaces' radiant temperature. Radiative heat exchange is dependent on optics—in other words, surfaces will exchange heat in this manner only if they "see" each other. We make use of this fact to control the amount of cold or hot sensations that visitors experience throughout the room. Just like an op-art installation, where different colors are revealed as the position of a person changes in space, so would the amount of radiation change in relation to a person's position in the room. Infrared camera projections will make this hidden play visible to the human eye.

Radiant heating and cooling systems leverage the ability to shift thermal perception, while also operating more efficiently with system temperatures much closer to room air. These systems can integrate with the architecture to activate surfaces—typically ceilings or floors— creating an alternative experience of thermal comfort. Thanks to the larger surface area of heat exchange into the room, the system can transfer heat into the room with much lower temperatures than in an air-based heating system, or vice versa for cooling with much higher temperatures. This greatly improves the performance of the system, as these temperatures are much easier for the system

to deliver, so even if two buildings have the exact same shell, creating the same heat losses and gains, that heat can be compensated for by the system with much less effort than if it is done at less extreme temperatures.

Performance is a second critical aspect of the exhibition, revealing the concept of exergy and the inherent low-exergy nature of building conditioning. Radiant heating and cooling can require the same quantity of heating or cooling demand, but the thermal potential to achieve that quantity is lower as the temperatures are less extreme. This added efficiency is shown by displaying the performance of an actual heat pump and a chiller as they operate, moving heat at different temperature levels to supply the heating and cooling, which will be linked to the operation of the hot and cold surfaces and space.

CREATING CLIMATE
Kipp Bradford

Heating and cooling are essential elements of modern life. The thermal environment determines our comfort and productivity—and sometimes even our ability to survive in a space. However, as vital as heating and cooling are, these systems are never part of our building aesthetic. They are designed to be out of sight and therefore out of mind. We take thermal systems for granted, only ever thinking about them when they don't work. Here, we subvert this norm by showing off the technology system and revealing the magic that we all depend on.

Modern life requires readily available cooling, but cooling is a contradiction: everything we do to make cold ultimately generates more heat. This is the reality of physics. It is not possible to conjure up cold the way we can conjure heat from a flame or friction, because cold is not the opposite of heat. Rather, it is the absence of heat—and heat will flow to where it is cooler. Thus, to cool a system, we must transport heat against its natural flow. This transport requires work, and work requires energy. The flow of energy and the technology system that generates it deserves to be seen and understood, which is why we're showcasing it here. This technology—the heat pump—is often listed as one of the most important inventions of humanity. Relentlessly compressing and condensing gas, then evaporating liquid to remove heat against its natural flow, heat pumps are so integrated into our lives that we often ignore the value of this technology and take it for granted. The effort required to maintain a controlled, comfortable thermal environment means that heating and cooling represent the majority of the energy flow in and around buildings. It should therefore also command a significant portion of our attention.

A NEW TYPE OF VENTILATION
Salmaan Craig & Forrest Meggers

Moving air is inherently complex. The flows are almost universally turbulent in buildings, and the exchange of energy is dependent on both the air temperature and its velocity. Supplying adequate air has driven much of the technological evolution of mechanical systems in buildings over the last century. Generally, the complex dynamics of air have been overcome with brute force rather than elegant designs. Natural ventilation is commonly used to passively ventilate buildings, yet one of the major challenges of natural ventilation is the unpredictable frequency, direction, and strength of the wind. Buildings can often receive enough fresh air exchange through their shells, but to achieve cool comfort, a certain

level of breeze is necessary. In the last decade, progress has been made in understanding a more reliable driving force—buoyancy. Buoyancy isn't powered by the wind; it's powered by the waste heat from occupants, computers, and other internal heat gains.

Hot air rises. We can design our buildings to exploit this fact. Heated by occupants and computers, the interior air rises naturally up a chimney that connects all the floors of an office building. As it escapes at the top, fresh air is pulled in from the windows and across the floor plates. With buoyancy ventilation, the fresh air is sucked in from the sides—by the warm air column rising up the chimney. On a hot day, when the occupancy is high, there may not be enough wind to flush out the interior. But buoyancy ventilation is different: as the occupancy rate increases, so does the driving force. In other words, buoyancy is a force you can engineer. By design, we can reliably sustain a "breeze" in the absence of wind.

How does one know how to size the chimney and the windows? If the openings are incorrectly sized, there will not be enough air flow, and the interior will overheat. This used to be a difficult problem, especially for multistory buildings. But new research has provided new insights. We now have simple mathematical models that retain the most important physics. Now design teams can easily decide if buoyancy ventilation is feasible, early on in the design process.

We have constructed two buoyancy ventilation stacks to show how adding heat can drive air upward and adding cool can drive air downward. This heat and cold are simply the residual energy from our heat pump installation and could represent any variety of sources available in the built environment. You can observe and feel the free movement of the air that, although seemingly complex, is now coaxed, not forced, into performing the ventilation and human conditioning we need without additional energy input.

RECLAIMING BACKLANES
Marcel Brülisauer

Shophouse clusters, built from rows of historic buildings with mercantile-type occupancy common in Southeast Asia, are increasingly the subject of urban regeneration, as they are often situated in prime areas of the city. The shophouses are grouped around and separated by small lanes at their back, which are noisy, dirty, and thermally uncomfortable because of the number of air-conditioning units, other infrastructure, and service functions. By extending a dialogue between heritage conservation, urban design, and building technology beyond the physical mass of shophouses, these back lanes offer a remarkable prospect to act as strategic urban attractors.

While the thermal conditions of the tropical climate require some sort of air-conditioning in these buildings, the prevalence of air-cooled split-type air conditioners results in entire façades being covered with this simplest and cheapest cooling equipment, at the lowest energy efficiency. The air conditioners also create a hotter urban microclimate, nudging the conditions of valuable urban spaces beyond acceptable outdoor thermal comfort, a visible and perceptible consequence of the energy used for air-conditioning.

A systems approach to building climatization through neighborhood-scale cooling systems not only would allow an increase in energy efficiency by up to 50% but also would free back lanes from excess heat, noise, and bulky installations on the back façades. A key element is to reject the heat in a centralized evaporative cooling tower on a rooftop, thereby reducing the temperature lift of the chillers and improving their energy performance. While shared cooling infrastructures—either district cooling systems with central chillers or heat bus systems, a combination of decentralized water-cooled split units connected to an evaporative cooling tower—are a novelty for low-rise neighborhoods in the tropics, our studies have demonstrated their technical, economic, and operational feasibility.

This technical refurbishment could be used as a trigger to improve the overall pedestrian connectivity, increasing the spatial quality and usability of the back lanes. While all these aspects have their value and justification on their own, only their synergetic combination can unlock the full potential hidden in these neglected urban spaces and reprogram the back lanes into a viable space. Originating from speculative, interdisciplinary studies at the Future Cities Laboratory, the design team uses the back lane model and its book to showcase visions for different back lanes in Singapore.

Do We Dream under the Same Sky?

Nikolaus Hirsch / Michel Müller with
Rirkrit Tiravanija

Do we dream under the same sky asks something obvious. Of course our sky is the same. But is it, really?

The Land is a self-sustaining environment that emerged from the artistic community initiated by Rirkrit Tiravanija and Kamin Lertchaiprasert. Located in the northern part of Thailand, near the village of Sanpathong, 20 km southwest of the city of Chiang Mai, it is intended to be cultivated as an open space free of ownership, an environment conducive to discussions and experimentation in the fields of culture. The Land is open to the day-to-day activities of local living (i.e., the cultivation of rice) and to the neighboring community. A hybrid of innovation and traditionalism, the Land juxtaposes contemporary materials and technologies with ancient forms of practice.

While the Land is inherently a rice field and a garden, freely accessible to all, it also supports architectural constructions that may be utilized in a variety of ways: from shelters for sleeping, to kitchens for cooking, to platforms for lectures or performances. A number of artists and architects are involved in this aspect of the Land's potential, though participation is not confined solely to those in the arts. The people who have contributed to the Land's structure thus far hail from both local and international backgrounds, with artists such as Kamin Lertchaiprasert, Tobias Rehberger, Philippe Parreno, François Roche, Angkrit Ajchariyasophon, Carl Michael von Hausswolff, Superflex, and Rirkrit Tiravanija. The most recent project at the Land is being designed by Frankfurt-based architects Nikolaus Hirsch and Michel Müller: a structure that comprises studios, workshop space, and shelter, and involves a number of international partners.

Exhibition as Component Development

Together with artist Rirkrit Tiravanija, we develop a new building component of our ongoing project that produces building elements for future edifices via exhibitions and collaborative work with architects, engineers, and artists. The first component of the building, a structural system consisting of a bamboo-steel roof and flexible columns, was realized on the occasion of Art Basel in 2015; the second element, a hanging façade structure, was constructed for the Garden Triennale in Aarhus (Denmark, 2017).

The third building component, integrating both a protective façade material and an energy-producing device, was developed for the Biennale in Seoul: a textile façade that produces electricity and emits light, using advanced organic photovoltaics (OPV) and organic light-emitting diode (OLED) technology. The shingle-like system includes 1250 OPV and 403 OLED modules (each 155 x 175 mm) suspended from a grid of bamboo tubes. The energy is produced during the day and emitted during night, highlighting the question "Do We Dream Under the Same Sky." The title refers not only to the commons of energy but also to the question of whether a universal culture exists in the context of rising national, ethic, and religious particularism around the globe.

Instead of focusing on the single-author figure of the architect, the project aims to highlight the multidisciplinary work and complex, often contradicting geographies of architectural and technological processes. As much as we are interested in the finished product, what we expose as an aesthetic question is the material history of a building component: its primary sources, its manufacturers, engineers, designers, locations, trajectories.

Rirkrit Tiravanija, Nikolaus Hirsch, Antto Melasniemi, Michel Müller: Do We Dream Under The Same Sky, Art Basel, 2015

Expansion and Contraction

The project aims to reflect on new forms of contemporary architectural practice. The focus is the increasingly broad, yet in its core expertise limited, often threatened role of the architect. We face a paradox: the field of architecture is both expanding and contracting. On the one hand, architects pride themselves on their multidisciplinary practice, and on the other—contrary to the classic self-image of the generalist architect-genius—they have become marginalized experts on formal packaging.

In this disciplinary context, the project aims to critically investigate the conflictual question of transdisciplinary collaboration. It will discuss the potentials and contradictions of the "architect in the expanded field" (to rephrase Rosalind Krauss). Squeezed between art and engineering, between an increasing number of consultants, controllers, developers, manufacturers, etc., the contemporary architect needs to search for a new position.

How to Lose Control

The classic self-image of the architect is someone who controls. Yet, how can an architect avoid the profession's ambitious yet problematic heritage, that is, its tendency to predetermine a future end state

(*telos*)? How can he or she counter the primacy of *telos* that is based on a procedure that determines and subordinates the place of the various parts?

One way to lose control while stressing the importance of a particular strategy is the concept of the exquisite corpse, which refers to the Surrealist drawing experiment: a collaborative drawing of the human body, fragmenting the human corpse into its parts and members, from head to feet, introducing a moment of chance and improvisation that questions the teleological masterplan. If we apply this logic to a building—what would it look like?

A Building as Exquisite Corpse

It is a banality to say that planning and building are the result of collaborative processes, involving many authors and reflecting on larger political, socio-economic, and cultural contexts. Yet, paradoxically, it is still broadly assumed that this complex spatial-physical entity called architecture must imply a coherent language conceived by a single author (usually, the architect).

Prototype of OLED facade element, 2017

Nikolaus Hirsch / Michel Müller with Rirkrit Tiravanija, Elevation of OPV-OLED facade, 2017

In contrast, our project for the Land proposes an approach that questions notions of coherence and homogeneity. Following the sequential and accumulative logics of the exquisite corpse, different partners, manufacturers, architects, engineers, and artists are selected to participate in the development of several building components that—when seen as a whole in a 22 x 22 meter building—make time and process visible. As a collective work, it will be reminiscent of a surrealist "exquisite corpse," a collective work that begins with a single contribution and continues to grow. Never finished, never complete, as an organic entity, it knows no endgame.

In this sense, *The Land Workshop* is both a building and a practice. The aim is to investigate new models of building that use the logics of a collaborative workshop as a trigger and to seek the therein appropriate architectonic, programmatic, and organizational languages. This "workshop of workshops" will itself be constructed through a series of sessions, hence reflecting on the potential and contradictions of a workshop as such. In each step, one spatial element will be added: foundation, structure, façade, energy, services, studios. Eventually the building will be readable like an exhibition that evolves in time.

Architects: Nikolaus Hirsch / Michel Müller
(Frankfurt)
Artist: Rirkrit Tiravanija
(Chiangmai, New York, Berlin)

In collaboration with Hannah Bürckstümmer, Michael Grund, Richard Harding, Martina Hüber, Hermann Issa, David Müller, Guido Olbertz, Ralph Paetzold, Pavel Schilinsky.

The project has been made possible through the generous support by Merck, Kolon, OLEDWORKS and OPVIUS.

Rirkrit Tiravanija, Nikolaus Hirsch, Michel Müller: Do We Dream Under The Same Sky, ARoS Triennial, Aarhus, 2017

Thermodynamic Urbanism

Philippe Rahm

The history of urban and regional planning for the past forty years has been written from a macroscopic and aesthetic point of view rather than a microscopic and physiological one. By re-analyzing this history according to a microscopic prism, we can discover other factors that have actually been efficient in the constitution of cities and their forms. This reassessment will allow us to propose a future alternative to current urban development which is based on an unbalanced and humanly unfair economic globalization phenomenon. Our ambition is to contribute to a more sustainable, humanist, and equitable planetary urbanization for all.

The popularization of the macroscopic and aesthetic analysis of the city was certainly helped by the Italian architect Aldo Rossi who, in the pages of his book *The Architecture of the City* (1970), denounces the "naïve functionalism" that would reduce the history of the city and its project to the physiological and the organic. Yet, from the very first page of Rossi's introduction, it is indeed a physiological reason that he places as the very origin of architecture: the biological and climatic necessity of humans to "construct an artificial climate" as an environment more conducive to their existence. Immediately ignoring this condition, he asserts that man has built his environment with aesthetic and civilizing intentions above all else. It is these superstructural intentions that he studies, deriding any more infrastructural approach as "naive." Without engaging in any polemic, and acknowledging the theoretical contribution of Aldo Rossi, we nevertheless place ourselves on the side of the naive and partially challenge this macroscopic approach in favor of a reversal of analysis that would proceed from the microscopic. Rossi could be so sharp in 1970 only because the use and distribution of antibiotics had become widespread in the West since the 1950s, making irrelevant the entire hygiene program of architectural modernity and its physiological language. When Le Corbusier denounces the narrow street and invents zoning with the Athens Charter, he did so to fight against the foci of bacterial infections, continuing the first hygienic measures of the eighteenth and nineteenth centuries, those of Rambuteau and Horne,[1] Maret and Soufflot,[2] to fight against the stagnant air of dark alleys and poorly ventilated rooms. And the formal language of modern architecture of the 1920s—the long window and bay window, balcony and solarium for air and sun cures, the reverberant whiteness of disinfectant lime milk—is a plastic declination of the design of Alpine sanatoriums, invented in the nineteenth century to fight tuberculosis and other bacterial diseases. All of this curative language suddenly loses legitimacy with the discovery of penicillin. What is the point of shaving the narrow, dark streets of the Middle Ages, and moving the dwellings into vast parks of greenery, if you can just get rid of the disease with an antibiotic to swallow twice a day for a week? And it must also be admitted that the sun and the pure air of modernity did not heal very well.

What Aldo Rossi took as a primary cause of urban history was perhaps only a consequence of the use of antibiotics: functionalism had preceded aesthetics, physiology had allowed the symbolic, the microscopic had induced the macroscopic. This reversal of the historical links that we propose by starting from the microscopic and the physiological in order to explain the history of the city and the planning of the territory is important for our ability to project the future. If the "Rossian" postmodernism of the years from 1970 to 1980 did not completely succeed, it is perhaps because forms were constructed without cause, while keeping only the consequences of the urban facts. As an example, these numerous new squares were charged with symbolism and morphology, but were devoid of their original physiological significance as the place where people of former times had to go to draw drinking water, and then established social bonds there. It is this reversal of precedence between cause and consequence that we propose to study in urban planning and spatial planning, starting with the contributions of the new schools of thought in history as well as in geography and economy.

In his books *Guns, Germs, and Steel* (1997) and *Collapse* (2005), Jared Diamond has popularized this reversal of the grasp of the sequences of human history by placing environmental factors, those of climate, geology, or virus, upstream of human events.[3] If it was the Spaniards who

1. J. de Horne, *Mémoire sur quelques objets qui intéressent plus particulièrement la salubrité de la ville de Paris* (Paris, 1788): "One of the principal points of the healthiness of a large city like Paris is to promote Free circulation of the air in which it breathes, by gradually destroying all the obstacles which can intercept it [...] and by removing all the centers of uncleanliness and corruption from cities." Quoted by Richard Etlin, "L'air dans l'urbanisme des Lumières" [The air in the urbanism of the Enlightenment], *Dix-huitième siècle*, no. 9 (1977): 123-134. French translation by Jacques Guillerme. Garnier Frères, 1977.

2. Alain Corbin writes in *Le miasme et la jonquille*: "Soufflot has designed a vaulted room whose elliptical shape makes it possible to eliminate the stagnant corners and to establish ascending air currents." Alain Corbin, *Le miasme et la jonquille* (Paris: Flammarion, 1986).

3. Diamond writes: "History followed different courses for different peoples because of differences among peoples' environments, not because of biological differences among peoples themselves." Jared Diamond, *Guns, Germs, and Steel: The Fates of Human Societies* (New York: W. W. Norton, 1997).

conquered South America, and not the Aztecs who conquered Spain, it is because the viruses brought by the handful of conquistadors were far more proliferating and deadly than the viruses carried by the millions of Aztecs.[4] The writing of the History of America as revealed by Jared Diamond thus appears to be much more the consequence of the virulence of a virus than that of a political or religious program that would have been written upstream. Similarly, the American scientist explains the apogee and decline of civilizations such as those of the Vikings or Easter Island in relation to phenomena of climate change and soil erosion. In line with this new school of thought, some researchers have shown more recently that the moments of change in Chinese civilization correspond to periods of climatic aridity.[5] Or that the periods of great cold during the Middle Ages in Europe correspond with a rise of the religious era.[6] One might think that the history of civilizations would gradually free itself from this climatic influence with modernization, but on the contrary, it is an inverse trend, as described by Harald Welzer in *Climate Wars*. Welzer shows that climatic events lie behind the wars taking place in the twenty-first century. He writes: "Climate change is a social hazard that is underestimated and it seems that we refuse to imagine that this phenomenon, although

scientifically described, can generate catastrophes such as the implosion of social systems, civil wars, genocide."[7]

In his book *Trois leçons sur la société post-industrielle*, economist Daniel Cohen proceeds in a similar way to describe surprising reversals between what was believed to be the cause when it was actually a consequence. Thus he explains the phenomenon of the disappearance of social diversity in the city during modernity as being due not to the charter of Athens, which proposed to separate work districts from housing districts, but to the invention of the elevator first and then the RER, the express regional subway for suburban Paris: "Yesterday, in a normally constituted city, the rich lived on the second floor, the poor at the last. Rich and poor met on the stairs, and even if they did not talk, their children sometimes attended the same schools. Since the elevator has become widespread, buildings are frequented by the rich or the poor, but never again by the two at the same time, rich and poor living in distinct neighborhoods. Social diversity." As for the RER, Cohen explains that it is less a means of transport that would bring people closer together than a way to separate them even more: "Even worse, with the RER, the suburbs tend to move further away from the districts. Yesterday the workers' suburbs were

<hr>

4. Jared Diamond, "Guns, Germs, and Steel " (1997) "Far more Native Americans and other non-Eurasian peoples were killed by Eurasian germs than by Eurasian guns or steel weapons. Conversely, few or no distinctive lethal germs awaited would-be European conquerors in the New World." Ibid.

5. Hai Cheng, "Les variations de la mousson et la société chinoise depuis 1800 ans" [Changes in the monsoon and Chinese society over 1800 years], in *Des climats et des hommes* (Paris: La Découverte, 2012). "Thus, the collapse of some Chinese dynasties is related to periods of abnormal dryness."

6. Emmanuel Le Roy Ladurie and Daniel Rousseau, "Fluctuation du climat en France du Nord et du Centre au temps du Petit Âge glacière," in *Des climats et des hommes*, op. cit.: "In 1315 (the year of the great famine during the Little Glacial Age 1300-1350), there were few riots, but many prayers. Then there will be less devotion and more revolts."

7. Harald Welzer, *Climate Wars: What People Will Be Killed For in the 21st Century* (Cambridge, UK: Polity, 2012).

never very far from the city centers, and the workers had to walk to their place of work, and the distance could increase with the RER. … The inhabitants of the suburbs come to town Saturday nights, fill up images, and go home."[8]

Endocrine Development of the Territory in the Nineteenth Century

Rethinking the History of Urbanism to the prism of microscopy, that of the endocrine in the nineteenth century and bacteriology in the twentieth century, leads to surprising re-evaluations of the processes of making landscapes and cities. The medical role of iodine was identified in the first part of the nineteenth century and was popularized by English doctors, who began sending their patients to the seaside or to thermal spring areas where iodine was in liquid form; it appeared in water, as a gas, in marine spray,[9] or in solid form in fish or algae. The result of this discovery was the construction of the railway network and the urbanization of the seaside, with the invention of new seaside or spa towns such as Biarritz, Brighton, Spa, Ostend, Vichy, Arcachon, and Évian-les-Bains. At the scale of the territory, the urbanization of Europe in the nineteenth century and the invention of tourism are formal and programmatic consequences of the discovery of iodine (I) and its medical prescription. This discovery also plays a major role in the shaping of European cities, which from then on turned towards the beaches and shores, extended and opened to the sea or to the lake water, to those "real open-air sanatoriums where the fortunate patients come to enjoy the balsamic and iodized air coming from the ocean and the scents of pines." The morphology of the Swiss villages, for example, was totally reversed for this reason in the nineteenth century. The Swiss fled the shores until the beginning of the nineteenth century. Up to that time, the side of the houses facing a lake was considered the back of the building where the garbage was dumped, whereas the opposite side of the houses opening towards the mountains, with their back to the lake, was considered the beautiful facade. We then witnessed the complete reversal of this urban morphology. Indeed, once the water was recognized for its iodized value, new building constructions were turned towards the lake, such as the large hotels of Montreux. And the main street that was formerly set back from the lake was doubled by the construction of new docks

8. Daniel Cohen, *Trois leçons sur la société post-industrielle* (Paris: Seuil, 2006), XX. All translations mine unless noted otherwise.

9. See A. A. Boinet, *Iodothérapie* (Paris: Victor Masson et Fils Editeurs, 1865): «Chemical analysis, by discovering iodine in a crowd of mineral waters, where formerly there was no suspicion of its presence, has come to furnish the explanation of the ancient healing powers of these waters in the affections where the Iodic acid are indicated today with success. But it is to Dr. Goindet of Geneva that the honor of having introduced iodine and consequently its compounds into the medical field belongs. In seeking a formula from Cadet de Gassicourt, he found that Russell advised the burnt fucus against goiter. Suspecting then that the sponge which was then used against goiter and fucus might well owe their medicinal properties only to the iodine of which Courtois had proved the existence in the mother waters of the soda of kelp, [he] tried [it] against the hypertrophy of the thyroid gland and had the happiness to succeed. A year had elapsed since the beginning of his experiments when he communicated his discovery to the Helvetic Society of Natural Sciences assembled at Geneva, on July 25, 1820. Two other memories of Coindet appeared some time after, to prove that iodine was the true specific of goiter, and that it was a sovereign remedy for the treatment of scrofula and some diseases of the lymphatic system.»

that offered a promenade by the water. Thus all the European shores are now urbanized near lake water and the sea, rehabilitated thanks to iodine.

Later in the century, around 1860, Louis Pasteur discovered that the air we breathe is not empty but contains bacteria, and has less bacteria in the mountains.[10] This medical knowledge, combined with the so-called microbicidal power of solar radiation to fight tuberculosis,[11] led to a tremendous development in the urbanization of the Alps with the creation of Leysin, Davos, and Gstaad. Whereas, earlier, people had fled from the mountains as places of extreme poverty and degenerate populations,[12] once Maugiron of the Société des Sciences de Lyon in 1838 and Saussure in his *Journey to the Alps* recounted first the discovery of iodine and then the promotion of sunbathing,[13] or heliotherapy, by Doctors Bernhard and Rollier in Switzerland, the mountains turned into desirable places for holiday. Just as the theses stated by Aldo Rossi in *The Architecture of the City* are a consequence of the discovery of penicillin, those stated by Le Corbusier in *Towards an Architecture* or The Charter of Athens are a consequence of the discovery of iodine, the microbicidal power of the sun, and a decline in microbial presence in less polluted air.

Thermodynamic Planning in the Twenty-first Century

It is important to understand the direction of these mechanisms of causality. An analysis by microscope very often reverses the order: what one takes for a cause on the macroscopic scale proves to be a consequence at the microscopic scale. If we want to define an urban and territorial strategy for the future, we must therefore analyze whether they are really the efficient causes at work in the transformation of territories. In this analysis, the climatic and energy parameters, which are strongly linked between architectural and urban factors, appear to be the main vectors that act and will continue to act on the renewal of spatial planning. The term "thermodynamic urbanism" that we are going to define here could cover all the active criteria that can be mobilized in a renewal of global urbanization.

If we look for a microscopic cause that would be upstream of the major architectural and urban decisions to come in the twenty-first century, carbon dioxide (CO_2) is certainly felt to play the leading role. Over the past two decades, we have become aware of the negative consequences on the climate of the increasing presence of this gas in the atmosphere caused by the consumption of fossil fuels such as gas, oil, and coal.

10. See Louis Pasteur, *Oeuvres*, vol. 2 (Paris: Masson et cie, 1922): «And first, are there germs in the air? Nobody denies it, because we understand that it cannot be otherwise.»

11. «One will continue as in the past to live in the darkness. The sun will not be able to penetrate the dwelling and dislodge the exterminating bacillus. In short, lack of aeration and sun in the accommodation, lack of sun especially. In summary, one can formulate the result of this research by saying that tuberculosis is above all the disease of darkness. « In Congrès international de la tuberculose, Paris, 2–7 October 1905, *Rapports présentés au congrès*, vol. 25 (Paris: Masson et cie, 1905).

12. See E. Esquiral, *Des maladies mentales*, book 2 (Brussels: Librairie médicale et scientifique de J. B. Tircher, 1838): «The names of cretins are given to idiots and idiots who usually inhabit the gorges of the mountains. Is it not endemic in the gorges of mountains more or less marshy and exposed to moist air?»

13. J. Malgat, «Cure solaire de la tuberculose pulmonaire chronique,» in Congrès international de la tuberculose, Paris, 2–7 October 1905, *Rapports présentés au congrès*, vol. 25 (Paris: Masson et cie, 1905).

Burning fossil fuels releases CO2 into the atmosphere, which has the disadvantage of constituting a kind of lid that prevents heat from escaping the earth's atmosphere. The result is a warming of the atmosphere which disrupts the climatic equilibriums on which the urbanization of the planet was built for centuries, causing catastrophes and migrations. The energy consumed by building techniques (heating, ventilation, air conditioning, hot water production) is responsible for almost 50% of the release of these greenhouse gases, so architecture and town planning are directly involved in ecologists' and citizens' mission for a reduction of these emissions. The discovery of the role of CO2 in global warming and its popularization by the IPCC of 1988 certainly marks the end of postmodernism and renders obsolete the study and design of an architecture that is only aesthetic and symbolic. The need to combat global warming assigns new responsibilities to architecture and town planning, as it is an emergency similar to that experienced in the face of bacteriological diseases in the nineteenth century.

The nuclear crisis following the Fukushima accident (2011) is expected to lead to a gradual abandonment of this energy source. Without fossil energy or nuclear energy, and without the possibility of immediately replacing them with renewable energies such as solar or wind, cities at the beginning of the twenty-first century must immediately reduce their energy expenditure. It is in this context of the current need to save energy that the notion of thermodynamic planning can begin to be defined as taking advantage of local natural energy resources to build architecture that has been called green, solar, ecological, or meteorological.

Thermodynamic urban planning would be a new way of envisaging globalization, through a redeployment of industrial production, on a global scale, based on energy and climatic rather than economic criteria. We are in the midst of a crisis in the "post-industrial" model of society, which was based on a global distribution of labor between the skilled work of designing ideas, software, design, and marketing in the North and the unskilled labor of manufacturing objects, computers, and clothing in the South. Until 1960, the South exported only raw materials which were then manufactured in the North. Since the 1960s, the industrialization of the South led to the deindustrialisation of the North, and the South now exports the finished manufactured product directly, leaving to the North the design and the marketing of this product. This situation is risky because the technological advance of the North vis-à-vis the South is reduced every year; we can predict that soon the South will be producing as many ideas, designs, and concepts as the North, which will lead automatically to a drop in work and employment in the North, in Europe in particular. From this perspective, what becomes of Europe and especially France? With few industries and only some state-of-the-art technological know-how (in nuclear or TGV), which tends to be surpassed by the arrival of new technologies developed in the United States such as Google or Facebook, what will happen to France if it no longer produces or designs products? There is still the luxury industry, of course, and the cultural and gastronomic tourism that Michel Houellebecq describes so well as the industrial future of a France that would fall back on the "magic of the terroir" of its countryside: cheeses, Palombes, snails, Massif central, and Relais et Châteaux chains.[14] Indeed, putting aside cynicism, certain products belong to an inalienable specific terroir linked to a particular climate, to a mineral quality of the soil, which confers a unique taste to a product, such as the

14. Michel Houellebecq, *La carte et le territoire* (Paris: Flammarion, 2010).

contribution of limestone soil and sun to the great wines of Bordeaux. There is no question here of know-how or cultural traditions that globalization will inevitably copy, hybridize, or relocate, but only certain geographical, geological, and climatic conditions, unique to a place that is not national, as Houellebecq says, but regional. For although it is impossible to relocate Bordeaux to China or Bangladesh, this does not prevent new terroirs from appearing in the Napa Valley in California or in Ningxia in China, with wines that were rated as the best in the world (in 2011).

To begin to explain the concept of thermodynamic planning, we will rely on three examples, each revealing a particular way of exploiting the energy resources that are unique to a specific geographical location. The first example is the relocation of Facebook servers from California to the Arctic Circle in Lulea, Sweden. Computers that store the gigantic amount of digital information overheat and require enormous energy to be cooled. Since the annual average temperature of Lulea is 2 degrees Celsius, it is therefore easy to understand the savings that will be realized by the US company (which amount to several tens of billions of dollars) by relocating their servers to Lulea from the Mediterranean climate of California, whose annual temperature is 19.5 degrees Celsius. The second example is the village of Trient in Switzerland. This small village of 150 inhabitants deep in the steep mountains of the Valais, without even a ski slope, will receive in the years to come several million Swiss francs of hydraulic royalty because it owns a glacier that provides water to the dam that produces electricity for the entire Swiss rail network. The third example is the German Desertec project, which aims to cover part of the Sahara desert with solar power plants to supply all the electricity requirements of North Africa and Europe.[15] These three examples reveal astonishing new places of urbanization that were almost uninhabited and are in the great north, the desert, and high mountains, places that have had nothing to do with urbanization since the beginnings of humanity. The twenty-first century will see a radical change in the criteria of geographic value. We could witness a relocation of human geography that will lead to the birth of new cities and the decline of old ones.

Climate can thus play an essential role in the future urbanization of the planet according to global thermodynamic values linked to the parameters of geographical positioning, latitude, and altitude. It could be a solution for a globalization that would rely no longer on wage injustices or an international division of labor but on ecological and climatic criteria in the direction of a general ecology at a human scale.

Three Projects Based on Thermodynamics

Climate could also play a major role in the design of the morphology of the city and in the choice of its materiality. Three recent projects by our office are challenging the climate as the major factor for urban design. The first one is a study for the city of Copenhagen in Denmark, the second is a new park under construction for the city of Taichung in Taiwan, and the third is an urban competition for the city of Samara in Russia. Copenhagen and Samara are situated in a cold and dry latitude, while Taichung is in a humid and warm climate. For these three projects, we try to create a good quality of life in public space. But we think that the quality of public space is not only about the conviviality of

15. "All kinds of renewables will be used in the DESERTEC Concept, but the sun-rich deserts of the world play a special role: within six hours deserts receive more energy from the sun than humankind consumes within a year. In addition, 90 percent of the world's population lives within 3,000 km of deserts." http://www. desertec.org/fileadmin/downloads/desertec_foundation_flyer_en.pdf

the program and the size of the space, but it also concerns the notion of comfort in all senses— that is, thermal comfort, health comfort, silence comfort, etc. By starting to design a public space by focusing on its climate, we will give sensorial qualities to the city while simultaneously meeting the new targets of energy savings and sustainability. In Copenhagen, we propose to define a new urban circulation network that is no longer based on cars and visual representation, but is based on sound quality, the reduction of air pollutants, and the natural increase of heat in the outdoor space. In Taiwan, we propose an urban park with its composition based on a real site analysis of the repartition of the temperature, humidity levels, and pollution rates. In Samara, we propose to design a dual-season geometry in new blocks of the city using the wind, in which fresh air will be increased in the summer by allowing cold wind in and the cold wind will be blocked during the winter.

PUBLIC AIR, COPENHAGEN, DENMARK (2013-14)

A collaboration between Philippe Rahm architectes & Frans Drewniak
Supported by The Danish Arts Foundation & Dreyers Fond

The "Public Air" project for the City of Copenhagen aims to rethink the formal and technological heritage of the twentieth century in favor of new physiological criteria, to mitigate the air and noise pollution brought on by automobiles and industrial processes. To this end, cycling has recently become very popular in Copenhagen, despite the city's vehicle-centric design and materials. Consequently, cyclists in Copenhagen share the roads with cars, a result of twentieth-century urban planning. Further, the physical exertion necessary for riding a bike causes bicyclists

to breathe deeper, inhaling the air pollution given off by automobiles. Because it is both socially and politically impossible to ban the use of cars in the city, the City of Copenhagen has recently proposed a "Green Bike Network" to be developed in the near future. This proposal comprises a network of paths specific to bicycle and pedestrian traffic, and parallel to roadways used by automobiles. The plan, already in progress, navigates parks and vacant spaces in order to avoid crossing streets used by motor vehicles, and the air pollution therein. Rather than fighting against air pollution and the automotive-centric design of the twentieth century, this project proposes the creation of a new physiological vocabulary for the Green Bike Network. By analyzing and reconceptualizing each element of the twentieth-century built environment that contributes to undesirable physiological consequences, we can return to the causal relationship between physiological necessity and the impulse to build. Based on a study of urban forms and materials, focusing on how they contribute to air pollution, noise pollution, and heat gain, we have reconsidered each element of the built environment in terms of its ability to negate undesirable physiological consequences caused by the current built environment and climate of Copenhagen. Soil, façade material, street furniture, street layout and orientation, air, light, sound, and smell are elements that can be specifically implemented to create a more comfortable city air quality, noise threshold, and atmospheric temperature, in the cold climate of northern Europe.

Our goal is to provide a comfortable street network and atmospheric quality for cyclists that protects them from cold winds, utilizes light to simulate the warmth of the sun, and minimizes air and noise pollution. In a way, the new street, a public space, will have the comfort and quality of life—specifically, heat, clean air, and silence—that are usually exclusive to private space in a house or inside a car.

To optimize the comfort of pedestrians and cyclists, we are offering research and ideation towards conceiving a new street layout, construction, building orientation, and material usage. To do so, we have analyzed each physical component of the proposed Green Bike Network according to the following criteria:

HEAT

To bring heat into the cold Northern European climate of Copenhagen, we propose the following:. Use low-albedo (nonreflective) street materials to transform the visible and invisible rays of the sun into heat energy through contact with absorptive, non-reflecting surfaces like dark and porous asphalt. Within a short zone of influence, these materials will conduct and radiate heat to human bodies. Use high-albedo (reflective) façade and signage materials to reflect heat downward, towards the absorptive, low-albedo street materials. Further, reflective building and signage orientation should be angled to catch sunlight and reflect it downward.
— 1. Materials will be made to protect cyclists from wind chill. The wind increases heat loss from the body faster because it convects and conducts heat energy away from the skin, which increases the feeling of cold.
— 2. The street orientation and programmatic clustering that accommodates specific activities throughout the day is based on the sun's position in relation to the streets. For lunch breaks, streets used to travel to food outlets and restaurants will be oriented in a north-south direction to absorb maximal sunlight. For the commute to and from work, in the late afternoon and early morning, the streets used to go to work are oriented from east to west to absorb maximal sunlight.
— 3. Geothermal heat pumps can be used to extract or dissipate heat from the ground, in order to heat the air above.
— 4. Street and façade materials will be made with a high thermal conductivity can rapidly absorb sunlight and transfer heat to bodies and the air during times of day and seasons with little to no sunlight. This will maximize the amount of heat that can be absorbed from what little sunlight there is during the day.

DEPOLLUTION

To create better air quality, we will use pollution-absorbing street and façade materials, especially in areas near major roads, industrial processes, and power plants.
— 1. Recently developed depolluting street and façade materials formulated with titanium dioxide (TiO_2) can be used to attract and decompose nitrogen oxide (NO_x)—a harmful pollutant put into the air by vehicles and industrial processes—into harmless nitrate (NO_3).
— 2. nontoxic street and façade materials that will not add more pollutants, specifically aerosols, to the atmosphere.
— 3. The absorption of dust can be achieved by some trees with downy leaves, as well as some materials.

NOISE

To create quieter public spaces in response to car noise, we propose
— 1. To use soft, porous soil and vegetation, as well as sound-absorbing façade materials, to absorb, diffract, and dissipate noise coming from the streets. . To plan a drawing and cutting profile of the streets in order to optimize the sound quality in public spaces, like theaters, using nonparallel store fronts.

JADE METEO PARK, TAICHUNG, TAIWAN (2012-15)

A collaborative project between Philippe Rahm architectes, Mosbach paysagistes, and Ricky Liu & Associates for the Government of Taichung City, Taiwan

The ambition of our project is to give the outdoors back to inhabitants and visitors by proposing to create exterior spaces where the excesses of the climate of Taichung are lessened. The exterior climate of the park is thus modulated to propose spaces that are less hot (cooler, in the shade), less humid (by lowering humid air, sheltered from the rain and flood), less polluted (by adding filtered air from gases and particulate-matter pollution), less noisy, and with less mosquitoes. The design composition principle of the "Taichung Jade Meteo Park" is based on climatic variations that we have mapped by computational fluid dynamics simulation (CFD): some areas of the park are naturally warmer, more humid, and more polluted, while others are naturally cooler (because they are in the route of cold winds coming from the North), drier (because protected from the Southeast wind that contains the humidity of the sea in the air), and cleaner (far away from the roads). We have augmented these differences of climates in order to increase the coolness, dryness, and cleanliness of places that are naturally cooler, less humid, and less polluted, in order to create more comfortable spaces for visitors. Beginning with the existing conditions as a point of departure, we have defined three gradation climatic maps following the results of three computational fluid dynamics simulations. Each map specifically corresponds to a particular atmospheric parameter and its variation of intensity throughout the park. The first one corresponds to variation in the heat on the site, the second one describes the variations in humidity in the air, and the third one the intensity of the atmospheric pollution. Each map shows how the intensity or strength of the respective atmospheric parameter is modulated through the park. By doing so, the maps keep areas within the park from reaching excessive natural conditions while making the experience of changes in climate much more comfortable in the areas where we will reinforce the coolness, dryness, and cleanness. The three maps intersect and overlap randomly in order to create a diversity of microclimates and a multitude of different sensual experiences in different areas of the park that we could freely occupy depending on the hour of the day or the month in the year. At a certain place, for example, the air will be less humid and less polluted but it will still be warm, while elsewhere in the park, the air will be cooler and drier, but will remain polluted. The three climatic maps vary within a gradation, which ranges from a maximum degree of uncomfortable atmospheric levels that usually exist in the city (the maximum rate of pollution, humidity, and heat) to areas that are more comfortable, where the heat, humidity, and pollution are lessened.

To materialize these climatic maps, we invented a catalogue of climatic devices (natural and artificial) that reinforce areas that are already more comfortable by lowering, reducing, inverting, and diminishing the heat, humidity, and pollution. These devices are classified in three categories: the cooling devices, the drying devices, and the depolluting devices.

The natural cooling devices are trees with specific qualities for cooling the atmosphere because they

Jade Meteo Park, Taichung, Taiwan (2012-15)

have lots of leaves or big leaves that create heavy shadows, or white flowers and waxy leaves that reflect the warm sun rays, or trees that produce a strong evaporation with the consequence of cooling the air around them because of the physical change of phase from liquid to gas. The artificial cooling devices are apparatuses working on meteorological phenomena like convection, conduction, evaporation, or reflection in order to cool the air or to cool the human body directly. The convective cooling devices are named "Anticyclone" or "Underground breeze," and they blow cool air chilled by underground heat exchange. The conductive cooling devices are named "Night light" or "Vertical night," and expose black and cold surfaces chilled by cold water where human skin can be cooled by touching them. The evaporating cooling devices are named, for example, "Stratus cloud" or "Blue sky drizzle," and by emitting mist or rain, they refresh the surrounding air temperature by their change of phase from liquid to gas. The reflective cooling devices named "Moon light" or "Long wave filters" are apparatuses that filter or reflect the sunlight and the heat carried by it.

The second category of climatic devices are the drying climatic devices whose objectives are to protect the body from the rain and to reduce the excessive humidity in the air that amplifies the discomfort by an unfavorable influence on the human body in the thermolysis process by blocking perspiration. The first objective is reached by artificial shelters and trees with dense fronds that protect visitors from the rain. The second objective is reached by natural drying climatic devices that absorb the humidity in the air with their floating roots and by artificial drying devices that blow air dried by silicate gel exchangers named "Dry cloud" or "Desert wind."

The third category are the depolluting climatic devices. They reduce the atmospheric pollution in the air, excessive noise, and the presence of mosquitoes. The natural depolluting devices are composed of trees with the capability of absorbing oxides of nitrogen and other aerosols, to make effective sound barriers. The artificial depolluting devices such as the "Ozone eclipse" blow into the park filtered air without gaseous pollution like NO_x, O_3, or SO_2. The "Preindustrial draught" blows into the park air that doesn't have particulate matters PM10 and PM2.5 emitted by industry and cars. The Ultrasound Repellant device repels mosquitoes by emitting waves above the human auditory range (>20kHz), and at the same frequency as the beat of a dragonfly's wings. This will repel mosquitos by using the sounds of their predators.

According to the density and quantity of climatic devices in a given area, we create spaces more or less enjoyable, and more or less comfortable. Thus, the different climatic properties sometimes overlap, separate, regroup, densify, or dilute, generating a variety of atmospheres which visitors can choose from and appropriate as they see fit.

With these two projects, we argue that the climate could be the main focus in the design of a city. We know that global warming phenomena creates anxiety about the future of the planet. Our argument is that if the climate is the problem, it could be also the tool for rethinking the urbanization of the planet and the city in a more ecological and sustainable way that could also provide to the inhabitant a new quality of life that is more comfortable, more sensual.

Seasonal City, Samara, Russia (2013)

SEASONAL CITY, SAMARA, RUSSIA (2013)

Philippe Rahm architectes

In Samara, we propose to create a city that contains a double public network distribution system: one mainly for cars (that nevertheless keeps sidewalks for pedestrians), and the other exclusively for pedestrians and cyclists who can cross the city entirely away from pollution and noise. The road networks, separated from each other, create two distribution systems in which we strengthen the qualities of climatic comfort based on whether the majority is using it more or less depending on the season. Thus, we focus on the automotive network more diligently in the winter when it's cold, when more people take refuge in the heated interior of the car, while on the pedestrian promenade, which is less commonly used because more unpleasant, we induce special treatment of the ground, facades, and street furniture to enhance the warmth in winter. Because this automobile street network and surrounding places will be used in the winter, we give it the name "Winter Network," and it is the first distribution system in the area.

On the other hand, the pedestrian and bicycle networks will be used more often in the summer when it's hot, when people can walk outside without the discomfort of cold and snow.

We enhance the effects of fresh air, shade, and the absorption of light to prevent overheating of its spaces. This pedestrian network of streets and squares is named the "Summer Network." The two networks of streets each has a place towards which all of its streets converge. The streets in the Winter Network converge at the "Winter Place," a more urban area, with cars, which is linked directly to the city center, at the south of the new district. The "Summer Place," where all the summer pedestrian streets converge, is located at the north of the district, directly on the river, so people can enjoy its spaces for walking and relaxing.

Thermal Mass

Stoss Landscape Urbanism,
(Elaine Stokes, Katherine Harvey,
Amy Whitesides, Chris Reed)

Subterranean soil systems have a profound impact on the habitats occupying the earth's surface. As urbanization continues and anthropogenic processes output carbon dioxide, soil absorbs and holds thermal mass in new patterns. Heat sinks, in turn, creating conditions that contribute to the urban heat island effect while also forcing the migration of plants to cooler regions. Moving beyond surficial design, landscape architects must consider the deep section and choreograph the subterranean conditions that impact the organisms occupying its surface. By drawing, mapping, and modeling subsurface soil types and thermal mass, we acknowledge that these factors play an essential role in the health of the habitats above them. Activating new design methodologies that pair thermal mass assessment with large-scale open space initiatives will allow soil to take a more active role in the design of cities, landscapes, and environments.

Soil as an Active Material for Design
Heat Sources and Sinks

The urban heat island effect is frequently addressed as a surficial issue; surface materials and the impermeability of land attract most of the attention when discussing it. However, urban heat islands result from the interface between atmospheric and subterranean heat sources and sinks. Soil is the second-largest carbon sink on the planet,[1] with cities augmenting thermal mass in the soil below them. In urban areas, subterranean hotspots evolve over decades or centuries, originating from anthropogenic heat sources leaking into the soil.[2] Subterranean transportation systems, sewage systems, geothermal energy plants, and heated basements are just a few of the sources that release heat into

1. European Environment Agency, "Soil and Climate Change," *Signals—Towards Clean and Smart Mobility* (2015): 5.

2. Kathrin Menberg et al., "Subsurface Urban Heat Islands in German Cities," *Science of the Total Environment* (9 October 2012): 123.

the soil. The urban heat island effect results in micro-climates that are warmer than the surrounding rural areas, which has a significant impact on the well-being of the humans, flora, and fauna occupying cities.

The City of Seoul presents a valuable case study of the urban heat island effect and the role that soil and open space play in the overall energy of the city. Situated in a valley, Seoul's densest areas occupy some of the lowest elevations in the city, while the mountainous northern and southern peripheries of the city transition to forest. Belowground, Seoul's extensive subway system spans 200 kilometers and has been steadily expanding for over four decades. Within an area of 600 square kilometers, the landscape transitions from river valley to mountain edge, from dense urban to open rural space. These topographic and anthropogenic conditions result in intense temperature variations within the city. A study by Yeon-Hee Kim and Jong-Jin Baik of Seoul National University found that the low-lying densely urban areas experienced an average annual temperature 3 degrees Celsius warmer than elevated, open spaces elsewhere in the city.[3] While causality was not proven in this research effort, correlation between warmer temperatures and level of human activity was clearly demonstrated: city centers became warmer on weekdays than on weekends, when human occupation of downtown was lower[4]. Continued exploration of cities like Seoul and their heat sources and sinks will provide key insight into design methodologies to cope with the urban heat island effect.

Distribution of average air temperature in Seoul, March 2001 through February 2002. Numbers indicate degrees Celsius. Excerpt from: Yeon-Hee Kim and John-Jin Baik, "Spatial and Temporal Structure of the Urban Heat Island in Seoul," *Journal of Applied Meteorology* 44 (May 2005): 594

Advocating for Soil through Representation

The incorporation of soil into the urban planning process requires a shift in representational method when drawing the urban fabric. While city planning has traditionally been concerned with the urban surface at the macro-scale and the seemingly omniscient plan view, this approach overlooks the subterranean processes that impact the urban environment above them. If city planners switch to alternative representation methods that acknowledge the sectional nature of cities, the subsurface space will become an essential aspect of the urban environment to include in the design process.

3. Yeon-Hee Kim and Jong-Jin Baik, "Spatial and Temporal Structure of the Urban Heat Island in Seoul," *Journal of Applied Meteorology* 44 (May 2005): 594.

4. Ibid., 603.

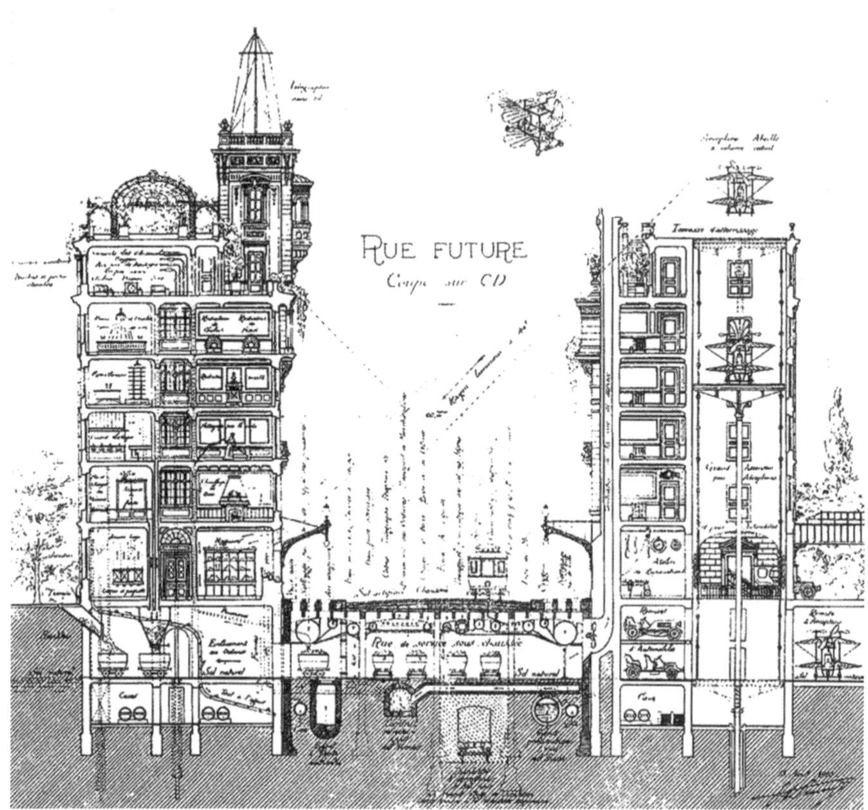

To get a complete picture of the urban heat island effect, we must shift our perspective in visualizing the city. Rather than accepting the plan view as the most efficient method of capturing the urban environment, we must recognize the plan's tendency to obscure the systems operating below the urban surface. New modes of dissecting the city through section and three-dimensional modeling allow subterranean networks to be foregrounded. This approach to drawing the subsurface in detail became a more common practice by architects in the early twentieth century. As underground transportation systems gained prevalence, subterranean networks made their way into design representation, thickening the sectional drawing. In his section "La Rue Future" Eugène Hénard activates the transportation systems below the surface with greater detail than the ground's surface, marking a shift in the design field towards recognizing the potential for below-ground human occupation. Similarly, realized transportation networks like Grand Central Terminal in New York and the multilevel street system in Chicago increasingly engaged the volume below the city surface. However, these projects and representations predominantly indicated the anthropogenic impact into the subsurface, rather than indicating the impact of soil and stored heat upon the surface above it.

La Rue Future by Eugène Hénard, presenting subsurfaces' volumes with the same weight as supersurface spaces.

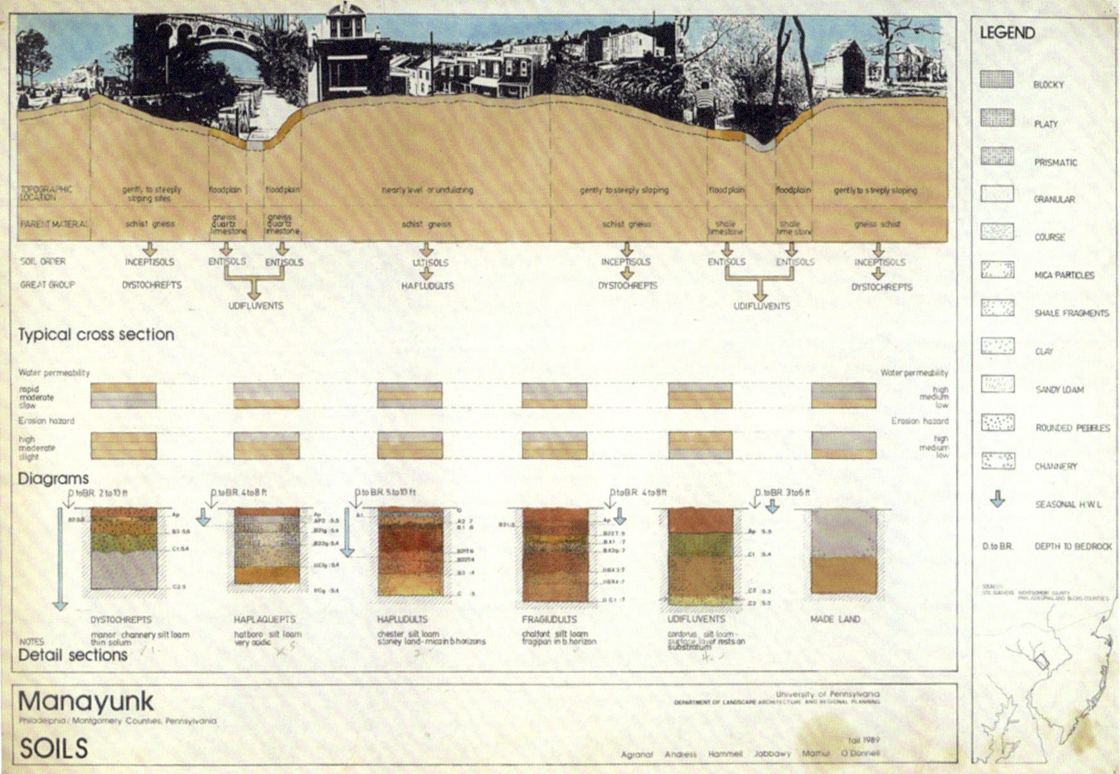

Ian McHarg turned the deep section into a tool for demonstrating the existing natural conditions that influence human occupation, rather than the inverse. In his section of Manayunk, Philadelphia, McHarg employed collage, diagram, and section to characterize the subterranean soil characteristics of the site. By translating this type of section with embedded soil information into a planning tool, designers can create more informed strategies for planting and human occupation that complement the specific soil conditions below. Soil types, water content, and temperature gradients, which each have significant impact on the flora and fauna occupying the soil's surface, take form in overlaid plans, the exploded axon, and especially in the deep section. Through these methods, heat sources and sinks can be directly incorporated into the dialogue influencing urban development patterns.

Soil-based Tools

Climate change has already had significant impact on the growth patterns of flora. As precipitation patterns shift and temperatures become more extreme, plants are migrating to new geographies that better accommodate their needs. Cities are particularly critical in demonstrating the new ecologies that form as plants adapt to evolving environments.

Sections and diagrams by McHarg (and his students) documenting soil types below the city of Philadelphia.

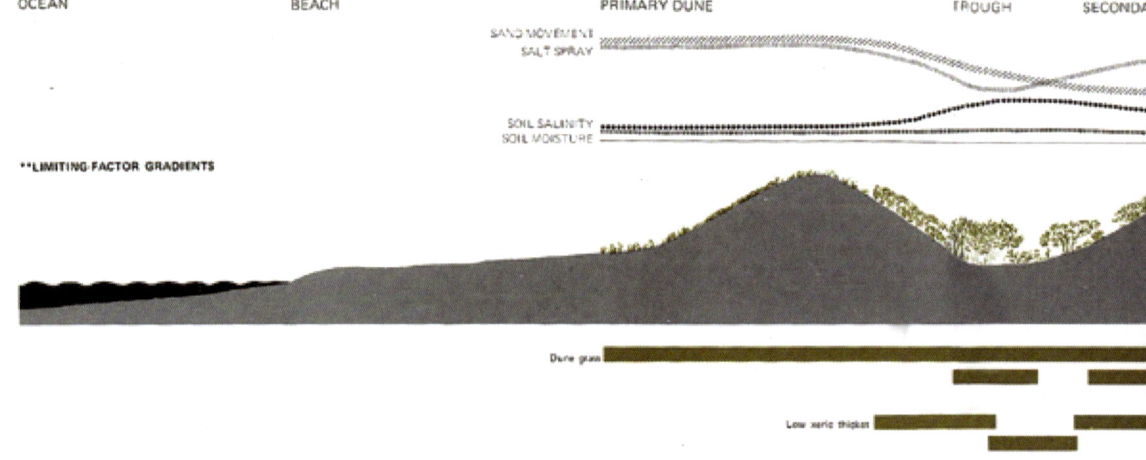

Section by McHarg, illustrating the fluid nature of dunescapes.

Given the uniquely warm soil in cities caused by the urban heat island effect, urban cores act as epicenters for novel ecologies. A new body of research exploring the impact of new environmental conditions on plant communities has flourished in recent years, shifting landscape priorities away from preserving prior ecological conditions and instead understanding plant communities as fluid, ever-evolving compositions.

In particular, the influence of urban soils on the plants that occupy them has gained greater attention. Peter Del Tredici has written extensively on the "novel ecosystems" arising within urban contexts. Rather than glorifying the native plant, Del Tredici studies "invasive" species with equal attention and acknowledges the critical ecological functions that spontaneous vegetation serves. Most importantly, he credits the variation in urban soil as a driving factor in determining which plants will thrive in a particular site. Certain plant species have developed characteristics that allow them to occupy contaminated and compacted soils that characterize ruderal landscapes.[5] Rather than allowing preconceived notions of landscape typologies to guide his analysis, Del Tredici considers the particular traits of a plant species that allow it to adapt to anthropogenic landscapes. This methodology could similarly be applied to studying the particular traits of soil that accommodate plant communities.

Laura Solano has recently advanced the perspective that soils deserve equal attention to the plants that occupy it. Since "healthy soils beget trees that live longer and grow bigger, enabling them to cast more shade, and absorb more CO2, and runoff," Solano advocates

5. Peter Del Tredici, "The Flora of the Future," *Places Journal* (April 2014), https://doi.org/10.22269/140417, accessed 15 June 2017.

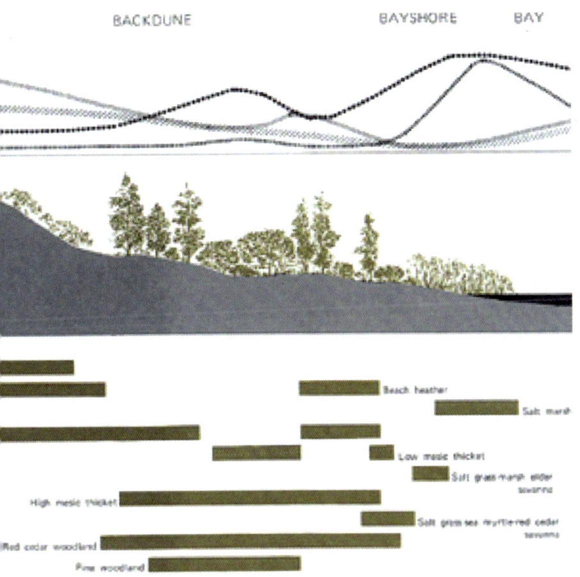

for investment in urban soils as a crucial step towards cultivating a healthy urban plant community.[6] A robust vegetal network increases shade and reduces carbon dioxide, which in turn mitigates the urban heat island effect; thus, soil serves a foundational role in this process.

In order to design with these new conditions, we need to develop tools for assessing evolving contexts. By adapting to new environmental conditions and by better understanding the factors that cause plant migration, we can capitalize on beneficial factors while also mitigating anthropogenic processes that would hinder plants' ability to thrive in future environmental conditions. While planting plans normally take into account factors like sun, water, and soil acidity, additional factors have a profound impact on a plant's ability to grow in a particular site.

As we evolve the landscape profession to work with new environmental conditions, we have the opportunity to develop additional site assessment tools focused on soil and thermal mass and their impact on the longevity, maintenance, and resiliency of what we see expressed on the surface.

One method of incorporating subterranean systems into the design process is conducting thermal mass assessments of landscape sites. The thermal mass of soil has a significant impact on plants' ability to absorb nutrients, thereby influencing their growth patterns; for example, the onset of photosynthesis has been observed to occur concurrently with the end of soil thawing.[7] Given this, if soil retains a higher level of thermal mass later into autumn or begins absorbing thermal mass from the atmosphere earlier in spring, plants' photosynthesis cycles will likely extend throughout a longer portion of the year. However, extreme heat can reduce plant fertility, potentially causing a rapid decline in the population of certain plant species. Therefore, by assessing a site's thermal mass, we can capitalize on plants that will respond with an extended growing season, thereby creating more productive year-round landscapes.

In addition to assessing the thermal mass of a landscape prior to implementing a design, the continued monitoring of a site's ground surface temperature provides insight into the design's effectiveness at reducing the urban heat island effect. While *greening* of urban space has long been known to create cooler microclimates, recent studies have illuminated some nuances to this theory. Studies demonstrate that non-domestic areas covered in trees and shrubs keep

6. Laura Solano,

7. Satyen Mondal et al., "Impact of Elevated Soil and Air Temperature on Plants' Growth, Yield, and Physiological Interaction: A Critical Review," *Scientia Agriculturae* 14 (3) (5 May 2016): 293–305.

soil surface temperature several degrees cooler over an eleven-month period than similar residential green spaces.[8] Additionally, the location of public green spaces in relation to one another must be choreographed. The monitoring of ground surface temperature indicates that the ecological principle of "single large over several small" (SLOSS) guides the organization of urban open space. In the context of the urban heat island effect, single large vegetated spaces have a greater impact in decreasing urban temperature than several small vegetated spaces scattered throughout a city. According to a study of Phoenix, Arizona, "clustered or less fragmented patterns of vegetation lower seasonal [land surface temperature] more effectively than dispersed patterns."[9] Such research indicates that the relationship between open spaces is more important than sheer quantity of spaces, and as a result landscape architects must operate at the macro-level planning scale to most effectively relieve urban centers of the negative effects of global warming.

Soil-based Design

While designers certainly have a responsibility to minimize anthropogenic impact on climate change, a certain degree of global warming is inevitable. In addition to capitalizing on methodologies that decrease the urban heat island effect, we can curate novel successional landscapes that cope with warming environments while also improving quality of life for the city's occupants. Landscape is a unique medium due to its dynamic nature; a landscape design evolves continuously, achieving a certain level of maturity several decades after its conception and continuing to experience phases of succession afterwards. It becomes the responsibility of the landscape architect to account for evolving climatic contexts that the design will experience in the coming years. In particular, plant migration due to warming climate and shifting precipitation patterns will create novel successional landscapes. If designers only look at current conditions, their projects will likely not be able to adapt to warmer, drier, or wetter conditions that will occur in the near future. However, by understanding the relationships between soil, water content, thermal mass retention, and plants, designers can create self-sustaining landscapes that will flourish as the climate shifts.

Seoul presents a compelling study site within the context of global warming and the urban heat island effect to explore how plant communities might shift in response to these factors. Because Seoul's urban center experiences higher average annual temperatures than its surrounding environment,[10] the city can serve as a case study for the warmer temperatures that may migrate north as general global warming occurs. Plant migrations respond to a multitude of environmental factors, including soil type, elevation, water access, and temperature. Each of these conditions varies significantly across the area of Seoul, making this city a unique testing ground for evaluating plant adaptation strategies within a small geographic range.

8. J. L. Edmondson et al., "Soil Surface Temperatures Reveal Moderation of the Urban Heat Island Effect by Trees and Shrubs," *Scientific Reports* (19 September 2016):

19. Chao Fan et. al. "Measuring the Spatial Arrangement of Urban Vegetation and Its Impacts on Seasonal Surface Temperatures," *Progress in Physical Geography* (March 2016): 215–16.

9. Yeon-Hee Kim and John-JinBaik. "Spatial and Temporal Structure of the Urban Heat Island in Seoul." *Journal of Applied Meteorology* 44 (May 2005): 594.

While research into plant migrations in response to global warming is a relatively new field, with most studies arising within the past few decades, landscape architects can begin testing the design implications of such migrations by employing soil-based tools in urban environments. By assessing a site's soil type and its ground surface temperature before and after design implementation, we can increase our understanding of how particular species adapt to specific soil conditions and build a body of knowledge that informs how we implement landscapes most effectively to cool urban centers.

More projectively, landscape architects can capitalize on the intensity of warming temperatures in city centers by creating landscapes that highlight its thermal qualities. Innovative avenues of design exploration can be tested in relationship to soil and thermal mass. By focusing on these factors, we can move beyond formal attributes as the guideline for design and focus instead on the sensory, experiential qualities of landscape. Rather than perceiving formal output as the aim of our work, landscape architects can look at their efforts as an experimental feedback loop. Urban sites should be conceived of as testing grounds embedded with ever-shifting data points, which landscape designs can push in a particular direction. With this understanding, the thermal mass of soil serves as an essential variable that requires careful monitoring and deserves thoughtful representation. Increasing our discipline's knowledge of soil's influence on surface conditions, both through our own design explorations and by marrying ecological and geological research to design, will allow landscapes to become increasingly effective at coping with shifts in climate. Acknowledging soil as a material equally as fluid as the plant species and human processes we work with will allow the discipline to ultimately achieve a deeper understanding of the landscapes we craft.

References

Del Tredici, Peter. "The Flora of the Future." *Places Journal* (April 2014).

Edmondson, J. L., et al. "Soil Surface Temperatures Reveal Moderation of the Urban Heat Island Effect by Trees and Shrubs." *Scientific Reports* (19 September 2016): 1.

European Environment Agency. "Soil and Climate Change." *Signals—Towards Clean and Smart Mobility.* 2015: 5.

Fan, Chao, et al. "Measuring the Spatial Arrangement of Urban Vegetation and Its impacts on Seasonal Surface Temperatures." *Progress in Physical Geography* (March 2016): 215–16.

Kim, Yeon-Hee, and Jong-Jin Baik. "Spatial and Temporal Structure of the Urban Heat Island in Seoul." *Journal of Applied Meteorology* 44 (May 2005): 594.

Menberg, Kathrin, et al. "Subsurface Urban Heat Islands in German Cities." *Science of the Total Environment* (9 October 2012): 123.

Mondal, Satyen, et al. "Impact of Elevated Soil and Air Temperature on Plants' Growth, Yield, and Physiological Interaction: A Critical Review," *Scientia Agriculturae* 14:3 (5 May 2016): 293–305.

Solano, Laura.

Beyond Mining—
Urban Growth

The architectural innovation of cultivated resources through appropriate engineering

Dirk Hebel, Philippe Block, Felix Heisel, and Tomás Méndez Echenagucia

Steel-reinforced concrete is the most common building material in the world. However, very few developing countries have the availability or economic capacity to produce their own steel or cement. They become easily trapped in exploitative import relationships with the developed world in their efforts to adapt to this globally standardized yet unsustainable building practice. Materials that were previously considered unwanted and/or low-strength may present possibilities to end this undesirable state of affairs. Building with materials that can be effectively cultivated on site or nearby and/or designing in compression to produce structures that can span space despite the low tensile capacity of their components may bring about changes that are desperately needed.

Furthermore, the twenty-first century will face a radical paradigm shift in how we produce materials for the construction of our habitat. The linear concept of "produce, use, and discard" has proven itself unsustainable in the face of scarce resources and largely urban populations that are increasing exponentially. Instead, to achieve a cycle of production, use, and re-use, we must explore alternative materials and approaches to construction that strive for creative innovation using the latest available technologies, tools, and methods. Professor of Sustainable Construction Dirk E. Hebel at the Karlsruhe Institute of Technology and the Block Research Group (BRG) at the Swiss Federal Institute of Technology (ETH) Zürich are combining their knowledge in materials, construction, structures, and geometry to address the problems posed by inefficiency in the realms of design and material use.

While Hebel's team explores the cultivation of natural, regenerative materials and their use in construction optimized for the challenges presented in global urban environments, the BRG researches how methods from the past, including building in compression to span space and the technique of graphic statics, can be revived to take advantage of today's technological and digital advances. The advent of computation and the use of sophisticated design tools present opportunities to create efficient and expressive structures. This opportunity enables us to realise the potential of "low-strength" materials as structural elements, and designing with the flow of forces enables their use in construction.

Utilizing regenerative materials such as bamboo and mycelium and a design based on form and force diagrams to show the geometry of the structure's forces, Professor Hebel and the BRG present the first full-scale structure designed using 3D graphic statics. It represents a vision for the ways we may move beyond the mining of our construction materials to their cultivation and growth. It suggests ways that efficiency of digital design and engineering and efficiency of (scarce) resources can combine forces to question current practice and to propose alternative, more sustainable approaches.

The status quo

As urban populations grow, so does the demand for materials and resources to support them. Although such resource demands were once satisfied by local and regional hinterlands, they are becoming increasingly global in scale and reach. This phenomenon has generated material flows that are transcontinental and planetary in scope, and has profound consequences for the sustainability, functioning, sense of ownership, and identity of future cities. However, the global concentration of the construction industry on a few selected materials puts great pressure on our natural resources. For example, aquatic sand used as an aggregate in concrete mixes is scarce. In Southeast Asia, islands disappear due to landslides caused by ocean sand mining to satisfy the industry's hunger. North African countries are losing their beaches due to illegal scraping practices. The state of Florida is testing the use of recycled glass as a sand replacement in order not to lose their image as a tourist destination. If we talk about the future city, it is clear that it cannot be built with the same resources as the existing cities. Seen from this perspective, the project for urban sustainability cannot be a matter of applying a universal set of rules, as we see it happening currently around the globe. Rather, sustainability requires a decentralized approach that both acknowledges the global dimension and is sensitive to the climatic, social, cultural, aesthetic, economic, and ecological capacities of particular places, so they can not only endure but flourish and thrive.

Professor of Sustainable Construction Dirk E. Hebel at the Karlsruhe Institute of Technology (KIT) with their engagement at the Future Cities Laboratory (FCL) in Singapore, together with the Block Research Group (BRG) at the Swiss Federal Institute of Technology (ETH) Zürich, try to adapt such thinking to the areas of urban development and construction in various scales. Sustainability is an open system that must be capable of being positioned in its respective contexts. In recent years, the teams have concentrated their research on common interests in alternative, often weak construction materials and their application in specific contextual

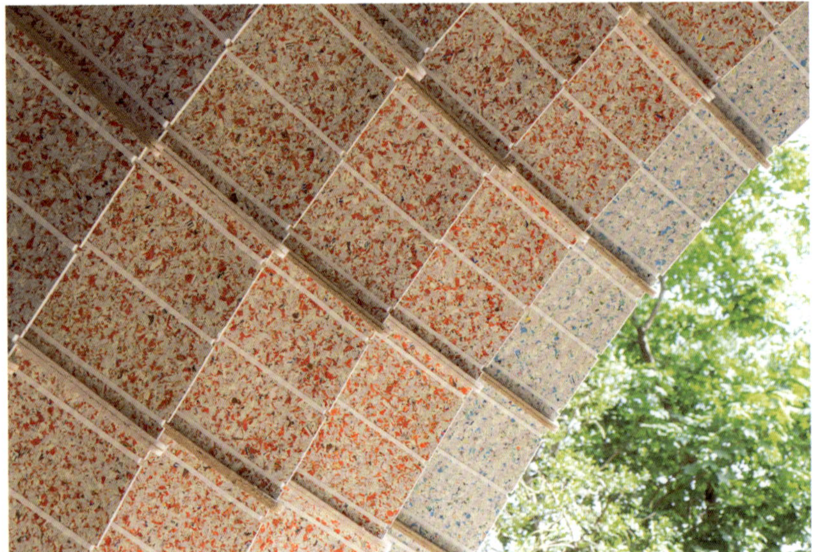

settings, taking into account the availability of materials, human resource capacities, and skills. Projects like SUDU—The Sustainable Urban Dwelling Unit in Addis Ababa or the Waste Vault in New York City (pictured above) are just two of their common engagements in the past years (Hebel, Moges and Gray 2016; Heisel 2015). The "alternative" aspects of these projects emerge from a shared exploration of innovative and applied thinking. This approach has informed and continues to inform a laboratory to test new ideas on how to combine already existing materials and knowledge with cutting-edge research. It is the declared aim of the collaboration to widen the palette of available architectural instruments and tools and therefore to question the global monopoly of material and conceptual choices.

Can a grass replace structural elements made out of steel or timber? Can building materials made out of mycelium structures or hardened by bacteria be a widespread, alternative building technology? Can a "three-story-city" be built with locally available materials, and can the resulting neighbourhoods be as dense as high-rise typologies suggest? Could waste be a future resource for the building sector? What engineering principles have to be discussed and applied? Next to empirical research, that is, gaining knowledge through observation, Hebel's team has quantified these hypotheses through scientific engineering

Waste Vault – the ETH Pavilion activated one of New York City's waste resources, discarded beverage cartons, as a building material for a temporary exhibition structure at the IDEAS CITY Festival in 2015.

and the establishment of new and specialized laboratories. Along with other partners, test scenarios and standards have been developed to compare the results to already established building substances. The research has focused on full-scale material applications based on workshop environments, including students and other researchers from various fields and backgrounds.

A paradigm shift

The twenty-first century will face a radical paradigm shift in how we produce materials for the construction of our habitat. While industrialization has resulted in a conversion from regenerative to non-regenerative material sources, our time will experience the reverse: a shift towards cultivating, breeding, raising, farming, or growing future resources (Hebel and Heisel 2017). These can be cultivated either within the conventional, soil-based agricultural framework or in breeding farms, using microorganisms that thus far were not even considered useful for the energy or building industry. In our view, both cultivation scenarios are important. The latter approach is additionally an elegant response to the current trend of small-scale industrial and agricultural production units within urban environments.

When considering the use of natural and organic raw materials in the current framework of digitalization, prefabrication and mass production, the imperfections of living materials and the ways engineering principles need to react to those become key aspects in material development and application. An underlying effort, next to a continuous interest in advancing material properties, is a form of standardization of such natural resources and their respective industrial production processes in order to

guarantee predictable and controllable properties in every material lot.

Some of the suggestions in the research work of Hebel's team operate with ideas and organisms that were previously seen as unwanted or labelled as repulsive. For example, while the pharmaceutical industry uses bacteria with undisputed success, architecture and construction so far have not activated or exploited bacteria's capacities. The same is true for other organisms, such as mushroom mycelium or bamboo, which will be further discussed below.

For centuries, the linear thinking of "producing, using, and discarding" was the dominant method of any industrialized value chain. Only recently, terms such as recyclability, embodied or grey energy, acceptability for repositioning, and sorted reassembly, have become evaluation criteria for an increasingly sensitized society. A new generation of cultivated building materials easily adopts such a model: not only can a house be grown, it could also be composted after its use.

The cultivation of building materials requires a sustainable and ethical economic model. Especially when addressing soil-dependent cultivated materials, there are significant side-effects to an uncontrolled and profit-driven agricultural model. A cautionary tale can be seen in the palm oil industry, in which natural forests are burned in order to gain more area under crops. On the other hand, one positive effect is the changing profil of building experts. In the work of FCL, multidisciplinary teams are engaged in future development: biologists, bioengineers, ecologists, chemists, and material scientists cooperate with architects and civil engineers to create a broader understanding of how to approach complex tasks. Supplemented by economists, this multidisciplinary work also holds the promise of sharpening our view of alternative urban models, where production is an integral part of a future urban society, requiring new types of spaces and infrastructures.

Learning from the past

Since the nineteenth century, the construction industry has relied heavily on the bending capacity of materials such as steel and reinforced concrete for their structures, because they have the necessary tensile capacity to span space in bending by using rectilinear elements such as columns and beams. These simple geometries are convenient and efficient for their fabrication and repeatability, making them cheaper and faster to produce. As a consequence, the construction industry became accustomed to the inefficient use of large amounts of non-renewable and energy-demanding materials. This problem continues to this day, and it is further reinforced by industrialization, building codes, and architecture and engineering practices. Furthermore, modern engineering relies heavily on stress-based methods for the sizing of structural elements. This results in a mentality that is geared towards the materialization of bad structural geometry and away from the design of efficient geometries.

However, this scenario of inefficiency is relatively recent. Before the widespread use of steel, reinforced concrete, and other "high-strength" materials became standard practice following the Industrial Revolution, buildings were designed to span space with compression. The vaulted roofs of Gothic cathedrals or the arches and domes of the Italian Renaissance provide instructive examples of compression-only structures built using materials with no tensile capacity. The structural principles and methods of the master builders who created these historical precedents are a rich source of inspiration and knowledge.

The material and construction constraints that the master builders faced in the past put them in a position to develop methods for generating sound structural geometry. Their structures follow the flow of forces; that is, they placed masonry elements where the forces wanted to go in compression, from the roofs down to the foundations. These sound structural principles remain as valuable today as they did then, regardless of the materials used.

Of course, today's construction industry is now very different. The availability of modern materials and advanced construction methods allow us to build almost anything, leaving us with the question of whether we should build just anything?. However, if we consider our current environmental challenges and the accelerated population growth we face now and in the future, we can argue strongly that the constraints these master builders had to face are again highly relevant. The importance of learning from their structural principles and methods and building in a more responsible way has never been greater. The environmental cost of materials should now become more valuable than their strength. Grown or recycled materials usually have small compressive strengths and little or no tensile capacity. As a result, they are often labeled as "low-strength" materials.

Graphic statics: From 2D to 3D

One of the most useful historical methods to revive is graphic statics. From Varignon in 1725 onwards, an increasing wealth of knowledge formed around the subject of finding the equilibrium of forces based on dual diagrams (Varignon. 1725). Many important figures, like James Clerk Maxwell and William Rankine, added to this knowledge base over the centuries, publishing books and articles on the subject (Maxwell 1864; Rankine 1864). Later on, this knowledge was largely abandoned in the twentieth century by engineers who favoured equations of the theory of elasticity over geometrical drawings. These methods are only recently being rediscovered because of their capacity to relate geometry to force equilibrium.

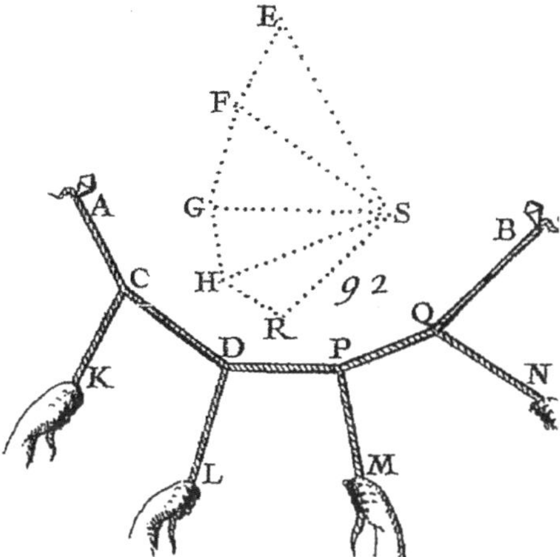

Indeed, graphic statics allows designers to have an explicit representation of the relationship between the geometry of a two-dimensional structure and the equilibrium of the forces acting on it (Block et al. 2016). The magnitudes of these forces are represented in the so-called force diagram, which is made up of connected lines, each of which represents one force acting on a node. The equilibrium of a node in a two-dimensional structure is represented by a

closed polygon in the force diagram. A long line represents a large force, giving designers a clear understating of the structural behaviour.

Enhanced through modern digital technologies and computational methods, form and force diagrams can be used to design a structure by designing or constructing the geometry of its forces. The BRG works extensively in providing and teaching graphic-statics-based tools for structural design, including RhinoVAULT, a freely available plug-in for the design of compression shell structures.

William Rankine was the first to propose a method for three-dimensional graphic statics (Rankine 1864). If the equilibrium of a node in a 2D structure is represented by a closed polygon in the force diagram, in 3D it is represented by a closed polyhedron. In 2D, the magnitudes of the forces are represented by the lengths of the lines; in 3D, they are represented by the areas of the faces of the polyhedron. Rankine described this principle in a short two-paragraph article more than 150 years ago, and yet it was never used until very recently. The BRG has been working on deciphering and understanding Rankine's method with the purpose of extending graphic statics to three dimensions and achieving very efficient structures in an intuitive and visual design environment. This exhibition presents the first full-scale structure designed with this method.

Because the equilibrium of a spatial system of forces can be represented geometrically through force polyhedra, 3D graphic statics allows designers to explicitly control both the geometry of the structural form and the geometry of the internal forces. This unique quality enables

Form and force diagrams (Varignon 1795)

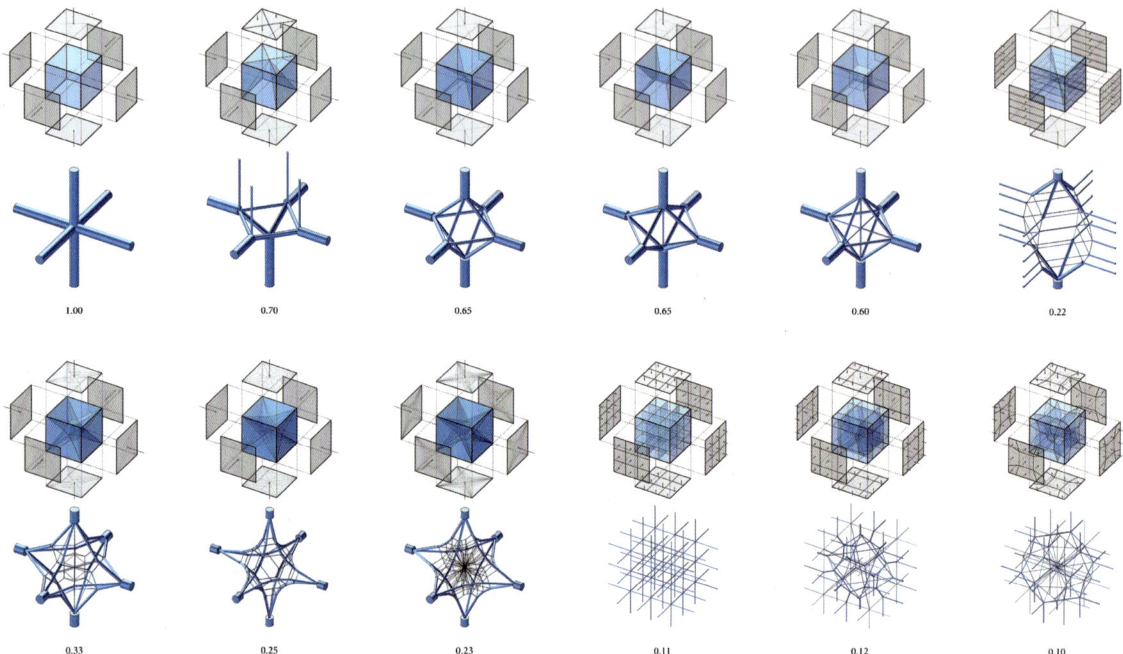

the generation of complex spatial geometries in an easy and controlled manner while structural equilibrium is constantly enforced. Through various stereotomic operations on the solid geometries of force polyhedra, new structural forms can be discovered and previously unimaginable architectural expressions can be explored.

Structural geometry for "low-strength" materials

The advent of computation and sophisticated design tools are an opportunity to create efficient and expressive structures, not an excuse to indulge in empty architectural gestures that make irresponsible use of precious materials and energy. This opportunity enables us to realise the potential of "low-strength" materials as structural elements.

Structural geometry had an important moment of development with the thin shell structures of the 1950s and 1960s, when mathematicians and engineers devised ideal and optimized shapes for these shells. Currently there is an even higher potential for efficient and expressive structural shapes. Fuelled by computation and knowledge of historical principles and methods, the BRG has been developing structural systems for different environmental contexts and needs (Block 2016). A prominent example among these is the funicular floor system (Liew et al. 2017). The funicular floor system is made up of a thin, funicular, unreinforced concrete vault supported at its four corners; a series of stiffening fins on the vault's extrados; and tension ties connecting the four support points. The introduction of vaulting to floor systems,

Exploration and refinement of structural forms through geometric transformations of force polyhedra (Lee et al. 2016)

inspired by masonry vaulting systems, results in a system that does not rely on the tensile capacity of its materials. This means it can be made of unreinforced concrete, and it does not require additional concrete to cover the steel rebar, resulting in a material reduction of 70% in comparison to an already optimized, traditional concrete slab. In addition, the use of compression forces and tension ties allows us to go beyond concrete to experiment with different materials for the floors.

Designing with the flow of forces allows not only for significant material reductions but also for the use of "low-strength" materials. The funicular floor system is also being developed as a 3D printed object (Block et al. 2017). A powder-based, 3D-printed floor system is being developed, which has the advantage of being bespoke. Furthermore, it is highly precise and does not require a mould. On the other hand, 3D printing comes with disadvantages; the available printing materials are usually very weak, it does not allow for the introduction of reinforcements, and printing sizes are usually limited. However, these issues can be resolved by using funicular geometry and by designing pre-cracked structural systems with discrete parts.

3D printed funicular floor system (Block et al. 2017)

New Structural Bamboo Materials

Many so-called "low-strength" materials belong to a group that has been known for centuries as reliable and accepted resources for construction, yet they have never advanced to the level of an industrialized product—as if they were locked in a box called "vernacular." The use of bamboo as a construction material is the perfect example: high-rise scaffolding structures in Hong Kong, traditional buildings in Southeast Asia and Japan, or highly individual signature architecture come to mind. In contrast, our point of departure is that the potential of bamboo lies not in applications of the raw material, but in its extremely strong fibre. The approach of extracting and reconfiguring bamboo fibres is suitable to prompt the industry to develop new industrialized production methods.

Steel-reinforced concrete is the most common building material in the world, with developing countries using close to 90% of cement and 80% of steel consumed by the construction sector globally. However, very few developing countries have the ability or resources to produce their own steel or cement, forcing them into an exploitative import relationship with the developed world. Bamboo, an alternative to steel, grows in the tropical zones of our planet and coincides with developing regions. The plant belongs to the botanical family of grasses and is extremely resistant to tensile stresses. In fact, bamboo is one of nature's most versatile products.

The Advanced Fibre Composite Laboratory in Singapore produces and tests bamboo composite materials for high-performance applications

Bamboo is also a highly renewable and eco-friendly material. It grows much faster than wood, is relatively easy to obtain, and is available in large quantities. Furthermore, it is known for its unrivalled capacity to capture carbon and could therefore play an important role in reducing carbon emissions worldwide. The great social, economic, and material benefits of bamboo are currently not reflected in the demand for the material, despite its abundant availability.

Professor Dirk E. Hebel is working to tap bamboo's potential by exploring new types of composite bamboo materials. Investigations have focused on the tensile strength of bamboo; they have explored possibilities for extracting and transforming fibres into a manageable industrial product, a viable building material with the ability to rival steel and timber on residential and commercial scales. This composite bamboo material can be produced and applied in any of the familiar shapes and forms common to traditional construction, but it can also be tailored for specific applications that best take advantage of the material's tensile strength, such as newly developed reinforcement spanning systems for ceiling and roof structures.

Mycelium materials

A cutting-edge approach in the building sector might be summarized with a bold statement: "Grow your own house." Previously misunderstood as hazardous waste, microorganisms have recently been rediscovered as a rich resource with the potential to redefine the categorization of renewable building materials, the important distinction being their unique self-growing capabilities. Research is underway to develop methods of implementation within the construction sector.

Mycelium is the root network of mushrooms, a fast-growing matrix that can act as a natural and self-assembling glue. Digesting plant-based waste products, such as saw dust, mycelium's dense network of hyphae binds the substrate into a structurally active material composite. The advantages of such products are significant: As mycelium follows a metabolic cycle, building elements or whole constructions may be composted after their original use. In their second phase of life, they become a fertile matrix for subsequent generations. Under the correct conditions, the material may be grown locally,

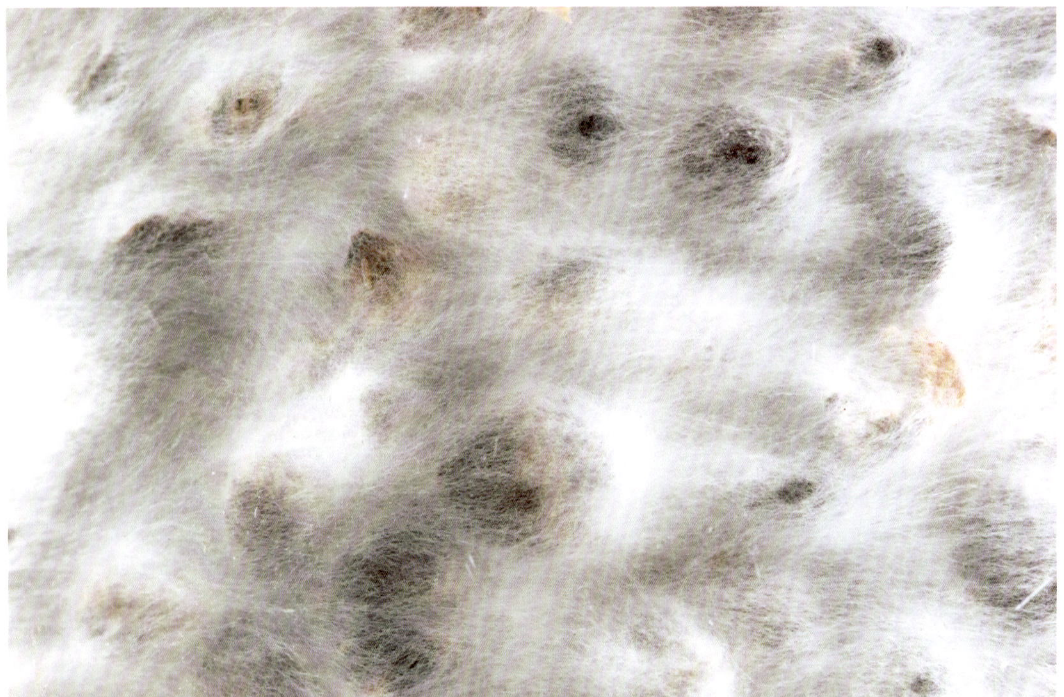

reducing both the energy and time required for transportation. Finally, as they are organic matter, they act to reverse carbon emissions through the absorption of carbon.

Mushroom mycelium is able to digest cellulose and transform it into chitin. To initiate the growth process, sterilized wood chips (or other plant waste) are mixed with mycelium tissue. Over the course of days, the fungi will start to digest and transform the nutrients and grow into a dense, spongy substance of interlocking hyphae. In a second step, this mass can then be "cast" into almost any form or mould. Left for another few days, the cast mycelium further densifies into its final shape. In a last step, the resulting building element can be dried out in order to stop the growth process and effectively kill the organism.

A controlled environment is required to grow mycelium materials. Initially, the space must be dark, and moist, and provided with the right organic nourishment. A change in environmental conditions, such as altering the humidity levels or exposing the material to a different light or temperature, can deactivate the growth process at any chosen point in time. Due to their spongy rhizomatic and fibrous nature, the mycelium produces a lightweight and insulating material considered very desirable by the building industry. In combination with innovative engineering, we believe that such organically grown substances have the potential to become a very real alternative to established, even structural, materials within the building industry, as the exhibition by the two teams demonstrates expressively at the 2017 Seoul Biennale.

References

Block, Philippe. 2016. "Parametricism's structural congeniality," In "Parametricism 2.0: Rethinking Architecture's Agenda for the 21st Century." ed. P. Schumacher Special issue *AD Architectural Design*, 86(2): 68-75 (March/April).

Block, Philippe, Matthias Rippmann, and Tom Van Mele. 2017. "Compressive assemblies: Bottom-up performance for a new form of construction," In "Autonomous Assembly: Designing for a new era of collective construction," ed S. Tibbits, special issue, (In preparation), *AD Architectural Design*.

Block, Philippe, Tom Van Mele, and Matthias Rippmann. 2016. "Geometry of Forces: Exploring the solution space of structural design," *GAM* 12: 28-37 (April). *Issue on Structural Affairs.*

Hebel, Dirk, and Felix Heisel. 2017. *Cultivated Building Materials: Industrialized Natural Resources for Architecture and Construction.* Birkhäuser: Berlin and Basel.

Hebel, Dirk, Melakeselam Moges, and Zara Gray. 2016. *SUDU—The Sustainable Urban Dwelling Unit, Research and Manual.* Ruby Press: Berlin.

Heisel, Felix. 2015. "Waste Vault—The ETH Zürich Pavilion at the IDEAS CITY Festival in New York City." "Constructing Alternatives. Future Cities Laboratory, Singapore." Special issue, *FCL Magazine.*

Lee, Juney, Tom Van Mele, and Philippe Block. 2016. "Form-finding explorations through geometric manipulations of force polyhedrons," *Proceedings of the International Association for Shell and Spatial Structures (IASS) Symposium 2016*, (September). Tokyo, Japan.

Liew, Andrew, David López, Tom Van Mele, and Philippe Block. 2017. "Design, fabrication and testing of a prototype, thin-vaulted, unreinforced concrete floor," *Engineering Structures* (In press).

Maxwell, James. 1864. "On reciprocal figures, frames and diagrams of forces." *Phil Mag* 27:250–61.

Rankine, W. J. Macquorn. 1864. "Principle of the equilibrium of polyhedral frames." *Phil Mag* 27:92.

Rippmann, Matthias, Lorenz Lachauer, and Philippe Block. 2012. "Interactive Vault Design," *International Journal of Space Structures*, 27(4): 219-230 (December).

Varignon, P. 1725. *Nouvelle mécanique ou statique.* Paris: Claude Jombert.

Seoul Agro-City in 2050: Proposal on Food Security in Seoul

Turenscape
(Dr. Kongjian Yu and Stanley Lung)

Urban agriculture is not new to Seoul, but the practice is facing huge challenges in the locality. Land shortage, limited skills and technology, piecemeal operations, and limited investment incentives are major problems despite the municipal government's strong efforts to promote urban agriculture since 2012. This proposal is made as an analytical framework for the following purposes: first, to investigate whether Seoul can be self-sufficient enough to provide the city with food security, and second, to determine how this practice can be integrated into other urban strategies.

Learning from Cuba, the United States, and China, we attempt to summarize a list of ways to influence policy-making and urban farm operations for the future Seoul. To gather information, we are examining the existing agricultural system in South Korea, crops consumption, and production patterns.

Summarizing what we learned from overseas examples and our understanding of the current agricultural system in Seoul, this proposal is provided as a groundwork for setting up a top-down strategy on urban agriculture. Three milestones were set towards the goal of Seoul transforming into an Agro-city—2030, 2050, and beyond. Decisions were made to determine locations suitable for urban farming, space requirements for growing respective crops, the service area of urban farms, and the scale of urban farms and the actors involved.

Urban agriculture is known for its importance in providing food security to the local area. Apart from the top-down strategy, this proposal also experiments with the applicability of integrating urban agriculture with other urban systems. Precisely, we look at the social, economic, and ecological values which accompany urban agriculture.

1. Seoul Solution, https://www.seoulsolution.kr, accessed 2016.

2. According to the Food and Agriculture Organization of the United Nations, "food security exists when all people, at all times, have physical and economic access to sufficient, safe and nutritious food to meet their dietary needs and food preferences for an active and healthy life." See Food and Agriculture Organization of the United Nations, "World Food Summit: Rome Declaration on World Food Security," 13 November 1996, http://fao.org.

SECTION 1: The Rationale of Urban Agriculture

Urbanization and food security

By 2050, the world's population will have increased to be three times higher than today (FAO 2012). About 70% of the people will be living in urban areas, creating a greater demand for food. FAO suggested raising food production by 70% in order to feed this expanding urban population. Seoul, one of the cities experiencing rapid urbanization, is now facing a challenge to its food security by 2050. Its population has increased tenfold from 10,000 in 1973 to 10,969,862 in 1992. Population density is currently 17,473/km2, exceeding that of New York, Paris, and Tokyo.[1]

Definition of Urban Agriculture

Urban agriculture is part of the urban ecosystem. It is defined by RUAF as "the growing of plants and the raising of animals within and around cities" (RUAF 2017). It is "integrated into the urban economic and ecological system: urban agriculture is embedded in and interacting with the urban ecosystem."

Urban agriculture can make great contributions to people living in the city. In terms of social impact, it contributes to the local community by involving disadvantaged groups in the city—women, the unemployed, immigrants, etc. In terms of food security[2] and nutrition, urban agriculture offers citizens a wide range of locally produced food, securing them a healthy diet and a local food supply. The local economy also benefits from having a self-sufficient food supply. Apart from this, urban farms offer city green spaces that reduce urban temperatures and opportunities to recycle urban waste and wastewater.

The RUAF writes that "urban agriculture is embedded in—and interacting with—the urban ecosystem. Such linkages include the use of urban residents as laborers, use of typical urban resources (like organic waste as compost and urban wastewater for irrigation), direct links with urban consumers, direct impacts on urban ecology (positive and negative), being part of the urban food system, competing for land with other urban functions, being influenced by urban policies and plans, etc." (RUAF 2017).

	United States	Cuba	China
Rationale of urban agriculture:	The practice of urban agriculture in American cities is grounded in the basis of promoting health and equality, especially in low-income and minority areas.	The goal is to achieve self-sufficiency in food supply after independence from Soviet rule. Cuban agriculture used to depend highly on oil. When the Soviet Union collapsed in the early 1990s, Cuba lost access to the inputs required to sustain their agriculture system. The Cuban food supply relied heavily on imports.	Urban agriculture is mainly practiced to shorten food miles and make fresh food accessible to major cities.
Legislation:	Urban Agriculture Ordinances The importance of urban agriculture is highly recognized and addressed in the legal framework in terms of permitting urban agriculture land uses and height limit exemptions. According to Trish Popovitch (2014), American cities demonstrate various different ways to support the practice. Detroit in Michigan saw population decline as an opportunity to develop urban agriculture, by adopting a comprehensive urban agriculture ordinance and detailed zoning focused on local food production.	The Havana Urban Agriculture Policy was officially launched in 1998 to govern and promote urban agriculture. The National Urban Agriculture Group was set up to resolve the food crisis experienced during the "Special Period" after the fall of socialist rule. It demonstrated a successful case of making it possible to foster urban food production via top-down policy making.	There is increasing attention to the importance of urban agriculture as an ecological protection and urban-rural interchange, but legislation and action plans are still being developed. Scientific research was carried out with the establishment of the Key Laboratory of Urban Agriculture within the Ministry of Agriculture.

	United States	**Cuba**	**China**
Implementation:	**Seattle** The Seattle City Council adopted land-use code changes to grant permission for community gardens in all zones. In residential zones, larger farms require an administrative conditional use permit, while small farms are permitted if they are up to 4,000 square feet in area. In commercial zones and industrial zones, urban farms are allowed as a principal or accessory use, including the tops and sides of buildings. Height-limit exemption is granted up to 15 feet if the top floor is dedicated to greenhouse food production (Cohen 2011). **Chicago** Community gardens and commercial urban farms became legal land uses by adding onto the city's zoning ordinance in 2010. Gardens and farms would become legal provided that they meet the requirements outlined in the zoning ordinance. This includes size, location, and operational parameters. The "Go To 2040" plan suggests the conversion of vacant and underutilized lots, spaces, and rooftops into agricultural uses. Under this ordinance, community gardens were defined as community-based developments. Commercial gardens and greenhouses (i.e. growing beds, hoop houses, greenhouses, vertical farms, and hydroponic systems) are growing locations set up for propagation, processing, storage, and sale. In order to close the nutrient cycle, the ordinance also restricts composting with the use of organic matter generated on-site (Cohen 2011). **San Francisco** In San Francisco, the threshold of urban farming sites is clearly defined. "Neighborhood agriculture" sites are less than 1 acre, and include community gardens, community-supported agriculture, market gardens, and private farms (Cohen 2011). **New York** In New York, the zoning code allowed "truck gardens" and farmstands in residential and commercial districts. Urban agriculture is permitted land use inside manufacturing districts (M1, M2, M3). The code also addresses nuisance control and sales restrictions (Cohen 2011).	Instructed by the Ministry of Agriculture, vegetable production was organized "in order to achieve no less than 300 grams per capita per day, and to meet the demands of social consumption, tourism and exports." The Provincial Administration Councils were responsible for organizing production and identifying areas available for production. In 1999, the land-use plan produced by the Provincial Physical Planning Authority included urban agriculture as an ongoing activity. The plan also provided details of the spatial distribution of urban agriculture subprograms. Forestry in urban parks in the central area; organoponic farms, nurseries, plots, and courtyards for growing vegetables, herbs and spices, flowers and ornamental plants, rabbit and poultry farming in the intermediate zone; and suburb farming on the outskirts of the city. Other key issues cover the transfer of vacant land to urban farmers, legislation on pig breeding on the outskirts of the city, pig farming, and the promotion of urban forestry.	**Shanghai** demonstrates a case where urban agriculture was upgraded from an individual business to a top-down government strategy. According to Yue-man Yeung, United Nations University, Shanghai has established a unified, coordinated regional food system to replace the fragmented individual operations. The city is divided into two zones, the inner zone and outlying zone. The inner zone produces vegetables all year supporting consumption within a 10km circle from their point of sale. It guarantees fresh vegetables are available within 10 to 15 hours of being harvested. Shanghai is a leading city in urban agriculture in China. With strong support from the local government, district administration is responsible for a minimal quantity of vegetable production. Quality assurance is clearly regulated. Subsidies are also provided to farms of over 2mu in size at a rate of RMB76/mu. In Beijing, urban agriculture is incorporated into urban planning. According to Beijing Agriculture (农业 2007), urban agriculture is divided into five concentric zones. Within the fifth ring, livestock raising and food crop production is not encouraged, but ornamental elements like flowers and lawns are allowed. Between the fifth and the sixth ring, areas close to the rural fringe, flowers, seedlings, and food grains are grown for weekend leisure or scientific research. Outside the urban zone, the third zone will be used for growing high-value crops. Farms are practiced in large-scale along with processing industries. Further away, the fourth zone is used to develop eco-agriculture and agritourism. The fifth zone will be small towns surrounding developing agriculture based on the availability of local resources. Apart from Shanghai and Beijing, other regions are catching up with urban agriculture. Chengdu is attempting to develop the image of an Agro-city in 20 years' time. Major strategies include developing high technology, intensive farming, organic farming, agritourism, and increasing farmers' income. In Guangzhou, 11 km2 (16,500mu) orchard land was taken as an ecological barrier in 2012.

	United States	**Cuba**	**China**
Implementation:			Successful precedence can also be seen in landscape design to integrate planning and ecology into landscape design. Shenyang Architectural University Campus in Liaoning Province (Figure 1) provides an example of making efficient use of open space left over from new development for growing rice paddies. Quzhou Luming Park (Figure 2) in Zhejiang province is a dynamic park incorporating the agricultural strategy of crop rotation and low-maintenance meadow, preserving the remnant landscape and riparian flood plain amid a dense urban context. Suqian Santaishan Flower Quilt (Figure 3) demonstrates another example of converting subtle terrain into productive landscape that is functional and aesthetically pleasing.
Funding:	For financial support, the United States Department of Agriculture (USDA) has provided a range of funding available to new urban farmers. There are loans—namely, the Farm Loan Programs, the Organic Cost Share Programs, Value Added Producer Grants, and Farm Storage Facility Loans—and some funding for research. Technical supports were given through the Noninsured Crop Disaster Assistance Program and Conservation Technical Assistance. There are also a range of marketing and promotion programs like the Farmers Market Promotion Program, Local Food Promotion Program, and Environmental Quality Incentives Program (USDA 2016).	It is financed partly from public funds and partly from the work of urban farmers. Over the years it has received funding from several international development cooperation agencies and institutions.	
Effectiveness:	Compared to many cities in the world, US cities have made urban agriculture possible by means of a supportive legal framework. Because local governments have granted permission to urban farm operations, ownership can be secured and larger farm inputs have resulted.	The policy benefits 22,700 urban farmers and the nation's food supply, providing 285,166 tons of vegetables produced in 2009. The enactment of 18 Ministerial Resolutions, Decrees, Circulars, and laws established a legal framework to make future practice easier. The results include a range of programs and activities, in the categories of livestock raising, vegetable gardens, fruit and ornamental flower production, and forestry. Around 22,700 urban farming jobs were created.	Urban agriculture in Shanghai has proven successful. According to Shanghai Agriculture (2012), Shanghai has achieved a self-sufficiency rate of 20% in food with annual production exceeding 1 million tons in 2011, regardless of the scarcity of less than 544,500 mu agricultural land. In 2011, vegetable fields increased to an area of 542,000 mu. Shanghai can sustain itself on its supply of local leafy greens (90%). The success in urban agriculture benefited the local economy by stabilizing the price of leafy greens at RMB2.1/kg. With 50% of finance supported by local government, farmers are given strong incentives to operate their farms.

	United States	**Cuba**	**China**
Effectiveness:		The policy was very successful in (i) bringing together production and environmental components (i.e. emphasis on increased productivity based on a free scheme for synthetic chemical suppliers); (ii) facilitating skilled labor and the organization of urban farmers in start-up and operation; (iii) identifying the need to include urban agriculture as a permanent land use; and (iv) identifying the importance of high-quality food in key areas like children's and mothers' nutrition.	Urban agriculture in China was made possible given the strong support from the state government. Its large workforce, high capital inputs, and land availability should have provided China a good foundation. However, according to the Ministry of Agriculture of the PRC (2012), urban agriculture is not clearly defined under the governance of modern agriculture (现代农业发展规划 2011-2015). In many cities, there is no clear role or responsibility outlining who should practice urban agriculture and where, leave it hanging and not implementable. Agriculture remains a kind of secondary production commonly abandoned from major development strategies. Secondly, capital and manpower are shifting towards the urban center instead of investing in farms. With growing scarcity of space, many farms have to give way to other development goals. The current operation of urban farms remains small scale and fragmented. Small individual ownership makes it difficult to self-finance and sustain in the long run. In Shanghai, land ownership is temporary for a maximum of three years. Short-term ownership cannot attract big investment nor develop into a larger-scale business.
What can Seoul Learn from this Country:	The United States is a developed country where urban agriculture is introduced mainly to eliminate the urban poor and to supply healthy food for minority groups. The program not only benefits the city by providing healthy food, but also helps to resolve social problems and promote equality. The introduction of a height-limit exemption is also applicable as a way to provide developers the incentive to integrate urban agriculture into their properties.	Urban agriculture contributes to the local economy by safeguarding the local agricultural system from an import-oriented economy. The leading practice introduced land-use governance and spatial decisions necessary for urban agriculture to develop in scale.	Urban agriculture in China has received top-level government support including planning and subsidies. It is practiced within and around the city. Strong government support is the key to success. The case in Shanghai demonstrates how urban agriculture fits in the process of urban sprawl. To determine what crops to be grown through zoning control is also a lesson to learn. By incorporating urban agriculture into planning, resource allocation can be made better to minimize nuisance and encourage collaboration among different farmers' groups.

SECTION 2:
The Basis of Urban Agriculture in Seoul
Overview of Korean agriculture

Agricultural industry has been an important sector contributing to South Korea's economy. Under the threat of urbanization and industrialization in the past 30 years, Seoul is losing her competitiveness in agricultural production. The percentage of agricultural GDP in proportion to total GDP dropped from 40% to 5% (KRET 2013). While rice cultivation has been an important sector in our agricultural production and export trade, the share of agricultural exports in proportion to total exports declined significantly since the early 1960s. The figures fell from 40% in the 1960s to less than 1% in 2014 (KRET 2013).

Unequal trade balance

In fact, other than major export items like rice, ginseng, and vegetables, South Korea's reliance on imports has continued to increase. Beef, pork, dairy products, tropical fruits, and vegetables are imported. Figures show a diminishing trade balance over the past twenty-four years, where import outweighs export by 4.5 times in 2014 (KRET 2013).

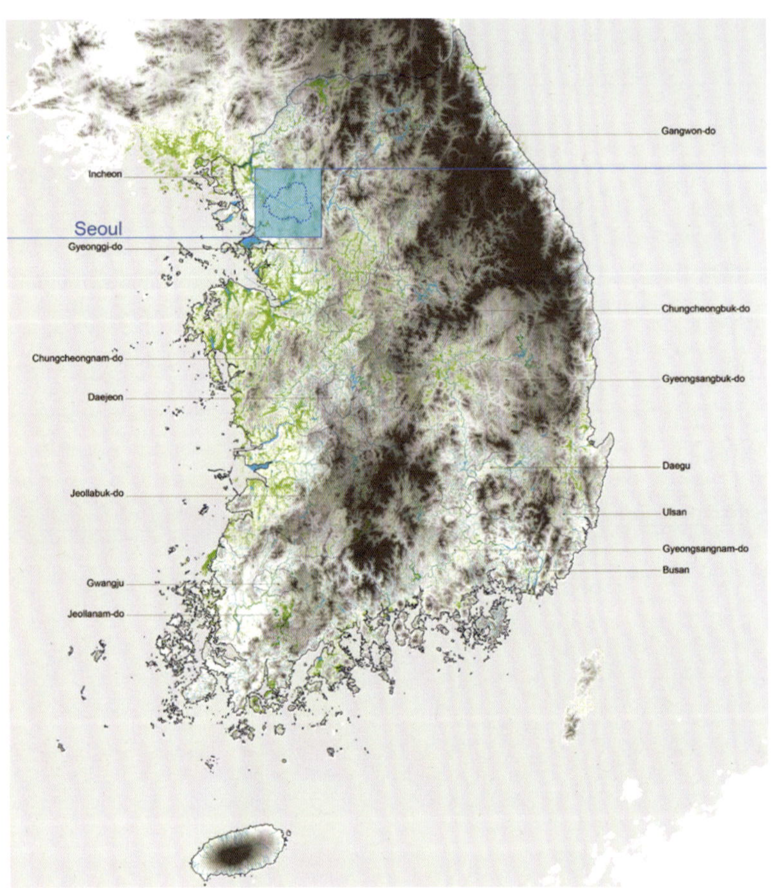

Farm location across South Korea

Decline in arable land

Korean farmland accounts for only 17.1% of the nation's land; the rest is left as forest (63.5%) or is urban land (19.4%). The supply of arable land has shown a decrease of 24% over the past 30 years, in which 40,000 ha of land has turned idle every year and 15,000 ha of land has been converted into other uses (KRET 2013). Owing to the hilly landscape and temperate climate, the supply of arable land is limited, let alone the diversity of crops suitable to this weather, with annual temperature ranging 6°C to 16°C and precipitation not more than 1500mm per year.

Decline in rural workforce

Rapid urbanization contributed to a sharp decline in the rural workforce. South Korea used to have around half of its population working on farms, declining to only 5.7% in 2014 (KRET 2013).

Local food consumption

Local food consumption is summarized as follows, showing the consumption pattern of food in relation to Korean cuisine.

1. Grain Rice is a major food in Korean cuisine. It continues to be the most consumed crop,

1. Korean Trade Balance. Extracted from "Agriculture in Korea", KREI, 2014.

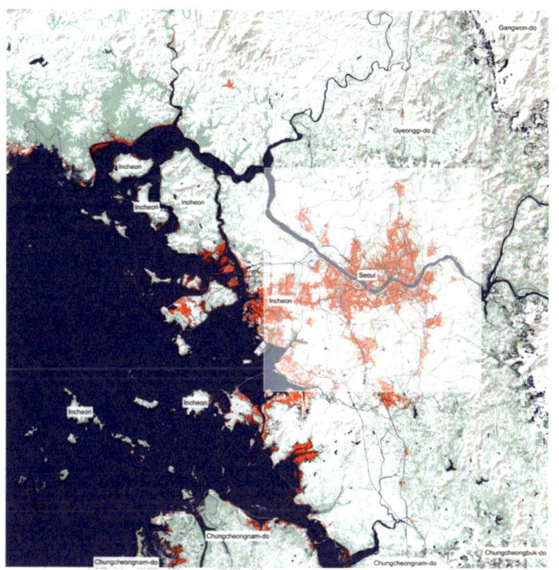

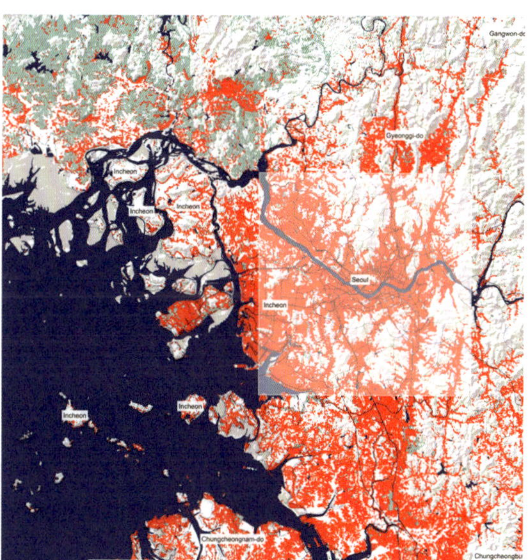

with over 4 million tons consumed in 2014. Comparatively, corn has shown large figures of 9.8 million tons, but a majority is used in feeding livestock. (See table 1 in appendix.) Examples: Dolsotbap, boribap, kongbap, bimbap, japchae

2. Vegetables and fruits Chinese cabbage, onions, and radishes are the most popular vegetables across South Korea, with 2.7 million tons, 1.3 million tons, and 1.2 million tons, respectively, consumed in 2013. (See table 2 in appendix.) Likewise, apples, tangerines, and grapes have a high demand of over 0.3 million tons consumption in 2014. (See tables 2 and 3 in appendix.) Examples: Miyeok guk, chwinamul, kimchi

3. Meat Milk and dairy products continue to be the largest demand in this category, with over 1.5 million tons consumed in 2014. Pork comes second with a figure of 1.6 million tons. Other than that, there is a growing consumption of chicken to over 1 million tons in 2014 (double the figure consumed in 1995). Beef and chicken have shown great increases, with an extent of 80% and 62%, respectively. (See table 4 in appendix.) Examples: yukpo, samgyetang, samgyeopsal

Urbanization in Seoul, 1999, 2009, 2016

Food pyramid

Consumption:	Grain: 58%	Production:	Grain: 26%
	Livestock: 6%		Livestock: 9%
	Vegetables: 25%		Vegetables: 50%
	Fruits: 9%		Fruits: 14%
	Specialty crops: 1%		Specialty crops: 0.25%

Local food production

1. Grain Barley suffers from a sharp decline in local production, losing around 80% of cultivated areas from 1990 to 2014. Corn production also suffered a decline of more than 30% in local production. (See table 5 in appendix.)

2. Vegetables and fruits

The kinds of vegetables suffering the greatest decline in local production between 1990 and 2013 are Chinese cabbage and radishes, with -29% and -26% in local production, -32% and -41% decline in cultivated area. For fruits, apple production is declining (-25%) with a smaller cultivated area (-37%). (See tables 6 and 7 in appendix.)

3. Meat

Beef production is under threat, with a huge decline in cultivation area (from 2,500,000 tons in 1995 to 480,000 tons in 2013). Comparatively, dairy farms and chicken farms are becoming more intensive. (See table 8 in appendix.)

Trade balance and Self-sufficiency

Revealing the import volumes of respective crops, we can conclude that the following items are not self-sufficient in South Korea. Among the grains, corn, wheat, and soybeans rely heavily on imports, as is revealed by their figures of 10 million tons, 0.36 million tons, and 0.13 million tons, respectively, in 2014. Korea is also a big importer of flavored vegetables, especially chili (172,700 tons), with a growing demand for carrots (99,400 tons), grapes, and tropical fruits. Besides all this, there is an increasing import of dairy products and chicken. (See table 9 in appendix.)

Summary

The proportion of crops being consumed and produced can be summarized as follows:

Import:	Grain: 1%
	Livestock: 0.02%
	Vegetables: 0.01%
	Fruits: 99%
	Specialty crops: 0.001%

Review on Current Practice in Seoul

Rationale of urban agriculture:

According to the city government, Seoul set herself a vision of transforming into an Agro-City. The official website[3] demonstrates their goal to form 3.3 square meter vegetable gardens per 1 million city farming houses for the provision of 3,201,000 tons of local food (Seoul Metropolitan Government 2014).

Legislation:

The legal framework in Seoul has developed only to the phase of promotion. In 2012, an Urban Agriculture Ordinance was enacted together with the Urban Agriculture Committee. The Korean Association of Urban Agriculture Development was relied upon for the duties of promotion. The Seoul Metropolitan Agricultural Technology Center was set up to offer technical help and training.

This is a list of legislation set up for the purpose:
1. Act on Promotion and Support of Urban Agriculture, 2013
2. Enforcement Decree of the Act on the Promotion and Support of Urban Agriculture, 2013
3. Ordinance on support for the promotion of special environmental agriculture and weekend experience farming in Seoul, 2013
4. Ordinance on Support for Eco-Friendly Farming and Weekend Experience Farming in Seoul, 2009

Implementation:

According to Chang-Woo Lee, Senior Research Fellow of the Seoul Institute, the movement on urban agriculture showed great success in 2012. He stated that in the performance of general categories of urban farms and programs, most of the listed projects have shown figures outweighing their goals. For example, there were 135 local community gardens (where the goal was 25), 104 small-scale rooftop gardens (the goal was 40), and the conversion of 3,398 leftover gardens (the goal was 2,500 plots). The list also highlights things that had already been done, namely:

1. Site provision (i.e. leftover gardens, box gardens, local community gardens, small-scale rooftop gardens, urban park model farms, the Kwanghwamun Rice Farming Project, Nodeul Island UA Park);
2. Promotion (i.e. urban beekeeping on the City Hall rooftop, exhibitions, school gardens, urban agriculture ordinance enacted);
3. Practices (i.e. the elderly, multi-cultural family farms, private farms, leisure gardens, the Hopeful Seoul Environmentally Friendly Farms);
4. Training (i.e. 52 urban agriculture expert training courses and 60 city farmers' schools).

An Agriculture Technology Center was set up to operate as a city farming school to train local city farmers. A city rice farming experience center was also formed to donate 200 boxes of rice to homes and welfare centers.

The plan has now added some new proposals, such as expanding the operation of Hope Seoul environment-friendly farms, and establishing themed farms and vertical farms. On research and training, there are proposals to organize an agriculture-farm village experience event, to draft city agriculture white papers, and to create a vegetable garden model for Seoul. In the area of promotion, there are proposals to open a city agriculture exhibition, a farmer's market, a city agriculture international interchange business, city agriculture festivals, bus for rice, workshops, seminars, etc.

3. Seoul Solution, https://www.seoulsolution.kr

Nodeul Island. Photo taken by Chang- Woo Lee (2013). Urban Agriculture Policy of Seoul.

In practice, four districts were selected as tests, namely Gangdong-gu, Nodeul Island, Dohong-gu, and Jongno-gu.

Funding:
About US$46 million to transform unused spaces at schools, parks, and apartment rooftops to activate urban farming (RUAF).

Effectiveness:
According to Lee's survey (2013), urban farming had already developed a level of popularity before 2012. The number of city farms increased from 691 in 1992 to 2,919 in 2002 across South Korea. In 2012, 3,596 municipal farms were established in 2010 based on the Act on Special Exemptions for Farmland Laws (Farmland

Jongno-gu. Photo taken by Chang-Woo Lee (2013). Urban Agriculture Policy of Seoul.

Loans Act) and the Citizen's Farm Maintenance Promotion Act. A total of 173,343 blocks and an area of 1219ha was established nationwide.

Urban farms are mostly owned by the government or corporations, and public participation is allowed via short-term lease. The farms mainly operate between March and April, and applications must be made one to three months ahead. In terms of lease period, 60% of these farms can operate for less than two years and 40% between two to five years. Fees applied, 50% are rented at 5000 won a year, 30% are rented between 5000 won and 10,000 won, and the rest are free of charge. Farm managers are allowed to sublease their farms, so most of them subdivided the farm and rented it out to normal citizens or experienced farmers. Normally, a person can get 10 to 15 square meters for one to three years. Experienced farmers can get more spaces in general.

Major challenges were addressed. According to Lee's survey (2013), key problems include the following:

1. It was not easy to secure farmlands due to high land prices in the urban areas
2. Short-term leases are difficult to sustain
3. Information on garden selling, agricultural materials, and cultivation techniques is insufficient
4. Social consensus on urban agriculture is insufficient
5. Policy, budgets, and organizations have not been prepared in a systematic manner.

Critique:
Urban agriculture is not new to Seoul, as can be seen from the government's efforts at promotion and its growing popularity since 2012. The majority of citizens are aware that food security is a result of urban agriculture. So, what was missing in Seoul to put urban agriculture into a new phase?

According to Lee's survey (2013), urban agriculture is facing a number of barriers. Site shortage remains a big problem for practicing urban agriculture within the city. Land prices are high, and short-term leases have difficulty providing investment incentives for farming. Insufficient information is another problem. There is also a lack of the expertise required to practice farming within an urban context. This includes farming techniques, crop selection within the urban context, having seed banks available, cultivars, marketing and finance options, etc.

Small-scale farming requires a high setup cost and is hard to sustain in the long run. Given that land is scarce and some vacant space is inaccessible, a considerable setup fee and operation fee are required, and the yield and crop quality are uncertain, urban agriculture is difficult for individuals to undertake. Many only operate the farm for leisure or retirement activities, instead of making it the only source of income.

For farm owners, although they have a better knowledge of how to run a farm and generally own greater resources to sustain it, challenges involve keeping the farm in business over the off-farm period and potential risk created by bad lessees. Cost-savings can be achieved from economies of scale, but space constraints in the urban context are always a problem preventing them from scaling up.

For local governments and corporations that have vital resources to start up urban farming, there is an ongoing struggle between development goals and retaining space for farming. To make a space available for urban farming involves substantial effort in terms of constructing irrigation systems and composting operations and guaranteeing the market for urban agricultural products. Considerable effort is also involved to eliminate the nuisance and minimize pollution created by raising livestock or farming.

As a result, although urban agriculture is practiced in many places, much is operated on an illegal basis in the form of guerilla gardens. Temporary ownership has been a problem keeping these farms from developing to scale. Few of them are successful later to receive government sponsorship; others are often left idle when farms cannot self-finance.

From a planning perspective, inadequate resources are allocated to establish a coordinated regional food system that binds together individual fragments. Urban farms are mainly operated at small scale and are randomly distributed across the city wherever space is available—some on rooftops and some on vacant land. Piecemeal distribution and separate ownership make central management difficult, and operation costs remain high when farm business cannot operate to considerable scale. It also makes it hard for local government to estimate farming needs and equip urban farms with logistical systems and other facilities.

SECTION 4:
Proposal
In line with the government's goal to develop Seoul as an Agro-city, a top-down strategy is proposed. This proposal is made as an analytical framework to investigate, first, whether Seoul can become self-sufficient to provide the city with food security and, second, how this practice can be integrated into other urban strategies. On top of what has been done recently, there is room to improve in terms of legislation, spatial planning, land-use governance, land ownership, and establishing independence in farm finance.

Planning:
Borrowing strategies from the Unites States, Cuba, and China, where spatial distribution was made successful by granting permission and zoning, zonal distribution of urban farming programs can be introduced in Seoul. Zoning in Seoul can be classified on the basis of urban density (i.e. space available for urban agriculture), water supply, and physical constraints to cultivation.

On urban density, the city of Seoul can be divided into three zones, programmed as follows:

1. Inner city: used for farming practices that can be intensified. For example, ornamental plants and flowers, urban forestry for fruit production, vertical garden for herbs and fresh vegetables, beekeeping and aquaculture.
2. Districts with more open space: for farming practices that require considerable space. For example, urban forestry for fresh vegetables, fruit production, beekeeping, livestock raising. Crop rotation is recommended to make efficient use of space.
3. Spaces around the municipal boundary: for farming practices that cannot be intensified, like food grain production, seedlings, and large livestock farming.

On water supply, estimation on water availability is calculated by considering water availability from natural sources and the municipal water supply. Seoul can be divided into three zones of high water supply, medium water supply, and low water supply, which provides a foundation for crop selection and information on whether extra facilities are required.

1. High water supply: rice paddy, fresh vegetables
2. Medium water supply: soybeans, fruits, and fresh vegetables
3. Low water supply: barley, corn, wheat

Besides urban density and water supply, physical constraints shall also be considered to minimize the requirement of extra infrastructure or site modification for farming practices:

1. Hilly regions: barley, millet
2. Gentle slopes: fresh vegetables and fruits
3. Low-lying regions: rice paddy and other crops with a high water need

Legislation:

Allowing guerilla gardens and vacant lot ownership will increase the number of urban farm ownerships and eliminate the current problem of temporary operations and piecemeal ownerships. With a stable land supply, larger investment and facilities will be attracted.

Converted vacant land to urban farms over development:

To increase the supply of space used for urban agriculture, it is proposed to safeguard abandoned space for use as urban farms. According to Lee (2013), 142 leftover gardens have already been converted for the use of urban farming. Though many of these spaces are temporary, they offer a chance for urban farming.

Landuse governance:

As in Cuba, land-use zoning is strongly recommended to guarantee space availability for farming in the long run. The principle is to address the importance of urban farming in planning so that space can be reserved while new development comes into place.

Funding:
Land ownership

Regarding the current problem in which land ownership granted on a temporary basis is unattractive to big investment, land-use governance on public parcels, private parcels, and the public realm not only benefits the industry with space available for the long term, but also provides investment opportunities to developers and urban farmers. When the problem of space limitation is resolved, it is hoped that urban agriculture can attract the biggest investment or even commercial sectors. Instead of the current practice which relies heavily on government subsidies and technical support, private ownership helps release the burden and offers bigger resources like centralized management and quality assurance.

In turn, urban agriculture can be practiced at scale instead of as piecemeal operations. Major benefits include but are not limited to technological advancement, better facilities for farm operations, marketing of urban farm outputs, better skills and management, productive workforce, and tolerance of potential financial risk and bad yield.

Providing incentives to integrate urban agriculture into large developments

Like Seattle, Seoul can also consider introducing a height limit exemption or financial benefits to provide developers incentives on urban agriculture. The practice can be integrated either horizontally on rooftops, podiums, or backyards, or vertically as green walls and other possible means.

1. Decisions on space requirement:

By comparing the existing supply of land and per capita consumption of each food category, a significant agricultural land shortage can be summarized as follows. In order to keep up with today's food consumption pattern, we need 500 times more agricultural land.

A ratio is developed reference from existing cultivation area of grain, meat, vegetables, fruits, and specialty crops.

In calculating the cultivation space required to achieve self-sufficiency, the per capita consumption and average space requirement for each item are used to make the estimation. The following figures summarize the local consumption pattern of each food item with reference to current statistics obtained from the Korean Statistical Information Service. A detailed breakdown is attached in table 10 appendix.

Annual per capita consumption:
> Grain: 350 kg
> Livestock: 128 kg
> Vegetables: 150 kg
> Fruits: 63.2 kg
> Specialty crops: 3.75 kg

Required cultivation area to sustain one-year of self-sufficiency for one person:
> Grain: 692 square meters
> Livestock: 451 square meters
> Vegetables: 57.78 square meters
> Fruits: 28.66 square meters
> Specialty crops: 0.78 square meters

2. Decisions on what crops to be grown:

To estimate what types of crops should be grown in South Korea, we used a statistical analysis of food crops and livestock in relation to their consumption, production, and import balance. Crops are selected on four criteria: (i) high local demand, (ii) decline in local production, (iii) heavy reliance on imports, and (iv) their relation to Korean food culture.

3. Decisions on urban farm locations:

A top-down planning approach is proposed to govern zonal distribution of urban farms. The following are three sets of analyses to recommend the location of urban farms and what should be grown.

4. Decisions on integrating urban farms into other landuses:

From the following calculations, we can determine what kind of land use can provide the best effectiveness if converted into productive landscape. Built-up areas (i.e. roof-top farming) reserve the highest potential, while infrastructure comes second. Open-space, educational ground follows.

5. Agencies to be involved

This section considers how each sector can contribute to urban agriculture in Seoul.

Recalling the examples in the United States, urban farms provide enormous social benefits while involving minority groups in the city. The participation of minority groups shall be promoted. In Seoul, these people can be new immigrants, the elderly, disabled people, or even students who offer their time to generate weekend profits.

The local government plays an important role in offering technical assistance and financial initiatives for urban farm start-ups. As in the United States, local government is the organizer of weekend farms. Other than this kind of pop-up event, local government can contribute more to the marketing of crops, facilitate the sale of urban crops by providing logistic facilities, and centralize the compost recycling system. By organizing composting and returning it as farm inputs, the government can largely reduce the cost of farm operations.

Apart from the local government, schools are the biggest sector to start urban farming. Considerable efforts were put into starting school gardens for educational purposes. This can be something to take on in the future.

Corporations play a part in providing financial support and organizing urban agriculture. Corporations are encouraged to integrate urban agriculture as part of their business strategy so skills and resources can be shared. It can be done simply by establishing a rooftop farm used as a lunchtime garden for their staff.

Collaboration between different production sectors shall also be encouraged. For example, livestock are fed on grains provided by corn fields, processing industries cooperate with those selling ingredients, fisheries collaborate with rice production. A sharing platform shall be established so those with different areas of expertise can find a common ground and generate mutual benefits.

Individuals are strongly encouraged to play a part by practicing farming in the nearby community gardens.

Existing condition:
According to Chang-Woo Lee's survey in 2013, urban agriculture has already developed considerable coverage in the following areas.

In 2013, urban farming achieved an area of 115 ha in total, including 135 local community gardens, 142 leftover gardens, 89 rooftop gardens, 3 urban park gardens, 16 public gardens, 55 private farms' leisure gardens, 29 Gu-government gardens, 30 city-supported school gardens, and 878 school gardens.

In addition to the area of existing agricultural land (i.e. dry paddies, rice paddies, orchards, pastures), we have an extra 2398 ha. Together with the land area of school gardens, 2411 ha, we have a total area of 4924 ha land used as productive landscape.

Goal:
The following milestones are proposed on the basis of short-term (2030), mid-term (2050), and long-term (beyond 2050) goals.

Short-term goal (2030):
Refine legislation to address urban agriculture in city planning; provide investment incentives for private farm ownership, large corporations, and small urban farmers. Secure existing urban farm sites, including school gardens, community farms, and existing farmland in the periphery. Provide these farms with legal support in terms of land permits, legalizing guerilla farms, providing water supply and necessary facilities. If possible, existing open space (i.e. recreational ground, gardens, and parks) shall all be converted into productive use. Along the river banks, reserve islands and both banks for urban agriculture.

It is assumed that 1230 square meters (0.123ha) of land is required to provide food for one person a year: see section above on decisions on space requirements.

Mid-term goal (2050):
Urban farm business grows in scale from current farm locations, with small urban farmers receiving

adequate support. To grow in scale requires urban crop production to either intensify or invade surrounding available space. Urban farming will be integrated into citizens' lives, supplying fresh crops easily accessible within a 1km service area. A logistical network shall be established to facilitate individual farms and encourage collaboration among farms. Spatial distribution of food crop production starts to develop.

It is assumed that 1230 square meters (0.123ha) of land is required to provide food for one person a year: see section above on decisions on space requirements.

Long-term goal (beyond 2050):

Urban farm business grows and becomes self-sustaining. Urban agriculture needs to be intensified to become the foundation of local agriculture and economy. Satellite farming plots are suggested to supplement the local food supply.

It is assumed that 1230 square meters (0.123ha) of land is required to provide food for one person a year: see section above on decisions on space requirements.

Experimentation in detail:

Three sites are suggested as examples to highlight the benefits of integrating urban agriculture with other urban strategies.

1. Yongsan Park—Urban agriculture as a social strategy

As discussed, urban agriculture helps resolve social problems. By shortening food miles, it makes fresh food easily accessible to the public. In the case of Yongsan Park, we will investigate how urban agriculture in a central park could benefit the surrounding neighborhood.

2. Teheran Valley—Urban agriculture as an economic strategy

By integrating urban agriculture into the IT hub of Seoul, we attempt to investigate how high technology and information sharing can increase the productivity of urban agriculture.

3. Nodeul Island—Urban agriculture as ecological protection

Growing food in the city not only contributes to the local economy, it also provides substantial ecological value. The practice can become a flood protection strategy by growing food around the river banks and flood-inundated areas.

Conclusion:

It can be concluded from the above analysis that urban agriculture can be further improved under a structured framework and supportive legal system. The following diagram summarizes how the proposed items respond to the studied obstacles and challenges.

References

Cohen, Nevin. 2011. *Urban Food Policy: Strategies for Sustainable Food Systems*. Blog. https://urbanfoodpolicy.com/author/nevincohen/.

FAO (Food and Agriculture Organization of the United Nations). 2014. "Cattle Housing." UN: Farm Structures in Tropical Climates. Rural Infrastructure and Agro-Industries Division. http://www.fao.org/3/ a-s1250e/S1250E11.htm.

Feifei, Zhang, Cai Jianming, and Liu Gang. 2007. *Emerging Migrant Farmer Communities in Periurban Beijing*. Beijing: Institute of Geographical Sciences and Natural Resources Research (IGSNRR), Chinese Academy of Sciences (CAS).

de Haen, Hartwig. 2002. *Enhancing the Contribution of Urban Agriculture to Food Security*, ed. René van Veenhuizen. Resource Centre for Urban Agriculture (RUAF). Urban Agriculture Magazine, The Netherlands.

Kim, Si Yeon, et al. 2014. "Food Consumption Trends in Korea." USDA Foreign Agricultural Service. Global Agricultural Information Network.

Kim, Wan Soon. 2013. *National Policy, Laws, and Institutions of Urban Agriculture in Korea*. Seoul: Agro City Seoul, University of Seoul.

KREI. 2014. *"Agriculture in Korea."* Korean Rural Economic Institute. https://www.krei.re.kr/web/eng/agriculture-in-korea.

Lee, Chang-Woo. 2013. "Urban Agriculture Policy of Seoul." Seattle: American Community Garden Association Conference. The Seoul Institute, Seoul, Korea.

Nam, Tae-Ho, and Tae-Yeol Jung. 2014. "The Distribution and Characteristics of Use of Urban Farms: A Case Study of the Siji Region in Daegu Metropolitan City." Dept. of Landscape Architecture, Kyungpook National University. *J. KILA* 42 (6) (December): 1–9.

Oberholtzer, Lydia, et al. 2014. "Urban Agriculture in the United States: Characteristics, Challenges, and Technical Assistance Needs." *Journal of Extension* (),a.https://www.joe.org/joe/2014december/a1.php.

RUAF Foundation, 2017. "Urban Agriculture: What and Why?" RUAF. http:// www.ruaf.org/urbanagriculturewhatandwhy, accessed 4 August 2017.

Santandreu, Alain. 2010. "Havana, Cuba: Urban Agriculture Policy." United Cities and Local Governments. Under the supervision of Dr. Stefania Barca at the Centre for Social Studies, University of Coimbra, Portugal. https://www.uclg-cisdp.org/sites/default/files/La%20Habana_2010_en_final.pdf, accessed 4 August 2017.

Seoul Metropolitan Government. 2014. "Seoul City Agriculture." http://english. seoul.go.kr/policy-information/economy/economy-for-the-people/2-seoul-city-agriculture/.

Sonaiya, E. B. 2004. "Small-scale Poultry Production: Technical Guide." FAO Animal Production and Health Rome, 2004 manual. http://www.fao.org/docrep/008/y5169e/y5169e05.htm.

Teaster, Sara, et al. 2009. "Regional Land for Food.", University of Virginia, Urban and Environmental Planning. http://www.virginia.edu/ vpr/sustain/foodcollaborative-wp/wp-content/uploads/2016/09/Land-Need-for-Producing-Food.pdf.

Yeung, Yue-man. "Examples of Urban Agriculture in Asia." United Nations University. http://archive.unu.edu/unupress/food/8F092e/8F092E05.htm, accessed 4 August 2017.

Yoon, Jeong-joong, et al. 2014. *National Report for Habitat III*. Seoul: Land and Housing Institute, Ministry of Land, Infrastructure and Transport.

农委信息中心. 2008. "农业布局确定五个发展圈"《农业. 2007 (31).23. http://www.agri.ac.cn/news/2008521/52022.html.

农业部. 2012. "农业发展情况的调研报告" 农业部市场与经济信息司. http:// www.moa.gov.cn/ztzl/jlh/xgzl/201204/t20120425_2610915.htm.

农业技术网. 2012. "现代农业的领跑者。" http://www.agri.sh.cn/njxw/ nyxw/201204/t20120423_214958.html.

Liveware: The Plug-In Ecology—Urban Farm Pod

Mitchell Joachim and Christian Hubert

At Terreform ONE, we are keen to understand more about the imminent interdependence between agriculture and cities. Many biological technologies that will change this relationship are ubiquitous and readily available. To us, architecture is biology. Organisms in some form or another created almost everything on earth. Consequently, how can new architectural methodologies play a helpful role in merging farms and cities?

Farming is like manufacturing—both have strictly coordinated procedures for creating dependable goods, impervious as far as possible from the impulses of the larger environment. In part due to an improved comprehension of DNA sequencing, the vegetation and mammals nurtured on a farm are also exactingly structured. Accurate genomic control, known as "gene editing," makes this a reality. Today it's practical to genetically alter a single characteristic in a crop or an explicit chromosomal element in an animal. This knowledge will be more suitable to customers than the kaleidoscope of entire genes between species that buttressed initial genetic engineering exercises. It's a process that merely emulates the procedure of transformation on which plant reproduction has always required but in a significantly more manageable way.

Fully understanding a plant's cellular hereditary material also means that propagation itself can be prepared more accurately. Now, it's not necessary to cultivate a plant species to adulthood to find the required characteristics show up. Instead, a rapid observation of its genome early on will reveal it. Such scientific high-tech revolutions are in effect turning plants and animals into "liveware." Research on the fusions of architecture and liveware is a far-reaching and critical point

of exploration. We created the Plug-in Ecology: Urban Farm Pod precisely for this reason.

The Plug-In Ecology is a number of things in one. It is a "living" cabin for individuals and urban nuclear families to grow and provide for their daily vegetable needs. Moreover, it is an adaptable interface with the city, potentially touching upon urban farming, air quality levels, DIY agronomy techniques in test tubes, algal energy production, and bioluminescent light sources, to name a few possibilities. It can be outfitted with a number of optional systems to adapt to different locations, lighting conditions, and habitation requirements. While agricultural food sources are usually invisible in cities such as New York, the pod archetype turns the food system itself into a visible artifact, a bio-informatic message system, and a functional space.

The Plug-In Ecology cabin sphere prototype uses a robotic milled rotegrity ball for the under-grid structure made of reclaimed flat packed materials. A fully operable sub-irrigation system and shaped foam panels serve as sleeves for the potted elements and agronomy tissue culture for micro-propagation. A digital monitoring platform relays information about specific plant health to the web. Our vision for future iterations of the pod is to naturally grow structures over time, within a new form of mediated arboreal culture, to integrate the biological and mechanical elements more closely, to transform the object into one that grows and changes symbiotically. The Plug-In Ecology project sets out a direction for healthy biological exchanges with urban inhabitants, and aims to contribute to the life of urban ecosystems that mediate between autonomy and community. Here, Terreform ONE's work is both technical

and symbolic in a distinctive and provocative way. Many of our objects and graphics are both representations of quantifiable processes (for example, the production of trash) and symbolic objects with suggestive and multivalent meanings. One project, for example, used the statue of liberty as a measuring device. But the Statue of Liberty itself is an object saturated with symbolic meanings. How many of those meanings are meant to attach themselves to that T1 project remains an open question.

The Plug-In Ecology and the more recent Cricket Shelter: Modular Edible Insect Farm are meant to address some of the crucial food issues of today: especially growing vegetal and alternative protein sources of food. Although traditional and artisanal techniques have won the hearts and minds of many well-meaning and environmentally conscious people who eat, highly rationalized, potentially automated, and intensive cultivation techniques lay claim to the future. New technoscientific processes, such as genetic modification (described above), are a controversial part of that same future, as is cultivation in new environments, from the oceans to outer space and other planets.

The spherical form of the Plug-In Ecology speaks to that kind of techno-futurism, and to its cosmological dimensions. In this respect, Buckminster Fuller serves as a role model, and indeed, its structure and fabrication processes are clearly indebted to his structural innovations, as well as to some of his symbolic archetypes. The spherical form speaks to "spaceship earth" and to the planetary experience conveyed, for example, by Fuller's observatory at Cornell. The Plug-In Ecology clearly needs to float off the ground.

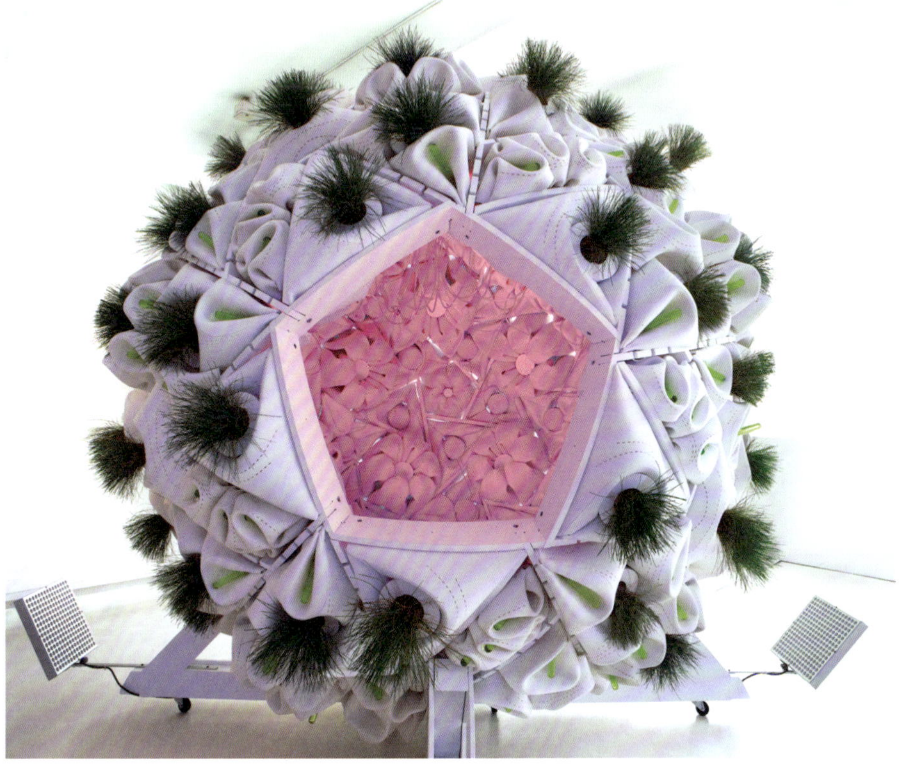

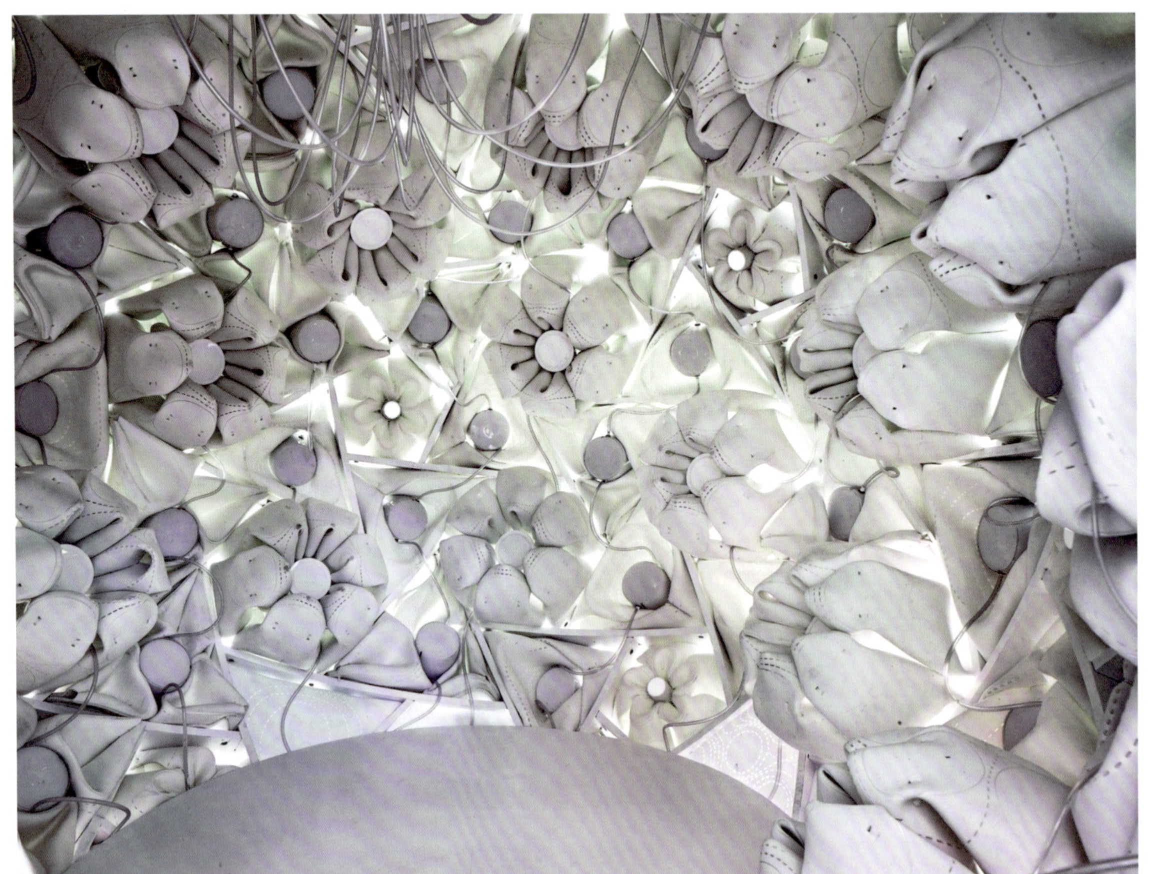

The orientation of the plants in relation to both gravity and sunlight are issues that could be developed—but for now, they defy both gravity and expectation.

In conclusion, what kind of object or architecture is this? It is not straightforwardly functional—at least for a terrestrial farm. It does not fly the banner of efficiency. The project itself is a hybrid of technical and biomorphic forms. The computer-milled plywood structure is rationalized into a soft and curved integument that holds the potted plants and fills the polygonal openings in the structure, hinting at a continuity between its making and the unfolding of a flower. The tectonic strangeness gives the ball an ambiguous living quality—and makes for a variety of programmatic and symbolic interpretations, from a nest to a teleportation pod, to a full-spectrum gardening/tanning salon and beyond. Is it animal, vegetable, or mineral, or all three merged cohesively as one?

The Flexing Room: Embodied Computation, Autonomy, and Architectural Robotics

Axel Kilian

Discussions about sensing and autonomy are becoming more common-place, prompted by the autonomy of everyday objects such as vacuum cleaners and on an experimental level in cars and in research in humanoid robots. In fiction, an increasing number of storylines based on autonomous robots from *blade runner* to *Ex Machina* have similarly moved questions of autonomy into the mainstream. However, there is an omission in the lineup of potentially autonomous constructs: architecture.

The Flexing Room installation aims to move forward our understanding of autonomous architectural robots through the concept of embodied computation. Embodied computation is an argument for a closer integration between the physical and material structure and the integration of computational control and sensors. A key aspect of embodied computation is a holistic sense of self, of existing with a body. Current architecture has limited self-awareness with few sensors compared to its large physical extents, and most are related to the conditioning of spaces. Autonomy is more than automation; it is more than interactivity, more than a smart room. The Flexing Room combines an active bending structure with sensors for controlling actuation pressure and motion tracking for capturing human actions. The building body acts as a bridge between the environment and its finite-state machine that makes the engagement of visitors with the structure visible for the Biennale public. The interaction between visitors and the structure is imagined to be open-ended, allowing for the building's response to human presence to evolve over time, adjusting actions based on the perceived responses of visitors. Visitors get a sense of acknowledgement of their presence through a series of posture

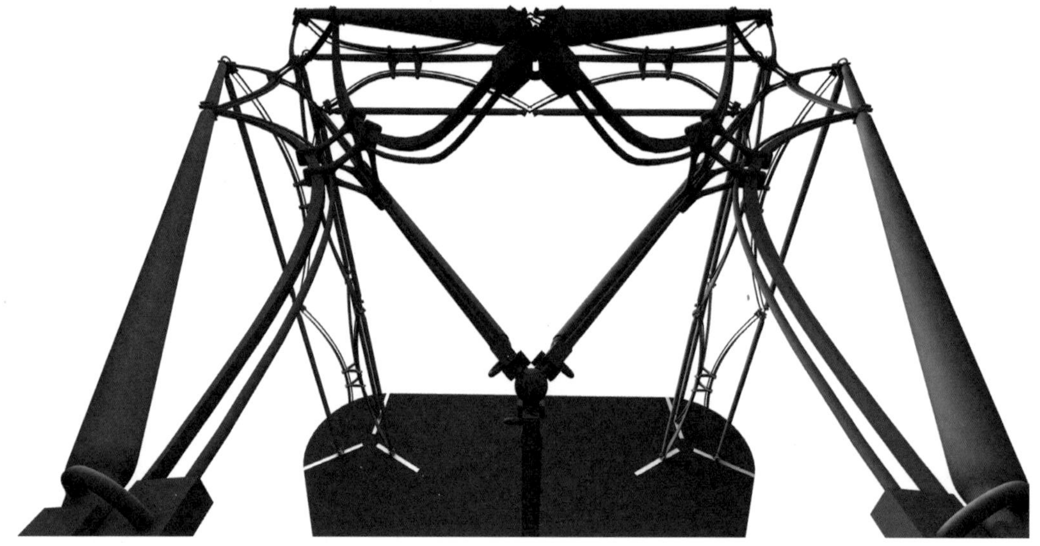

Close-up of the upper crossbeams of the experimental structure

changes of the structure based on the internal computational state and the sensor input. The map of state changes can be changed over time, letting the structure's behavior evolve over time. The physical posture of the building is in part computationally determined through the set pressures in the actuators, and in part resolved through the active bending response of the fiberglass skeleton, and is less predictable as it is soft and responsive to environmental forces. Through the sensed position of visitors, space becomes interface and building behavior communication. Motion is secondary to the notion of a holistic building scale awareness, which can be expressed in various other ways. Posture is chosen here for the relative ease it can be read in the likely short time a Biennale visitor spends with the structure. In structures with longer-term occupation, this can expand into all degrees of freedom of a building both with visible and invisible consequences. Ultimately the autonomy of a building allows it to pursue an agenda that becomes part of the design intent. In the context of embodied computation, autonomy allows for the continued design adaptation throughout the lifetime of the structure.

Introduction

Autonomy is slowly taking hold in our technology-driven lives as research pushes more objects from automatic to autonomous operation. Current examples all come from the object realm. From our social interactions and our experiences in the world, we are relatively familiar with the paradigm of moving objects from living things and fellow humans, and we have a relatively well-formed set of conventions shaped by experiences of how to interact and what to expect. In that sense, the introduction of autonomously acting, moving entities in the form of robots or self-driving cars is not fundamentally new but differs in how it is controlled. Autonomy in architecture in its non-object state is different. Architecture surrounds us, we inhabit it, it is always there.

Architecture is physical. Computation is abstract. Embodied computation is a concept that combines the two through a merged presence of computational control through the physical presence of the material artifact. Its material presence at full scale is crucial in its impact on the world. Computational processes have had a significant impact on the design process and the delivery of the design through digitally administered fabrication. However, I argue that computation needs to reach beyond the design and construction process into human occupation. I propose the concept of embodied computation to address this change and test it in the Seoul Biennale through an experimental structure, the Flexing Room. It is a sensing, actuated structure that can adapt to changing conditions. On a very simplistic level, it learns from the observed behaviors of its human occupants by adapting its behavioral scenarios in the form of its finite-state machine.

The problem statement of autonomy in architecture is a combination of two questions. First, how can the physical structure in its architectural scale be fully involved in the sensing and communication with its inhabitants? Second, how can the design process extend beyond the development and building of the physical structure into the evolving interaction between inhabitant and architecture throughout the lifetime of the structure?

To explore these concepts in the context of the Seoul Biennale, I developed a selective prototype, a prototype at human scale that explores a

select few of the key concepts in physically experienceable form. This "Flexing Room" senses people around it and their position in space through a Kinect sensor and, based on an internal finite-state automata and the sensory input determines its next action. Over time, this finite-state automata can adjust by reorganizing its connectivity to try out different response configurations. The construct is a selective prototype of an autonomous architectural robot. We view it as an experimental platform for future larger-scale autonomous architecture. The experimental structure is a sensing, actuated structure that can adapt to changing conditions.

A crucial element in doing so is to include the physical entity of the structure into the computational process. In the case of the Flexing Room, this happens through an active bent structure using pressure-based actuation that arrives at its physical posture through a combination of computationally controlled pressure settings in the actuators. The result is the deformation of the interconnected fiberglass rod structure. This is not a fully determined mechanism. It's resolving its state based on an equilibrium between environmental forces and the internal pretension of the active bent skeleton.

Background—Buildings as Robots

Architectural robotics in the past decade has been increasingly defined by the use of industrial robotic arms as manipulators for automated construction and digital fabrication (Kohler, Gramazio, Willmann, 2014). The Flexing Room, on the contrary, is architecture as robots, meaning it is an example of the development of buildings as robots with a level of autonomy and the basic ability to sense and respond to the world and its inhabitants. Architectural robots have precedents in Cedric Price's 1960s Fun Palace project (Hardingham 2016), an adaptable, open-frame work that configures itself to different user scenarios. However, the building in the Fun Palace proposal is more architectural machine and industrial armature than sensing body, a spatial enabler rather than a sensate architectural participant. Price's visions are essential, though, in establishing the concepts that followed. With the availability of affordable electronic controls and computing power and computational developments, architectural-scale interactive concepts have increasingly been experimented with in a field referred to as "interactive architecture" (Fox and Kemp 2010; Bartlett 2017). The Hyperbody group at TU Delft became a leader in developing such interactive architectures and referred to them in later iterations as "architectural robotics" (Bier 2014). Intelligent rooms were long a focus in research in artificial intelligence, for instance in project Oxygen (Oh et al. 2002) and in one of the most complex publically accessible installations, the 2002 expo Ada intelligent room (Eng, Mintz, and Verschure 2005), which placed particular emphasis on the tracking and active influencing of visitors' behavior in space through an interactive, lit floor pattern and surrounding screens (Eng et al. 2003). Tremendous progress in sensory processing power and data processing algorithms have made human sensing an affordable and robust endeavor (e.g.,Kinect). But still much active research remains to be done for the type of dense social interactions so crucial for understanding dynamic human social interactions in architectural spaces. Some very promising advances being made (Joo et al. 2015) using hundreds of overlapping video feeds for high-occlusion object tracking and detecting

subtle social cues based on the body language of interacting groups of individuals. The architecture of Joo's visual sensing space is a static video rig though using a geodesic dome geometry.

Buildings as robots is a concept that is only at the beginning of its development, and most sensing development is based on visual video feeds. But there is a wealth of sensory data that can be derived from the physical materiality of the architecture itself, from vibration patterns, flow of forces, and acoustics, to touch and environmental measures. This heterogeneous set of sensory data requires novel models of integration to derive decisions from the sensed states in the world. Ultimately the discipline of architecture will have to define an agenda on which to act to expand architectural design beyond the description of material form into the behavioral realm.

The sensing body

Currently the notion of the body of architecture is mostly synonymous with architectural form. But when comparing the notion of body and self-awareness with that of our own human body, it becomes clear that architecture has vastly fewer senses helping it to feel itself than humans do. Architectural sensory abilities generally do not go much further than the thermostat, and most other sensors in the home consist of accessories visually monitoring space more than being integrated with the physical structure itself. The 1930s discovery of somatosensory and motor cortex regions in the brain established the understanding of the sensory distortion with regards to the size of the brain regions attributed to their respective body regions. (Penfield and Boldfrey 1937). The human body as a living organism is densely packed with sensing cells, but also surprisingly varied in its sensing density, a fact that is also traceable to the somatosensory and motor cortex regions in the brain, where different body parts are represented disproportionally to their actual physical scale based on sensor density. This brain mapping theory has been studied critically in much more detail with much more sophisticated imaging techniques in recent years; those studies revealed a much more volumetric interconnected clustered mapping of the different regions in the brain (Graziano 2008).

What would the sensory map for architecture look like? How much awareness of self does a robotic building need? Should the focus be mostly on the human activities within or more on the state of the building in terms of temperature, structural behavior, and energy use? Likely it is a combination of factors. With the contextualized information about its own state, it can respond better to evolving situations.

How does an architectural response look? The most likely response in an anthropomorphic sense would be kinetic; many early proposals such as Price's Fun Palace, mentioned above, rely on kinetic components. But at the scale of architecture and engineering, kinetic elements quickly become massive and difficult to move, requiring large actuation systems to aid or replace human manipulation. Furthermore, there are other degrees of freedom in architecture besides the kinetic, including lighting and sound. There are also robust established mechanical systems as possible channels for expression, such as doors and windows and adjustable façade systems for sun control. Would it be possible to coordinate the opening and closing of windows in such a way that the building could capture an approaching breeze and allow it to flow through the building in a controlled fashion, opening and closing windows at just the right time to aid ventilation?

Sensing structures are still in early development at larger scales and mostly pushed through distributed devices and performance-related sensors related to mechanical functions. But such approaches could aid building-scale constructs to reach an awareness of self. In combination with space monitors, these approaches could provide a fine-grained enough resolution to perceive human intentions and the nuances of interaction. The ubiquity of relatively cheap sensors such as the Kinect and multi-camera visual tracking algorithms have improved things. Yet today these devices continue to be just accessories to already built spaces and have little to no architectural integration except in experimental smaller-scale work. Current sensing density at architectural scale is extremely low in comparison to that of living organisms and is almost entirely focused on the void spaces that can be occupied. Sensing is typically geared towards calibrating human comfort and sensing human presence but does not address the physical state of the architectural body itself. Examples from other industries are instructive as to possible directions. In the high-end sailing boats of the America's Cup, for example, sophisticated, integrated load sensors throughout the critical load-bearing structures monitor their load limits and influence maneuver decisions. But beyond the gathering of sensing data, for architecture the bigger challenge is to create a level of self-awareness for the architectural structure that allows for judgement at the overall building scale, but also offers enough granularity to engage with individuals at the human scale. Creating the sensing body is one part of design; developing the sensing integration and the learning of meaningful responses and cross connections is another open-ended design challenge that will increase in importance.

Space as interface for human–machine interaction: The challenge of scale

A fundamental and obvious difference between the established anthropomorphic approach to robotics and the challenge of autonomy in architecture is scale. It is necessary to rethink interaction fundamentally when human-to-object shifts to one large object containing the human. A building's scale makes it likely that many occupants want to interact with it simultaneously and spread out over large distances in distinct spatial settings, likely not connected to each other. The spatial distance complicates the relative contained nature of object-based interactions. But it also offers the possibility of a much higher position-based granularity by using relative position as a differentiator in interactions between the architectural constructs and its inhabitants.

It is an open question of how a building articulates itself to its inhabitants. Possible responses range from screens to acoustics such as speech and voice recognition. But there is something specific about the distributed nature of a larger building with respect to its inhabitants that makes things particularly challenging for expressing the building state. Is there a centrally shared state communicated consistently to all parties, or is there spatial resolution of states with respect to the specific location of the inhabitant? How can a building interface with its inhabitants? The scale difference between building and inhabitant opens the possibility of using spatial differentiation as the interface. The relative position of people in space and to each other over time offers a richer exchange but also the challenge of extracting and detecting the subtleties in the social interactions and their implications for the architecture they happen in. The spatial resolution of an inhabitant's position is a unique quality one can derive (only?) from architecture. Most established interaction conventions are based on object-to-human and mostly screen-to-vision exchanges. There is the potential for a distributed collective interaction model that leverages the spatial dimensions and minute differentiations in posture, gaze, and social constellations as cues for a building to respond to (Joo et al. 2015). Parallel interfacing between groups of people and a single building poses unique challenges and opportunities in both identifying channels of interaction and identifying new computational collective models with distinct spatial traits.

The Flexing Room is an exploration of interfacing through positions in space and building postures and motion. Change in the form of kinetic movement is an expression similar to a dancer communicating through movement. The Flexing Room selectively explores motion and posture as potential architectural expression.

Ultimately it will not be enough to use different entities in isolation—the challenge is to achieve a holistic expressiveness and variability across heterogeneous entities, joining tangible and intangible degrees of freedom. Also, the current approach of accessorizing existing buildings with intelligent gadgets such as Google's Nest will have to go further and integrate the different degrees of freedom of an "as is" building with relatively minimal interventions, such as retrofitting existing architecture and achieving more through algorithmic complexity of control.

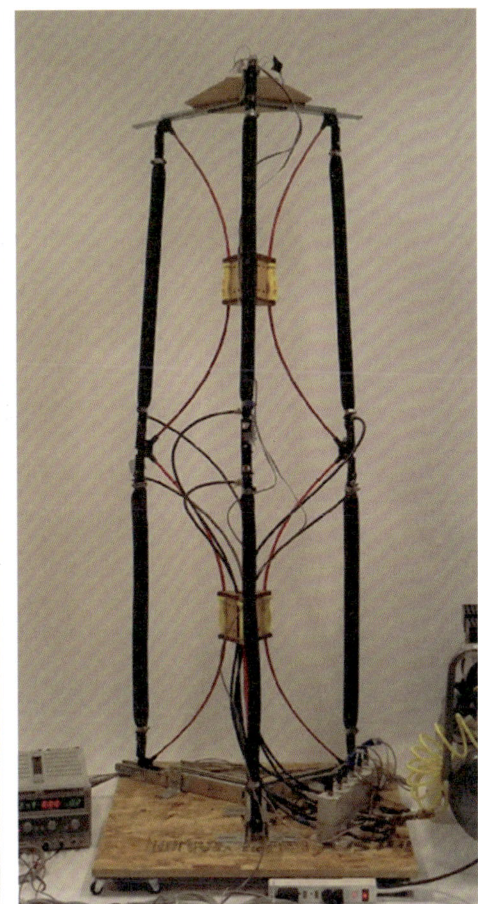

Imagine cutting individual building elements free and giving them more autonomy to operate independently within the overall structure.

The Flexing Room

The Flexing Room was developed as a selective prototype of an architectural robot, following the concept of embodied computation. It is based on the core unit of the earlier experiment of the Bow Tower, which established the base premise of an actuated active bending structural column. The Bow Tower allows for six degrees of movement of its column tip using a combination of contractions of its six fluidic actuators (Davis and Carlson 2003) to tilt its top in all three axes. In addition, it can also change its position in the xyz-directions by elongating and shortening the tower. The actuators are based on the fluidic muscle principle (Davis and Carlson 2003) using a mesh sleeve outer tension membrane and an inner stretching airtight tube to build up pressure. As the pressure builds up, the tube expands and rotates the outer fibers against each other up to 72 degrees. At this point, the maximum volume

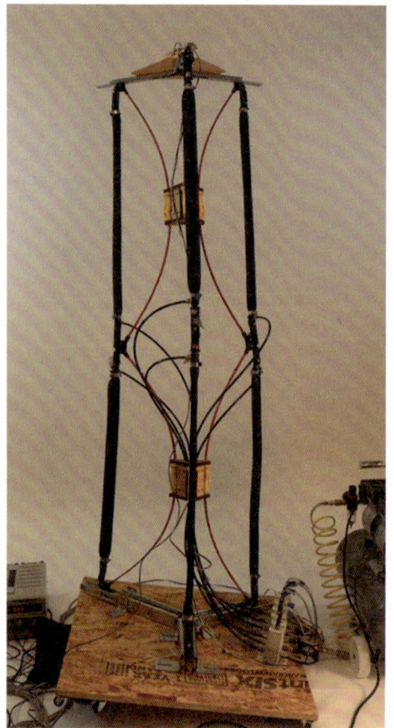
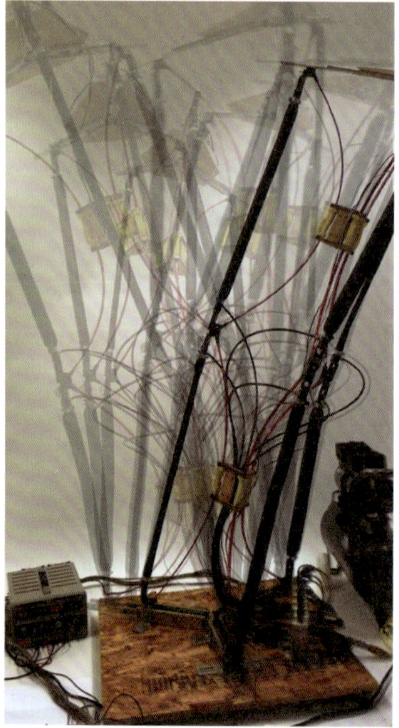

Single experimental column test showing actuation range and ability to compensate for uneven ground condition through sensor feedback from accelerometer on top of column.

3D printed connector detail

of a geodesic, fiber cross-wrapped volume and the geometric contraction limit is reached.

The pressure in each actuator is monitored through a differential pressure sensor that compares the external pressure against the internal pressure and an Arduino Nano board that operates two solenoid valves to increase pressure from a feed line or shed pressure when the target pressure set by the central control unit is reached. This pressure-based actuator is linked to a fiberglass bow that keeps the actuator under pretension at all times. This allows the unit

to both contract and expand despite the limitation of the actuator that can only contract. Three such bow actuator units are joined by a 3D printed joint that fuses them into one level capable of controlling all degrees of freedom within a limited range.

This unit is stacked into a Bow Tower-like column. The selective prototype mission is to encapsulate space, which is achieved by combining the minimum number of columns in a triangular configuration connected by horizontal double units at the top.

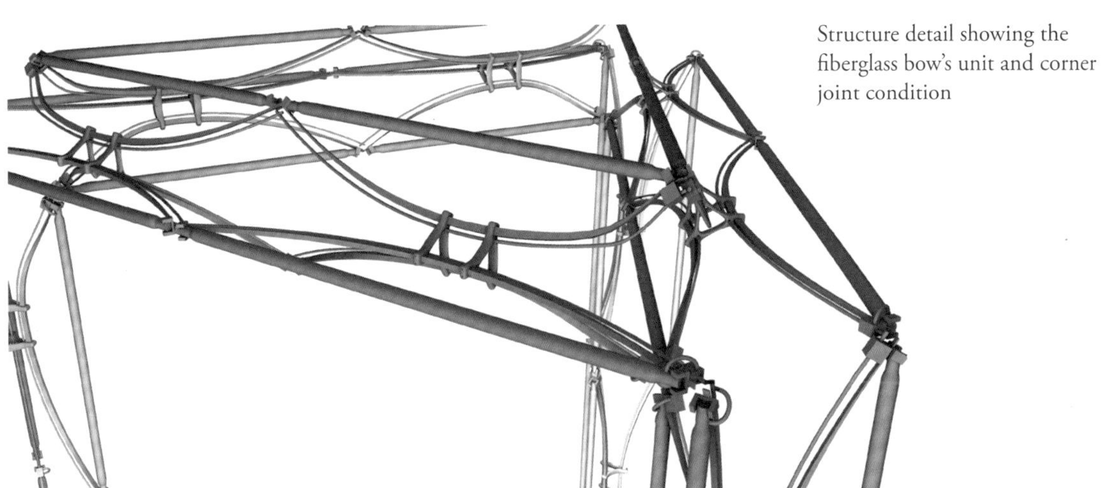

Structure detail showing the fiberglass bow's unit and corner joint condition

Architectural Robot in an idealized neutral state showing the part topology and base. Such a straight state does not occur in the physical actively bent structure.

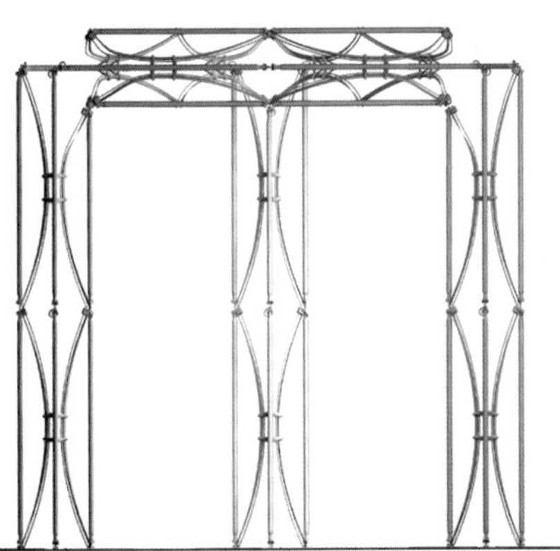

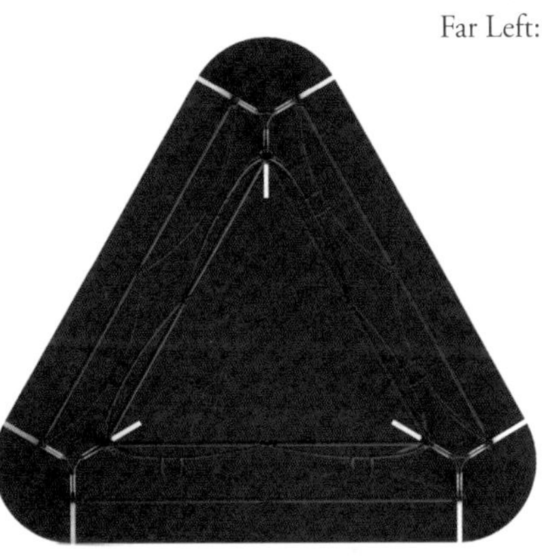

Left: Side view
Far Left: Plan view of the structure

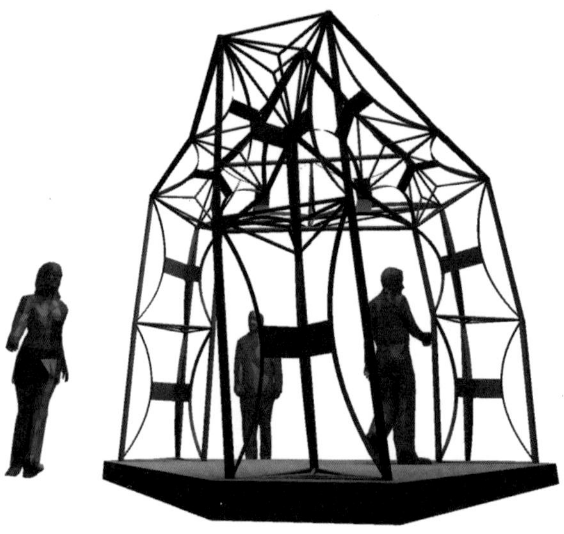

Posture response to human presence through distortion of the fiberglass frame. Both preconfigured postures and behavioral loops during idling are part of the repertoire.

One of the main challenges of this construction approach is that there is no set length for the structural unit, but a wide range of lengths and angles between base and top plane described by the respective three tips of the bow unit. This makes geometrically modelling the structure in a descriptive geometry sense useless as each unit's state influences the other in its connected structural state and requires a full structural simulation to determine the geometric state of the structure. Therefore, the detail figure of the overall structure shown above is simply an idealized geometric unactuated state for illustration purposes only. The posture states figures are derived from an approximate particle spring construct developed in kangaroo or grasshopper to test different actuation configurations and their posture response for the overall connected structure. The result is an undetermined structure that is difficult to simulate, but its physical state can be resolved through the actuation of the physical construct. Therefore, the physical construct is doing part of the computation in response to the computational actuation trigger, which is part of the experimental question of how to use the body of architecture as part of the physical computation.

The architectural structure is capable of different postures based on the combination of actuation pressures in its thirty-six pneumatic actuators. The active bending structure acts as a mediator between potentially contradictory actuation states in deforming in such a way to even out all actuation states throughout the structure into one cohesive posture. The posture is a form of interface of the structure to its environment and signals to its users the structure's awareness of human presence and also which state the architecture is in. Internal states are cross-referenced with physical states of the structures and connected with sensors that monitor outside movement. Based on the combination of external movement, internal state, and physical posture, a next course of action is determined by the architectural construct.

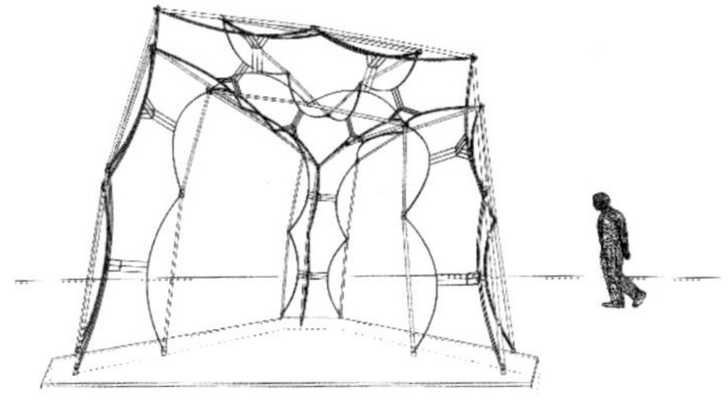

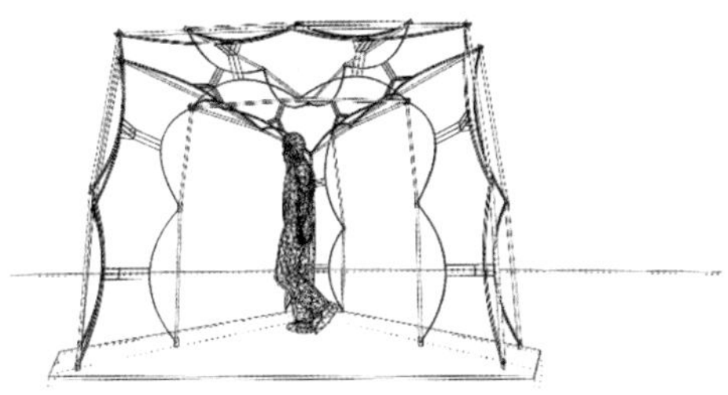

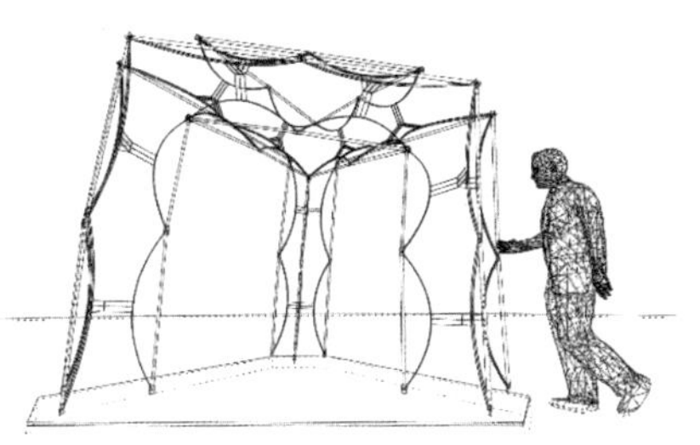

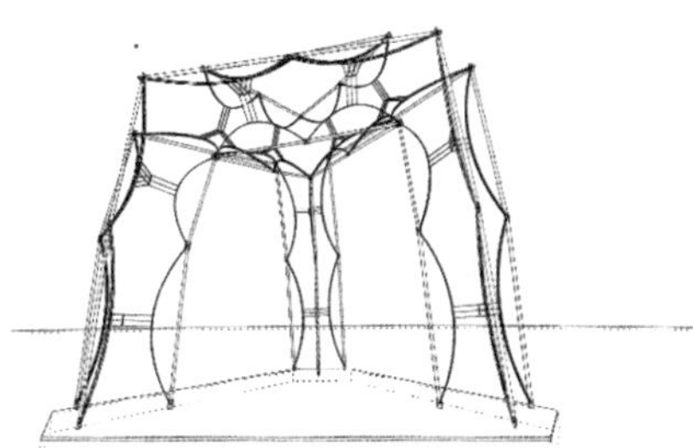

The internal states correspond with the physical states of the structure as it is sensed by its inhabitants. The architectural robot uses its physical structure state to correspond to its internal computational state, and through active bending the structural state is also directly connected to the environment in deforming due to wind, or limited human interference. Each posture is associated with a set of pressures. These sets can adjust over time based on sensor feedback and inhabitant behavior.

The structure has a number of postural responses to the sensed presence of people surrounding the structure. The structure has a series of internal states that it moves through based on the current state and the sensed external interaction. This finite-state machine is calibrated with the postures and refined based on the spatial context of the interaction. The structure is able to use the postures to attract attention if there is a lack of human activity and the structure moves into an idle or bored state.

The positioning of the sensors are on the one hand thirty-six pressure sensors directly in the actuator to control the fluidic actuators. The human tracking using a Kinect is difficult in that it requires a stationary position in order to process positions of humans in space consistently. Therefore it is connected to the static base plate with a viewing angle covering the internal space and the main approach to the structure. Additional local motion sensors are considered but will have to be tested for robustness in the final installation.

Architectural postures in response to human approach and during idling

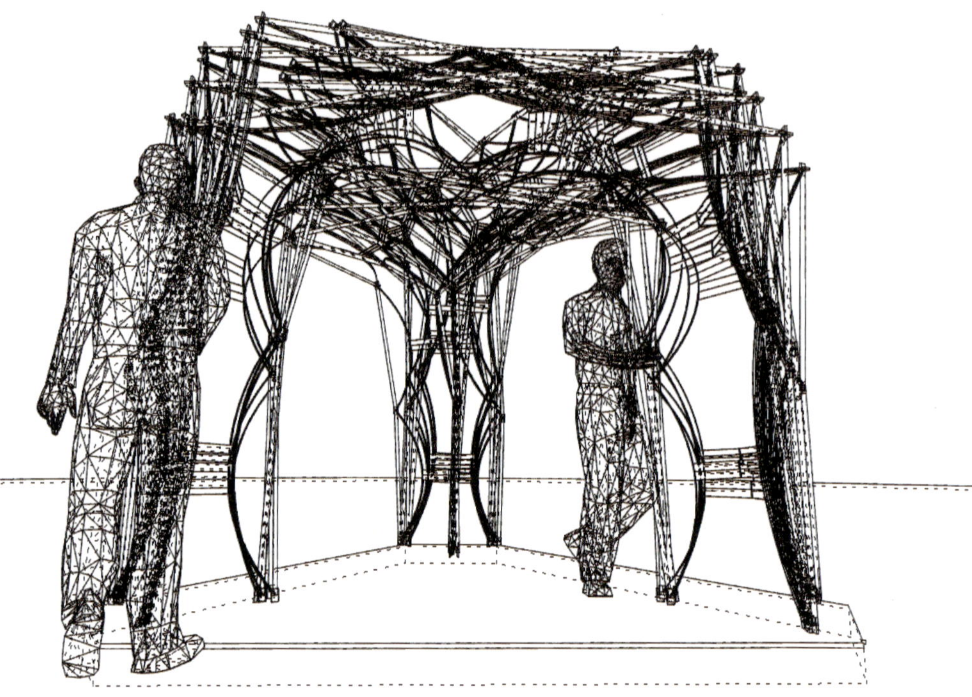

A scene showing the architectural robot amongst visitors

Conclusion

The development of autonomous architecture will be a long process and likely will have little directly in common with the installation experiment developed here. What the experimental structure offers is a changed expectation for architecture as a sensate and acting entity rather than a passive material form. Architecture has many ways through its spatial and compositional vocabulary to project intent without a technologically enabled autonomy; but as the rise of AI enabled handheld and home-based devices show, there is a large segment of design dealing with the continued exchange between human and artificial intelligences, and architecture has space to offer as an interface underrepresented in all other technologically enabled objects. In its physicality and scale, architecture's embodied computation is its greatest potential. Architectural expression ranges much wider than current interface paradigms of voice and image, and this is a continued design challenge. The experimental structure developed here as part of a search for communication bridges this challenge at the pace and scale of architecture with its occupants and ways to embed the seeds of design intent into those developing exchanges over the lifetime of the building. Giving sensing physical context and form and sensing through architectural constructs is at the core of the proposed embodied computation concept of autonomous architectural robotics.

The project was developed in the Embodied Computation Lab at the Princeton University School of Architecture as part of the Embodied Computation Group initiated by the author. The Embodied Computation Lab is itself an experimental architectural structure for experimenting on architecture at full scale, and was proposed and co-developed by the author.

References

Bartlett Interactive Architecture Lab, http://www.interactivearchitecture.org/lab-projects, accessed 2017.

Bier, Henriette H. 2014. "Robotic Building(s)." *Next Generation Building* 1:83–92, 83; DOI: 10.7564/14-NGBJ8.

Davis, Donald L., and Jeffrey A. Carlson. 2003. "Fluidic Actuators." US Patent US6868773, B2.

Eng, K., M. Mintz, and P. F. M. J. Verschure. 2005. "Collective Human Behavior in Interactive Spaces." International Conference on Robotics and Automation.

Eng, Kyan, David Klein, Andreas Baebler, Ulysses Bernardet, Mark Blanchard, Marcio Costa, Tobi Delbrueck, J. Douglas Rodney, Klaus Hepp, Jonatas Manzolli, Matti Mintz, Fabian Roth, Ueli Rutishauser, Klaus Wassermann, Adrian M. Whatley, Aaron Wittmann, Reto Wyss, and Paul F. M. J. Verschure. 2003. "Design for a Brain Revisited: The Neuromorphic Design and Functionality of the Interactive Space 'Ada.'" *Reviews in the Neurosciences* 14:145-180.

Fox, M., and M. Kemp. 2010. *Interactive Architecture*. Princeton, NJ: Princeton Architectural Press.

Graziano, M. S. A. 2008. *The Intelligent Movement Machine*. Oxford: Oxford University Press.

Hardingham, Samantha. 2016. *Cedric Price, Works 1952–2003: A Forward-Minded Retrospective*. London: Architectural Association.

Hyperbody Group, TU Delft, http://www.hyperbody.nl/research/projects/robotic-architecture, accessed 2017.

Joo, Hanbyul, Tomas Simon, Xulong Li, Hao Liu, Lei Tan, Lin Gui, Sean Banerjee, Timothy Godisart, Bart Nabbe, Iain Matthew, Takeo Kanade, Shohei Nobuhara, and Yaser Sheikh. 2015. "Panoptic Studio: A Massively Multiview System for Social Interaction Capture." 2015 ICCV.

Kapadia, A., I. Walker, K. E. Green, J. Manganelli, H. Houayek, A. M. James, V. Kanuri, T. Mokhtar, I. Siles, and P. Yanik. 2010. "'Architectural Robotics': An Interdisciplinary Course Rethinking the Machines We Live In." 2010 IEEE International Conference on Robotics and Automation, Anchorage, AL.

Kohler, Mattias, Fabio Gramazio, and Jan Willmann. 2014. *The Robotic Touch: How Robots Change Architecture*. Zurich: Park Books.

Oh, Alice, Harold Fox, Max Van Kleek, Aaron Adler, Krzysztof Gajos, Louis-Philippe Morency, and Trevor Darrell. 2002. "Evaluating Look-to-Talk: A Gaze-Aware Interface in a Collaborative Environment." *Proceedings of the Conference on Human Factors in Computing System* (CHI), 650–651.

Penfield, Wilder, and Edwin Boldfrey. 1937. "Somatic Motor and Sensory Representation in the Cerebral Cortex of Man as Studied by Electrical Stimulation." *Brain* 60(4): 389–443. doi:10.1093/brain/60.4.389.

OK, Computer: Opening the Black Box of Machine Learning, Algorithms, and Bias

David Benjamin

In May of 1997, the world's best human chess player, Garry Kasparov, sat down to play the world's best computer, IBM's Deep Blue. Ten years before, Kasparov had boasted, "No computer can ever beat me." But the recent progress of computation seemed impressive and potentially game-changing. In the lead-up to the competition, the battle had been dubbed Ali-Frazier.

Near the end of the first game, in the forty-fourth move, Deep Blue a made highly unusual play, sacrificing a rook while ahead, which seemed to hint at a sophisticated strategy of preventing countermoves. Kasparov was rattled. He could not comprehend why the computer made the move, and he feared that it demonstrated a superior intelligence. The game ended in a draw, but at the beginning of the next game, Kasparov made an unprecedented error, and Deep Blue went on to win the epic battle. According to a report in *Wired Magazine*, "The chess world found it devastating. 'It was too much to bear,' said grandmaster Yasser Seirawan. The cover of *Inside Chess* magazine read 'ARMAGEDDON!'"[1]

In 2012, long after computers asserted their dominance in chess, one of the inventors of Deep Blue revealed that the fateful forty-fourth move had been due to a software bug. According to writer Nate Silver, "Unable to select a move, the program had defaulted to a last-resort fail-safe in which it picked a play completely at random. … Kasparov had concluded that the counterintuitive play must be a sign of superior intelligence. He had never considered that it was simply a bug."[2] In the end, the computer won not because of an innovative strategy, but because the human was prone to worry and

---

1. Rudy Chelminski, "This Time It's Personal," *Wired Magazine*, October 1, 2001.

2. Nate Silver, *The Signal and the Noise: Why So Many Predictions Fail—But Some Don't* (New York: Penguin, 2015), 288.

doubt and self-destruction. The human assumed that machine intelligence worked like human intelligence—and therefore the unusual move must have been a rational strategy. But the computer had a different intelligence altogether, one that was subject to bugs, but not subject to weariness or worry.

Neurologist Robert Burton elaborates on the distinction between humans and machines, arguing that in the near future, "The ultimate value added of human thought will lie in our ability to contemplate the non-quantifiable. … Machines cannot and will not be able to tell us the best immigration policies, whether or not to proceed with gene therapy, or whether or not gun control is in our best interest."[3] In other words, since machines cannot worry, and since worry and doubt are productive in creating humanistic, fair solutions to the problems of our time, humans will never be replaced by machines.

Perhaps the most instructive message of the chess battle was that humans and machines should not be paired for competition, but instead they should be matched for collaboration, where each species of intelligence can complement the other.

Machine learning

In April of 2016, almost twenty years after the fateful computer victory in chess, Google's DeepMind defeated a human champion at the game Go. This was big. Go was once considered a game for uniquely human intelligence. It was thought that Go was impossible for a machine to win due to the nearly infinite number of outcomes and the difficulty of calculating which player is leading at any given moment. But Google's computer used a new version of artificial intelligence called machine learning, which involves machines deriving conclusions without being explicitly programmed. This technology made it possible for a machine to approach Go in a new way.

Machine learning is now being applied behind the scenes for financial trading, advertising, language translation, malware detection, computer vision, and countless other applications. These applications and DeepMind's victory may signal what Maksim Podolyak, a vice president of the Russian Go Federation, refers to as the birth of a "new age—an age of computers able to resolve specifically humanistic problems."[4]

Does the computer victory in Go change the idea that machines and humans have distinct kinds of intelligence, and that one cannot be easily exchanged for the other? It may shift the balance. But perhaps this is not the most relevant issue. Perhaps the battles of chess and Go—and the advance of machine performance that they represent—suggest that it is important for humans to become more fluent in algorithms. It is important to understand what's going on under the hood—including the bugs that algorithms contain, the data they are based on, and the rules that lead to their conclusions. The chess victory indicates that machine intelligence has distinct characteristics. The Go victory indicates that machine intelligence is advancing rapidly and can learn in ways beyond pre-programming. Both victories indicate that it is important to know about the algorithms as we use them with increasing frequency. This is crucial not just to be able to use the algorithms effectively, but also be able to guide, temper, and respond to their use. In other words, this is a political issue as well as a technical issue.

3. Robert Burton, "How I Learned to Stop Worrying and Love A.I.," *New York Times*, September 21, 2015.

4. Dawn Chan, "In the Age of Google DeepMind, Do the Young Go Prodigies of Asia Have a Future?" *New Yorker*, March 11, 2016.

Assumptions and bias

The rise and influence of algorithms is a story notably told by Michael Lewis in his book *Moneyball*, published in 2003. The story documents the use of data and algorithms in baseball in ways that seem almost magical and that produce bottom-line results. Yet in Lewis's most recent book—*The Undoing Project*, published in 2016—he addresses the way algorithms and human thinking relate to one another. Lewis documents the influence of two Israeli psychologists whose research initiated the field of behavioral economics, and who essentially concluded that the human brain is subject to misperceptions and false assumptions. Lewis goes on to say that recognizing this deficiency in humans led to the rise of algorithms—the rise of objective machines correcting subjective humans, as well as machines coming up with insights that would not have occurred to humans. Lewis proposes, "If a fresh analytical approach had led to the discovery of new knowledge in baseball, was there any sphere of human activity in which it might not do the same?"[5] But this argument may be missing something: algorithms themselves contain assumptions and biases, and algorithms can easily misperceive and be subjective, just like humans.

As with all technologies, algorithms—especially machine learning algorithms—involve assumptions and biases. But the biases of machine learning may be even more troubling than other biases because they are hidden, sometimes even hidden from their own inventors. According to writer Andy Greenberg, "Engineers often refer to the artificial intelligences they create as 'black box' systems: Once a machine learning engine has been trained from a collection of example data to perform anything from facial recognition to malware detection, it can take in queries—Whose face is that? Is this app safe?—and spit out answers without anyone, not even its creators, fully understanding the mechanics of the decision-making inside that box."[6]

The importance of recognizing how these algorithms are affecting our lives has been articulated by Kevin Slavin in his famous TED Talk, "How Algorithms Shape Our World." Slavin observes that algorithms are now automating many aspects of our life, without our quite realizing it. Algorithms are even influencing the production of culture. A related concept has been articulated in recent writing, including Cathy O'Neil's *Weapons of Math Destruction* and Kate Crawford's "Artificial Intelligence's White Guy Problem." O'Neil and Crawford show how the biases of algorithms can lead to racial profiling in policing, sexism in job listings, and uneven distribution of resources in urban neighborhoods. And their arguments imply that understanding algorithms requires understanding the humans who create them, the humans who are displaced by them, and the humans who are affected by their conclusions.

One way of understanding these developments is that algorithms are increasingly operating in more qualitative, social, and cultural domains. They are quantifying aspects of life that previously seemed uncomputable. And they are making decisions that previously seemed to require human judgment.

But of course, even when algorithms are operating in the qualitative domain, their decisions still involve human judgment, since humans are selecting data, deploying algorithms,

5. Michael Lewis, *The Undoing Project: A Friendship that Changed Our Minds* (New York: W.W. Norton, 2016).

6. Andy Greenberg, "How to Steal an AI," *Wired Magazine*, September 30, 2016.

and accepting the conclusions of these systems. Computer algorithms are written by specific humans with specific names and opinions. This is obvious yet worth noting, because it reminds us that algorithms are not neutral or objective. They have a perspective. They play out assumptions. And they have biases.

This also applies to data and algorithms in architecture. Design-related algorithms are created by specific people with assumptions and biases that condition what they produce. And if these assumptions were different, the designs produced through them would be different. In architecture, digital workflows and applications—such as software for parametric modeling, Building Information Modeling (BIM), building simulation, and optimization—push us in certain design directions. They play a significant role in architectural design, defining the design space of any project that uses them. Software has an enormous influence on the topological surface that describes any design problem. While end user input affects the features of this topological surface, software defines the type of topological surface. A change in software would mean a change in type. Yet, architectural software and the algorithms behind it are usually authored by teams of computer scientists, and they are usually opaque to architects. The assumptions and consequences of the algorithms are often difficult for architects to ascertain. As computer scientist Eitan Grinspun observes: "I think architects have been hijacked! The tools they are working with are written by programmers whose training, by and large, comes from a very scientific, engineering-based mindset. These tools provide the language that architects have to use, and as architects start becoming more proficient with the tools, they start adapting to the engineers'

language."[7] In other words, to simply launch and start using architectural software is to operate like an engineer.

The stakes get higher when algorithms are operating not just on geometry but on data about profit, public space, program, environmental impact, and individual and collective preferences and values. As with policing and job listings, the high stakes and the hidden assumptions of algorithms make it urgent for citizens—including architects—to become "algorithm literate."

Faces and facades

At first glance, human faces seem to belong squarely in the domain of humans, not computers. Faces are part of the organizing logic of human understanding. Instinctually, people are incredibly good at recognizing and distinguishing between faces—and even easily matching someone's older face to their younger face. Computers have a different logic. Historically, faces have stumped computers. But machine learning may be changing this. New algorithms and techniques are bringing machines closer to human capabilities of detecting and recognizing faces, even if most people have no clue how they do it, or exactly how good they are. And these techniques also offer capabilities beyond those of any human—most immediately the ability to catalog and recognize not hundreds of faces but hundreds of millions.

This project for the Seoul Architecture Biennale will make visible the characteristics and hidden assumptions of machine learning algorithms. It will explore implications for the process of design with algorithms, and it will also speculate about the impact on the built environment, specifically through prototyping a new building envelope.

7. Eitan Grinspun, from transcript of Columbia Building Intelligence Project, New York Think Tank, February 18, 2011.

The building envelope is a key site for the city's commons. While buildings are owned by specific people and institutions, building envelopes belong to the street, to the city, and to its citizens. In this way, building envelopes are a form of public space.

For most of architectural history, building envelopes *represented* culture, politics, and aesthetics through symbols and materials. In the past twenty years, building envelopes have come to life through *displaying* dynamic lighting and movement (used as decoration or occasionally as real-time information about the city, such as environmental quality). Now, with machine learning, it may be possible for building envelopes to *learn* and evolve over time with their own intelligence. This project explores this new direction for building envelopes.

The goal of this project is to create an installation that reveals both the power and limitations of state-of-the-art machine learning technology in an intuitive way to visitors of the Biennale. The project will use machine learning to recognize human faces and re-draw them on a building envelope in a way that describes both the individual and the collective. More specifically, the system will capture an individual face, compare it to a dynamic computer model of thousands of other faces, learn what makes this particular face unique, and draw a sketch of the 200 most essential line segments for this person. In order to reveal what is happening under the hood, the project will use not one but two "autoencoder" machine learning models running on a computer at the exhibit. This will reveal some of the assumptions of each model and indicate that the results are not neutral or inevitable.

In the physical exhibit, both models are connected to a camera that is able to recognize the faces of people who approach. Each model is also connected to a monitor that shows the real-time video of visitors' faces processed through each model. This creates a kind of "double mirror" which shows how the two models interpret the faces of Biennale visitors in different ways, and reveals the hidden biases within them.

The autoencoder model

An autoencoder is a type of machine learning model that can learn how to encode any information into a lower-dimensional form through a trained neural network. The information in this case is an image of a face taken from the camera feed at the exhibit. The network is composed of two parts—an encoder and a decoder—which are mirror images of each other. Both the encoder and decoder are convolutional neural networks composed of some number of convolutional and fully connected layers. The decoder is composed of the same number and types of layers as the encoder, except sequenced in reverse order. In the middle, between these two networks, is a single fully connected layer of neurons which contains the encoded information. The number of neurons in this layer specifies the extent to which the data is compressed.

The encoder network takes in an input image and processes it into a series of values in the encoder layer. The decoder layer can then take this encoding and work backwards to generate an image. The goal of the full autoencoder network is to tune the weights of all the parameters in both networks such that the image output from the decoder matches the input image as closely as possible. Since the middle encoder layer has

less dimensionality than the original input data, it forms a bottleneck between the input and output data. Thus, the autoencoder is trying to learn a way to compress the data into the lower-dimensional form such that it can be reconstructed into the full dimensional representation (an image) with a minimum of information loss.

Model training

The parameters of both models are initialized with random values, so that initially the autoencoder just creates random noise. The models are then trained simultaneously by feeding images from a training set into the encoder network, and comparing them to the results coming out of the decoder network. During each training step, the parameters of both models are tuned slightly so that the reconstructed image is closer to the original. Thus, both models are learning at the same time—the encoder is learning how to compress the image into a lower-dimensional form, while the decoder is learning how to take this compressed data and recreate the original image as well as possible. This training process is called "self-supervised" learning. As with supervised learning, the model is trained based on example data, but unlike supervised learning the model is not learning the relationship between the input features of the data and a target label. Instead, the network simply learns how to recreate the input while passing it through a lower-dimensional form. Thus, instead of being supervised according to target labels, we can say that the network supervises itself.

Installation design

While the training process can teach the autoencoder good strategies for compressing images, this strategy will be highly influenced by the images that it sees during training. For example, an autoencoder trained only on images of cars may do a good job of compressing other car images, but will likely perform poorly on images of other things. This bias is not unique to autoencoders, and is in fact a major limitation of any machine learning model based on training. In the field of machine learning, this bias is referred to as "overfitting" to the training data.

Although such biases exist in every machine learning model, including those built into tools that we interact with on a daily basis, they are typically hidden from the user. The goal of our installation is to reveal these inherent biases to visitors of the Biennale by allowing them to interact directly with two separate models which are both trained on different sets of data. The first model is trained before the event based on a "canonical" dataset of faces—the Labeled Faces in the Wild (LFW) dataset—which is commonly used for developing state-of-the-art facial recognition software. The second model will be trained during the course of the event based only on faces of people at the event.

The LFW dataset contains 13,234 images of faces, taken from 5,749 people who are mostly well-known politicians, athletes, or celebrities. The data was compiled by researchers at the computer science department at the University of Massachusetts in Amherst and released with a public license in 2007. Since then, over fifty academic papers have used the dataset to develop and test a variety of facial detection and recognition systems. The dataset's popularity among computer vision researchers has been driven by its ease of access, large scale, and clear organization. However, since the data is based on well-known people, it contains inherent racial and gender biases which may influence the broad applicability of the methods it helped to develop. By training two separate models on two completely different datasets, we hope to expose the inherent biases of any machine learning model which is trained on a limited and finite set of data.

Installation experience

As a visitor approaches the installation, OpenCV software running on the computer will recognize their face, and will pass the video through the two models before displaying both versions on a prototype building facade as well as on two monitors. At the same time, images of the visitor's face are used to train the second model in real time.

To the visitor, this will look like a "double mirror" with their image represented two different ways. The first model, which is pre-trained, will always have the same processing, and will reveal the biases in a model trained on "academic data." The second model will initially have a very poor representation (since it starts untrained), but over time will become better as it learns from images it gathers during the event. Although this model should be more related to the faces of the people at the event, it will contain its own biases since it will also be trained on a limited set of data.

In addition to the two displays in the gallery, the

images will be represented outside on a digital building facade. This installation will display three images—the actual face of the installation visitor, along with the two "likenesses." This exterior version of the installation can create more public engagement around the installation, and expose its concepts to a wider audience. There are several precedents of showing faces on large public video installations, including the display of faces on existing video billboards in projects by JR (New York, 2013) and Sebastian Errazuriz (New York, 2015), and the display of faces on custom video displays by Jaume Plensa (Chicago, 2004) and Asif Khan (Sochi, 2014). But this project will involve the first use of a dynamic machine learning model along with a large public display.

By giving people a real-time representation of two machine learning models—and actually training one during the course of the event—our installation will give people a more tangible experience of the types of algorithms that they are interacting with every day. At the same time, by training the models on two different sets of data, the installation will also reveal the inherent biases within such models in a direct and visual way.

**The urban commons, the Other,
and ourselves**

Overall, the project will create custom technology to draw automated collective portraits of the city on a building envelope. The technology will involve algorithms that can take a huge amount of image data, learn how to detect key patterns about urban life in the data, and identify features that are at once personal and public. When combined, these processes will allow us to create a bottom-up, layered, dynamic drawing of the city that reveals a new intelligence—a new computational agent in the city that is exciting, anxiety-provoking, and beyond our direct control.

This project involves a combination of human and artificial intelligence to explore the boundary between the individual and the collective within the urban commons. The project extracts crowd-sourced data from the urban commons by encouraging the audience to actively participate. This social engagement adds an uncertain and uncontrollable factor that is fitting for the inherently uncontrollable urban context. In addition, the machine learning neural network that forms the basis of the project's intelligence is a somewhat uncontrollable black box—analogous to our own human consciousness—that makes intuitive decisions about how to artistically represent a given subject. Like a human artist, it develops a unique style from biases in its training and limitations in its perception. It takes on a life of its own. We cannot completely control it, but we can still try to understand it. We can get to know the features and assumptions of its workings—its algorithms. Perhaps we can engage it the way we engage another person, and in doing so develop a new sense of the urban commons, the other, and ourselves.

Sensing Syntax

**Mark Wasiuta and Farzin Lotfi-Jam
with Jean Im**

Happy cartoons, dancing diagrams, and vast scale models animated by blinking LEDs; we are shuttled from one public relations nexus to the next. In Songdo, Korea's most enthusiastically promoted smart city enterprise, learning what makes the city smart turns out to be an arduous undertaking. Cisco's engineers refuse to speak to us, implying that what we are looking for is a trade secret. A strange, almost impossible contradiction starts to form around the perpetual exclamation of the innovations of this city and the secrecy of where this innovation lies. We start to suspect that the innovation belongs less to Songdo, than it does to a standard, rehearsed set of descriptions and platitudes about integration, intelligence, and urban life enhanced by data. In the numerous dead-ends of this informational terrain vague we seem to be repeating the experiences of other smart city pilgrims, researchers, and adventurers, lost in the zero panorama of the Songdo smart city tour.

The evasion we encounter in Songdo is entirely contrary to the reception at COR—the Center of Operations Rio—the stout mirrored building that is the pulsing cybernetic heart of Rio de Janeiro's smart city network. There, we are met by COR's director and a team of engineers and operators, who guide us through COR's history, its mission, the structure of its algorithms, and their assessment of the successes, failures, and limits of Rio's smart city experiment. It is an elaborate demonstration of COR's decision protocols and the possibilities of a city viewed and organized through data extraction and sensors.

These contrasting experiences of welcome can be explained by distinct forms of civic government, by the discrepant responsibilities of the agencies

Overall view of activity in the Mission Operations Control Room in the Mission Control Center during the Apollo 14 transposition and docking maneuvers, 1971.

"

in Songdo and Korea, and by different strategies for smart city implementation and integration. Yet, almost by chance, these two encounters illuminate ideas prevalent in smart city discourse. As the industry penetrates cities across Asia, Europe, and the Americas, it continues to predict massive growth and billions of dollars of smart city revenue. Grasped through this commercial logic, smart cities are proprietary technologies akin to industrial design artifacts—as Cisco insinuated—with complex supply chains, and whose technical composition and innovation paths are secrets to be protected from industrial espionage. The city appears much like a sales object, a total urban commodity, marketed through the jingoism of urban security and the jargon of urban sustainability.

The inverse of this economic logic is governmental innovation. Along with sensors and feedback channels, smart city algorithms are championed as components of an open source urban code that promises almost inconceivable citizen access to municipal data. In this argument, not only is the city enhanced, but so are the inhabitants. Smart cities engender better, more politically active and engaged citizens. The smart city is the aggregate of technologies that foster smart citizens.

This distinction seems noteworthy, as though these arguments—as well as Songdo and Rio—help us identify starkly different poles on a spectrum that spans civic benefit, global sales, and smart city hucksterism. Yet, despite the varied reception we have received, this helpful, diagrammatic opposition does not survive much scrutiny. Global commerce and municipal government, along with repression and agency, surveillance and security, efficiency and invasiveness, are neither positions nor ideas that remain stable or distinct in Songdo or Rio. They orbit around each other, leaving a comet trail of smart city concepts and clichés of interaction, responsiveness, and the social benefits of urban data.

Center of Operations Rio, Rio de Janeiro, June 2012

Whatever conceptual, operational distance these arguments, positions, and Songdo's and Rio's smart city installations retain, it collapses further at the moment we encounter their control rooms. For both Rio and Songdo the control room is the active demonstration of urban sensing, information extraction, feedback, and management. Titanic walls of data screens and camera feeds form a sublime image of urban omniscience, a proscenium of management in which the subdued theatricality of quotidian city routine is as much a rhetorical effect as it is the product of real operational drama.

The theatricality relies on the tracking, staging, presentation, and visualization of an event that can interrupt the banal data tableau of daily urban life. At COR, maps of the city are activated by the sudden appearance of street lines colored green, red, or yellow. Each color indicates a degree of traffic interruption and the level of algorithmically determined response. The strobing of these colored vectors is the visual corollary to a script of urban drama registered through traffic congestion and coordination.

In Songdo, the drama is more anticipatory. A network of cameras, vigilantly focused on apartment and office towers to catch the first sign of building fire, recompose the city into a grid of video feeds. Fixated on Songdo's architecture, the monitors seem to stretch the eight-hour duration of Warhol's *Empire* to infinity. The Songdo serial aesthetic is relentless. Other cameras catch and record the license plate of each car entering the city and track its movement through streets, intersections, and ubiquitous underground car parks. Another expanse of monitors shows the array of license plates as they are tabulated into Songdo's traffic-oriented database. In Songdo, the narrative arc of the control room is keyed to vibration

New Songdo City. View from Central Park to G-Tower, June 2017

sensors and vibration events. Sensors embedded in streets, fences, and building facades record patterns of movement and stasis, predict use cycles, and warn of transgression and invasion.

The drama performed in, and by, smart city control rooms is gripping, in part, because of its familiarity. The image of massive control screens and banks of glowing monitors has become a standard trope of cinema and an emblem of cold war computational technocracy. From NASA Apollo mission command centers to the war room in Kubrik's Dr. Strangelove, the control room has erupted as a dream image of twentieth century rationality. The smart city control room is the product of the world seen through space programs, defense systems, and the image of mega-death calculation meeting the everyday life of the city.

In alignment with their image inheritance, smart city control rooms exhibit and conflate at least two primary characteristics. The first is the rational administration of the city. Faced with intensifying density, complexity, and the striation of populations through wealth disparities and access to services, the control room promises a corrective process of municipal management. The second is through their association with urban emergency response centers, from which smart cities cathect an urban imaginary of failures, crises, and vulnerabilities. A sense of threat attaches itself to the smart city at its origins. Looming political instability, environmental catastrophe, financial precarity, infrastructural entropy, and other signs of urban apocalypse fuel the desire for smart city experimentation.

The theatricality of the control rooms extends to the scene of public presentation. On the 3rd floor of Songdo's G Tower we are led to a viewing room to watch a film that narrates the story of Songdo's sensor infrastructure and the

View of operator's desk at the Songdo Third Zone Automated Waste Collection Plant, June 2017

city's "Smart Environment," "Smart Home," "Smart Building," "Smart Health," and "Smart Learning" accomplishments. As the film reaches its climax, the "switchable smart glass projection screen" fades from hazy to transparent, revealing—like an apparition coming into view—the smart city operations center below. In keeping with the persistent secrecy of the Songdo operation, photography is prohibited and the length of our observation is tightly curtailed. We glimpse the control room in a flash, as a profane illumination of computational rationality.

In Rio, the performance strategy differs considerably. From an open balcony COR'S control room can be observed by Rio's citizens or any visitor, and can be viewed online through a camera serving as a permanent witness to COR's data collection and presentation. The implication is that COR's control mechanisms are components of the democratic city and, like the data, graphs, and charts they generate, belong to the citizens of Rio.

Whatever their differences, these approaches to visual access are attempts to ward off the common accusation that smart cities are merely population surveillance networks disguised as civic amenity. Moreover, through the forms of access they allow, they are strategies that draw their population into the logic of urban command and control.

In Songdo, smart city interpolation begins at home, where domestic sensors, automated waste retrieval, and interactive television education merge with the traffic cameras and vibration sensors on the streets of the city. Songdo's smart citizen identity is one in which a sense of domestic security permeates the city and ubiquitous street monitoring is as familiar as an apartment smoke detector. In Rio, the control room also doubles as a public relations space in which the city can show evidence of managerial competence. This is no small feat for Rio—its wild topography and aging infrastructure make it an improbable host to the smooth rationality of urban management that smart city rhetoric proclaims.

As they translate sensing operations and information extraction into a scene of representation and consumption, the control rooms demonstrate a new mode of urban vision while they alter the image of the city. In Songdo, and other smart cities, the conventions of urban formal organization—with their hierarchies of visual, spatial, perceptual, symbolic order—shift toward a new urban vocabulary comprising motion sensors, traffic cameras, and operational data maps. Written into smart city control algorithms, these newly significant urban elements produce an undifferentiated, non-hierarchical array of urban objects and actors.

The reformation of urban vision, the decision trees and algorithms that coordinate smart city operations, and the distribution, location, and saturation of the city with sensors and cameras together provide the physical, spatial, informational, and political armature of what we are calling smart city "control syntax."

The habituation to this syntax, the collating of city populations into the scenes and technologies

Songdo sensor and communications post, June 2017

of control, and the merging of citizen identity with smart city ideals of efficiency and security are the basis for an ever more pervasive, 21st-century version of a condition we identify as "computational governmentality."

Such computational governmentality—with origins in post-war command and control networks, in early experiments that integrated computers and urban planning, and in notions of the city as messaging system—involves citizens as sensors and treats them as informational units. Through expanding computational governmentality, the rationality of smart enhancement of the city and fantasies of the frictionless management of the city encounter the more complexly coded political, social, and topographic facts of the city. It is an informational feedback system of governance that interpolates viewers into its spectacular, optical logic, its techniques of urban regulation, and its scripted data scenography. The city as data-driven political configuration—configuring cities, streets, sensors, and data—is also the city as theater of control, a theater narrated and dramatized by control syntax.

B. Control Syntax Rio

Control Syntax Rio models a traffic route through Rio de Janeiro from Copacabana Beach to Maracana Stadium—beach volleyball and soccer competition sites for the 2016 summer Olympic games. Built in 2010, in reaction to a calamitous landslide, COR was planned to anticipate and respond to future disasters and infrastructure failures. Equally important, it was intended to assuage the International Olympic Committee by demonstrating Rio's commitment to improved urban administration and traffic management. To the IOC and Rio's citizens both, COR was heralded as an urban feedback system and control center that would combine disaster response, urban sensor monitoring, and a form of intelligent traffic administration that would unsnarl streets and speed circulation during the crush of the Summer Olympics and after. Along with the code for its decision matrix, the technical and conceptual armature for COR originated in IBM's "Smarter Cities" initiative. Supporting police and defense operations, a second command and control center in Rio conducts urban surveillance, face recognition sweeps, and crowd pattern evaluation. Segregating overt security and tracking tasks from COR's operations left IBM and COR with a relatively narrow mandate. COR amasses data on traffic flows, urban health, and weather patterns and responds to interruptions by changing traffic routes and by directing emergency teams to these sites of interruption. In short, COR's primary tasks are to monitor, assess, and represent the metabolism of the city and to respond to actual or potential interruptions that drain, slow, or block it.

COR determines if Rio's metabolism is normal or abnormal. Through the logic of the IBM code around which it is built, COR measures abnormality according to four escalating scales of intensity: incident, event, emergency, crisis. How this scale is registered and represented, and how it determines response, form the foundation of Rio's control syntax.

At first glance, COR's control syntax appears banal and managerial. Yet, it is also charged with potential crisis. For example, if protest erupts, an increasingly common event in Rio, then traffic will have to be redirected to avoid paralysis. If buildings explode, also not entirely uncommon in Rio, then routes will need to be cleared to usher response teams as quickly as possible. Explosions, fires, protests, landslides, rallies, and sudden tropical storms, combine with faulty

Control Syntax Rio, Storefront for Art and Architecture, March 2017

traffic lights, accidents, spilled trucks, burning buses, and quotidian congestion as elements of the COR control syntax.

COR and smart cities form an image of the city and initiate a new system of representation. This system encompasses how the city is seen through cameras, how it is registered through sensors and data, and how it represents what is happening in the city, as well as how the conditions of control, optimization, and algorithmic decision paths become the rationality of the city. The image appears in the coordinated impression of a city through this rationality. Through COR, and in its coding, we glimpse the current image of computational governmentality, not only blithely directed toward engineered efficiency, but also flooded by narratives of possible threat, risks, and disruption.

Overlaid on the traffic route from the beach to the stadium, *Control Syntax Rio*, also traces a decision path through COR's decision matrix. The model aligns the material traffic infrastructure of the city with the immaterial syntax of COR's urban management code. It allows us to see the physical city—its traffic apparatus of streets, lights, and sensors—organized through Rio's control syntax.

In the COR syntax, radically disparate modes of action or interruption are flattened and made equivalent. Protests and traffic jams occupy the same plane of meaning. This implies both the banalization of politics, through COR's algorithm, and the simultaneous elevation of traffic control to politics. *Control Syntax Rio* sees traffic engineering as urban politics haunted by potential catastrophe.

The conjoined flattening and elevating of events, urban politics, and traffic, is the myth of the smart city—its unresolved and unresolvable contradiction. The myth is the rational

management of the city in the face of what can't be managed: sources of conflict, urban inequities, and the division of cities into zones of affluence and zones of impoverishment. It transposes structural, social, and economical precarity onto the surface of geological, climatological, and technological fact. The theater of Rio's control room is the accomplice to this myth. It distracts from failing infrastructure, lack of political reform, and from all else the algorithm can't resolve, repair, or remedy.

C. Control Syntax Songdo

Control Syntax Songdo has two main components: a physical model and a sequence of 360º videos shot at principle Songdo intersections. The videos mark key sensor locations and illustrate the attentive, nervous ubiquity of Songdo's vision technologies. The model compresses Songdo into a single intersection, congested with compound traffic accidents, registering and cataloguing this sequence of accidents alongside the anxieties that lurk within the imaginary of smart city algorithmic control and regulation. In Songdo, there is a plan to geotag children to better monitor their movement and for fear they will be hit by traffic. Incoming cars are monitored to track drivers, check records, and to alert the city of possible criminal intrusion. Within a narrative of smart city civic life gone awry, each accident is the consequence of a particular system failure. Yet, the model is less a scene of spectacular catastrophe than an image of the predictive logic that forms the rationality of the smart city, of the computational governmentality through which Songdo both absorbs and limits urban life, and of the real and fabricated fears percolating through Songdo and similar smart city installations.

The sensors that saturate Songdo are both technical and expressive. In their technical mode, they monitor environmental conditions and

Stills from 360° video of Songdo intersection showing sensor and the environment it is monitoring, June 2017

traffic patterns, track vehicles, and record street and building vibrations to signal disruptions, anomalous events, and potential dangers. As expressive objects the sensors signal to Songdo's residents that the city is ecologically optimized as well as safe, controlled, and vigilant. The streetscape of sensors, the elision of traffic control and citizen identity, and the compaction of environmental, social, and urban threat are the informational and spatial matrix of Songdo's Control Syntax.

These threats and the fears they raise are not merely the product of solicitous municipal authorities; they are the constitutive feature of Songdo's smart urbanism. For the Songdo model to be sold as a successful urban product, it must first be recognizable as a city. Songdo's master plan—that places towers adjacent to its "central park," allocates space to global universities and charter schools, and inserts museums and cultural centers into the city grid—is designed to attract residents by generating a convincing image of city life. This is a spreadsheet urbanism, for which elements, buildings, programs, and amenities are determined by a serial logic of differentiation and are calculated to deliver an impression of programmatic and morphological diversity. Yet, the fully regulated city is also intrinsically fearful of the diversity, disorder, and social tensions that are among the most visible signs of urbanity.

The paradox of urban fear exaggerated and then dramatically controlled is as familiar to contemporary global rhetoric of national security as it is to Songdo's smart city syntax. In this sense, Songdo, like other smart city sales operations, is a byproduct of disinvestment in conventional public welfare programs and the inverse investment in border security, immigration, and other global population circulation controls and restrictions. Marketed as a "global city," Songdo's primary

global claim is its attenuation of an international logic of internalization and exclusion.

The global also appears in Songdo through implicit association with global climate change. The virtues of environmental climate monitoring, of which the urban network of air monitors are the pervasive reminders, help normalize and idealize a fully monitored city. Inside, automated waste extraction reinforces the link between environmental protection and domestic monitoring. Connecting apartment buildings to collection plants, a network of pneumatic tubes suck apartment waste beneath the streets to processing. Garbage is collected, compacted, and exported from the city in hyper-compressed containers. Residents are provided coded waste bags, deposited through the "smart" garbage portal on each floor of each building. Monitoring the disposal of domestic waste correlates to monitoring domestic energy consumption, and to the perpetual monitoring of particulates and contaminants in city air. The constant threat of climate catastrophe hovers over Songdo's monitoring regimes, lending them a sense of urgent necessity.

If environmental monitoring and domestic monitoring merge through waste disposal, Songdo's streets are the site of the most complete condensation. The habituation to monitoring on the inside extends notions of domestic security out onto the streets. In Songdo's control room—and in its imagination—the street persists as the image of both threat and control, the image of smart city efficiency and optimization, as well as the image of social fears and transgressions. As in Rio de Janeiro, traffic engineering in Songdo is politics. Here, it is also biopolitics: a metonomy of sensing operations connect city, street, camera, license plate, and particulate sensor to environmental threat and to new forms of monitored life.

Chronosphere: Experiments for the (IPv6) Sensor City

**Future Cities Lab
(Nataly Gattegno and
Jason Kelly Johnson)**

The emerging IPv6 (Internet Protocol Version 6)[1] protocol will allow for a staggering amount of the physical world to be dynamically addressed, located, and computed using the internet. This emerging communications protocol establishes a staggering 3,911,873,538,269,506,102 IP addresses per square meter of the surface of the earth.[2] Glance at a square meter of space immediately in front of you and imagine that every object in sight is potentially addressable, networkable, and sentient. Each object might also contain billions upon billions of addressable sub-objects, all too small to be seen with a naked eye. Coupled with the advent of massively distributed computing, imaging, and data-collection technologies, it is foreseeable that these computational sensing networks will rapidly expand and become defining features of our physical environment. The bits and atoms that define ecologies and cities (plants, animals, people, objects, buildings, pipes, wires, transportation networks, rivers, weather systems, and more) will increasingly have computational and generative potential for architects, designers, engineers, and others.

Chronosphere (/ˈkränəˌskōp/) noun - An immersive instrument for the precise measurement of small time intervals (as by means of a falling sphere, rod, released pendulum, or an electronic device); or for measuring a person's reaction time.

Future Cities Lab invented the Chronosphere Seoul Biennale installation as an instrument to explore these emerging conditions. The multimedia sensor-laden installation is composed of a

1. Portions of this essay were previously published and/or adapted in part from "Sensing the (IPv6) City" by Jason Kelly Johnson, published in the ACSA 101 "New Constellations/New Ecologies" proceedings, chapter entitled "Exchange Terminals + Interactive Technologies," edited by Ed Mitchell and Ila Berman, 2013.

2. Quoting figures from the IPv6 Knowledge Base website: *http://www.ipv6.sltnet.lk/know2-whatis.html*

digital projection system and suspended illuminated LED nodes. It serves as an immersive theater—a portal to interact with dynamic points, lines, variable forces, and gradients moving between different mediums of light and sound. These portals blend the digital realm with the physical one, creating a back and forth between a computational system and a public space or gallery where it is installed.

In this case, Chronosphere is driven by sensor data from Seoul's open data system (http://data.seoul.go.kr), offering an immersive glimpse into the dynamic and evolving sensor space of Seoul's Han River network delta. Future Cities Lab is interested in exploring Seoul's potential as one of the most networked and sensor-driven cities in the world. It is in many ways the pre-IPv6 sensor city par excellence. How can we begin to design, curate, choreograph, engineer with Seoul's sensor data so that it becomes productive, generative, creative, and inspirational?

It has been forecasted that every word you have ever spoken; every object you have ever looked at, touched, or smelled; and everything you have ever thought could someday be retrieved by supercomputers capable of processing, comparing, and visualizing massive repositories of so-called IPv6 enabled "big data."[3] Combine this with the exponentially increasing power and miniaturization of computers, the radical scale and scope of the so-called IPv6 "internet of things" will fundamentally alter how we interact with the world.[4] While it remains to be seen whether or not these protocols will be utilized for even a fraction of their potential, it is clear that IPv6 will have an increasingly profound impact on the future. It will challenge and inspire any field concerned with theorizing, visualizing, or constructing the physical environment, including devices, buildings, and cities.

Since the 1960s an avant-garde group of urban theorists, activists, architects, and artists has been exploring the political, social, ecological, and aesthetic dimensions of these emerging protocols. The pioneering work of theorists like Marshall McLuhan, collectives such as Archigram and Superstudio, and designers like Constant Nieuwenhuys foresaw cities defined by these artificially intelligent information networks. A half century before IPv6 was even conceived, Marshall McLuhan (who famously coined the phrases "global village" and data "surfing") theorized that, "The medium, or process, of our time—electric technology is reshaping and restructuring patterns of social interdependence and every aspect of our personal life. It is forcing us to reconsider and reevaluate practically every thought, every action, and every institution formerly taken for granted."[5] McLuhan, who critically explored the effects of media on our senses, was interested in how the human sensorium was fundamentally conditioned and extended by emerging technologies: "All media are extensions of some human faculty … the wheel is an extension of the foot; the book is an extension of the eye; clothing, an extension of the skin; electric circuitry, an extension of the

3. For more detail on this subject, see Ray Kurzweil, *The Singularity Is Near* (New York: Penguin Books, 2006).

4. For more detail on this subject, see William J. Mitchell, *M++: The Cyborg Self and the Networked City* (Cambridge, MA: MIT Press, 2003).

5. Marshall McLuhan, *The Medium Is the Massage: An Inventory of Effects* (Corte Madeira, CA: Gingko Press, 1967).

6. Ibid.

central nervous system."[6] Today, the most visible manifestation of these extended protocols is the rapid emergence of sensor-packed smartphones and wireless devices enabling real-time geo-location, social networking, banking, navigating, voting, and more. In many ways the continuous and networked cities theorized in the 1960s are now manifest in the way that many government agencies now essentially resemble computing platforms, entire libraries are accessible virtually anywhere anytime via handheld devices, and the great trading floors of the New York Stock Exchange[7] have evolved into virtual interfaces guided by mathematical algorithms housed in remote data farms. With the emergence of IPv6, these manifestations will only be intensified.

We also now see massive corporations (IBM's Smarter Planet Initiative) and entire nations (China's State Grid Corporation) investing billions in IPv6 infrastructure and cloud-based "big data" technologies.[8] In an essay published in 2012, IBM described exactly how ambitious their investment is and just how pervasive their technology has supposedly become: "Today we are capturing more data more quickly than ever before: about buildings, roads, cities; about people, our habits, passions, needs; about transactions, workflows, markets; right down to the temperatures, location, and condition of a single item in the global supply chain. … Nothing challenges an unexamined way of doing things like a daily rush of data and analytic insight."[9] IBM, like Google, Amazon, the US Government (with its recent "Big Data" initiative), and others, are betting that data will eventually replace many human transactions, including everyday observations, decision making, and even scientific method.

The technology writer Chris Anderson explores this notion in his controversial article, "The End of Theory: The Data Deluge Makes Scientific Method Obsolete." He wrote: "This is a world where massive amounts of data and applied mathematics replace every other tool that might be brought to bear. Out with every theory of human behavior, from linguistics to sociology. Forget taxonomy, ontology, and psychology. Who knows why people do what they do? The point is they do it, and we can track and measure it with unprecedented fidelity. With enough data, the numbers speak for themselves."[10] As Anderson implies, every field will be destabilized by these emerging protocols. Similarly, in a 2010 paper entitled, "Sensors and Sensibilities," the University of Pennsylvania Wharton School professor and technology analyst Kevin Werbach wrote that this focus on data and analytic insight will fundamentally "challenge hidden assumptions in a bewildering array of doctrinal fields."[11]

7. Based on the research by Kazys Varnelis, "Space Finance and New Technologies" in *Sentient City*, ed. by Mark Shepard (Cambridge, MA: MIT Press, 2011), 200.

8. For more detail on this subject see "Sensors and Sensibilities: A Smarter World Faces Many Hurdles". *Economist Magazine* Special Report on "Smart Systems," 4 November 2010, http://www.economist.com/node/17388338

9. IBM, "The More We Know The More We Want to Change Everything," (2012), www.ibm.com/smarterplanet/

10. Chris Anderson, "The End of Theory: Big Data Makes Scientific Method Obsolete." *Wired* 16.07, http://www.wired.com/science/discoveries/magazine/16-07/pb_theory

11. Kevin Werbach "Sensors and Sensibilities: A Smarter World Faces Many Hurdles." *Economist Magazine* Special Report on "Smart Systems," 4 November 2010, http://www.economist.com/node/17388338

Architecture, built upon thousands of years of aesthetic doctrine and technical knowledge, is one of the fields that will increasingly face these challenges. Increasingly we will have to address the shifting role humans will play in the design, construction, and maintenance of these devices, buildings, and cities. How much agency will humans be willing to relinquish?

Past installations by Future Cities Lab have sought to explore the issue of design agency through physical installations situated in urban environments. The facade installation Lightswarm[12] sensed sound and vibration data from the city through window-mounted sensors that used a 3D live simulation model to drive a 15m tall swarm of light. Design agency was in many ways a co-production between fixed elements (the suspended LED modules), the computational systems and sensors, and the sounds of the city itself. Another installation, Datagrove, used text-to-speech synthesizers to whisper trending social-media hashtags to visitors who entered the installation shaped by its lattice of steel and acrylic. Most recently, the Chronoscope installation created an immersive cloud of projected dynamic data. The installation allowed gallery visitors to occupy, interact with, and manipulate a suspended cloud of continuously flowing data.

The Chronosphere installation exhibited at the Seoul Biennale was developed to further explore these questions. It is a raw "work-in-progress" spatial prototype that can be reconfigured to explore different datasets or locations. A 5x5x5 km cubic space of Seoul's Han River network delta creates a foundational underlay for the installation. Mounted to the installation's structural scaffolding are networked projectors which are mapped to project onto the floor, creating the illusion of being immersed in floating swarms of dynamic data flows. A series of 3D scanning sensors (in this case we integrated an X-Box Kinect) are mounted to the scaffolding to allow the entire system to react to the movement and gestures of visitors. As visitors inhabit the space of the gallery, their interactions influence the magnitude and direction of these three-dimensional forces. These motions leave dynamic contrails, each with their own unique velocity, trajectory, and duration. These contrails stream from a high-resolution floor projection, up to a series of physical illuminated LED tapestries that surround visitors in vibrant light and sound. The installation harvests databases from Seoul's open data system (http://data.seoul.go.kr). The installation cycles through data related to air quality, sound quality, temperature, transportation flows, and other openly accessible datasets.

Chronosphere is a prototype for a larger spatial construction consisting of sixteen networked stacked modules. These modules will form an immersive and synthetic "theater-in-the-round" for experimenting with the interplay of the physical and digital worlds. This deployable construction, a cross between a lunar landing module and an underwater observation gallery, will serve as a hub for exploring the complexity of a range of dynamical systems and data visualizations from evolving structures of the internet and social media, to simulations of swarming urban flows, to live footage of biological or weather systems. As we proceed deeper into the research, we hypothesize that these temporary constructions will shift from being classified as mere experimental prototypes

12. For more information about previous work referenced here, please visit www.future-cities-lab.net/datagrove.

or instruments, to being a new kind of architecture with its own classifiable attributes, distinct design methodologies, pedagogies and disciplinary classifications.

As our contemporary design tools such as GIS, CAD, and parametric models increasingly become informed by both IPv6 protocols and big data, what role will human subjectivity play in design? How do we ensure that the less linear and unpredictable aspects of design practice are not lost in a world defined by artificially intelligent networks and machines? Theorist Sanford Kwinter forecasts that "a type of world emerges whose material, technical, and architectural manifestations—no longer simply objects, structures or "buildings" but indeed electro-material environments at all scales—manifest themselves in a soft, perhaps insidiously holographic, manner, a world where everything flows together in real time."[13] How can we render these real-time invisible flows and processes of the city visible, meaningful, and perhaps tangible? How can we encourage citizens to participate in the making, marking and activation of urban space with emerging technologies, social media, big data, and more? When the IPv6 sensor enabled city truly becomes *sentient* and is woven with artificial intelligence, how will architecture become an active participant?

13. Quoting Sanford Kwinter, "Soft Systems," in *Culture Lab*, ed. Brian Boigon (Princeton, NJ: Princeton Architecture Press, 1993) p.227

SMELL = INFORMATION

What Could Happen When Invisible Information—from Smell Molecules—Is the Starting Point for Acting and Reacting

Sissel Tolaas

We can potentially read the physical world with all of our senses. Unfortunately, today we are surrounded by clinical and desensitized environments filled with unresponsive objects and finished with protective coatings to create a barrier between us and our environment, the things we live with. This makes us passive and vulnerable so that we are quite literally becoming disembodied.

The nose is the most advanced human interface. When you smell something, signals from the odor receptors in your nose reach your amygdala first, producing an immediate, visceral reaction. No other sense is directly wired to this emotion-processing part of the brain. When using all of the other senses, you think before you respond, but with smell your brain responds before you think. Smell is our chemical alert system.

Smells are used constantly, consciously or subconsciously, to communicate among plants, animals, and human beings.

Smells are a *very* crucial component in the definition of, understanding of, and orientation to an environment. Smells surround us all the time. Every day we breathe 23,000 times and move 12.5 cubic meters of air. With every breath we take, smell molecules flood through our bodies. Because they permeate the immediate environment and penetrate the body, our response to them is likely to be very strong. Even when we sleep, we smell.

The sanitation imperatives in contemporary culture seek the removal of all environmental smells, contributing to a desertification of our experience.

Because not all environmental smells can be pleasant, the consequence could be that we will have none at all! This has to change.

The most important and crucial question about the smells that surround us is what constitutes an acceptable smell environment? Who makes those rules? What justifies the existing rules and their definitions of bad and good? Is it not time to redefine these rules and relearn our approach to them?

Smells are important because they are instrumental in generating what is considered to be appropriate activity. While smell settings may be taken for granted in an unreflective manner, they are nonetheless cues to particular modes of involvement within that setting.

In cities, the places, neighborhoods, and people are characterized individually by smells. This needs to be recognized as the immensely valuable quality that it is. Social and cultural preconceptions to a large degree predetermine people's range of movement, level of engagement, and experience in cityscapes. Sensory interaction allows humans to experience their own self-image and presence in the city, unlocking the potential for creativity and empathy.

Historical, sociological, and religious reasons have pulled the contemporary human being into almost ignoring the sense of smell. *Only* education can revive these hidden capacities, since the hardware and software still function in the healthy human body, but only if they are consciously trained and used. There is a whole world to educate and a whole world to smell!

There is a playful aspect about discovering the world through smells.

Challenging people to use their noses gives them new methods to approach their realities, different from those methods they learn from watching their smartphones and TV. I think we need more optimism and positive attitudes to be able to understand the seriousness of what we face: new challenges, new methods, new methodologies, new tools. The *nose* is the key here.

CITY SMELLSCAPES 1998–2017

I have completed fifty-two City SmellScapes in cities including Mexico City, Nuuk, London, Kuwait, Berlin, Singapore, Cape Town, and Istanbul. I performed them for various reasons and for various clients. The process I use while working applies to them all.

The following pages will demonstrate:

— **Fieldwork phase 1: analogue smell site and source identification**
— **Fieldwork phase 2: digital smell site and source sampling**
— **Smell site and source sampling analysis**
— **Future database**
— **Smell replication: chemical reproduction**
— **Smell execution and implementation**
— **Smell education**

Smells are (chemical) signals arising out of our surroundings, from the animate and inanimate things around us. It is part of their escaping substance, the volatiles, that are the smell molecules that I identify, collect, and replicate.

Fieldwork Phase 1: Analogue Smell Site and Source Identification

Walking and smelling, using my own nose. Visiting the smell site and its sources at different times of the day and year, if necessary. This is required to reassure myself that the smells at the site are permanent.

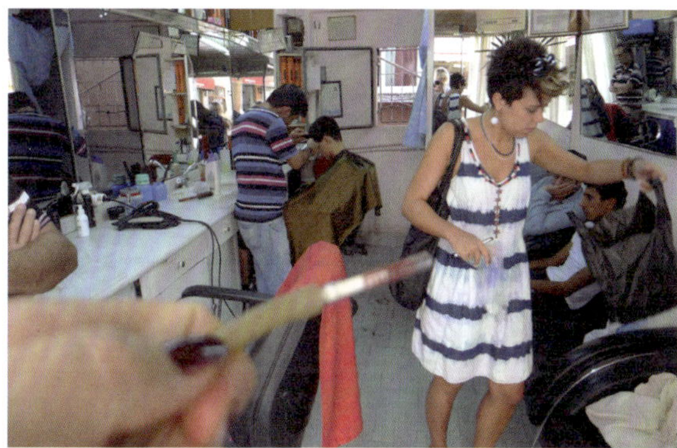

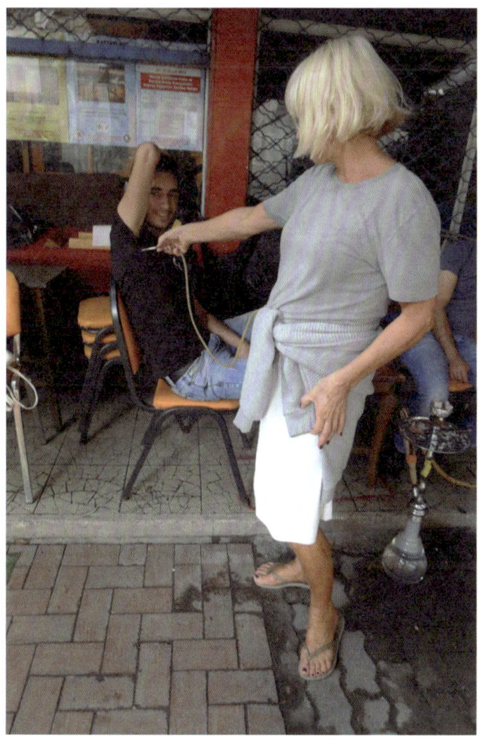

Fieldwork Phase 2: Digital Smell Site and Source Sampling

Visiting the same smell sources and sites that
I visited during the analogue phase, but now
collecting the smell molecules emitting from
them. The collecting time needed for each smell
is dependent on the strength of the source and
the scale of the site.

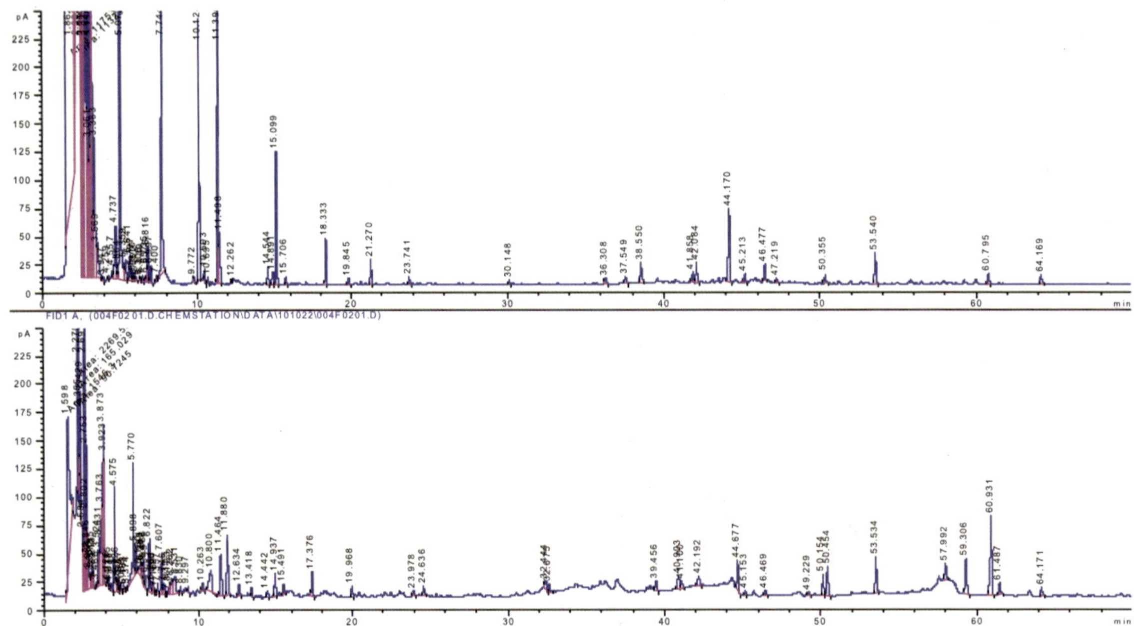

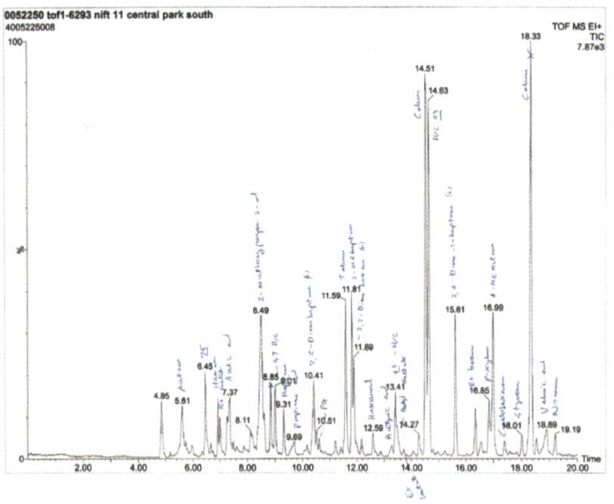

Smell Site and Source Digital Sampling Analysis, Future Database

The analysis is performed in close cooperation with IFF, the company that has been supporting my work since 2004. I work actively with the chemists in their lab in the United States. The results are sent to me in the form of data, which is added to the existing database.

Sample Information				
Request Number	**Run Number**	**Date Modified**	**Mass Spec Run**	**I&A Number**
RD88944	7	30-Nov-2015	4005225008	
Sample Name				
CENTRAL PARK (SISSEL TOLAAS)				
Notes				
Central Park South				

Peak Number	I. E.	Retention Time	Component Name	pp1000	CAS Number	CID Number
1	0.76	5.61	acetone	12.65	67-64-1	4779
2	1.44	6.45	unknown bp-75 ov1 1.44	11.22		
3	1.82	6.93	hexane	4.84	110-54-3	8226
4	1.89	7.01	ethyl acetate	5.50	141-78-6	4139
5	2.09	7.37	acetic acid	13.75	64-19-7	6301
6	2.54	8.49	propylene glycol monomethyl ether	38.93	107-98-2	12524
7	2.74	9.01	unknown hydrocarbon bp-57 ov1 2.74	6.93		
8	2.86	9.31	heptane	5.17	142-82-5	8093
9	3.01	9.69	propionic acid	3.96	79-09-4	9913
10	3.20	10.41	2,5-dimethylhexane (t)	12.43		
11	3.23	10.51	propylene glycol	2.75	57-55-6	10162
12	3.52	11.59	toluene	20.12	108-88-3	8234
13	3.58	11.81	2-methylheptane	18.47		
14	3.60	11.89	2,3-dimethylhexane (t)	9.57		
15	3.79	12.59	hexanal	3.30	66-25-1	1330
16	3.97	13.27	butyric acid	2.64	107-92-6	6302
17	4.00	13.41	unknown hydrocarbon bp-43 ov1 4.00	7.70		
18	4.03	13.56	butyl acetate	4.84	123-86-4	6299
19	4.06	13.71	ethyl lactate	1.10	97-64-3	4347
20	4.22	14.63	unknown hydrocarbon bp-43 ov1 4.22	45.41		
21	4.39	15.61	2,4-dimethyl-1-heptene (t)	18.25		

Smell Replication: Chemical Reproduction

I execute the replication of the original smells in
my lab in Berlin (also supported by IFF). This
lab is a proper smell chemistry lab where I have
up to 4,000 individual chemical components at
my disposal.

The replication process involves very precise
work such that every nano-unit of a chemical
being added can change the smell outcome
of the replication. Each unit is recorded so
that the final formula allows the smell to be
reproduced endlessly for the intended purpose,
i.e. preservation, conservation, information.

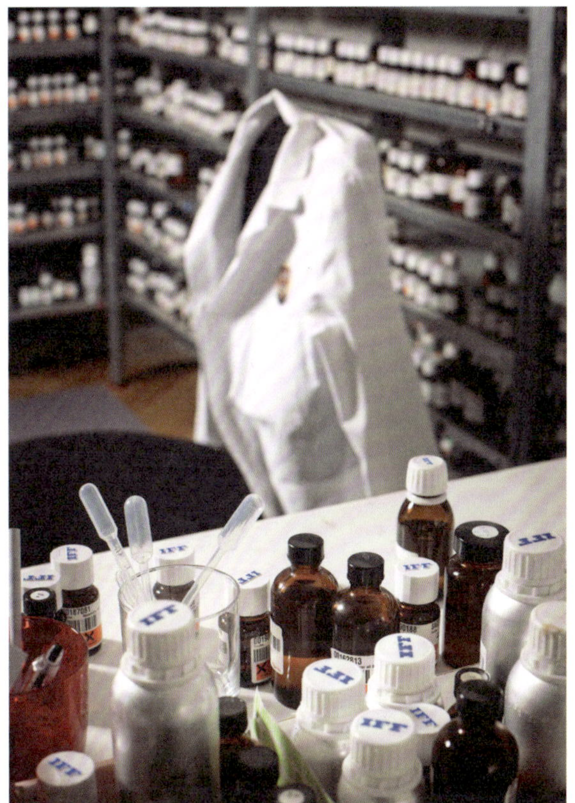

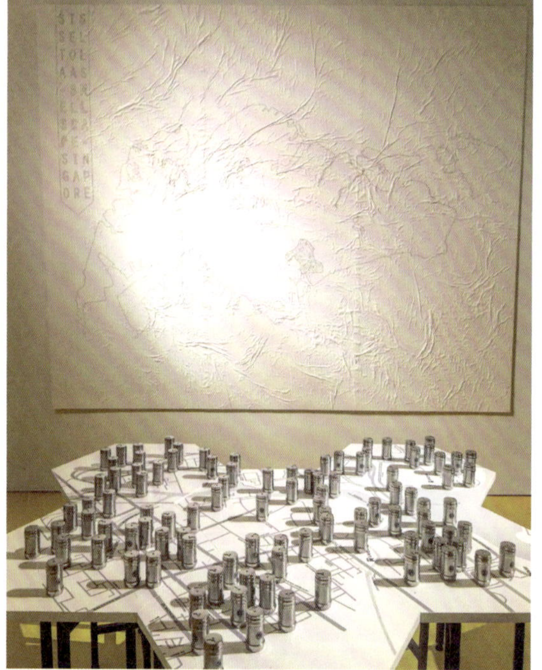

Smell Execution and Implementation
SmellScape Displays from Different Cities:
Mexico City; Amman; Singapore; Kansas City,
KS/MO; Shanghai

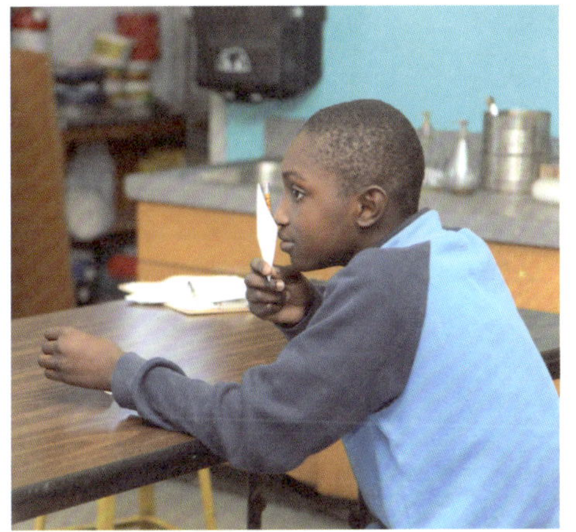

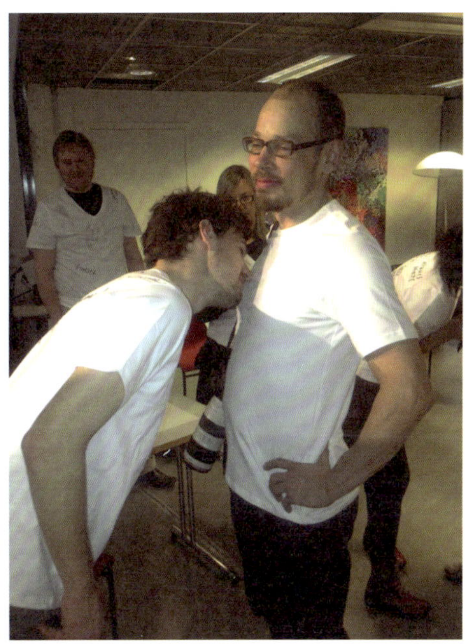

Smell Education

There is a whole world to smell and a whole world to educate how to smell.
Every City SmellScape has an important element called EDUCATION.

SmellScape Seoul 2017
Inside ⇄ Outside

What could happen when invisible information becomes the starting point for understanding, acting/reacting, navigating, tolerating, and communicating in and about Seoul?

All cities—as built environments—contain accidental and overlooked smells as part of their identity. Nevertheless, these smells shape spatial perception much more powerfully than light or sound. Our olfactory systems navigate using our subconscious and memory as much as they navigate through cultural stereotypes and recognizing urban structures. They reveal unexplored layers of existence in the different areas of the 605 km² of the Seoul Special City, helping us to tell alternative narratives.

SmellScape Seoul 2017 Inside ⇄ Outside (SSS) connects the Donuimun Museum Village (DMV) to the Dongdaemun Design Plaza (DDP) in an unconventional way: through overlooked *smells*.

In between the Donuimun Museum Village and the Dongdaemun Design Plaza, important overlooked smell sources were found, collected, and replicated. This amplifies the effect of the original smells beyond their original sites and sources.

Inside the Donuimun Museum Village the decontextualized and replicated smells from various sites around Seoul are displayed in the context of a large map of Seoul highlighting the neighborhood of concern. The focus is on the nature of the specific smells and why they were chosen to represent the DMV; this is because the displayed smells and their sources are not directly identified.

SmellScape Seoul 2017_Inside ⇄ Outside *invites* visitors to smell the displayed city smell sources (boxes with numbers). Then by looking at the indoor map, they will know in which locations in the city the displayed smells were collected. Visitors participates actively inside the exhibition by adding personal comments near the numbered smell jars; these will then be added to the database. Visitors is also encouraged to add comments to their own personal handout map, which includes an invitation to visit the original smell source locations in the real, outside neighborhoods in Seoul.

Only by visiting the smell source locations can one get to know what the smells are and what causes them.

In the Village there are signs indicating where the smell sources can be found. By following the handout map, visitors can move around, also aided by the signs. Upon finding a smell source, they will see and experience the context from which the smells were collected and potentially solve the puzzle. Comments from visitors to the site are very welcome.

Conclusion

In a world with significant greater global instability, it is important that we carefully consider and rethink our conventional modes of communication and our decision-making biases. We need to undertake a sensory reboot. The time is right to relearn how to understand our responses to sensory inputs in a constructive and scientifically validated manner.

And we need to educate our children to use all their senses so that they can understand the complex world they are living in.

It has been my experience that people all over the world really get challenged when they are seriously asked to use their noses properly. It doesn't even matter what they are asked to smell. What matters is that they start to rediscover the overlooked common environment, the air that surrounds them, whether its smells come from other human beings, places, or the city. They then start to approach it differently. If people get the messages through the nose, they really get it. And above all, smelling is joyful, meaning that people who use their noses more consciously add joy and playfulness to their lives, qualities that will improve life in the cities.

If we train our noses to navigate properly in the urban setting, we make progress in tolerating each other.

"Tolerance" is the keyword for a new approach to our surroundings. Tolerance starts with how things smell. I believe we have to relearn how to be tolerant, starting with using our senses actively. Only in this way will it be possible for us to coexist and live together in a different way. This process starts with the NOSE!

SmellScape Seoul 2017_Inside ⇄ Outside
is supported by
IFF Inc. USA
OCA, Norway

AN ATLAS OF MACHINE LANDSCAPES

A tour through the post human architectures of machine vision

Liam Young

Hurtling above us at almost 7,000 miles per hour is an improbable creation. Delicately dancing with gravity, a WorldView-3 satellite is looking down at the earth, beaming back images that Google algorithms will tile together to create a digital map of its surface. At the resolution of these images, a pixel is less than half a meter in scale, just a bit bigger than the width of our bodies. Ancient craftsmen once measured the world using parts of the human body: the cubit is based on the length of a forearm; the inch, the length of a thumb. Le Corbusier designed his buildings based around the Modulor, a scale he derived from the proportions of the human body. We once understood our world through systems founded on human size, vision, and patterns of occupation. In a culture of the digital, however, the body is no longer the dominant measure of space; it is instead the technologies through which we see and experience the world that now define how we navigate and build it. In this context we must begin to imagine new design sensibilities legible across both human and machinic experience.

Machines see the world through coded sets of rules. Whether through a camera lens, sensor, or scanner, they search for particular configurations of data, sets of predefined relationships, patterns, and geometries. Machine vision abstracts the nuances and complexity of our cities so they can be efficiently calculated, identified, and processed. Faces register as patterns of light and dark pixels that are based on a picture cropped from the centerfold of a 1972 issue of Playboy. In fact, this photo, of Lena Söderberg, has been used to test the rule sets of some of the most common facial recognition algorithms employed around the world today — a ghost in the machine, just one example of how machine vision is neither neutral nor objective but rather encoded with bias, privilege, and ideology.

In these autonomous vision systems a fiducial is a calibration pattern or marker that is created to be recognizable to scanning machines. As the pixel has come to define a new 'modular' we are witnessing the emergence of a new architecture: a fiducial architecture. A posthuman architecture designed to be read by machines yet sited both in the digital spaces of the network and on the physical ground of the earth. An architecture whose form and materiality is configured to anticipate the logics of machine perception, to either announce itself to the lens of the machine or to disappear, to either flare up or dissolve, to register as permeable or solid, understood or corrupted. An architecture encoded with digital information so that it may serve as a marker for computer calibration or a locative point for anchoring a luminous augmented-reality structure of intricate detail and immeasurable complexity. An architectural vocabulary that, in plain sight, may read one way to the human eye while signifying something completely different to the machine lens.

The infrastructures of the digital world have extraordinary implications for material existence.

These are the architectures behind the screen and beyond the fog of the cloud, the physical consequences of our digital enterprises. Architecture has always been defined by the prevailing means of production. Stonemasons once carved column capitals and modern architects harnessed the prefabricated components engendered by industrialization. The Atlas of Machine Landscapes is a journey through a catalogue of structures that suggest an emerging design language conditioned by these new forms of computational infrastructure. This collection of posthuman architectures and spaces reverberates across multiple forms of site and experience. It is an atlas of a world where the terms virtual and real no longer apply but where a luminous architecture can cast shadows across both physical and digital spectrums alike.

We can tour this digital skin of the earth, visiting sites and structures that are made for and by machines but that evidence alternative modes of spatial perception. We can trace their edges, glitches, and anomalies and see where the digital bubbles to the surface, congealing into an atlas of fiducial territories, landscapes, and architectures.

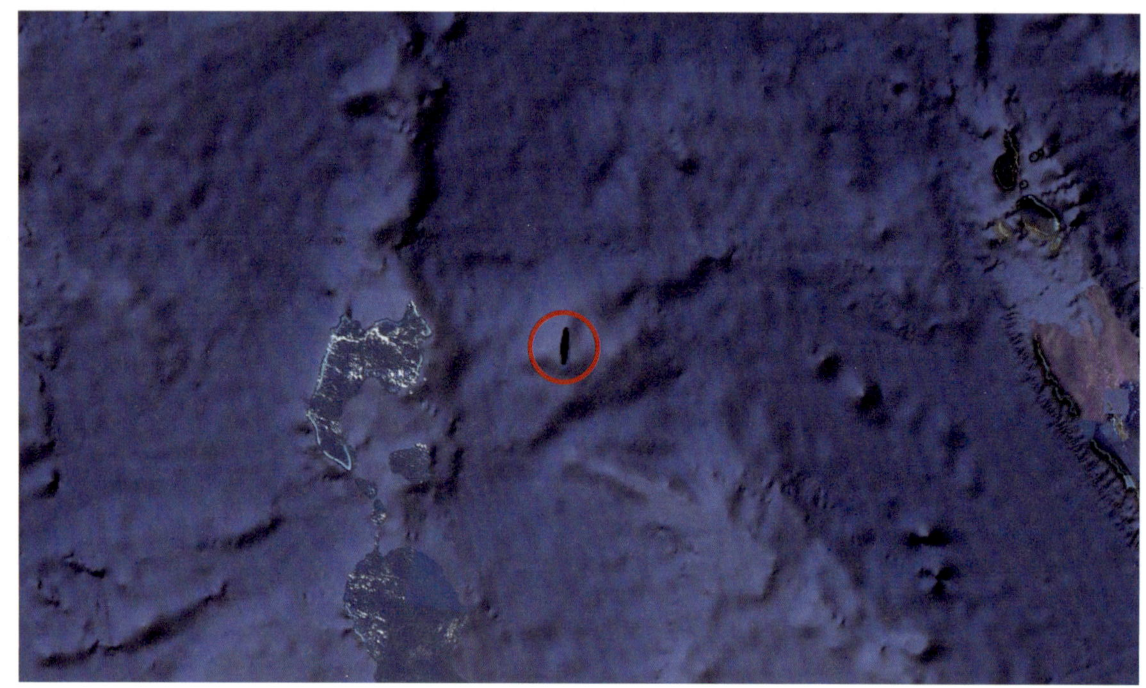

SANDY ISLAND 19°13'12"S, 159°55'48"E

Travelling acrossthe pixel sea of google earth, we wash up on the shores of a Sandy Island, just off the coast of Australia. Sandy Island is a collection of dark pixels, GPS coordinates, hyperlinksand stories. Originally charted by the whaling ship 'Velocity' in 1876 the island has long been an 'evidence doubtful' landmass, a place perhaps originally recorded to be a trap to supporta maps copyright or a mislabelled pile of volcanically ejected pumice that was seen drifting on the horizon. This cartographic apparition remained visible in Google Earth until an Australian research vessel confirmed its nonexistence during a 2012 expedition to survey the ocean floor. Up until that point, to a world of Google explorers and hyperlinkadventurers Sandy Island was just as real as any other place they visited online. If places and spaces exist in the mediums through which we experience them then they become just as real as any other. We can design in these digital landscapes, conjuring architectures of code, GPS tags and metadata, to be read and disseminated by machines, experienced and inhabited by us.

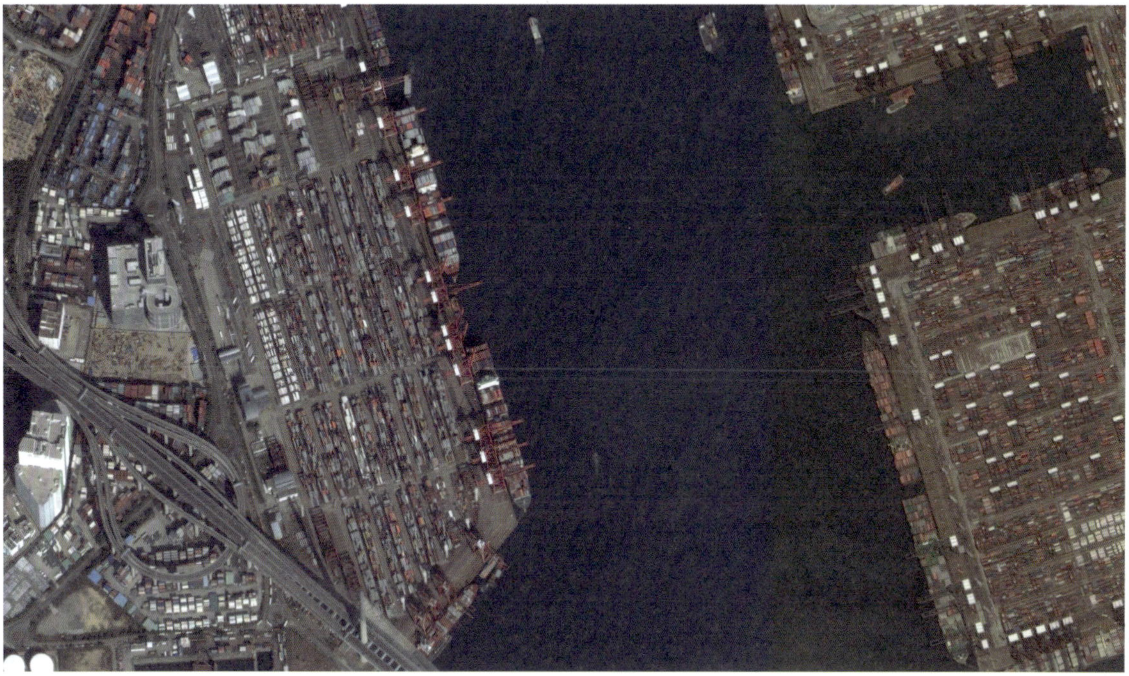

PORT OF HONG KONG 22°20'03.2"N, 114°06'59.5"E

Drifting within this sea of GPS islands is the computer controlled container fleet of the mega shipping industry. The paper sea charts and maps once scribbled over by captains have now been sucked into the screen and the ships now navigate autonomously based on traffic algorithms, efficient route processing and satellite positioning. To these digital captains any feature that appears on its screen is just as real as anything in the water. When the ships dock they are met by the portside cranes that are also driven by these same company algorithms. A boat used to moor in poor for week as every object, crate and barrel was carried onto the ship by hand. Now, autonomous creatures roll across the tarmac surfaces of markings and painted lines, their operators just passengers in the machine, their bodies repurposed as a component in the landscape scaled robot that stacks the containers ready for delivery.

SATTELITE CALIBRATION TARGET, GOBI DESERT 40°27'07.6"N, 93°44'31.6"E

Deep in the Mongolian desert huge landscape scaled fiducial markings are focused on by the same machines watching over the container ships. Not evidence of some ancient culture the or forgotten versions of the Nazca lines they are the traces of the new tribes of the digital, the animal tracks of orbiting machines. This is a satellite calibration target, a machine vision graphic etched into the earth and supporting the precision this whole system relies on. These patterns were created to give aircraft and satellite-mounted cameras something on which to calibrate their lenses, allowing them to test resolution and their ability to take clear pictures at high speeds. The surface of the earth is a digital test pattern, as our landscape is scored with the traces of a new kind of autonomous aerial infrastructure.

PINEWOOD FILM STUDIO 51°32'53.0"N, 0°32'04.7"W

When a machine system is properly calibrated and understands its position in physical space the digital can be collocated with our own physical experience. This is the commodity of the film studio, where physical emptiness is the critical asset, spaces designed to be as open as possible to reimaging so as the same space can be for one week, a hellish landscape on an alien planet and the next a rainy New York street ready for the last kiss of a ditzy rom com. Onto these blank spaces stage sets of pixels are projected. Behind the film fantasy they are just green screen structures adorned with black cross hairs, calibration markers and ping pong ball body suits. Modern film studios are a new kind of architecture, stripped back to become scaffolds and infrastructure for a digitally constructed world. As augmented reality explodes the CG experience from the cinema screen to the city street an emerging form of architectural ornament is beginning to be defined by machine vision and camera tracking algorithms. This will be the physical world left behind when everything disappears into the lens of Google Glass or Oculus Rift. When we turn off the bespoke billboards of Minority Report's urban spaces, the tailored ads, navigational prompts, tinder profiles and tracked status updates of our sci fi cityscapes, we will see a world where everything has become a screen. An architecture that is lying in wait, ready for the premiere of a million animated movies that will illuminate its surfaces with colour, detail and specificity.

VOLKEL AIR BASE, NETHERLANDS
(51°39'16.6"N, 5°41'11.4"E)

In southeast corner of the Netherlands appears a strange field of hexagons. It is made up not of trees or manicured lawns but of pixels – a digital camouflage cloak draped across Volkel Air Base, home to the 703rd Munitions Support Squadron. Beneath this Google Earth apparition is believed to be 22 tactical nuclear weapons belonging to the United States, a legacy of Cold War rapid-response strategies. While on the ground this site is hemmed in by a nondescript fence, on Google Earth it manifests as a distortion, a glitch, a 404 error in the geographic data set. A similar ghost territory can be found in Google Street View at 2208 Seymour Avenue in Cleveland, Ohio, another stealth site, where a decisive blur masks what was once the home of kidnapper Ariel Castro, in which he imprisoned three women for a decade. These sites suggest a new form of camouflage, imposed not to confound the human eye but to evade virtual scrutiny. But perhaps we can imagine designing stealth buildings to preempt the post hoc process of reporting "inappropriate" images to Google, with their own geometric and material rules that exploit the gaps, cracks, and blind spots of machine vision: mirrored surfaces to scatter the laser light of lidar scanning systems, radically curved forms to evade edge-detection algorithms, copper-mesh Faraday cages to block electromagnetic signals, and other yet-to-come architectural technologies to create exuberant glitches, distortions, and disturbances in the data set. Hidden within these stealth buildings may be sensitive services, abortion clinics, underground hacker spaces, preschools, or backyard meth labs. Architectures with a new kind of political agency, evading algorithmic detection, no matter how exuberant in plain sight, but invisible to the algorithms mapping the city. If it doesn't exist to the machine, then perhaps it doesn't exist at all.

CHERNOBYL EXCLUSION ZONE, PRIPRIYAT 51°22'52.2"N 30°07'02.4"E

Once called 'the City of Tomorrow' the Chernobyl nuclear zone is now a seeminglyabandoned post-human landscape. In March 2002 a group from GSC Game world travelled to the Chernobyl exclusion zone. Armed with cameras and sketchbooks they meticulously documented the landscape that would soon become the photorealistic environment of their video game S.T.A.L.K.E.R.Now, security guards here tell stories of their nights in the zone, as they chase STALKER fanboy gamers that break into the restricted city to re-enact their digital characters and plot lines. Pixels give way to radioactive particles as they wander the city, airsoft rifles over their shoulders, hand stitched uniforms and surplus gas masks keeping out the toxic dust. STALKER has transformed this place into a hyperlink landscape, still and quiet but at the same time filled with a thousand footsteps and digital gun shots echoing from distant weapons. Here are two superimposed cities, like an urban moire effect, constantly shifting between one world and the other. It is a mirror site, both its digital self and its physical self, a new type of city distributed across the planet into flickering constellations of luminous rectangles.

AIRBNB APARTMENT, NEW YORK CITY
(40°43'51.7"N, 73°59'14.7"W)

Neighborhoods in New York have become, for all intents and purposes, atomized hotels, their vacancies distributed across the floors of many buildings. But this hotel architecture exists only for the registered users of Airbnb; for everyone else these spaces remain private apartments, anonymous and inaccessible. This is a new type of building – a "smart" building enabled by the sharing economy. It is a sequence of spaces that coalesce like a cloud, inhabited for a single night before returning again to the grain of the city. Areas of the New York, once catering to a resident population, are now managed by proprietary software systems focused around tourists and public services are disappearing into the network and the magic of the screen. In this "Internet of architectures," are we customers or citizens? What other programs might be monetized and distributed through the unoccupied spaces of the city? An empty office reactivated after workers log off, a nightclub–cum–daytime classroom. A collection of latent rooms, nothing but space and an interface, become an amenity when logged on but vanish when the plug is pulled. Everything is connected to everything, appliances hum, cooling fans whir, LEDs blink, and babies drift off to sleep to white-noise lullabies. Our apartment crashes, and we can't get in or turn the heat on. We are all tired, but the bedroom is buffering.

AMAZON FULFILMENT CENTRE,
SWANSEA. 51°37'27.0"N, 3°51'45.6"W

Stretching out before us in the Atlas is the endless shelves and storage bins of the Amazon Fulfilment Centre. When we send an order to Amazon this is where it goes. As the digital leaves the screen it's patterns and code restructure architectural spaces in ways it is difficult to comprehend. The Amazon bookshelves are stacked based on a complex sorting algorithm engineered around sales frequencies and complex buying patterns. The search terms and suggested readings lists of the web crystallise into unintelligible juxtapositions and calculated adjacencies. Amazon workers rush through the stacks, navigating from book to book, filling orders by following the most efficient route generated for them by thebespoke tabletsthey constantly carry. Through this interface they are able to make sense of this system but it is not organised for them, it is a space organised by digital logics and inhabited by their bodies repurposed as machines. Our cities are starting to be organised by similar algorithms of big data efficiencies. Like the fulfilment centre we can imagine emerging urban form designed around satellite sight lines orcities impossibly intricate and dense as we locate ourselves in space not through sight lines and visual orientation points anymore but the pulsing blue dot of a live updating Google map.

FACEBOOK DATA CENTRE, PRINEVILLE.
44°17'44.9"N, 120°53'01.1"W

Terms like cloud, wifi and web are suggestive of something omnipresence, emphemeral, everywhere and nowhere yet these structures are supported by an extraordinary, planetary scaled physical infrastructure. In Prineville Oregon, a sleepy, unremarkable town, at the confluence of cheap hydro energy and tax incentives are the data servers of Facebook, Google and Apple. Everylike, love letter and ironic update, every photo that's been taken, every photo that ever will be taken is stored in these purring machines. At a time when our collective history is digital, this is our generations great library, our cathedral, our cultural legacy. Is the internet a place to visit, are they sites of pilgrimage, spaces of congregation to be inhabited like a church on Sundays? Would we ever want to go and meet our digital selves, to gaze across server racks, and watch us winking back, in a million LEDs of Facebook blue? Every age has its iconic architectural typology. The dream commission was once the church, Modernism had the factory, then the house, in the recent decade we had the 'starchitect' museum and gallery. Now we have the data centre.

KALGOORLIE SUPERPIT, WESTERN AUSTRALIA 30°46'26.2"S, 121°30'00.1"E

It is in the massive mining excavations, carved out of the wilds of Outback Australia that our new digital reality begins and ends its life. The material from this site, now one of the largest unnatural holes on the planet, is embedded in all the objects of technology we carry around with us now. With every tech gadget we buy, with every choice to upgrade, we dig a little deeper. The computer models of mines are now linked live to the fluctuations of metal prices on the stock market. It is a landscape of data geology. If gold is priced high, it becomes cost effective to mine lower concentrations of ore, if the price is low, the weeks excavation plans focus only on richer ground. Every modern mine site can be read as a kind of data visualisation etched into the earth at the scale of the Grand Canyon. As explosives, diggers, and drills have replaced the slow erosion of rivers and earthquakes we are scoring our economy into the archaeological record, a chronicle of the digital permutations that drive the modern world.

TRANSURBAN LOVE
The architecturalization of romance

Office for Political Innovation
(Andrés Jaque) and Miguel Mesa

In the last decades, four simultaneous phenomena have revolutionized the way architecture participates in the making of LOVE: 1. The development of location-based dating media (such as Grindr); 2. Monopolized control on the distribution of adult films (MindGeek); 3. The financial crisis; and 4. The money-storing condominium towers with "helicopter views". These four emerged in 2008 as a coordinated process that produced an unforeseen outcome: a shift from the desire for true love to the collective assessment of verified lovability. Post-2008, LOVE has progressively stopped being an interpersonal human transaction (in the U.S., interhuman intercourse has decreased at a consistent 5 percent rate per decade; in Japan, half of the adult population claimed not to have engaged in interhuman intercourse in the past month) and has instead become an architectural business. This started as a process of urban atomization. At the height of the HIV crisis, humans were distributed in bubbles of confortable prophylactics, and risk was surrogated to pockets of recorded promiscuity. Thirty years later, this has resulted in a process in which romance has progressively been embodied in architectural devices that no longer provide accommodation for LOVE, but have become LOVE itself.

0. Antecedents: Air-Filled Urbanisms: Surrogating Risk Into The Unlatexed

LOVE was radically changed by the 1984 Beta-max Case, and so did its urbanism. That year, the US Supreme Court ruled in favor of Sony Corp. that VCR users had the right to make copies of complete TV shows as a way to achieve a new media experience: "television time shifting." [1] In four years, the percentage of US homes equipped with VCRs raised from 19% to 88%, as revenues from film studios drastically shrank. [2] VCRs allowed many people stay to at home, instead of going to the movies.

1. Sony Corp. v. Universal City Studios 464 U.S. 417 (1984)

2. Asa Briggs and Peter Burke, *A Social History of the Media: From Gutenberg to the Internet* (Cambridge, UK ; Malden, MA: Blackwell Publ, 2010). 262.

"Watch Whatever Whenever." 1978, Sony Betamax SL-8600
Video Recorder Ad

Something was already happening to the
architecture of homes. In 1969, the Monroe,
Michigan-based company La-Z-Boy patented
the first upholstered reclining chair. Promoting
the predominance of latex-made rubber foam in
domestic furniture, the company, in a single year,
absorbed many of its competitors in the U.S.
furniture market by massively rendering domestic
interiors upholstered. Its sales grew from 150
million in 1981 to 500 million by 1983.[3]

A year later, General Mills developed the
first mass-produced microwave popcorn with
butter flavoring, which shifted the $53 million
home-popcorn market of 1983 into a $250
million market ten months later.[4] VCRs and
couches came with fat. In 1985, Tom and James
Monaghan's Domino's Pizza opened franchises
in Japan and the UK in a transoceanic expansion
that, ten years later, brought their "mouth
watering" meals to five continents.[5]

Air-filled-latex-couches make love go home. La-Z-Boy.
A chair by any other name is just a chair.

3. "La-Z-Boy Feels Energetic about Future: Company Is Restructuring to Return
the Brand to Profitability." *Winston-Salem Journal* (Winston Salem), August 30,
2006, sec. D.

4. "Microwave Key to Popcorn War," *The New York Times*, June 22, 1987.

5. Sean Farrell, "The Rise and Rise of Domino's Pizza," *The Guardian*, January 9,
2014, sec. Business.

The transnational retreat of the social to fat-retaining-homes synchronized with the transnational HIV crisis, that resulted in the disappearance from cities of spaces where love was staged and negotiated, a regime that established the fear of fatless bodies. The architectural socialization of movies left theaters to circulate within the connected but isolated, sweet, homey couches of the living room, where hyper-caloric food was delivered.

"Lovers at the Palace Theatre". c.1940, Weegee

Whereas Weegee's photographs exposed the bodily experience of love as something happening in the collective spaces shaped by projection beams, in the VCR era, love was surrogated to a distributed architectural network of foam rubber fluffiness, time shifting, and fat gaining. Since the 1920s, most condoms have been made of latex. So, too, is foam rubber whose air-filled matrix is made of latex and is the same material used in furniture upholstery. Architecture brought prophylactics and comfort together. If latex condoms were used to introduce a clinical regime of sexual vigilance, it was also latex—air-filled latex—that isolated homes in their access to fictional media and body-transforming fat.

The use of the two latex byproducts, condom and upholstery, grew exponentially at a time when the architecture of love was spatially becoming an air-filled matrix. Not an urban —because it transited from urban to rural and suburban—but a transurban evolution, by which the greatly rhetorical architecture of big spaces for social summing evolved into a prophylactic, networked architecture made out of something different from construction; it was the creation of a network of homes, territorially dispersed, working as an air-filling strategy through which a different form of LOVE was enacted.

Facing the big studios' massive firing (desperately intended to reduce their profit drain), their unemployed technicians and the independent companies depending on the film industry found a fresh place to work in San Fernando Valley.[6] In 1984, the first non-professional camcorders, JVC GR-C1 and Sony Betamovie-100P[7], rapidly propelled the industry of adult video films. Director Harold Freeman, accused of pandering, won the appeal to the California Supreme Court in what was in fact the legal recognition of adult filming in California as a practice detached from prostitution.[8] The then-depreciated real estate market of suburban San Fernando Valley made it possible to deploy a mirrored transurbanism; a film industry that,

6. Melia Robinson. "How LA's 'Porn Valley' Became the Adult Entertainment Capital of the World." *Business Insider*, March, 2016.

7. New York Times, *The New York Times Guide to Essential Knowledge: A Desk Reference for the Curious Mind*, Edition: 3 Rev ed. (New York: St Martin's Press, 2011).

8. People v. Freeman, 758 P.2d 1128, 46 Cal. 3d 419, 250 Cal. Rptr. 598.

rather than occupying monumental architectural compounds like Universal and Disney studios did, could be enacted through the architecture of a constellation of interconnected small warehouses and reappropriated dwellings.

thousand actors working in San Fernando, as a means to keep industry workers safe from HIV, chlamydia, gonorrhea, and syphilis.[9] Latexed prophylactics, were both responded and served by a trust-based love-making community.

"Tasha's Third Film from The Valley." 1998, Larry Sultan

VCR camara becoming a love-making device. "JVC Hold Everything video camera with VHS tape deck." 1984

In a mix of subversion and service to the 1980s latex prophylactic reurbanization of love, San Fernando became a non-latexed community, living collective forms of non-latexed love. It was the milieu to which the air-filled transurbia surrogated its risk. In 1998, a former adult film actress, Sharon Mitchell, founded the Adult Industry Medical Health Care Foundation, an organization that tested monthly an average of more than one

Monthly tests and strict protocols produced a database that comprehensively accounted for thirteen years of intercourse within the adult entertainment industry. An invisible reality, only visible through fictional sexualized video-recorded scenes, developed to collectively a surrogated manage a surrogated risk, had been constructed. No single case of HIV contagion was reported for more than four years.[10] Community-making and laboratized bodies, were simultaneously forms of counter-latex resistance and allies in the making of the air-filling society. Politics were contained in a mirrored risk-zoning society.

9. Terrell Tannen, "Sharon Mitchell, Head of the Adult Industry Medical Clinic," *The Lancet* 364, no. 9436 (August 28, 2004): 751, doi:10.1016/S0140-6736(04)16921-3.

10. Susan Abram, "Founder of Clinic for Porn Actors Fights Back." *Los Angeles Daily News,* December 19, 2010.

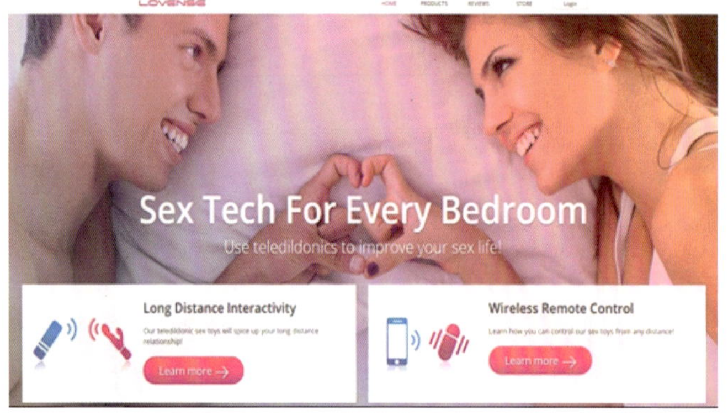

Lovensense. Teledildonic. 2016

I. The Network is a Rapist. Urbanism Goes Genital

In September 2016, a person registered as "N. P." sued Standard Innovation Corp., alleging that its collection of "sensual lifestyle products," in particular its latex-free We-Vibe digital dildo, "secretly collected and transmitted highly sensitive personally identifiable information (including heat level and vibration level) about the consumers using them." The product could only operate if paired with a smart phone with the company's *teledildonic* software, We-Connect, and it is through the phone that orders, data, and videos were transmitted between distant devices. The online mediation was built as a space that convened companies, multiple users and infrastructures in a shared interaction. A form of collective saloon made of loving and connected genitals, mediated by digital technologies. Being online, made it possible for sensual lifestyle products to be hacked. According to John Banzhaf, a law professor at George Washington University, "Unauthorized entry into a vagina may be rape even if she cooperates, provided that her consent was obtained by fraud or trickery."[11] N.P. claimed that it was the networked collective space itself, controlled by Standard Innovation Corp., what was emerging as a rapist subject, by

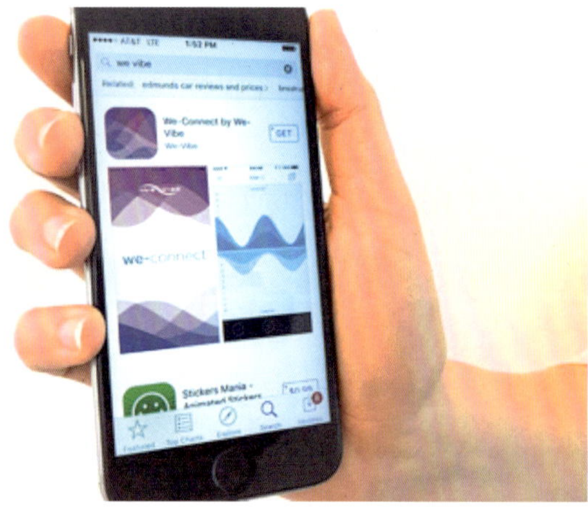

We Vibe 4 Plus app for smartphones. 2016

collecting and filing intimate data. Besides legal judgment, the argument succeed in detecting the way bodily love is no longer accommodated, but mediated. The urbanism of *teledildonic* is no longer made out of space, nor can be described as a "city", "landscape," "room," "building," or "typology." It became a subject itself; a non-human subject, founded in the connection of distant interacting genitals, in the search for an ethical constitution.

11. Chris White, "Lawsuit Alleges 'Smart' Vibrator Illegally Transmits Intimate User Data Back to Company," Law Newz, September 15, 2016.

Launched in 2011, Chaturbate, with four million visits per month, has become a voluntary space for intimacy to circulate in form of orders, data, and videos. At every moment, thousands of amateur models expose themselves from the upholstered intimacy of their post-VCR homes. Many have temporarily installed inside their bodies devices similar to We-Vibe that allow anonymous cybernauts to have access to their bodies and to activate their teledildos at a distance.[12] Thirty-three years after the VCR urbanism, a new latex-free society of connected-at-a-distance domesticities has been added together in platforms of sensual life and shared risk.

II. (In The Era of Grindr) LOVE IS BODIES RENDERED ARCHITECTURAL

The average number of time American adults have romantic intercourse per year has dropped a whole 15% since the 1990s.[13] It is even more pronounced in those born after 1990, among whom the number of non-active adults doubles the numbers previous generations presented at the same ages.[14] Even though it is generally assumed that interpersonal intimacy among young people has multiplied in an era of digital interaction, social media and location-based apps, it is definitively not the case. In the U.S., the number of eighteen-year-olds who have never experienced intercourse has constantly grown, adding a total 13%, since 1991,[15] and only 43% of college students claim to engage in genital penetration

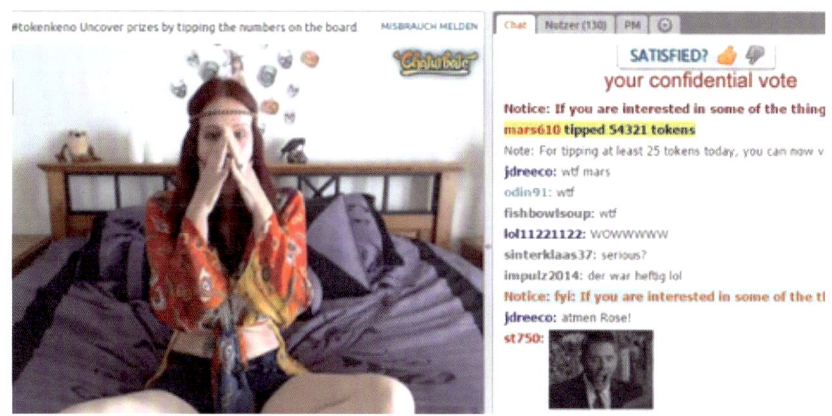

Cam-girl Germanflavor2 performing at Chaturbate from her home. 2017

12. Jamie Bartlett, *The Dark Net: Inside the Digital Underworld*, Reprint edition (Brooklyn, NY: Melville House, 2016).

13. Matthew Haag, "It's Not Just You. Americans Are Having Less Sex." *The New York Times*, March 8, 2017.

14. Burns, Janet. "Millennials Are Having Less Sex Than Other Gens, But Experts Say It's (Probably) Fine." Forbes, August 16, 2016.

15. "YRBSS | Youth Risk Behavior Surveillance System | Data | Adolescent and School Health | CDC."

in their sporadic relationships.[16] It is even more extreme in Japan, where in 2016,[17] half of the adult population claimed to not have engaged in bodily love in the previous month. Ai Aoyama, a Tokyo-based expert on relationship counseling, said: "(Young people) come to me because they think that by wanting something different, there is something wrong with them." But it evinces a significant shift in contemporary modes to construct love and desire.[18]

Landis Smithers, Grindr's marketing strategist, said: "I was looking at my Tumblr feed and I realized that it is basically fashion, fashion, porn, porn, interior design, art, porn, porn. This is just how we absorb things these days. And (on Grindr) I would like to find a tool where I can do that in real life."[19] Love is no longer genitally constrained, nor happening among univocal bodies, but an activity that registers and promotes subjects as multiple, composed out of the association of numerous versions of beings, constellations of heterogeneous entities. Since the 1980s, love is no longer happening just among people; it is also the interaction of multiplicities composed by cloths, art, images, technological mediation, architectural settings and interiors. In the urbanism of love, it is love itself that has been urbanized. Love is no longer a body-constrained business, but rather an architectural setting.

III. Locative Media, Or The Birth Of The Alkali-Aluminosilicate ZONE

Joel Simkhai was born in Tel Aviv in 1976 and soon migrated with his family to the conservative New York suburb of Mamaroneck. As a teenager in the 1990s, he started participating in what was the then-emerging world of online chat services, which he would use to meet guys. In the dark of his bedroom, with his parents watching TV in the next room, he would access the CB simulator's multi-user chat channel 33 and A.O.L.'s instant messaging service to immediately connect to a multitude of distant gay guys. "I was gay-born online," Simkhai said. "It was great, but most of the time I would end up talking to guys in places like Wyoming, Minnesota, or Washington, D.C. It was impractical."[20]

When he was twenty-one, and still closeted, he lived for one year in Paris as an NYU exchange student. Disappointed by the limited options he found at the gay bars in Tel Aviv, where he spent his summers, he was amazed at the effect that a pioneering communication system called MINITEL had on Paris, whose population density is 21,000 inhabitants per square kilometer, which is about twenty-seven times the density of Mamaroneck. With 9 million users, MINITEL,[21] the French predecessor to the Internet, had already produced a digital language

16. Arielle Kuperberg and Joseph E. Padgett. "Partner Meeting Contexts and Risky Behavior in College Students' Other-Sex and Same-Sex Hookups." *The Journal of Sex Research* 54 (2017): 55-72.

17. Jiji. "Abstinence on rise as nearly half of Japanese report no sex." *The Japan Times*, January 19, 2015.

18. Abigail Haworth, "Why have young people in Japan stopped having sex?" *The Guardian*, October 20, 2013.

19. Emma Hope Allwood, "What's grindr's new agenda?" *Dazed*, June 2016.

20. Vernon, Polly. "Grindr: a new sexual revolution?" , July 4, 2010.

21. "An encounter with Joel Simkhai, founder of Grindr." *Numéro*, August 25, 2016.

Joel Simkhai (right) with
his family in Mamaroneck,
NY. 1980s

for online dating. It consisted of a videotext
system that provided interactive content that it
displayed on a video monitor. Even though it
required its users to engage with an unwieldy
device that had to be wired to a fixed phone
line and placed in the user's room, the high
number of MINITEL users made it possible to
extend the text-screen conversations into offline
encounters and sexual intercourse.

Spending his Summers in Tel Aviv, he had the
chance to know WAZE, the location based
social media developed to enable drivers lost in
traffic jam to avoid bad traffic in the congested
Israel road system. What WAZE had done for
lost drivers, he could do to lost gay men in the
search for love.[22]

In 2008, as cell phones with GPS were being
launched by Apple, Samsung, and Nokia,
Simkhai, Morten Bek Ditlevsen, and Scott
Lewallen developed over six months the first
version of a location-based application that they
called Grindr, a portmanteau of *guy* and *finder*.
It was designed to help gay men easily find other
gay men in close proximity. In June 2009, on
the BBC-2 show *Top Gear*, the British actor
Stephen Fry showed Jeremy Clarkson how easy

22. Joel Simkhai in conversation with Andrés Jaque. Los Angeles, 2016.
Included in "Intimate Strangers" video installation by Andrés Jaque / Office for
Political Innovation, included in Fear And Love, 2017 exhibition at the Design
Museum, London.

Grindr Operational Center in Los Angeles. A. Jaque 2016

Grindr made it to cruise nearby gay men. A week later, 40,000 men had downloaded the app.[23] For Jaime Woo, "it was like gaining Superman's X-ray vision, and suddenly being able to peer through brick and steel to reveal all the hungry men around. People use the term 'gaydar' to refer to a queer man's ability to sense another man as a fellow queer. Grindr felt like a literal radar…"[24]

In its free version, Grindr opens with a display of twelve photographs of the closest individual users, with their names on the lower left corner. The profiles shown can be filtered by age, body metrics, ethnicity, relationship status, and also by the way users define themselves as aligned with one of twelve "tribes": bear, clean-cut, daddy, discreet, geek, jock, leather, otter, poz, rugged, trans, twink. Scrolling down reveals up to one hundred nearby users.

The alkali-aluminosilicate glass screen of cell phones provides a texture similar to smooth skin, so that as you rub your thumb down the display of Grindr users, it is like touching the young, hairless skin of a naked body.

Finger caressing alkali-aluminosilicate sking glass. Grindr, 2010

The display promotes interaction: blocking, favoriting, and messaging are the next steps. When a user's picture is tapped, his profile grows to occupy the whole screen. A user's profile consists of the guy's distance, his age, body metrics, and intentions, a headline, and a 120-character "About Me" section.

23. Vernon, Polly. "Grindr: a new sexual revolution?" *The Guardian*, July 4, 2010.

24. Woo, Jaime. *Meet Grindr: how one app changed the way we connect*. Canada, 2013.

These are the features guys use to construct themselves on Grindr (or that Grindr uses to online construct them). Photographs mainly show sexualized versions of users, in desirable interiors, with carefully selected outfits. Less than five percent of the conversations happening on Grindr end up in offline encounters.[25] Grindr provides a new mode of romantic experience, not meant to promote love forever nor genital interaction, but rather the desire-driven journey from profiled assemblages of porn, fashion, and interior design. The bodily experience of the finger-scroll on the alkali-aluminosilicate surface is a tiny gesture repeated all over the world for an average total time of ninety minutes every day that requires and triggers important architectural transformations.

What's up? What're you up to? What u into? Where u at? Trying to meet people. Are u interested? What are you looking for? Visiting. Looking for someone to show me around. Have more pics? How old are you?

As one Grindr user put it: "Nothing matters on Grindr besides the picture." Grindr conversation tends to be simultaneously casual and intimate. It accelerates romantic serendipity by creating a space of *visually driven* pre-agreed normativity. The 3.0.9 version of the app, released in October 2016, removed the orange frame in its interface to avoid users being exposed when checking Grindr by the orange glare coming from their cell phone's screens, coloring their faces. Grindr is an online architecture that enables offline spatial over-layering.

Grindr is a zone of its own, one different from cities, enacted more than constructed, but one that is also part of the way our offline world is happening now. Predictions made in the 70s on the way digital interaction would result in the unimportance of proximity have been proven false. It is rather that proximity has become multiple and technologically manageable. With ten million users in 192 countries, growing at a rate of 10,000 daily downloads, Grindr produces a flow of more than seventy million messages a day. It is not only in the dark of bedrooms, but in offices, bars, streets, trains, factories, gyms, and colleges that people inhabit it.[26]

User Jeff Ferzoco said he needs Grindr to have a sense of who is in the room.[27] For people like Ferzoco, architectural experience is no longer possible without the X-ray vision locative media provides. Grindr is the contemporary melting of architecture and urbanism. If places (bars, clubs, saunas, cruising spots…) used to be what produced LGBT scenes, it is now the self-reconstruction of subjects, through online editing and circulation, that host gayness.

Grindr constitutes a transnational urbanism, made in the intersection of bytes and flesh, that comprises five trillion bytes of data in use, stored in servers located in twenty-three sites in only two countries: the U.S. and China.[28] The management of functional dispersion and bodily reconstruction is actually concentrated in a binational location. Grindr pioneered what became a diverse context of proximity-based social media, including Badoo, Blender,

25. "Intimate Strangers" video installation by Andrés Jaque / Office for Political Innovation, included in Fear And Love, 2017 exhibition at the Design Museum, London.

26. Ibid.

27. Ferzoco, Jeff. *The you-city: technology, experience & life on the ground.* San Francisco: Outpost19, 2012.

28. Grindr Development Team in conversation with Andrés Jaque. Los Angeles, 2016.

Blued, Down, Glimpse, Happn, Hinge, Jack'd, JSWipe, Nuh Lang Nah Lang, Pure, Tinder, and Scruff among many others, that have not only radically changed the way sex and love are currently understood and experienced, but have also altogether enrolled more that 360 million people around the world in a process by which self-construction replaces building and intimacy among strangers reinvents urbanity.

Similar to what happened in the 1980s to movie-theaters with the emergence of VCRs, cruising spots and dark rooms all around the world have seen their constituencies reduced and aged in the last years, when younger generations abandoned them and found digital spaces to flirt and negotiate love. In London, historical gay venues like Black Cap and Joiner's Arms awoke media concern when they where demolished to make room for apartments. In New York, West Village's Westway club closed in 2015 to be replaced by condominiums. Sayvon Zabar, owner of the Latino gay club La Escuelita, claimed that his club had been shut after forty-five years because "minorities did not fit into the gentrification plans of the city."[29] In 2016, the apartment towers of Chelsea, East Harlem, and Greenpoint were Grindr users' favorite locations to find lovers worldwide, and Saturday noon was the preferred time of the week. Historical 1980s and 1990s match-making disco venues, such as La Escuelita, were replaced by apartment towers, just as smoky, lofty, night interiors were replaced by open-plan apartments as the number one desired architecture for love. Whereas the erotic industry used to occupy economically depressed parts of a city, now places like rent-spiking

Greenpoint and Chelsea have become the place of popular adult studios like Burning Angel and Cocky Boys. These are gentrified parts of the city that have attracted investment while at the same time becoming a laboratory for romance among urbanized multi-bodies.

In May 2015, Grindr went through a ten-month integral reconstruction orchestrated to turn the app into an expanding milieu for a total experience. Step one: Grindr hired Raine Group LLC to find a buyer, so the company could raise capital to develop. Eight months later, Grindr sold 60 percent of its stake to the Chinese gaming company Beijing Kunlun Tech.[30] Step two: Lukas Sliwka, Grindr's chief technology officer, launched a new Grindr software stack. Initially, Grindr's digital infrastructure was composed of customized solutions, which kept their in-house engineers' time fully compromised since only they could do the updates. The new stack used off-the-shelf components, which made updates easy to outsource. This way Gindr's engineers could concentrate on expanding the app by finding new ways to cater to its users. Whereas apps like Uber, which had eight million active users in 2016, are valued at more than 25 billion dollars, Grindr, with ten million users, stays within the 155 million dollar range. For the programmers forum Venture Beat,[31] this is how Grindr continues to expand, by introducing value-adding services, transforming itself into a broader gay lifestyle platform. Step three: In September 2015, Smither was appointed as Grindr's vice president of marketing. During London fashion week in January 2016, Grindr gave its users a code to access an exclusive live-

29. Musto, Michael. "Let's Dance. But Where?" *The New York Times*, April 28, 2016, New York ed. Sec. D.

30. Isaac, Mike. "Grindr Sells Stake to Chinese Company." *The New York Times*, January 12, 2016, New York ed., sec. B.

31. VB Staff. "Mobile app analytics: How Grindr monetizes 6 million active users (webinar)." VentureBeat. April 11, 2016.

stream of JW Anderson's autumn/winter 2016 menswear show,[32] in an act Smithers described as "pok[ing] fun at the fussy establishment a little bit."[33] In April 2016, *Paper* magazine announced that the male models for its summer issue would be cast from Grindr. Fashion magazines became an extension of Grindr's trans-media urbanism. Many potential young, fit, healthy, affluent models were right there, a few feet away from users' cell phones, where they might be available for chatting or even for love. Nicola Formichetti, Diesel's creative director, who decided to advertise on Grindr, believes that "social media is where people are now. We live on our phones. I want to go where people are. Tinder, Grindr and Pornhub might appear a little left-field. But it's Diesel. We are not scared of these places. We are street."[34]

Cities do not accommodate Grindr; Grindr is the city itself. It is an actor as much as the effect of night venues being replaced by condominium towers. It is composed of the way apartments, clothing, pornified versions of people, and urbanized bodily assemblages are mobilized through the sexual activity of rolling fingers on cellphone screens. It is the mode of romance urbanized bodies play, at a time when social media is "street." It is in itself a form of architecture, one based on the collaboration between diverse technologies at different scales. One that has redefined what being in a room means, the notions of proximity we live by, what density is about. One that requires aesthetics, interfaces, and memberships to be sensed. One so successfully integrated in daily life that is often not even paid attention to.

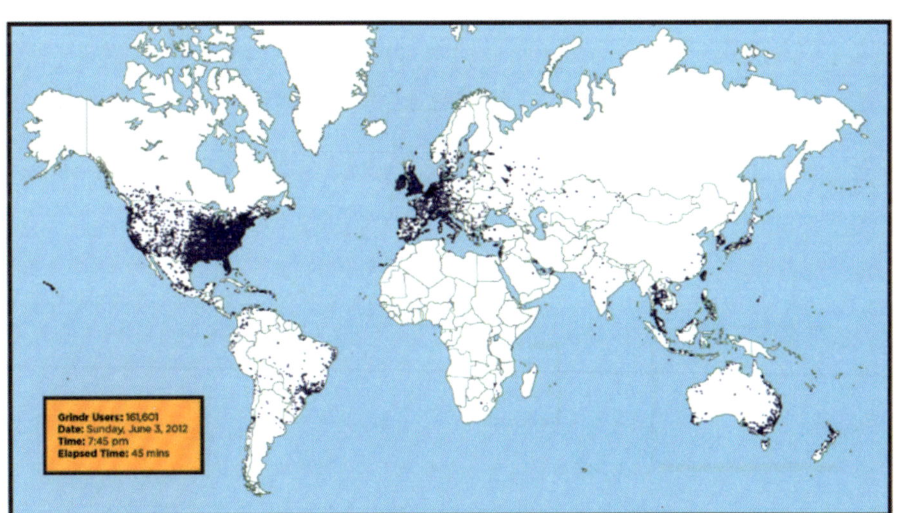

Grindr transnational location-based urbanism. Distribution of the 161.601 Grindr users on June 3, 2012 at 7:45 pm Los Angeles time

32. Cochrane, Lauren. "JW Anderson mixes mundane and strange in fashion show streamed on Grindr." The Guardian. January 10, 2016.

33. Allwood, Emma Hope. "What's grindr's new agenda?" *Dazed*, June 2016.

34. Salter, Steve. "why you'll soon be seeing diesel ads on grindr, tinder, pornhub and youporn | read." I-D. January 10, 2016.

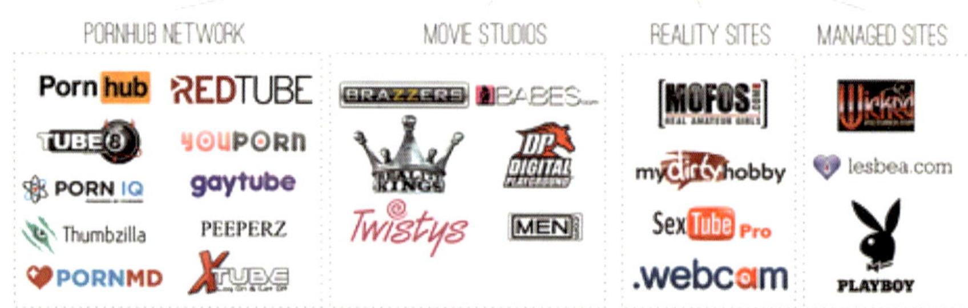

Mindgeek Business porn monopoly. 2017

If clubs and gay venues in the 1980s provide love experience, condo towers and fashionable profiling adds value. The architecture of contemporary love is no longer intended to maximize experience but value-addition. Love is no lived, but assessed.

V. Real Estate Became LOVE.
How LOVE Became Real Estate At The Age of Value-Addition

In 2007, Stephane Manos and Ouissam Youssef founded the Canadian company Manwin (later renamed MindGeek), which would soon become the world's biggest adult online platform. Perceived as a fragmented context of more than one hundred competing "tubes" (Pornhub, YouPorn, RedTube, Tube8, XTube, ExtremeTube, SpankWire…), Mindgeek operated as an aggregator platform providing free adult video content in a way so far unavailable, which rapidly mobilized more that one hundred million visits per day, far bigger than Amazon, Facebook, and Twitter, as the world's third biggest concentration of bandwidth.[35]

Progressively, the MindGeek platform grew as social media. Pornhub made it possible to follow the professional evolution of models and enabled users to produce their own movies and even to animate their bodies with Snapchat-like features.[36] MindGeek has also been seen as the promoter of a new accessibility to adult movie models, in what is a growing practice for adult films models to work as escorts through online agencies where they link their personal profile to MindGeek-hosted adult movies in which they starred.

MindGeek and the 2008 financial crisis are simultaneous phenomena. The financial crisis happened while senior staffers at the Securities and Exchange Commission were surfing pornography when they were supposed to be policing the financial system. A senior attorney was reported to be spending an average of eight hours per day browsing and downloading porn. This was not an exception in the commission. The dimension of the activity forced the SEC to install a blocking system for sexual content, and one of their employees, an accouter, was reported to be blocked more than 16,000 times in only one month. Between 2007 and 2008, seventeen high profile senior employees were admonished for this reason.[37]

35. "Mindgeek.com Traffic, Demographics and Competitors - Alexa."

36. Mix, "Pornhub Launches 'Snapchat for Nudes' so You Can Put Filters on Your Genitalia," *The Next Web*, April 18, 2017.

37. Daniel Indiviglio, "Did Porn Cause the Financial Crisis?" *The Atlantic*, April 23, 2010.

In the early 2000s, a combination of, one, a new way for air-rights to be traded between lots with at least a ten-foot adjacency; two, the public acceptance of the use of limited liability companies in New York as shell companies to hide the identity of real estate owners; and three, the 421-a New York Exception Program,[38] which reduced the tax imposition of top-prized apartments to 1/100 of the average New York property-tax payment[39]—all of these brought to New York a new typology of residential towers. Super slender residential towers (reaching a slenderness rate of 1:14) with "helicopter views"[40] meant to take advantage of the post-2008 difficulty in find financially stable locations to secure investment portfolios. In 2013, New York mayor Michael Bloomberg stated: "If we could get every billionaire around the world to move here, it would be a godsend." [41]

432 Park Avenue can be seen as the most refined outcome among these towers. Its design is the result of the collaboration of three architectural firms: Rafael Viñoly Architects (in charge of the overall structure), Deborah Berke and Partners (apartments layout), and Dbox (similar to Grindr in rendering 432 Park Avenue as a broader lifestyle platform). According to *NY Magazine*: "In the past few years, architecture has become the sexiest of arts. Keith Bomely and his colleagues at Dbox are its pornographers."[42] They were hired by CIM Group and Marklowe Properties to develop, through movies, photography, and online circulation, a post-2008 fictional society for the 432 Park Avenue high-end condominium tower.

In their four minute, one million dollar[43] movie *Before Night Falls*,[44] there is a scene where the 2016 *Sport Illustrated* bathing-suit model Christina Makowski travels from the UK to be introduced by Philippe Petit at a party at a 432 apartment wearing an Armani version of Kim Kardashian's famous Lanvin shirtless suit. According to Mathew Bannister, founding partner of DBOX, the important part of the scene is in the background, in that of a male character in his 70s called by Bannister and the DBOX team "the Danny-DeVito-Guy,"

Park Avenue, New York

38. Evan Bindelglass, "Everything You Need to Know About NYC's 421-a Tax Program, Poised to Expire Today," *Curved* (New York), January 2016.

39. Kriston Capps, "Why Billionaires Don't Pay Property Taxes in New York - CityLab."

40. Harry Marklow, CEO of Marklowe Propperties, codeveloper of 432 Park Avenue in association with CIM Group, claims to have invented the concept "helicopter views" as the main feature of a real estate product meant to create a high profile condo market based on "uniqueness."

41. Michael Kimmelman, "Seeing a Need for Oversight of New York's Lordly Towers —*The New York Times.*

42. Published, "The Influentials: Architecture & Design," *NYMag.*

43. Julie Satow, "Selling Park Avenue Condos at $250,000 a Minute," *The New York Times,* June 21, 2013, sec. Real Estate.

44. "DBOX › 432 Park Avenue," *DBOX.*

Romantic scene between the triple composed by Sport Illustrated model Christina Makowski (wearing an Armani version of Kim Kardashian's Lanvin shirtless), the Danny DeVito Guy and the 432 helicopter views. New York. 432. Park Avenue. Before Night Falls. By DBOX, New York

who is not played by an actor, but by a New Jersey-based businessman who is close friends of the towers' co-developer Harry Marklowe.[45] The movie presents this character as someone who, through the mediation of the tower, could romantically engage with Makowski's character.[46] Bannister meant to channel through architecture a form of sexual achievement and the confirmation of self-value though acquisition.

In 2004, George W. Bush stated in front of the US National Association of Home Builders that "(The government is) creating an 'Ownership Society' in this country, where more Americans than ever will be able to open up the door where they live and say 'welcome to my house, welcome to my piece of property.'"[47] "Owning a home is part of the American experience." [48] According to Michel Feher, contemporary love is shaped by the way financial strategies jumped into the making of subjectivity.[49] Financial credit become more important than commercial revenue. Rating agencies epitomized neoliberalism. For Feher, "Tinder is the Standard and Poor of love." The enactment of credited value has become the ultimate form of love. In the post-2008 era, love-yearning subjects, looking for satisfaction, have been replaced by vulnerable subjects dependent on the permanent capturing of self-esteem.

In the post-2008 era, verifiable lovability, replaced true love.

45. Mathew Bannister in conversation with Andrés Jaque and the Columbia GSAPP advanced studio "Revolting Apartments". New York, 2015.

46. Marjorie Garber, *Sex and Real Estate: Why We Love Houses*, 1 (New York: Schocken Books, 2000).

47. "George W. Bush: Remarks to the National Association of Home Builders in Columbus, Ohio," accessed June 19, 2017, http://www.presidency.ucsb.edu/ws/?pid=64585.

48. "George W. Bush: Remarks at the Plenary Session of the President's Economic Forum in Waco," accessed June 19, 2017, http://www.presidency.ucsb.edu/ws/?pid=73101.

49. Michel Feher, "Self-Appreciation; Or, The Aspirations of Human Capital," *Public Culture* 21, no. 1 (December 21, 2009): 21–41, doi:10.1215/08992363-2008-019.

References

Abram, Susan. "Founder of Clinic for Porn Actors Fights Back." *Los Angeles Daily News,* December 19, 2010.

Allwood, Emma Hope. "What's grindr's new agenda?" *Dazed*, June 2016.

Bartlett, Jamie. *The Dark Net: Inside the Digital Underworld*. Reprint edition. (Brooklyn, NY: Melville House, 2016).

Bindelglass, Evan. "Everything You Need to Know About NYC's 421-a Tax Program, Poised to Expire Today." *Curbed NY*, January 15, 2016.

Briggs, Asa, and Peter Burke. *A Social History of the Media: From Gutenberg to the Internet.* (Cambridge, UK ; Malden, MA: Blackwell Publ, 2010).

Burns, Janet. "Millennials Are Having Less Sex Than Other Gens, But Experts Say It's (Probably) Fine." *Forbes*, August 16, 2016.

Capps, Kriston. "Why Billionaires Don't Pay Property Taxes in New York - CityLab."

Cochrane, Lauren. "JW Anderson mixes mundane and strange in fashion show streamed on Grindr." The Guardian. January 10, 2016.

Farrell, Sean. "The Rise and Rise of Domino's Pizza." *The Guardian*, January 9, 2014, sec. Business.

Feher, Michel, "Self-Appreciation; Or, The Aspirations of Human Capital," *Public Culture* 21, no. 1 (December 21, 2009): 21–41, doi:10.1215/08992363-2008-019.

Ferzoco, Jeff. *The you-city: technology, experience & life on the ground*. (San Francisco: Outpost19, 2012).

Garber, Marjorie. *Sex and Real Estate: Why We Love Houses*. Edition: 1. (New York: Schocken Books, 2000).

"George W. Bush: Remarks at the Plenary Session of the President's Economic Forum in Waco."

"George W. Bush: Remarks to the National Association of Home Builders in Columbus, Ohio."

Grebowicz, Margret. *Why Internet Porn Matters*. 1 edition. (Standford, California: Stanford University Press, 2013).

Haag, Matthew. "It's Not Just You. Americans Are Having Less Sex." *The New York Times*, March 8, 2017.

Hauskeller, M. *Sex and the Posthuman Condition*. 2014 edition. Basingstoke, Hampshire. (New York: Palgrave Pivot, 2014).

Haworth, Abigail. "Why have young people in Japan stopped having sex?" *The Guardian*, October 20, 2013.

Indiviglio, Daniel. "Did Porn Cause the Financial Crisis?" *The Atlantic*, April 23, 2010.

Isaac, Mike. "Grindr Sells Stake to Chinese Company." *The New York Times*, January 12, 2016, New York ed., sec. B.

Jacobs, Katrien. *C'lickme : A Netporn Studies Reader*. (Amsterdam: Institute of Network Cultures, 2007).

Jiji. "Abstinence on rise as nearly half of Japanese report no sex." *The Japan Times*, January 19, 2015.

Kimmelman, Michael. "Seeing a Need for Oversight of New York's Lordly Towers - *The New York Times*."

Kuperberg, Arielle, and Joseph E. Padgett. "Partner Meeting Contexts and Risky Behavior in College Students' Other-Sex and Same-Sex Hookups." *The Journal of Sex Research* 54 (2017): 55-72, doi: 10.1080/00224499.2015.1124378.

"La-Z-Boy Feels Energetic about Future: Company Is Restructuring to Return the Brand to Profitability." *Winston-Salem Journal* (Winston Salem), August 30, 2006, sec. D.

Levy, David. *Love and Sex with Robots: The Evolution of Human-Robot Relationships*. (New York: Harper Perennial, 2008).

McCormick, Joseph Patrick. "Gay Dating Apps Hornet and Blued Enter Global Partnership." *PinkNews*. December 18, 2016.

"Microwave Key to Popcorn War." *The New York Times*, June 22, 1987.

"Mindgeek.com Traffic, Demographics and Competitors - Alexa."

Mix, "Pornhub Launches 'Snapchat for Nudes' so You Can Put Filters on Your Genitalia," *The Next Web*, April 18, 2017.

New York Times, *The New York Times Guide to Essential Knowledge: A Desk Reference for the Curious Mind*, Edición: 3 Rev ed. (New York: St Martin's Press, 2011).

Ogas, Ogi, and Sai Gaddam. *A Billion Wicked Thoughts: What the Internet Tells Us About Sexual Relationships*. (Plume, 2012).

O'Toole, Laurence. *Pornocopia: Porn, Sex, Technology and Desire*. (London: Serpent's Tail, 1998).

Paasonen, Susanna. *Carnal Resonance: Affect and Online Pornography*. Cambridge, Mass. (London: The MIT Press, 2011).

"People v. Freeman, 758 P.2d 1128, 46 Cal. 3d 419, 250 Cal. Rptr. 598 – CourtListener.com." *CourtListener*.

Published. "The Influentials: Architecture & Design." *NYMag.com*.

Robinson, Melia. "How LA's 'Porn Valley' Became the Adult Entertainment Capital of the World." *Business Insider*, March, 2016.

Salter, Steve. "why you'll soon be seeing diesel ads on grindr, tinder, pornhub and youporn" I-D. January 10, 2016.

Satow, Julie, "Selling Park Avenue Condos at $250,000 a Minute," *The New York Times*, June 21, 2013, sec. Real Estate.

"Sony Corp. v. Universal City Studios 464 U.S. 417 (1984)." *Justia Law*. Accessed June 18, 2017.

Tannen, Terrell. "Sharon Mitchell, Head of the Adult Industry Medical Clinic." *The Lancet* 364, no. 9436 (August 28, 2004): 751. doi:10.1016/ S0140-6736(04)16921-3.

Tarrant, Shira. *The Pornography Industry: What Everyone Needs to Know*. 1 edition. (New York, NY: Oxford University Press, 2016).

VB Staff. "Mobile app analytics: How Grindr monetizes 6 million active users (webinar)." VentureBeat. April 11, 2016.

"We're casting a big photoshoot on grindr." *Paper Magazine*, April 27, 2016.

White, Chris. "Lawsuit Alleges 'Smart' Vibrator Illegally Transmits Intimate User Data Back to Company," Law Newz, September 15, 2016.

Woo, Jaime. *Meet Grindr: how one app changed the way we connect*. (Canada, 2013).

"YRBSS | Youth Risk Behavior Surveillance System | Data | Adolescent and School Health | CDC."

Gig Faces, Gig Spaces is an installation using videos of MTurk (Amazon Mechanical Turk) workers performing small tasks—"gigs"—for money. It is an array of videos made by the workers themselves using computer webcams. We can't see the tasks they are performing, but we see the faces and spaces of new labor: domestic settings all around the world, with workers' faces locked in the view, eyes darting around their screens as they earn cash for tasks.

Gig Faces, Gig Spaces

Pablo Garcia

"Going to work" used to mean commuting: wake up in a domestic space, travel to an office space, then return to the domestic space. Sleep, repeat. This age-old arrangement created a functional division: work spaces are for earning while domestic spaces are for living.

For nearly 30% of American workers, this is an antiquated notion. According to think tank McKinsey Institute, between 54 million and 68 million US laborers are "independent workers."[1] They define this as "someone who chooses how much to work and when to work, who can move between jobs fluidly and who has multiple employers or clients over the course of the year." This is the "gig economy": workers who supply services—"gigs"—typically powered by online networks and platforms.

Some of these workers are traditional freelancers—professionals who take on clients and perform services. But many of these are a new type of worker: the gig worker takes advantage of new labor technologies and platforms. To do this, they leverage existing assets into profit-making services. Own a property? Rent it out on Airbnb. Own a nice car? Pick up passengers with Uber or Lyft. In recent years,

1. McKinsey Global Institute Report, *Independent Work: Choice, Necessity, And The Gig Economy*, October 2016

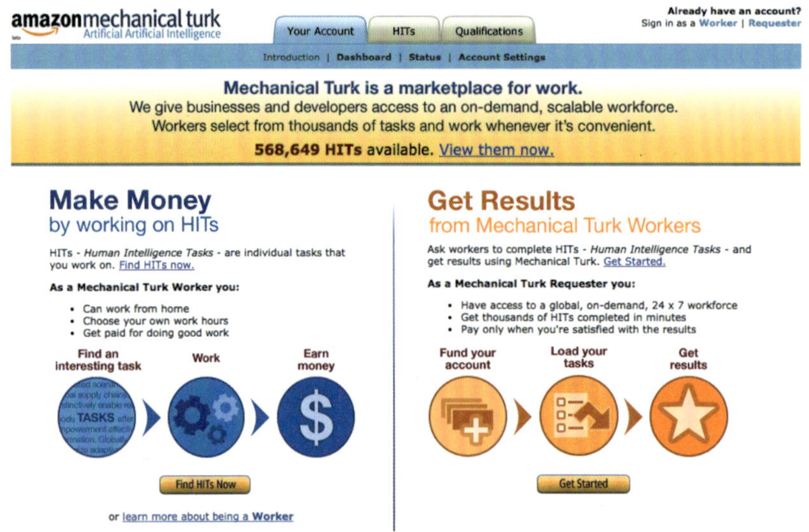

Amazon Mechanical Turk's landing page (https://www.mturk.com/mturk/welcome) offers a simple choice: Choose blue and "make money," choose orange and "get results."

these crowd-sourcing sharing platforms have received a lot of attention as visible ways people are shifting their income models.

Quietly, for over twelve years, Amazon has empowered anyone with a computer and an internet connection to earn income. Called "Amazon Mechanical Turk," or MTurk, the online retail giant connects workers (affectionately referred to as "turkers") with requesters to perform "Human Intelligence Tasks" (HITs). The idea is to crowdsource tasks that prove challenging to computers but are simple for humans.

Typical tasks involve basic data entry, transcribing text from audio clips, categorization tasks, or providing up-to-the-minute pricing information on eCommerce sites. These are tasks that still require human skill to process at a high success rate.

In some cases, a computer cannot simply provide context for information that humans can.

When Twitter's internal systems discover a popular new search query, the company automatically sends a job to Mechanical Turk, where it asks humans to categorize or provide additional information on the term. One example Twitter gave was that of Big Bird, the *Sesame Street* character who became a hot topic during the (2012) presidential debates. Twitter was able to find out the context for searches on Big Bird was more political than childrens'-TV-related and avoid sending out Dora the Explorer ads instead of ones by Barack Obama or Romney."[2]

2. Holt, Kris, "11 absurd Mechanical Turk Tasks You Can Do For Pennies", *The Daily Dot*, last updated 11 December, 2015 (http://www.dailydot.com/business/11-absurd-mechanical-turk-tasks-pennies/).

For your effort, you earn money. The HIT may only take seconds, up to a minute or two, and for the work you can earn between US$0.10 - to US$0.25 (Amazon charges the requester 20% of the "wage" for the platform service). This makes MTurk workers depend on speed and volume: take as many jobs as you can and pound away on your computer as you accrue pennies for somewhat mindless tasks.[3]

Odds are you don't know about MTurk. The work is tedious and seemingly inconsequential to everyday life. By completing surveys or doing data entry, turkers help companies refine their marketing strategy and improve their databases. Turkers' tasks amount to program debugging: incremental, tiny improvements to boost system performance. Important, but not glamorous. Uber and Airbnb, however, get a lot of attention these days. Their services are more visible and accessible to the general public. They behave more like peer-to-peer services: a person offers another person a ride in their car.

But not just anyone can provide services on these newer crowdsharing platforms. Uber requires a nice, clean car; Airbnb a nice, clean apartment. You're not gonna last as an Uber driver if you own a run-down 1995 Toyota hatchback. You have to own something of value to monetize, and that means you are likely middle class.

And since this "disrupts" the traditional narrative of the middle class—the dutiful employee who goes to an office to earn money to buy things—media focuses on this sea change.[4]

Nobody calls MTurk "disruptive." MTurk only requires a computer and internet connection, but it doesn't require any pretense other than completing the task. Computer costs have plummeted in the last decade, allowing anyone with US$200 to buy a working PC. This is a small investment to get started; a few weeks on MTurk and the computer is paid for. Working anonymously from home for pennies doesn't upend classic economic narratives. If anything, it reinforces it: this is a labor force of people willing to work for low wages to complete tedious tasks.

It's the economics of outsourcing. It's not particularly innovative to have cheap labor do tedious tasks for low wages. It's Capitalism 101.

A half-million workers worldwide toil away on MTurk. Launched in 2005, it's older than Airbnb (launched 2008), Uber (2009), and Lyft (2012). In fact, MTurk is more of a contemporary with more well-known sites utilizing the internet for social interaction, like Facebook (2004), MySpace (2003), QQ (2005), and Twitter (2006).

3. For a deep dive into the world of Mechanical Turk jobs and culture, visit http://turkernation.com/. This forum site posts job leads, advice to requesters and workers, and labor advocacy discussions.

4. Tech journalism, in particular, enjoys writing about the "next big thing" and definitive proclamations about the demise of tradition. Just for a few examples, see Larry Alton, "How Purple, Uber and Airbnb Are Disrupting and Redefining Old Industries", *Entrepreneur*, 11 April 2016, https://www.entrepreneur.com/article/273650, and Mathew Ingram, "Airbnb, Coursera, and Uber: The Rise of the Disruption Economy", *Bloomberg.com*, 25 October 2012, https://www.bloomberg.com/news/articles/2012-10-25/airbnb-coursera-and-uber-the-rise-of-the-disruption-economy.

Wolfgang von Kemeplen's Mechanical Turk, as described in Karl Gottlieb von Windisch's *Inanimate Reason; or a Circumstantial Account of that Astonishing Piece of Mechanism M. de Kempelen's Chess-Player* (1784).

Who are the turkers? There isn't a lot of data available, since Amazon keeps much of that information secret, and access to turkers is limited to requesting work through anonymized job requests.[5] Request work, results appear—as if by magic—in your MTurk interface. Unlike crowd-sourced gigs based on sharing like driving and accommodations, MTurk doesn't put faces to the service providers. Service and personal interaction is a feature of Uber and Airbnb. For MTurk, results are the feature. The providers are invisible. Amazon hints at the invisibility of the worker in the platform's name: Mechanical Turk. In 1770, Hungarian inventor Wolfgang von Kempelen stunned Europe when he exhibited an automaton capable of defeating most challengers in a game of chess.[6] Dressed as an Eastern mystic in a turban and robes and seated at a large cabinet with a chessboard, the robot was known as the Mechanical Turk. The Turk defeated master chess players and luminaries like Benjamin Franklin and Napoleon I, drawing audiences until it was destroyed in a fire in 1854. The Mechanical Turk was a marvel of engineering. Not only did it win almost all of its matches,[7] it was far more complex than any of the popular automata of the day.[8]

5. The most ambitious attempt in recent years to profile the MTurk labor force is from Pew Research Center. See Paul Hitlin, *Research in the Crowdsourcing Age: A Case Study*, Pew Research Center, 11 July 2016, 15.

6. Tom Standage, *The Turk: The Life and Times of the Famous Eighteenth-Century Chess-Playing Machine* (New York: Walker & Co., 2002)

7. In an 1819 tour of the United Kingdom, the Turk won forty-five matches, lost three, and drew twice.

8. For a thoroughly excellent survey of automata throughout history, see Minsoo Kang, *Sublime Dreams of Living Machines* (Cambridge, MA: Harvard University Press, 2011).

There's just one little problem: the Mechanical Turk was a hoax. Hidden inside the cabinet of gears and machine works was a space for a chess master to sit and control the Turk. Like a good magician, Kempelen would begin demonstrations by opening the cabinet to show the inner workings, a dense set of cogs, gears, and springs. And just like a magician, he showed it in such a way as to misdirect from part of the cabinet where the chess master sat. When Kempelen closed the cabinet, the chess master would slide out from his hiding spot and sit directly under the chess board. Using mechanical linkages and magnets, the chess master would operate the Turk to victory.

The original Mechanical Turk was a human simulating a machine simulating a human. Amazon's MTurk is a little different: it's (many, many) people simulating a machine. But both Turks leverage a strange contradiction in our computerized world: it's just easier to pay humans to do the work than it is to develop the machine that can do the same thing. We've all seen images of auto factories where there isn't a single human around as a phalanx of robot arms spot weld car chassis on an assembly line. Most of us assume that modern industry is robots in massive factories with a single human in a lab coat and a clipboard overseeing production.

The Turk, revealed. As Kempelen would open the cabinet to reveal the inner mechanism, the chess master would move to avoid the open doors. When Kempelen closed the cabinet, the master would get into position to remotely play the match. From Robert Willis, *An Attempt to Analyse the Automaton Chess Player of Mr. von Kempelen* (1821). Willis was among a few clever skeptics to deduce the actual workings of the Turk before it was confirmed as a hoax in 1854. Along with Willis, Edgar Allan Poe, then a young journalist, also debunked the Turk's performance in "Maelzel's Chess Player" (1836).

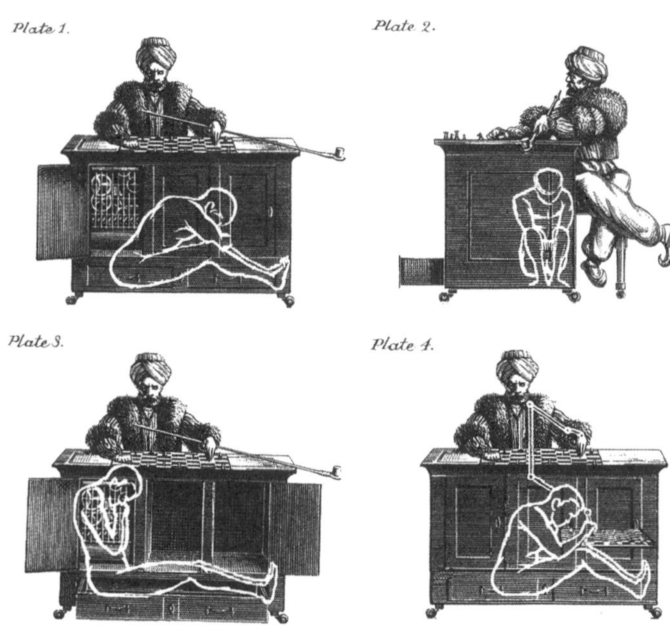

Gig Faces, Gig Spaces: Turkers recording themselves working on Human Intelligence Tasks.

That may be true for certain industrial fields, but the reality is that most of our goods—appliances, durable goods, electronics, and more—are "hand made." Industrial processes, especially in China and India, leverage inexpensive labor to produce vast quantities of products for international consumption. Sure, you could create a robot assembly line to build iPhones, but it's cheaper and less prone to error if you just throw tens of thousands of workers at the task. It's hard to imagine, given the sterile shrinkwrapped packaging and precise tolerances, but hundreds of invisible pairs of hands touched your smartphone before you broke the seal on the box. The invisible labor force is surprisingly efficient, precise, and adaptable to almost any industry. Sounds like a robot! But, especially in the technology hardware sector, it's actually humans simulating robots.

Investigative journalism has shown us the Chinese factories where iPhones and Samsung phones are made, especially after well-publicized worker suicides drew attention to working conditions. Tens of thousands of workers, in identical uniforms, work along conveyor belts. Machines and computers assist the workers in their tasks, but it's still humans directing machines and not the other way around.

What about the MTurk workers? They are just as invisible, just as machine-like in their performance, as the iPhone laborer. But they don't go to a factory. They work at home. They transform their domestic space into the invisible labor space, quietly supporting massive industries with their human hands mimicking computer actions. They are distributed all over the world with only one common feature: a computer with an internet connection. Who are they?

Gig Faces, Gig Spaces reveals the spaces of labor hidden inside MTurk. A young woman in Seattle working on her laptop in bed. A middle-aged gentleman in a home office in India. Canadian students in their kitchen; Bangladeshi workers in their living room. This is the invisible labor world made visible.

Using MTurk, I post requests for work. I ask laborers to make a video using their computer webcam of them working. They are to record how long it takes to make one US dollar. For this, I pay them one US dollar, effectively doubling their pay for the time it takes to do the work. Depending on the task, some can be finished in mere seconds, others can take several minutes to earn the dollar. As the workers complete their tasks, a counter totals the earnings, showing how much money they make during the run of the Seoul Biennale.

No matter the task, the videos are of framed faces staring at glowing computer screens. Eyes dart back and forth, mouths are muted as these invisible workers perform unseen tasks. The face of this new labor is, quite literally, just faces.

References

Alton, Larry. "How Purple, Uber and Airbnb Are Disrupting and Redefining Old Industries." *Entrepreneur*, 11 April 2016. https://www.entrepreneur.com/article/273650.

Chandler, Adam. "What Should the 'Sharing Economy' Really Be Called?" *The Atlantic*, 27 May 2016. https://www.theatlantic.com/business/archive/2016/05/sharing-economyairbnb-uber-yada/484505/.

Hitlin, Paul. *Research in the Crowdsourcing Age: A Case Study*. Pew Research Center, 11 July 2016.

Holt, Kris. "11 Absurd Mechanical Turk Tasks You Can Do for Pennies." *The Daily Dot*, 14 January 2013, last updated 11 December 2015. https://www.dailydot.com/business/11-absurd-mechanical-turktasks-pennies/.

Ingram, Mathew. "Airbnb, Coursera, and Uber: The Rise of the Disruption Economy." *Bloomberg.com*, 25 October 2012. https://www.bloomberg.com/news/articles/2012-10-25/airbnb-coursera-and-uber-the-rise-of-the-disruption-economy.

Kang, Minsoo. *Sublime Dreams of Living Machines*. Cambridge, MA: Harvard University Press, 2011.

McKinsey Global Institute. *Independent Work: Choice, Necessity, and the Gig Economy*. October 2016.

Poe, Edgar Allan. "Maelzel's Chess Player." *Southern Literary Messenger*, April 1836.

Smith, N. Craig. "Who's Responsible? The Ethics of the Sharing Economy." *The Huffington Post*, 1 February 2017. http://www.huffingtonpost.com/alliance-for-research-oncorporate-sustainability-/whos-responsible-the-ethi_b_14553878.html.

Standage, Tom. *The Turk: The Life and Times of the Famous Eighteenth-Century Chess-Playing Machine*. New York: Walker & Co., 2002.

Willis, Robert. *An Attempt to Analyse the Automaton Chess Player of Mr. von Kempelen*.

The City of Social Media

Beatriz Colomina

Perhaps the most important transformation in the social, cultural, and economic life in the twenty-first century has been the arrival of social media. With it a new space for design has opened up. Indeed, social media is the ultimate space for design, a space where design happens really quickly by an unprecedented number of people. Through its multiple channels we not only communicate and collaborate with wider and wider groups, but we refashion ourselves. Images, videos, texts, emojis, stickers, tweets, gifs, memes, comments, posts, and reposts are deployed to construct a very precise image, not necessarily matching our real-life person, an avatar launched with seemingly independent thoughts, looks, and actions—a perfected self, perhaps the image of whom we would like to be, that becomes real online. And there is no limit to how many digital personalities we might maintain at the same time, including "anonymous."

There was no social media before 2000. Friends Reunited was launched that year in Great Britain to help people locate old school friends. This was the first successful online social network, and by the end of the year, it had 3,000 users; a year later, it had 2.5 million. In 2002 Friendster got 3 million users in three months; 2003 was the year of MySpace. In 2004 Facebook started at Harvard as a collegiate version of Friendster; within a month, half of the Harvard College population was on it. Soon it expanded to other colleges, and in 2005 Facebook opened to high school students; 2005 was also the year in which YouTube was launched with an invitation to "Broadcast Yourself." The year 2006 was Twitter, as well as the year in which Facebook opened to anybody above thirteen years old.

Default profile pictures from different platforms

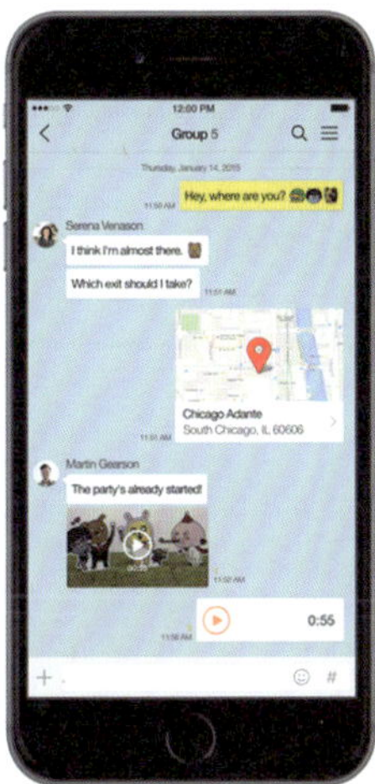

Official screenshots of social media apps on the App Store

Kakao Talk friends

WhatsApp arrived in 2009 and is the most globally popular messaging app, with 800 million users. KakaoTalk, based in Korea, was launched in 2010 and has now 140 million users. The app is used by 93% of smartphone owners in Korea. Instagram, launched in October 2010, had 300,000 active users as of December 2014 and 400 million in 2015. It is one of the social networks that has risen more rapidly in popularity: 53% of 18-to-29-year-olds use it and only 26% of users are older than 29. It is the more "urban," the one most used by women, Latinos, African Americans, and designers. Line, a messenger service for instant communication on electronic devices, was launched in Japan in 2011 and is also extremely popular in South Korea. It has 700 million users worldwide. It was designed by fifteen members of the NHN (New Human Network) in response to Japan's devastating Tohoku earthquake in March 2011, which damaged telecommunications infrastructure.

Mark Zuckerberg under map showing Facebook friendship connections at Mobile World Congress, Barcelona, February 2016

This short history could continue on and on. There has been an exponential acceleration of the number of available channels for broadcast of the self, matched by an accelerating number of people using them. There are social networks for practically everything. To find work: LinkedIn. Location-based dating apps: Tinder and Grindr. Video: Vimeo and YouTube. Mood boards: Tumblr, Pinterest. The network that has risen more rapidly among young people recently is Snapchat, where users program how long their photos and videos will be visible to other users—between one and ten seconds— until permanently erased from the system. A few seconds has become a space for design.

A map of Facebook users in 2010 showed 700,000 active users; there are now about 1.6 billion. It is estimated that 4 billion people—60% of the world population—are already connected to the internet, with 70% of them engaged in some form of social media, mainly through cell phones.

This represents a complete transformation of the way we live, with huge implications for architecture and design. Social media is not simply about what occurs in digital space— constructing a new kind of virtual city that has taken over many of the functions of the traditional city. We now inhabit a kind of hybrid space between the virtual and the real. Social media also redefines and restructures physical space, the space of our homes and cities. As with the arrival of mass media in the early twentieth century, social media redraws once again what is public and what is private, what is inside and what is outside. Design in the age of social media is not just what occurs in the space of a little screen. Social media redesigns the space we live in.

Early twentieth-century architects lamented the effect of photography and the illustrated journal on architecture. Adolf Loos, for example, criticized his contemporary and rival Austrian architect Josef Hoffmann because in Loos's view his houses appeared to be made for the camera. They were two-dimensional and had lost all tectonic qualities. It was difficult to tell them apart in photographs from their cardboard models. Loos was proud of the fact that his clients could not recognize their own houses in photographs.

A new generation of architects is now being asked by their young clients to design spaces that will look good on Facebook, Instagram, YouTube, etc. Even competitions, such as the MoMA PS1 Young Architects pavilion, take into consideration how "Instagramable" the winning design will be. Any building will be experienced far more often in social media than in the streets, and the encounter in the street is already shaped by social media. Social media is not simply the posting and sharing of things that have occurred. Rather, the experience occurs within the environment of sharing. While a generation ago design concerned itself with its reception in the printed press (newspapers, professional journals, magazines), now the concern is instead its reception in social media. How many tweets, how many likes, how many followers, how many reposts: the ultimate goal is design going viral.

It is not simply the expansion of reception that matters here. The internet and social media are fundamentally redefining the spaces in which we live, our relationship to objects and to each other. Social media is a new form of urbanization, the architecture of how we live together. In what is probably now a conservative estimate, the *Wall Street Journal* reported in 2012 that 80% of young New York City professionals work regularly from bed. The fantasy of the home office has given way to the reality of the bed office. The very meaning of the word "office" has been transformed. Millions of dispersed beds are taking over from concentrated office buildings. The boudoir is defeating the tower. Networked electronic technologies have removed any limit to what can be done in bed.

How did we get here?

In his famous short text "Louis-Philippe, or the Interior," Walter Benjamin wrote of the splitting of work and home in the nineteenth century:

Under Louis-Philippe, "the private citizen enters the stage of history. . . . For the private person, living space becomes, for the first time, antithetical to the place of work. The former is constituted by the interior; the office is its complement. The private person who squares his accounts with reality in his office demands that his interior be maintained in his illusions . . . From this spring the phantasmagorias of the interior. For the private individual the private environment represents the universe. In it he gathers remote places and the past. His living room is a box in the world theater.[1]

---

1. Walter Benjamin, "Louis-Philippe, or the Interior," in *Reflections: Essays, Aphorisms, Autobiographical Writings*, ed. Peter Demetz, trans. Edmund Jephcott (New York: Schoken Books, 1978), 154.

COLLABORATE IN BED

"Collaborate in Bed," Bluebeam Advertisement

Industrialization brought with it the eight-hour shift and the radical separation between the home and the office or factory, between rest and work, night and day. Postindustrialization collapses work back into the home and takes it further into the bedroom and into the bed itself. Phantasmagoria is no longer lining the room in wallpaper, fabric, images, and objects. It is now in electronic devices. The whole universe is concentrated on a small screen, with the bed floating in an infinite sea of information. To lie down is not to rest but to move. The bed is now a site of action. But the voluntary invalid has no need of their legs. The bed has become the ultimate prosthetic and a whole new industry is devoted to providing contraptions to facilitate work while lying down—reading, writing, texting, recording, broadcasting, listening, talking, and, of course, eating, drinking, sleeping, or making love, activities that seem to have been turned, of late, into work itself. Waiters in restaurants in the United States ask if you are "still working on that" before removing your plate or your glass. Endless advice is dispensed about how to "work" on your personal relationships, "schedule" sex with your partner. Sleeping is definitely hard work too, for millions, with the psychopharmaceutical industry providing new drugs every year and an army of sleep experts providing advice on how to achieve this apparently ever more elusive goal— all in the name of higher productivity, of course. Everything done in the bed has become work.

This philosophy was already embodied in the figure of Hugh Hefner, who famously almost never left his bed, let alone his house. He literally moved his office to his bed in 1960 when he moved into the Playboy Mansion at 1340 North State Parkway, Chicago, turning it into the epicenter of a global empire and his silk pajamas and dressing gown into his business attire. "I don't go out of the house at all!!! . . . I am a contemporary recluse," he told Tom Wolfe, guessing that the last time he was out had been three and a half months before and that in the last two years he had been out of the house only nine times.[2] Fascinated, Wolfe described him as "the tender-tympany green heart of an artichoke."[3]

Playboy turns the bed into a workplace. From the mid-1950s on, the bed becomes increasingly sophisticated, outfitted with all sorts of entertainment and communication devices as a kind of control room.

2. Tom Wolfe, "King of the Status Dropouts," *The Pump House Gang* (New York: Farrar, Straus & Giroux, 1965).

3. Ibid., 63.

Hefner was not alone. The bed may have been the ultimate American office at midcentury. In an interview in the *Paris Review* in 1957, Truman Capote is asked, "What are some of your writing habits? Do you use a desk? Do you write on a machine?" To which he answers: "I am a completely horizontal author. I can't think unless I'm lying down, either in bed or stretched on a couch and with a cigarette and a coffee handy."[4]

Even architects set up office in bed at midcentury. Richard Neutra started working the moment he woke up, with elaborate equipment enabling him to design, write, or even interview in bed. As his son Dion Neutra revealed:

"Dad's best time for creative thinking was early in the morning, long before any activity had started in the office below. He often stayed in bed working with ideas and designs, even extending into appointments which had been made earlier. His one concession to convention was to put on a tie over his night shirt when receiving visitors while still propped up in bed!"[5]

Neutra's bed in the VDL house in Silver Lake, Los Angeles, included two public phones; three communication stations for talking with other rooms in the house, the office below, and even another office 500 meters away; three different call bells; drafting boards and easels that folded down over the bed; electric lights and a radio-gramophone controlled from a dashboard overhead. A bedside table rolling on casters held the tape recorder, electric clock, and storage compartments for drawing and writing equipment so that he could, as Neutra put it in a letter to his sister, "use every minute from morning to late night."[6]

Postwar America inaugurated the high-performance bed as an epicenter of productivity, a new form of industrialization that was exported globally and has now become available to an international army of dispersed but interconnected producers. A new kind of factory without walls is constructed by compact electronics and extra pillows for the 24/7 generation.

The kind of equipment that Hefner envisioned (some of which, like the answering machine, didn't yet exist) is now expanded for the Internet and social media generation, who not only work in bed but socialize in bed, exercise in bed, read the news in bed, and entertain sexual relationships with people miles away from their beds. The *Playboy* fantasy of the nice girl next door is more likely realized today with someone on another continent than in the same building or neighborhood—a person you may have never seen before and may never see again, and it is anybody's guess if she is real (as in, exists in some place and time) or an electronic construction. Does it matter? As in the recent film *Her*, a moving depiction of life in the soft, uterine state that is a corollary to our new mobile technologies, the "her" in question is an operating system that turns out to be a more satisfying partner than a person. The protagonist lies in bed with Her, chatting, arguing, making love, and eventually breaking up still in bed.

4. "Truman Capote, The Art of Fiction No. 17," interviewed by Patti Hill, *The Paris Review* 16 (Spring–Summer 1957).

5. Dion Neutra, "The Neutra Genius: Innovation and Vision," *Modernism* 1, no. 3 (December 1998).

6. Richard Neutra to Verena Saslavsky, 4 December 1953, Dion Neutra Papers, quoted in Thomas S. Hines, *Richard Neutra and the Search for Modern Architecture: A Biography and History* (Los Angeles: University of California Press, 1982), 251.

If, according to Jonathan Crary, late capitalism is the end of sleep, colonizing every minute of our lives for production and consumption, the actions of the voluntary recluse are not so voluntary in the end.[7] The nineteenth-century division of the city between rest and work may soon become obsolete. Not only have our habits and habitat changed with the Internet and social media, but the predictions about the end of human labor in the wake of new technologies and robotization that were already being made at the end of the nineteenth century are no longer treated as futuristic. Thirty-five years ago, the late economist Wassily Leontief said, "They replaced horses, didn't they?" and the business section of *The New York Times* recently reconsidered his idea of the end of the "human workhorse":

"Horses hung around in the labor force for quite some time after they were first challenged by "modern" communications technologies like the telegraph and the railroad, hauling stuff and people around farms and cities. But when the internal combustion engine came along, horses – as a critical component of the world economy – were history. . . . Humans as workhorses might also be on the way out."[8]

Economists wonder what kind of economic model this reality will lead to: from growing inequalities with vast amounts of people unemployed to large-scale redistribution in the form of Universal Basic Income, which was recently considered in a referendum in Switzerland and rejected. The end of paid labor and its replacement with creative leisure was already envisioned in utopian projects of the 1960s and 1970s by Constant, Superstudio, and Archizoom, including hyperequipped beds.

Meanwhile the city has started to redesign itself.

In today's attention-deficit-disorder society, we have discovered that we work better in short bursts punctuated by rest. Today many companies provide sleeping pods in the office to maximize productivity. Bed and office are never far apart in the 24/7 world. Special self-enclosed beds have been designed for office spaces—turning themselves into compact sealed capsules, mini-spaceships, that can be used in isolation or gathered together in clusters or lined up in rows for synchronized sleep—understood as a part of work rather than its opposite.

Between the bed inserted in the office and the office inserted in the bed, a whole new horizontal architecture has taken over. It is magnified by the "flat" networks of social media that have themselves been fully integrated into the professional, business, and industrial environment in a collapse of traditional distinctions between private and public, work and play, rest and action. The bed itself—with its ever more sophisticated mattress, linings, and technical attachments—is the basis of an intrauterine environment that combines the sense of deep interiority with the sense of hyperconnectivity to the outside.

What is the nature of this new interior in which we have decided collectively to check ourselves in? What is the architecture of this prison in which night and day, work and play are no longer differentiated and we are permanently under surveillance? New media turns us all into inmates, constantly under surveillance, even as we celebrate endless connectivity. We have all become "a contemporary recluse," as Hugh Hefner put it a half a century ago.

7. Jonathan Crary, *24/7: Late Capitalism and the Ends of Sleep* (New York: Verso, 2013).

8. Eduardo Porter, "Contemplating the End of the Human Workhorse," *The New York Times*, 8 June, 2016, B1 and B6.

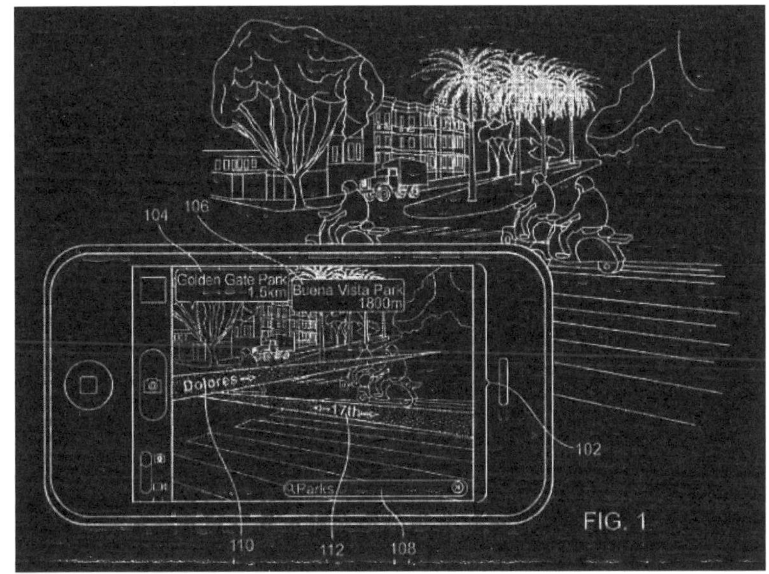

Patent drawing for navigating the city through augmented reality

In Laura Poitras's film *Citizenfour*, we see Edward Snowden close up, sitting on his bed in a Hong Kong hotel for days on end, surrounded by his laptops, communicating with journalists in the room and around the world about the secret world of massive global surveillance. The biggest invasion of privacy in the history of the planet is revealed from bed and dominates all media. The most public figure in the world at that moment is a recluse. Architecture has been inverted.

Writers and artists in the twentieth century worked from bed, from Proust to Matisse, to Truman Capote, who couldn't even think unless he was lying down. Today everybody is an artist, a writer, a curator, a designer. . . . If Walter Benjamin thought the arrival of the printing press made everyone a critic, the arrival of social media makes everyone an author, an artist, a self-designer. One of the paradoxes of the age of social media and the sharing economy is the extreme cultivation of the sense of self. Everybody has the fantasy of being an independent producer, self-employed in the permanent project of constructing oneself. Self-design has become the main responsibility and activity. As Boris Groys writes:

"With the death of God, design became the medium of the soul, the revelation of the subject hidden inside the human body. Thus design took on an ethical dimension it had not had previously. In design, ethics became aesthetics; it became form. Where religion once was, design has emerged. The modern subject now has a new obligation: the obligation to self-design, an aesthetic presentation as ethical subject."[9]

But are we so independent in the end? Aren't we still working for the man? Sacrificing all privacy to produce big data in return for the illusion of independence?

9. Boris Groys, "The Obligation to Self-Design," *e-flux* (November 2008), http://www.e-flux.com/journal/the-obligation-to-self-design/.

An Architect's Contract for Outcomes

**Dark Matter Laboratories, UK
(Dr. Orestes Chouchoulas,
Prof. Indy Johar)**

Current models of urban change are failing to address the big and complex challenges we face in our cities. The marginalisation of urban disciplines like architecture and city planning in the drive to create positive change is largely due to inherent limitations in the institutions that underpin the production of the built environment. We propose an alternative vision to structure the procurement of the built environment around the production of positive social outcomes, with architectural contracts potentially leading the charge. This possible future is made more plausible by a host of recent advances in financing, design, computation and data, policy, regulation, and governance. We propose that a new prototypical architect's contract for outcomes can become a key component of this vision, driving a realignment of the architectural profession with the needs of citizens and society at large. This could foster a fundamental transformation of the institutional infrastructure of how we build (and rebuild) cities. Such a prototype contract should be able to define and measure impact while bringing together a large number of diverse parties. To conclude, we explore what this could mean for professional practice and the design of cities.

The Marginalisation of Urban Professions

It is not news that cities are facing rapidly evolving challenges. As cities grow and change at an accelerating pace, they present new problems and complicate existing ones. Historically, both government and the built environment professions have tended to see these as discrete problems, addressable at the level of distinct policy fields, including urban planning, architectural design, and physical infrastructure. Many of us have been labouring under the assumption that improving the built environment is sufficient to drive positive change.

But the fast evolution of our cities is driven by global, co-dependent complex systems, from "hot global money" and disruptive technological advances to climate change and its impact on migration streams. Such systems and trends are often not amenable to traditional methods of analysis and manipulation. Our shared public institutions, still rooted in industrial age paradigms of central control and discrete top-down hierarchies, are repeatedly proven inadequate. They move too slowly and their power is too dispersed, and they cannot affect the entire system with sufficient agility to address the scale of the challenges at hand—"wicked" challenges like poverty, social exclusion, inequality in health outcomes, ageing, and environmental degradation.

Architecture and urban design, the disciplines traditionally responsible for delivering city-level change, are not coping well with these challenges. It is becoming increasingly evident that current models of developer-led urban production seldom result in positive place-based change—and that when they do, this happens in spite of the forces driving the market and not because of them.

More particularly, architectural fees, due largely to the legacy of the profession's history of patronage, have to date been associated with the capital costs of the commission, varied to a degree to account for programmatic complexity. In essence, the capital costs act as a viable proxy for the scale and complexity of construction, and therefore for the architects' contribution. In addition, contractual obligations make architects primarily answerable to their paymasters, though in many countries professional bodies and standards have always upheld architects'

obligations towards site safety and long-term soundness of construction—a more limited but nevertheless powerful version of the Hippocratic oath sworn by medical professionals.

The limits of this model of contracting are well-known: it discourages thinking beyond the site boundary, whether physically or socially, environmentally or economically; it encourages short-term profit-led strategies, potentially compromising professional ethics; it constrains the potential for building the collective knowledge of the profession, with postoccupancy data collection and evaluation seen as an unnecessary burden if not an outright liability; design becomes an instrument of seduction, and designers the celebrated creators of cultural accoutrements glamourised in global media. Taken in aggregate, these limitations have systematically distorted the accountability of the profession of architecture as a public good.

In this current model, developer profits are increasingly the engine that shapes most of our built environment, taking precedence over the goals of other stakeholders: architects become instrumentalised service providers; municipalities defer to developers' viability projections; users get cookie-cutter spaces to live, work, and play in, designed as financial assets with often the lowest common denominator provisions despite their glitzy looks; and the wider community is treated as an irrelevance or annoyance, if necessary to be appeased with token consultations.

These effects are the result of the existing financial, legal, and regulatory frameworks on top of which the urban disciplines operate, and are encapsulated in architects' services agreements and building contracts. It should be more surprising that we still have so many good buildings and masterplans than that the impact of most urban interventions is so poor. Where we see success, it is more a testament to the professional and human ethics of individual architects and clients than due to the way the legal cards are stacked. The nature of the environments we build is perhaps most fundamentally defined by the nature of the contracts we employ. To paraphrase Louis Sullivan, *form follows contract*.

An alternative vision for outcome-driven city hange

Let us then imagine an alternative model, one that begins with long-term, shared outcomes, impacting the full complexity of issues we face in fostering people's well-being and flourishing, from improving educational attainment to enhancing creativity and productivity, and from addressing older-age loneliness to the growing obesity crisis. The building procurement process would then have to be framed around the creation of common value, both in its incentive structures and in the capacity of its delivery agents. It should target issues emerging within communities, and it should be measured against its ability to effect positive change.

Let us be clear: this is not about rolling back the role of private developers and investors—cities need their money, their dynamism, and their wits. And in fact, looking beyond the boundary of a building site may enable them to benefit from investing in such outcomes. The point is that this could happen if built environment contracts would enable them to do so. The growing world of impact investment shows that where we create clear pathways for connecting

investment with positive outcomes, finance does indeed follow. So we are now proposing a grand transition. From a preoccupation with the organisation and measurement of the bricks and mortar that form walls and roofs, architects have progressed to valuing and understanding the production of space as the key focus of their profession. The next transition is to an architecture for outcomes, a practice that recognises what we all intuitively know and what is increasingly backed up by solid evidence: masterplanning and building are tools for nudging behavioural patterns, creating opportunities, and encouraging positive change.

Outside the world of architecture and urbanism, this transition has already begun. We are witnessing the emergence of outcome-based financing in public service procurement, social network tuning, "Hippocratic" oaths for MBA graduates, design studios for entrepreneurs, data science for predictive models and prescriptive action guidelines, behavioural economics in the field of policy intervention, and co-design and co-production processes to unleash the collective intelligence and engagement of stakeholders. These advances have so far eluded the building professions, hobbled as they are by their current business plans and operating assumptions. These changes in other professions will eventually reconfigure our towns and cities, and they *could* drive change in the professions of architecture and urban design. So how can architects and urban designers be part of, if not *lead,* this shift and avoid letting their role be marginalised even further? This necessitates a paradigm shift in which the social utility of architecture becomes quantifiable, comprehensible, comparable, and communicable, providing a new viable lens for understanding value through all levels of the system, including banking, public services, and architecture. This presents an opportunity for the architectural profession to take a moment for critical reflection, to consider its position and responsibility for the twenty-first century, and to address the excitement of complex problems head-on—not something architects have shied away from in other aspects of their work.

Through that lens, architects, as part of their contractual responsibility (to clients who themselves would be incentivised to focus on long-term public value), would be focused on delivering and curating the *outcomes* enabled by the built environment. For example, workspace design contracts would build in performance criteria for enhancing innovative thinking, encouraging creativity and empathy, improving staff retention rates, reducing sick leave, and ensuring the integrity of business decisions. Through a thoughtfully considered contract, architects would take responsibility for building the multi-layered environments to produce or accelerate these strategic outcomes. Accordingly, architects' fees would be connected to advancing these strategic outcomes and creating system-wide value, as opposed to being remunerated for organising the commodity of building materials. Clearly, the architect's responsibility would not end when the building is completed—ongoing postoccupancy evaluation becomes a crucial tool to assess impact, manage risk, and gain insights.

Opportune advances in institutional infrastructure

It may sound like a pipe dream, but this is becoming an increasingly plausible vision. We live in a moment of great opportunity that could allow this radical reinvention of the architectural contract and thereby the profession's business model, fundamentally reconnecting it to the public good. It is worth digging deeper into the trends that will enable this to happen, in particular the convergence of recent advances in six areas: financing, design, computation and data, policy, regulation, and governance.

Financing

In the realm of the financing common good, we have seen the emergence of impact-driven instruments, like social impact bonds, which predicate repayment to investors on the basis of the project achieving results. Their targets, such as reducing recidivism, strengthening early learning, and improving youth employment, are all connected to the public purse as well as directly impacting human lives. These instruments have given us the conceptual and systematic framework to understand costs and risks associated with social and environmental degradation but also have enabled the creation of mechanisms to naturally hedge against those future risks. They have given viability to investing in the preventative economy, driving outcomes that reduce future social liabilities. When preventative investment structures are combined with the recognition that the "wicked" challenges we face cannot be addressed in isolation or by selecting single points of intervention, then we can start to imagine a typology of instruments for funding multi-actor movements for change.

So far, impact investing has been mostly contained to a relatively niche part of the financing market which adds in social impact as a small, "nice-to-have" part of a standard decision making framework. However, we could easily imagine a new class of derivatives, *impact derivatives*, that are designed to fuel collaborative

Outcome-driven design and development
• Integrated design and planning model for place-making and infrastructure
• Dynamic cycles for design-based mass public engagement
• Design impact assessment of distributed infrastructure on precincts
• Emerging models of affordable housing (co-living, inter-generational, modular, prefabricated, self-build)
• 4D BIM showcase (from Building Information Modelling to Precinct Information Modelling)
• Continuous human capacity building via visionary learning and training strategies
• Open knowledge exchange platform

New financial instruments for system change
• Smart contracting and procurement
• Impact investment that rewards outcomes to reduce future social liabilities
• Risk and reward through intelligent value capture models
• Real time simulation for risk-based investment profiling

Shifting from control regulation to feedback-driven regulation
• Citizens and users at the centre of regulating city development
• Distributed digital-driven regulation
• Protocols for data validation and certification of trusted data sources
• "Hippocratic" oath for partners engaged in urban change

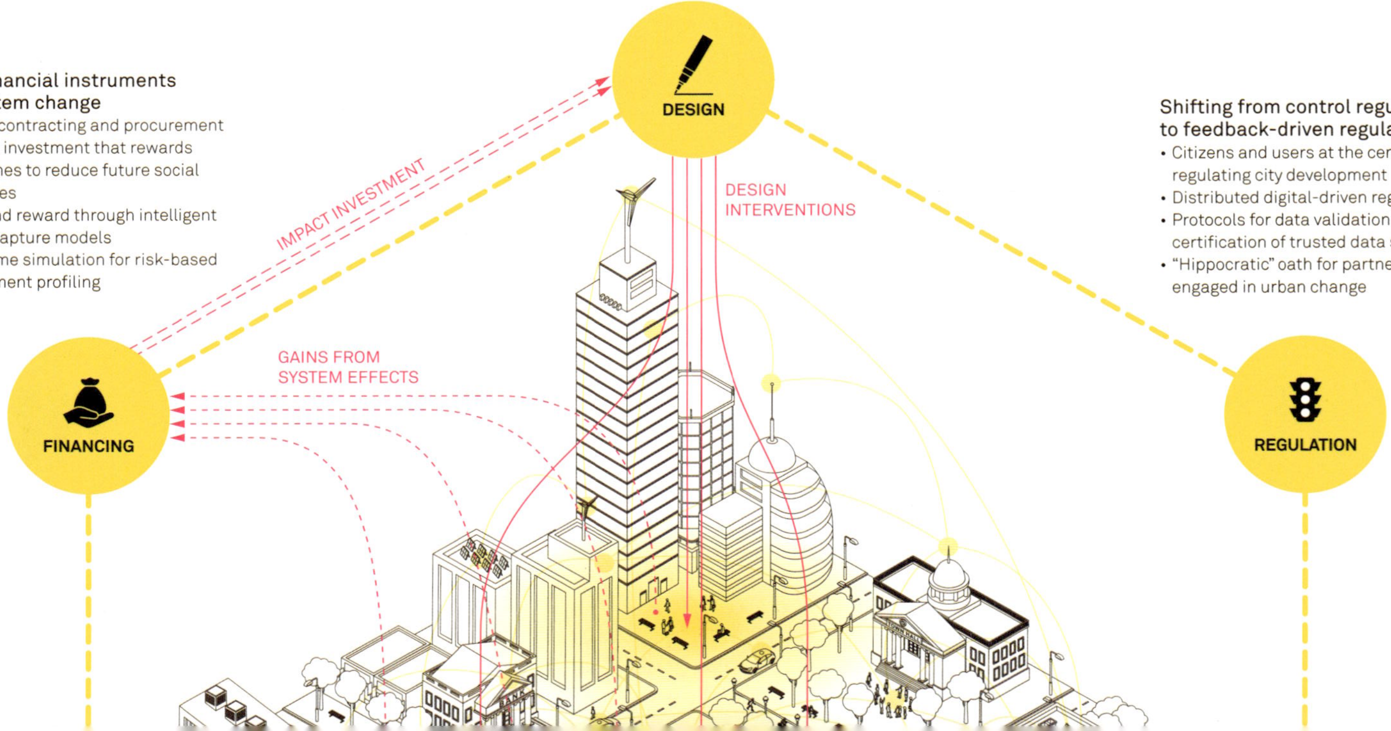

DESIGN
FINANCING
REGULATION
IMPACT INVESTMENT
DESIGN INTERVENTIONS
GAINS FROM SYSTEM EFFECTS

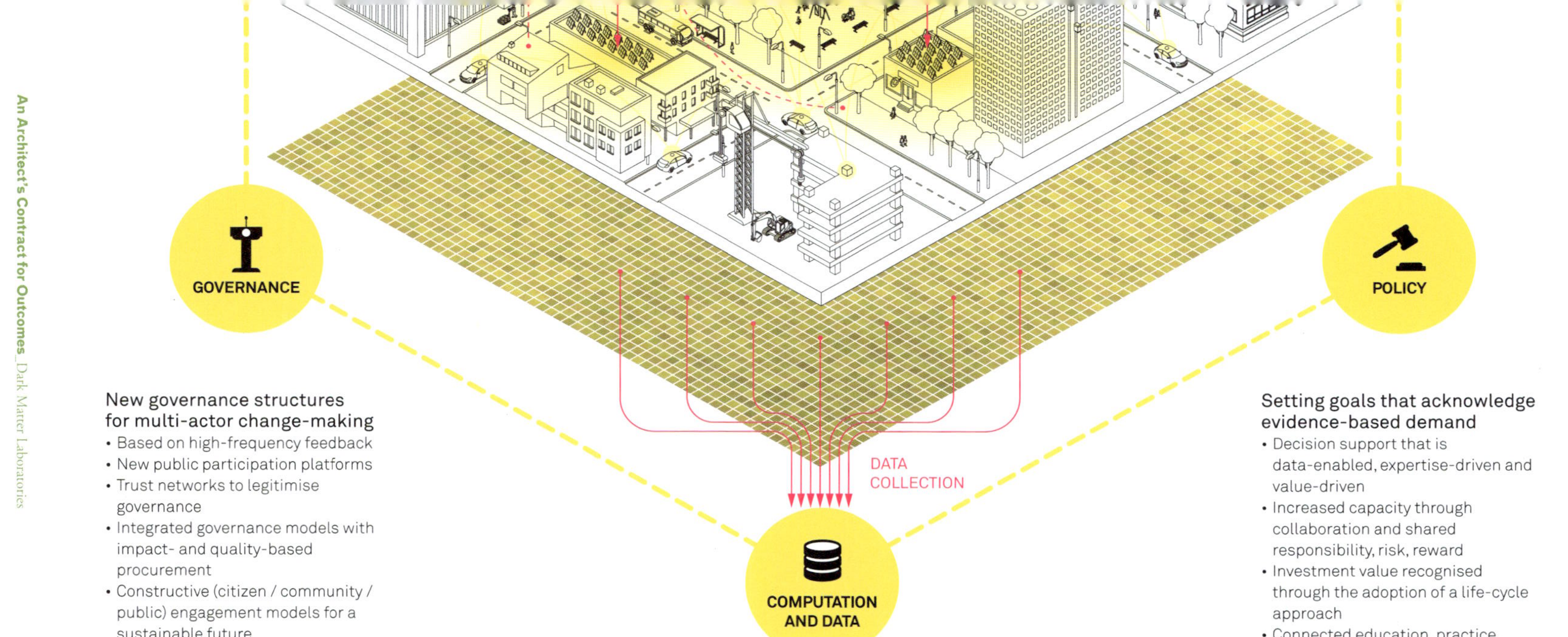

New governance structures for multi-actor change-making

- Based on high-frequency feedback
- New public participation platforms
- Trust networks to legitimise governance
- Integrated governance models with impact- and quality-based procurement
- Constructive (citizen / community / public) engagement models for a sustainable future
- Transparent and open administration protocols

Setting goals that acknowledge evidence-based demand

- Decision support that is data-enabled, expertise-driven and value-driven
- Increased capacity through collaboration and shared responsibility, risk, reward
- Investment value recognised through the adoption of a life-cycle approach
- Connected education, practice, research, and innovation with high industry impact

Datascape providing evidence base for policy and outcome evalution

- Real-time data collection through new sensor technologies
- Big, open, and rich data initiatives
- Open APIs to encourage broad use of current information
- Continuous improvement of data quality and integrity
- Use of data science and AI techniques to develop shared predictive models

The confluence of advances in financing, design, computation and data, policy, regulation, and governance allow us to imagine a future architecture for outcomes.

projects for common benefit instead of merely dealing with the management and diversification of risk. This is financing focused on system change—a synthesis of direct, oblique, and outcome-based returns, fusing traditional finance tools like equity, debt, and grants with outcome delivery contracts. Impact derivatives could account for the second-order value creation in the system and unlock access to cashflows associated with market failures that all too often are ignored in our current thinking.

Design

Supporting the urban design process towards positive city outcomes requires new tools as well as the repurposing of existing ones. For example, advanced computational design tools, such as parametric design and evolutionary algorithms, that are already widely employed to generate novel sculptural forms can attain their full potential when used instead to optimise for building performance against social outcomes. We can move from Building Information Modelling (BIM) to Precinct Information Modelling. Geographic Information Systems (GIS) can integrate multi-layered city-wide knowledge, enabling design impact assessment of system-scale distributed infrastructure. A great example is Flux (flux.io), a tool that allows visualising and designing directly to site conditions like building regulation constraints, view corridors, and planning restrictions, all built on a collaborative design platform.

We are also seeing progress in design away from professionals' desks. Social architectural practices have pushed forward with innovative methods for ongoing mass public engagement in the design of our cities that go beyond one-off appeasement exercises. And the area of affordable housing has seen the invention of new approaches, including co-housing, intergenerational accommodation, modular, prefabricated, and self-built houses. These advances are enabling highly responsive design processes, focused on outcomes, at scales previously unimaginable.

Computation and data

Blockchain (technology that allows decentralised secure transactions through a shared ledger) and smart contracts (executable automatically through digital platforms) are harnessing the effects of Moore's law and the ubiquity of cloud computing to permit secure transactions and the execution of legal agreements between thousands of parties and at incredibly high frequencies. With contracts for city-wide outcomes, these digital protocols can dynamically accommodate the thousands of stakeholders vested in the process, not just the few who can fit in a boardroom.

Technological advances in data collection and analysis are critical to build the assessment and evidence apparatus for this vision of the future. New types of sensors open up the potential for real-time measurement behaviours and system flows. Open data initiatives are creating protocols for sharing up-to-date information between collaborating parties. Rapid progress in the field of data science has produced new machine learning techniques that could help develop shared predictive models to unlock preventative interventions. The real-time feedback mechanisms based on these technologies can inform behaviours of enlightened self-interest in the private sector and responsive policies to benefit the public sector.

Policy

As the scope for sustainable, forward-looking innovation extends past the boundaries of corporate entities and persists beyond the re-election cycles of city officials, the city itself emerges as the new persistent social structure, defined by the the culture and missions of its institutions and its residents. City policy and strategy should therefore encompass all interrelated actors, and act on the timeline of the city itself. It is thus buoying to see the increasing interest in decoupling policy making from short-term dependencies and in couching policy in evidence-based demand, driven by data, expertise, and the creation of shared value in ways that create new types of public accountability. Adopting an assessment approach that acknowledges value generation throughout the life cycle of the built environment enables this longer-term view and the recognition of the effects of impact investment. In parallel, collaborative approaches with shared responsibility, risks, and rewards, help increase the capacity of policy making institutions, supporting the increased scope demanded for system-wide change.

Regulation

New protocols of validating and certifying trusted data sources are driving a shift from centralised control regulation to distributed and responsive feedback-driven regulation. This has so far been motivated by the potential efficiency gains in the planning process, but they also show the promise of putting citizens and users back at the centre of regulating city development. Supported by a "Hippocratic" oath for all partners engaging in urban change, a distributed system can connect citizen-led initiatives with city-wide strategy and accelerate development geared towards the public good.

Governance

At the heart of this version of the future is the idea of strengthening citizen agency— engendering a democracy of action and not only of representation. It is about creating the institutional infrastructure through which citizens, for-profit businesses, and the public sector can collaborate for outcomes that benefit all stakeholders as much as their local communities in aggregate.

As we observe the diminished capacity of the traditional democratic apparatus to respond in agile ways to our current challenges, we also see the beginnings of new models for bolstering citizen agency and harnessing energy at the grassroots level. These new public participation platforms rely on constructive engagement methodologies, trust networks, and radically transparent administration to legitimise the leadership and contributions of all actors. Multiplying and scaling up these early prototypes could lead to a transformation of city governance for multi-actor change-making informed by broadly sourced high-frequency feedback, unleashing and democratising the power to co-create society.

Prototyping a new architect's contract for outcomes

It may seem daunting to imagine a future that depends on ongoing innovations across all six of these areas achieving critical mass. But the time is right to start prototyping one of the key components of this future: an *architect's contract for outcomes* that brings together the necessary ingredients of legitimacy, accountability, finance, regulation, design, and evaluation. Unless we imagine, debate, and test it now, it will not exist when the future knocks on architects' doors.

This new contract must be designed around two core principles: first, it must effectively include city-wide objectives arrived at through democratic means and openly define the metrics of success; second, it must enable the accommodation of a large number of potential stakeholders and beneficiaries, reflecting that all of them need to be involved in future governance. The prototype contract should be informed by precedents of contracts that are already in use, including various flavours of Performance Based Contracting (PBC) that are typically used in the defence sector, as well as multi-party contracts such as the alliance contracts gaining popularity for large-scale construction projects.

Defining and assessing outcomes
Put simply, the function of a contract is to provide a structure of mutual reliance between participants. Contracts operate by engineering incentive structures that are sufficiently aligned to allow parties to proceed with the confidence that a successful conclusion to the agreement benefits all, while a breach will result in costly ramifications to the offending party.

It would be tempting to argue that when the objective of the contract is to implement positive change at the city scale, all parties are thereby automatically incentivised. But to act as a rigorous mechanism for accountability, the contract must also clearly define the desired outcomes, linking incentive mechanisms directly to them. Such contracts could be drafted for any existing Key Performance Indicator (KPI) that can be tracked at the right spatial scale and temporal frequency, but also for any aspect of urban activity that can be measured by emerging data collection methodologies. We could therefore envisage contracts written for:

• green spaces that enhance activity levels, resulting in less obesity and an increase in fitness,
• school facilities to drive an increase in educational attainment or accelerate innovation,
• civic halls that increase civic engagement and administrative transparency,
• workspaces that lead to an increase in productivity and work satisfaction,
• residential neighbourhoods that foster social networks, and neighbourhood satisfaction, and decrease crime rates,
• transport infrastructure that reduces pollution while shortening journey duration,
• hotels that increase city revenue from tourism,
• industrial facilities that increase recycling rates and reduce CO_2 emissions.

It follows that the necessity for measurement of the metrics of success must be stipulated in the contract, making long-term post-occupancy data collection a requirement for all newly procured buildings. In the absence of direct measures of success or unambiguous causal relations (which will often be the case), peer-validated data science techniques could be used to generate viable proxies. The methodology for the measurements and target values should also be debated by all parties and seen as a desirable part of the contract negotiation process, ensuring broad trust in the terms of the agreement.

It also becomes clear that to allow enthusiastic adoption of this potentially risky new type of contract, incentives cannot be binary, with full payouts only if ambitious targets are fully attained. The agreements should therefore include payout matrices or proportional formulas that acknowledge and incentivise the difficulties in pursuing projects of worthwhile ambition.

Finally, the agreements need to include provisions that outline the processes of review, enforcement, and dispute resolution, with an emphasis on serving the delivery of the target outcomes rather than on penalising or compensating individual parties.

Accommodating multiple parties

Successful outcomes are not only contingent on a successful conclusion to the construction process, but also on effective operation and responsible use of the building in the long term. This implicates not only all building and construction professionals, but also the financial and legal professionals around them, the commissioners, the planners, the local authority, the building users and guests, the service providers tasked with the building's maintenance and operation, and even the neighbours. The resulting problem of tracking the accountability of the huge number of parties responsible for a building's performance during its occupation is clearly not trivial.

Computable smart contracts could offer a solution. These are digitally encoded contracts that can be entered into by filling an online form and executed without legal oversight, for example by authorising payments on the condition of specific metric thresholds having been achieved. Automating the process of entering into and completing an agreement is a necessary step towards prototyping the contractual collaboration of thousands of parties. While smart contracts are a relatively new technology, progress has been rapid, with Monax (monax.io) and R3 (r3cev.com) leading in their commercial implementation.

Additionally, the possibility of contracts that mature at periods in the order of magnitude of building lifetimes suggests that a flexible approach would be needed. In this we can look to alliance contracts, which have been used with success in recent years to deliver large collaborative projects, particularly in construction and the IT industry. The benefit of the alliance approach is that it can be used to address a specific problem without specifying a priori what the solution looks like. As such, it creates the space for stakeholders to innovate cooperatively towards a shared mission even in the face of changing and unpredictable conditions, in a spirit of shared accountability and liability. This flexible approach motivates parties towards a reduction in costs and project duration, which are otherwise not specified in a fixed way.

Implications for the professions

A rigorous application of this type of contract will by necessity have significant implications on the building professions. It would signify a need to reframe the standard schedule of works to encompass user behaviours and building performance data. Our architectural codes of conduct would become irrelevant unless they change to reflect architects' renewed responsibility towards outcomes. The planning and regulation frameworks would need to be rebuilt around citizen-driven collaboration and outcome delivery. Our insurance infrastructure would have to keep pace with system accountability. Fundamentally, the nature of architectural and urban practice and the capabilities demanded of these disciplines would need to change, resulting in a rethinking of the curricula of our schools of architecture.

The following are seven institutional infrastructure propositions for the profession, stemming from the potential impact of this new architect's contract for outcomes.

1. Introduction of a "Hippocratic" oath for architects, with ensuing liabilities in reference to the long-term social and environmental performance of the built environment they design.

2. Shift the business model of architecture from its current base as a percentage of the cost of construction towards being priced on the basis of outcome performance.

3. Reimagine the process of building to unleash the collective knowledge, intelligence, innovation, and engagement of all stakeholders, including building users and other citizens.

4. Develop a new field of evidence and hypothesis-driven urbanism by establishing new public procurement requirements on the demand side and by investing in an open-source evidence base on the supply side.

5. Establish a data commons for all registered architects and their design data and knowledge, based on the typology and licensing agreements of open-source code repositories like GitHub, and powered by a viable open-source file standard for design data with versioning and forking control.

6. Refocus the performance metrics of architecture and the built environment on their social and environmental outcomes.

7. Seed a new generation of architecture schools as advanced polytechnics built around a live project framework and delivering a curriculum focused on a systems approach to place-making, including data-driven design, behavioural economics, social physics of place, econometrics, politics of change, impact analysis, and ethnography.

This is a transition that places architecture on the verge of unleashing a data-driven future—an architecture which can quantitatively justify its impact and thereby assert its capacity to take on our biggest challenges. It is a micro-massive architecture of many small-scale interventions powering massive effect, driving a fundamentally different economy of design, predicated on the awareness that investment in design can be leveraged to produce 800 times its value in human outcomes. This is an architecture that moves beyond the seductive image and towards making sustainable long-term contributions to human progress.

Implications for the city and its citizens

What effect can we expect adoption of this new contract to have on the design of our cities? The hope is that we can put human experience back at the heart of future urban development.

The demand for this realignment is readily evident in South Korea. After the end of the Japanese occupation and the subsequent Korean War, South Korea experienced a period of rapid economic growth. This "miracle on the Han River" saw the country transform from one of the poorest countries in the world to a member of the G20 within sixty years. This tremendous expansion—still ongoing—caused a process of accelerated urbanisation, resulting in the forward-looking and sprawling metropolis that is Seoul, but with a prevalent feeling that the advancing economy left quite a number of people behind.

This is an experience that is shared by other cities that underwent rapid spurts of development, leading to the sense that dynamic cities can be dehumanising environments beyond the control of their residents. Still, in recent years

there have been examples of enterprising citizens
who managed to shape their cities for common
benefit in spite of unyielding institutions.

In Portland, Oregon, seventy-five volunteers
removed the pavement from the parking lot of
the Escuela Viva Community School, turning
10,000 square feet of concrete into a planted
playground (depave.org/escuela-viva/). This is
only one of many such interventions facilitated
by the Depave organisation in Oregon.

In the wake of Superstorm Sandy hitting
New York in 2012, members of the Occupy
movement swiftly refocused their activism and
became a disaster relief organisation, providing
early assistance to victims. Occupy Sandy
(occupysandy.net) was able to respond with
greater agility than the state, offering aid and
organising collaborative rebuilding efforts.

In North London, a group of women over fifty
have just built a co-housing community inspired
by another Dutch example. Older Women's Co-
Housing (owch.org.uk) managed to overcome
significant institutional obstacles, forging a path
for other such shared housing projects to follow.

These are certainly remarkable and exceptional
projects—and that is the problem. We cannot
rely on black swans to address the issues we face
in cities around the world. By establishing a new
architectural contract for outcomes and building
the congruent institutional infrastructure around
it, projects like these would get the systemic
support they require to become the default
method for improving our cities.

Seoul: Genealogy of a Logistical Ecosystem

Clare Lyster

Introduction

There is increasing discussion in the design fields about how logistical systems are re-shaping lifestyles and cities. I'm defining logistics here as a specific set of time-space networks that combine emerging technologies (from algorithmic supply chain inventories to apps to high speed fiber) with post-Fordist production and consumption practices. Controlled (for good or bad) by popular, neo-liberal corporate actors from *Amazon* to *FedEx*, from *Facebook* to *Grub Hub* and from *Instagram* to *Uber*, to name but a few, these communication systems increasingly manage the accelerated provision of information, services, food and goods across the world each day, and by extension are altering how and where people work and live.

If the Swiss historian and theorist, Sigfried Gideon charted the evolution and subsequent impact of mechanization on everyday life [1] and the architectural critic, Reyner Banham explored the spatial impact of automation;[2] then today we must concern ourselves with a third phase of industrial production, that being logisticalization, and how its transforming the built environment, particularly the city. Logistics are increasingly embedding themselves into the fabric of our cities as well as our culture. Many of us shop via Amazon.com as well as a wide range of other online retailers (from Target to Apple) in the U.S. and have products delivered directly to our home, sometimes within hours of ordering;[3] Courtesy of apps, we can have food cooked by willing chefs, to match our culinary desires and, in a whim, have it delivered to our table; We can stream movies and games from media networks via high

1. Sigfried Giedion, *Mechanization Takes Command: A Contribution to Anonymous History* (1948; repr., New York: W. W. Norton & Company, 1969).

2. Reyner Banham, "A Home Is Not a House," *Art in America* 2 (1965).

3. For more information on the most popular e-retailers, see "Most Popular Retail Websites in the United States as of September 2015, Ranked by Visitors (in Millions)," Statista, www.statista.com/statistics/271450/monthlyunique-visitors-to-us-retailwebsites/ (accessed 9 February 2016).

speed fiber; We can send a document around the world via priority shipping within 48 hours and track every moment in its trajectory; We upload millions of videos and images in servers in large data centers so that others can download them in micro-seconds, and we can video-chat a friend in real-time despite being 5,000 miles apart. We can arrange for a driver to pick us up; meet up with a stranger; share a car; live in someone else's apartment; rent books and borrow bikes. The almost simultaneous delivery of a plethora of services and experiences to fulfill every desire and need we might have, produces a new form of urbanity, here characterized as the logistical city.

While synonymous with excessive consumption and neoliberal ideology in the west, nonetheless the logistical city, as a concept exists everywhere, even as small pockets in less affluent regions. The agency of mobile technologies and smarter governance protocols in large African cities without reliable municipal infrastructure is evidence of this[4], as is the increasing presence of medical drones and micro-financing in rural and underserved regions.[5] Even, sociologist Manuel Castells highlights that urban areas, or parts

thereof, outside the list of elite world-cities, can be participants in the "space of flows", for example, he cites La Paz, Boliva, as having a role in global financial networks.[6] Suffice to say that since the 1970s, logistical technologies have become persistent in their reach to format territory across the world.[7]

In tandem with the territorial smoothing made possible by logistics, there are sites that stand out as archetypes of logistical urbanism, each having their own unique identity:

Special Economic Zones (SEZs) are uniquely created logistical districts for packing, assembly, processing and research that lie adjacent many manufacturing zones and container ports in cities all over the world from Panama to Shenzen. Derivative of international production protocols, tax incentives and real estate formulas, these apolitical enclaves, emerge as either new ground up urban areas or are formed within existing urban contexts. Operating as mini cities, with their own rules and regulations outside of the nation state in which they find themselves, they nimbly foster trade flows and attract investment.[8]

4. Joe K. Mensah, Country General Manager, IBM Ghana, "Cloud, Social, Big Data and Mobile Technology Reshapes One African City" (Sponsor Content), *The Atlantic*, 12 December 2013, http://www.theatlantic.com/sponsored/ibm-cloud/cloud-social-big-data-and-mobile-technologyreshapes-one-african-city/80/ (accessed 19 January 2017).

5. I cite Zipline and Kiva as logistical systems operating in less affluent and rural areas, for more information on this see Rohini Nambiar, "How Rwanda Is Using Drones to Save Millions of Lives," CNBC, 27 May 2016, http://www.cnbc.com/2016/05/27/how-rwanda-is-using-drones-to-save-millions-of-lives.html, and Jessi Hempel, "Peer-to-Peer Site Kiva Is Finally Offering No-Interest Microloans in the US," 9 December 2015, https://www.wired.com/2015/12/peer-to-peer-site-kiva-is-finally-offering-no-interest-microloans-in-the-us/ (accessed 21 January 2017).

6. Manuel Castells and Martin Ince, "Conversation 3: The Space of Flows," in *Conversations with Manuel Castells* (Cambridge: Polity Press, 2003), 55.

7. See the introduction of my book, *Learning From Logistics: How Networks Change Cities* (Birkhäuser, 2016) pp 1-14, for a brief history of the circumstances that fostered the rise of logistical networks and why the early 1970s emerged as a pivotal moment in the popularization of logistics in culture.

8. For more information see Keller Easterling, *Extrastatecraft: The Power of Infrastructure Space* (New York: Verso, 2014), and Deborah Cowen, *The Deadly Life of Logistics: Mapping Violence in Global Trade* (Minnesota: University of Minnesota Press, 2014).

Global capitals such as London and Paris that are the nexus of financial trade, are logistical cities because they are places where international markets and their affiliated services aggregate.[9]

Backstage cities like Memphis, Tennessee and Louisville, Kentucky in the U.S., which are home to sorting and storage facilities for large shipping networks (for example, Fed Ex and UPS respectively), highlight how logistics, in the form of freight flow is a catalyst for urban development.

Technopoles, from Silicon Valley to Tel Aviv, illustrate how IT economies combined with institutional research and venture capitalism articulate the logistical city as an entrepreneurial ecosystem.

Lastly, sites from The Pearl River Delta in S.E. China to Mumbai, exemplify how logistics, in this case, the procedures of transnational manufacturing and business, is responsible for the restructuring of existing and the emergence of new urban formats, in the case of the former, a regional city and, in the case of the latter, the mega-city.

Seoul: The Paradigmatic Logistical City

In this context of logistical paradigms, there exists an even more illustrative case of the logistical city; where logistics has a much more robust role in the daily routines of its inhabitants. Seoul, South Korea, one could argue is the world's paradigmatic logistical city because of the way that new technologies have not

9. SaskiaSassen, *Cities in a World Economy*, 1st ed. (Newbury Park, CA: Pine Forge Press, 1994), 1–8.

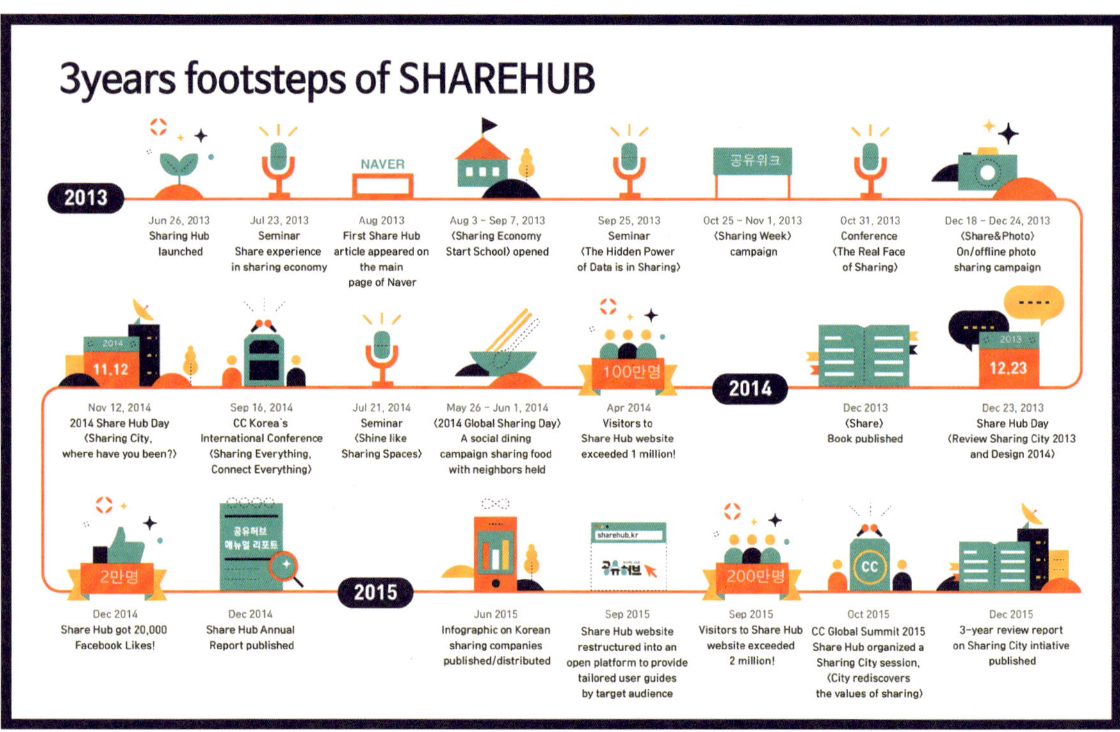

Sharing City Seoul: 3 years' Footsteps, infographic.

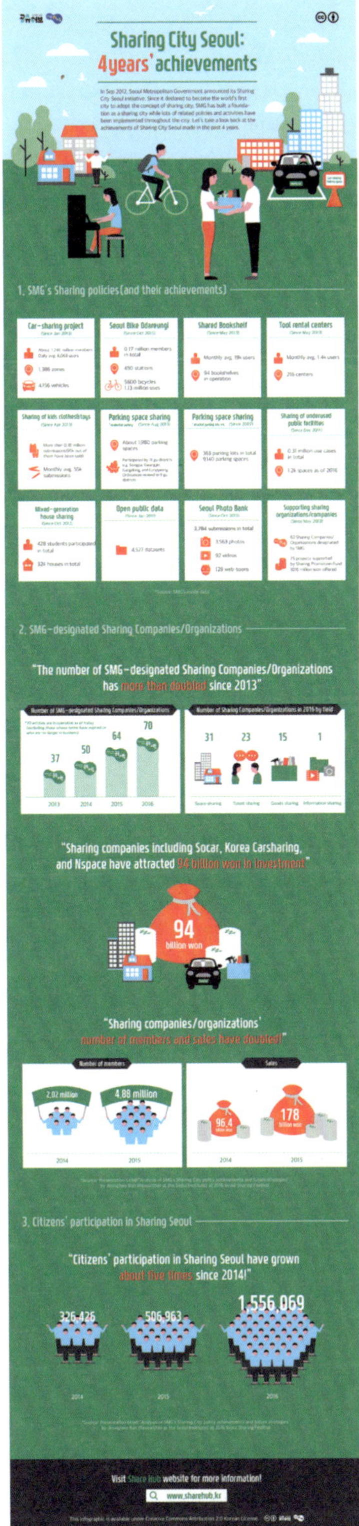

only infiltrated and accelerated international production and economic growth since the 1960s--in 1960, South Korea's GDP was that of a third world country but by 2016 it had a GDP of 1.4 billion, the 11th highest in the world,[10] but more significantly for this study, how logistical systems have infiltrated the "everyday" of the city's lifestyle and imaginary. A recent article in the *New York Times*, argues that Seoul is a rival to Silicon Valley[11] and Forbes describes it as "wealthy, wired and dense."

Shared Web: For one, the sharing economy, a phenomenon traditional in older communities but now capable of full optimization as a result of logistics, is well advanced, with citizens sharing everything from housing to parking, while second-hand mobile devices are passed on to the needy. The mayor of Seoul, Park Won-soon, relies on feedback from the public courtesy of Twitter and "Sharing City Seoul," an initiative in collaboration with the Seoul Metropolitan Government that began in 2012, with the mission to share urban resources. It has resulted in the allocation of tool libraries, lending libraries in apartment buildings, and shared gardens, and matches students with isolated seniors, for multi-generational domestic collectives. (South Korea has an aging population and one of the highest incidences of suicide. As many as forty people take their own lives each day in Korea.)[12]

10. https://knoema.com/nwnfkne/world-gdp-ranking-2016-data-and-charts-forecast, accessed January 28, 2017.

11. https://www.nytimes.com/2015/06/07/magazine/what-silicon-valley-can-learn-from-seoul.html?_r=0 and "Was 2016 the Worst for South Korea's Startups?," *Forbes*, 6 January 2017, https://www.forbes.com/sites/elaineramirez/2017/01/06/was-2016-the-worst-for-south-koreas-startups-survey-says-nope/#dc043544e701.

12. Duncan McLaren and Julian Agyeman, *Sharing Cities: A Case for Truly Smart and Sustainable Cities* (Cambridge, MA: MIT Press, 2015), 71–136. See also, Dieter K. Schneidewind, *Economic Miracle Market South Korea: A Blueprint for Economic Growth in Developing Nations*, (Singapore: Springer, 2016) pp 243.

Sharing City Seoul: 4 years' Achievements, infographic

All this is controlled through a centralized agency called *Sharehub*. Despite a very efficient public transport system, car sharing is on the rise courtesy of the city's two services Socar and Green Car, with the knowledge that for every shared car, there is a reduction of 125 vehicles on the road. A wave of startups, some of which have been financed by the initiative, include *se-Poomasi*, a bartering platform; Kiple, a children's clothing exchange, and Zipbob, a meal-sharing platform that allows you to connect with others and eat home-cooked food socially.[13] While Airbnb, Relayrides, Snapgoods, and Zip Car are still the predominant shared platforms available in many American cities, Seoul leads the way in deploying the sharing economy as a social web at many different scales.[14]

New Economies: Beyond sharing networks, both access to, and use of, e-commerce is relatively advanced in South Korea, particularly in Seoul. The city has seen a wide range of big and small startups come into operation over the last six to ten years. The number of American and international venture capitalist and investment firms sponsoring Korean startups attests to this. In 2012-13, South Korea's president Park Geun-hye pledged her support for a "startup ecosystem" that would provide an alternative economy to the *Chaebol* (large, hierarchical family-run corporations) and a more diverse employment sector in the aftermath of the 2008 crash. She promised "that anyone with good ideas would be able to get funding," a promise now being played out in the concentration of IT industries in the Gangham area of Seoul. Yello Mobile, a mobile platform company hailed as Asia's most exciting startup, is one of the success stories.[15] Building on this, Google opened its Campus Seoul in 2015, which can only be described as a school for startup entrepreneurs.[16] The *New York Times* proclaims, "American investors have begun to think of Seoul as a sort of crystal ball. In it, they can glimpse a future where the most ambitious dreams of Silicon Valley—a cashless, carless, everything-on-demand society—have already been realized."[17]

On Demand: This enthusiasm has served not only to cultivate the new ecosystem but to bolster online platforms that were already in operation. Ticket Monster (TMON), founded in 2010, is an entertainment, goods, travel, and lifestyle company partly owned by Groupon.[18] Coupang was also founded in 2010, by Bom Kim, a Korean native educated in the United States, and considered the Jeff Bezos of South Korea. Originally modelled on Groupon's "deal of the day," it has since moved to e-retail and specializes in rapid delivery of goods. It's the fastest-growing

13. http://www.shareable.net/blog/sharing-city-seoul-a-model-for-the-world and http://english.sharehub.kr.

14. http://www.economist.com/news/leaders/21573104-internet-everything-hire-rise-sharing-economy.

15. http://www.koreaobserver.com/yello-mobile-perhaps-asias-most-exciting-startup-story-in-2014-24332/.

16. https://www.techinasia.com/guide-to-south-korea-startup-scene.

17. "What Silicon Valley Can Learn from Seoul." https://www.nytimes.com/2015/06/07/magazine/what-silicon-valley-can-learn-from-seoul.html?_r=0 and http://www.forbes.com/sites/elaineramirez/2017/01/06/was-2016-the-worst-for-south-koreas-startups-survey-says-nope/#dc043544e701

18. http://www.wsj.com/articles/nhn-entertainment-invests-in-south-koreas-ticket-monster-1460282444

Coupang Rocket Delivery Men

e-retail company in South Korea, if not the world. Coupang focuses on expedited delivery (same day and sometimes same hour), courtesy of its 3,600 drivers known as Rocket men. This delivery force is the public face of the company and has somewhat of a reputation (all good) for kind service, an important quality, given that most of Coupang's customers are young mothers. (While there is not quite gender equality in South Korea, nonetheless women control household finances.) Even Amazon does not have its own last-mile integrated delivery infrastructure up and running yet (drones are still in the testing phase), and instead relies on offloading its delivery to other networks, from Uber to FedEx to the United States Post Office (USPS). Coupang's network currently comprises twenty-one warehouses in South Korea, including one at Incheon International Airport.[19] According to an article by *Forbes*, the success of Coupang is helped by a pre-established delivery culture in Seoul, where "people are accustomed to having couriers meet them at the subway station near their homes to deliver their dry cleaning and, occasionally, their dinner."[20] Coupang's own marketing claims, "Our vision is to create a world in which customers ask, 'How did I ever live without Coupang?'"

Polyvalent Platforms: Vying with Coupang for the top spot in online retail is Gmarket, which predates some of the newer companies, having been founded in 2000. Gmarket differs from the Coupang/Amazon model insofar as it's really just a virtual department store. It does not stock goods itself but links with different vendors to supply the customer, manage payments, and organize delivery, prices for which are sometimes set via auction. It also offers food (fruit, vegetables, and dry goods). It was purchased by eBay in 2009 for US$1.2 billion, and Yahoo has a 9% share.[21]

19. http://blogs.wsj.com/briefly/2015/06/03/5-things-to-know-about-south-koreas-coupang/.

20. http://www.forbes.com/sites/ryanmac/2016/04/13/coupang-south-korea-amazon-bom-kim/#68e7eac818c8.

21. http://newsok.com/article/2949535 and http://www.koreaittimes.com/story/50391/what-motivates-softbank-invest-coupang.

In 2011, the British retailer Tesco (called Tesco Homeplus in Korea) installed virtual shopping aisles in a total of twenty-two public spaces including bus and train stations, anticipating that busy lifestyles necessitated a new way for customers to shop. Using a smartphone and a QR code, customers could order food from a vertical interface akin to a digital mural comprising about 500 products.[22] By 2015 it had become the most popular retail app in Korea.[23] Homeplus became a model for similar experiments around the world: Peapod, the food delivery network based in Illinois, US, attempted similar pilot projects at train stations in Philadelphia and Chicago, and Tesco also ran the service at Gatwick Airport to enable people to fill their refrigerator on the way home from a business trip or vacation. Not only are these practices evidence of how goods are leaving the supermarket and coming into the city, but they exemplify how metabolic flows in the city are increasingly manifested as spatial platforms—the hybridization of virtual processes with physical artifacts and space. Baedal Minjok is a food delivery startup operated by the Woowa Brothers that began in 2010, and now has a library of 140,000 restaurants with 99% of orders placed through apps. The company is a host for

Baedal Minjok, Korean food app

Tesco Homeplus virtual storefront, Seoul, South Korea, 2011

22. http://www.businesstoday.in/magazine/lbs-case-study/case-study-tesco-virtually-created-new-market-based-on-country-lifestyle/story/214998.html and http://www.telegraph.co.uk/technology/mobile-phones/8601147/Tesco-builds-virtual-shops-for-Korean-commuters.html and http://tracks.lionel.com/going-virtual-the-worlds-first-virtual-store-was-in-the-subway/, accessed September 7, 2016.

23. https://www.theguardian.com/business/2012/aug/07/tesco-virtual-supermarket-gatwick-airport, , accessed September 4, 2016.

many small South Korean food outlets, each focusing on a particular Korean favorite, including fried chicken, which is a popular late-night snack.[24] Naver is the nation's top web portal with its own search engine that supports Naver Line (a text-messaging platform invented by Navar Japan) as well as Kakao Talk, a multifunctioning message service that is supposedly found on 93% of Korean phones, which also allows one to read news, chat with friends, order food, or play games.

Common to all these platforms is the sheer numbers of people who access many of them. Smartphone use is high and so it's no surprise that delivery apps are really popular in Seoul; for example, TMON claims 70% of its sales are via its phone app, 25 million people use the Coupang app, while Baedal Minjok processes four million orders a month. What we learn from Seoul is that urbanity is no longer a destination in the habitual sense; it is recast as a multilayered organism of exchange—a service platform that augments the needs and experiences of everyday routines.[25]

Genealogy of a Logistical Ecosystem
Seoul is an urban Petri dish for examining the proliferation of logistical platforms in the built environment, and by extension, how logistics emerge as a new paradigm for urbanism. Yet, every ecosystem has its own unique habitat, and within this context, it's worth speculating on the social, technical, and cultural circumstances over the past forty years that have steered Seoul toward this unique condition.

PPerfect Figures: Fifty million people live in South Korea. Ten million live in what constitutes the political boundary of Seoul (Seoul Special City), while an excess of 25 million live in the metropolitan area (Seoul Capital Area). That half the nation's population is tied to one city makes the greater Seoul area the third-largest urbanized area in the world (after Tokyo, with nearly 40 million, and Jakarta with 30 million, according to 2014 stats).[26] While rural migration is still expected to continue, since 2011 the city has actually been declining in population, however, owing to lower birth rates and young couples fleeing the expensive city to live in outlying areas. Thus, increases are minimal compared to those seen from circa 1955 to 1980, the height of the population boom. Still, estimates predict that by 2039 the SCA is expected to accommodate 31 million.

Other demographic statistics are also significant here. First, density in Seoul is high, at 27,000 per square mile. *New Geography,* an online platform, states that "Seoul is more than twice as dense as Tokyo-Yokohama, three times as dense as Paris and four times as dense as Los Angeles or Toronto, the densest urban regions in North America."(27) Secondly, the number of single-person households in Seoul has almost doubled between 1995 and 2010, with the total figure today being in the region of 4 million people. Many new services and goods have been developed for single-family households, from mini pack meals to mail delivery services such as that offered by CJ GLS, a logistics and shipping company that offers door-to-door delivery as well its Parcel Box service, located in

24. https://techcrunch.com/2014/11/27/baedal-minjok/ and https://techcrunch.com/2014/03/06/flare-up-over-food-delivery-fees-has-south-koreans-debating-uber-like-marketplaces/.

25. Despite the high use of the Internet, South Korea has also been accused of censoring material online. For more information on this, see http://www.economist.com/blogs/economist-explains/2014/02/

26. http://worldpopulationreview.com/world-cities/seoul-population/.

27. http://www.newgeography.com/content/002060-the-evolving-urban-form-seoul.

apartment buildings and in the Seoul subway.
(28) Lastly, it's important to note that 60% of the
population lives in apartments.

South Korea is small and dense, and such
thick proportions make the distribution of
communication infrastructure and services
efficient and plausible as well as a perfect base
condition for logistics to proliferate unhindered.
Furthermore, that half the nation's population
lives in the SCA suggests that the city of Seoul
contributes as much to the Korean identity as
the nation state. City and nation have merged
as one and the same territory: the nation is a
city and the city is a nation. From a conceptual
perspective, this means that South Korea can
be mentally imagined as a large national-urban
scape, capable of fast and easy connections.

Long Days: According to the OECD, South
Korean is the second-hardest working nation
in the world (after Mexico). Put it this way:
Koreans work four months a year more than
Germans.[29] On average, a typical South Korean
works 354 hours more than the 1,1770 hours per
year average for the thirty-four OECD member
countries.[30] Also of interest is that Korean women
work about 10 hours per week more than the
OECD average of 34.3 hours, while Korean men
average about 48.3 hours per week[31] In a 2015
article in *The Economist*, Eric Surdej, the first
non-Korean to join the upper management of
LG, the multinational conglomerate and popular

electronics company, wrote of fourteen-hour
workdays.[32] Not unlike other Asian countries,
long hours are ingrained in the Korean psyche,
and the time spent working seems to conflict with
contemporary sociological theory that professes
an overall reduction in labor hours in the post-
Fordist era—the estimated average workweek
in the United States in 1880 was sixty hours per
week; today, in Sweden, a six-hour workday is
becoming popular[33]. In Korea, it's no wonder that
companies are quick to capitalize on the limited
time employees have to shop, eat, and socialize.

Home Grown: What the proverbial "coal is to
Newcastle," electronics are to South Korea.
Samsung, one of the world's largest technology
companies, resides in Seoul. While the company
dates from 1938, it emerged as an electronics
producer in the late 1960s/early 1970s, producing
its first black-and-white TV in 1970, followed
by washing machines and refrigerators in 1974,
microwave ovens in 1979, and air conditioners in
1980. It was in the 1980s that Samsung began to
emerge as a leader in digital products, with its first
PC computer in 1983; a VHS machine in 1984;
and in 1991, it launched its most famous product
yet, the mobile handset. This was followed in
1995 by MPEG technology; in 1996, the world's
fastest CPU, and in 1999 the smartphone.[34]
LG (founded 1947),a multinational firm also
known internationally for consumer electronics,
especially TVs and plasma screens, is also a local
company, while Hyundi (founded 1967) is the

28. http://www.koreatimes.co.kr/www/news/biz/2013/10/330_131393.html.

29. http://www.koreaherald.com/view.php?ud=20151102001240.

30. https://economix.blogs.nytimes.com/2010/05/12/s-koreans-put-in-most-hours/?_r=1.

31. http://www.vagabondjourney.com/south-korean-work-hours-highest-in-oecd/.

32. http://www.economist.com/news/business/21679214-punishing-work-culture-
gradually-being-relaxed-loosening-their-ties.

33. http://fortune.com/2015/10/06/sweden-6-hour-work-day-what-u-s-can-learn.

34. http://www.samsung.com/us/aboutsamsung/corporateprofile/history06.html.

fourth-largest auto company in the world after GM, Volkswagen, and Toyota (inc. 33% of Kia). In December 2016, it unveiled its prototype for an autonomous car in a demo in Las Vegas; it hopes the vehicle will be commercially available by 2021. Given Korea's penchant for adopting new technologies ahead of the rest of the world, it would come as no surprise if Seoul was one of the first designated cities for autonomous driving. Seoul University has already deployed self-driving taxis—*Snuber*—on its campus.

These companies and others provide investments and infrastructure to spur digital innovation, and Seoul is a willing and able test-bed for a wide range of logistical research and design. Logistics is a home-spun enterprise in South Korea, and so it's no wonder American VCs are heavily investing in Korean research and startups. South Korea might also explain Castells' theory of "clustering" as a spur for technological innovation, a theory he deploys to explain why Nokia emerged in Finland and why the IT industry evolved in Silicon Valley.(35) In fact, many post-Fordist theorists acknowledge similar paradoxical dualisms. On the one hand, globalism cultivates homogeneity across the world, but in other instances, it foregrounds hyper-specificity (clustering), such as the intensification of certain production processes and research in specific areas. If this is true, one can only expect further aggregation of South Korea's digital ecosystem, given that its technological past presents a fertile habitat for further growth. For example, a second phase of the Korean Wave, since the mid 2000s, known as Hallyu 2.0 (K-Pop including fashion, music and gaming) is perfect evidence of how Korea is combining information technologies with local creative industries as a cultural export.[36]

Cultural Gizmos: The Samsung Galaxy, launched in 2009, is one of the world's most popular mobile phones. Its numerous offspring are akin to characters in a sci-fi graphic novel: the S, the Ace, the Fit, the Gio, the Mini, the S2, the R, the W, the Y, the XCover, the Stratosphere, and the Galaxy Nexus. Then came the Ace Plus, the Beam, the Pocket, the Stellar, the Reverb, the Rugby Pro, and the S4. Samsung's Galaxy S4 sold 80 million units in 2013, while the Samsung Galaxy E1100 is eighth in the list of best-selling phones, selling 150 million units in 2009.[37]

Then there is the phablet, sold by none other than Samsung, of which the Galaxy Note 7 was the go-to device, that is, until it began to explode (its battery was too big and prone to overheating, a problem now solved). The phablet, which is nothing more than an oversized phone, was chosen by 41% of phone users in South

35. Maunel Castells, *The Rise of Network Society*, 1st ed. (Hoboken, NJ: Wiley-Blackwell, 1998), 40–60.

36. http://www.economist.com/news/books-and-arts/21611039-how-really-uncool-country-became-tastemaker-asia-soap-sparkle-and-pop. For an excellent summary of the two phases of the Korean Wave, see Dal Yong Jin, "Hallyu 2.0: The New Korean Wave in the Creative Industry," available online at //quod.lib.umich.edu/i/iij/11645653.0002.102/--hallyu-20-the-new-korean-wave-in-the-creative-industry?rgn=main;view=fulltext, accessed 23 March 2017. Thanks to Patrick Finn for pointing me to the K-Wave phenomenon.

37.http://www.telegraph.co.uk/technology/2016/01/26/the-20-bestselling-mobile-phones-of-all-time/samsung-e1100/ and http://www.digitaltrends.com/android/history-of-samsungs-galaxy-phones-and-tablets/#ixzz4VORQk2gi.

Commuters using their mobile devices
on Line 5 of Seoul's subway system

Korea. Samsung has sold 10 million of them domestically.[38] No surprise, since over 70% of Koreans use mobile apps to purchase goods and services online. Samsung even has a museum dedicated to its phone archive in Gimu, South Korea, supporting the notion that the phone is not merely a technological device, but is a cultural icon. Akin to Banham's gizmo (or is it more like McLuhan's prosthetic?), the phone allows the urban subject the freedom to run his or her own life and to fulfill a plethora of desires. Instead of the American frontier, which was the context in Banham's essay, the city is the backdrop to this logistical gizmo—or is it that the smartphone has replaced its context and emerged as the de facto space of urbanity on its own? Unlike Banham's examples (from radio transistors to outboard engines), this gizmo cannot get by without infrastructure, but that's not a problem, as South Korea has that in abundance.[39]

Fibrous Web: South Korea has the most internet users per capita and the heaviest data usage of any other nation. Fiber cables even run in subway tunnels, allowing passengers high-speed internet while travelling. According to a 2015 feature by CNN, the government in South Korea is sinking $1.5 billion into upgrades to data infrastructure for a 5G network so that mobile communications can run as much as 1,000 times faster by the year 2020.[40]

"When I was in S.F., we called it the mobile capital of the world," he said. "But I was blown away because Korea is three or four years ahead." Back home, Kim said, people celebrate when a public park gets Wi-Fi. But in Seoul, even subway straphangers can stream movies on their phones, deep beneath the ground. "When I go back to the U.S., it feels like the Dark Ages," he said. "It's just not there yet." [41]

38. http://www.phonearena.com/news/Samsung-confirms-Korea-is-the-home-of-the-phablet-10-million-Notes-sold-since-launch_id51474.

39. Reyner Banham, "The Great Gizmo," in *Reyner Banham: Design by Choice*, ed. Penny Sparke (New York: Rizzoli, 1981), 108–114.

40. http://www.cnn.com/2014/01/22/tech/mobile/south-korea-5g/

41. "What Silicon Valley Can Learn from Seoul." https://www.nytimes.com/2015/06/07/magazine/what-silicon-valley-can-learn-from-seoul.html?_r=041.

Data compiled in 2015 by Akami Technologies (one of the world's largest cloud-computing platforms and Content Delivery Networks, based in Boston) reveals that the average internet speed in South Korea was 21.1 Mbps above the global average.[42] Furthermore, Akami highlights that 62.6% of internet connections in South Korea are at speeds higher than 15 Mbps (this compares with 31% in the US), while 80.5% of connections have an average speed faster than 10 Mbps (almost double the global average). According to OECD, 94% of Koreans have what is classified as a high-speed connection. Supposedly, the city of Cheongju, south of Seoul, has an average internet speed of 124.5 Mbps and one gigabit per second plans are available for just US$20. (This would allow you to download a two-hour movie in eight seconds.) No wonder the same article presents South Korea as the "most plugged-in place on the planet."[43]

At the same time, widespread internet use is not just a result of good infrastructure but also occurs because large-scale use of online platforms was encouraged in every aspect of society, from the beginning of the digital age. After switching from dial-up to broadband in 2005, the South Korean government subsidized low-income groups across the nation (not just in Seoul) to improve their access to infrastructure, and focused on teaching housewives to use the web.[44] Rob Atkinson, president of the Information Technology and Innovation Foundation (the internet policy think tank), argues that Koreans' fixation on education has also served to bolster internet literacy, thus incentivizing competition between providers in the commercial realm. (According to the National Center on Education and the Economy, Koreans spend 7.6% of GDP on education, which is the third highest among OECD countries after Denmark and Iceland; and parents are known to spend over 20% of their household income on schooling, including schools, tutors, and other aids.)[45] Internet speeds also explain why Korean apps and mobile platforms are often ahead of their European and American counterparts. An article in *The Economist* serves to remind us that Cyworld (1999), a social media platform in Korea, was operating years before Faceboo*k*.[46] Moreover, faster internet connections in Korea allow apps much more bandwidth than their western counterparts, enabling them to host multiple functions. They are thus conceived as polyvalent platforms rather than mono-functioning devices. For this reason, Korean apps don't transfer well beyond their own context. For example, when Band, a multi-operational South Korean mobile-messaging app, was exported to Silicon Valley in 2014, users found the number of functions too confusing to handle.[47]

42. https://www.fastmetrics.com/internet-connection-speed-by-country.php.

43. http://au.pcmag.com/networking/30145/feature/fastest-isps-2015-south-korea#) and https://www.fastmetrics.com/how-fast-is-fiber-optic-internet.php.

44. Heejin Lee and Bob O'Keefe, "The Growth of Broadband Internet Connections in South Korea: Contributing Factors,"https://domino.fov.unimb.si/proceedings. nsf/0/fa0fcb8fecb778fbc1256e9f0030a71f/$FILE/27_Lee.pdf.

45. http://ncee.org/what-we-do/center-on-international-education-benchmarking/ top-performing-countries/south-korea-overview/south-korea-system-and-school-organization/.

46. http://www.economist.com/blogs/economist-explains/2014/02/economist-explains-3.

47. "What Silicon Valley Can Learn from Seoul."

Hanjin cargo ship at the Port of Long Beach in
Long Beach, Calif., on September 15 2016

Flow Hub: Global shipping is often a measure of
a nation's position in the realm of logistics, since
the flow of materials is a critical component in
the logisticalization of space. Before its demise in
August 2016, Hanjin (1949–2016) was the world's
seventh-largest container shipping network,
operating ninety-eight container ships. Sadly,
now bankrupt, the company will be disbanded,
and the final delivery of goods currently on ships
around the world is still in dispute at the time of
writing this document. Nonetheless, for over sixty
years, Hanjin's blue container, emblazoned with
a white logo, was surely one of the most legible
symbols of global logistics. Much has been written
on the history and role of the shipping container
and its impact on globalization, a topic that needs
no revisiting here, except to say that Hanjin was
a significant player in the industry, with twelve
terminals worldwide (Seattle and Long Beach in
the US; Antwerp and Algeciras in Europe and the
Mediterranean region; Osaka, Tokyo, Vietnam,
and Kaohsiung (Taiwan) in Asia, as well as seven
locations in South Korea) that combined for
an annual handling of 10 million TEUs (Twenty
Foot Equivalent Unit, the industry name for
a container unit).

One of Hanjin's main terminals is located at
Busan International Port, South Korea's largest
facility, located on the southeastern coast of the
country. Busan, South Korea's second city and
located on the Naktong River, is dominated by
the port, which is currently sixth in the ranking
of global facilities and anticipates handling
up to 20 million TEUs by 2017. Like many
traditional port cities, such as Hamburg, Busan
commenced construction of a new, larger port
landscape (Busan New Port), 20 kilometers to
the west of the city, in 1997. The old facility
(North Port) is now undergoing redevelopment
with a high-end mixed-use program, a new
passenger ferry terminal, and the all essential
eco-friendly waterfront that, according to
brochures, allows "nature, culture and luxury to
coexist side by side."[48] Busan is a popular ferry
stop for cruises and is known for its giant fish
market. Planned in multiple phases, Busan's
New Port, which actually comprises four ports
and forty-two container berths, opened in 2006.
With its automated facilities, quay cranes with
large outreach that are capable of receiving
and handling both Super-Panamax and Post-
Panamax container ships, as well as unmanned

48. 2014_Busan%20New%20Port%20Distripark%20Brochure%28English%29.pdf.

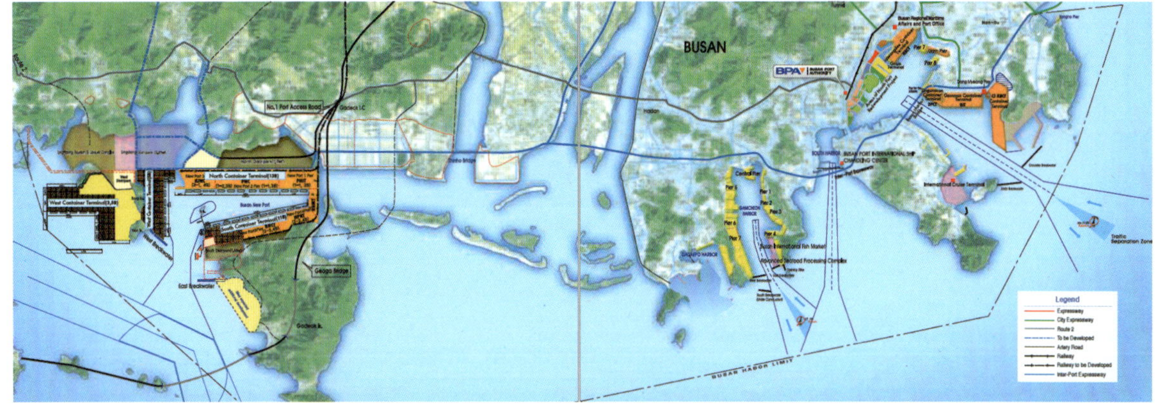

Busan Port Diagram

gate systems and a new Distripark (none other than a free-trade zone) for warehousing, assembly, and manufacturing, New Port is being marketed as the logistics hub of Northeast Asia.[49]

South Korea can also boast another global hub in Seoul Incheon International Airport, which was opened to great acclaim in 2001. Famous for being built offshore, the result of filling and reclaiming the space between two islands in the Yellow Sea, Incheon Airport has emerged as a fully fledged urban entity in and of itself. Apart from its world-renowned passenger facilities, which in 2015 catered to almost 41 million travelers, the airport also includes a golf course, an ice skating rink, nap rooms, and a medical center catering to the medical tourism trade. It is regularly acclaimed as one of the world's best terminals. While located 27 km west of Seoul, the airport is linked to the capital by AREX, a train line, and in February 2016, a 6 km Maglev train began a new service between the terminal and the AREX connection as well as to the southwest of the country, the first of a three-phase Maglev

loop linking Incheon to the mainland. Incheon is also home to the fifth-largest cargo airport in the world after Hong Kong, Shanghai, Memphis, and Anchorage. In 2015, the airport handled 2.6 million metric tonnes, but future expansion to the airfield including a dedicated runway for cargo will allow the airport to serve 7 million metric tonnes of cargo by 2020. In the airport's free trade zone, Fed Ex, the world's largest express transportation company, has announced it will upgrade its facilities with a new sorting facility in 2019 capable of processing up to 9,000 packages per hour.[50]

Seoul has its own plans for an airport city at Incheon. A series of plans for a resort with hotels, a casino, shopping, and entertainment facilities as well as expansion to the existing water park facilities are being considered in tandem with the expansion of the Maglev.[51] This is amplified via the Incheon Bridge, a 12 km infrastructure that in fifteen minutes links the airfield to another offshore urban landscape that is best described as the icing on the logistical cake.

49. http://www.ship-technology.com/projects/portofbusan/.

50. http://about.van.fedex.com/newsroom/asia-english/fedex-to-operate-at-new-cargo-terminal-at-incheon-international-airport/.

51. http://www.airport.kr/co/en/3/4/1/index.jsp.

Aerial of Incheon Airport

New Songdo is a 1,500 acre (2.34 sq. miles) ground-up city of the future being built by Kohn Penderson and Fox, an architecture firm from New York, to the tune of US\$40 billion, and is being pitched as the business center for the Incheon Free Trade Zone. It is currently 60% complete with 70,000 inhabitants, about a third of its expected population at full build out. At its inception, New Songdo was hailed by the *New York Times* as a "high tech utopia"[52], while *The Atlantic* characterized it as a space for a future that had not yet arrived.[53] Conceived as the ultimate smart city, New Songdo boasts on-demand videoconferencing, smart key cards, RFID technologies, censored infrastructure, shared data systems, and a garbage disposal system that sucks refuse into underground tubes (this conjures images of pneumatic tube networks found in many European cities at the turn of the twentieth century). Not unlike its corporate kin from Amazon to FedEx, New Songdo is a platform built on knowledge and information and other surveillance technologies; Cisco has even developed micro-chips in bracelets to track children. While it might be sustainable (well over 100 buildings are now LEED certified), it presents an uncomfortable reality—a glimpse of what happens when logistical abstraction and efficiency are pushed to the extreme.

End note

Hubs, gizmos, webs, and platforms are the new fundamentals of the city. It's no wonder that South Korea, in particular Seoul, has emerged as a paradigm of logisticalization and as a seedbed for a range of new online markets and information platforms that continue to advance how people live in the city. While some of these fundamentals are making a big impression on Seoul's urban ecosystem, others challenge the

52. http://www.nytimes.com/2005/10/05/technology/techspecial/koreas-hightech-utopia-where-everything-is-observed.html.

53. https://www.theatlantic.com/international/archive/2014/09/songdo-south-korea-the-city-of-the-future/380849/. See also http://www.worldfinance.com/inward-investment/could-songdo-be-the-worlds-smartest-city and John D. Kasadra and Greg Lindsay, *Aerotropolis: The Way We'll Live Next* (New York: Farrar, Straus and Giroux, 2012).

U-city Operation center

behavior of its base habitat. For example, food delivery networks are having a negative impact on the popular micro-restaurant economy that was already well established in Seoul, while the startup economy is having its own effect vis á vis gentrification in some neighborhoods. New Songdo claims a futuristic vision for urban life, but at the time of writing this essay, it has been described as a ghost town. No one wants to live there. Furthermore, that the leader of New Songdo's U-city planning (U is for "ubiquitous") is a former employee of Yahoo says a lot about the agency of the architect in the era of the logistical city. However, it's comforting to learn that the most popular feature is not the technology or the tracking but a 101-acre public landscape modelled on New York City's Central Park, a spatial typology from the mid-nineteenth-century industrial city. The lessons learned from Seoul are certainly mixed.

Despite this, Seoul is presented here as a productive prototype for the adaption of urban technologies into the fabric and lifestyle of a city. In tandem with our fascination, however, we must be careful not to either forget or fetishize the exclusions and abstractions of neoliberalism that many argue are responsible for the expansion of logistics in the first place. In an era of increasing urbanization, Seoul offers many clues about how logistics might be deployed to transform collective space through shared communities, new social spaces, and online platforms, as well as to remedy many urban problems, such as limited resources, loneliness, and an aging population. The question for Seoul (and other cities) is how to utilize logisticalization to improve the urban environment for all, not just to emulate a faster and more fulfilled one. To borrow and alter British architect Cedric Price's reflection on technology in a lecture from 1966, "Logistics is the answer, but what was the question?"[54]

54. Cedric Price, *Technology Is the Answer, But What Was the Question?*, audiobook, World Microfilms Publications Ltd. (December 1979).

Between Friction and Fulfillment

Jesse LeCavalier

"Fidget Spinners A Over," declares a June 2017 headline from the statistics website fivethirtyeight.com.[1] A fidget spinner is a palm-sized novelty toy consisting of weighted lobes that spin freely around a central bearing. Contrary to fivethirtyeight's assessment, Amazon's best-seller charts suggest that the toy's popularity far from "over," as versions of the device occupied eighteen of the top twenty spots on the company's "Hot New Releases" category for the same month.[2] The origins of the toy are contested—some versions credit a nervous tech industry worker looking to focus during long meetings, while other accounts point to a chemical engineer who was disturbed by the sight of children throwing rocks at Israeli police and set out to design something "as a way of promoting peace … something that was very calming."[3] The toys are touted, dubiously, to have relaxing properties and to help relieve anxiety. Even though there is no substantial evidence yet to support such claims, products sold on Amazon still use them in their titles. For example, one product's official name is "UFO SPINNER Fidget Spinner Toy Ultra Durable Stainless Steel Bearing High Speed 3-5 Min Spins Precision Metal Hand spinner EDC ADHD Focus Anxiety Stress Relief Boredom Killing Time Toys."[4]

One of the top-selling fidget spinner toys available on Amazon.com

1. Walt Hickey, "Fidget Spinners Are Over," fivethirtyeight.com, June 16, 2017 (https://fivethirtyeight.com/features/fidget-spinners-are-over/).

2. "Amazon Hot New Releases," Amazon.com, accessed June 25, 2017 (https://www.amazon.com/gp/new-releases/toys-and-games/ref=zg_bs_tab_t_bsnr).

3. Kenny Malone, "Fidget Spinner Emerges as Must-Have Toy of the Year," All Things Considered, npr.com, May 4, 2017 (http://www.npr.org/2017/05/04/526931943/fidget-spinner-emerges-as-must-have-toy-of-the-year). For more on the invention of the toy, see Jennifer Calfas, "Meet the Woman Who Invented Fidget Spinners, the Newest Toy Craze Sweeping America," *Time*, time.com, May 3, 2017 (http://time.com/money/4762207/fidget-spinner-inventor-catherine-hettinger/), and "Millions Sold: Was the Original Fidget Spinner Made in Suquamish?" *Seattle Times*, Seattletimes.com, May 17, 2017 (http://www.seattletimes.com/seattle-news/our-high-end-fidget-spinner-will-beat-the-competition-local-makers-say/).

4. Jennifer Calfas, "Do Fidget Spinners Really Help with ADHD? Nope, Experts Say," time.com, May 11, 2017 (http://time.com/money/4774133/fidget-spinners-adhd-anxiety-stress/).

The popularity of the device suggests that something is motivating its rapid spread, perhaps a reflection of an increase in collective anxiety as people desperately seek out sanctioned ways to relieve stress. The effortless action and comforting weight of the device has soothing properties, even if the scientific evidence is not conclusive. In fact, it is the humble ball bearing, the central assembly of rings and metallic spheres, that is the real hero of the fidget spinner's success and the element that allows them to function as they do. The bearing has contributed significantly to processes of industrialization and has been a key point of military and geopolitical strategy exactly because of its ability to reduce friction so that motion may occur more smoothly, more quickly, and for greater duration.[5] As fidget spinners, and their central bearing, find their way into the hands of millions, it is possible to see this success as a small triumph for the ball bearing as millions of individuals perform infinite aspirational gestures of friction reduction in their own lives. And, if the origin stories of the device are true, they are voluntarily enrolling themselves in a behavior modification program in the process. The fidget spinner as friction reducer, as self-medicating stress reliever, and as device of control and discipline, would not be out of place in the worlds of materials handling and logistics, concerned as they are with similar issues of behavioral regulation, control, and friction. But, as the fidget spinner suggests, the worlds of logistics are more ubiquitous than might be immediately evident and we are more logistical than we might think.

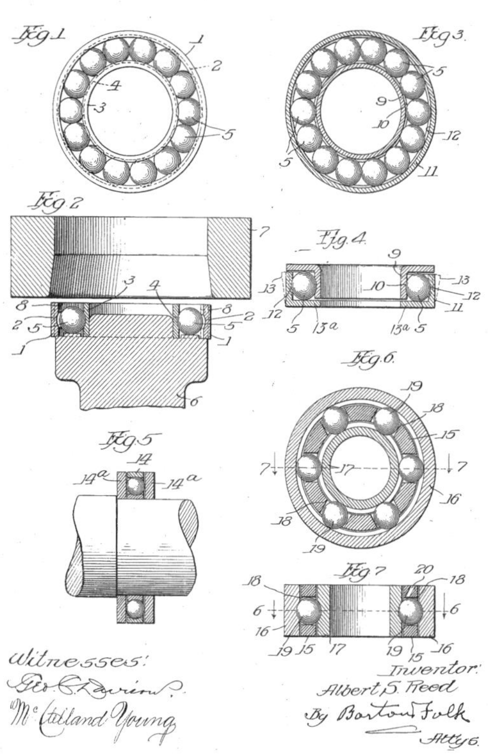

Plan view of a patent drawing for a "Ball Bearing Construction" from A. S. Reed showing balls in place between grooved inner and outer rings. USPTO 1,080,169, December 2, 1913.

Friction is the enemy of fulfillment

The operations of the logistics industry, the area of work and body of knowledge concerned with moving things in time and space, do their best to overcome problems created by things like the shape of the planet, its gravity, and the friction that ensues. Too much and nothing can move,

5. Peter Galison, "War against the Center," *Grey Room*, no. 4 (2001): 7-33.

not enough and we lose control. In the quest to facilitate infinitely lubricated movement of things and people, logistics companies continually seek out ways to overcome friction and its effects. Through a diverse collection of technologies and instruments, enterprises concerned with the movement of objects through space aspire to greater levels of control and speed. Some of these technologies comprise vast and sophisticated networks of tightly calibrated command and communications systems that govern with exacting detail the location of an item in space and time. Other technologies are simpler in their mechanism. For example, a single ball transfer unit—effectively a lone ball bearing—is insufficient to offset the weight of an air cargo container. However, thousands of them assembled together lower the coefficient of friction sufficiently to allow a lone human to physically move something that would otherwise be impossible to handle. The bearing once again triumphs, this time by transforming the architecture itself. By transforming the floor of the fulfillment center into an effectively frictionless surface, logistics companies create a new kind of environment that hints at the transformations wrought by the industry, at the ways that human mobility is affected, and at an expanded set of design possibilities for creating program or atmosphere.

In the case of a distribution building, operated by Amazon or FedEx or UPS or Walmart, for example, lubricating technologies like the ball transfer unit floor accelerate the work of routing merchandise along its trajectory. However, this process does not happen automatically, and without such augmenting technologies, humans who find themselves inhabiting these environments, out of choice or necessity, can hardly function. Indeed, such technologies become a form of life support for an environment increasingly hostile to human life. In the automated warehouses of Amazon.com, the area of the fulfillment centers dedicated to moving and storing of inventory is described as the "Human Exclusion Zone."[6] Are there possibilities for discovery in these environments designed by us but hostile to us, or must we adopt a more defensive posture as we brace for their imminent ubiquity?

"Ballmat" roller platforms allow workers to glide air containers weighing several thousand pounds into and out of UPS aircraft

6. "The Window—High-Speed Robots, Part 1: Meet BettyBot in "Human Exclusion Zone," Warehouses," amazon.com, accessed July 9, 2017 (https://www.amazon.com/Window-High-Speed-BettyBot-Exclusion-Warehouses/dp/B00UUK3IN6).

While the environments I am describing are generally contained within the warehouse landscape of light industrial ex-urban development, it requires little imagination to conjure a world where the logistical landscape spills out into everyday life. The emergence of Amazon Dash or Prime or Alexa are just a few examples that point to the increasing integration of fulfillment, both personal and logistical, into the built environment, not to mention the tiered systems of access that comes with them. The challenge of making sense of architectures of logistics—of fulfillment, in other words—is an urgent one. It points to how we collectively imagine our social and political patterns, to how we might see each other as part of a collective or, instead, as a collective of consuming individuals. Some of that is influenced by the built environment and is supported or reinforced in overt and subtle ways.

Visualizations of logistics naturalize its operations

In the popular imagination of logistics, as evident in things like television commercials, the metaphor of "flow" emerges as a dominant trope. Scholarly approaches use similar language, influenced by Manuel Castells's distinction between the space of places and the space of flows. By imagining that all the things swept up in global supply are somehow flowing suggests that they are moving of their own volition or are being propelled along by some distant force. By alluding to the movement of liquids, the metaphor suggests a kind of physical inevitability and makes it easier to overlook the enormous effort it takes to move things (and people) through space. If everything in the supply chain flows, questions of access to mobility resources can be construed as the responsibility of the participants, suggesting that somehow all should be able to partake, even though this is a highly tiered system and access to mobility resources can contribute significantly to uneven development and increasing polarities and inequalities. When deployed in the context of global logistics, the metaphor of flow can work to naturalize the idea that commercial inventory, like rivers or waterfalls, must continue to be in motion and that these streams of goods move of their own accord. Indeed, if one beholds footage of fulfillment centers in action, the automated environments of materials handling can create such an impression. When these mechanical systems are accelerated, through the cinematic technique of the time lapse, for example, the images blur together into a single stream. Hilary Harris was an early pioneer of the technique and used his 1975 film, *Organism*, to make connections between the metabolism of the human body and that of the city. The film intersperses footage of microscopic physiological systems with accelerated images of New York City to establish links between the functions of an organism and that of a city. Through the blurred effects of time-lapse film, cars become pulsing streams of red and white, not unlike a circulating bloodstream.

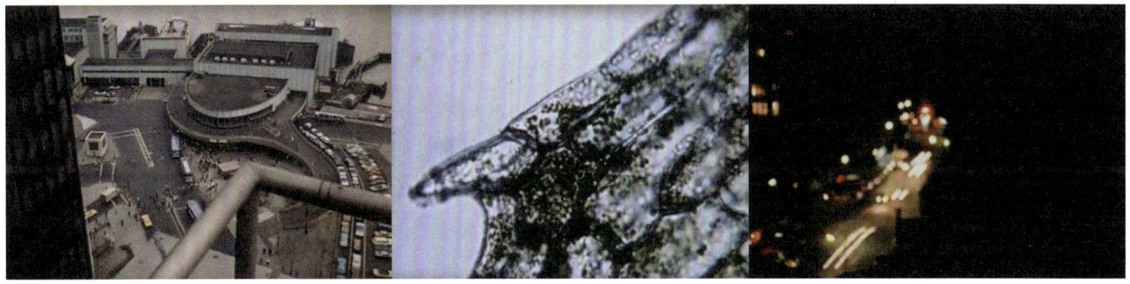

Frames from the short film *Organism* (Hilary Harris, 1975).

The metaphor offers a model of urbanism underpinned by movement, circulation, and exchange but also as a self-regulating system that seeks equilibrium. In the 1983 film *Koyaanisqatsi*, director Godfrey Reggio also alludes to similar ideas, translating his title as "life out of balance." The film devotes much footage to processes of logistics, and while the imagery creates similar effects, Reggio's outlook is less optimistic than Harris's.

Reggio's *Koyaanisqatsi* is a non-narrative film that takes viewers along a global itinerary using a variety of techniques, including aerial footage, time-lapse, and slow motion, all set to a score by Philip Glass. In a number of scenes, the position of the camera places the body in a range of mechanical mobility systems and conflates the eye of the lens with that of the viewer. By switching from an omniscient position to a "first-person" view, the film produces different associations with the viewers. One particularly dense sequence, "The Grid," begins with workers leaving a Lockheed factory and then proceeds to describe a series of entanglements with mechanical control including a string of access points, from subway doors, to turnstiles, to revolving doors—each a moment of delay in pursuit of control and management. From these shots, the camera switches to a point of view from the front of a vehicle, allowing viewers to see what a car might "see" as it races at high speeds along the freeways of San Francisco and Los Angeles. The position changes again but this time the view is not from the front of a car but from inside a television in an assembly plant, looking out from the carapace that will eventually receive the tube assembly. As the conveyor moves the camera along, one can discern the various stages of process, including

Frames from *Koyaanisqatsi* (Godfrey Reggio, 1983).
These are from the section of the film called "The Grid."

the housings and monitors. Following the trajectory of a gravity-fed conveyor, the camera shifts to a vertical tracking shot downward through crisscrossing mall elevators, only to jump to a view from the conveyor of a snack cake production line and then the equally propulsive and jerkily disorienting path of a supermarket shopping cart. As the Glass score continues to build, Reggio presents a mother and two children indifferently watching one television amongst a bank of them, organic creatures embedded in and seduced by an environment of their own making. The film then turns to the object of their gaze and presents an escalating succession of rapid images from news, advertisement, and entertainment. This instantaneous array of images is then punctuated with images of people walking in slow motion towards the camera, slowly acknowledging the presence of the camera with looks of self-satisfaction, curiosity, or suspicion. The sequence concludes with a return to a view from a car—either from the back seat of a convertible or from a position in front of the hood—a view from the machine's perspective. As the camera speeds through Las Vegas, the city disappears into nigh as viewers seem to be propelled along tunnels of light made from the traces of the long and accelerated exposures.[7] Interrupted briefly by a view from inside what appears to be a religious procession, the camera continues to speed up such that the streams of lights consolidate around a single vanishing point before a cut to an aerial view of downtown Los Angeles and the next movement. The moment of chaos within the procession is a counterpoint to the portraits of individuals walking towards the camera. The focus on individual specificity in a film about infrastructure and logistics prefigures the construction of the isolated consuming subject by companies like Amazon. In the crowd, individuals are difficult to discern, awash in a blur of adjacency and contact. In the context of logistics regimes in which friction is the enemy, the presence of humans becomes a special kind of irritant, as we grow increasingly incompatible with the systems and spaces we have designed for our fulfillment.

Frames from *Eagle Eye* (D. J. Caruso, 2008) during a chase scene
in an automated distribution center

7. Reggio explains his intentions with the film thusly, "What I did was try to eradicate all of the foreground of traditional film and take the background, or what's called 'second unit' and make *that* foreground, give *that* the principle focus. We were trying to look at buildings, masses of people, transportation, industrialization, as autonomous *entities* … in the synthetic world the presence of a different entity, a consuming and inhuman entity." Quoted in Scott MacDonald, *Avant-Garde Film: Motion Studies* (Cambridge: Cambridge University Press, 1993), 140.

Humans are incompatible with the operating systems of logistics

In the 2008 film *Eagle Eye*, a key chase scene takes place in a contemporary automated distribution hub at an airport.[8] In the space of the film, two strangers are brought together to deliver a mysterious briefcase, guided by an equally mysterious computer system and on the run from the FBI. In the protagonists' attempt to escape, the computer system guides them into an automated distribution facility at an airport, effectively inviting them into the world of the machines. In exchange, the computer system reads them as inventory and thus as incompatible elements within the system. Indeed, one overhears a voice in the background exclaiming, "Hey! You're not allowed to be in here." As they tumble down a series of belts and rollers, the heroes' poor fit is initially an asset. In a bout of slapstick, a low beam clocks the pursuing FBI agent and sends him sprawling backward on the belt, enough time to gain some ground. However, it is the computer system that ultimately controls the outcome as it takes command of the sliding shoe sorters to divert the agent to another part of the warehouse.[9] These elements are a common feature of an automated distribution system and allow packages to be diverted from the trunk line to various branching gravity-driven rollers. Telling in the film's production design is the way in which the bodies are rendered in the computer's "vision"—not as bodies but as boxes with a pop-up annotation that reads "Error: No bar code, destination unknown." This suggests that all elements that pass through the computer's gaze are understood as inventory and that the task of the system is to sort and direct. While *Eagle Eye* is a product of Hollywood, logistical vision shares the tendency to treat all material within the system as data points to be managed. The industry produces habits of mind that imagine material as data while nonetheless finding ways to physically manage it. By seeing the world thusly, such abstraction accelerates processes of externalization, as all decisions become problems of management and allocation. To an inventory control system, every *thing* and every *body* become both a parcel and a data point.

Frames from *Eagle Eye* (D. J. Caruso, 2008).
Automatic sliding shoe sorters help the protagonists escape

8. For an in-depth description of the interior of a UPS sortation centers, see John McPhee, "Out in the Sort," in *Uncommon Carriers* (New York: Farrar, Straus and Giroux, 2006), 176.

9. "Dematic FlexSort SL2," dematic.com (http://www.dematic.com/en-us/flexsort-sl2/).

As the technologies and practices of logistics, as well as the habits of mind that attend them, increasingly spill out of the enclosed worlds like those depicted in *Eagle Eye*, we humans will be challenged to make our way alongside them and not always with the controlling system looking out for us.[10]

To overcome these escalating incompatibilities, we have developed augmenting technologies that help us to cope with the demands of a logistical environment. To meet order fulfillment quotas, warehouse employees rely on a host of mobility augmentations to increase both their speed and their range. So-called Automated Storage and Retrieval Systems (ASRS) create a human-machine assemblage in which the automated order fulfillment systems transport human "pickers" to the right location in space, at which point they select the appropriate items to be added to the order. The logistical environment is also an encrypted one and to navigate its illegible surfaces, technologies like wearable computer-scanners are required by the contemporary fulfillment center worker. Voice-directed picking systems subject pickers to the demands of software protocols as managers and company owners seek ways to increase output and profit. With these systems, language is no longer a barrier because the software can be programmed to communicate in the native tongue of the person whom it is directing, creating both an

environment in which those humans in it can neither read, because of barcode-encrypted surfaces, nor communicate. Kiva systems, now Amazon Robotics, creates a condition in which workers are stationary while small robotic drive units bring shelves to them for order assembly, effectively acting as organic valves mediating between the automated inventory floor and the awaiting delivery vehicles.[11] As the spaces of logistics continue to transform from mechanized to entirely automated, the ability to interact with these environments becomes increasingly dependent on mediating and decrypting technologies. Even if these environments are products of human ingenuity and even as their contents reflect some idea of fulfillment, access to them becomes more remote. If the habits of mind that form in the space of logistics are biased towards control and efficiency and as the industry spreads and serves as a training ground for those seeking power or influence, similar thinking will likely try to assert its values on spaces not designed to be efficient or profitable.

The freeze-frame turns organisms to machines, the time-lapse turns machines to organisms

There is an absurdity to the scene described above from *Eagle Eye*. Though the humans moving through the automated system are not presented for humorous effect, it nonetheless conjures canonical scenes of human and

10. *Eagle Eye* is based loosely on the Isaac Asimov story "All the Troubles of the World," in which an omniscient computer regulates society and preemptively stops crimes through predictive modeling. Issac Asimov, "All the Troubles of the World," in *Nine Tomorrows: Tales of the Near Future* (New York: Fawcett World Library, 1959), 137-153.

11. For further discussion, see Jesse LeCavalier, "Bodies: Coping with Data Rich Environments," in *The Rule of Logistics: Walmart and the Architecture of Fulfillment* (Minneapolis: University of Minnesota Press, 2016), 151–178.

Frame from *Modern Times* (Charlie Chaplin, 1936) in which the Little Tramp
is ingested by the machinery of a modern factory

technological entanglement. A familiar example is Charlie Chaplin's maceration in *Modern Times* in which he is unwittingly pulled into the inner workings of the factory machinery. By compelling line workers to perform the same repetitive tasks, shop floor managers forced human workers into a machinic mode; and as Chaplin is swallowed up and processed through the gears of the factory, that absorption is rendered literal and comic at the same time. Chaplin was also responding to the emerging field of Scientific Management and its attention to the minute human gesture. Scientific

Management deployed disciplinary mechanisms to micro-manage human workers and offer constant feedback while also assessing their fitness in order to match them with the task deemed most suitable to their abilities. With the emergence of mechanization, in which human workers labor alongside machines, efforts to monitor and improve efficiency remain, but, in the case of manufacturing, more of the tasks are performed by machines, with humans only performing crucial steps for which their affordable dexterity makes them especially qualified.

THE MIDVALE STEEL CO.

Form D—124. Machine Shop........................18..........

ESTIMATES FOR WORK ON LATHES

OPERATIONS CONNECTED WITH PREPARING TO MACHINE WORK ON LATHES AND WITH REMOVING WORK TO FLOOR AFTER IT HAS BEEN MACHINED

OPERATIONS	TIME IN MINUTES
Putting chain on, Work on Floor	
Putting chain on, Work on Centers	
Taking off chain, Work on Floor	
Taking off chain, Work on Centers	
Putting on Carrier	
Taking off "	
Lifting Work to Shears	
Getting Work on Centers	
Lifting Work from Centers to Floor	
Turning Work, end for end	
Adjusting Soda Water	
Stamping	
Center-punching	
Trying Trueness with Chalk	
" with Calipers	
" with Gauge	
Putting in Mandrel	
Taking out "	
Putting in Plug Centers	
Taking out " "	
Putting in False Centers	
Taking out " "	
Putting on Spiders	
Taking off "	
Putting on Follow Rest	
Taking off " "	
Putting on Face Plate	
Taking off " "	
Putting on Chuck	
Taking off "	
Laying out	
Changing Tools	
Putting in Packing	
Cut to Cut	
Learning what is to be done	
Considering how to Clamp	
Oiling up	
Cleaning Machine	
Changing Time Notes	
Changing Tools at Tool Room	
Shifting Work	
Putting on Former	
Taking off "	
Adjusting Feed	
" Speed	
" Poppet Head	
" Screw Cutting Gear	
SIGNED TOTAL	

NAME ....
Sketch .... Number...........
Order............... Weight..........
Metal................ Heat No. ....
Tensile Strength.... Chem. Comp.......
Per cent. of Stretch ....
 HARDNESS, Class ....

OPERATIONS CONNECTED WITH MACHINING WORK ON LATHES

OPERATIONS	Speed	Feed	Cut	Tool	Inches	Minutes
Turning Feed In						
" " "						
" Hand Feed						
" " "						
Boring Feed In						
" " "						
" Hand Feed						
" " "						
Starting Cut						
" "						
Finishing Cut						
" "						
Fillet						
"						
"						
Collar						
Facing						
Slicing						
"						
"						
Nicking						
"						
Centering						
Filling						
Using Emery Cloth						
" " "						
TOTAL						

Machining — Two Heads Used
" — One Head Used
Hand Work
Additional Allowance

TOTAL TIME
HIGH RATE
LOW RATE

Remarks

Time actually taken

FIGURE 6. — INSTRUCTION CARD FOR LATHE WORK

Example of an instruction card from F. W. Taylor, in this case a description of lathe work for the Midvale Steel Company with every step broken into its smallest component. From F. W. Taylor, *Shop Management* (New York: Harper & Brothers, 1912), 171

The industrialized factory housed workers who were subjected to motion studies that sought to root out inefficiencies. Such efforts persist in contemporary automated environments, including the space of fulfillment centers, but the corresponding analytical-visual mode is not the same. Scientific Management, as championed by figures like Ford and Taylor, found technologies for considering the micro-management of human movement in the development of photography and especially the high-speed photography of Eadweard Muybridge and Etienne-Jules Marey. These photographs effectively slow down time in order to understand aspects of motion inaccessible to regular vision. In these studies, the human body is captured and analyzed at the granular level; its motion slowed to understand aspects of motion not available to unaided observation. From the point of view of the managers charged with improving efficiency, these techniques allowed for the hyper-management of each gesture, subjected workers to increasing scrutiny, and gave managers license to intervene at the bodily level in pursuit of greater efficiency (i.e. productivity). Subjected thusly, the human figure becomes an object of analysis and a site of engineering—a machine whose performance demands monitoring, maintenance, and improvement.[12]

If the freeze-frame was symptomatic of mechanization and Scientific Management, the time lapse might be better suited for the worlds

12. For more detailed discussions, see Hugo Kijne and J.-C. Spender, "Introduction," in *Scientific Management: Frederick Winslow Taylor's Gift to the World?*, ed. J.-C. Spender and Hugo Kijne (London: Kluwer Academic, 1996); James R. Beniger, *The Control Revolution: Technological and Economic Origins of the Information Society* (Cambridge, MA.: Harvard University Press, 1986); and Anson Rabinbach, *The Human Motor: Energy, Fatigue, and the Origins of Modernity* (Berkeley: University of California Press, 1992).

of automation and logistics. Indeed, in the long exposure, the movement of humans tends to register only as blurs, effectively removing them from the frame, leaving only the machines. The same kind of thinking is used to consider the management of cities. However, the freeze-frame proves a difficult format for assessment. Instead, city managers must develop a more complete picture, which tends to produce a metabolic version of the city in which, like Harris's *Organism*, the city is imagined as a kind of body whose healthy equilibrium must be maintained. Cities in their modeling of mobility and movement (e.g. smart city monitoring) use both the physiological model of the time lapse, monitoring metabolism, input, output, monitoring "flow" (e.g. of traffic, pedestrian movement, etc.) and the freeze-frame to micro-manage productivity.[13]

As the frozen frame of the high-speed photograph turns bodies to machines and time lapse turns machines to organisms, all become available for forms of management, leaving little space for the unexpected or the irrational. Which is why Plate 176 from Muybridge's *Animal Locomotion* series stands out. Muybridge's studies of human motion tend to focus on feats of athleticism, work, or everyday activities like walking, running, standing, sitting, throwing, etc. Even within the structured space of his photography studio, the models still appear to be performing their assigned motion with some degree of naturalness. However, Plate 176, described as "Woman Falling onto Mattress" creates a condition in which the model must act out an unnatural and irrational action, one that typically happens by accident, not on purpose. The resulting images have an awkward humor to them, partly because they exist at odds with

apparent purposes of the photographic enterprise. Not being a "productive" action, falling is not necessarily something that would be the subject of an efficiency study, which makes this freeze-frame deconstruction all the more compelling. Frozen in a state of near collapse, and having just overcome the self-preservation impulse, the model's position is awkward and humorous because it defies expectations and allows a view of a body in a rare state and one impossible to maintain without the technology of the camera. Part of the absurdity of this image lies in the tension between the body in motion and the analytical grid in the background, designed to support an understanding of human movement as mechanical and capable of quantity-based assessment and modification, as if seeking the most perfect way of falling to the ground. Such pursuit of an absurd efficiency suggests a productive realm of aesthetic exploration with the emerging dominance of logistical regimes of efficiency. As fulfillment becomes calculable and formulaic and predictive analytics can anticipate our next purchase before we know what it is that we desire, it seems useful to continue calling attention to these tendencies.

Absurd efficiencies and the possibilities of para-logistics

If the effects of logistics tend to be naturalized and also expand to influence other forms of management, the drives to rational management and efficiency that characterize e-commerce fulfillment or retail logistics start to show up unexpectedly elsewhere. Speed and efficiency increasingly govern a range of interactions and exchanges, and even the ways in which these processes are articulated and communicated suggest a degree of inevitability or "naturalness"

13. For an overview of literature on smart cities see Robert Hollands, "Will the Real Smart City Please Stand Up?" *City* 12, no. 3: 303—320. See also Nerea Calvillo, Orit Halpern, Jesse LeCavalier, and Wolfgang Pietsch, "Test-Bed as Urban Epistemology," in *Smart Urbanism*, ed. Simon Marvin and Andres Luque-Ayala (London Routledge, 2016).

Eadweard Muybridge, "Woman Falling onto Mattress" from Eadweard Muybridge, *The Human Figure in Motion* (New York: Dover, 1955, reprinted selection of plates from *Animal Locomotion*, 1887), plate 176

(e.g. flow). Cities become modeled on the machines they increasingly house. This is an argument not against efficiency but rather against the narrowing of criteria that admits efficiency as its sole metric, thus foreclosing on much of what is thought of as having cultural value. In Keller Easterling's study of Benton Mackaye and his ideas for rethinking terrestrial connectivity in the United States, she writes, "Whatever remains eccentric to a culture's boundaries and brackets is more likely to cross-reference its intelligence."[14] Such eccentricities might allow consideration beyond symmetrical modes of conflict. They also might offer ways to deal with the questions of scale and connectivity that are part of any consideration of networks of global mobility. As Bernes argues, modes of subjugation and alienation function differently in the global shipping instances he analyzes.[15] To "seize" the apparatus is simply to replace one form of power with another. From the perspective of the logistics revolution, the labor at the port facility is connected to a much larger, globally attenuated system of indenture.[16] Logistical technologies of circulation and management allow processes of extraction, production, and exploitation to be generally externalized from the majority of consumers, leading one to wonder to what degree logistics is something we can escape, and to what degree we might be able to think logistics *outside* capitalism. A counter-logistics might advocate for bringing production and circulation to a halt in order to restart them on different terms.[17] But what would a *para-logistics* look like? It could be something alongside the normal channels that would use the same tools and processes of logistics but direct them elsewhere. The prefix itself is hard to nail down. The Greek root *para-* means "alongside, beyond; altered; contrary; irregular, abnormal," while the Latin *parare* is "to be ready" and suggests "defense, protection against; that which protects from." In this sense, a para-logistics might be imagined as both an alternative space of logistics and a pre-emptive response to it. As one example, Cameron looks at instances that link the urban with its hinterland through community-supported agricultural initiatives to better understand how "community economies" take shape. Standing outside of normative systems but also poised to respond to them, para-logistical systems might contribute to a diversity of multiple ways forward.[18]

14. Keller Easterling, *Organization Space: Landscapes, Highways, and Houses in America* (Cambridge, MA: MIT Press, 1999), 4.

15. Jasper Bernes, "Logistics, Counterlogistics and the Communist Prospect," *Endnotes* 3 (2013)

16. W. Bruce Allen, "The Logistics Revolution and Transportation," *Annals of the American Academy of Political and Social Science* 553 (September 1997): 108.

17. Bernes, "Logistics."

18. J. Cameron, "Enterprise Innovation and Economic Diversity in Community Supported Agriculture: Sustaining the Agricultural Commons," in *Making Other Worlds Possible: Performing Diverse Economies*, ed. Gerda Roelvink, K. St. Martin, and J.K. Gibson-Graham (Minneapolis: University of Minnesota Press, 2015), 53–71. See also Anna Lowenhaupt Tsing, *The Mushroom at the End of the World: On the Possibility of Life in Capitalist Ruins* (Princeton, NJ: Princeton University Press, 2015).

Friction is a necessity of fulfillment

Proximity and the contact that often follows
create friction as surfaces encounter each
other and irregularities produce drag, slowing
or preventing unencumbered movement.
Anna Lowenhaupt Tsing describes friction
as "encounter across distance" and uses the
concept to better understand both the sources
and effects of different cultural movements
within the regimes of global capital. As an
example she uses shifts in the substance we call
"coal" along its journey—a journey sometimes
described as a supply chain or a commodity
chain—from element of the ground to a
part of an energy production mechanism.
She describes how a lump of coal "rubs
up against other participants in the chain:
unhappy villagers, conveyor belts, contracts.
In its shape, its cost, and its composition,
coal is made in the friction of the commodity
chain."[19] In Tsing's reading, friction is a
generator and a necessary action out of which
new forms emerge. Let's continue to explore
the productive dimensions of friction and the
aesthetic possibilities of absurd efficiencies.

19. Anna Lowenhaupt Tsing, *Friction: An Ethnography of Global Connection*
(Princeton, NJ: Princeton University Press, 2005), 51.

Moving Parts: How the Design of Vehicles Shapes Cities

Philipp Rode

The modern motor car is an astonishing machine. The average 1.5 tonnes vehicle accelerates from 0 to 100 km/h in less than 14 seconds; has a comfortable cruising speed of 140 km/h; and is fairly versatile, easily outperforming mountain bikers on a steep uphill gravel road. With an average inside noise level of about 50dB at urban speeds, the automobile's interior is among the most silent environments in cities; occupants usually profit from full control of ambient air temperature, and can take advantage of an ever-increasing entertainment suite. Furthermore, interior space for transporting stuff is enough to make for permanent storage space. And as the modern car is designed to be driven by almost any adult person, it is prepared for impact: hitting an inflexible structure at 50 km/h still leaves you with a 70% likelihood of survival.

At the same time, the car, as we know it, faces an existential crisis. It is, in fact, an urgently needed and long overdue crisis which should be a cause for optimism, imagination, and creativity—above all for the future of cities. This is why: Irrespective of the long list of qualities of the modern car, its design has failed societies on two critical accounts. First, it has ultimately been unable to account for human health, ecological constraints, and its operational context and environment. Second, and due to the latter ignorance, the required adjustments of the built environment to accommodate conventionally designed cars have had additional adverse effects on socio-economic well-being and environmental sustainability.

Evidence for the first point is overwhelming. Vehicle design, operation, and technology has been identified as critical factors for many of the

most pressing twenty-first-century challenges: motorised road transport accidents are estimated to account for 1.3 million deaths per year (Bhalla et al. 2014); car use is the single largest contributor to transport carbon emissions globally (IPCC 2014); motorised transport generates much of outdoor air pollution, leading to an estimated 3.2 million deaths a year across the world (OECD 2014)—a public health emergency according to the World Health Organisation—and increasing levels of motorisation have led to a reduction in total physical activity levels, in turn elevating risks of cardiovascular problems, cancer and diabetes (WHO 2014).

The second point, on changes to the built environment induced by car design, becomes most obvious when considering the case of cities. It is a well-established fact that the design of transport systems has a considerable impact on the shape and life of the city. What

is, however, less well understood is the extent to which the narrower design of vehicles— the moving parts of transport systems—is driving this relationship. As New York's former transport commissioner Janette Sadik-Khan put it: "Urban development in the second half of the twentieth century was basically determined by mechanical engineering from Detroit."

Over the last century, the mechanisation of transport and the associated reduction in mobility costs relative to incomes have allowed cities to de-densify and expand horizontally, resulting in the substitution of access by proximity with access by movement. Initially, starting well before the turn of the last century, this was driven by the introduction of streetcars, metro, and regional rail systems (Heinze and Kill 1991; Gayda et al. 2005; Knoflacher et al. 2008). But public transport, including commuter and metro rail networks, still played a complementary role to the pedestrian city and generally re-enforced its structures. It served longer distances in a wider network of urban relationships at extremely high efficiency levels with regards to space and energy consumption. The initial introduction of mechanized public transport also maintained the need for social interaction as people continued to travel collectively. As a "closed transport system" with a high degree of control, public transport further allowed for integration with the overall planning of urban structure when, for example, decisions on locations of stops and stations had to be made.

Towards the end of the nineteenth century, the first automobiles appeared in the public arena and shortly after the turn of the century, the car's presence—both moving and stationary—in public spaces increased. By law, pedestrian movement became restricted to sidewalks, if not banned altogether in certain areas. Owning and driving a car became the ultimate symbol of freedom of movement, constrained only by the lack of space within city centres. But car drivers found places to live and work outside the traditional city borders, and this allowed them to significantly increase their average amount of personal living space.

Over the last half of the twentieth century, this had a dramatic effect on the urban structure of cities, mainly in the industrialized world. Space-consuming traffic moved economic, cultural, and leisure activities away from urban centres and transformed cities into nondescript agglomerations—an effect that has become known as urban sprawl. City-making in the twentieth century was dominated by a single paradigm: optimising conditions for the movement of cars. Large areas in and around the city were paved for motorways and parking in public spaces, while pedestrian space was reduced to a minimum, or even zero. "Transport" in its original sense lost its meaning, and the quality of car traffic flows, measured in terms of "level of service," became the dictating parameter for planners and decision-makers. The free movement of cars was given priority over the quality of urban life.

Optimizing traffic flows meant not only dedicating large amounts of space to the high-speed movement of machines, often occupied by a single driver, but also adopting urban design solutions that corresponded to the new requirements of speed—linear, monotonous structures lacking any human-scale design quality. Ironically, in cities built around cars and their movement, efficient access to urban space was often drastically reduced, not only because cars require significantly more space for their movement than other modes (at 50 km/h, cars require more than 160 sqm per person to operate, compared to 4 sqm for buses [Rode and Gipp 2001]—the primary reason for road congestion), but also because of the very systemic character of car traffic: roads act as major barriers in cities. This is exemplified by the well-researched fact that increasing traffic flows significantly reduces the social interaction of residents living on opposite sides of the same street. Moreover, there is a massive storage problem for cars which, on average, sit unused for 96% of the time (Heck and Rogers 2014) resulting in aggregate parking space in car-oriented CBDs such as in Los Angeles of more than 80% of the CBD land area (Manville and Shoup 2004).

Given the above, it is now widely accepted that car design and operations have failed the city on

an unimaginable scale. It is in cities where many of the general car problems accumulate and where concerns about air pollution, road accidents, and limited public space have created a potent political force challenging car-oriented futures. Public opinion has forced even Chinese cities to restrict vehicle use, courts across the world have put new pressures on local and regional governments to act, and mayoral campaigns in cities globally are won based on promises for better air quality and more sustainable travel. Even car companies, some by manipulating emissions standards of their vehicles, are driving this shift away from the traditional car as they have actively destroyed the trust of the general public in their ability to drive necessary change.

In fact, many commentators have been irritated for some time by the fairly stagnant design approach to the motorcar, which has remained more or less the same for more than half a century. This, however, is now beginning to change as a result of the increasingly pressing problems discussed above and of an impending socio-technological transition. Recent developments in vehicle technology, above all electrification, digitalisation, automation, and new materials, are now accelerating design change and are challenging conventional design paradigms linked to the internal combustion engine. BMW's i Series, Tesla, Renault's Twizy, and new autonomous car designs by Google and Apple are just a few prominent examples.

Vehicles as "computers on wheels" are increasingly becoming the norm: lane-keeping, cruise control, and autonomous parking are already integrated in today's car. Some projections assume that fully autonomous vehicles may enter markets already by the early 2020s and may reach market shares of 15% to 40% in advanced economies by 2035 (Trommer et al. 2016). Niche vehicle manufacturers such as Local Motors have already shown how to use 3D printing technology to successfully re-imagine, engineer, and produce urban vehicles. Other startup companies are changing design paradigms around autonomous driving by concentrating on low-speed, ultra-light urban vehicles. For the first time, such innovation may also seriously change the efficiency of car use: new autonomous vehicles may be able to travel closer together, be designed for a wider range of passenger numbers, and not require a crumple zone, thus increasing utility, and effective use of space and energy. And autonomous vehicles could overcome the 90% of accidents caused by human error, considerably increasing road safety (Fagnant and Kockelman 2015).

At the same time, the trend towards larger, heavier, and gas-guzzling cars and SUVs not only challenges the integration of these vehicles as part of an urban transport system but defies any serious attempt at addressing the global urban transport challenge. Besides ignoring the resulting environmental and health problems, these vehicle designs only further exacerbate congestion costs. As the *Guardian*'s George Monbiot put it, "The undercapacity of the roads arises from the overcapacity of the vehicles that use them" (Monbiot 2016). Rather than confronting this, there are serious risks that the future automation of driving may further exacerbate overcapacity by enabling zero-occupants travel or by transporting children alone. Furthermore, driving may simply increase overall with greater willingness for longer commutes as people are able to take their hands off the wheel and engage in other activities than steering the car.

Similarly contradictory trends can be observed with regards to the operation of vehicles in cities. On the one hand, conventional car ownership is exponentially increasing in urban China, India, and many other emerging economy countries. On the other hand, a pronounced shift away from conventional car use and towards multi-modal, public, and shared mobility has been observed in many OECD country cities (Rode et al. 2015). Based on the mobile internet, mobility services such as Bridj, Lyft, and Uber,

alongside car sharing by Zipcar, Car2Go, and DriveNow, have become a clear alternative to conventional car ownership. In the future, autonomous vehicle-on-demand services may be able to provide "taxi-quality" travel at costs as low as €0.30/km and for autonomous car pooling even around €0.10/km, which is similar to public transport (Trommer et al. 2016). Cities such as Helsinki, Paris, and Amsterdam are experimenting with possibilities for de-privatising road traffic, while others including Pittsburgh, Tokyo, and London have become centres for testing autonomous taxi services.

Regardless of the great socio-technological uncertainties which these contradictory trends represent, there is little doubt with regard to the transformative forces impacting cities today as a result of the changes to their "moving parts." And at a time when cities are beginning to grasp the enormity of these changes ahead, critical questions need to be asked about the design dynamics that are at play within the wider car and urban vehicles complex:

Can the design of vehicles, the moving parts of the city, be understood as a form of city design? To what extent are designers of cars and urban road vehicles considering the conditions presented by the environments they need to operate in? How much is this adjustment to "operational environments" addressing specific urban conditions? How are vehicle designers adapting to the socio-technological change which we can now detect in many cities? What are competing design objectives that may prioritise goals which imply compromising a fit for urban operations? What are the laws and regulations of relevant case study countries and cities that manage the relationship between vehicle design, operation, and the built environment? What vehicle design inputs have been underrepresented (majority of trips below 7km, most car journeys are driven solo, etc.) versus those that are overrepresented (acceleration, top speed, etc.)?

These questions may well position vehicle designers far above their actual sphere of influence. Vehicle design is a dependent discipline, contingent upon consumer preference, cost effectiveness, technological possibilities, government regulation, marketing strategies, system engineering, and many other contextual factors. And car design, in particular, is stuck with a conventional ownership model in mind in which exceptional rather than ordinary use dictates vehicle shapes: top speeds, off-road use, five passengers, holidays, moving stuff, etc. Unfortunately, most of the latter considerations have to be traded off against adjusting vehicle designs to urban conditions which in turn would enable better urbanism and quality of life in cities. But there is a parallel story of a dependent discipline where design responsibility for the city as a whole is more frequently demanded and accepted: architecture, urban design, and planning. The above discussion suggests that the current technological disruption in the transport sector presents a unique opportunity to advance a similar design ethos for those involved in imagining and creating the moving parts of cities.

References

Bhalla, Kavi, Marc Shotten, Aaron Cohen, Michael Brauer, Saeid Shahraz, Richard Burnett, Katherine Leach-Kemon, Greg Freedman, and Christopher J. L. Murray. 2014. *Transport for Health: The Global Burden of Disease from Motorized Road Transport*. Global Road Safety Facility. Washington, DC: Institute for Health Metrics and Evaluation and World Bank.

Fagnant, Daniel J., and Kara Kockelman. 2015. *Preparing a Nation for Autonomous Vehicles: Opportunities, Barriers and Policy Recommendations. Transportation Research Part A: Policy and Practice* 77: 167-181.

Gayda, S., G. Haag, E. Besussi, K. Lautso, C. Noël, A. Martino, P. Moilanen, and R. Dormoi. 2005. *SCATTER—Sprawling Cities And Transport*. Brussels: Stratec S.A.

Heinze, G.W., and H.H. Kill. 1991. "Chancen des ÖPNV am Ende der autogerechten Stadt. Verkehrspolitische Lehren für einen traditionellen Verkehrsträger im Strukturbruch." *Jahrbuch für Regionalwissenschaft*, 12/13: 105-136

IPCC (Intergovernmental Panel on Climate Change). 2014. *Climate Change 2014: Mitigation of Climate Change—Transport*. Potsdam, IPCC—Working Group III.

Knoflacher, Hermann, Philipp Rode, and Geetam Tiwari. 2008. *How Roads Kill Cities*. In Ricky Burdett, and Deyan Sudjic (eds.), *The Endless City*. London: Phaidon. 340-347.

Monbiot, George. 2016. "Our Roads Are Choked. We're on the Verge of Carmageddon." *The Guardian*, 20/09/2016.

OECD. 2014. *The Cost of Air Pollution: Health Impacts of Road Transport*. OECD.

Rode, Philipp and Christoph Gipp. 2001. *Dynamische Raeume: Die Nutzungsflexibilisierung urbaner Mobilitaetsraeume am Beispiel der Berliner Innenstadt*. Technical University Berlin. Berlin.

Rode, Philipp, Christian Hoffmann, Jens Kandt, Andreas Graff, and Duncan Smith. 2015. *Towards New Urban Mobility: The Case of London and Berlin*. London: LSE Cities, London School of Economics and Political Science, and Innoz, Innovation Centre for Mobility and Societal Change.

Trommer Stefan, Viktoriya Kolarova, Eva Fraedrich, Lars Kröger, Benjamin Kickhöfer, Tobias Kuhnimhof, Barbara Lenz, and Peter Phleps. 2016. *Autonomous Driving: The Impact of Vehicle Automation on Mobility Behaviour*. Munich: IFMO (Institute for Mobility Research).

WHO. 2014. *Physical Activity* [Online]. World Health Organization. http://www.who.int/mediacentre/factsheets/fs385/en/, [accessed 12 June.]

The Dabbawala—Informality Leveraging Formality

Rahul Mehrotra and Michael Jen

Introduction

Today, Indian cities include two components occupying the same physical space: the static city and the Kinetic City. The static city, built of more permanent materials such as concrete, steel, and brick, is perceived as a monumental two-dimensional entity on conventional city maps. Meanwhile, the Kinetic City—incomprehensible as a two-dimensional entity—is perceived as a city in motion, a three-dimensional construct of incremental development. The Kinetic City is temporary in nature and often built with recycled materials: plastic sheets, scrap metal, canvas, and waste wood. It constantly modifies and reinvents itself. The Kinetic City is not perceived as architecture, but in terms of spaces, which hold associative values and supportive lives. Patterns of occupation determine its form and perception. It is an indigenous urbanism that has its particular "local" logic. It is not necessarily the city of the poor, as most images might suggest; rather, it is a temporal articulation and occupation of space that not only creates a richer sensibility of spatial occupation, but also suggests how spatial limits are expanded to include formally unimagined uses in dense urban conditions.

In fact, Kinetic City presents a compelling vision that enables us to better understand the blurred lines of contemporary urbanism and the changing roles of people and spaces in urban society. The increasing concentrations of global flows have exacerbated the inequalities and spatial divisions of social classes. In such a context, an architecture or urbanism of equality in an increasingly inequitable economic condition requires a deeper exploration to find a wide range of places to mark and commemorate the cultures of those excluded from the spaces of global flows. These do not necessarily lie in the formal production of architecture; rather, they often challenge it. Here the idea of a city is an elastic urban condition—not a grand vision, but a "grand adjustment."

The dabbawalas of Mumbai are an example of the intertwined relationship between the formal and informal city. The tiffin delivery service, which relies mainly on the train system for transportation, costs approximately 300 rupees (4.5 euro) per month. A dabbawala (literally translated as "tiffin man") picks up a lunch tiffin from a house anywhere in the city. Then, through a complex system, he delivers the tiffin to one's place of work by lunchtime and returns it to the house later in the day. The dabbawalas deliver hundreds of thousands of lunch boxes every day. The efficiency of Mumbai's train system—the spine of the linear city—enables such a complex informal system to work. The dabbawalas have set up an innovative network that facilitates an informal system to take advantage of a formal infrastructure. The network involves the dabba or tiffin being exchanged up to four or five times between its pickup and return to the house in the evening. The average box travels about 30 kilometers each way. It is estimated that approximately 200,000 boxes are delivered across the city every day, involving around 4,500 dabbawalas making 400,000 deliveries. In economic terms, the annual turnover amounts to roughly 50 million rupees, or about a million euros![1]

Mumbai
The dabbawala service is an enterprise which is unique to the city of Mumbai.[2] This may be in part because the service requires the fundamental linearity of the train system and of the city itself in order to operate. This particular geography of Mumbai and the manner in which the train network is embedded in this geography creates efficiencies in terms of distance that makes this delivery system possible. Furthermore, there is a cultural aspect regarding the movement of food that is integral to the character of Mumbai and its streets, where food is continuously being prepared, eaten, and distributed. The relationship between the fixed infrastructure of the trains and the street, with the temporal aspects of people and food, is a defining characteristic of the city. What is most interesting about the movement of food in Mumbai is the scale at which it happens. For one of the largest cities in the world by population, food is often moved at the scale of the carrying capacity of a single person, or of a bicycle, or a hand-pushed cart. All of these forms of transportation are utilized to staggering effect by the dabbawalas.

The demand for the dabbawala's service is revealing about certain larger social aspects of food in the Indian context, and specifically in Mumbai. The most obvious societal quality is the preference for hot, homemade meals. The many rural migrants to the city bring with them a preference for their own regional cuisine, often driven by dietary restrictions due to religious beliefs.[3] There is also a prevalence of people available to cook from home, either wives, mothers, or hired staff; however, due to the length of time required to prepare an Indian meal, as well as the unreliability of another civic infrastructure—the water supply—the meal may not be ready by the time that the worker leaves home. The density of the commute makes

1. Vinay Venkatramam, and Stefano Mirti, "Dabbawallas." Domus 885 (December 2005): 85.

2. Ibid.

3. Jacobson "Doing Lunch." *Natural History* 1 (March 2000): 66.

carrying one's own lunch with them on the crowded trains extremely cumbersome.[4] Finally, the low cost of labor in the service industry makes it economically feasible for the middle class to pay for this service.

Moving

Due to the linear shape of Mumbai, the train can be used efficiently for travelling the longer distances in the north-south direction. Bicycles and handcarts can be used to cross the shorter east-west distances between the railway stations and the home or office. Since the dabbawalas appropriate existing infrastructure and utilize simple forms of transportation, using only rudimentary forms of technology, the operating costs are very low.

The network begins every day with the dabbawala reporting to his designated train station in the morning. He then rides to about thirty residences on a fixed route, starting with the location furthest from the originating train station. Each customer knows exactly when the dabbawala will arrive in order to have the food ready. The tiffins are then delivered to the railway station where they are sorted based on the train station of destination. Once sorted, crates containing about forty tiffins are loaded into the luggage compartment of the train. After arriving at the station of destination they are re-sorted and delivered to each individual office before lunchtime. After lunch, the entire sequence runs in reverse to return the empty tiffins to the originating residences. Within about six hours each tiffin has completed its full daily cycle and has been returned to its originating home.[5]

If a dabbawala gains a new customer within his collecting area, he will make the complete journey to check the address of delivery and to co-ordinate with the dabbawalas along the way who will have a free place to carry an additional tiffin. Once the railway stations and the system of exchanges have been decided, it is possible to add the code to the tiffin.

Connecting

The coding system of symbols on the tiffins is different than a typical postal address; it is both more rudimentary, and infinitely more complex. Instead of marking the exact locations of the starting and ending points of delivery, the codes indicate the people, routes, and points of exchange. A standard address would often be useless, as the majority of dabbawalas are poorly educated and often illiterate, at least in a traditional sense. However, instead of being handicapped by this weakness, the dabbawalas have leveraged the weakness into strength, developing their own language of signs, which facilitate the process of delivery much more efficiently than a standard address could. The code acts as a sort of organizational map of the entire delivery system.

A simple but comprehensive system of codes is universally used by the dabbawalas; it consists of colors, characters, and well-known symbols. The code does not need to contain all of the information necessary to make the delivery; the gaps are filled by the dabbawala's memory. The code on each tiffin contains three main markers. The first is a large bold number in the center, which indicates the neighborhood to which the lunch box needs to be delivered. Second, on the edge of the lid, is a number which indicates the identity of the dabbawala who will make the delivery, as well as a code for the name of the

4. Venkatramam, and Mirti."Dabbawallas," 85

5. Stefan H. Thomke, and Mona Sinha, "The Dabbawala System: On-Time Delivery, Every Time." Harvard Business School Case 610-059, February 2010 (revised January 2013): 6.

building, and a number for the floor to which it is to be delivered. Third, also on the edge of the lid, is a combination of colors and symbols which indicate the station of origin, to which the tiffin will be returned on its afternoon journey.[6] Before the end of the day, all of the tiffins are delivered to their original stations where they are again sorted, taken by their specific dabbawala, and delivered back to their respective homes.

Rather than being written on the tiffin, the exact address of the home and the place of work are remembered by heart by the dabbawala who is responsible for each tiffin. Sometimes the customer's name is also written on top of the tiffin; this is not for the dabbawala, who can identify each of his tiffins on sight; rather it is so that the customer will recognize his own tiffin when it arrives at his place of work.

Dabbawalas: A social history
Around the year 1885, a British banker in Mumbai hired a man to pick up a lunch from his home, deliver it to his office, and to return the empty lunch box home each day. An early deliveryman and entrepreneur saw an opportunity and the dabbawala service was born.[7] He started the lunch delivery business with a number of farmers from his village near the city of Pune, eighty miles southeast of Mumbai.[8] To this day nearly all of the dabbawalas are migrants from these same few farming villages. The CEO of one of the dabbawala's associations has claimed that all but six of the 5,000 dabbawalas come from these particular communities of Maharashtrians.[9] Historically, the service actually stopped for a week each year during the harvest, as most of the dabbawalas returned home at this time to help their families with the farming. Naturally, this has changed slightly now with greater demand on their services as their popularity has grown.

Another factor which lends itself to the dabbawala's legendary reliability is the social cohesion of the group. Their service is a monopoly and only works because the members are totally interdependent. The system requires the solidarity and social control that exists within the group. New employees are recommended for employment by a personal guarantee of an existing member, often a family member.[10] Trainees from the villages belong to the family of an older dabbawala who will assist in their training. Within the dabbawalas there is a special group called muqaddams who are each responsible for small segments of the city and the customers within that area. The muqaddam of each group is the oldest member and is not paid any extra.[11] Each muqaddam has a number of workers and trainees under him—typically between six and twelve workers—who work together to deliver their group of lunches. These teams of dabbawalas are necessary as one dabbawala cannot be responsible for the tiffins all the way from the house to the office, because

6. Ibid. 8.

7. Ibid. 2.

8. Jacobson, "Doing Lunch." 68

9. "Importing Efficiency: Can Lessons from Mumbai's Dabbawalas Help Its Taxi Drivers?," Knowledge@Wharton, The Wharton School, University of Pennsylvania, 12 October, 2011, Web, 16 July 2012.

10. Ibid.

11. "TEDxSSN—Dr. Pawan Agrawal—Mumbai Dabbawalas" online video clip, Youtube, 24 February 2011, Web, 13 May 2013.

the city is too large and timing is critical. In this way the system works as a sort of relay race. The dabbawalas know that they can count on the timeliness of each member of their team in support of the delivery of every lunch.

Sharing

While there is a financial impact to the customer and the worker of the dabbawalas' resourcefulness with limited resources, the environmental impact is of much greater importance. The dabbawalas use of manual forms of transportation, as well as pre-existing public transportation, means that the 400,000 daily deliveries are made while polluting very little, adding almost no fossil fuel consumption to the city. The city's willingness to share its infrastructure is evident in the train cars specifically devoted to the dabbawalas. This management and sharing of resources is beneficial to the dabbawalas, their customers, and the city at large.

Beyond their own impact, the dabbawalas offer an example for other businesses and services in the city, as a model for a sustainable and just urbanism.

Adapting

One thing which is always evident in Mumbai is that things are constantly changing. Today, fewer people at home are available to cook the lunches in the morning due to the increasing number of women entering the workforce and the rise in the number of nuclear rather than extended family residences. Increased security concerns after the 2008 terrorist attacks in Mumbai have led to further changes to the dabbawala system. In a system which is fundamentally based on trust, dabbawalas' now need to verify new customers more carefully as a result. For fear of unknowingly delivering bombs instead of

lunches, the tiffins' may only be delivered to the security check in many buildings, which slows the process and can result in errors in the delivery.[12]

However, the dabbawalas have demonstrated that they are adaptable to change. In a recent development, some private meal suppliers have begun to use the dabbawala network to deliver meals to their customers. With both members of the family leaving home every day for work, this arrangement retains the personal delivery of the food while adapting to changing societal norms. At least fifteen to twenty such meal suppliers are using the dabbawala network currently. Another thing which is evident through these private meal suppliers is that the character and history of the dabbawala delivery system has a strong symbolic currency in Mumbai. One such private meal supplier packs their lunches in spill-proof throwaway containers using modern technology for hygienic reasons. However, this container is then packed into a traditional metal tiffin, which is still used for the delivery, retaining the symbolic nature of the movement of food on the street.

Conclusion

Entrepreneurship in the Kinetic City is an autonomous and oral process that demonstrates the ability to fold the formal and informal into a symbiotic relationship. The dabbawalas—like several other informal services, ranging from banking to money transfers, couriers, and electronic bazaars—leverage community relationships and networks to deftly use the static city and its infrastructure beyond its intended margins. These networks create a synergy that depends on mutual integration without the obsession of formalized structures. The Kinetic City is where the intersection of need (often reduced

12. Thomke, and Mona Sinha. "The Dabbawala System."

to survival) and the unexploited potentials of existing infrastructure initiate new innovative urban experiences. The trains and streets of Mumbai are emblematic of a kinetic space supporting and blurring the formal and the informal, slicing through these worlds while momentarily collapsing them into a singular entity. Here, any self-consciousness about modernity and the regulations imposed by the static city and its globalized counterparts are suspended and redundant. While the static city aspires to erase the local and re-codify it in a written "macro-moral" order, the Kinetic City carries local, often traditional, wisdom into the contemporary world without fear of the modern. These tactics have the potential to change the way we live in the city and, paradoxically, may present the most hopeful outcome for contemporary cities. This transformative urban process presents a model for new, more equitable forms of urban experience.

*In the film, humans, animals, and machines
come together in solidarity*
Leo Carax

Driver-less Vision:
Learning to See
the Way Cars Do

**Fake Industries Architectural Agonism,
Guillermo Fernandez-Abascal, and
Perlin Studios**

Recent developments in driverless technologies have brought discussions around urban environments to the forefront. While developing the actual vehicles, major players such as Waymo (Google), Volkswagen, or Uber are equally invested in envisioning the future of cities. Yet, the proposed scenarios tend to emphasize consensual solutions in which idealized images of the streets seamlessly integrate driverless technology. Avoiding the immediate future, these visions focus on a distant time in which the technology has been hegemonically deployed: Only driverless cars circulate while humans, city infrastructure, and autonomous vehicles have learned to live together.[1]

1. Future scenarios tend to focus their predictions on how driverless cars combined with a sharing economy could reduce drastically the total amount of cars and on the implications of this reduction in urban environments. Brandon Schoettle and Michael Sivak of the University of Michigan Transportation Research Institute foresee a 43% contraction. (Brandon Schoettle and Michael Sivak, "Potential Impact of Self-driving Vehicles on Household Vehicle Demand and Usage," http://www.driverlesstransportation.com/wp-content/uploads/2015/02/UMTRI-2015-3.pdf ([accessed February 2017]). Sebastian Thrun, a computer scientist at Stanford University and former leader of Google's driverless project predicts a 70% ; see "If Autonomous Vehicles Rule the World," *The Economist*, http://worldif.economist.com/article/12123/horseless-driverless (accessed February 2017)). Matthew Claudel and Carlo Ratti anticipate an 80% reduction (Matthew Claudel and Carlo Ratti, "Full Speed Ahead: How the Driverless Car Could Transform Cities," Mckinsey.com, http://www.mckinsey.com/business-functions/sustainability-and-resource-productivity/our-insights/full-speed-ahead-how-the-driverless-car-could-transform-cities, accessed January 2017). Luis Martínez of the International Transport Forum expects a 90% decline in his study of Lisbon mobility (Luis Martínez, "Urban Mobility System Upgrade: How Shared Self-driving Cars Could Change City Traffic," CITF, OECD, http://www.itf-oecd.org/sites/default/files/docs/15cpb_self-drivingcars.pdf, accessed January 2017). In a similar exercise, Dan Fagnant of the University of Utah forecasts a 90% decline for the city of Austin (Daniel James Fagnant, "Future of Fully Automated Vehicles: Opportunities for Vehicle- and Ride-sharing, with Cost and Emission Savings," Ph.D. diss., University of Texas, https://repositories.lib.utexas.edu/bitstream/handle/2152/25932/FAGNANT-DISSERTATION-2014.pdf?sequence=1 (accessed February 2017). All of these hypotheses operate in a distant future when the technology has been fully implemented. IEEE predicts up to 75% of vehicles will be autonomous in

This paper argues instead that the conflicts untapped by the new technology's disruptive effects will trigger the most meaningful transformations of the city and that these changes they will happen in the near future. The fast deployment of driverless technology does not preclude a specific urban solution. Rather, it requires our imagining how the cohabitation of humans and cars is going to be discussed. Our hypothesis entails that, in the short term, the urban realm will be the place where the negotiation will take place and that the differences in the ways cars and humans sense the city will define the terms of the discussion.

After successful deployment of autonomous vehicles in close circuits and major non-urban areas, the city has become the ultimate frontier for driverless technologies. Personal rapid transit systems (PRT) operating in closed systems like the self-driving pods in Heathrow Airport have been successfully running since the end of yhe last century.[2]

Adaptive Cruise Control, Automatic Emergency Braking, or Automatic Parking are widely available in commercial cars. Tesla, BMW, Infiniti, and Mercedes-Benz offer models with Automatic Lane Keeping that guides the car through freeways and rural roads without relying on the driver's hands, eyes, or judgment.[3] Yet the city seems to resist the wave of autonomous cars. Several reasons explain why. Urban environments multiply the chances of unforeseen events and dramatically increase the amount of sensorial information required to make driving decisions. The quality and amount of data is directly proportional to the price of the technology and to the chances of the car's successfully resolving difficult situations. It also is inversely proportional to the car's processing and decision-making speed.

2040 and IHS forecasts that almost all of the vehicles in use will be driverless by 2050; see IEEE, "Look Ma, No Hands!," http://www.ieee.org/about/ news/2012/5september_2_2012.html (accessed February 2017) and IHS, "Emerging Technologies: Autonomous Cars—Not If, But When," http://www. ihssupplierinsight.com/_assets/sampledownloads/auto-tech-report-emerging-tech-autonomous-car-2013-sample_1404310053.pdf (accessed February 2017).

2. Personal rapid transit (PRT) was developed in the 1950s as a more economical response to the conventional metro system supported by the Urban Mass Transportation Administration (UMTA). Originally they had similar capacity to cars but as they evolved into bigger vehicles they lost these advantages. As a result only one PRT was built, in Morgantown, WV (USA). It has been operating successfully since then. We can position Heathrow's pods, the Sky Cube in Suncheon (Korea), or Masdar Abu Dabhi pods as their latest implementations of this technology.

3. In January 2014, SAE International (Society of Automotive Engineers) issued a classification system defining six levels of automation, spanning from no automation to full automation (0 to 5), with the goal of simplifying communication and collaboration among the different agents involved. The classification is based on the amount of driver intervention and attention required instead of the vehicular technological devices. The characterization sets a crucial distinction between level 2, where the human driver operates part of the dynamic driving task, and level 3, where the automated driving system carries out all dynamic driving task. SAE., "Automated Driving. : Levels of Automation Are Defined in New SAE International Standard J3016"," https://www.sae.org/misc/ pdfs/automated_driving.pdf (accessed February 2017)). Later in 2014, Navya launched a self-driving vehicle (level 5) which has been performing successfully in different closed environments from Switzerland to France, the United States,

The equilibrium between these two opposed parameters defines different approaches to the driverless cars.[4] Eventually, it will also define how the streetscape needs to change to accommodate the cohabitation of autonomous vehicles, regular cars, pedestrians, and other forms of transportation.

The presence of self-driving cars in urban environments also challenges accepted notions of safety. Accidents involving self-driving cars are well documented. Google issued a public report monthly until November 2016. Tesla and Uber are more secretive, but their accidents tend to become media events.[5]

England, and Singapore. Arma, their latest carrier, is operating trials under fixed routes in urban scenarios. The shuttle can transport up to 15 passengers and drive up to 45 km/h. Other major players have been testing vehicles in closed environments and on public roads under special circumstances. When driven on public roads, the cars require at least one person to monitor the action and assume control if needed. Some of the more popular testing programmes involve companies such as Waymo (Google), Tesla, or Uber. Google has been testing their cars since 2009 on freeways and testing grounds. In 2012, they shifted to the city streets, identifying the need to do tests in more complex environments. In their latest published monthly report, in November 2016, their vehicles operated 65% of the time on autonomous mode. Along the lifespan of the programme they have accumulated more than 2 million self-driven miles.(Waymo, "Journey," https://waymo.com/journey/ [accessed February 2017]).

Tesla started deploying their Autopilot system in 2014, with a level 2 automated vehicle. In October 2016, Tesla announced that their vehicles have all the necessary hardware to be fully autonomous (level 5 capabilities). However, as they clearly state, its functionality depends on extensive software validation and regulatory approval. They currently offered multiple capacities such as adaptive cruise control or autosteer. Initially, the systems could only be deployed on specific highways but at as of February 2017, they also perform in some urban situations. (Tesla, "Full Self-Driving Capability," https://www.tesla.com/autopilot [accessed February 2017]).Uber joined the race in 2016. Their controversial programme offered, right after nuTonomy's pilot scheme, to carry fare-paying passengers in cars that have a high level of autonomy. The vehicles deploying this service have two employees in the front seats to monitor and take control in case of problems.

4. Tesla's current sensing system arrays eight cameras that provide 360 degrees of visibility with a range of 250 m. Twelve ultrasonic sensors and a forward-facing radar complement and strengthen the system. However, Waymo and most of the other competitors follow a different approach. (Tesla, "Advanced Sensor Coverage," https://www.tesla.com/autopilot [accessed February 2017]).Waymo's most advanced vehicle, a Chrysler Pacifica Hybrid minivan customised with different self-driving sensors, relies primarily on LiDAR technology. It has three LiDAR sensors, eight vision modules comprising multiples sensors and a complex radar system to complement it. (Waymo team, "Introducing Waymo's Suite of Custom-built, Self-driving Hardware," Medium, https://medium.com/waymo/introducing-waymos-suite-of-custom-built-self-driving-hardware-c47d1714563 [accessed February 2017]).

5. Tesla's fatal accident occurred on 7 May 2016 in Willston, Florida, while a Tesla Model Selectric car was engaged in Autopilot mode; see Anjali Singhvi and Karl Russell, "Inside the Self-Driving Tesla Fatal Accident," *New York Times*, 1 July 2016, https://www.nytimes.com/interactive/2016/07/01/business/inside-tesla-accident.html

The majority of these events involve single vehicles or collisions between two or more vehicles. Urban environments increase the chances of accidents involving pedestrians and other forms of non-vehicular traffic. The ethical implications of this scenario have been popularized by MIT's interactive online test, Moral Machine.[6] Self-driving technologies imply a transfer of accountability to the algorithms that guide the vehicle. Most legal experts predict a trend towards increased manufacturer liability with increased use of automation. Major players such as Volvo, Google, or Mercedes already supported this solution in 2015. Car manufacturers will accept insurance liabilities after full automatization (level 5) is a reality.[7] But safety goes beyond the insurance conundrum. In *Aramis, or the Love of Technology*, Bruno Latour proves how the success of a new technology is deeply connected with the perceived dangers it entails.[8]

To share the streets with cars driven by computers shakes collective notions of acceptable risk. The technology needs to prove trustworthy. And trust, in this cases, results from a combination of scientific evidence, storytelling, and public demonstrations constructed by the engineers, economies, and populations involved in their development. When common agreements regarding trust and responsibility shift, the way we will live together needs to be settled, again.[9]

(accessed February 2017). Uber's most recent accident happened on 24 March 2017. Although they were not accused for being responsible of the accident, they temporarily suspended their programmes in their three testing locations: Arizona, San Francisco, and Pittsburgh. See Mike Isaac, "Uber Suspends Tests of Self-Driving Vehicles After Arizona Crash," *New York Times*, 25 March 2017, https://www.nytimes.com/2017/03/25/business/uber-suspends-tests-of-self-driving-vehicles-after-arizona-crash.html.

6. Iyad Rahwan, Jean-Francois Bonnefon, and Azim Shariff, "Moral Machine: Human Perspectives on Machine Ethics," http://moralmachine.mit.edu/ (accessed January 2017).

7. Kirsten Korosec, "Volvo CEO: We Will Accept All Liability When Our Cars Are in Autonomous Mode," *Fortune*, 7 October 2015, http://fortune.com/2015/10/07/volvo-liability-self-driving-cars/ (accessed February 2017), and Bill Whitaker, "Hands off the Wheel," *Sixty Minutes*, CBS, http://www.cbsnews.com/news/self-driving-cars-google-mercedes-benz-60-minutes/ (accessed February 2017).

8. Bruno Latour, *Aramis, or the Love of Technology* (Cambridge, MA: Harvard University Press, 1996).

9. Charles Perrow analyzes the social side of technological risk. He argues that accidents are normal events in complex systems; they are the predetermined consequences of the way we launch industrial ventures. He believes that the conventional engineering approach to ensuring safety, building in more warnings and safeguards, is inadequate because complex systems assure failure. Charles Perrow, *Normal Accidents: Living with High-Risk Technologies*. (Princeton, NJ: Princeton University Press, 1999). Hod Lipson, professor at Columbia University and co-author of *Driverless, Intelligent Cars and the Road Ahead*, advises that the Department of Transportation should define a safety standard based on statistical goals, not specific technologies. They should specify how safe a car needs to be before it can drive itself, and then step out of the way.(Cited in Russ Mitchell, "Why the Driverless Car Industry Is Happy (So Far) with Trump's Pick for Transportation Secretary," Los Angeles Times, 5 December 2016, http://www.latimes.com/business/autos/la-fi-hy-chao-trump-driverless-20161205-story.html.

If dense urban environments intensify the conflicts between technology, ethics, economy, and collective safety, the realm of sensing renders the conflicts public. The arrival of autonomous vehicles entails the emergence of a new type of gaze that requires the negotiation of existing codes. Currently, human perception defines the visual and sonic stimuli that regulates urban traffic. The transfer of information has been designed, with few exceptions, to be effective for human vision and in some cases for human audition. Driverless sensors struggle with these logics; e.g., redundancy, used to capture drivers' attention, often produces a confusing cacophony for autonomous vehicles. Dirtiness on the road graphics, misallocations of signage, consecutive but contradictory traffic signs, or even the lack of proper standardization of traffic signs and markings are the reasons behind some of the most notorious incidents involving autonomous vehicles.[10]

Assuming that driverless cars will adapt to these conditions implies a double contradiction. It forgets the history of transformations of streetscape associated with the changes in vehicular technologies.[11] But more importantly, it ignores

10. Several relevant figures in the field such as Elon Musk from Tesla, Lex Kerssemakers, the North America Volvo CEO, and Christoph Mertz, a research scientist at Carnegie Mellon University, have pointed out the problem of faded lanes in the current development of the technology. Paul Carlson, from Texas A&M University, aims for consistency in signage along American roads in order to accommodate automation favorably. The agency Reuters also points out that the lack of standardization in the US compared to most European countries, which follow the Vienna Convention on Road Signs and Signals, causes a big problem. At the same time several researchers at Sookmyung Women's University and Yonsei University in Seoul are focusing on how current automated sign recognition systems detect irrelevant signs placed along roads. This problematic cacophony is dramatically amplified in urban scenarios. See Alexandria Sage, "Where's the Lane? Self-driving Cars Confused by Shabby U.S. Roadways," Reuters, http://www.reuters.com/article/us-autos-autonomous-infrastructure-insig-idUSKCN0WX131 (accessed December 2016); Andrew Ng and Yuanquin Lin. "Self-Driving Cars Won't Work Until We Change Our Roads—And Attitudes," *Wired* https://www.wired.com/2016/03/self-driving-cars-wont-work-change-roads-attitudes/ (accesed December 2016); and Signe Brewster, "Researchers Teach Self-driving Cars to 'See' Better at Night," *Science*, http://www.sciencemag.org/news/2017/03/researchers-teach-self-driving-cars-see-better-night (accessed March 2017).

11. The relationship between the transformations of the streetscape and the arrival of new vehicular technologies also places driverless cars at the center of the history of architecture. Since its inception, the car has often played a central role in architects' urban visions. The precepts of the Athens Charter and the images of the Ville Radieuse were an explicit responses to the safety and functional issues associated with the popularization of car. Its implementation, with different degrees of success, during the post-war reconstruction of Europe and the global explosion of suburban sprawl, fueled architectural controversies that questioned the role of cars in the definition of urban environments. Ian Nairn's *Outrage* (1955), Robin Boyd's *Australian Ugliness* (1960), Appleyard, Randolph Myer, and Lynch's *The View from the Road* (1964), Peter Blake's *God's Own Junkyard* (1965), Reyner Banham's *Los Angeles: The Architecture of Four Ecologies* (1971), Venturi, Scott-Brown and Izenour's *Learning from Las Vegas* (1973), and Alison and Peter Smithson's *AS IN DS: An Eye on the Road* (1983) are not only some well-known examples of these debates; they also show how the topic lost traction in architecture debates at the end of the last century.

the fact that self-driving cars construct images that are barely comparable to human perception.[12] Driverless cars take in real-time data through different on-board sensors. Although there is not an industry standard yet, certain trends are ubiquitous. The vehicles use a combination of radars, cameras, ultrasonic sensors, and LiDAR scanners to get immediate information from the external environment.[13] The resulting perception differs greatly from a human one. Driverless cars do not capture environmental sound. Colour rarely plays a role in the way they map the city. And, with various degrees of resolution, their sensors cover 360 degrees around the vehicle.

At the same time, car sensors and human senses share a logic of specialization. The human sense of hearing tends to recognize exceptional and abrupt changes in the sonic landscape—a siren, a claxon, a change in the sound of the engine. Even if human peripheral vision operates in a similar fashion, attention is essential for eyesight. Human vision requires continuity and focusses on subtle changes. Thus fog or darkness decrease the eye's ability to discern difference and decrease its effectivity. Similarly, the way self-driving cars' sensors function defines their potentials and limitations. Some sensors detect the relative speed of objects in close range while others capture the reflectivity of static objects far away. Some are able to construct detailed 3D models of objects no farther than a meter away while others are indispensable for pattern recognition. Human drivers combine eyesight and hearing to make decisions and driverless cars' algorithms use

information from multiple sensors in their decision-making processes. Yet, autonomous vehicles' capacity for storing the information their sensors capture makes a big difference. As each of the four types of sensors in a driverless car captures the area they circulate, they also produce a medium-specific map of their environment.

Radars are object-detection systems that use radio waves to determine the range, angle, or velocity of objects. They have good range but low resolution, especially when compared to ultrasonic sensors and LiDAR scanners. They are good at near-proximity detection but less effective than sonar. They work equally well in light and dark conditions and perform through fog, rain, and snow. While they are very effective at determining relative speed of traffic, they do not differentiate colour or contrast, rendering them useless for optical pattern recognition. They are critical to monitoring the speed of other vehicles and objects surrounding the self-driving car. They detect movement in the city and are able to construct relational maps capturing sections of the electromagnetic spectrum.

Ultrasonic sensors are object-detection systems that emit ultrasonic sound waves and detect their return to define distance. They offer a very poor range, but they are extraordinarily effective in very-near-range three-dimensional mapping. Compared to radio waves, sound waves are slow. Thus, differences of less than a centimetre are detectable. They work regardless of light levels and also perform well in conditions of snow, fog, and rain. They do not provide any

12. Uber's arrival is linked to the famous Google lawsuit against Uber that position LiDAR technology at the centre of the dispute. Again, this legal battle locates the discussion of the car's ability to see the world. See Alex Davies, "Google's Lawsuit Against Uber Revolves Around Frickin' Lasers," *Wired*, https://www.wired.com/2017/02/googles-lawsuit-uber-revolves-around-frickin-lasers/ (accessed March 2017).

13. For a detailed list of the the onboard sensors used by different self-driving car brands, see footnote 4.

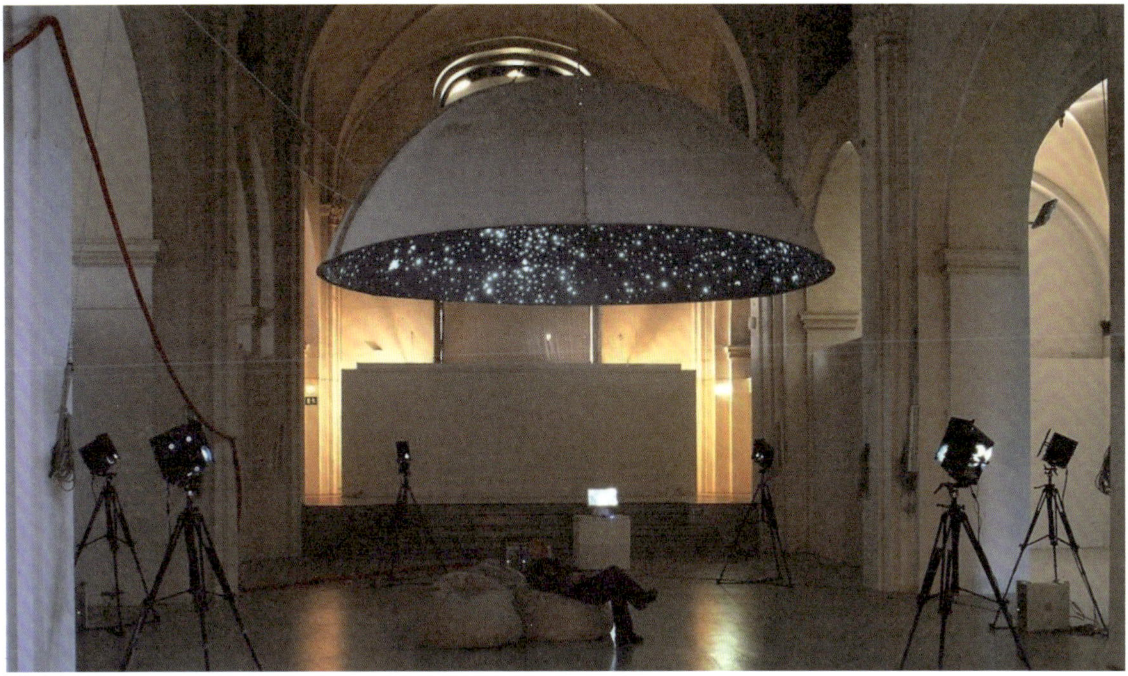

Up to the left:
360 immersive projection in the dolby
dome for Vivid 2016 Festival

Up to the right:
Black Shoals Dome exhibited at
Nikolaj Copenhagen Contemporary
Art Centre

On the left:
Still from "Where the City can See"
a LiDAR film by Liam Young

colour or contrast or allow optical character recognition, but they are extremely useful to determine speed. They are essential to for automatic parking and to avoid low-speed collisions. They construct detailed 3D maps of the temporary arrangement of objects in the proximity of the car.

LiDARs (Light Detection and Ranging) are surveying technologies that measure distance by illuminating a target with a laser light. They are currently the most extended object-detection technology for autonomous vehicles. They generate extremely accurate representations of the car's surroundings but fail to perform in short distances. They cannot detect colour or contrast, cannot provide optical character recognition capabilities, nor they are effective for real-time speed monitoring. Light conditions do not decrease their functionality, but snow, fog, rain, and dust particles in the air do. Due to their use of light spectrum wavelengths, LiDAR scanners can sense small elements floating in the atmosphere. They produce maps of quality of air quality.

RGB and infrared cameras are devices that record visual images. They have very high resolution and operate better in long distances than in close proximity. They can determine speed, but not at the level of accuracy of radar. They can discern colour and contrast but underperform in very bright conditions and also as light levels fade. Cameras are key for the car's optical-character recognition software and are *de facto* surveillance systems.

This proliferation of sensors in the environment is a defining factor of the imminent urban milieu. Environmental sensors connected to cars distribute instant remote sensing, enabling the constant flow of information on the urban environment while at the same time radicalizing issues of privacy, access, and control. They simultaneously react to and change the urban pattern, generating an unprecedented environmental consciousness. The resulting image of the city cannot differ more from human perception. It is a combination of sections of the electromagnetic spectrum, detailed 3D models around cars, detailed maps of air pollution, and an interconnected surveillance system. It is not the city as we see it.

And yet interconnected sensors can create a new common, a ubiquitous, global sensorium that obliterates further the distinction between nature and artifice. While the city is managed by non-human agencies, it continues to be designed around the assumption of a benign human-centered system. Engaging citizens in this new sensorial environment makes them aware of the necessity of a new sensorial social contract.[14] It embeds the judgment of society, as a whole, in the sensorial governance of societal outcomes. The city is therefore the space where we can gain mutual confidence trust, generating the necessary relationship for coming scenarios of coexistence. In other words, driverless vision isn't just about cars, rather it is more akin to the interaction between a government and a governed citizenry. Modern government is the outcome of an implicit agreement—or social contract—between the ruled and their rulers, aimed at fulfilling the general will of citizens.

14. "Algorithmic Social Contract" is a termed coined by MIT professor Iyad Rahwan and develops the idea that by understanding the priorities and values of the public, we could train machines to behave in ways that the society would consider ethical. See Iyad Rahwan, "Society-in-the-Loop: Programming the Algorithmic Social Contract," www.medium.com https://medium.com/mit-media-lab/society-in-the-loop-54ffd71cd802 (accessed March 2017).

Cyclopean Cannibalism, or, Taming Rubble with Robots

**Matter Design
(Brandon Clifford, Wes McGee)**

Cyclopean /ˌsīkləˈpēən,sīˈklōpēən/ *adj.* (1) often capitalized: of, relating to, or characteristic of a Cyclops; (2) huge, massive; (3) of or relating to a style of stone construction marked typically by the use of large irregular blocks without mortar[1]

Cannibalism /ˈkanibəlizəm/ n. (1) the usually ritualistic eating of human flesh by a human being; (2) the eating of the other flesh of an animal by another animal of the same kind; (3) an act of cannibalizing something[2]

Cyclopean Cannibalism: construction technique consisting of the re-appropriation of pre-existing building for the assembly of 'new' buildings // *harnesses robotics to site, scan, and minimally carve stock to re-construct architecture at a full scale*

Abstract

The myth of Cyclops is described in Hesiod's *Theogony*[3] as a race of giants, known for constructing massive stone walls. Cyclopean masonry, then, consists of massive stones that fit together, despite their diverse sizes and shapes. Their assembly is so dramatic that it seems feasible only by the hands of a mythical race of giants. Of the numerous civilizations that produced these megalithic stone works, the Inka constructed without a preconceived design. This architecture emerged through a sequential logic informed by the constraints of resources. *The Inka stone works were computed.* When materials were scarce, stones were readapted into new works. *They consumed their own cities.*

In today's urban context, we generate unprecedented quantities of waste. There is an impending crisis hinging on how we deal with this debris, specifically from buildings. In order to

Figure 1. Cyclops (illustration by Joshua Longo)

1. *Merriam Webster Dictionary*, https://www.merriam-webster.com/dictionary/cannibalism

2. *Merriam Webster Dictionary*, https://www.merriam-webster.com/dictionary/cyclopean

3. Hesiod, *Theogony* (New York: Liberal Arts, 1953).

Figure 2. Concrete, concrete, and more concrete

more intelligently reconsider the existing building stock, the profession could learn a great deal from the Inka and other cyclopean builders. Their methods force us to relinquish predetermined design composition in exchange for a systemic, intelligent design, capable of responding to unknown conditions. ***Cyclopean Cannibalism*** deciphers the Inka method and translates it into a possible contemporary method. Future cities demand a creative cannibalization of their accumulating debris and stagnating structures. Can urbanism of the near future be reimaged as architecturally self-sustaining? Can our future cities disassemble, devour, and reassemble themselves?

Introduction: A persistent problem

Our cities are ticking time bombs. They are developing at an unprecedented, uncontrolled rate. By 2050, the majority of the world's population will live in urban centers.[4] The rapid growth of urban centers leaves little room and time to adequately receive the impending population influx. Buildings are demolished and rebuilt, while informal communities burgeon with new dwellers. The construction debris generated in the wake of redevelopment projects is exponentially increasing, in some cases annually resulting in millions of tons. This rate of dangerous development begs for a relinquishing of totalizing design control.

4. "By 2050, this percentage will increase to 86% in advanced countries, and 64% in developing nations." Seoul Biennale Description and "World's Population Increasingly Urban with More than Half Living in Urban Areas," accessed 7 February 2017, <http://www.un.org/en/development/desa/news/population/world-urbanization-prospects-2014.html>.

We position Seoul as a case study in our urban exploration. Seoul embodies the new global city—it is increasing in both population and quantity of buildings. And yet the lifespan of buildings in Seoul is shockingly low. The average life of a Seoul building lasts a mere twenty-two years.[5] That is a quarter of the average lifespan of South Korean citizens.[6] Like the US paradigm, existing structures are demolished and materials are shipped off-site. The most ideal scenarios of this process allow for material to be recycled, downgraded, and shipped back to site. Still, the amount of rubble waste generated from these perpetual demolitions demands upheaval of current construction and material paradigms.

Past civilizations were adroit in readapting previous built structures into transformed environments. Their methods of re-appropriation reduced waste and transportation efforts. They prioritized a craftsman's ability to template and customize stones. The Inka Empire devised an alternative technique to managing developmental waste. The Inka integrated found stones into their constructions, drawing from their immediate surroundings to constitute new structures. Inka stone works adapted harmoniously to nature, both drawing from resources and formally mirroring them.[7] Their system, in a morbid-poetic way, consumed both the pre-existing and the found. The Inka construction system was also capable of responding to unknown conditions, prioritizing technique over a final form. Their cyclopean stones, working in aggregate, flexed to any environment, consuming any adaptable masonry to grow.

Figure 3. Detail of the Inka Roca, Cusco Perú. This detailed image contains draft re-direction, a Utah stone, as well as a nub detail.

Which brings us to cannibalism. The act is in dire need of some good press. We're taking the bad reputation that cannibalism has made for itself, and adapting it to an urban context. The future city is forced to build upon itself. Existing structures are destroyed, and debris is summarily removed. The site is treated as a *tabula rasa*, with

5. Seongwon Seo and Yongwoo Hwang, "An Estimation of Construction and Demolition Debris in Seoul, Korea: Waste Amount, Type, and Estimating Model," in *J. Air & Waste Manage Association.* (1999): 980-985.

6. http://www.cnn.com/2017/02/21/health/life-expectancy-increase-globally-by-2030/

7. Inka works often frame or mime views, naturally found "structures," and anthropomorphic stone works. They celebrate and augment the pre-existing, natural beauty of an adjacent landscape. Carolyn Dean, *A Culture of Stone: Inka Perspectives on Rock* (Durham, NC: Duke UP, 2010).

existing buildings as undesired marks to be erased. But existing buildings and their leftovers beg fo re-assembly. The promise of the digital era will be to robotically scan and consider these existing materials as stock to construct future architectures.

This project picks up where the Inka left off. It begins at the end of Inka civilization and, in a way, our own. It offers regeneration within the context of demolition and rampant urban inflation. It seeks to learn from both crises and construction techniques of the past. This project unearths the "primitive" Inka technique to postulate a new, material paradigm. *Cyclopean Cannibalism* seeks to reclaim the remains of demolished buildings within the urban fabric. It harnesses the craft of stone cutting to assemble a structural system out of ruin. This act straddles two time periods. The project cannibalizes the waste of demolished Seoul buildings, today. It employs the cyclopean, Inka stone-cutting techniques of the distant past. What may read as an anachronistic technique, we see as a means of sustainable assembly. This method is not motivated by a romantic viewpoint, but rather by a recognition that cyclopean cannibals understood this crisis better than we do.

We foresee a future city that is forced to build upon itself. We pose Cyclopean Cannibalism as the solution.

Assessing our urban reality

Our systems of urban development lurch in haggard strides. Concrete is being poured at an unprecedented rate. [8] Meanwhile, we generate construction waste that is sent directly to landfills.

While steel is typically recycled, leftover masonry negates facile re-assembly into new systems. In many developing urban contexts, re-appropriation practices of past civilizations have been lost. Buildings are sooner obliterated—the land they occupy deemed more valuable than retaining the structure(s) that stand on them—than modified, added on to, or 'readjusted.' Cities seem to generate construction waste faster than the city can responsibly and sustainably control.

Figure 4. Demolition

We are confronted with the evidence of our daily trash. We go through the empty pizza boxes, the used products, the leftover plastic packaging, etc. etc. ...but we are largely unaware of the sheer quantity generated. This mundane waste is about

8. David Harvey highlights growing concern, stating, "Concrete is everywhere being poured at an unprecedented rate over the surface of planet earth. We are in the midst of a huge crisis—ecological, social, and political—of planetary urbanization without, it seems, knowing or even marking it." David Harvey, "The Crisis of Planetary Urbanization," In *Uneven Growth: Tactical Urbanisms for Expanding Megacities* (New York: Museum of Modern Art, 2014), 27.

254 million tons of municipal waste in the United States each year.[9] And this is our *visible* waste, the trash that we *know* we generate. Meanwhile, the construction and demolition debris (CD) is less visible to society. CD debris is moved around the city in autonomous trucks and trains, out of sight, yet the debris is in fact much more prevalent. There is *double* the amount of CD debris as there is conventional trash—about 534 million tons per year.[10] A recent report in the *Journal of Nature* attempted to put such vast numbers into perspective, stating, "[t]he average person in the United States throws away their body weight in rubbish every month."[11] Put in context, we throw away two body bags of trash each month—one filled with our own trash, the other with construction debris.

Of this vast construction and demolition debris, the stark majority is concrete. Seventy percent of construction debris, or 375 million tons, is generated per year.[12] In other words, there are 1.17 tons of concrete being taken to landfill per person in America, each year. The principal source of this concrete is the demolition of roads and bridges (150 million tons), and then buildings (84 million tons).[13] While a significant proportion of this debris has its origin in the city, the landfills where demolished concrete ends its lifecycle are often in far removed. For example, Tunnel Hill Partners operate a waste management service in the northeast of America, which transports CD debris from New York and Boston by train to two landfill sites in Ohio.

People pay to dispose of concrete debris, and the industry of demolition has in recent years seen the emergence of larger companies which manage waste at the scale of entire regions. Tunnel Hill Partners account for just 1.2% of all the CD debris in America. Yet they operate a collection of around 400 wagons shifting 140,000 tons of debris from urban areas to landfills in Ohio *each day*.[14]

Strategies for recycling concrete exist, yet they take energy and labor. The most common strategy is to crush concrete into fine aggregates. Only companies in Japan have developed technologies to re-use these aggregates in structurally load-bearing roles. Instead, these aggregates are commonly used as an underlay in asphalt road surfaces.[15] Papers on the recycling of concrete make no reference to the idea that one could take a block of concrete from the construction site and use it as a load-bearing brick.

9. U.S. EPA, "Municipal Solid Waste Generation, Recycling, and Disposal in the United States: Facts and Figures," 2015.

10. U.S. EPA, "Construction and Demolition Debris Generation in the United States, 2014," 2016.

11. D. Hoornweg, P. Bhada, and C. Kennedy "Environment: Waste Production Must Peak This Century," Nature (2013).

12. U.S. EPA, "Construction and Demolition Debris Generation in the United States, 2014."

13. Ibid.

14. Tunnel Hill Partners, http://tunnelhillpartners.com/.

15. V. Tam, "Comparing the Implementation of Concrete Recycling in the Australian and Japanese Construction Industries," Journal of Cleaner Production (2009).

Figure 5. Demolition

We seem to omit our own, ancestral knowledge in managing this problem. We forget that past cultures built on top of one another. The litany of models points to a natural affinity to retain what already exists. So why are we now negating this tendency? Perhaps when working with stone, the idea of re-use is appropriate. Today, however, we tend to operate in three categories: (1) re-appropriation—we try to simply fill an existing structure with a new program; (2) re-use/expansion—we try to keep parts of an existing structure, but build around it; (3) recycling—we demolish a structure and start over, and in the best cases, parts of the structure are recycled. These categories operate within a "mature" urban framework.

Reviving the 'primitive': Cyclopean methods

With rapid urban expansion, the future city will inevitably face a mountain of irregular demolition debris. As we have proven, this is not a new problem. A plethora of early cultures created incredible architectures from this very constraint, polygonal masonry (Fig. 8) being one example. This category of masonry does not rely upon standard units of construction. Rather, it lives in the possibilities of randomness. It assumes the assembly of irregular shaped stones, occasionally fitting them together as found, and often carved slightly to ensure a better fit. This category of masonry is broad. It covers a litany of assembly types, from dry stacking to rubble-fill, from imprecise to precise, and from manageable in scale to the megalithic (Fig. 6).

Figure 6. Megalith – (Big Stone) Baalbek, Lebanon

Figure 7. Dry Stone – Rapa Nui

Figure 8. Polygonal Masonry – Tarawasi, Perú

Figure 9. Cyclopean Masonry – Inka Roca, Cusco Perú

Polygonal masonry is also practical and provincial. It focuses on assembly over fit, often filling gaps between stones with smaller stones (Fig. 7). Others explore a unique character of fit and shape, as in the Temple of Apollo at Delphi in Greece. While these seem to speak to explainable differences in means, methods, resources, or perhaps cultural inclination, one category of polygonal masonry is uniquely shrouded in mystery—cyclopean masonry (Fig. 9).

Hesiod's *Theogony* references Cyclops as part of a race of giants. Who are the authors of megalithic stone works. Massive stones assembled dry are composed into a cohesive, compressive system. The stones project the illusion that they have been squeezed together by giants, given their precise assembly. The stones also appear to be assembled as found, as the stones still retain a rounded character. The attribution to Cyclops is no mistake. A mythical race of giants is the closest "rational" explanation for such an architectural feat—so rational, in fact, that the ancient Greeks and Romans are not the only cultures to arrive at this explanation. Though this form of masonry bears a Eurocentric title, it is anything but.

Similar stone structures are found around the world among cultures that have never encountered each other. Of these cultures, the Quechua (commonly Inka) people of the Andes produced the most complex and copious amounts of cyclopean architecture.

Similar structures are also found on Rapa Nui (Easter Island) at the Ahu Vinapu (Fig. 10). This resemblance is uncanny. So much so, it fooled the famed adventurer and amateur archaeologist Thor Hyerdahl. He falsely proposed the Inka had previously colonized Rapa Nui.[16] This colonialist viewpoint has been detrimental to the pride of the Rapa Nui people, not to mention the Inka, given Hyerdahl's additional speculation that the Inka themselves were taught by a prior race of Europeans. While careful work by archaeologists Carl Lipo and Terry Hunt[17] debunked these claims, the theory is pervasive. Falsities such as these are not unique with regard to these cyclopean structures. It is perhaps no surprise that the idea of a primordial giant race is also not unique to Mycenae. The Inka myth was that their god Viracocha created a race of giants as a first attempt at human creation. He then destroyed that race with a flood in order to breathe life into smaller stones.[18]

These cyclopean works of architecture evade a linear history. Despite eager attempts to attribute these wonders to a single culture, a people, or a myth, these works are not the result of an architect. They are the *inevitable* result of a resource and a technology (or lack thereof). Whenever a similar set of resources and technology overlap, *this architecture re-emerges*, engendering new but similar myths about its miraculous appearance. Cyclopean masonry appears across varied geographical and time scales, tied only to the very limitations that generate it.

16. Thor Heyerdahl, *Aku-Aku: The Secret of Easter Island* (Chicago: Rand McNally, 1958).

17. Terry L. Hunt, and Carl P. Lipo, *The Statues That Walked: Unraveling the Mystery of Easter Island* (Berkeley: Counterpoint, 2012).

18. Kenneth McLeish, *Myth: Myths & Legends of the World Explained & Explored* (New York: Bloomsbury Publishing, 1996).

Figure 10. A comparison of Inka and Rapa Nui masonry.
(lef) Machu Picchu
(right) Ahu Vinapu, Rapa Nui

Hammerstones

Each of these cultures share the same resource of dense stone (often granite), but do not have the technology of metal tooling, resulting in a shared technology—the hammerstone. Though a number of theories suggest the Inka used a variety of techniques to carve stone, scant evidence exists to prove this. With the information we have, we know that the Inka were carving stones with other stones. The use of a hammerstone is difficult to claim as carving. It is more akin to sanding than cutting. In fact, the Inka didn't call this carving. As Carolyn Dean explains, "the Inka referred to the working of finely joined masonry as *canincakuchini,* which is derived from the verb *kanini (canini),* meaning to bite or nibble."[19]

Blows from a hammerstone at angle close to an edge can rapidly draft away large chunks of material. When hit perpendicular to a face, they peck and dress the stone. This act of pecking is tedious, but as a result extremely precise. Imagine asking a carpenter to craft a table, but remove their usual suspects of steel tools. Only hand the carpenter a pile of lumber and some sandpaper. It will take them some time to create a table, but that table is likely to be round with any joints precise. Hammerstones do act differently on different types of stone. Some stones carve more rapidly and roughly, while others, like granite, carve more slowly. An interesting tendency of the Inka stonework is the harder the stone, the larger the stones are in the assembly, and the tighter the fit.

Quarrying and selecting

The use of hammerstones is laborious, and requires a shift in our contemporary way of thinking about stone construction. While most stone construction is quarried from a site, typically in block form, and transported to a stone-cutter to carve that block into a unit of

19. Dean, *A Culture of Stone.*

construction, the restriction of the hammerstone forces these cultures to look at stone sourcing in a different way.

As a result of the hammerstone technology, the Inka (and other cyclopean constructors) dressed their stones instead of carving them.[20] Because their subtractive method was so slow, it made more sense to devote time to properly selecting the appropriate shape to fill a hole and only work on that stone minimally to fit, carving that rock into a rectangular block. This process of selection then leads to another way of thinking about stonework. Though the standard masonry module of the brick is universally determined by the mass a single hand can hold and place, or perhaps a CMU is the result of two hands, the hand is not the limiting factor in creating cyclopean architecture. Cyclopean architecture is the result of selecting the proper shape to fill a hole from irregular geometries. Time is the rate-limiting step. The fewer the stones, the less selection takes place. Thus, megalithic stones commonly emerge when this conflation of resources and constraints exist.

Fitting methods

Given the hard stone and hammerstone resources, the resulting massive and precise cyclopean architectures emerge with similar patterning. The design of these assembled stones is not predetermined because it is the result of "sequential assembly."[21] This process is a form of minimal nesting, the act of finding the closest fit, and then removing the least amount of material in order to make that fit perfect. While a number of theories propose how the Inka carved their stones to fit, the general agreement is that there were two dominant procedures—templating and dry fitting.

Templating: This common theory suggests that a wooden template is constructed to scribe the existing condition of either the assembled wall or the quarried stone. This template is then translated onto the stone that will be dressed to fit and used as a guide to approach the desired profile geometry (Fig. 11). This process is ideal for stones that are too large to maneuver over and over again, but does not produce the same precision of the dry fitting approach.

Dry Fitting: One byproduct of the carving method of nibbling with hammerstones is a great deal of stonedust. In the dry fitting theory, this stonedust coats the set stones while the loose stone is set into place. This stone is then removed and where the stone is touching the existing condition, the dust is compacted and visualizes where material needs to be removed. This is a tedious process and limits the size of the stones to something easily maneuverable. While this fit is more precise than the templating approach, it is also more laborious.[22]

20. "In the quarries of Kachiqhata, the In[k]as did not practice quarrying in the technical sense. The stone was neither split off a rock face nor detached from bedrock by undercutting. The quarrymen simply went through gigantic rockfalls, carefully selecting raw blocks that met their specification. As far as I can ascertain, once a suitable block was located, it was roughed out before it was sent on its way to [the site]. Protzen." Jean-Pierre Protzen, *Inca Architecture and Construction at Ollantaytambo* (New York: Oxford University Press, 1993), 165.

21. "The configuration of these stones is not pre-determined, but the result of a sequential assembly from the bottom up of irregular forms that are scribed and minimally carved to align with their neighbors." Brandon Clifford and Wes McGee, "Digital Inca: An Assembly Method for Free-Form Geometries," *Modelling Behaviour* (2015): 173-186.

22. Ibid.

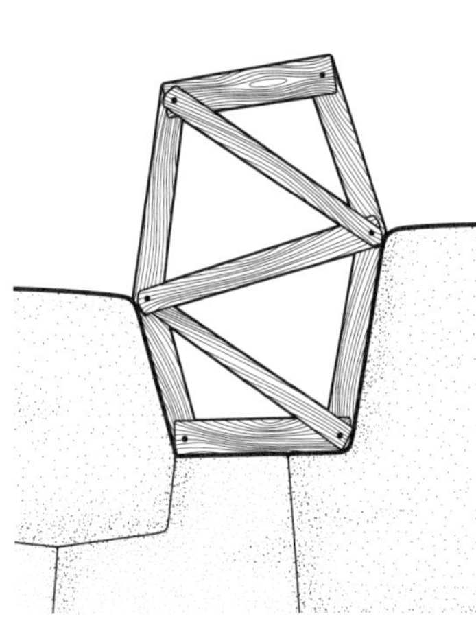
Figure 11. Templating Diagram.

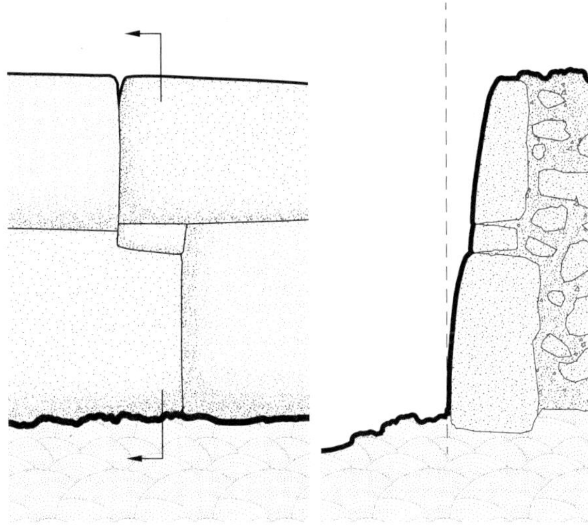
Figure 12. Elevation and Section through Ahu Vinapu of Rapa Nui showing the angle and depth of stones

Details and sequence

Yet these constructions are the result of a procedure, a code (or in contemporary terms, a script). It is possible to reverse engineer their sequence (Fig. 17). A few key details allow for this inverse decoding. For instance, bed joints clearly define intention. The Inka would carve the bottoms of the stone intended to be placed, and leave the tops uncarved. Once set, those tops would be carved in-situ to receive the stone above them, resulting in Utah-shaped stones (Fig. 13). While this rule is common, it is not religiously followed. Another telling detail is draft re-direction (Fig. 14). Stones often shift their vertical edges when engaging a different stone. These seams kink immediately. This is the result of necessarily lowering stones from above. The angle determines the draft. If it is a positive angle, the stone is able to be dropped in from above. If it is a negative angle, the stone is not able to be lowered in. Finally, there is the wedge stone (Fig. 15). The wedge stone[23] is similar in approach to a keystone. It is the last stone set in a wall. Instead of being dropped in from above, particular details allow it to be tilted in from the face. In addition to these sequential details, a number of strange details also describe how stones were placed. These handle details can describe whether a stone was lowered in from above with ropes, or tilted up from below with sticks (Fig. 16).

Translating past to present

So how do we begin to translate these primitive methods into a contemporary language? Recent advances in robotics and scanning allow us to dislodge the technique from its roots within the contemporary context of the economy of labor. They provide an original framework, upon which we can explore new treatments to demolition debris. While there has been significant interest in

23. Protzen, *Inca Architecture and Construction at Ollantaytambo*, 195-197.

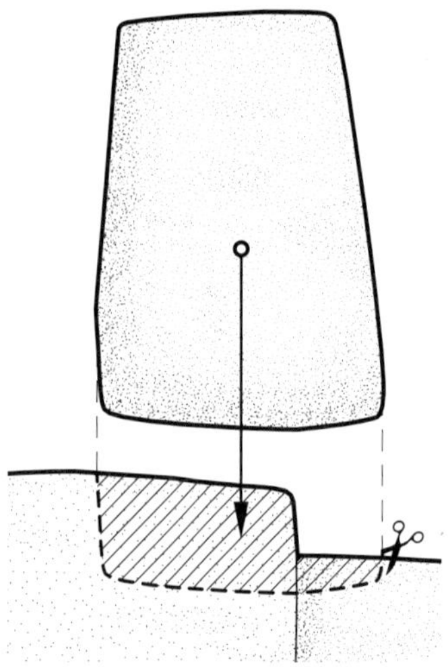

Figure 13. Diagram of the Bed Joint
Process resulting in Utah Stones

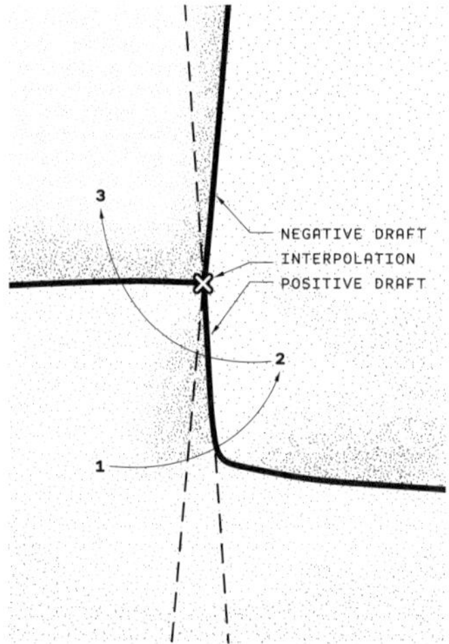

Figure 14. Diagram of Draft Re-Direction

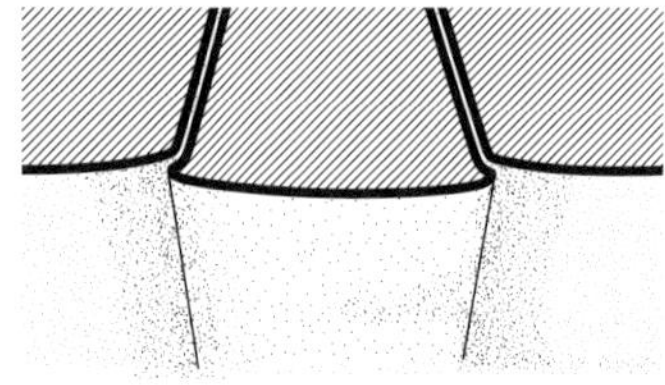

Figure 15. Figure 15. Plan Diagram of the
Inka Wedge Stone

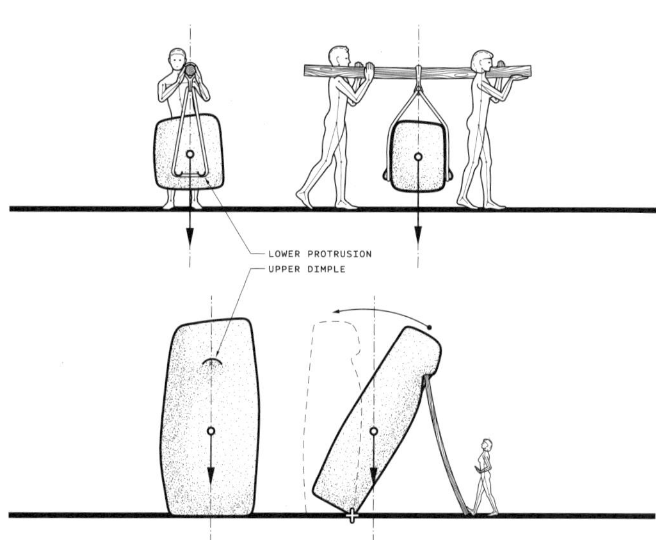

Figure 16. Detail Diagram of the lower protrusions and upper
dimples commonly found in Inka cyclopean masonry

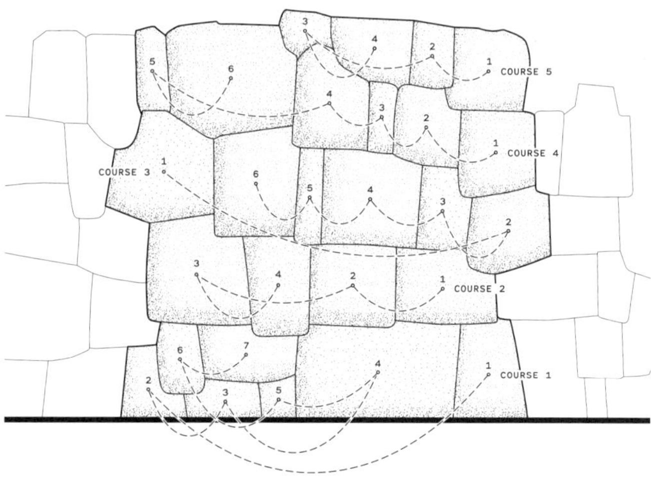

Figure 17. Diagram of Sequence and Coursing—
deciphered from the Inka Roca of Cusco, Perú

the development and adaptation of robotic fabrication techniques to architectural applications, it is the more recent move towards implementing adaptive processes that holds the most potential to disrupt the typical digital fabrication paradigm. The incorporation of sensor feedback into a production process can occur at multiple levels. A typical sensing system might include a one- or two-dimensional laser, or a three-dimensional time-of-flight camera such as the Microsoft Kinect.[24]

Industrial manufacturing processes often use a variety of sensing and gauging techniques to insure part accuracy, especially in processes where tool wear or variability in work holding could compromise the desired tolerances. By integrating the sensing process tightly within the production workflow, this can be extended to the concept of "Adaptive Part Variation,"[25] whereby sensors are utilized to provide real-time feedback to robotic fabrication and assembly processes. This feedback can be used to make online corrections to the geometry of future components to adapt to deviations between a master digital model and a constantly updated as built condition. Within the context of mobile robotics, sensors can be used to provide feature based localization, for example in-situ assembly processes utilizing mobile robot manipulators[26].

In this research we propose to utilize scanning processes in order to explore potential new efficiencies in the design and fabrication stages of the process. It is also important to recognize that we do not see the translation from design to production as a linear, one-way flow of information. Instead, the process is a bidirectional flow of information, whereby the overall design can adjust to results or in-progress changes to the as-built system. One stage of scanning will be utilized to analyze the existing geometry of found stone. An algorithmic design process will then analyze these geometries to determine best-fit conditions for producing specific adjacencies with minimal material removal. This process must consider a range of inputs, including structure, fabrication constraints, and formal considerations. Another potential application of scanning is to analyze the as-built condition of the overall assembly of stones as the structure progresses, allowing for adaptive customization of future components.

"Reincarnation out of willful destruction"[27]

It seems that we are forging a friendship between the primitive past and the robotized future. A rich body of precedents frame our translation process. Lebbeus Woods's *Radical Reconstruction* questions normative means of building and occupying space. His projects offer a new way of building and inhabiting space, one that is

24. Carlo Dal Mutto, Pietro Zanuttigh, and Guido M Cortelazzo, Time-of-Flight Cameras and Microsoft Kinect™, *SpringerBriefs in Electrical and Computer Engineering* (2012).

25. Lauren Vasey, I. Maxwell, and D. Pigram. "Adaptive Part Variation: A Near Real-Time Approach to Construction Tolerances," *Robotic Fabrication in Architecture, Art and Design* (2014): 291-304.

26. Katherin Dorfler, and T. Sandy, M. Giftthaler, G. Gramazio, M. Kohler, and J. Buchli, "Mobile Robotic Brickwork: Automation of a Discrete Robotic Fabrication Process Using an Autonomous Mobile Robot," *Robotic Fabrication in Architecture, Art and Design* (2016): 204-217.

27. Lebbeus Woods, *Radical Reconstruction* (Princeton, NJ: Princeton Architectural Press, 1997).

premised as "reincarnation out of willful destruction."[28] Material debris is readapted to become entire buildings or armatures on existing structures. This move, while varied in contexts, retains a connotation of reassembled memory. The appropriated debris embedded in his drawings—rubble left over from warfare, economic stagnation, and earthquakes—raise questions about the entrenched, past experiences of readapted materials. It questions what these memories carry into the reassembled structure.

Architects have recently taken up Woods's assertions, operating within the framework of digital fabrication. Greg Lynn and Gramazio Kohler have expanded our vocabulary of design uncertainty through advances in scanning and robotics. Greg Lynn's "Blob Wall" (2005) employed "reinvented," hollow plastic as robotically molded bricks, or individual components assembled to form a 'blob' wall. This inventive project reconsidered the potentials of selectively carving complex intersections via robotics. This process knows the geometries prior to the digital Boolean operation, illuminating the problematics of compacting the units to ensure collisions occur. Gramazio Kohler's "Endless Wall" (2011) also utilized robotics in the construction process to assemble individualized components into a single wall. While this project contributes to resolving unknown conditions through scanning, it maintains stacking without indexing or carving. These explorations underscore the burgeoning confluence between construction processes, robotics, and masonry.

Manual for reassembly

We also draw from peripheral studies in vernacular architecture to shape our process. Bernard Rudolfsky's *Architecture without Architects*

places design in the hands of the anonymous participant. His text proposes "to break down our narrow concepts of the art of building by introducing the unfamiliar world of non-pedigreed architecture."[29] It is within such a framework that we seek to position *Cyclopean Cannibalism*. Building off of Woods's "ambiguity," we intend for this project to function as a liberation of choice. We rely on the user, the participant, to imbue meaning into the system.

As a product of this investigation, we present *The Cannibal's Cookbook: Mining Myths of Cyclopean Constructions*, a Do-It-Yourself Manual on *Cyclopean Cannibalism*. The manual places the opportunities embedded in the technique in the hands of the urban *polis*. Our manual will contain instructions for assessing and creating one's own structure out of demolition debris. We see this publishing of information as a move to democratize the technique. Perhaps the manual could mitigate the lack of affordable housing. The exponential rise of informal housing across the globe demands attention. The publication of sustainable and accessible construction techniques like *Cyclopean Cannibalism* acknowledges this shifting urban context.

In praise of destruction

There is an urgent, overwhelming urban crisis that demands our attention. Our current paradigm of construction, as evidenced by past civilizations, is a path to slow suicide. Despite the body of knowledge we have accumulated regarding the extinctions of past civilizations, we ignore its application within our own, contemporary reality. Our urban centers are no better than Rome. Like our ancestors, we are incessantly biting off more than we can chew. And not in the cannibalistic sense.

28. Ibid.

29. Bernard Rudolfsky, *Architecture without Architects*, (New York: MoMA, 1964), 1.

We will keep biting—it is inevitable, clearly it
is human nature. But by acknowledging this
tendency, we can also embrace it. Let's celebrate
our utter inability to take care of ourselves.
Our destruction can be harnessed. *Cyclopean
Cannibalism* is a reimagined trajectory for
future urbanism that extols our propensity for
self-annihilation. It proposes the conversion of
a worldwide problem into a localized solution.
The macro-scale abuse of urban demolition and
importation of new materials can be resolved
at the micro-scale of the demolition zone. Why
look outward when we can—and *should*—look
very, very inward?

By proposing a system that relies on its own,
internalized logic, we offer a panacea that
adapts to variable contexts. Our project and
its manual affords a diverse audience the
access and opportunity to engage in this urban
transformation. It is a bottom-up solution—by
both builder and material—embracing a top-
down problem. It's time to dine on what already
exists, what we already have. Dear city dwellers:
dinner is served. *Bon appétit.*

Figure 18. Cyclops (illustration by Joshua Longo)

Strange Weather

Ibañez Kim
(Mariana Ibañez and Simon Kim)

Within room G7.1 in the East Gate complex of the Seoul Biennale, visitors enter a space defined by a ceiling grid occupied by volumetric tiles, and floor tracks with movable modules. The ceiling tiles and the movable modules are networked so that citizens and visitors alike affect, and are subject to, an indoor meteorological system.

Unlike a typical suspended grid found in office environments, the ceiling tiles of *Strange Weather* do not conform to human-centric occupant expectations. Whereas the normative ceiling grid supplies conditioned air, humidity control, and lighting, the *Strange Weather* grid produces a more exo-environment that is not predictive nor subservient to human desires.

Vaporizers, high-lumen LEDs, and heaters are placed in the ceiling grid within the tiles. Each ceiling tile is made of either densely wrapped carbon fiber in lieu of acoustic ceiling tiles and air diffuser units, or translucent polyethylene for ceiling lights. They are actuated by a multiagent system programmed so that each node works together with ascending orders. Different combinations of moisture levels, temperature, and lighting produce a range from dry and unnaturally bright, to dark and clouded.

Visitors physically interact with the modules that are located on the floor. These ground modules move on tracks, thus allowing flexibility in rearranging the space, and in forming different seating/climbing assemblies.
As visitors sit, lounge, and socialize, their patterns of play are measured and entered within the multiagent system.

The electronic systems are ESP8266 wifi modules with Arduino microprocessors that

are continually sensing and signaling different outputs of the Strange Weather system vis-à-vis real-time human input.

What the visitor understands from this exchange is the artificial distinction between inside and outside. Human-centric, controlled interior environments are not easily separable from the natural world, and that anthropocentric intervention has consequences across scales in nature.

Strange Weather

Weather is a phenomenon that is both local and shaped within an encompassing global system. Its behavior and logics are nearly impossible to describe with certainty and only with recent mainframe computation has it become a model for simulation and prediction. Weather and climate have also given form to political endeavors tethered to socioeconomic conditions. The climate of Korea, for example, brings a summer with heat and humidity that is stifling. Following the Annexation by Japan and the Korean War, this climate, paired with the introduction of electric fans and a government fear of overtaxed power stations in a recovering economy, led to the dissemination of Fan Death. Fan Death is the sudden and inexplicable respiratory failure of people young and old brought about by sleeping near an electric fan. It is an occurrence only found in Korea, and is a myth that has been reported in Korean news media and in government-funded research.[1]

The influence of weather and climate has been the subject of negation in the modern era. As interiors expanded and buildings were enveloped in glass, artificial lighting and air conditioning gave rise to cycles of labor and living that are untethered to the sun and the climate.

The idea of climate that is controllable and bent to human requirements is only one century old (Willis Carrier, invented artificial refrigeration in 1902), yet its results are ubiquitous in modern cities and buildings. This brought about Cold War research into exerting human control on weather systems (e.g., a May 28, 1954, cover of *Collier's* magazine—described button-controlled seasons), such as cloud seeding for rain or modifying fog to cloak military movement.

To renovate the classical hierarchy of human-above-all, the idea of nonhuman agency in has become a prevalent discussion. The break from a chain of command to a flattened network of agents—of which humans are a node—that work in an ecology is finding ascendance in design and architecture. This agency follows the dual arguments of emergent authorship brought on by computation and synthetic biology from the late twentieth century, with the recognition of the Anthropocene and global conservation. For architecture and urbanism, the resultant ideology is one of duration or longevity within systems and environments. This agency enables a design strategy of time and interaction, and not necessarily a dependence on formal generation based on reading and legibility. Rather than relying on a syntax and curated meaning found in type, agency is fluidly adaptive to its own logics and independent from human expectations or hierarchies.

The formal structure of *Strange Weather* consists of three core elements: a ceiling, a tapered column, and the ground condition. The ceiling is made up of multiple 2' x 2' wound carbon fiber (CFRP) hanging modules on a 14'x24' grid. The ceiling meets the ground in a tapering stalactite and stalagmite column, where the transition from

1. "Beware of Summer Hazards!," press release, Korea Consumer Protection Board (KCPB), 18 July 2006; archived from the original on 27 September 2007.

ceiling to ground is seamless. The structure is a lightweight, self-similar family of monoliths (each module is a disformed dimension of about 2 cubic feet) that assemble into a whole. The ground is a maze of two static (CFRP) and five kinetic modules (milled MDF) whose arrangement is left up to the visitors. Each ceiling tile is made of either densely wrapped carbon fiber (in lieu of acoustic ceiling tiles) or translucent polyethylene for ceiling lights or air diffuse units.

Ibañez Kim has used carbon fiber in multiple research projects via academic work by Simon Kim and Immersive Kinematics, and in its own publications and ongoing research. Carbon fiber skin is derived from the amalgamation of layered vectors that allows for a new tectonic language of visual and tactile merits to arise within the design of inhabitable spaces. References to prove carbon fiber's applied performance can be found in educational/institutional research and recent robotically fabricated projects. Institutional research of the use of carbon fiber has been demonstrated by Simon Kim's seminar at the University of Pennsylvania School of Design called Immersive Kinematics[2] that is co-directed by Professor and Director of Integrated Product Design Mechanical Engineering and Applied Mechanics Mark Yim.[3] Kim and Yim have been researching and using wound carbon fiber to demonstrate action and behavior in composite

modules. References to robotically fabricated projects include Ibañez Kim's collaboration with Andrew John Wit and Tyler School of Art's (Temple University) *rolyPOLYGON* (2016)[4] and Ibañez Kim's *Confessional* (2016).[5] Projects that have used wound carbon fiber, such as *rolyPOLYGON* (see Figure 1) and *Confessional* (see Figure 2) have an underlying geometry that is a unique polygon that allows for packing (see Figure 3). The geometry allows these polygons to aggregate with others in new, informal communities, as will be applied and demonstrated in *Strange Weather.*

The same process of fabrication that was used in *rolyPOLYGON* will be applied in *Strange Weather.* The CFRP will be wound around a sacrificial frame (see Figures 4 and 5), and baked into structural rigidity.[6] The use of pre-impregnated carbon fiber strands yields a flexible platform for research and design. Simon Kim and Immersive Kinematics group has been working on innovative weaving techniques that allow for self-supporting carbon fiber structures (see Figure 6). The weaving patterns of the carbon fiber strands inform apertures, structural integrity, rigidity, and densities all with the use of a singular medium.

The process of weaving carbon fiber begins digitally, where three-dimensional massing geometries are developed to suit the needs of

2. Simon Kim, "Polyhedra," Immersive Kinematics, http://www.immersivekinematics.com/polyhedra-1.

3. "Mark Yim, Professor and Director of Integrated Product Design Mechanical Engineering and Applied Mechanics," Penn Engineering, The Trustees of the University of Pennsylvania, https://www.seas.upenn.edu/directory/profile.php?ID=107.

4. Mariana Ibañez, Simon Kim, and Andrew John Wit, "rolyPOLYGON," Ibañez Kim, http://www.ibanezkim.com/work#/rolypolygon/.

5. Mariana Ibañez, Simon Kim, "Confessional," Ibañez Kim, http://www.ibanezkim.com/work#/confessional/.

6. Andrew John Wit and Simon Kim, "rolyPOLY. A Hybrid Prototype for Digital Techniques and Analog Craft in Architecture." Education and Research in Computer Aided Architectural Design in Europe Conference (eCAADe), Oulu, Finland, August 22-26, 2016, pp. 631 – 638.

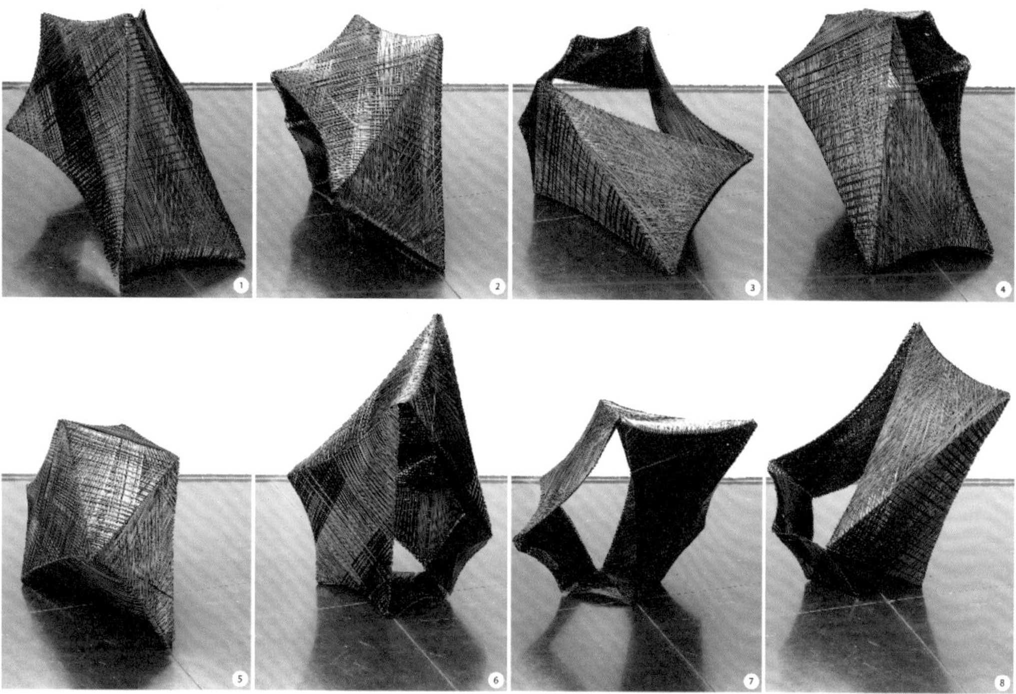

Figure 1. Ibañez Kim, Andrew John Wit, and Tyler School of Art's (Temple University), *rolyPOLYGON,* 2016

Figure 2. Ibañez Kim, *Confessional,* 2016

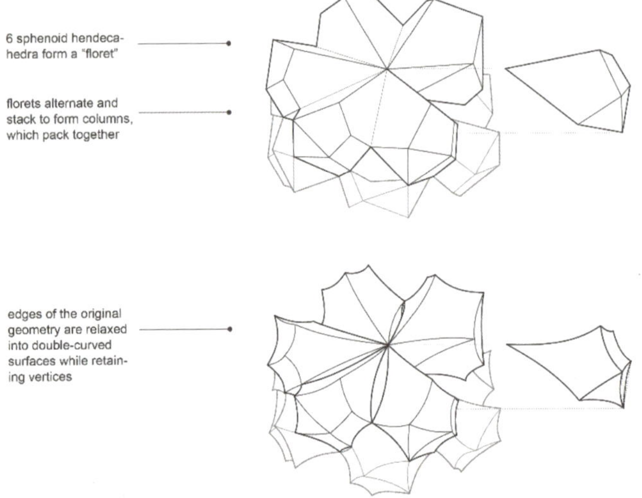

Figure 3. Packing capabilities of modules, *rolyPOLYGON*, 2016

Figure 4. Constructing the frame, 2016

Figure 5. Sacrificial frame for winding carbon fiber, 2016

Figure 6. Immersive Kinematics Seminar, programmed behavior,
University of Pennsylvania School of Design, Fall 2016

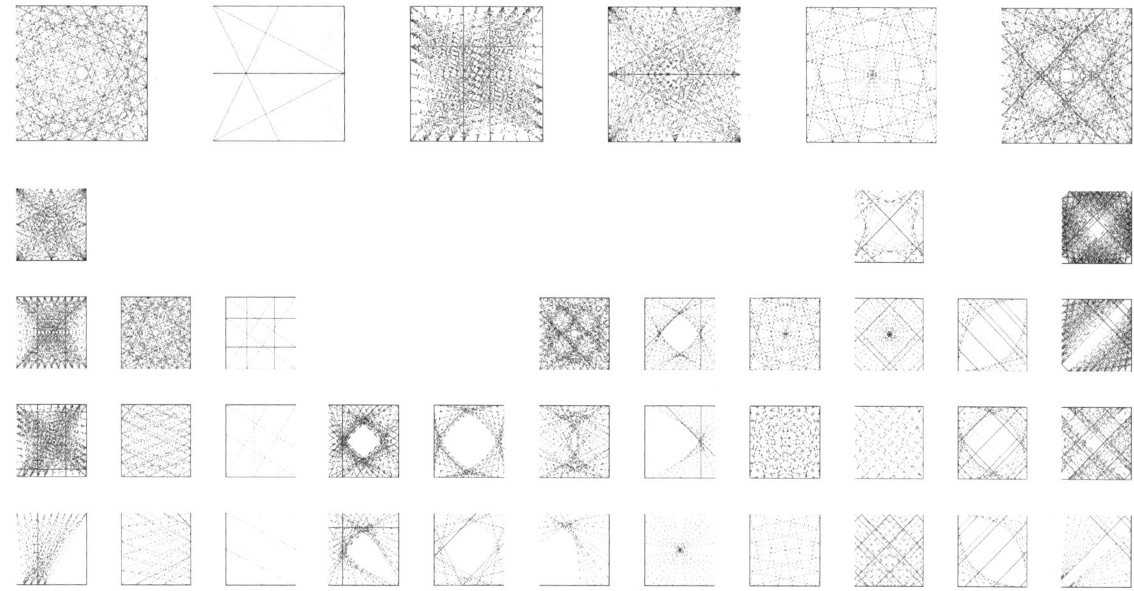

Figure 7. Digital carbon fiber weaving studies, 2016

specific projects. Next, digital weaving patterns are applied to the model parametrically to test the fitness of multiple weaving patterns in relation to functionality and design aesthetic. Several iterations are tested prior to moving into physical prototyping and mockups (see Figure 7).

Once the digital prototype successfully achieves the design criteria, the physical work can begin. The first step is to develop a physical framework for construction. Ibañez Kim has developed a low-cost adjustable frame that allows one frame to create infinite amounts of different objects. By using two different sized galvanized steel conduits, Ibañez Kim can create telescoping members that are adjustable and removable (see Figure 8). The digital model becomes the instruction set to which the steel frame will conform. The telescopic function allows the frame to change forms from one iteration to the next. Each telescoping member of the frame has two swivel joints at either end; the swivel joints can be adjusted to nearly any angle allowing the most system flexibility. To maintain rigidity of the structure to allow for precise weaving, each swiveling member end is mechanically fastened to a static node. When the frame has been assembled into its final form, the "weaving teeth" can be affixed to the steel structure.

The "weaving teeth" are laser cut strips of medium-density fiberboard (MDF). Each laser-cut strip of MDF matches to a specified member's length in order to maintain accuracy between the computational model and the physical model. The spacing of the teeth is determined during the

Figure 8. Galvanized steel conduits: telescoping members that are adjustable and removable, 2016

digital weaving iterations. Distance between teeth can influence multiple variables, for instance density of the weave and the structural integrity of a given face. Once the weaving teeth are cut and matched to the referenced steel member, they are mechanically fastened to the frame using common conduit hangers. Once all the MDF strips have been securely fastened to the frame, the winding can begin.

Winding the carbon fiber at Ibañez Kim is primarily done by hand with two people. Winding by hand allows for greater control of the final product. A typical weaving workflow would normally be one person pulling carbon fiber from a larger spool while the other weaves the fibers around the MDF teeth following the computational patterns that have been generated. It is important to note that although the

computational model is important and necessary, it is not a rigid requirement. The person weaving can change weaving strategies in real time if the computational model falls short of a superior idea.

The second to last step of the weaving process is to bake the carbon fiber while on the fame. After the carbon fiber has been baked for several hours, the pre-impregnated epoxy is activated and allows the carbon fiber strands to become rigid. Once the frame and carbon fiber are cooled, the frame can be dismantled, the teeth can be removed, and the carbon fiber will exist singularly as a hardened shell.

The process will produce a lightweight mono-coque structure that will house the mechanical atmosphere-producing devices that allow pattern interference and visual effects. The *rolyPOLY-*

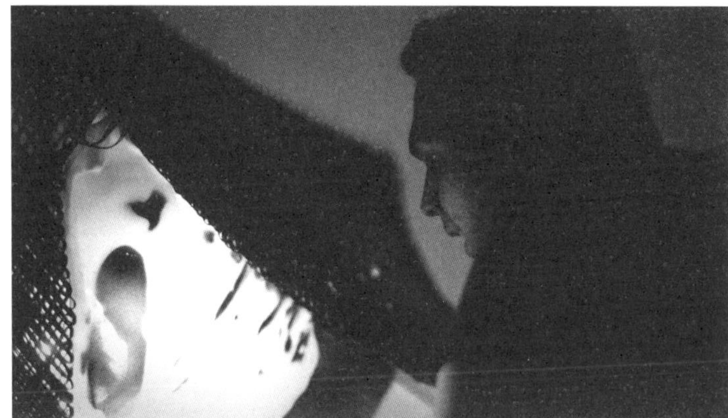

Figure 9. Confessional speakers and LED lights, 2016

GON provided an internal space for one person, and the *Confessional* has a matrix of LED lights, flex sensors, and speakers controlled by a microprocessor stitched into its surface (see Figure 9).[7] *Strange Weather* is a challenge and progression of previous work, whose design will provide internal space for devices that summon fog, invoke heat, filter the air, dehumidify moisture, make ambient sound, or create wind. Those mechanical devices will be housed in the extruded ceiling grid, and the ground modules will take on an external function of sitting and rearrangement (as opposed to *rolyPOLYGON* and *Confessional's* internal, shelter-like functions). As research and invention continue to evolve the potential of the monocoque polygons, Ibañez Kim continues to push the boundaries and re-invent its use and appropriation in the field of design.

Ibañez Kim's goal is to ignite an internal mechanical ambience of external environmental conditions via man-made environmental controllers. Through the disruption of the human desire to block outside discomforts (and occasional terrors) of nature (natural disasters, humidity, cold, noise, etc.) via advancements in building technology, Ibañez Kim inverts this idea of nature on the outside and brings the discomforting forces of nature inside. However, they are not just bringing nature inside; they are simulating discomforting, as well as comforting, aspects of external climates via mechanical devices. They are placing the control of external forces on the interior into the hands of visitors to play with and manipulate the conditions of the gallery space. Imagine visitors entering a space defined by a collection of ceiling units. The ceiling grid is occupied by volumetric tiles. Tracks on the floor create a grid for moving and rearranging the ground condition. The static ceiling tiles and kinetic ground modules are networked so that citizens and visitors alike affect and are subject to an indoor meteorological system. Unlike a typical ceiling grid normally found in office environments, the ceiling tiles of *Strange Weather* do not conform to human-centric occupant expectations. Whereas the normative ceiling grid supplies conditioned air, humidity control, and lighting, the *Strange Weather* grid describes an external natural environment that is not predictive or subservient to human desires.

7. Mariana Ibañez and Simon Kim, "Confessional," Ibañez Kim, http://www.ibanezkim.com/work#/confessional/.

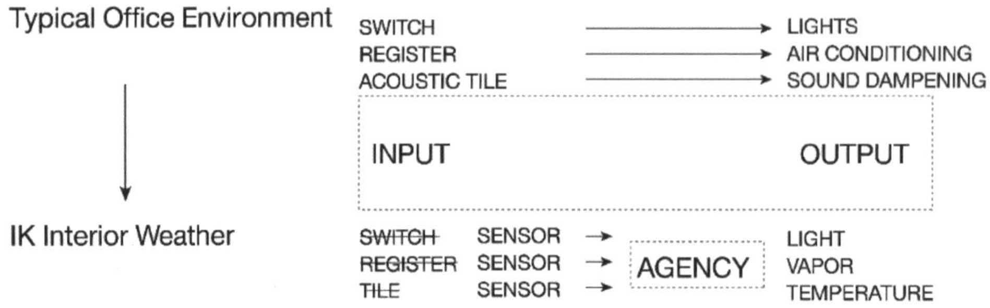

Figure 10. Ibañez Kim, *Electronic Programming Diagram*, 2017

Mechanical devices are programmed to create unpredictable atmospheric ambience in the East Gate Complex. Where a typical office environment has inputs (i.e. a switch contributing to the output of a light turning on or off), Ibañez Kim inserts sensorial agency in place of a typical office environment input. This applied sensorial agency allows the outputs to have an unknown and surprising outcome (see Figure 10). Ibañez Kim is demonstrating the manipulation of light, sound, climate (humid and conditioned air), and temperature (cool and hot). When triggered (via mobile app and/ or switches), the ceiling will eject a mystifying result. Visitors will be unaware of the multitudes of patterns that the ceiling can emit. The ceiling behavior is triggered by a ground module reorganization or vice versa. Coded scenarios include a sensor where all the lights in the space turn off, and the visitor is consumed by a feeling of warm or cold air blowing on their skin. In another experience, the room could be cloaked in darkness and the sound of air hissing through a mister overtakes the space. LED lights blink and shine on floor patterns, and a light turning on can trigger a temperature shift, or variations of sounds. These coded conditions can be controlled as well as unpredictable. Human intervention creates a series of patterns of differing experiences and behaviors.

Strange Weather is a crowd-made "weather-maker" that will create a unique experience allowing visitors to participate in creating environmental conditions. *Strange Weather* expands upon Ibañez Kim's ability to create interactive and programmable data within varying scales of architectural design. Smart modules will hang from the ceiling. Visitors to the space will be able to piece together the suspended components to form larger suspended clouds. These clouds will be activated via sensors to release atmospheric conditions housed by the community of polygons previously described. Like Programmable Matter,[8] each component snaps or clicks with other components. When visitors put a certain number together, an atmospheric condition is created. Our exhibit is essentially a maker of atmospheres: the audience can summon fog, invoke heat, filter

8. Mark Yim, "Programmable Matter Creating Systems that Can Think, Talk, and Morph Autonomously," Massachusetts Institute of Technology, Cambridge Office Of Sponsored Research. September 2011. http://www.dtic.mil/docs/citations/ADA584792

the air, dehumidify moisture, make ambient sound, or create wind. Modules on the ground glide on tracks that allow for desired patterns or conditions that can be continuously regrouped by people visiting the Biennale. Ibañez Kim supplies a half-dozen patterns (via an app), and then each additional weather module can be designed by the public on a digital interface (tetra and cube) with face-matching components. Once printed, hung, and embedded with a simple sensor, they can be connected to each other like programmable matter or modular robotics. Visitors can create a variety of clouds, depending on the number of modules used, desired outcomes, and the configurations in which they come together. Where precedents of Ibañez Kim's work, such as *Confessional*, allow the occupant to choose different interactive behaviors (i.e. to whisper their secrets and desires in anonymity, or to communicate with others) and create a community among clustered cocoons near or far away by filling them with light and broadcasting wirelessly to other *rolyPOLYGONS* at the command of voices or gestures, *Strange Weather* will be activated by different sensors and create a community of atmospheres. They are actuated by a multiagent system programmed so that each agent works together with ascending orders. Different combinations of moisture levels, temperature, and lighting produce a range from dry and unnaturally bright to dark and clouded. The end goal is to bring a consciousness of the individual impact on the urban environment and atmosphere. *Strange Weather* should be a unique experience that allows visitors to participate in creating environmental conditions, and that either draws excitement in the mastery of local weather, or tempers our demands and expectations of city life.

References

Ibañez, Mariana, and Simon Kim. 2016. "Confessional." Ibañez Kim. http://www. ibanezkim.com/work#/confessional/.

Ibañez, Mariana, Simon Kim, and Andrew John Wit. "rolyPOLYGON." Ibañez Kim. http://www. ibanezkim.com/work#/rolypolygon/.

Ibañez, Mariana, Simon Kim, "rolyPOLYGON: Confessional." https://vimeo.com/169560349

Kim, Simon. "Polyhedra." Immersive Kinematics. http://www.immersivekinematics.com/ polyhedra-1

Wit, Andrew John, and Simon Kim. August 2016. "rolyPOLY: A Hybrid Prototype for Digital Techniques and Analog Craft in Architecture." Education and Research in Computer Aided Architectural Design in Europe Conference. Oulu, Finland: eCAADe. pp. 631–638.

"Yim, Mark. Professor and Director of Integrated Product Design Mechanical Engineering and Applied Mechanics." Penn Engineering, The Trustees of the University of Pennsylvania, https://www.seas.upenn.edu/directory/profile. php?ID=107.

Yim, Mark. September 2011. "Programmable Matter Creating Systems that Can Think, Talk, and Morph Autonomously." Massachusetts Institute of Technology, Cambridge Office of Sponsored Research. http://www.dtic.mil/docs/citations/ ADA584792.

Adaptive Assembly: Collaborative Robotic Reuse in Construction

Ryan Johns and Jeffrey S. Anderson

A new era of automation in which humans and small-scale industrial robots work side-by-side on the same tasks has the potential to bring high-value production back to urban cores. New forms of urban metabolism in which materials are processed, used, and reused in creative ways by both humans and machines are establishing "Making" as a new urban common. This project explores the potential of using robots and computer vision to assemble a structure of irregular parts using a human operator in concert with adaptive assembly algorithms. By developing software and hardware interfaces which incorporate machine vision, structural intelligence, and interactive visualizations, it is possible to create a collaborative construction process which balances the aesthetics and efficiency of natural materials with algorithmic intelligence, robotic dexterity, and human creativity. We have developed an intelligent system that operates with a fixed logic, but can be modified with material variation and strategic offerings, allowing us to use both the strengths of the robot (precision, stamina, and computational intelligence) and the strengths of the human operator (creativity, decision making, spontaneity) to achieve a shared goal. Further, by using found materials to assemble our structure, this project appeals to the light manufacturing industries already in place in Seoul, demonstrating the possibility of reusing scrap materials with low embodied energies and site-specific materiality in construction. By demonstrating principles of collaboration, reuse, and adaptability in the context of urban production, this project is a first step in understanding the potentials and limitations of collaborative robotics.

The making common and Seoul

The advent of new technologies for sharing knowledge and producing goods has blurred the historical boundaries of urban production. After having been exiled from urban cores for decades, industrial production is seeing a resurgence in urban areas, partly due to an influx of new technologies for one-off production and an increasingly competent do-it-yourself culture. Where the means and methods of the production of goods were once tightly kept secrets, the ideas, technologies, and techniques of making are now spread freely across a cosmopolitical, open-source community, and the intelligences behind making have become a common resource from which anyone can draw. This pool of knowledge, the technologies which make it possible, and the culture which promotes it have become an integral part of contemporary urbanism.

In light of high-value, small-scale production technologies, cities must now consider how to incubate entrepreneurship and cultivate a culture of sharing knowledge rather than focus on designating arbitrary boundaries for working, living, leisure, and industrial activities. It is clear that lightweight fabrication technologies such as collaborative robotics and 3D printers have become key technologies of urban areas, allowing industrial production to occur in nearly any space. However, what is less clear is how urban areas will adapt to incorporate these technologies and how humans will learn to live with them. Rather than focus on creating boundaries for human activities, contemporary cities need to consider how to incorporate non-human agents such as robots, communication technologies, and networks for sharing materials into their master plans. How does a city promote cross-disciplinary innovation? How can new fabrication technologies be integrated into the city? How can humans work with these fabrication technologies toward productive ends? How can people and robots efficiently and intelligently use materials for construction? How will bubbles of research and production within cities help them grow and diversify? These are the crucial questions when thinking about a new urban metabolism: the production, consumption, reuse, and disposal of resources in the city mediated by both humans and machines.

Efforts to modernize industrial infrastructure in South Korea have been seen as a threat to light manufacturing in Seoul, particularly in the craft, fashion, and clothing industries clustered around the Dongdaemun and Namdaemun markets. Through its "Manufacturing Industry Innovation 3.0" plan launched in 2014, South Korea aims to set up thousands of smart factories by 2020 to upgrade industrial infrastructure with a focus on the convergence between software and hardware technologies.[1] The computerization of industry represents a risk to manufacturing jobs, particularly in dense urban areas where many believe their jobs may be taken over by robots.

However, upgrades to industrial infrastructure do not imply replacing human workers with robots, particularly in light manufacturing applications where complicated and dynamic tasks need to be completed to develop a product. Robotics companies have begun developing reprogrammable machines which can work in close quarters with humans through the use of soft materials, smaller payloads,

1. Dr. Suk In Chang, "Reshaping Innovation Strategy for the Fourth Industrial Innovation in South Korea: Beyond the Manufacturing Innovation Strategy 3.0.," International Conference on Industry 4.0: The Time to Act by HK Industry Is Now, held by Hong Kong Productivity Council (IIKPC), 26 July, 2016, Korean Institute for Industrial Economics and Trade.

and elastic joints. These are designed to be easily programmed in real time with physical human interaction. The goal is not to replace human labor, but to offload the tedious and mundane tasks of manufacturing to machines, freeing the human to complete skilled and creative tasks which are difficult for robots to do autonomously. A new era of collaborative robotics in which humans work side-by-side with robots will revolutionize light manufacturing in urban cores.

By focusing human labor on creative tasks, the aim of collaborative robotics is to improve, not replace, manufacturing jobs, adding value to products through craft and creativity, not monotonous fabrication operations. Dangerous, large-scale industrial robotics have been used for decades in fixed automation applications where robots and humans are separated for safety. The goal of these collaborative robots is to interact with humans directly in highly flexible environments, while improving the speed and quality of production. The potential of robotics to enrich high-value production in urban cores (where labor forces and expertise are already dense) is great, and Seoul is a perfect case study for this research. However, the question remains: What will collaboration between humans and robots look like and how can we leverage the intelligences of both to produce a more sustainable and equitable future?

Introduction

In the two decades since the first "digital turn" in architecture, the increasing utility of computational design and fabrication tools has dramatically altered the process of design development and building construction.[2]

Parametric computer-aided-design tools (CAD) and computer-assisted-manufacturing equipment, (CAM) have provided architects, engineers and contractors with the ability to plan and construct with previously unfathomable levels of complexity and variation. While such algorithmic design tools have provided methods for enriching the aesthetic and performative aspects of the built environment, they have also served to make architects—a notoriously obstinate and narcissistic bunch to begin with—even more stubborn. Precision surveying tools and robotic actuators have resulted in "zero tolerance" design methods,[3] with the expectation of sub-millimeter precision for both the digitization of the physical environment and the actualization of the digital. Designs are conceived in a digital realm of seemingly infinite conceptual freedom, but are materialized with tightly constrained toolpaths into a world bound by dimensionally standardized, industrial materials (blanks, bricks, bars, and sheet stock). This expectation of exactitude comes at the expense of material and energy efficiency, improvisation, and the aesthetic advantages of natural variation.

Reclamation

The mass-produced standard components of the first industrial revolution and the mass-customized components of the digital revolution both share the economic reality of centralized production and the economy of scale. The common claim is that "digital fabrication tools can produce variations at no extra cost," and that "economies of scale are irrelevant in digital production processes."[4] In practice, however, designers and fabricators need supply-chain and

2. M. Carpo (ed.), *The Digital Turn in Architecture* 1992–2012: AD Reader (Hoboken, NJ: Wiley, 2013).

3. B. Sheil (ed.), *High Definition: Zero Tolerance in Design and Production*, Architectural Design (AD) Profile no. 227 (Hoboken, NJ: Wiley, 2014).

4. M. Carpo, *The Alphabet and the Algorithm* (Cambridge, MA: MIT Press, 2011), 41.

profit models that work, and the time spent sourcing materials and writing code for truly "one-off" products becomes infeasible. The practicality of "nonstandard-seriality" or "mass-customization" is derived not from deviation, but abundance (*-seriality, mass-*): making many slightly differentiated products from one algorithm or many differentiated panels for one large architectural project. Both machinic reproduction and parametric fabrication enable designers by minimizing the costs associated with onsite, skilled labor.

Digital projects tend to emulate the variability of natural systems in their logic, but produce a discrete, selected set of objects for production. In such work, there is always a moment where the infinite potential of the multi-variable parametric model is locked into place, and an entirely deterministic fabrication process begins. What seemed boundless on the computer screen becomes a rigidly fixed collection in reality.

An alternative to this top-down approach of obtaining substantive variation is to creatively employ and organize the variety that is inherent in naturally produced raw material, found objects, and reclaimed building materials shaped by architectural entropy (rubble, salvage, construction remnants, etc.). While the systemization and assembly of such materials requires onsite skilled labor and some relinquishing of architectural authority, it is environmentally economical in its sustainable use of local materials, and benefits from the aesthetic attributes of "beauty's found geometries."[5]

Given the lack of transportation and manufacturing energy, the use of unprocessed rock or recycled aggregate materials has practically nonexistent embodied energy when compared to more common building materials.[6] The practice of building using local materials is also culturally sustainable, as the site-specific materiality can exhibit a cross section of regional trades, vernacular building methods, local industry (building with manufacturing waste), architectural history (building with architectural salvage) and consumer trends (building with refuse).

A number of notable architectural projects have encouraged a recent revitalization or reinvention of traditional vernacular building techniques by using low-cost, locally available materials. (Figures 1-3). Such projects showcase the wide potential for creative reuse of local materials, but generally also tend to be located in regions with relatively inexpensive, semi-skilled labor (Sub-Saharan Africa, China, the rural American South). Developing strategies for coupling new sensing and fabrication technologies with traditional and locally-oriented building methods has the potential of expanding the reach of these projects to economies in which the additional labor would make them cost prohibitive in comparison to large-scale, repeated-detail, centralized-manufacturing-based construction models.

Adaptability

Materially aware and regional approaches to architectural assembly can often seem at odds with digital design methods. Such was the case with the recent Venice Biennale "Reporting from the Front" (curated by Alejandro Aravena), in which work by designers such as Aravena, Max Lamb, and Rural Studio highlighted the potential of highly tailored adaptive reuse.

5. J. Enns, "Beauty's Found Geometries," M. Arch Thesis (with Axel Killian, advisor), Princeton University, 2010.

6. A. Alcorn, "Embodied Energy and CO_2 Coefficients for NZ Building Materials," Centre for Building Performance Research, Victoria University of Wellington, 2001.

Figure 1. The Ningbo Museum of Amateur Architecture Studio (Wang Shu & Lu Wengyu) stands as an archeological assemblage of various stone and tile building blocks from razed farmers' dwellings

Figure 2. Rural Studio's work in Hale County, Alabama, is known for using inexpensive and abundant reclaimed materials, such as salvaged automobile windows and tires

Figure 3. MASS Architect's principle of "lo-fab" (local fabrication) encourages the use of regionally sourced materials and labor, such as using volcanic stone for the Butaro District Hospital in Rwanda

Figure 4. (Left) Andy Goldsworthy, *Stacked Whalebones*, 2001. (Right) Andy Goldsworthy, *Roof*, 2004-2005

In contrast, the U.S. pavilion presented a number of projects by "American architecture's digitally savvy but ... politically illiterate parametric wing" which treated the struggling urban areas of Detroit as a digital tabula-rasa, and stood "blithely for everything Aravena wants to rail against: top-down and slickly rendered solutions shot through with disdain for the kind of expertise required to get architecture at this vast scale approved, financed and built."[7] Despite the desire of digital architecture to convey the lightness and adaptability of virtual design spaces, the rigid implementation associated with computer numerically controlled (CNC) fabrication and the unvarying smoothness of its variation can render it brutally immalleable and contrived. With many parametric projects, in short, the baby has been thrown out with the bathwater.

The careful arrangement of nonuniform "found" material collections, on the other hand, tends to convey a sense of natural belonging, despite requiring a great deal of concerted manual effort in their production (Figure 4). This is well demonstrated in the internet phenomenon of "flat lays" where carefully curated lifestyle objects are arranged against a neutral backdrop, photographed and shared (Figure 5). While heavy-handed in their production, these images catch the eye and convey an air of nonchalance: the flatlay is thus the Instagram-incarnation of Baldassare Castiglione's *sprezzatura*, or artful artlessness.[8]

Interestingly, the flat lay finds its origins in another term popularized by Tom Sachs, who worked at Frank Gehry's office in the late 1980s: "knolling" is a process of organization in which similar objects are grouped and arranged orthogonally (Figure 6).[9] It is not without some irony that such careful, unmodified curation of existing objects was born out of the office that developed and integrated many of the tools and systems which made top-down parametric architecture possible.

7. Christopher Hawthorne, "Review: A Grassroots, Handmade Venice Architecture Biennale from Alejandro Aravena," *Los Angeles Times*, 2016, http://www.latimes.com/entertainment/arts/la-et-cm-venice-biennale-review-20160530-snap-story.html.

8. Baldassare Castiglione, *The Book of the Courtier* (London: Penguin, 1976), 66-68.

9. *Business Insider*, 14 May 2015, http://www.businessinsider.com/instagram-flat-lay-trend-knolling-2015-5.

Figure 5. Flat lay

Digitally Integrated Adaptive Assembly

To overcome the lack of control in conventional construction sites, the vast majority of digitally fabricated structures rely on off-site prefabrication of building components in a controlled factory setting. This practice can reduce onsite labor costs, improve quality control, increase allowable complexity, and minimize material consumption when compared to similar methods of onsite construction. However, prefabrication can also be considered as a means of increasing the embodied energy associated with construction: materials are mass-produced in a centralized factory, and then shipped to a fabricator with the necessary computer numerically controlled (CNC) equipment and expertise in prefabrication. The fabricator post-processes this material into the required geometry, and again must transport the material to the site for assembly. Compared to traditional vernacular building methods which rely on locally available materials, this practice is incredibly inefficient in terms of

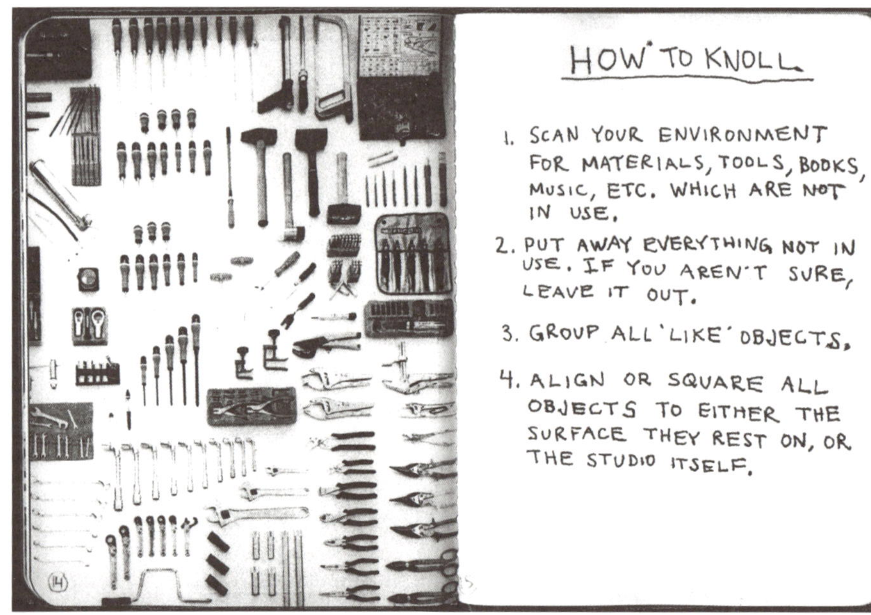

Figure 6. "How to Knoll," Tom Sachs, 2009

material consumption and transportation energy. Moreover, the tight tolerances associated with digital design methods have served to bring intelligent decision making even farther from the place of construction, and thus also make it less tolerant of change. While most constructs must become fixed at some point in their materialization, pushing some amount of decisions back towards the construction site has the benefit of mitigating material and energy waste, while also working to make the completed structure appear less contrived. Architects often alter their fuzzy design concepts based on the limitations of their software and fabrication processes (i.e. changing curvature to meet ruled surface requirements); allowing design details to continue to take shape on the construction site (i.e. based on material limitations) should similarly be considered as a necessary aspect of design.

Robotic fabrication processes and machine intelligence have the potential to unite the previously incongruous concepts of regionally oriented adaptive assembly with digitally assisted design and manufacturing. Rather than working entirely top-down from custom components, recent work with industrial robotics has explored the potential of developing construction processes which begin with material understanding.

Gramazio and Kohler's "Stratifications" project demonstrated one of the first examples of robotic construction using bricks with variable thicknesses.[10] GREYSHED's "Bandsawn Bands" technique works to fabricate doubly curved surfaces from live-edged wood slabs by bounding the initial design concept within the constraints of naturally occurring, 3D scanned geometries (Figure 7). Similarly, the *Woodchip Barn* was constructed using digitally scanned tree fork sections culled from the surrounding forest and modified robotically.[11] By understanding the "material morphospace" of selected material subsets, computational methods can begin to prescribe methods for organizing, modifying, and aggregating found objects.[12] This capability will become increasingly available to architects with the continued development of onsite robotic systems,[13,14] improved sensing technologies, and machine learning.

Adaptive Assembly is intended to convey the potential of integrating variable material properties with onsite robotics and collaborative/ augmented design techniques. The project was developed with close connection to an ongoing research initiative at Columbia University's Graduate School of Architecture, Planning and Preservation (GSAPP) which focuses on robotic

10. Gramazio and Kohler, ETH Zurich, "Stratifications," Fabricate Conference, UCL, London, 2011.

11. M. Self and E. Vercruysse, "Infinite Variations, Radical Strategies," in *Fabricate 2017* (London: UCL Press, 2017), 30–35.

12. R. Johns and N. Foley, "Bandsawn Bands: Feature-Based Design and Fabrication of Nested Freeform Surfaces in Wood," in W. McGee and M. Ponce de Leon (eds.), *Robotic Fabrication in Architecture*, Art and Design (Berlin: Springer, 2014), 17–32.

13. M. Giftthaler, T. Sandy, K. Dörfler, I. Brooks, et al., "Mobile Robotic Fabrication at 1:1 Scale: The In Situ Fabricator; System, Experiences and Current Developments," *Journal of Construction Robotics*, 2017.

14. S. Keating, J. Leland, L. Cai, and N. Oxman, "Toward Site-specific and Self-sufficient Robotic Fabrication on Architectural Scales," *Science Robotics* 2 (5) (26 April 2017).

Figure 7. "Bandsawn Bands" by GREYSHED, 2013

assembly using rejected and repurposed materials. Student projects in the course "Assembling All Sorts" (led by Ryan Luke Johns) have worked to develop custom computer vision strategies and robotic workflows for creating constructs from materials ranging from lightbulbs to rubble, dried food and broken glass (Figure 8).

Collaboration

The ability of designers and builders to work collaboratively with robots is a key component in the development of functional and materially empowering onsite robotics. While "collaborative robotics" has become a catchphrase used by technologists to quell neo-Luddite fears of human obsolescence, the nature of such collaborations is still largely undefined.

It is essential, for example, to distinguish between collaborative projects which bridge short-term robotic inadequacies with human skill, and those which seek to develop a codependency which will not disintegrate as better actuators, sensors, and software are released.

Collaborative projects currently range from those which use human dexterity and mobility to augment shortcomings in robotic capabilities (for example, tying a knot,)[15] and those in which robotic dexterity augments human shortcomings (in strength, stamina, speed, patience, or precision) to produce works which are otherwise defined by human creativity and improvisation (for example, the gestural design of a robotically built brick wall).[16,17]

15. B. Lafreniere, T. Grossman, F. Anderson, J. Matejka et al., "Crowdsourced Fabrication," in *UIST 2016 Conference Proceedings, ACM Symposium on User Interface Software and Technology,* 2016.

16. A. Kondziela, V. Helm, R. Bärtschi, R. Johns, and D. Weber, "The Endless Wall," by Gramazio & Kohler, Chair of Digital Fabrication, ETH Zurich, *Scientifica,* 2011, http://gramaziokohler.arch.ethz.ch/web/e/forschung/216.html.

17. R. Johns, "Augmented Reality and the Fabrication of Gestural Form," *Rob|Arch 2012* (Vienna: Springer, 2013), 248–255.

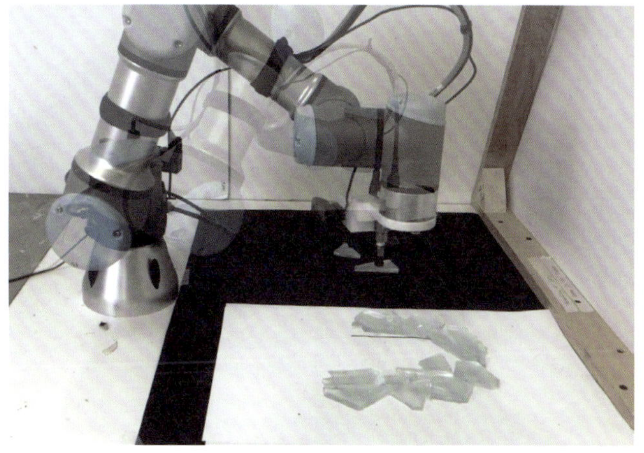

Figure 8. Student work from "Assembling All Sorts" at Columbia GSAPP.
(Top) Ruomeng Wang, Constructing a wall from broken glass along a drawn curve (2016)

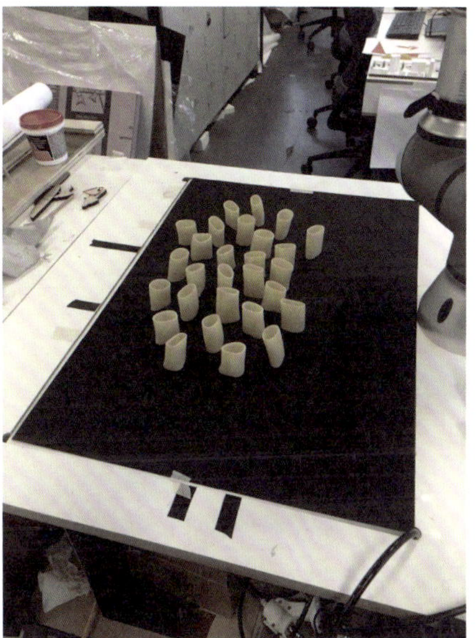

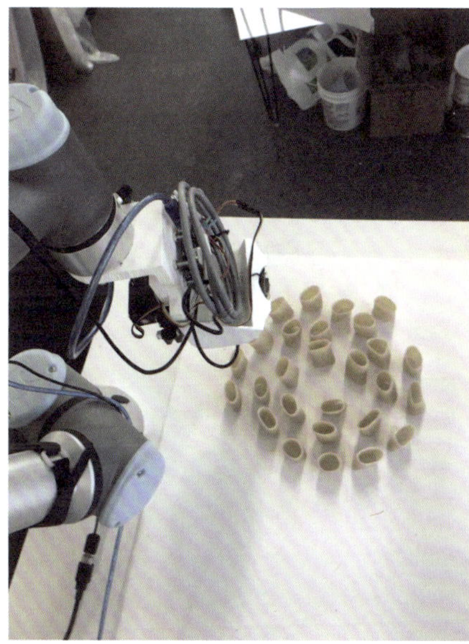

(Middle) Eugene Chang, Spiral of scanned and robotically sorted pasta (2017)

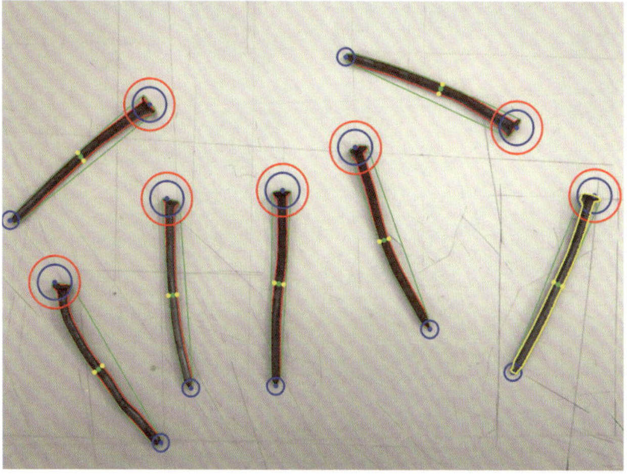

(Bottom) Tianyang Xie, Computer vision analysis of reclaimed nails, identifying bend angle and head location (2017)

Figure 9. Projecting acoustic information onto the robotic arm during the *Machine Yearning* performance, 2014

It is essential to develop collaborative processes where the unique skills of both robots and humans are utilized to produce works which could not be produced by either party in isolation from the other. For such processes to work, it is necessary to develop clear lines of communication: software and interfaces must allow the human designer and to tell the robot what to do, but they must also work to show humans clearly what the robot is doing, and what it needs of them. By understanding and providing "social cues to people,"[18] we ensure that fabrication processes are not simply informed by the human operator, but that they can also inform him or her.[19] By projecting information about the computational decision making process and the robot's awareness of human desires directly onto the worksurface[20] and onto the body of the robot itself,[21] it is possible to create a bidirectional communication flow which allows true collaboration to take place (Figure 9).

Through the development of software and hardware interfaces which incorporate machine vision, structural intelligence, and interactive visualizations, we can create collaborative construction processes which balance the aesthetics and efficiency of natural materials with algorithmic intelligence, robotic dexterity, and human creativity. Such robotic processes do not produce a single outcome, but are highly variable and dependent on site-specific materials, performance requirements, and designer intent. By recognizing the "sign

18. C. Breazeal and R. Brooks, "Robot Emotion: A Functional Perspective," in *Who Needs Emotions?: The Brain Meets the Robot*, J. M. Fellous and M. A. Arbib (eds.), Oxford Scholarship Online, 2005.

19. R. Johns, A. Kilian, and N. Foley, "Design Approaches Through Augmented Materiality and Embodied Computation," in McGee and Ponce de Leon (eds.), *Robotic Fabrication in Architecture*, Art and Design, 319–332.

20. R. Johns, "Augmented Materiality: Modelling with Material Indeterminacy," in F. Gramazio, M. Kohler, and S. Langenberg (eds.), *Fabricate* (Zurich: Verlag, 2014), 216–223.

21. J. Snyder, R. Johns, G. Kogan, C. Avis, and A. Kilian, "Machine Yearning: An Industrial Robotic Arm as a Performance Instrument," Proceedings of the International Conference on New Interfaces for Musical Expression, Baton Rouge, LA, 2015.

22. J. L. Gould and C. G. Gould, Animal Architects: *Building and the Evolution of Intelligence* (New York: Basic Books, 2007).

Figure 10. Hubert Duprat, Caddisfly larvae with shell of gold, pearl, turquoise, 1980-2012

stimuli"[22] that trigger certain robotic behaviours, designers can adapt their actions to better take advantage of the robot's capabilities. Just as Hubert Duprat leverages the caddisfly's tendency to build by offering it selective materials (Figure 10), so can we study and alter the inputs of robotic assembly processes to creatively orient their outcomes. By working within the constraints of design objectives, machinic and material morphologies, it is possible to produce designs which are closer to the intent of the designer and material, while more clearly illustrating the adaptability and variation enabled by digital design tools.

Conclusion

This research proposes a shift in the notion that computational design must always precede and exist separately from material reality. Our project demonstrates a real-time collaboration with a robot in which irregular, found materials offered by a human are processed by an adaptable assembly algorithm and positioned by a robotic arm to build a structure. By using non-standard materials that are typically perceived of as waste, we hope to engage in a discourse about adaptive reuse in architecture and the possibility of a digitally augmented craft culture. By using computer vision and an adaptable assembly logic, "waste" can be redeployed as a structural element (here, a stand-in for an architectural building element) which can be precisely placed into a stable construct. We propose a construction process and architectural language of discarded parts which allow for material and energy efficiency, improvisation, and the aesthetic advantages of natural variation. Though this is research, our goal from the beginning was to engage the public with an interactive exhibition. To do this, we have allowed visitors to engage with the robotic assembly system directly, permitting them to leave their own mark on the construction of a collective structure. By generating an interactive demonstration of collaboration, adaptation, and reuse in robotic construction, we hope to engage the public in the first steps of understanding what is at stake for collaborative robotics.

The Ideology of Sharing Culture:

Open-Source Architecture as a Design Factor and Research Tool

Husum & Lindholm Architects
(Sine Lindholm and Mads-Ulrik Husum)

The growing ideologies of local production, the maker movement, and the sharing culture are starting to challenge the way we think about products, design, and architecture. With shared data (the open-source movement), a new worldview has arisen that challenges many of our conventional ideas about patents and ownership. This also changes the way we think about products, design, and architecture. Architects could play an important and responsible role in this matter because designs must, in this context, operate on very different parameters than before.

We see tendencies in the world, as expressed by strong voices like that of Jeremy Rifkin, who envisions a not so distant future where global societies must address the potentials and limitations of the open-source movement. This movement is flourishing in the era of the internet of things, resulting in global communities online.

Public fabrication labs with advanced production tools are spread throughout the world, making it possible for people to produce, share, and develop ideas locally, at a limited cost. Open-source architecture is not only benefitting the user, but the designer can use it as a tool for investigating the needs and behaviors in local societies.

The sharing culture within the open-source movement has resulted in the idea behind Growmore. Based on giving and sharing knowledge, improvements and ideas are developed in an open productive environment.

Sharing Culture

We are moving towards an open-sourced global society, an ideology that is moving out of the basements and hobby rooms and into the market of professionals, requiring new business models to prevail. The movement is embarking on a paradigm shift in the way we understand production, goods, and customers, turning consumers into prosumers (Rifkin, 2011).

The reason this major shift is possible is due to the web 2.0,[1] as David Gauntlett elaborates in his book *Making is Connecting* (Gauntlett, 2011 3-5).

The ability to receive and share information, articles, videos, etc., has created a movement of people sharing and learning from others around the world. It distorts the boundaries of religion, nationality, and community, as we create bonds with people with entirely different backgrounds over common interests.

We share stories and knowledge in a way that is so fast that the information industries are unable to compete with it, something that shatters their standard business models and forces them to alter the way they think and provide and sell news. An interesting aspect is that sharing information is not happening vertically— from the top of the chain down to the passive consumers—but laterally, due to individuals documenting and sharing information and news via the technologically advanced mobile devices in their pocket. In this sense, the open-source movement is the ruling part of the internet, as we share, collaborate, and tell other peoples' stories combined with our own, in writing, images, video, etc. Jeremy Rifkin describes this shift in his book *The Third Industrial Revolution* (Rifkin 2011), and coins this as one of the five

pillars of the third industrial revolution that is going to have a great impact in altering the governmental and economical structures in the coming decades.

What is happening now, and has been going on for a while, is that the open-source ideology is moving hastily into the physical scene.

A New Paradigm

From the web 2.0, we are moving into the era of the Internet of Things[2] (Rifkin 2011, 193-270) connecting the internet to machines, fabrication labs, products, sensors, etc. The IOT allows us to move our information sharing into the physical world, with a great impact on the way we live, work, and commute. Jeremy Rifkin augments this in the following citation:

> *It isn't just technology. What it (the IOT) does is it democratizes the economy. And hopefully you'll be in a world in 2050 where it won't be the 1% and 99%. It will be a shared economy, a sustainable good quality of life, where no one's left behind. Now is it utopian? No. We need to change the human narrative. We need a new story for the human race to go with the technology. We have to move from geopolitics to biosphere consciousness in one generation. Everything we do intimately impacts some other human, some other ecosystem, some other species on this earth. We got a young generation that's beginning to see that we live in one indivisible community, the biosphere.* (Rifkin 2015)

Previously, produced goods were bought as an already made object, like the newspaper, from a dealer, and we used this product as it was intended. Production was in the hands of industrious

1. https://en.oxforddictionaries.com/definition/us/prosumer

2. https://en.oxforddictionaries.com/definition/internet_of_things

companies and organizations, using advanced and expensive technology and equipment to produce goods for the intended consumer.

What we are seeing now is that the production technology is improving rapidly, making the costs of machinery drop, and the quality rise. Just as we all now have advanced mobile devices that can document and frame our surroundings with a quality that was impossible to carry and pay for a decade ago, production technology is increasingly becoming available to the general population. This goes hand in hand with the paradigm shift of consumers turning into prosumers—from passive costumers to active consumers—experts within various fields.

This paradigm shift is resulting in a new kind of community that exists in the span between the online world and the physical realm. We share and improve our knowledge, information, and skills online and in the physical world and hereby have the possibility to produce our own devices, ideas, and products ourselves and together with others, at a minimum cost. What drives this whole revolution is a lateral drift powered by a communal passion, not equity. This change is going to shatter the economical and governmental institutions across the globe, as they witness a generation of makers, caring more about sharing, developing, and producing along with others, rather than defining their quality of life in ownership and wealth. As David Gauntlett puts it:

Living a creative life can encompass all areas of our family life—from our hobbies, to the ways we connect in our community, to the ways we celebrate our days together, and to the ways we celebrate each other. (Gauntlett 2011, 67)

Sharing Architecture

Open-source ideology contributes to design processes

With the Internet the world has gotten a lot smaller, and we have the opportunity as architects and designers to get involved and making change. (Sinclair 2016)

Architects and designers get innovative ideas and create beautiful and visionary concepts and related visualizations. However, the construction of the design and architecture is often not an integrated element from the beginning, and is often developed later in the process. In this sense the design and architecture is often not reflecting the construction, and in many cases the construction is hidden, because it is not incorporated to be a part of the aesthetic.

A changing society calls for new ways of making. Defined by the relationship between man and machine, craft has always operated at the interface of cultural, economic and social contexts. New technologies not only alter the way we make things, they also influence the way we think about production. (Bauhaus Dessau, 2017)

The construction and how elements are assembled is the most vital part when developing open-source architecture and design. The production and assembly has to be as intuitive and simple as possible, in order for the user in the other end to understand, create, replicate and develop the design. If not, the idea of open-source ideology will find it difficult to flourish. For instance, the construction and choice of material in open-source architecture is a crucial part of the design and aesthetics. This requires a need for sharing knowledge, in this case a combination of the disciplines of architecture, engineering, and other relevant branches.

It requires different demands of the designer and gives an entirely different meaning for the design, the development process, the design parameters, and the aesthetics.

These new ways of making have started a new design thinking—an honest design with transparency in the construction structure. The construction has become a part of the design and the aesthetics—the design is the construction.

Open Source Architecture as an Investigation of Needs
When designs are open-sourced, they become a research tool

There are several advantages when deciding to open-source a design. It is not only beneficial for the people who decide to download and build the design, but it is also benefitting the designer. The internet works both ways; a designer can upload and open-source a design, and the design can be downloaded and built all over the world. But at the same time the designer will receive feedback, and get ideas for improvements, when observing how people are deciding to produce it, their choice of materials, its functionality, etc. Social media like Instagram is a great channel for collecting and investigating feedback. This also means that the design doesn't have to be "perfect" when it is open-sourced, but can be improved constantly when using the world as a collaborating partner, thereby supporting a flourishing community.

"If we accept that improvements can always be made then there is no limit to what we can measure and do. If we accept that no product is perfect, then we open up the opportunity and welcome the idea of continual improvement." (Baker 2017)

Another advantage and maybe an even more important and interesting observation about open-sourcing is that open-source architecture and design can be used as an investigation of the needs and behaviors of local communities. When actively observing the end-users' use of the open-sourced design, they can act as sounding boards and test subjects for anthropological studies.

In this sense open-source architecture and design is like planting the same seed in different arenas, and seeing how it will grow up differently. We can analyze the development and add-ons of the original open-source element and how it reflects a need in the specific arenas.

These observations can be explored in different matters, such as the functionality and flexibility of the structure: is it being used as intended or has the functionality changed? What sorts of materials have been used and why? Is the scale fitting the functionality of the structure? In which context do people decide to place and use the design?

All solutions and needs are local, and by using open-source as a tool for investigation, it will be possible to collect information about needs and behaviors, and thereby fine-tune the design, and rethink flexibility and changeable ideas or add-ons.

Developing Growmore—an open-source investigation

The development of Growmore can be viewed as a case in using open-source architecture as a research tool.

Growmore is a further development from the open-source edition of the Growroom that was released in February 2017, which was created in collaboration between the Future Living Lab SPACE10[3] and architects Husum&Lindholm (see Figure 1). The Growroom is an Urban Farming Pavilion and the design was based on spatial experimentation with the Urban Farming concept. The concept of the pavilion was to point in a direction of local food production and bringing vegetation back into the urban scene. The pavilion, designed as a sphere, had the intention of invoking the idea of a vibrant cosmos—a green globe. Inside the pavilion visitors share the same seat as the plants; in this sense people and vegetation become equals and coexist in the same cycle. In this enclosing garden people could connect with nature and use all their senses to smell, taste, and feel the abundance of herbs and plants.

People throughout the world are now building their own personal Growrooms and are posting their results on Instagram with the hashtag #space10growroom (see Figure 2). People have contacted Space10 and Husum&Lindholm with ideas and suggestions for further developments. This gives a wide range of insights into how people use it, build it, add elements to it, and in what context they place it.

The result of this experience sparked the development and idea behind Growmore.

Growmore is based on the ideology of sharing and improving together with peers around the world, and is in that sense to be seen as a living laboratory.

At its core, the Growmore is a flexible structural design that can be altered and transformed to any given context and use (see Figure 3).

The idea was to minimize the complexity and make it as simple, intuitive, and cost efficient as possible while elaborating on the use of technologically advanced machinery and materials.

Growmore is still developed to be an Urban Farm but could be used for other purposes as well.

We see the need for green spaces in the quickly expanding cities, and the idea of the design is for it to act as small oasis structures that can be scattered around in the urban scenery, to be used as shared human rechargers in the expanding cities. With its great flexibility, we see the structure as a temporary plugin or an ad-on in the in-between spaces in the city scenery.

With the visual honest expression of Growmore, the simple design is referring to the open-source and maker movements. The construction and design go hand in hand with the flexible function of the structure in an exploration of a new aesthetic, rooted in the open-source ideology (see Figures 4 and 5).

In this way Growmore is not just an urban garden but, as mentioned, a living lab where all the elements of a future garden system are incorporated in the structure, and offer transparency in the construction and function.

3. https://www.space10.io

Figure 1. Pictures of the Growroom: building parts, assemby detail, and the completed construction

Figure 2. Selected pictures, collected from Instagram from the hashtag #space10growroom, show how different people decided to use the Growroom

Figure 3. Visualization of Growmore by Husum&Lindholm

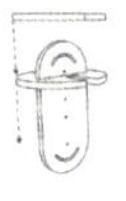

Pivotal link with stabi-
lising disks

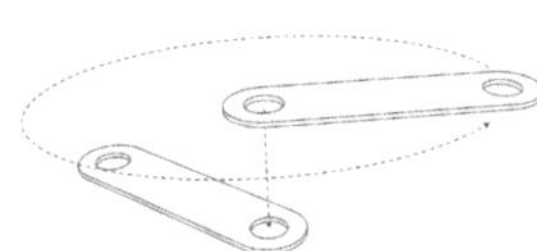

Horizontal elements are put
on top of each other, able
to rotate freely around the
pivotal link

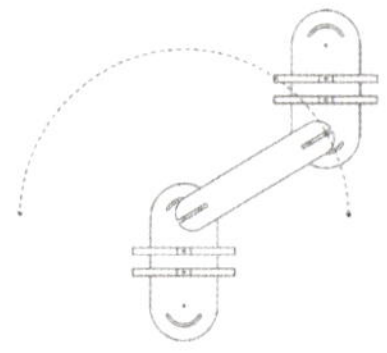

The vertical element is mounted
to the pivotal link and can rotate as needed as well as slide in
and out of the pivotal link prior
to fastening. In this way, the
same kind of vertical element
can be used for all levels

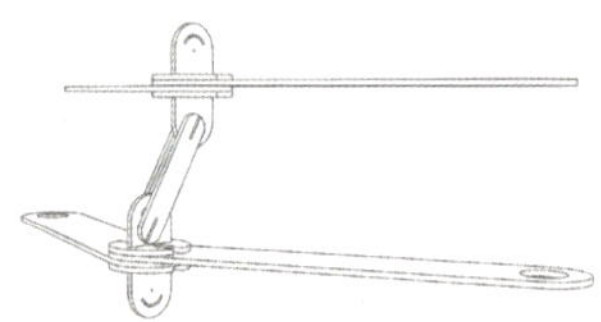

All the elements in one
connection put together, ready
to have additional level above,
below and to each side.

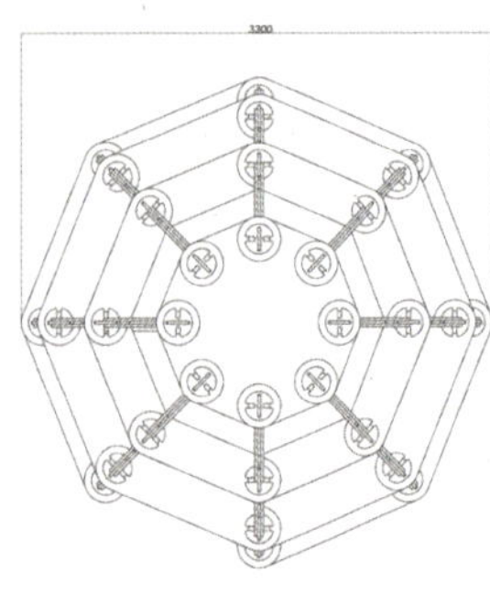

Plan

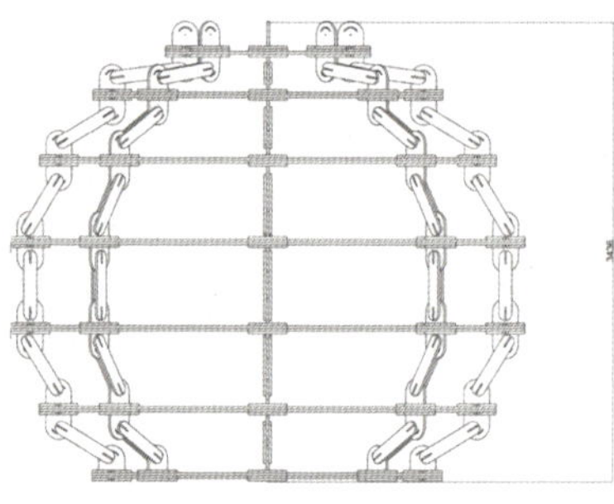

Elevation

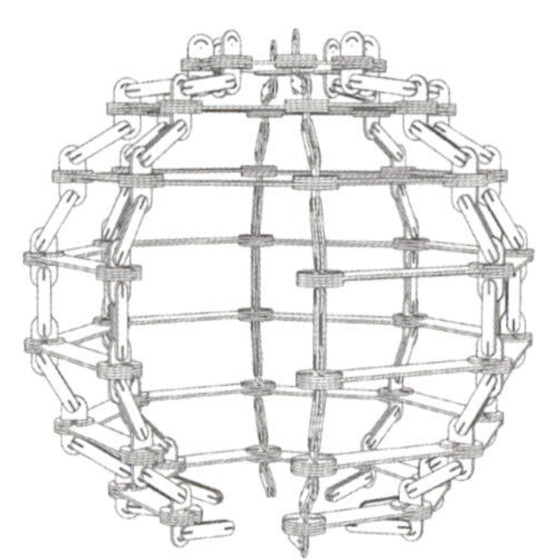

Perspective

Figure 4. Construction details of Growmore

It can be used as small vertical urban farms, public meeting places, public libraries, or exhibition arenas—thereby the name Growmore.

Architecture reflects the world we live in, using the means available, and as Cameron Sinclair puts it: *"architecture is not just about solutions, but also about raising awareness"* (Sinclair 2006). When knowledge is shared as a common resource, we can develop designs and technologies much faster and easier than with conventional R&D processes, benefitting communities of all sorts.

The open-source movement in all its branches is creating a whole new range of possibilities and challenges. Within our field it calls for architects, designers, and makers of all kinds to take part in the movement. It alters the way we think about design. Through online platforms and advanced shared production facilities throughout the world, we are looking at a different approaches for designing and creating—not for costumers, but for each other. Our peers are not passive consumers, but active, innovative participants, who produce and adapt our shared vision, creating a wide range of possibilities. We are still in the early stages of this new era, but the more we elaborate on and develop this new approach, the further we can reach out.

As more people all over the planet take part in the sharing culture ideology, the weight of it will create an impact on the financial and governmental institutions that define and rule our way of life. Living will no longer be based on personal wealth and isolated vertical careers, but rather on a lateral, shared global community growing on living, sharing and producing together with each other as equals.

This is not a far-off dream. This is a reality in a future not so far away.

References

Baker, Ben. 7 April 2017. "Continuous Improvement over Delayed Perfection." Open Desk. https://www.opendesk.cc/blog/continuous-improvement-over-delayed-perfection.

Bauhaus Dessau Foundation. "When Craft Becomes Modern: The Bauhaus in the Making," BauhausDessau exhibition, 13 April 2017–7 January 2018, http://www.bauhaus-dessau.de/en/exhibitions/craft-becomes-modern.html.

Gauntlett, David. 2011. *Making Is Connecting*. Cambridge, UK: Polity Press. 286.

Rifkin, Jeremy. 2011. *The Third Industrial Revolution*. New York: St. Martin's Press. 291.

Rifkin, Jeremy. 2015. "Jeremy Rifkin: Zero Marginal Cost Society." Youtube. https://www.youtube.com/watch?v=MBlWEOHqdOU

Sinclair, Cameron. 2006. "My Wish: A Call for Open-source Architecture." TED. https://www.ted.com/talks/cameron_sinclair_on_open_source_architecture.

Trash Peaks

Design Earth
(El Had Jaziary and Rania Ghosn)

The space of trash has become increasingly complex, with factors extending beyond traditional limits of the city. In the context of South Korea, the intense demographic transformation over the past four decades—with over half of the population now living in the Seoul metropolitan area—has posed significant challenges to the management of waste volumes, its technologies of disposal, and the question of landfill areas that will be exhausted in a matter of time. These realities of space and resources have pushed the city to actively engage the lifecycle of waste beyond landfilling, and has shifted public awareness towards waste disposal and the urgency of waste reduction.

Trash Peaks seeks to engage the public on the issue by placing the undesired matter of waste and its associated logistics, economics, and ecologies at the center of the "theater of the world." The project composes a geographic imaginary of trash in Seoul: it foregrounds a scale, a representational view, a speculative practice, and an aesthetic. In a world where there is no longer an environmental outside, *Trash Peaks* articulates the interrelated acts of representing and projecting geographies of trash. First, it maps the materialist, political, and economic geographies of waste: of regulation changes, new processing facilities, change of sanitary landfill size, the emergence of recycling systems, the isolation of waste streams, and the emergence of waste-to-energy systems, amongst others. Second, it projects alternative imaginaries that aspire to shift public debates from their focus on positivist solutions to "garbage crises" to reconfigurations of the cultural assumptions upon which trash—its systems and symbolism—rests. In this respect, the project proposes five speculative yet generic projects that bring to visibility disciplinary controversies on the relations of technology, space, and politics.

The installation deploys the three objects of the carpet, the folding screen, and the tea table as devices to represent, project, and assemble a space of discourse and speculation. The carpet weaves an actor-diagram network of trash systems in Seoul. The folding screen appropriates the object of the irworobongdo, which traditionally symbolize a mythical place of mountain peaks in a royal court, to compose a highly stylized landscape of waste heaps that places the subject of trash at the center of conversation and the imaginary. The table hosts a series of miniature ceramic models involving the ceremonial preparation and presentation of the project.

Introduction

On November 21, 2013, the South Korean monitoring microsatellite, Science and Technology Satellite 3 (STSat-3), was launched to provide imagery for earth's environmental monitoring and land classification research as well as that of the galaxy and the cosmic background. After a little over a year in orbit, communications surfaced that STSat-3 was on course with a high probability of colliding with a piece of space debris left behind after a 2009 collision between a deactivated Russian communications satellite and an operating American commercial satellite. US scientists realized the likelihood of an upcoming collision and warned South Korean officials. After a narrowly avoided collision, officials of Korea and the United States governments held their first annual meeting on space policies to share common concerns about increasing space waste and to jointly take measures in response to the rising risk of possible future collisions with space debris.[1]

Simultaneously, back on the ground 40 miles southwest of the capital of Seoul, the Korean government was overseeing the transformation of a 600-hectare marshy stretch of tidal flats at the Yellow Sea over the course of three years with 500 million tons of sand to build the new "smart city" of Songdo International Business District. Designed for a population of roughly 70,000, there are no garbage trucks or outdoor waste bins in the city, and only seven employees are said to operate the entire waste system.[2] Trash from apartment buildings and offices is sucked directly into a system of underground pipes and transported to Songdo's "Third Zone Automated Waste Collection Plant" under the city. Waste is automatically sorted and recycled, burned for fuel, and buried deep underground.

Above and below the surface of the earth, these two cases exemplify the expanding scalar and technological complexity of managing the space of trash. South Korea, with a population of 50 million, has undergone intense transformation in the past four decades. More than half of the population lives in the Seoul metropolitan area alone. The realities of waste volumes, the major challenges of disposal, and limited landfill areas that will be exhausted in a matter of time, have called for new imaginaries of waste management in Seoul. Ambitious national targets for Seoul to be the "World's Cleanest and Best Resource-recirculating City," and a "Waste-Zero City" by

1. "South Korean Satellite Faces Collision with Space Junk: Reports," *Sputnik International* (January 3, 2015).

2. Ross Arbes and Charles Bethea, "Songdo, South Korea: City of the Future?," *The Atlantic* (September 27, 2014).

2020 without direct landfilling of household waste, requires inventive means to relocate the waste of over 25 million people.[3] Following the geography of this waste once it is "put away" is the stream of inquiry for this work.

Construct:
The externalization of trash

The approach to the question of trash speaks to the geographic scale of waste flows, representing and speculating on the territories over which the negative effects of urbanization extend, or what David Harvey refers to as an "externality field."[4] Much urban analysis fails to address or acknowledge how garbage shapes our geographies. Indeed, "clean" urbanism has rested on the city's capacity to divest itself of the environmental costs of rapidly expanding consumer culture by relegating responsibility for the inevitable "dirty" waste products to political and geographic entities beyond city jurisdictions. Waste-processing practices continue to manage obsolescence as "matter out of place"—the containment of which reaffirms the purity of what remains without. Because such spaces are beyond the city, their sites and forms are an out-of-sight-out-of-mind entity for the public as well as for architects, urban planners, and urban theorists.

The rise of environmentalist constituencies has invited us to account for all environmental externalities of the urban process, be they resource extraction, waste disposal, water management, nuclear testing, or the logistics of circulation. Such worldviews brought to public consciousness the ethics of the distribution of matter and the realization that there is no outside in which the unwanted consequences of our collective actions could be allowed to linger and disappear from view. That there was, in Bruno Latour's words, "no zone of reality in which we could casually rid ourselves of the consequence of human political, industrial, and economic life."[5]

Trash as matter-in-place

Given that we cannot stop being involved in the world we create, political ecology has the obligation to internalize the externalities that it has viewed up until now as an outside world, and to adopt our environmental technologies with patience and commitment. In "Love Your Monsters" (2011), philosopher Bruno Latour deploys Victor Frankenstein's creature as a parable of political ecology. Like a Frankensteinian monster, waste is an emblem of fear of the nature–technology entanglement and a symbol of guilt over the unintended consequences of our ever-increasing environmental actions. Latour observes,

Written at the dawn of the great technological revolutions that would define the 19th and 20th centuries, Frankenstein *foresees that . . . we have failed to care for our technological creations. We confuse the monster for its creator and blame our sins against Nature upon our creations. But our sin is not that we created technologies but that we failed to love and care for them.*[6]

3. Seoul Metropolitan Government, "Seoul, A Resource-Recirculating City" (June 20, 2015), https://seoulsolution.kr/en/content/seoul-resource-recirculating-city.

4. David Harvey, *Social Justice and the City* (London: Blackwell, 1973), 57-60.

5. Bruno Latour, *Politics of Nature: How to Bring the Sciences into Democracy* (Cambridge, MA: Harvard University Press, 2004), 58.

6. Bruno Latour, "Love Your Monsters: Why We Must Care for Our Technologies as We Do Our Children," The Breakthrough Institute, Winter 2012, http://www.bruno-latour.fr/sites/default/files/downloads/107-BREAKTHROUGHREDUXpdf, 20.

"What, then," Latour asks, "should be the work of political ecology?" For him, it is the work of mixing many more heterogeneous actors, at a greater scale and at an ever-tinier level of intimacy with the new natures we are constantly creating.[7] What we need is not to isolate once again the worlds of science, politics, and space. Instead of distinguishing that which can no longer be distinguished, Latour invites us to ask these key questions: "What world is it that you are assembling, with which people do you align yourselves, with what entities are you proposing to live?"[8]

Trash at the center of the theater of the world

How can we reclaim the forms, technologies, economies, and logistics of waste systems in the production of urbanism? If the externalization of trash has placed it beyond the agency of design, can the expansion of urban analysis and speculation on the geographic reinscribe municipal waste management as "matter in place"? In order to do so, we must shift public debates on trash and the environment away from positivist solutions that treat garbage as a factually repugnant entity to be kept out of sight. Rather, we must adopt a worldview on externalities that, in Latour's words, "adds to it its whole scenography, much like you would do by shifting your attention from the stage to the whole machinery of a theatre."

DESIGN EARTH has engaged the expanded environmental imagination in a series of projects that make visible the geographies of waste systems and chart their material, political, and scalar attributes.[9] The research proceeded through the interrelated acts of representing and projecting geographies of trash. Designers are increasingly compelled to transform larger contexts and to address problems that had been confined to the domains of engineering, ecology, or regional planning. From the Greek *geōgraphia* (geo 'earth' + -graphia 'writing'), the geographic embodies the concomitant acts of re-representation (mapping the earth) and re-forming (writing the surface of the earth)—and which, by making space visible and formal, seek to bring it back into public debate. The proposed projects aspire to shift public debates from their focus on what Bruno Latour calls matters-of-fact: that is, positivist solutions to "garbage crises," which continue to insist that garbage must be kept out of sight as a factually repugnant entity.[10] Instead, our practice seeks to draw attention to Latour's matters-of-concern: arguments that accept the fact that trash creates problems that we must address, yet seek creative, alternative, and realist solutions through the grounding of research and design in political, economic, and geographic specificities.

1] To Represent: The Carpet

The carpet becomes a physical device construct showing the constellation of actors and networks in Seoul's systems of waste management. The actor-network diagram depicted in the carpet maps the materialist, political, and economic

7. Ibid.

8. Bruno Latour, "Waiting for Gaia: Composing the Common World through Arts and Politics, November 2011, 7, http://www.bruno-latour.fr/sites/default/files/124-GAIA-LONDON-SPEAP_0.pdf.

9. Rania Ghosn and El Hadi Jazairy, *Geographies of Trash* (New York: ACTAR, 2015).

10. Bruno Latour, "Why Has Critique Run Out of Steam?," *Critical Inquiry* 30(2) (2004): 225-248.

geographies of waste. The mapping endorses Latour's "assembly of entities," which "extend the number of parts necessary for the gathering of the [thing] and then multiply the number of assembling principles that gather them together in a functioning whole."[11] In this framework, Latour takes the word network not to describe things in the world that have the shape of a net but "to designate a mode of inquiry that learns to list the unexpected beings necessary for any entity to exist." The notion of networks," Latour adds, "points to a transformation in the way action is located and allocated, and, what had seemed self-contained is now widely redistributed."[12] Each element is assigned a role and then placed into relation with one another on a grid. Over the course of this reconstruction, "you discover a swarm of entities that seem to have been there all along but were not visible before, and that appear in retrospect necessary for its sustenance."[13] What is produced on the ground is a dynamic assemblage. Trash-space is totally transformed once it is portrayed within a vast network of technologies, sites, actors, and regulatory bodies. From this perspective, waste management is not matter-out-of-place. Rather, trash sites are territorially embedded in the ground plane. The action of mapping out knowledge forms a space of political, social and creative discourse.

The carpet shifts the attention of the visitors to a visual and tactile experience that lies below their feet. Through a new application of the rich history of Korean embroidery, the tool of embellishment also becomes the representation of waste as a surplus of the city. All stitches across the field playfully lead back to the central knot of the 37,843 tons of waste that is produced every day in Seoul (as of 2012).[14] Variations of standard embroidery stitches (the chain stitch, satin stitch, blanket stitch, back stitch, feather stitch, knotted stitch, running stitch, cross-stitch, etc.) extend beyond the moment of discard at construction sites, through the daily activities of citizens, and at their workplaces, to chart out a full-bodied geography of waste in and around Seoul.[15] Like traditional embroidery that alternated threads of silk, cotton, gold, and silver, the material of the carpet threads differentiate between waste streams, rendering them separate as well as connected to the whole of the cloth.

Embroidered streams in Seoul

The carpet will chart out regulation changes and the development of new processing facilities that have transformed the landscape of waste management in the recent history of Seoul. As with many cities, operations were heavily reliant until the 1990s on sanitary landfills, which appeared as the first formalized dumping sites three decades prior. Over time, landfills were phased into larger, consolidated sections of land located further outside the space of the city. Initially smaller and dispersed at the outskirts of the city, landfills constructed between 1964 and 1970 were used to bury general waste until the mid-1980s. When the acquisition of large-scale

11. Bruno Latour, "Can We Get Our Materialism Back, Please?," *Isis* (2007): 138–142, 140.

12. Bruno Latour, "Networks, Societies, Spheres: Reflections of an Actor-network Theorist," *International Journal of Communication* 5 (2011): 796–810.

13. Latour, "Can We Get Our Materialism Back, Please?," 140.

14. Seoul Metropolitan Government, "Seoul, A Resource-Recirculating City."

15. Ibid.

landfill sites in the vicinity of Seoul became a pressing urban issue to move away from the developing city, the island of Nanjido was selected by the Seoul Metropolitan Government and it accepted 78% of the total waste produced in the city between 1978 and 1992.[16] Recognizing a need for even more space, the Sudokwon Landfill site was acquired in 1987, further from the city, as a shared agreement between the Seoul metropolitan area, the Incheon Metropolitan area, and Gyeonggi-do. Seoul has a share of 44.5% in this agreement. Although the scale of Sudokwon Landfill, with an estimated capacity of 228 million tons, seems large, the first of its four sites reached capacity in 2000. As the limits of continually acquiring more space to dispose of waste becomes more apparent, methods to extend the effective lifespan of existing landfills has risen to be a top priority. Today, landfilling has become a last resort in the waste management system. As a result, actively engaging in the lifecycle of waste beyond storage in a landfill has become a necessary next step for Seoul.

Increasing the amount of recycling has been a straightforward means to extend the lifespan of landfills by reducing the amount of trash entering waste bins across the city. Recycling rates in Seoul remained relatively low, around 5% until the late 1990s, after the 1995 introduction of a "volume-based waste collection fee system" by the Ministry of Environment.[17]According to this system, households and businesses purchase bags, with a fee for collection and disposal of garbage included that can recirculate to garbage collectors and processing centers. Each district in Seoul has individual color-coded garbage bags available at convenience stores and supermarkets in incremental sizes. This system, the first of its kind to be adopted at a national level, shifted public awareness toward waste disposal and the urgency of waste reduction.

The effective isolation of waste streams has significantly increased the amount of recycling occurring in Seoul, and has influenced many to reduce their trash output through related fees. Stemming from issues of exposed food waste, there has been a nationwide ban on the discarding of food waste in South Korea landfills and waterways.17,100 tons of food waste was generated each day in South Korea.[18] All households and businesses in Seoul are now legally required to separate food waste and dispose of it in either pre-paid plastic garbage bags, small waste containers, or a series of Radio Frequency Identification System (RFID) disposal containers that were installed across the city in 2012. RFID bins charge each resident a fee calculated based on the weight of the food waste they discard. Seoul has one of the highest percentages of restaurants per square mile in the world, and the food waste has a moisture content of approximately 80%.[19] Removing organic waste from the inorganic waste stream has redirected a major contributor of environmental leachate contamination into

16. Jae Min Song, "Smart Waste Management in Seoul: From Waste to Resource-Sanitary Landfills," Seoul Solution (May 27, 2014), https://www.seoulsolution.kr/en/content/smart-waste-management-seoul-waste-resourcesanitary-landfills.

17. "Recycling (Smart Waste Management in Seoul)," Seoul Solution (November 21, 2014). https://seoulsolution.kr/en/content/recycling-smart-waste-management-seoul.

18. Karim Chrobog, "South Korea: Cutting Back on Food Waste" (November 12, 2015), http://pulitzercenter.org/reporting/south-korea-cutting-back-food-waste.

19. Ibid.

a new waste stream that can be recycled. Over 90% of South Korea's food waste is recycled into biofuel, animal feed, or fertilizer. Isolated collection of food waste does not come without a cost to government, composing 5-6% of the government's annual budget.[20]

Since recycling surfaced in Seoul in the 1990s, beginning at apartment complexes, and gradually spreading to detached houses and commercial buildings, other waste streams for recycling have emerged, such as urban mining. E-waste is the fastest growing solid waste stream. Today, circuit boards can contain higher amounts of gold and other precious metals that can be mined from earthen ores, providing the required economic incentives to collect and dismantle the objects, and sort their component parts. Landfill mining has also emerged as a process of re-entering closed landfills to find e-waste from past decades that is now considered valuable.

Burning waste has become a means to reduce the physical volume of waste, and increase diversion from landfill sites. In 1991, the Seoul Metropolitan Government signaled a transition in waste management policy from landfilling to resource recovery. The total amount of ash produced through incineration ranges from 4–10% by volume and 15–20% by weight of the original quantity of waste. South Korea also imports approximately 97% of its primary energy demand due to its minimal natural energy reserves, making the waste-to-energy stream economically appealing.[21] Out of the eleven facilities that the City of Seoul Waste Disposal Plan initially outlined, only four were constructed between 1996 and 2005. The facilities were sited in four separate districts including Nowon-gu, Yangcheon-gu, Gangnam-gu, and Mapo-gu, with a total processing capacity of 2,850 tons of municipal waste per day.[22] Energy from these facilities are shared with twenty-two of Seoul's twenty-five administrative districts.

The relationship between these transitions to waste streams and the actions of the public is critical to the operation of the overall network. Informal waste management has been important to many citizens, with thousands living or earning extra income through the collection and recycling of plastic, paper, and metal waste. Employed waste-monitoring personnel now inspect, scan, and collect food waste containers, while those who disregard waste policies face potential fines. Elderly citizens are employed to sort through growing accumulations of e-waste for valuable resources, and appointed honorary citizen monitors receive education to help guide citizens in adapting to new modes of waste disposal as technology plays an ever-increasing role in waste processing.

2] To Project: The Folding Screen

The Korean illustrated folding screen, known as irworobongdo, has been a key element in both ritual and domestic environments of the peninsula. The traditional abstract scenography, placed behind the throne of the king, depicts a symmetrical balance between two celestial bodies

20. Ibid.

21. "South Korea Energy Profile: Heavily Relies on Imports to Meet Total Primary Energy Consumption—Analysis," *Eurasia Review: A Journal of Analysis and News* (October 6, 2015).

22. "Smart Waste Management in Seoul," Seoul Solution (November 24, 2014), https://seoulsolution.kr/en/content/smart-waste-management-seoul-resource-recovery

above the landscape, the sun and the moon.
The red sun symbolizes the king and yang,
associated with a positive principle in nature
with geographical reference to openness, the
south side of a hill, and the north bank of a river.
The white moon inversely symbolizes the queen
and yin, associated with a negative principle in
nature with geographical reference to a shaded
orientation, the north side of a hill, and the
south bank of a river. Closely tied to geography,
the two together reference the cycle of the earth
and "the workings of the universe" that "result
from the interplay of these two principles."[23]

The proposed projects reimage the landscape
and the five peaks to articulate and discuss the
present controversies of waste management in
Seoul. Emblematic of the major mountains that
surround the capital city in all directions, the
new peaks recompose the historical geography by
engaging alternative imaginaries for landfilling,
recycling, burning, reusing, and reducing within
the form of the mountain. Trash is put at the
center of the theater of the world, with the
public as the body of the sovereign. When the
king sat in front of this screen, he became the
central point of the composition and the pivotal
point from which all force emanated and to
which all returned.[24] Here, the king is replaced
with the public, and the representational
landscape they occupy is operationalized with
trash concerns that propose situated architectural
strategies to engage issues implicit in the
socialization of trash, such as value, scales of
management, social relations, ecology, and
geography. By overlaying the speculative and the
public, the space explores design's agency and
seeks to open up disciplinary and public debates
on the geographies of urban systems.

Methane forest

A post-extraction landscape of landfill methane
gas pipes creates a woven ecology of artificial
and natural habitats. The vertical pipes were
once the buried circulatory system of Seoul's
Nanjido landfill, a great artificial mountain built
from thirty years of waste collection from Seoul.
Limited area for storage caused the mound to
swell beyond its planned limit of 45 meters
high. Briquette ash and construction debris walls
were built to allow it to rise doubly to hold over
90 million cubic meters of trash, thirty-four
times larger than The Great Pyramid of Gyza.
Historically, Nanjido, or Mushroom Island,
was an island habitat for a diversity of water
fowl along the Han River. In a remarkable three
decades after a dike was constructed at the edge
of Nanjido to retain waste, the island witnessed
a rapid geomorphic transformation into an
artificial mountain that smothered surrounding
habitats with its toxic leachate. The mountain
was short-lived, soon excavated to grade in order
to extract its valuable metal ore. The exposed
methane pipes, at intervals of 120 meters, were
left intact as they continue to channel methane
from the aging waste that remains buried below
the surface. In a country with high import rates
of energy and raw materials, the landfills have
become a manufactured resource over time for
public facilities, offices, and households. In an
effort to reestablish canopy habitat for Seoul's
native birds, the pipes were retrofitted with an
aviary cap. Each aviary contains fragments of
the excavated trash that have been repurposed
into a diversity of nesting boughs suitable for a
particular species. The aviaries form a forest canopy that filters sunlight to foster a natural, emergent understory ecosystem. Nanjido is returned
to an aviary habitat after its brief geomorphic
history as a toxic mountain.

23. "Sun, Moon, and Immortal Peaches," *HKMJ* 2 (3) (September 1996), 234.

24. "Sun, Moon, and Five Peaks," *HKMJ* 4 (2) (June 1998), 114.

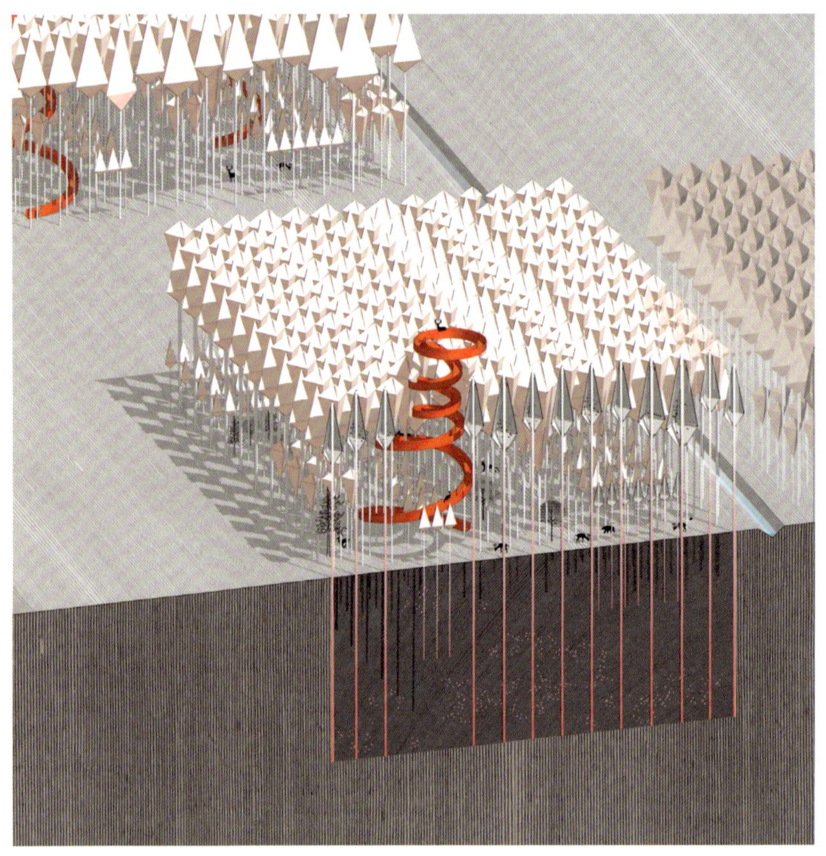

Methane Forest

Peak 1: The Tower

The Tower is sited on Mount Namsan, a peak valued for offering panoramic views of the city. This project responds to construction waste related to urbanization in Seoul, that as of 2012 constituted 71% of the daily waste generated.[25] The mountain is a contradiction: it is a historic icon with parkland, symbolic of Korea's natural imagery, as well as a host for Namsan Seoul Tower, a modern tourist destination and glowing beacon of technology. The project capitalizes on this relationship to make a visual commentary about urban development and modernization, and its resulting construction waste. Metal from demolished structures wraps around the mountain in an ever-spiraling "tower." As metal enters the waste stream, the tower builds on itself becoming more unstable. This communicates to Seoul the state of development at the compensation of nature. In the Tower, glass geometric rooms rotated and housed a venue for legislature, executive government, and information distribution. People within the trains rotate around the mountain and through

25. Seoul Metropolitan Government, "Seoul, A Resource-Recirculating City."

Tatlin's Tower

the voids. The chambers are made of the city's three major construction waste materials: concrete, brick, and wood. The rectangular chamber made of concrete houses a cemetery of deconstructed buildings. The pyramidal chamber made of wood holds the now preserved Gyeongbokgung Palace, and the dome made of brick holds the South Korea National Assembly.

Peak 2: The Leachate Amphitheater

The Leachate Amphitheater is sited within the 20 million square meters of reclaimed land that compose Sudokwon Landfill, one of the world's largest sanitary landfills. The monumentality of the project is expressed as a series of colossal excavations or voids in the form of a field of subterranean, spherical amphitheaters. Leachate from the ground below is filtered to remove organic contaminant and ammonia concentrations. The venues house purified leachate lakes on which there are stages for theater and music. The project is symbolic of the ecological loss of the original wetlands that has been the result, directly and indirectly, of waste production and storage in Seoul. They are monuments to remediation and progress, as the lakes sit center-stage giving the treatment of leachate a position of reverence.

The tops of the spherical venues peek out above the decommissioned landfill in a manner that is meant to evoke the domed form of traditional Korean burial mounds. The structures are also an ode to Boullée's Newton's Cenotaph—another grave. Hammams are referenced through the lighting and allusion to cleanliness. The lighting also evokes the cosmos, adding to the monumentality of the theater and reflecting off of the leachate. A visitor to the venue would descend underground through long tunnels, feeling the depth of their journey. They emerge from the tunnel in the void and are confronted by its scale and beauty.

Peak 3: Pseudo Volcano

Embedded deep into the Jurassic granite of Bukhansan Mountain, a great incinerator converts consumer waste into energy and building material for Seoul. This second face of Bukhansan looks away from the city, emerging from the mountain as a solitary monument to future energy. From the city, the incinerator reveals its activity only through the faint hint of smoke rising from a reinterpretation of the mountain's historic signal beacon. The project, which can output enough energy to power approximately one-quarter of the metropolis, is the latest achievement in a national effort towards energy independence.

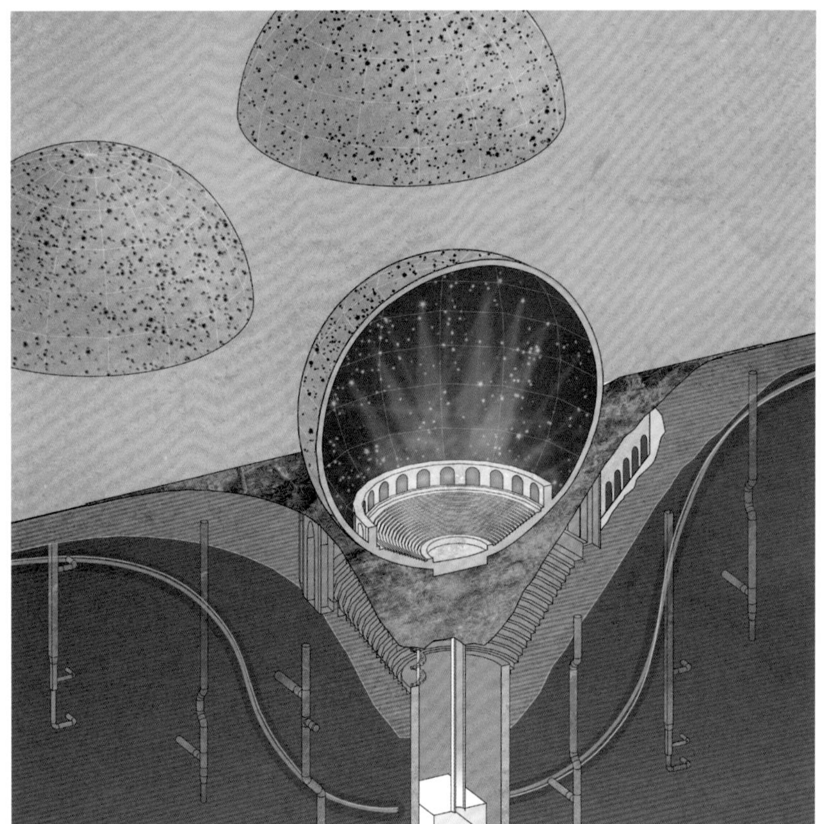

The Leachate Amphitheater

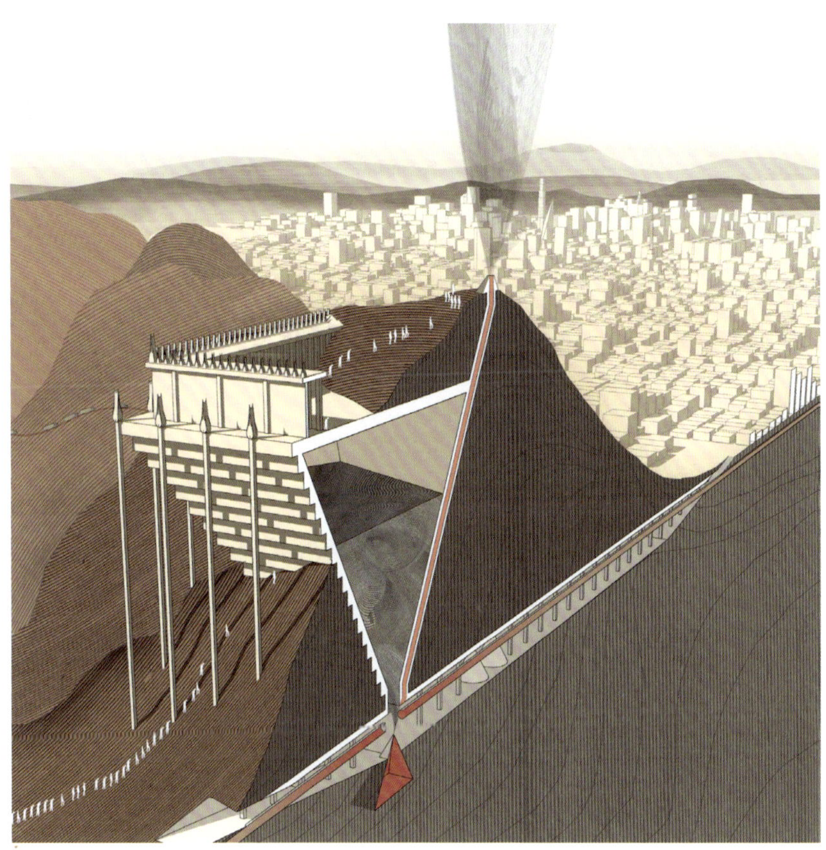

Pseudo Volcano

And now, after a century of trash exportation outside of the city, Seoul imports more waste than it produces in order to meet the ever-growing energy demands of the city. Old waste from decommissioned landfills is mined as feedstock for the mountain. A pyramidal collection chamber channels waste to an incinerator that produces four output streams from the furnace to the stack: Non-Ferrous Metals (Bottom Ash); Ferrous Metals (Bottom Ash); Bricks/Concrete (Fly Ash); and Electricity/Heat (steam). Each output stream radiates orthogonally from the point of incineration into great halls under the mountain where it is processed, developed into commodities, and distributed back to the city.

Peak 4: Plastic Mountain

In Changsin Dong, a dense hill neighborhood in Seoul where urbanization has claimed every landform, a suspended plastic mountain reforms a lost landscape. The global plastic waste epidemic is so pervasive that the substance has been discovered in the systems of most living organisms on earth. Microplastics, less than five millimeters in length and coming from a range of sources, infiltrate the composition of water and soil. Larger pieces sit idle, waiting out the centuries it will take to degrade to the size of these tiny pollutants. Plastic waste centers operate around the clock each day to sort plastic by type and color. In response, the Korean government initiated a

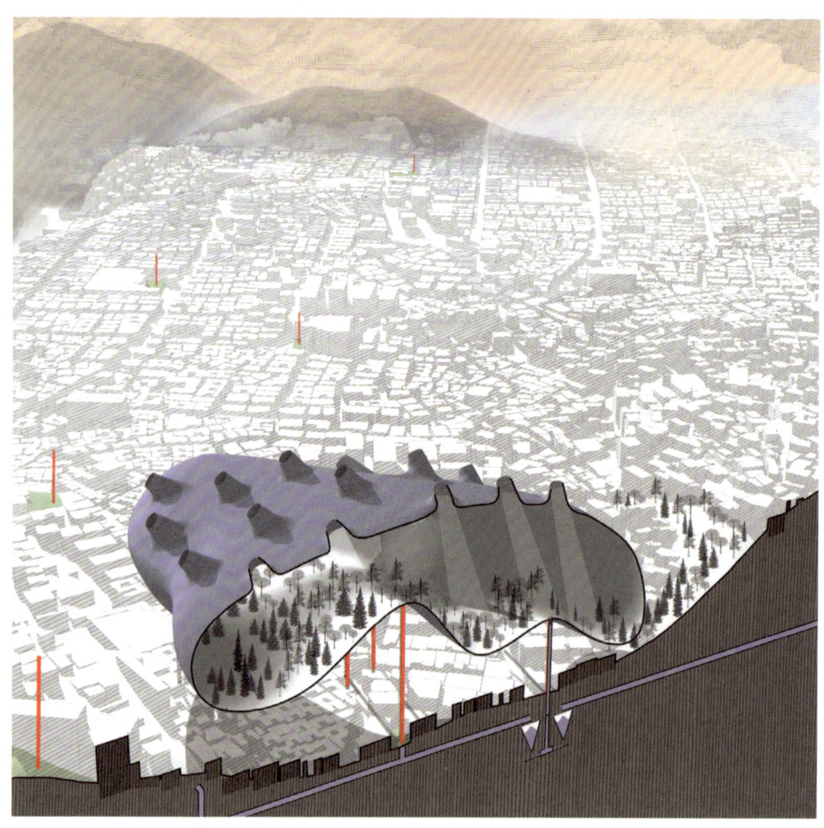

Mt. Plastic

project that localizes the recycling process and channels its output into a local, public amenity. Changsin's famous hilltop toy market becomes the site of a plastic recovery project that recycles obsolete toys and other plastic waste into an artificial, suspended pedosphere that supports plant growth. Localized plastic collection points throughout the neighborhood distribute plastic waste to a centrally located, subterranean processing plant where a great plastic extruder reforms the plastic into various components for the mountain. The suspended landscape adjoins a nearby hill and continues an artificial rolling topography internally. The enclosed plastic form regulates sunlight and air pollution to create a tropical biome that is enjoyed by local residents year-round.

Peak 5: E-Waste Valley

A great precious metals mine is erected over the obsolete 45-acre Yongsan Electronics Market in downtown Seoul. In a geographical area where natural resources are largely imported, recycling minerals already within the urban environment—concealed inside the plastic, glass, and metal casings of discarded electronics—is becoming increasingly valuable. Most e-waste was previously redirected to underdeveloped countries where ineffective extraction processes are conducted informally, exposing workers and their environments to damaging toxic chemicals. New advances in biotechnology utilize fungi to efficiently extract precious metals from e-waste. The new employment of fungi mimics the pulloch'o, or "long-life fungus," often illustrated

E-Waste

on the irworobongdo in bright red and yellow, sprouting from rock faces.[26] In an effort to become a negative-waste city, Seoul redirects the global e-waste stream to its Yongsan Mine where it employs fungal extraction at a grand scale. The mine is organized vertically into five levels that each processes a specific artificial ore: mobile devices, computers, TVs, small appliances, large appliances. Each level connects to the exterior of the mine where its altitude supports a specialized ecosystem that develops the fungi used in the extraction process. Long in need of renewal, the Yongsan electronics market now is witness to a rebirth of technology industry—a silicon valley reborn—that feeds off the extracted metals from its new mine.

3] To Assemble: The Table

The table holds miniature models of each of the six projects in a ceramic tableware set. Familiar and approachable, the tea ceremony ritual initiates a conversation about future waste management through the sharing of a cup of tea and a meal. The monolithic wood table-top represents the city of Seoul and is carved to provide contextual niches for each trash monument.

The tableware set includes six elements. The first is a utensil stand related to the project Methane Forest. Ceramic chopsticks are niched into the table in a gridded layout reminiscent of the methane gas pipes buried in the Sudokwon landfill. The next element is a set of nested dishes. A five-piece ceramic bowl set rests together in a conical miniature of E-waste Mountain. Each bowl has an identical volume, but is a unique diameter and depth. Next, a tea cup set inspired by the historic Korean covered tea cup is designed

with a removable lid reminiscent of the dome of the Leachate Amphitheater. The cup sits in a niche carved into the table referencing the theatre component of the project. A ceramic water pitcher that sits as the table centerpiece is reminiscent of Tatlin's leaning steel tower, forming the Parliament of Trash. A serving bowl reinterprets the inverted pyramidal collection chamber of Pseudo Volcano and niches into the side of a carved, wooden mountain. Lastly, a pair of salt and pepper shakers take on the amorphous form of Plastic Mountain.

The miniature forms sit on the table in front of the folding screen. They operate at different scales. They are both the three-dimensional taxidermied foreground of the diorama and a tool to welcome visitors to dwell in the space of trash.

Conclusion

Beyond a binary of purity and despoilment, *Trash Peaks* deploys uncomfortable yet oddly constructive relationships with geography's marginalized externalities. It attempts to reconfigure the cultural and aesthetic and assumptions upon which the management of the disappearance of undesired matter rests. It maintains as such the position that aesthetic reform is an agency for political action. Thus, the challenge of a geographic imagination is not simply to represent these systems and their futures but to render visible the inequality between the promises of technological fixes and the distribution of geographic externalities.

26. "Sun, Moon, and Immortal Peaches," 234.

Three Ordinary Funerals

Common Accounts
(Igor Bragado and Miles Gertler)

Broadly speaking, death is a wasted effort. Decades of technological progress have distanced the material business of death from everyday life; sanitization, disease control, and the funeral industry have kept it neat and tidy, and out of sight. The contemporary city has eradicated, modified, and restricted many of the urban typologies that once played host to the social activities surrounding death. Still, death is visible in home decor, in fitness programs, and in virtual space, yet architecture has failed to acknowledge the potential posed by the latent social situations and infrastructural networks around death, and failed to recognize these entities as a site for action. Further, cities can no longer afford to keep the material business of death at arm's length. New technologies present unique opportunities for the production of value—material, ceremonial, virtual, and ecological—to be ignored only at their own peril, while the traditional means of human disposition are threatened by diminishing land availability, environmental concerns, and the prospect of a digital afterlife.

Today the realities of the urban ecosystem have made the sites of death more ubiquitous yet potentially less evident. Death's atomization presents opportunities for its reintegration into everyday life.

For this, few cities present as fertile a test ground as Seoul. It is archetypal in its scarcity of available land, but also home to a population that in the last two decades has exhibited great flexibility in its attitudes toward death, the redesign of the body, and architectures of ceremony.

In upgrading death's productive potential, one might first consider the augmentation of existing city infrastructures. Techno-urban interventions could create robust societies through more immediate access to processes surrounding death. For instance, the heat of the crematorium can be used to fry your eggs (a reliable new power source?).[1] The internet has the potential to be a new site for memorial (provoking real engagement with the virtual afterlife?).[2] The state of the environment can be improved by adjusting remains disposition methods (a new arena for environmental activism?).[3] And the sale of your skin could pay the mortgage on your house (a new frontier for bio-capital?).[4] It is the role of the designer in the death-savvy city to negotiate the sensitivity to death that has thus far inhibited our ability to enrich our urban existence in these ways, through the careful calibration of its presence and visibility in daily life. Further, design can ensure the provision of choice: that multiple modes of disposition are made available to those facing death and that each technological option—indeed, each possible reconstitution of the body—is delivered through cultural experience (i.e. ceremony). But not only could death be more useful and customized: we could also welcome micro-scale memorial of the material and virtual substance of the urban dead to one's day-to-day navigation of the city, re-equipping death with greater social significance.

The deceased no longer occupy only a metaphysical space of remembrance. They are still our friends on Facebook, can be sent direct messages on Instagram, and are our followers in KakaoStory; they live on in new channels of existence; and the conditions of ceremony can no longer be limited to traditional funerary rites. The latent potential of the cadaver—its inherent energy, its material worth, and its political agency—no longer remains hermetically sealed in the coffin. New technologies and the logistics of global death networks complicate the status of the body and positions death as more of an inflection point than a full stop.

*****

A History with Organs

The last half-century of architectural discourse has contributed to the distancing of death from the daily urban, elaborating the metaphysical poetics of death as an island, apart from the everyday. Analogizing the corpse of high modernism, cemeteries and mausoleums proliferated amidst the new stance that architecture took to its own history from the mid 1960s. Architects like Aldo Rossi, Enric Miralles, and John Hejduk explored the sites of death with

---

1. Like the inter-building energy transfer observed at Redditch Community Centre, England

2. Much in the way that a John Berlin, a bodybuilder from Missouri, prompted the introduction of memorialization of user accounts of Facebook after his viral YouTube plea to the giant social media company.

3. Alkaline hydrolysis, for instance, demonstrates a marked decrease in carbon footprint and in the release of airborne mercury particles in comparison to cremation.

4. The human epidermis has been valued at up to US$80,000.

5. George Nelson in the CBS television special *How to Kill People: A Problem of Design* in 1961.

Redditch Crematorium begins to heat town pool

28 June 2013   Hereford & Worcester

A Worcestershire swimming pool is now being heated by a nearby crematorium.

Abbey Stadium leisure centre is finally using waste heat diverted from Redditch Crematorium after the project was **hit by delays due to extra work**.

Redditch Borough Council expects the scheme to reduce the centre's gas bill by aver 40%, equating to a saving of about £15,000 a year.

The heat of the crematorium in Redditch, England, is redirected to heat the community pool nearby

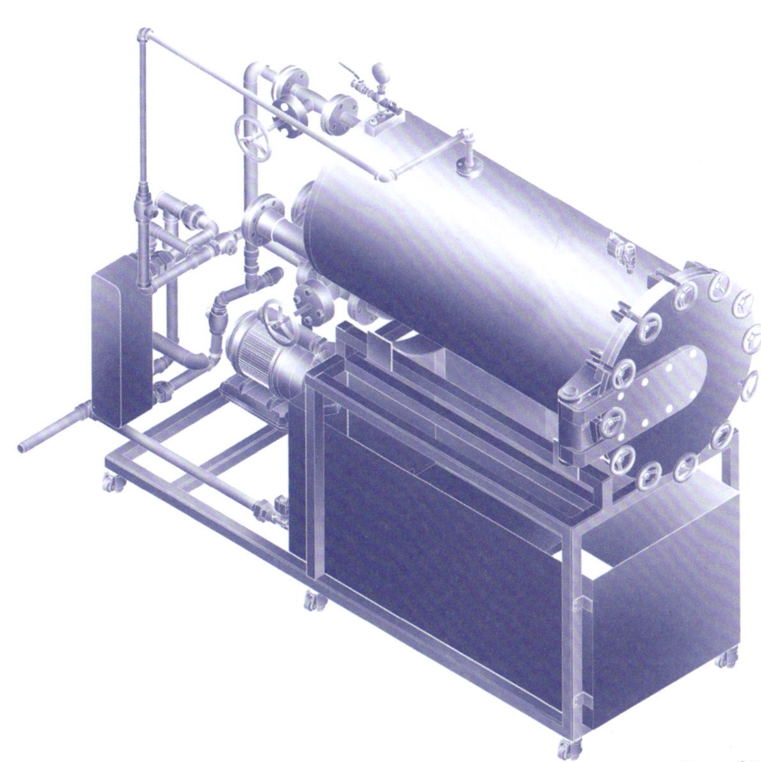

One of Supreme Thermal Instrument's alkaline hydrolysis systems: a new means of remains disposition

special attention to romance and aesthetics, obviating the ritualistic potential of material, logistical, and technological realities.

In contrast to these kinds of postmodern attitudes, Sigfried Giedion's (1888–1968) chapter on death in *Mechanization Takes Command* (1948) portrayed the techno-social and urban implications of the development of industries around death. He is arguably the first architectural historian to acknowledge the role of death industries as critical contributors to the construction of the modern landscape of the urban West, as was the case with nineteenth-century Paris or rural America. It was in this spirit that architecture could most meaningfully promote its own intervention. The account of Giedion is relevant to us for two reasons: first, because he considers death as a *theory* with implications for a historical conception of architecture, and second, because it has ramifications in the realm of the domestic and the mundane, rather than the spectacular. Through his lens, the fridge, washing machine, and canned food are laced with death. These are the kinds of domestic objects which the progress of mechanization has radically detached from the organic entities they deal with, and which have induced on humans a neutrality towards the reception of the processed bodies they conform to. In this way, death becomes domesticated. This observation is critical for those who wish to intervene in the traditions and systems that manage death in society. It articulates a theory of the mechanical dislocation of experience and perception of even the most

visceral aspects of human life. It is exactly this kind of reasoning that underlies the modernization of funerary tradition for institutions like funeral directors' associations and the military.

*****

"It was in a way a sad story when my father died... Because my mother called me on the phone and she said: 'You know? Your dad died.' And this was exactly two months before contest. She says: 'You come home to the funeral?' And I said: 'No. It's too late, you know? He is dead, there's nothing to be done, and I'm sorry, I can't come, you know?' And I didn't explain to her really the reasons why. Now, I had other excuses to her ... because how do you explain a mother whose husband died, you know ... you trip! I didn't bother with it."[6] **Max Out. Live On**

The political power of ceremony must not be underestimated. Ceremonial practices augment the ordinary as cultural experience. Ceremony bestows credibility, grants visibility, and articulates the political in formal and performative modes. In this way, ceremony is architecture and belongs within the domain of the discipline.

One of the most active agents in the extension of the life of the dead and experts in the construction of media-savvy ceremony may well be the military, and no armed force is as large, as extensively distributed, and as well funded as that of the United States.[7] The American military

6. Arnold Schwarzenegger in an interview for the movie *Pumping Iron*, 1977.

7. Global Firepower (*globalfirepower.com*) ranks the United States as first in military capacity, taking into account scale of force, geographical factors, infrastructure, natural resource reliance, naval capacity, access to water, and economic health of the nation state. See www.globalfirepower.com/countries-listing.asp. Business Insider (*businessinsider.com*) cites the Peter G. Peterson Foundation's 2013 study that shows that the United States' military's 2012 defense budget (US\$682 billion) surpassed that of the next ten best-funded state militaries combined (US\$652 billion). www.businessinsider.com/chart-of-defense-spending-by-country-2014-2.

is expert in the processing and transmutation of the human body in life and in death. Its global reach is matched by an infrastructural protocol that co-opts the body as a logistical unit and in so doing, invests in it a political, ceremonial, and virtual value. An examination of the US military's method of basic training and its department of Mortuary Affairs exposes the processes by which the military produces a *perfect* body: an *American* body.

Those soldiers who die on duty—53,402 in World War I; 291,557 in World War II; 58,220 in Vietnam; 4,410 in Iraq[8]—are retrieved, identified, catalogued, returned, processed, and ceremonialized according to the protocol of the department of Mortuary Affairs (MA). A department diagram articulates the order of things: storage; photography; personal effects; finger/foot printing; full body x-ray; dental oral surgery; dental x-ray; dental exam; pathological autopsy exam and records analysis; identification; cleaning and preparation; embalming; casket; holding; uniform; storage; shipment. The list only provides a schematic outline of the processes involved and neglects the details of the stages therein.

To render the experience whole, one must piece together the technologies, vehicles, architectures, choreographies, and scenarios produced by the industrial military apparatus that ensures the body's transmission from the theater of war to the funeral director.

Activities at the US military's lone port mortuary at Dover Air Force Base in Delaware reinforce the concept of the infrastructural body, and lace logistics with ceremony towards the production of a virtual subject. An official video of the Dignified Transfer of fallen Army Staff Sergeant William R. Wilson III exhibits exactly this.[9] "Dignified Transfer" is an appropriate neologism—"Dignified," denoting themes of honor and emotion; "Transfer," conveying technicality and the bureaucratic—that describes the process in which an honor guard unloads a casket from the cargo bay of a Lockheed Martin C-5 Galaxy transport aircraft, redirecting it for further processing to the Port Mortuary.

In the first stage, the casket—which is no ordinary coffin, but an aluminum "transfer case" draped in an American flag—is loaded onto a skyjack from the plane's cargo ramp. Each technological function is understood as a ceremonial process. That is, the skyjack's lowering of the body doubles as a moment of silence as the lift operator stands vigil in salute next to the case. The height of the lowered skyjack aligns with the height of the truck parked 50 feet away, so the pallbearers carry the coffin not on their shoulders, as they might at a funeral, but with arms extended downward, the body level with their hips.

The casket is there loaded onto a conveyer belt shelf. The video of Staff Sergeant Wilson shows a number of vacant shelves in the back of the truck for instances where a transport jet delivers more than a single body. This disrupts the myth of singularity of the hero but more accurately describes the military's mass production of the hero—of heroism as a virtual, mediatic image or protocol. Again, the techno-procedural is

8. Jeremy Bender, citing the US Department of Veterans Affairs and US Department of Defense, "The Number of US Soldiers Who Died in Every Major American War," *Business Insider*, May 28, 2014.

9. Staff Sergeant James Jackson, "Dignified Transfer of Army Staff Sergeant William R. Wilson III," *YouTube*, April 9 2012, www.youtube.com/watch?v=Ol6cOtykcRM.

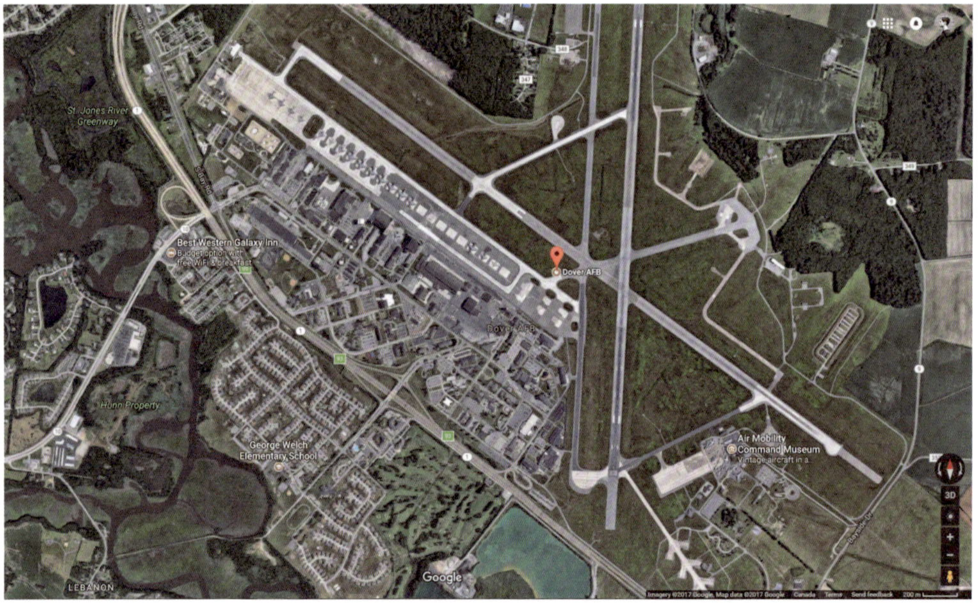

Dover Air Force Base: The US Military's lone port mortuary

An arsenal of semi-automated casket transport vehicles awaits new arrivals at Seoul Memorial Park: an 18,000 sq.m facility on a 36,000 sq.m site

Automated vehicles deliver bodies to crematorium retorts at Seoul Memorial Park

translated into ceremony. The closing of the truck doors is slow and measured, completed by gloved hands, one door at a time, on the Dover tarmac.

Tarmac constitutes the circulatory and philosophical culture at Dover. Military and mortuary facilities are positioned within the demonstrably logical network of highly articulated asphalt surfaces for maximum efficiency. The Joint Personal Effects Depot is located adjacent to Mortuary Affairs, which in turn is located near the end of one of the narrow taxi runways so that bodies can be immediately ushered to the MA loading dock without interrupting air traffic. A major parking lot and a number of smaller ancillary lots and staging areas serve each cluster of buildings. The Air Force Base flower shop—the stop for those looking for a memorial bouquet—is located one lot west of the mortuary cluster.[10] The base's streets are merged with parking lots and turning radii, and in some cases, they take the names of the defense infrastructure of the military network. The Lockheed Martin's transport aircraft lends its moniker to "Galaxy Street," and further north you may find yourself on "Chevron Ave."[11] In this way, instruments of the technological paradigm are honored as we might honor a fallen general or head of state.

At Dover, infrastructure is indiscernible from daily life, which is in turn indiscernible from urbanism. Rather, the infrastructural *is* the urbanism.

*****

"I'm in two minds, in an awkward situation, I just stare and say ba-ba-ba-baby. I'm going crazy. […] Slap slap slap the innocent doll, I sit and lie down all day, and time flies, flies, flies. What's with the dull skin again?"[12]
Seoul and Its Fluid Funeral Attitudes

In a country of roughly fifty million people, one-fifth of the population lives in Seoul, and 82.5% live in cities countrywide.[13] Although 75% of the population identifies as Christian or atheist, many of South Korea's cultural traditions are still informed by the country's Confucian heritage.[14] Cremation is the most popular form of human disposition, with roughly 90% of South Koreans today preferring the method for their disposal post-mortem. However, only twenty-five years ago, according to the Bureau of Statistics of South Korea, the incineration of the body was a dubious form of remains disposition. In direct confrontation with the country's rapid urban development and the shortage of available land, the Confucian traditions of burial and ceremony at home could no longer be supported in urban South Korea.[15] In recognition of rising land value and the need to house the newly urban, the government-funded Korean National Council for Cremation Promotion embarked on an aggressive public relations campaign in 2000 in hopes of popularizing

10. "Dover Air Force Base, Dover, Delaware," Google Maps, http://tinyurl.com/h3toy5m

11. Ibid.

12. Lyrics for the song *TT* by the K-pop band Twice, https://www.youtube.com/watch?v=ePpPVE-GGJw.

13. CIA World Factbook, https://www.cia.gov/library/publications/the-world-factbook/geos/ks.html.

14. Ibid.

15. "In Korea it is traditional to conduct funeral ceremonies at the home of the

cremation as an alternative solution requiring less space in the city.[16] In some cases the effort even adapted the form of Confucian burial grounds to the new material state of the urn-encapsulated, cremated body, converting the domed architecture of ancestral cemetery sites into icons of the columbarium.[17] In 2015, the president of a Korean funeral worker's association, Lee Sang-jae, told *The Korea Herald* that "the limited cemetery space and financial burden of purchasing land for graves contributed to the rise of cremation. Managing the grave also requires a lot of time, which poses challenges to the increasing number of nuclear families."[18]

The campaign—which included the normalized portrayal of the newly designed ceremony for cremation in multiple South Korean television dramas—was successful in its popularization of the new disposal system. Cremation rates exceeded 75% in 2014,[19] but plans to build crematoria faced steep opposition from anxious neighbors. Eventually, large-scale disposition infrastructures were built in relative isolation: what is now the Seoul Memorial Park took twenty-four years to open from the project's initiation due to fierce protest from the surrounding area.[20] These facilities help process the 22,000 Koreans who die each year countrywide,[21] but contribute to a range of other issues, not least among them the carbon footprint that results from incineration and the unregulated release of emissions like airborne mercury. As of 2015 there were fifty-five crematoria operating in Korea, sharing among them the roughly six hundred cremated daily.[22] This level of demand has already put a strain on the system, and the conditions are worse in areas where there are no crematoria close by.

deceased in accordance with Confucian ethics. However, urban expansion has meant that it is no longer possible to hold funeral or wedding ceremonies in the family home. The situation has led to the emergence of a funeral industry proposing a vast array of services, from the provision of mortuary accessories to the organization of all stages of the funeral by undertakers." Shi-Dug Kim, "Overview of Korea's Funeral Industry," in *Invisible Population: The Place of the Dead in East Asian Megacities,* ed. Natacha Aveline-Dubach (Plymouth: Lexington Books, 2012), 192.

16. Lim Yun Suk, "Shortage of Cremation Facilities in South Korea," Channel News Asia, November 22, 2015, www.channelnewsasia.com/news/asiapacific/shortage-of-cremation/2282306.html.

17. Shi-Dug Kim, "Overview of Korea's Funeral Industry," 192-206.

18. Lee Hyun-jeong, "More Koreans Cremated," *The Korea Herald*, November 9, 2015, www.koreaherald.com/view.php?ud=20151109001075.

19. Unclassified Memorandum, US Embassy Seoul, Korea, April 2015, 3.

20. Lim Yun Suk, "Shortage of Cremation Facilities in South Korea."

21. In 2016, there were 5.8 deaths/1000 population, according to the CIA World Factbook, https://www.cia.gov/library/publications/the-world-factbook/geos/ks.html.

22. Ibid.

Today, death makes itself visible but is restricted from having a material impact on the city. Any evidence of the material business of death, including the presence of bodies, embalmed or otherwise, is mostly absent from typical Korean funerals.[23] During a memorial, a photo portrait is usually displayed in the body's absence. As an extreme example, at the Seoul Memorial Park, technologies detach the workers and mourners from having much direct contact with the body itself. Automated carts ferry bodies around the building and, eventually, deposit the cadaver in the cremation retort. That experience, too, is mediated by technology for the family, who observe from another room on screen via CCTV camera.[24] Even the collection of ash is an automated process, carried out by a robotic proxy.

Spaces for death, on the other hand, restricted in access as they may be, are visible throughout the city. Most of Seoul's hospitals are equipped with funeral halls, often plugged into floors serving living patients too.[25] Many funerals still last for the traditionally observed three days of mourning, and as such, a wide range of family, friends, and associates are expected to visit and pay their respects. This expands some of the visibility of death in spaces and modes pre-designated by the protocols of the medical and funeral industries.[26] However, funeral parlours[27]—designed and operated by hospitals and professional funeral directors—foster an industry-specific culture of death in the absence of the other cultural paradigms once attached to long-established ways of life. As a measure

23. Even the floral arrangements are interspersed with a selection of eternally resplendent artificial flowers: "at least ten different varieties" for each funeral, as if to keep the prospect of death at bay. Shi-Dug Kim, "Overview of Korea's Funeral Industry," 195.

24. In some cremation centers elsewhere, like the Mount Pleasant Group facility at Elgin Mills outside of Toronto, family members are provided a lounge-like space to observe the body's entry into the retort and are even granted access to an adjacent space where they can witness the back-of-house of the cremation operations and the ash collection and emissions capture machinery.

25. Hospitals nationwide account for 70% of the country's total number of funeral parlours with 570 facilities across Korea. Shi-Dug Kim, "Overview of Korea's Funeral Industry," 195.

26. "The term 'funeral industry' *(jangrye saneop)* has been included in Korean industrial classifications since 1997. Alterations were subsequently made in 2007 to take into account the diversification of the industry. Moreover, the Korean Agency for Technology and Standards (affiliated to the Ministry of Knowledge Economy) has created a national standard for funeral parlours, ossuaries, crematoria and cemeteries with the aim of standardizing services within the industry and thus safeguarding national culture." Shi-Dug Kim, "Overview of Korea's Funeral Industry," 192.

27. The hiring of funeral parlours was first legalized by government decree in 1973, "introducing surface area standards and making the running of these facilities dependent on receiving authorization. In 1993 this authorization was abolished and replaced by a simple declaration: hospitals were also authorized to

of this change, Hyun-dong Song notes in his dissertation, "Changes and the Social Meaning of Modern Korean Funeral Ritual," that in 1994, only 22.6% of Koreans held funerals in hospital funeral halls, while in 2001, the figure had risen to 53.9%.[28] This means that the urban spaces occupied by death have moved, from peripheral cemeteries and ancestral burial grounds outside of the city, to the more central but tightly controlled money-making funeral halls attached to the city's medical infrastructure.[29]

*****

"Bobbi Kristina Brown, the only child of the pop star Whitney Houston [...] who set off a media frenzy after she was found unconscious in a bathtub on Jan. 31, died on Sunday. [...] The circumstances were reminiscent of those surrounding her mother's death; Ms. Houston was found submerged in a hotel bathtub in Beverly Hills, Calif., on Feb. 11, 2012."[30]
Preserve, Transform

Since processes of improvement, conservation, and destruction lie on a fluid scale between death and healing, we could form an understanding of each of these as instances of body processing or design. Tracing the origin of the sarcophagi and the bathtub in *Style in the Technical and Tectonic Arts*, Gottfried Semper (1803–1879) points to the reciprocity of origins between the tub for regeneration and the vessel for the dead body.[31]

A structuring cloud diagram for Hans Hollein's (1934–2014) *MAN transFORMS* exhibition of 1976 featured a central figure of the "BODY." Among the few "interrelated subjects" that orbited around this concept of the human body were "redesigning the man," "bodybuilding," and "death."[32]

Even if these subjects are presented as pivotal conceptual elements, they function merely as rhetorical devices, holding a minor presence in the actual exhibition. Bodybuilding and death do not have a strong presence in the show. It is unclear

run funeral parlours *(jangryesikjang)*, and in 1996 the government agreed to provide financial assistance for their construction." Shi-Dug Kim, "Overview of Korea's Funeral Industry," 195.

28. Hyung-dong Song, "Changes and the Social Meaning of Modern Korean Funeral Ritual," diss., Graduate School of Korean Studies, The Academy of Korean Studies, Seongnam, Korea, 2003.

29. South Korea's funeral industry is estimated to be worth US$2.3 billion "and up to 5,000 billion won (US$4.6 billion) if the cost of funeral parlours and other establishments is factored in." Shi-Dug Kim, "Overview of Korea's Funeral Industry," 201.

30. From "Bobbi Kristina Brown, Daughter of Whitney Houston, Dies at 22," *New York Times*, July 26, 2015.

31. Gottfried Semper traces the origin of the sarcophagi in the bathtub. In his "Style in the Technical and Tectonic Arts," he writes: "The oldest examples of these vessels are the Egyptian labra that were used as sarcophagi—or rather, that survived in the form of sarcophagi modeled after them." Gottfried Semper, *Style in the Technical and Tectonic Arts, or, Practical Aesthetics* (1860; repr., Los Angeles: Getty Research Institute Publications, 2004), 486.

when the aforementioned exhibition diagram was conceived, but the dislocation between the general framing of the exhibition and this representation is significant. Therefore in order to understand what correlation Hollein envisioned between the transformations of the human body and death, we must rely heavily on his texts.

In the catalogue of the exhibition Hollein writes: "An Exhibition on DESIGN needs necessarily to be an exhibition on life and death, because that is the reason why we engage with design, to live and to die, and possibly to live beyond death." He adds: "There are mainly two fields of man's activity: to survive during life and to survive after life." Self-design, or rather self-DESIGN,[33] according to the frame of the exhibition, is among those transformations which provide the extension of life after death—the *survival of death*.

The idea of self-design as a tool for the extension of life after death was not an isolated thought since it was also present in a previous exhibition by Hollein. Six years before the opening of *MAN transFORMS* at the Cooper Hewitt Museum, the Austrian architect curated a more modest exhibition called *Everything Is Architecture, an Exhibition on the Theme of Death*. The main space of the exhibition was a fake half-excavated ruin that contained ancient elements as well as objects of the recent past and more contemporary elements, like a golf club. The idea that for Hollein "transformations" were an "extension" of life after death is here reiterated in the catalogue of the 1970 exhibition, where "transformations" are listed as a *concept* of death.[34] According to Johannes Cladders, who wrote the introduction of the catalogue of *Everything Is Architecture*, for Hollein transformations are not intended for a takeover of the self, but they represent an addition—an implementation.

32. The topic of the exhibition *MAN transFORMS* was DESIGN. In a letter sent to the director of the Cooper Hewitt Museum Lisa Taylor in 1974, Hans Hollein writes: "The show will deal with design in the broadest sense. Product design will be included as well as city planning, it will present design as an approach towards dealing with situations, problems, human conditions, and not as a concern for the object alone. It will show that design lies at the basis of human activity and creativity (...)" Hans Hollein, *MAN transFORMS: Concepts for an Exhibition* (Vienna, Locker Verlag, 1989), 17.

33. The capitalization of words might cast light on the intentions behind the exhibition and the conceptualization of the terms. Generally speaking, a capitalized word has notoriety compared to a lower-case word. Both signifier and signified are enhanced. "DESIGN" is not "design." One is the bulked brother of the other. It is therefore paradoxical that the capitalized "DESIGN" refers in this exhibition to the objects of daily life not assumed by a general public to be produced by designers, that is, not assumed to be designed. So here "DESIGN" constitutes "design" in the face of its apparent inexistence. Similarly, we could question if "MAN" and "FORMS" are also entities to be subject to a different gaze in the face of their annihilation.

34. The catalogue of the exhibition *Everything Is Architecture, an Exhibition on the Theme of Death* itself is a vessel for the transition from live to death—a vessel for the survival in death. Flowers were introduced in the 550 copies of the catalogue wich was designed in the form of a black box. Hans Hollein, *Alles Ist Architektur, Eine Ausstellung Zum Thema Tod*, Stadtisches Museum Monchengladbach, Spring 1970. Consulted version at the Art Library Rare Books Collection, Princeton University.

Facebook answers grieving dad's emotional plea

John Berlin's viral YouTube plea to Facebook in 2014 marked the launch of the social media giant's policies around the memorialization of the accounts of dead users. Berlin's request to see the content on his deceased son Jesse's page was granted after his video received over one million views in its first day online.

This might all be a meaningless exercise altogether, but let's for a moment believe that there is more than mere mysticism in Hollein's words, and that our interpretation got somewhat close to his understanding of death. What are the manifestations in the world of death as an *implementation*? What does it mean for Hollein that the design of the body provides the extension of life after death—that self-transformations are a *survival of death*?[35]

Let's take the case of John Berlin: a middle-aged, overweight, married father of three living in a trailer home in Arnold, Missouri. On January 28, 2012, his twenty-one-year-old son Jesse died unexpectedly.

That year, John Berlin started a YouTube channel and began posting videos from day-to-day activities, many featuring his kids. *Experiments with Traffic Control* (*"Just another day at work,"* 300 views, Feb. 15, 2012), *Trippy Cat* (*"She's cool man, she just kinda trippy,"* 1,087 views, July 23, 2012), and *Rubber Face* (*"Just me and a leaf blower,"* 6,334 views, Oct. 22, 2012) documented the months following Jesse's death and the subtle ways in which it started to mobilize changes among the Berlins.

Shortly after Jesse's death, John discovered the Insanity physical fitness program, developed by Santa Monica–based Beach Body LLC. Confronted with death, Berlin turned to fitness, to reverse the effects that a sedentary lifestyle had had on his forty-four year-old body. On September 15, 2013, John posted his first fitness-oriented videos. It shows him, in nine separate clips, competing in the 2013 St. Louis edition of the Toughmudder team-based obstacle course race. A slimmed-down, athletic looking John runs, crawls, and climbs through the Mud Mile, Kiss of Mud, and Funky Monkey. One month later he began posting videos of Insanity workouts in his trailer home living room (5,315 views). By December, he announced he was taking on clients as a trainer in that same living room (21,766 views), now outfitted with a memorial to his son, Jesse, on the wall.

35. We need to thank and cite here Bart-Jan Polman for his input provided from his own unpublished research on Hollein.

Two years after his son's death, John posts his first viral video. In it, he makes a plea to Facebook to allow him the right to a "Look Back" video for his dead son's account. The Look Back video format was a product of Facebook's tenth-anniversary celebrations and created a slideshow of greatest hits from a user's virtual material. An emotional Berlin wanted to produce such a video from the material he didn't have access to on his son's account, and after logging 2 million YouTube views in a couple of days, he received a call from Mark Zuckerberg, granting his request and announcing an immediate change in Facebook's policy toward memorialization.

In the background of the plea video (now at 3,041,801 views, 60,584 likes, 631 dislikes), Berlin's living room had been further transformed. His son's memorial wall has been replaced by floor-to-ceiling mirrors, and sports equipment appears here and there. All this to confirm and legitimize the space as a gym—and Berlin as a trainer—for the viewer. The viewer, in turn, became a participant in Berlin's mourning. Through messages, requests, and attention to John's feed, the anonymous commentator produced, accelerated, and in many ways determined the activity and architectural behaviors in the trailer home. Furthermore, Berlin's Facebook page and his YouTube videos now operated as a social platform for other families to mourn their own children's death.

Berlin's body—in transformation—mirrors the programmatic promiscuity of his living room, itself belonging to an architectural vehicle (the trailer home). This programmatic substitution—living room for gym—and the physical improvement it promoted is, effectively, a means of memorialization. In the collapse of family structure brought on by death, social politics are up for reformation with architecture as correlative. Death produces new bodies, political transformations, social platforms, micro-economies, and home décor. Death, most importantly, sows further transformation, in line with Hollein's model of design as implementation.

Hollein's theoretical propositions on death, design, and the body seem to predict the current condition in a broader, metaphysical sense, just falling short of painting a full picture of the technical reality that augments his assertions from poetic speculation to post-digital contemporaneity.

That being the case, how can death be actively evolved as a catalyst for architectural technology to more fully serve society? In bringing death back into the city, we must refocus the lens of design on *both* digital and virtual channels—understanding that both bear material consequence—and be sensitive to the activity born of their interstices. This means that transmutation, the situation, or behavior itself is the most urgent site of architectural operation. This places operativity on the user: the avatar whose consciousness and substance is the dual currency of the post-digital city. In circumstances of ceremony and disposition, architecture engages the transmutation of bodies as a mechanism for the production of value, ritual, and the city as a combined action.

Reclaimed Resources:

Transforming Urban Waste into Architecture through Human Capabilities

Yusuke Obuchi with Deborah Lopez and Hadin Charbel

Sustainability and recycling, while commonly understood in terms of familiar and accepted ideas like reuse of materials or reduction of waste, must undergo a shift. Despite awareness of sustainability at individual, community, and corporate levels, material consumption continues, and with that consumption comes waste. We are also now at a time in history when human jobs are being replaced by automation; robots present value for their accuracy and efficiency, and humans with skillsets that can be replaced by computers (or may be replaced in the future) face uncertain times. This situation suggests that a transformation of the notions of sustainability and recycling is now required—a transformation that can no longer be limited to material use, but also applied to human resources. As more and more jobs begin to be transferred to robots, an increasing number of people will be equipped with skills for which there are no longer positions.

We must now consider how computers and humans can work together. Computers, while fast, efficient, and accurate, lack the adaptability, creativity, and problem-solving skills of humans. We consider the ways the strengths of humans and computers might be integrated to produce an output which would serve a function, but would also utilize available materials and available human resources. In this research, we present an approach to architecture-scale fabrication that allows participation of individuals with little to no architectural or construction experience. Teams of workers contribute to the creation of a structure produced with materials gathered from building demolition sites. Our proposal consists of (1) assessments of worker strength, (2) a panelized geometry for construction, (3) components made from a recycled material

The outcome of the described research: a temporary pavilion

collected from an existing urban network, (4) a scanning and guidance system which suggests appropriate workers based on strength tests and provides real-time instruction, and (5) a scanning and assembly system which optimizes and updates the target geometry to integrate human errors. The output of this research, exhibited in the form of a temporary pavilion, showcased how available human resources could be utilized along with available deformable urban resources to create structures from materials previously understood merely as "waste." The recycled material chosen for the project, woodchips, is collected from building demolition sites. It is combined with resin to create a malleable panel that can be shaped by pairs of workers before being assembled into an arch, multiples of which are combined to create a global form. Workers create panels in pairs off-site, following real-time color-mapped instructions. On-site, the panels are assembled with a separate guidance and optimization system. The research initiates one step towards a new understanding of the notion of a "resource," suggesting that the difference between "waste" and "resource" may be a matter of networking, in terms of both materials and humans.

Introduction

In recent decades, sustainability has been presented as something which individuals, communities, and corporate entities should aspire to achieve. It has been accepted across fields as an essential topic of consideration for ensuring a future for the planet and its inhabitants. Citizens in developed countries are not only familiar with daily sustainability-related practices (such as material recycling, power-use awareness, and pollution reduction efforts), they have integrated such practices into their lifestyle choices. The sustainability movement and related environmental protection movements have been easy for the average person to understand, prompting participation and community contributions in everyday life with the intention of bettering local and global communities.

Despite this awareness and these widespread efforts, however, consumption continues. Waste is still produced in astronomical quantities. Landfills grow in size, and questions of where to put waste remain. The flow of waste remains unchanged; products move from manufacturer to consumer, and finally to landfills or to processing facilities when their lifecycles have ended. Present sustainability practices have not addressed this material flow in its entirety. They have only provided an additional way of handling materials in the final stage of the flow.

We therefore propose a rethinking of the notion of waste and its relationship to urban networks. Cities produce huge amounts of waste materials each day, but because the materials are classified as "waste," their future is limited only to destruction or to a form of recycling. Depending on the material in question, recycling the material may actually require more resources than simply destroying the material, an additional factor indicating the ineffectiveness of the existing sustainability strategies. These need not be the only two options for dealing with waste materials. We propose a material transformation; the material is reused, but in a new form and with a new purpose. We suggest creating new links between communities and materials so that

elements previously only understood as waste could become understood as new resources.

This proposition comes at a time in history when robots are beginning to replace human jobs. As technology continues to advance in an effort to provide improved efficiency, convenience, and speed (which computers excel in), certain skillsets are becoming obsolete. We are already beginning to see that individuals without highly developed, specialized skillsets are replaceable by computers. Given the exponential rate at which digital capabilities are advancing, this could result in a growing number of people without work and without a way to sustain their lives or to contribute to their communities. Unlike robots, humans have unique capacities for creativity, problem-solving, and adaptation. How could these qualities be combined with computational capabilities to produce something which reflects the strengths of both humans and robots? How might our networks and our relationship to technology be shifted such that humans, with their unique capacities, never become "waste" and are never cast aside, as are products at the end of their lifecycles?

This key question of sustainability, applied both to materials and to humans, is the catalyst for our present research. We examine the ways in which human capacities might be combined and coordinated with robotic capacities. The present research proposes an approach to architectural fabrication that allows the participation of workers with no construction experience. The approach factors in the actual physical capacities of available workers and generates a geometry for the workers to create that has been optimized for the given material resource. The materials used to produce a pavilion-size exploration of this concept were woodchips and resin. The woodchips were collected from construction companies in the Tokyo area; the chips were the result of building demolition activities, and would otherwise have been disposed of.

We present a real-time feedback process for handmade construction. Outputs are imprecise, but with structural analysis of the entire assembly being conducted regularly throughout the fabrication and assembly processes, adaptation and readjustments are possible, through computational generation of new target geometries that integrate human-introduced errors. The optimization processes not only intend to address structural stability issues, but are also understood as a creative process wherein participants can be included in fabrication of a unique output.

The approach contributes a solution for improved networking of materials and also provides a participatory activity for unskilled workers wherein a community contribution could be made. It removes the idea that construction and architecture can only be designed and built by specialists; by factoring in individual workers' unique capacities into the form, it creates a more democratized output, and suggests that anyone can be a builder.

Related Works

The present research was inspired by and seeks to expand upon research conducted in 3D printing fields and computational science fields. It is a progression of the University of Tokyo's recent Advanced Design Studies program works. An initial inspiration for the current agenda was the Sculpting by Numbers project (Rivers et al., 2012), in which humans are guided in the shaping of a sculpted object via a color map projected onto a work in progress. The Projector-Guided Painting study by Flagg and Rehg (2006) uses a layered guidance system to support users in creating a target painting, with optional modes for different levels of detail. These studies led to questions about the applicability of such technologies at the architecture scale, an idea explored through the projected guidance-based aggregative construction method proposed by Yoshida et al. (2015), in which teams of workers drop materials (in the case study, chopsticks and glue) in accordance with a color map generated with a real-time scanning and analysis system. While the project indicated the feasibility of scaled-up 3D printing and potentials relating to human-machine coordination, it also revealed the challenge of integrating worker-introduced errors.

These challenges led to explorations of human-driven fabrication, including the FreeD project by Zoran and Paradiso (2013), in which a handheld milling device was guided computationally to reduce human-introduced mistakes. The authors of the FreeD research further explored the topic in an additional research study wherein the system included an ability to update the digitally defined target model during fabrication. Similar to the question introduced by precedent projection mapping and guidance system studies, these studies in user-centric fabrication inspired interest in architecture-scale explorations. In combination with the knowledge obtained in the study conducted by Yoshida et al. (2015), a human-error integrating fabrication and geometric optimization system (Lopez et al., 2016) was developed. The case study, named TOCA (Tool Operated Choreographed Architecture) examined how human movement could be a driver for the architectural fabrication process, and could be supported with an optimization system designed to absorb errors and generate an updated target geometry.

Material and component studies

The case study pavilion was composed of a panelized geometry made up of 11 arches, each fabricated panel by panel. This section will describe the processes used to create panels.

Woodchips and resin

The selected materials used to create these panels were woodchips and resin. The woodchips were collected from local construction companies and were the product of building demolitions. All other building materials (concrete, steel, platsterboard, plastic, etc.) are recycled and turned into new building materials. These woodchips were combined with an epoxy resin (at a 2:1 ratio) and were shaped into target panel geometries by workers using the developed guidance system (described in the Guidance System section). Panel shaping took place thirty minutes before the resin began to cure, when the components were malleable. After shaping, the components were allowed to solidify, after which they were assembled together to create arches.

Panel creation

Panels were created one by one in x-shapes before being manipulated by workers with the guidance system.

To create each panel, two thin sheets of plastic (an inner layer and an outer layer) are first prepared on a tabletop. Next, a frame for the x-shape panel is placed on top of the plastic sheets, and the woodchip-epoxy resin mixture is poured into the frame. An additional two layers of plastic sheeting are placed on top of the frame; the outer plastic sheet is fitted with a nozzle for attachment to a vacuum pump. These final sheets are sealed to the bottom two sheets to create a bag around the component. A vacuum pump is attached to the bag to remove air; the level of suction applied can affect the stiffness of components (suction can create a panel soft and malleable, or stiff and solid). Once all air is removed, the panels are ready to be shaped under the guidance system.

Guidance system

This research utilized a camera and projector-based scanning and guidance system to aid unskilled workers in panel shaping and construction processes. To accommodate worker capacities, prior to beginning fabrication, all worker strength capabilities were tested and recorded. This section will describe these factors of the research.

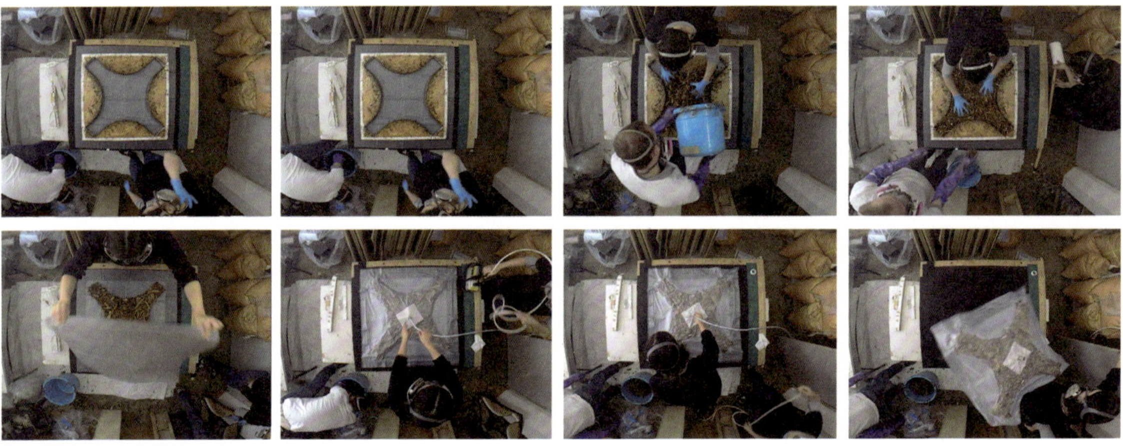

Panel creation process (from top left to lower right)

Worker strength tests

Prior to all construction processes, worker strength tests were conducted to determine the physical capabilities of each worker and to supply the developed guidance system with data that would facilitate worker suggestions during the panel shaping process. To accomplish these force tests, we created a glove outfitted with force sensors. Workers put the glove on (one hand only) and pressed against a surface, exerting as much strength as possible.

A worker wearing a glove equipped with force sensors presses against a panel. The sensors on the glove capture the amount of strength exerted against the surface.

The force sensors recorded this data, and worker strength was cataloged. This was done in an effort to ensure effective time management and efficiency during the fabrication process; panels requiring less extreme curvatures could be produced by workers with lower levels of strength, but panels requiring large degrees of curvature would require workers with a greater level of strength. Making certain that a few workers are not creating all panels required for construction helps ensure that workers will have enough energy and will be able to work more efficiently.

Projector-scanner system

A projecting and scanning system, developed and expanded upon based on the knowledge gained from the aggregative construction studies conducted by Yoshida et al. (2015) and the human-movement dependent fabrication studies by Lopez et al. (2016), was used to guide workers in both panel shaping and in assembly of the panels into a completed pavilion structure. The projectors and scanners/cameras were connected to a computer, and a target geometry for fabrication was defined. In this system, the scanner scans a panel as it is fabricated and compares it to the predefined target geometry. Differences between the target and the actual output are analyzed and converted to a color map (shown on the surface of the panel in progress). The results of the analysis are also converted into push/hold points, which are projected onto the actual panel as worker guidance. Workers push and hold these points, following the computer-provided visual directions, until the panel matches the target geometry to a sufficient degree (within 30 mm of the target geometry, for this case study).

Panel-shaping system

Panels were shaped on a tabletop setup. Prior to beginning panel shaping processes, the projectors and cameras (one on each side of the panel shaping setup) required calibration, to ensure accuracy in analysis of target form and real form, and to ensure accuracy in provided worker guidance. To do this, a prism-shaped calibration object was placed in the panel shaping area on the tabletop setup. Reflective markers were attached across the surface of this object. With a known origin point defined at the center of the table, the cameras used for this study (Kinect) then located the reflective markers, providing the camera positions and orientations.

To calibrate the projectors, however, a separate system was required. After setting up the projectors above the panel shaping space, we projected dots with known digital environment coordinates onto the workspace. We placed reflective markers on these dots on the workspace, which were then scanned and analyzed in comparison to the coordinates of the dots in the digital environment. Following this, we solved the projection matrix, and completed projector calibration.

Panels to be shaped were then placed one by one into the calibrated workspace on the tabletop, with the lower left corner of each panel secured in place with a clamp. The target panel, digitally defined, was then matched to the panel for fabrication, workers were suggested, and the guidance was projected onto the surface of the panel, as seen below.

Given the target geometry and the curvatures required to produce that geometry, the system suggests that two workers to create the panel, using the data obtained in the pre-fabrication stage worker-force strength measurement tests. One worker is positioned on each side of the panel shaping setup. Each worker follows the visual guidance of projected square points, which indicate locations to push/hold (push/hold actions depend on the side of the panel the worker is on). Larger squares indicate a greater degree of force is required; smaller squares indicate less force is necessary to achieve the target. When the two workers have successfully shaped a panel (within 30 mm of the defined target model), the panel is left to cure, which takes approximately thirty minutes.

Sequence for panel shaping (left to right). First, panel is placed on mount. Next, panel is matched to digitally defined panel for shaping. Finally, two workers shape the panel in accordance with projected guidance

Assembly and optimization systems

Once all panels in an arch have been fabricated, they can be assembled together with on-site assembly guidance. Arch assembly begins from the two root panels. When these panels are placed, they are scanned with an on-site scanning system (separate from the off-site panel shaping system).

For this system, researchers used an ASUS Xtion camera to scan the positions of the panels, and compare them to digitally defined targets. A marker for the scanner to detect is attached to each panel, as seen below.

On-site scanning of global form

To ensure structural stability, we examined three different approaches to assembly and optimization of the structure: panel by panel, arch by arch, and staggered. In the panel-by-panel approach, the initial root panels were placed in their designated locations, scanned, and compared against their target geometries.

Following analysis of this scan, the geometries of the subsequent panels were then updated to integrate the inaccuracies introduced by humans in the panel fabrication process. This generated an optimized target panel geometry for workers to fabricate and assemble. The process proved quite time-consuming, however, and for this reason, we also explored arch-by-arch assembly and optimization. The steps for this kind of optimization were the same as those described for panel-by-panel optimization, except that the scans did not happen after assembly of each panel in its designated position; scans of the global structure occurred after each individual arch was assembled, and the optimization system updated the geometry for the next arch (fifteen panels). While this system proved much more efficient in terms of time, the degree of human error introduced through this approach made it difficult to precisely assemble the panels. To address this, we utilized a third, staggered approach, in which all odd panels in a given arch were first fabricated and attached to the growing structure. The odd panels (and the global structure) were then scanned, and the even panels were then optimized and their target geometries regenerated. This staggered approach presented an acceptable balance between time required and achievable accuracy.

Case study pavilion

The case study pavilion developed in an effort to test the proposed system was created over a period of fifteen days on the University of Tokyo campus. Fifteen graduate students participated in the process of constructing the pavilion, creating 165 panels and 11 arches. The site for the pavilion was an outdoor location open to the public for viewing (both during the construction period and during the display period).

Completed case study pavilion structure composed of 165 panels and 11 arches

Panels were fabricated in a laboratory near the construction site and were carried to the site for assembly. The pavilion was exhibited for a period of twelve days.

Conclusion

This research proposes both a shift in the notion of recycling and an approach to fabrication and construction that integrates and accommodates the capacities of average humans. The developed system begins with an assessment of the strength capacities of the available human workers. The data collected from the assessment is used in coordination with projected visual guidance; workers cooperate to shape panels by pushing and holding indicated locations on the panel surface until the guidance system informs the users (via color) that they have achieved the target shape. On-site assembly follows a similar, if sep-arate process; workers position the created panels following computer-provided guidance. Once assembled, the entire form is scanned, and the next round of panels for fabrication is generated.

The case study successfully utilized an urban material previously understood as "waste" and transformed it (through application of resin and through physical manipulation) into a component for production of an architecture-scale object. The workers who participated in the project varied in strength and in construction experience, but all were able to contribute to the building process in an efficient manner due to the integrated worker candidate suggestion capability in the guidance system. In contrast to previous computationally guided architecture-scale fabrication investigations, this research provides users with instructions for *how* to produce an output (as opposed to simply learning whether or not an output matches a digitally defined target). Additionally, with the real-time scanning and structural analysis systems, new target geometries can be generated for fabrication. All geometrical inaccuracies caused by hand-making processes are absorbed and readjusted computationally.

This research indicates potential for other architecture-scale objects, but produced with different deformable materials. Materials currently only understood as "waste" in urban environments are being collected on a daily basis, but could have potential for transformation into a material resource for fabrication. Following examination of material properties (in combination with an adhesive), a variety of forms with different aesthetic and environmental properties could be created. While the present research examined the idea of recycling materials with the intent of producing architecture, it also suggests applicability for smaller scale object fabrication.

Limitations to the fabrication system include a constrained degree of possible curvature in the panelized component geometries; beyond a certain point, panels break, rendering them useless. Additionally, extreme degrees of curvature would be difficult for weaker workers to produce. Therefore, the geometries for production are limited to panels which do not require exceptional amounts of strength to create.

Through this research, we created an accessible, adaptable method of fabrication and construction which utilized both the available urban material resources and the available human resources. The result is an output which transforms waste into an architectural resource, and also creates an engaging, participatory experience for workers.

References

Flagg, Matthew, and James M. Rehg. 2006. "Projector-Guided Painting." In *19th ACM Symposium on User Interface Software and Technology (UIST 06)*.

Lopez, Deborah, Hadin Charbel, Yusuke Obuchi, Jun Sato, Takeo Igarashi, Yosuke Takami, and Toshikatsu Kiuchi. 2016. "Human Touch in Digital Fabrication." In *2016 Association For Computer Aided Design in Architecture (ACADIA) Conference*.

Rivers, Alec, Andrew Adams, and Frédo Durand. 2012. "Sculpting by Numbers". *ACM Transactions on Graphics* 31 (6): 1. doi:10.1145/2366145.2366176.

Yoshida, Hironori, Syunsuke Igarashi, Takeo Igarashi, Yusuke Obuchi, Yosuke Takami, Jun Sato, Mika Araki, Masaaki Miki, Kosuke Nagata, and Kazuhide Sakai. 2015. "Architecture-Scale Human-Assisted Additive Manufacturing." *ACM Transactions on Graphics* 34 (4): 88:1-88:8. doi:10.1145/2766951.

Zoran, Amit, and Joseph A. Paradiso. 2013. "FreeD – A Freehand Digital Sculpting Tool." In *The 31st International Conference on Human Factors in Computing Systems (CHI '13)*.

Zoran, Amit, Roy Shilkrot, and Joseph A. Paradiso. 2013. "Human-Computer Interaction for Hybrid Carving." In *The 26th Annual ACM Symposium on User Interface Software and Technology (UIST '13)*.

A Back-to-the-City Movement:

Some Proofs and Potentials of New Eco-Villages in American Cities

Sarah Mineko Ichioka

Ours is the time of the Great Turning (Macy 2011) or Great Disruption (Gilding 2011), when human societies must transition from extractive to regenerative systems if they are to survive. While international cooperation is essential to fully enact this shift, neighborhood-scale initiatives also play an essential role.

Academic and popular cultural interest in intentional communities has traditionally prioritized settlements of like-minded individuals who—driven by land values, ethos, or compound factors—have tended to locate in low-density, rural areas. The "eco-village" movement, a loosely organized global phenomenon with roots in the 1960s, which has become more clearly articulated since the 1990s, has likewise had more rural than urban manifestations. In recent years, however, several aspiring eco-village communities established within mature American cities have seen existing neighborhoods progressively activated by groups of people seeking ways of life that prioritize environmental integrity and social connection over material consumption.

When such shared, sustainability-focused modes of habitation are applied in the context of preexisting urban neighborhoods, which may be economically distressed and culturally diverse, they contend with distinctive challenges and opportunities. These can include the adjacencies of idealistic community-builders with neighbors who may be grappling with histories of structural inequality and disinvestment, and the need to confront the risks of gentrification and displacement, alongside the need to retrofit older buildings and to remediate contaminated brownfield land. Of necessity, and often by design—including governing principles of justice and education—such urban eco-villages exhibit social

and economic engagement with individuals and institutions beyond their self-selected residents.

This essay focuses on two case studies: the Enright Ridge Urban Ecovillage in Ohio and Los Angeles Eco-Village, in California. A detailed exploration of the origins and evolutions of these two, relatively new developments—in particular how their social and ecological priorities have influenced their reinterpretation of inherited physical spaces and their creation of new systems for decision-making, resource-sharing, and the like—aims to offer inspiration for the propagation of such communities elsewhere in the United States, and for the progressive retrofitting of cities in other advanced economies.

Seoul

The aim of the inaugural Seoul Biennale of Architecture and Urbanism is to address the myriad and interconnected human-made conditions that presently threaten the stability of our societies and—in the longer term— the viability of our species. The Biennale's commissioners and directors suggest that solutions commensurate to these existential challenges may be incubated in Seoul through the exchange of practical ideas for the radical (and suitably swift) transformation of how human settlements are built and lived in.

If we accept the escalating urgency of our collective circumstances—that we are depleting or destroying ever-greater amounts of the earth's land, water, and air, with existential risks for ourselves and other life forms—it stands to reason that any material resources invested in international participation in this project must offer a tangible benefit to Seoul itself. That is, it should make a locally relevant contribution

beyond the rolling global discourse between built environment theorists and practitioners; or else why waste the carbon necessary to manifest it physically in this particular place?

In autumn 2015, as part of the symposium that initiated this Biennale, I had the honor of moderating a public conversation through which four Seoul-based experts shared their knowledge of the city's historic development and contemporary conditions. When I asked these local experts[1] to identify specific challenges and opportunities for Seoul's near-future development, they articulated a range of compelling (and often interrelated) imperatives, which included the needs to

— Address citizens' perceptions of reduced social mobility, including through tangible actions such as improving the tenure security and affordability of housing;
— Integrate into a relatively homogenous society an increasing number of foreign residents;
— Accommodate the changing needs and benefit from the contributions of the rapidly aging population;
— Create appropriate building stock and social programs for the increasing number of single-person households;
— Prioritize smaller-scale infill sites for the creation of new housing, a process that should involve resident participation and integrate opportunities for job creation in its completed product.

At a systems level, some of the local experts identified the need to approach Seoul's aging building stock as an asset rather than a liability, one which offers the potential for remodeling and regenerating existing urban spatial structures; and to shift the spaces of the city away from capitalist models of consumption,

1. The participants were Choi Mack Joong, Cho Myung Rae, Byun Miree, and Byeon Chang Heum, along with Biennale co-director Alejandro Zaera-Polo.

congruent with a recent local policy shift towards qualitative (more than quantitative) growth. Perhaps most radically from a political perspective, one contributor urged Seoul to seek the "co-prosperity of humans and nature" rather than simply human-centric urban development aims (Ichioka 2015).

In pursuit of these identified agendas, and despite significant trans-Pacific cultural differences, I believe that study of some of the neighborhood-scale intentional communities that have emerged in a number of American cities over recent decades may yield useful ideas for Seoul's citizens and policy and planning professionals alike.[2]

The global and the local

Globally, the current political moment sees the a transnational rejection of social diversity linked with a denial of environmental accountability. In multiple parts of the world, efforts to cultivate nativist resentment on the part of historically empowered groups by scapegoating racial, ethnic, and cultural minorities has provided political cover for the deregulation of markets, industries, and agencies. These actions in turn are hastening climate catastrophe and deepening inequality.[3]

In perhaps the most prominent case, the United States of Donald Trump and Paul Ryan is characterized at the federal level by the normalization of social intolerance, endorsement of environmental exploitation, and withdrawal from multilateral international cooperation. The situation leads many would-be progressives to search anxiously for solutions: How best to restore our

planet and detoxify our politics at personal and collective levels? How to reconcile our behaviors with our beliefs in effective and enjoyable ways? And how to persuade others to join us, at scale? It is an urgent task to enact and articulate the stories of the things we stand for rather than simply resisting those that outrage us. In the spirit of Naomi Klein's crowd-sourced "beautiful solutions" to the climate crisis, I see some hope in identifying and broadcasting proven, and appealing (or as Klein puts it, "contagious") alternatives (Klein 2014).

Ten years ago, in his *Real American Ethics*, philosopher Albert Borgmann wrote of the need to define a model of the "good life" that would appeal to "decent" centrists. Borgmann asserted that the "most glaring blank" in the American approach to morality was "unconcern with Churchill's principle,"[4] namely:

> *The ways we are shaped by what we build are neither neutral nor forcible, and since we have always assumed that public and common structures have to be one or the other, the intermediate force of our building has remained invisible to us, and that has allowed us to ignore the crucial point: We are always and already engaged in drawing the outlines of a common way of life, and we have to take responsibility for this fact and ask whether it is a good life, a decent life, or a lamentable life that we have outlined for ourselves. [...]*

> *If we are unaware of how the shaping of our household[5] typically shapes our practices ... it will only create frustration and resentment*

2. And vice versa. South Korea is host to its own nascent eco-village movement, which the exhibition that derives from this research seeks to engage with.

3 I am particularly grateful to Cassim Shepard for helping me to articulate this line of thinking.

4. Winston Churchill: "We shape our buildings and then our buildings shape us."

5. Borgmann also repurposes several common terms: using "economy" to denote the ordering of the domestic sphere (returning to its etymology, *oikos* = "home" + *nomos* =

unless our home is so arranged that dong the right thing comes naturally or at least does not require heroic self-discipline.
(Borgmann 2006, 6-10)

The applied mathematician Lee Worden has identified the evolution of American "countercultural ambitions" from "the back-to-the-land shift of the late '60s [to] the replacement of systemic critique by self-realization in the '70s, to reabsorption by mainstream business in the '80s, and into the digital utopianism of the '90s and beyond" (Worden, 2012, 212). In the present moment, the internet has arguably proven more polarizing than it is unifying, an omnipresent yet uncertain terrain of fungible facts and suspect statistics.

In contrast, place-based stories—grounded illustrations of the good life—may assume a new rhetorical importance within civic discourse. As Borgmann suggests, "We have to locate the places where face-to-face communities, and at length the moral community of this country, may begin to prosper again" (Borgmann, 17).

Eco-Villages: Definitions and Origins

In one definition, an intentional community is a "group of people who have chosen to live together with a common purpose, working cooperatively to create a lifestyle that reflects their shared core values." As one long-time observer of intentional communities comments, "community is not just about living together, but about the reasons for doing so"; and these reasons are often reactive: "A community's ideals usually arise from something its members see as lacking or missing in the wider culture" (Christian 2003).

The eco-village[6] movement, comprising several hundred active communities around the world, seeks to build community in the context of concern for wider human society and its place within planetary systems. An influential definition of eco-villages describes "human-scale, full-featured settlements in which human activities are harmlessly integrated into the natural world in a way that is supportive of healthy human development, and which can be successfully continued into the indefinite future" (Robert and Diane Gilman, cited in Christian 2003). One seasoned practitioner describes the movement as modeled on a "three legged stool" of principles, comprising the "personal," the "social," and the "ecological"(Bang 2005, 59).[7]

Developments vary widely in how they manifest these principles, but in general, they tend to be characterized by an ethos of *interdependence* (see for example Litfin 2014, 4), in marked contrast to some other intentional communities' existential drive for isolation and independence. On an applied front, practices that seek to simplify and to share are common (see for example Walker 2005, 213). As an expansion of the sharing principle, eco-villages tend to be committed to the dissemination of ideas, through training and outreach programs.

Eco-villages' diverse intellectual and practical roots include ashrams, monasteries, camphills, kibbutzim and the appropriate technology, community land trust, and co-housing movements (see for example Bang 2005). Litfin credits the contemporary articulation of eco-villages as a global movement to the thinking

"management") and "design" to mean political economy. In this light, intentional communities can be said to offer examples of how economies can be designed to shape specific practical and ethical behaviors.

6. Punctuation varies: the Enright Ridge community uses "ecovillage," for example.

7. It is interesting to compare with the more commonly used tripartite definition of sustainability as comprising economic, social, and environmental elements.

and advocacy of two couples—Ros and Hildur Jackson (Gaia Trust, Denmark) and Robert and Diane Gilman (In Context, USA)—at a conference in Denmark in 1991, where the definition described above was first shared. At a subsequent international eco-village conference hosted at the influential Scottish eco-village of Findhorn, participants founded the Global Ecovillage Network, which has grown through the present day to incorporate various regional networks (Litfin 2014).

The movement has a wide geographic range, with presences on all inhabited continents, and its physical manifestations are as varied as their locations. It is important to note that eco-villages in poor countries and affluent countries will have different goals (Litfin, 16). To maintain relevance to Seoul, this research focuses on eco-villages' actual and potential contributions within affluent countries, although not necessarily the most affluent neighborhoods or regions thereof.

Rural locations dominate the roster of self-described "eco-villages" currently active around the world from Auroville (India) to Findhorn (Scotland) and Damanhur (Italy) to Konohana (Japan). Open-source databases (such as that found on the Fellowship for Intentional Community website) are not an entirely reliable source of comparative data, but a tally of the geographic locations of international eco-villages profiled in two case study based books showed a similar distribution, with city-based communities the clear minority:

Rural: 17/24; Suburban: 6/24; Urban: 1/24 (Bang 2005)
Rural: 10/14; Suburban 2/14; Urban 2/14 (Litfin 2014)

These ratios are consistent with an older survey that featured American intentional communities (not specifically eco-villages) in the following proportions: Rural (5/7); Semi-rural (1/7); Urban (1/7) (Christian 2003). In the U.S., they also reflect historic patterns, wherein intentional communities have tended to establish themselves in rural areas. This preference for rural areas may be attributed to a range of practical motivations, including more affordable land values, and the ability to build anew. From a cultural perspective, a desire to escape conventional social systems associated with cities, and the ethical valorization of "self-sufficient" agrarian lifestyles have their lineage in American thinkers and practitioners from Henry David Thoreau through to Helen and Scott Nearing and the "back to the land" movement of the 1960s and 1970s.

Back to the city?
If we aim to survive the Great Disruption, we will work within our cities, not try to flee them. Because they are where most of us already live, and—having already stripped the earth of so many of its limited material resources to construct them—they're what we've got to work with.[8] As the UN reminds us, "providing public transportation, as well as housing, electricity, water and sanitation for a densely settled urban population is typically cheaper and less environmentally damaging than providing a similar level of services to a dispersed rural population" (United Nations 2014). In the post-cheap fossil fuel period, a nation like the United States that has generally underinvested in its infrastructure in recent decades, and actively *disinvested* from its public transport networks, with a bias towards private cars, is going to be particularly challenged (see for example Kunstler 1994), but arguably will still be most likely to

8. Nearly 54% of the world's population, 80% of OECD member populations, and 82% of the U.S. population lives in cities (United Nations, World Urbanization Prospects, 2015, http://data.worldbank.org/indicator/SP.URB.TOTL.IN.ZS).

succeed by working within the framework of its, existing cities.

Several recent American intentional communities have chosen to embed themselves within existing city structures, embracing both the challenges and benefits of urban life. A closer examination of two such communities—Enright Ridge Urban Ecovillage ("ERUE") in Cincinnati, Ohio, and the Los Angeles Eco-Village ("LAEV") in California—suggests that there are diverse ways to pursue intersecting agendas of environmental restoration, human fulfillment, and social and economic inclusion within America's urban neighborhoods. This research is distilled from a year-long project that examined a range of urban intentional communities across the United States.[9]

Both of these communities, incipient in the 1990s, but formalized in the period since 2000, originally arose within neighborhoods grappling with disinvestment and economic stress, depopulation, and—in the latter case—overt social unrest. In more recent years, LAEV has emphasized the maintenance of affordability and economic inclusion in the context of rapid gentrification in its surrounding area and a socially and environmentally progressive state, while ERUEV continues to seek to stabilize asset values and advocate for inward investment in a Republican-governed state that remains more economically challenged.

Enright Ridge Urban Ecovillage, Ohio

A self-proclaimed "urban retrofit ecovillage," Enright Ridge Urban Ecovillage comprises approximately eighty detached houses located along and around Enright Avenue, a 3/4-mile-long street running north-south along the

top of a ridge in Price Hill, an "inner ring" neighborhood on the West Side of Cincinnati.

ERUE is one of several Cincinnati non-profit organizations with its origins in Imago, an environmental education organization founded by a local couple, Jim and Eileen Schenk.[10] The Schenks, both social workers, began Imago in 1978 with the mission "to foster a deeper harmony with Earth by providing educational experiences, creating opportunities for discussion and community building, and conserving natural areas" (Imago 2017). Anchoring Imago's various activities is the Earth Center, a 16-acre nature preserve (some of is land reclaimed from dilapidated buildings) and educational facility. The Schenks' vision of creating an eco-village in Price Hill had an initial false start in the late 1990s; despite receiving grant funding, the area they were looking at proved too large to handle (Tyrell 2016). In 2004 Imago succeeded on a smaller scale, bringing together 17 residents to establish the Ecovillage in seven houses in the area immediately surrounding the Earth Centre; the ERUE formally registered as a non-profit organization in 2009 (Fellowship for Intentional Community 2016).

ERUE "seeks to be an ecologically responsible community sharing ideas, resources and a reverence for earth." Imago owns 36 acres of land within the community, the rest of the property belongs to individual homeowners. As such, the Ecovillage operates an inclusive definition of its territory. Of the neighborhood's estimated ninety households (the majority of its eighty some buildings are single-family homes), ERUE's organizers estimate that 40% are "involved"

9. Other communities visited for the project included: Eco Village at Ithaca, New York, Detroit Shoreway Eco Village, Cleveland, Ohio; Daybreak Cohousing, Portland, Oregon; Swan's Market Cohousing and Mariposa Grove, both in Oakland, California.

10. Imago has incubated three other non-profits serving the Price Hill neighborhood focusing variously on economic regeneration and biodiversity (Imago 2017)

with the eco-village activities such as shared monthly meals at the Imago Center, while 30% are "open" and a further 30% "indifferent." It charges a modest $15 annual membership fee (Fellowship for Intentional Community, 2016), but the benefits of shared infrastructure, notably the interstitial green spaces, are accessible to all.

The properties in the neighborhood are majority owner-occupied, single-family homes; the ERUE also includes about ten rental units, allowing for some diversity of income level amongst resident households. Ranging from one to three stories, most houses date from the end of the nineteenth to the beginning of the twentieth century.

The rear yards of all of the houses back onto ERUE-owned woodland, and are connected by hiking trails, one of the first initiatives of the Ecovillage community. A number of the yards have been landscaped according to permaculture principles, for example incorporating bioswales to manage rainwater and growing organic food crops, and some are used to raise chickens and goats. The community also benefits from adjacency to St Joseph's Cemetery, a large, grassy expanse along the western side of Enright Avenue. Two additional parks and nature reserves to the south of Enright Avenue's cul-de-sac terminus provide additional green space and biodiversity amenities.

In a region that has struggled to recover from the Great Recession of 2008, ERUE has saved eighteen buildings from dilapidation or speculation. These include a corner building with a storefront (rented by the Cincinnati Zen Center), and five apartments opposite. The Ecovillage also acquired a commercial unit across from the Zen Center that previously housed a problematic bar (reportedly a drug hotspot), and rehabbed it to house Common Roots, a newly opened organic pub, cafe, general store, and performance space. The remainder are single-family homes, purchased when in foreclosure. These rescue-transformations have been enabled through small, low-interest loans from the Cincinnati-based Ed and Joann Hubert Family Foundation, financing the purchase and rehabilitation of each house in sequence (and repaid upon its resale) (author correspondence with Schenk 2017). Employing the services of a local contractor, they have rehabilitated each house to high environmental standards (i.e. high insulation, efficient appliances and lighting) and resold (or in a few cases, rented) it, mostly to buyers who are seeking to live in alignment with the stated intentions of the community.

ERUE members initiated a composting and recycling system, which apparently helped to persuade Cincinnati to adopt a similar program for the whole city (Christian 2014). Since 2008, the Ecovillage has had its own community supported agriculture (CSA) business, which employs local residents to grow food on reclaimed lots within the neighborhood. Its seventy-five-odd members, who live both within and outside the ERUE neighborhood, each pay a small fee—which can be reduced through sweat equity—at the start of the growing season, and collect a box of fresh produce every Saturday between May and November.

ERUE is governed by a four-member elected board, who use consensus to reach decisions. Various volunteer committees are responsible for areas including outreach and communications, conducting monthly tours of the eco-village, maintaining the website, and promoting available properties to potential new residents.

Enright Village Urban Eco-Village

ERUE's "intentional" residents may not necessarily be fully representative of its surrounding communities. A survey administered by the Ecovillage several years ago found that 92% of its 193 residents were white, and 8% black, compared with 53% white and 39% black in its encompassing East Price Hill neighborhood (Schenk correspondence 2017, US Census 2010). This is an area that would benefit from further exploration, to better understand if and how the socio-economic profiles of ERUE residents compare (by income, education, etc.) with their neighbors', and what implications this has for assessment of the community's success, beyond its evident successes in stabilizing real estate and creating new enterprises locally. Our second case study puts more overt emphasis on social and economic inclusion.

Los Angeles Eco-Village, California

The Los Angeles Eco-Village's core is a two-block area between the northern end of Koreatown/Wilshire Center and East Hollywood neighborhoods, about three miles west of Downtown Los Angeles. LAEV's declared purpose is to "demonstrate the processes for creating a healthy neighborhood ecologically, socially and economically. The strategy is to reduce environmental impacts while raising the quality of neighborhood life" (LAEV n.d.). LAEV dates its foundation to 1993. Originally, its founders, led by activist Lois Arkin, had planned to build an 11-acre "ecological village" on the edges of the city (Litfin 2014, 30). But the Los Angeles riots of spring 1992,[11] which destroyed multiple properties in the area around Arkin's home, persuaded them that it was more important to work locally. Arkin says that, in response to the riots, she and her fellow activists "unanimously and enthusiastically decide[d] not to start a new construction project, but to plant seeds of cooperative community where people already lived—in this case, in the heart of" her own neighborhood (Christian 2014). A commitment to social justice has been a core driver of the LAEV ever since (Litfin 2014, 30).

The community's approximately forty "intentional" residents (i.e. people who have moved to the area specifically to join in LAEV's stated aims) live in three main residential buildings: one two-story U-shaped pre-war garden apartment block—a common Southern California typology—a smaller two-story apartment block of similar vintage directly to its south, and a four-unit building located across the street.

The larger apartment block's lobby and central courtyard have both been retrofitted to encourage more sociable and sustainable activities. The lobby is full of comfortable second-hand sofas, to encourage informal socializing as well as host a regular program of education and outreach activities: workshops, lectures, film screenings. One corner houses a give-and-take area, where residents can give new life to usable yet no longer needed household items. On a nearby table, literature for local sustainability and cultural causes is displayed for reference and dissemination. Two ground floor rooms have been converted to communal use: one for bike parking, and another for a bulk food store and "shop," staffed by residents. One of the upstairs apartments has been converted

11. Public demonstrations, in response to the acquittal of policemen who had been filmed in the act of beating African American Rodney King, flared into a nearly week-long, city-wide period of violence, looting, and arson. Amongst other underlying factors, the riots highlighted social and economic tensions between Los Angeles's African American residents and Korean American merchants in the area of today's LAEV.

Los Angeles Eco-Village

into a common room that is also used for the community's regular governance meetings and social activities.

The central courtyard of the largest building hosts an outdoor kitchen, with grey water recycling facilities, and is densely planted with drought-resistant plants, many of them edible. Some of the owners of ground floor apartments have enlarged the original courtyard-facing windows into doors so that they can use the courtyard as a front garden. Adjacent open areas host compost piles and a timber play structure for residents' children. A run of low sheds that were originally private car garages have been converted into storage and workshop spaces.

Eco-Villagers have worked with the City of Los Angeles to calm the traffic on Bimini Place, the street running to the east of the two main apartment buildings. This includes the widening of the sidewalk outside of the LAEV's main entrance to accommodate planting beds, permeable paving, and colorful artwork on the street surface, incorporating designated pedestrian crossings. The lot on the opposite side of the street has been transformed into a shared garden that is used by both LAEV residents and the Los Angeles School District for educational visits from nearby schools, and acts as a buffer between the Eco-Village and a substantial surface car park immediately to the east.

The properties within LAEV have been acquired and transformed through the collaboration of several interrelated not-for-profit organizations. The two apartment buildings were purchased in 1996 and 1999 through an Ecological Revolving Loan Fund conceived for this purpose. The ERLF, still in use to finance various LAEV projects, comprises a collection of small, no-collateral investments from lenders known personally to its organizers, mostly individuals (e.g. members, neighbors, friends, and family) alongside a few institutional lenders such as Denmark's Gaia Trust—a long-term supporter of the Global Ecovillage Network, whose values aligned with LAEV's mission.[12] The ERLF was incubated by Cooperative Resources and Services Project (CRSP), a non-profit that Lois Arkin founded in 1980. In less than ten years after the first building's purchase, sufficient rental income from the units had paid off the ERLF loans, funded hire of professional management, and supported the buildings' physical refurbishment—all while maintaining apartment rents at approximately half of comparable market rates (Christian 2014).

Another tax-exempt non-profit, the Beverly-Vermont Land Trust, was founded in 2006 with the mission "to exercise land stewardship as the basis for creating pedestrian-centered neighborhoods emphasizing affordable housing, work and recreational spaces that are economically and socially sustainable, and that integrate urban living with nature" (Beverly-Vermont Land Trust n.d.) In 2010, several LAEV members founded the Urban Soil/Tierra Urbana Limited Equity Housing Co-op, which in 2012 purchased the two apartment buildings. At the same time, the BVLT received ownership of the land beneath the buildings, in order to remove them from the conventional property market and safeguard their affordability in perpetuity. The four-unit building across the intersection has been jointly owned by CRSP and BVLT since 2010. The co-op's stated mission foregrounds affordability, diversity, and the public demonstration of "higher quality

12. Disclosure: in an exercise of practicing what I preach, I invested a small amount of money to this fund in 2016.

living patterns while minimizing negative environmental and social impacts" (LAEV n.d.). At present, some of the units are owned by co-op members (those LAEV members who bought shares), while the balance are rented from the co-op, by both "intentional" residents and long-term tenants who have stayed on since before the LAEV was founded.

Remarkable in infamously traffic-ridden Los Angeles, the LAEV has managed to maintain relatively low private car ownership: about one car for every five members, approximately 30% the regional average. Benefitting from easy access to the Vermont/Beverly Metro station two blocks north, it actively promotes cycling and offers a discount on rent to those tenants who choose to remain car-free. A non-profit called Bicycle Kitchen, which provides walk-in maintenance and repair advice, tools, and refreshments, was incubated by an LAEV member in the kitchen of an empty apartment; the activity was so successful that it has expanded to its own building off-site, and inspired other similar workshops around the Los Angeles area (Litfin 2014, 65).

Like Enright Ridge, the LAEV has birthed a number of such initiatives and businesses whose benefits extend beyond its immediate residents. In addition to many cultural and educational initiatives connected to its non-profit organizations, these include a cooperative organic produce and bulk food buying scheme that supports regional farmers and operates on a sweat equity membership model, and a worker cooperative, living wage, affordable childcare center, open to families from the local area (LAEV n.d.). Using its revolving loan fund, the eco-village has recently acquired a quarter-acre

of adjacent commercial property with the aim of building a "mixed-use, permanently-affordable, ecologically-sensitive, culture-changing cohousing" development (CRSP 2016).

The community's physical and institutional infrastructures are matched by and interwoven with social and cultural practices. Most community decisions are taken at a weekly meeting, through a consensus process. These are supplemented by "many standing and ad hoc" committees, and a "conflict resolution team." Members eat shared meals once or twice a week, as well as celebrating holidays and life events and participating in working parties together (LAEV n.d.).

LAEV's organizers estimate that of the approximately 500 people living within the two-block area, 75 of them actively participate in Eco-Village activities. The neighborhood contains "a diversity of households" comprising an estimated fifteen ethnic groups with incomes in the"very low to middle but primarily lower" tiers (LAEV n.d.). An LAEV visitor familiar with the international intentional communities movement calls it the "most multi-racial, multi-cultural ecovillage" she has encountered (Christian 2014).

In keeping with its mission to "demonstrate processes," the LAEV and its associated non-profit organizations emphasize transparency, knowledge sharing, and outreach about their activities. Nearly all of their governance documents are available online, with information about processes, e.g. how to join as a new member, clearly outlined. They are active on social media and host weekly public tours (on a pay-what-you-can donation basis), which over the years have included universities, schools, and private and public sector organizations, both American and international.

One observer attributes some of LAEV's "huge ripple effect" to the fact that many of its intentional members are employed as "full-time environmental and social justice advocates" (Litfin 2014, 30). In this way, the community offers a model of embedded professionalism, where many of its intentional residents' jobs blend into their abilities and activities as neighbors and community members, whether their expertise is bike repair or non-profit management.

Through explicitly extroverted agendas and the implementation of systems and practices that allow for more inclusive definitions of community membership and benefits, urban eco-villages such as these in Cincinnati and Los Angeles demonstrate a promising model of intentional sustainability. This contrasts with both ecologically focused communities that are more geographically isolated, and with forms of "sociable," yet internally focused developments that may sit within city centers yet eschew broader neighborhood engagement.

While at their respective foundations, both communities depended upon charismatic leadership, which is still in evidence,[13] they have subsequently invested in institution-building. Each has helped to generate and is in turn enabled by a small constellation of non-profit organizations and social enterprises with distinctive aims yet complementary functions. Although the legal structures and stakeholder compositions of these micro-institutions vary between the two cases, both serve to link their respective residential communities with local social processes and economic markets.

Future researchers visiting these case studies and others may wish to source more quantitative data on community impacts such as levels of social cohesion, carbon footprint per person, socio-economic mix, etc. On the other hand, as one architectural critic has observed of the current socio-ecological crisis, "what we lack is not facts, but an answer to the far more difficult question of human behavioral change" (Farrelly 2017).

Potentials

Enright Ridge Urban Ecovillage, Los Angeles Eco-Village, and their peers demonstrate practical lived responses to generic characteristics of the post-war American model of development (e.g. built form dependent upon private cars, economies reliant upon escalating consumerism). Such eco-villages located within contemporary American cities (and beyond) appear well-positioned to

— Demonstrate and share their benefits beyond their "intentional" memberships, through both incidental and structured means;
— Connect with, and contribute to, infrastructural systems sustained by the density of urban populations (e.g. public transportation, a community-supported agriculture scheme);
— Reinterpret standard building typologies, to increase their ecological and social values. As with the back-to-the-city approach, the use of old buildings is driven not by a spatial aesthetic, but rather a pragmatic stance, because they are what is most easily to hand, and often cheapest, to work with. This low-cost approach conserves embodied energy and keeps prices accessible to increase the likelihood of economic inclusion.

13. Jim Schenk at Enright and Lois Arkin at LAEV still appear to play central roles in the operations and communications of their respective communities.

In this latter respect they contrast with the large-scale, *tabula rasa* approach of many developments that built environment professionals might more readily associate with the term "eco-city" (e.g. Dongtan in China and Masdar in the UAE), or green building standards such as *passivhaus*, which have tended to be used for new buildings. While they may lack architectural glamor in comparison with these better known examples, retrofit urban eco-villages may hold the potential for more rapid and more affordable implementation—cultivating networks of micro-communities across the terrain of large-scale cities. Such an approach is certainly better suited to the retrofitting of older neighborhoods and smaller-scale developments as identified as opportunities in Seoul.

Through the purposeful creation of new institutions (e.g. a no-collateral revolving loan fund, a community land trust), these communities may also be able to counter some of the negative characteristics of late twentieth century and early twenty-first-century urban regeneration, combatting both the displacement of lower-income residents through gentrification, and the homogenizing and polarizing effects of globalized finance. Such institutions and tools might address some of the challenges of affordability and insecurity of tenure currently faced in Seoul.

While the rural and the urban are of course interdependent and overlapping conditions, we see evidence of the many positive benefits that might accrue for the next communities emerging within the global eco-village movement to shift their tendencies from geographic and operational isolation—a rhetorical position of "self-sufficiency" and "back to the land"—to influence through integration with and productive physical and programmatic proximity to mainstream social, spatial, and economic systems. In terms of potential impacts, in many national contexts where political affiliations are increasingly divided along rural-urban lines, communities sited within cities may stand a better chance of benefitting from and contributing to progressive local politics (see for example Rodden et al 2016).

At the moment of writing it seems evident that, in order to survive the obliterating tendencies of populist plutocracy, progressive responses to urgent environmental and social challenges must be developed and implemented at a state, city, and neighborhood level. Reviving depressed districts while defending affordability, retrofitting standard building types to elevate their social and ecological values, and growing new enterprises of right livelihood on brownfield sites, these communities suggest practical ideas and appealing models for post-neoliberal urban development.

Taking root in our cities—the sites where "lifestyle" choices intersect with politics—an interdependent network of locally embedded urban eco-villages could provide an appealing alternative to technocratic sustainability and may even offer the potential for cultivating a "deep democracy" of the type described by political scientist David W. McIvor. This form of community development involves neither the nostalgic return to the greatness of a mythically homogenous, static past nor the naive expectation of effortlessly harmonious coexistence of diverse groups. Instead, whether in Los Angeles or Seoul, such deep democratic developments entail "a sophisticated orientation toward the common and commonality. The common is neither pre-existing nor always given, nor is it a place of frictionless togetherness. [...]

Commonality is discovered or forged through collective action; it does not exist as a reserve force or guaranteed background of public life. The common is better seen as a space around which people can gather in public, but only insofar as they labour to create and re-create the table itself" (McIvor and Hale 2016).

Acknowledgements

The original field work for this project was supported by a grant from the Graham Foundation for Advanced Studies in the Fine Arts. The author wishes to thank: Sarah Herda, Stephanie Whitlock, Fritz Haeg, Michelle Provoost, Cassim Shepard, Liz Ogbu, Grace Kim, Michael Pawlyn, Jack Stiller, Jeffrey S. Anderson, Green Kim, Mark Wee, Chai Yun Ray Chung, Hyewon Lee, Lois Arkin, Lara Morrison, Jim Schenk, and the many other eco-village hosts and teachers who shared so generously their time and ideas.

References

Bang, Jan Martin. *Ecovillages: A Practical Guide to Sustainable Communities*. Gabriola Island, BC: New Society, 2005.

Beverly-Vermont Land Trust. *http://www.bvclt.org/*. Not dated.

Borgmann, Albert. *Real American Ethics: Taking Responsibility for Our Country*. Chicago: The University of Chicago Press, 2006.

Chivian, E., and A. Bernstein (eds.). *Sustaining life: How human health depends on biodiversity*. Center for Health and the Global Environment. New York: Oxford University Press, 2008.

Christian, Diana Leafe. *Creating a Life Together: Practical Tools to Grow Ecovillages and Intentional Communities*. Gabriola Island, BC: New Society, 2003.

Christian, Diana Leafe. "Three 'Organized Urban Neighborhood'" (sic). *http://gen.ecovillage.org/en/node/4925*. Published 16 September 2014.

CRSP. "Opportunity to Be Part of Los Angeles History with Our New Acquisition." Email. 15 August 2016.

Donnally, Trish. "Growing Sociability: The Residents—and Their Connections—Are the Hottest New Features in Residential Communities." *Urban Land*. November/December 2014. pp 56-61.

Farrelly, Elizabeth. "Diller Scofidio and Renfro's Exit: decoding the data". http://architectureau.com/articles/exit/. 15 February 2017.

Fellowship for Intentional Community. "Enright Ridge Urban Eco-village." http://www.ic.org/directory/enright-ridge-urban-eco-village/. Last updated 1 March 2016.

Gilding, Paul. *The Great Disruption: How the Climate Crisis Will Transform the Global Economy*. London: Bloomsbury, 2011.

Ichioka, Sarah Mineko. "The Seoul Experiment." *Seoul, an Urban Experiment: Starting the Seoul International Biennale of Architecture and Urbanism*. Edited by Soik Jung and Green Kim. Seoul: Seoul Metropolitan Government, 2015. 31-39.

Imago. "History and Mission." http://www.
imagoearth.org/home/about_imago/history_and_
mission.html.

Klein, Naomi. *This Changes Everything: Capitalism vs.
the Climate*. New York, NY: Simon & Schuster,
2014. And the accompanying online database:
https://solutions.thischangeseverything.org/.

Kunstler, James Howard. *The Geography of Nowhere:
The Rise and Decline of America's Man-made
Landscape*. New York: Touchstone, 1994.

Litfin, Karen. *Ecovillages: Lessons for Sustainable
Community*. Cambridge, UK: Polity, 2014.

Los Angeles Eco-Village. *LAEV website*. http://
laecovillage.org/. Not dated.

Macy, Joanna, and Chris Johnstone. *Active Hope:
How to Face the Mess We're in without Going Crazy*.
Novato, CA: New World Library, 2012.

McCamant, Kathryn, and Charles Durrett. Second
Edition with Ellen Herdsman. *Cohousing: A
Contemporary Approach to Housing Ourselves*.
Berkeley, CA: Ten Speed Press, 1994.

McIvor, David W., and James Hale. "Common Roots:
Urban Agriculture's Potential for Cultivating Deep
Democracy" in *Growing Seeds in the City*, ed. Sally
Brown, Kristen McIvor, and Elizabeth Hodges
Snyder. Berlin: Springer, 2016.

Meltzer, Graham Stuart. *Sustainable Community:
Learning from the Cohousing Model*. Victoria, B.C.:
Trafford, 2005.

Olkowski, Helga, William Olkowski, and Tom Javits.
*The Integral Urban House: Self-reliant Living in the
City*. Gabriola Island, B.C.: New Catalyst, 2008.

Rodden, Jonathan (with Nolan McCarty, Boris
Shor, Chris Tausanovitch, and Chris Warshaw).
"Geography and Polarization." Stanford Spatial
Social Lab. Unpublished paper, current draft 16
June 2016.

Tyrell, Sarah. "Enright Ridge Urban EcoVillage: An
Urban Eden." Green Hawks Media. https://
greenhawksmedia.net/2016/02/14/enright-ridge-
urban-ecovillage-an-urban-eden/. 14 February 2016.

United Nations. "World Urbanization Prospects
2014." http://www.un.org/en/development/
desa/news/population/world-urbanization-
prospects-2014.html.

Walker, Liz. *EcoVillage at Ithaca: Pioneering a Sustainable
Culture*. Gabriola, BC: New Society, 2005.

Worden, Lee. "Counterculture, Cyberculture, and the
Third Culture: Reinventing Civilisation, Then
and Now." In *West of Eden: Communes and Utopia
in Northern California*, ed. Iain A. Boal, Janferie
Stone, Michael Watts, and Calvin Winslow.
Oakland, CA: PM, 2012.

States of Disassembly: Electronics, Toxicity, and Territory

Lateral Office
(Lola Sheppard and Mason White)

The Mine, the City, and the Dump

Our territories are, broadly speaking, made up of three general uses: sites of production, consumption, and waste. Naturally, we are most familiar with and dwell in sites of consumption. This is the site of social life – where we live, work, and play. The city, for example, is the preeminent site of consumption. In contrast to the consumption site, management sites are dedicated to extraction and production (pre-consumption) as well as waste (post-consumption) of these materials. Production and waste sites are often peripheral and located out-of-view of consumption sites. This distinct partitioning of land use separating consumption (clean) from production and waste (dirty) is a consequence of contemporary capitalist landscapes and a privileging of consumption spaces as the space of public realm. The cycle begins with the harvesting of a material toward manufacturing products; the consumption of this product within conducive sites; and, once the product has expired, we seek a place to dispose of it. Locating this cycle reveals three general spaces: the mine, the city, and the dump. Furthermore, we might distinguish these spaces as spheres, akin to Peter Sloterdijk's "spherology."[1] As spheres, these spaces catalyze communities centered around each site type. Just as communities associated with consumption have been recognized, there are communities associated

1. Peter Sloterdijk's trilogy of spherology consists of *Spheres I - Bubbles* (1998), *Spheres II - Globes* (1999), and *Spheres III - Foam* (2004). Its overall intent, in short, is to reveal the negotiation of spaces for the coexistence of life.

with production and even communities associated with waste. Communities forming from waste sites are both the least understood and the most emergent of the three.

The impact of late-20th century globalization on the logistics, politics, and economics of the waste stream is significant. Land use influences the organization of inhabitation and the proximity of management territories. The relationship of spaces of consumption (inhabitation) to spaces of production or waste (management) has been integral to territorialisation patterns. Prior to globalization, inhabitation sites sought to be close to management sites for convenience, but not too close to be a detriment to the land value. Planning and policy often attempt to negotiate the relative distance between these land uses, producing spatially distinct communities. Equally, infrastructure and logistics facilitate an increasing gap between inhabitation and management sites. With the proliferation of globalization and its attendant networks, the organization and proximity of production and waste to inhabitation sites now operates at the scale of the Earth and is entirely enmeshed within geo-politics, socio-economics, and available logistics. What was previously simply out-of-view is now completely far-flung. The 21st-century scale-shift in interactions between territories has generated complex geo- and bio-political impacts on the spaces and places of production and waste sites. While it is well-documented which nations and regions have emerged as haves and have-nots in terms of extractable raw materials for manufacturing, the same cannot be said for those nations and regions that are central to the waste stream. Very little is known, and even less is documented, on the geography of the waste stream, in part because it is not as tied to origins as sites of extraction. However, specific nations and regions have emerged as custodians of the world's waste. Waste streams tend to move toward struggling, unpredictable economies. Returning to the site types of the mine, the city, and the dump, it is the dump—and the cycles that lead to it—that has been most unpredictable and insidious. And increasingly, this waste cycle is congested with electronic waste, or e-waste, which is a toxic and colonial force on nations and cities.

Waste Commons

The 20th century has attempted to address unsustainable practices in global waste—organics, papers, plastics, etc.—through the introduction of recycling. Previously dependent on a "burn or bury" approach, the rise of recycling in many Western countries during the 1970s and 1980s yielded new infrastructure, landscapes, and architectures dedicated to recycling; these included sorting centers, materials recovery facilities, composting, among others. The transformation of the waste stream has reformatted territories and cities, and even changed perceptions of the value of waste. For example, Michigan imports a significant amount of waste—almost 17% of all solid waste in the state came from Canada, and 6% from other nearby states, according to a 2013 report.[2] Today, it is evident that the next waste-stream challenge is the burden of electronic waste. E-waste is the accumulation of discarded products that contain electrical systems. Today, a multitude of products such as computers and cellular phones contain electronics, but also an increasing number of common household products – from toasters to dishwashers to air conditioners – do as well. These products consist of various rare earth metals, lead, cadmium, phosphors, beryllium, or brominated flame retardants, much of which

2. "Report of Solid Waste Landfilled in Michigan," October 1, 2012 – September 30, 2013. Prepared by Michigan Department of Environmental Quality Office of Waste Management and Radiological Protection Solid Waste Section. February 13, 2014.

is deemed hazardous. Almost 50 million metric tons of global e-waste is discarded annually.[3] As e-waste enters the global stream, it is primarily in search of cheap labour and unregulated territories. How will society respond to this contemporary challenge?

Contrary to expectations, computers only make up a small portion of current e-waste, so far. As Jennifer Gabrys notes, the proliferation of microchips into common household and business products has "recast the extent of computing beyond the medium-sized memory machines that occupy our desktops."[4] The most common products now contain chips, motherboards, and electronic interfaces. In a 2014 study by the United Nations University, mobile phones, personal computers, and printers only accounted for about 7% of e-waste.[5] The bulk of this waste is discarded kitchen, laundry, and bathroom equipment, which often contain micro-computers, and are increasingly internet-connected and intelligent. Amplifying the unknown challenge of e-waste, it has been suggested that there is the phenomenon of personal hoarding, in which people hold on to equipment despite the inevitability that it will enter the e-waste stream at some point. This is often hoarded because people either do not know how to dispose of an singular product of e-waste or are concerned about safe disposal of personal data. For example, both personal credit card information and private contract documents have been found in recovered hard drives that surfaced in Agbogbloshie, an e-waste recovery district near Accra, Ghana.

Contemporary e-waste tends to accumulate into two landscapes: an "urban mine" of materials untouched and ripe for recovery, or a "toxic mine"—as in Agbogbloshie—of hazardous chemicals that pollute and pose a threat to human health. Both landscapes present material depots generating management sites (and new economies) within cultural contexts that value such materials and processes. With few regulatory policies in place, and with even fewer institutions to monitor those policies, these landscapes have become the unintended commons of the e-waste stream. While western nations lack the full and proper infrastructures needed to collect and deal with e-waste, many urban centers have salvage yards or other trade-oriented spaces (including online) to support a growing hacker and DIY culture seeking materials and components from these urban mines. These are the boutique landscapes of e-waste with its Silicon-Valley-like workers. On the other side, underpaid and un-regulated e-waste workers inhabit toxic mines and are essential to the disassembly and recovery processes to serve the bulk of e-waste. Developing nations and regions have become the stewards of ensuring materials re-enter the production stream. And they have often been unrecognized innovators with how to salvage and recover the west's production of e-waste.

Earth, Territory, Product

The scales of operation reveal three vantage points from which to observe the e-waste cycle: the Earth, territory, and product scale. The largest

3. Baldé, C.P., Wang, F., Kuehr, R., Huisman, J., "The Global E-Waste Monitor 2014: Quantities, flows and resources," United Nations University, Institute for the Advanced Study of Sustainability, Bonn, Germany, 2015.

4. Gabrys, Jennifer, *Digital Rubbish: A Natural History of Electronics*, (Ann Arbor, MI: University of Michigan Press, 2011), 3.

5. Baldé, C.P., Wang, F., Kuehr, R., Huisman, J., "The Global E-Waste Monitor 2014: Quantities, flows and resources," United Nations University, Institute for the Advanced Study of Sustainability, Bonn, Germany, 2015.

scale is an Earth-sized archipelago of nations that are the primary consumers, distributers, and managers of e-waste. The next scale reveals localized territories and regions that have become the focal point of e-waste management and processes. And the smallest is the scale of the product and its recoverable materials. Each scale reveals both the accumulation of objecthood and the formation of a distinct commons. In the realm of objecthood, there is the individual electronic product, such as the disused laptop; there is the collection of all similar disused objects, such as all laptops with their similar material assemblies; and there is the collection of all electronic items with their dissimilar material assemblies, or the larger assemblage of refrigerators, microwaves, cellular phones, and laptops. Each of these collections represents evidence of a strata of our consumption practices. We might also think of these accumulations as Timothy Morton's "hyperobjects." Morton identifies hyperobjects as "not just collections, systems or assemblages of other objects," but also "objects in their own right."[6] Morton's terminology is particularly apt in the sense that he identifies hyperobjects as viscous, meaning that they "stick to beings that are involved with them."[7] As discarded e-waste migrates in search of those places and people that address its recovery potential, it adheres to any carrier.

One extreme case that reveals the viscosity of e-waste is the incident of the Khian Sea cargo ship. The Khian attempted to find a site willing to take its shipment of 14,000 tons of incinerated waste—which included dangerous amounts of lead, mercury, arsenic, and dioxins— after the Philadelphia incinerators were no longer permitted to dump incinerated ash in a New Jersey landfill. It then tried international sites in the Bahamas, Dominican Republic, Honduras, Panama, and others with no success. It even tried to return the waste to Philadelphia, but was declined because of the toxicity of the waste. Finally, in January 1988, and under false pretenses that the material was "topsoil fertilizer," it struck an agreement for 4,000 tons to be dumped in Haiti. The ship then tried offload the remaining contents in farther destinations in Africa and Asia, before covertly changing its name twice and illegally dumping the material in open waters somewhere near Singapore in November 1988.[8] This global wandering for dumping sites reveals the politics and viscosity of the chemical waste cycle. We are content while we consume a product, but once a product becomes waste it is an undesirable we hope to pass off to others. And the perception of those whom waste producers see as deserving of their waste reveals a colonialist tendency. This incident is considered one of the catalysts for the important 1992 Basel Convention, which developed an international treaty to reduce the shipment of hazardous waste between nations, and sought to safeguard less developed countries from "toxic colonialism."[9]

6. Morton, Timothy, *Hyperobjects: Philosophy and Ecology after the End of the World,* (Minneapolis: University of Minnesota Press, 2013), 2.

7. Ibid., 1.

8. Reeves, Hope, "The Way We Live Now: 2-18-01: Map; A Trail of Refuse," *The New York Times Magazine,* February 18, 2001. http://www.nytimes.com/2001/02/18/magazine/the-way-we-live-now-2-18-01-map-a-trail-of-refuse.html. Accessed July 2, 2017.

9. The term "toxic colonialism" was thought to be introduced by Jim Puckett of Greenpeace in 1992. It refers to the practice of dumping hazardous industrial waste produced in the West on developing territories in an exploitive manner.

Meanwhile, the surge in "maker" and "hacker" culture in the West has become a cultural response to the complex cycle of contemporary electronics and the increased availability of e-waste. With more electronics and its components around, and with the individual desire to reclaim the manufacturing process from corporations, people are participating in manufacturing, repair, and recycling again. This shift in labour and entrepreneurship has made maker-spaces and technology-oriented businesses increasingly present in creative centers. These subcultures and their bottom-up organizations seek a renewed participation in technology. Simultaneously, however, manufacturers attempt to maintain control through product end-of-life cycles and planned obsolescence, leaving consumers with few recourses to repair or maintain technology. In most instances, it is easier and cheaper to throw away a technology product, such as an LCD monitor, that is not working or needs an upgrade, than to repair and maintain it. In combination with DIY aesthetics, hacker ingenuity has served as a catalyst for hackerspaces, fab labs, and other maker spaces.

While certain programmatic innovations are emerging in response to the growing desire to repair, reuse, hack, and remake their technologies, there has been little consideration of the landscapes and building types that might emerge in response to these new priorities. Landscape Architect Alan Berger's 2007 book *Drosscape* observed the "inevitable wasted landscapes within urbanized areas" (p.12) as a territory capable of reclamation for the city.[10] This notion is apt here. Deindustrialized landscapes emerged as critical new lands following shifts in economic and production practices. However, Berger's "wasted land" is better understood as under-utilized space, often the victim of de-industrialization or sprawl.

In the context of e-waste, landscape needs to be understood more literally as landscapes of waste management, or landscapes of disassembly.[11] How these landscapes can be integrated into our urban and post-urban imaginary, and what new building and landscapes typologies might emerge in the 21st century are key questions. If the twentieth century sought a response to the de-industrialization of the city — a challenge that led to renewed leadership among landscape architects — the twenty-first century seeks a response to our increasing waste management challenges, and its associated ecological and social impacts. And, in particular, a response to the mounting hyperobject of e-waste. But who will respond? The architectural possibility could be seen as a reconceptualization of the previous century's factory. In the case of e-waste, this architecture might suggest a factory of disassembly. If, in the past, the cathedrals of making were about assembly, today's factories will privilege dismantling, re-use, and reverse alchemy.

Three Techno-Commons

Commons I: An Ocean of WEEE
The geography of electronics material extraction, its subsequent product manufacturing, and ultimately its disposal reveal a fragmented globe. In the wake of increasing waves of e-waste, an archipelago of nations surfaces. Distinct leaders in extraction, manufacturing, consumption, and waste management corroborate economic and social disparity embedded in globalization. At each stage of the life cycle of electronics, nations emerge as primary contributors. Despite the passage of the Basel convention, few nations have the infrastructure in place to properly disassemble and dispose of their e-waste, in part because the cost of recycling is not yet offset by the value of the resources extracted.

10. Berger, Alan, *Drosscape: Wasting Land in Urban America*, (New York: Princeton Architectural Press, 2006).

11. Belanger, Pierre, "Landscapes of Disassembly," *Topos*, 2007, p. 83-91.

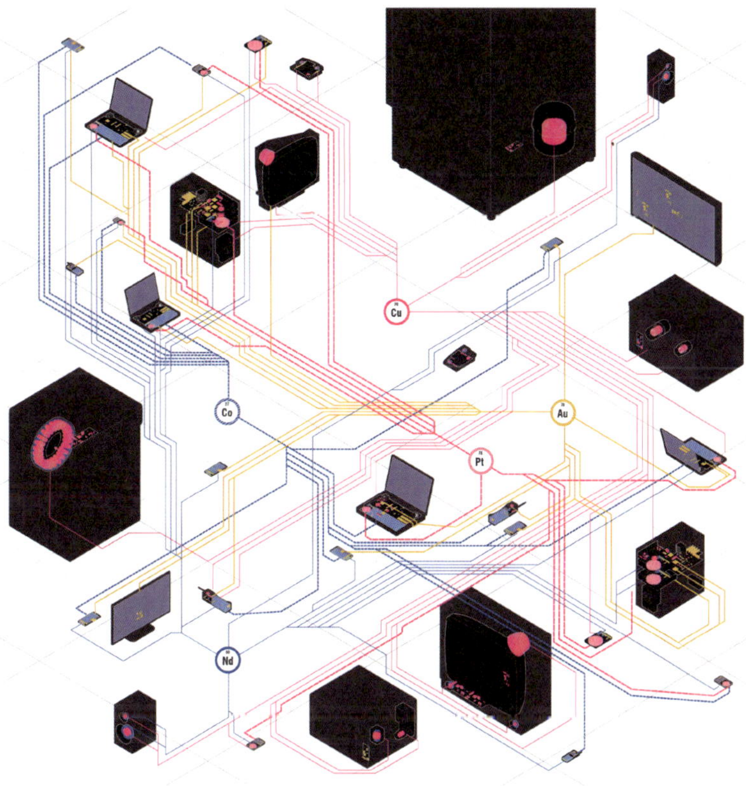

An Ocean of WEEE

This results the continued global shipment/transfer of waste from wealthier e-consumer nations to poorer e-waste receiver nations whose more informal economies, less regulated environmental controls and inexpensive labour forces renders the return on investment in disassembly viable. [12]

Commons II: Toxic Colonialism

The territories that form as part of the global archipelago of e-waste generate nodes of e-waste management, often in informal, un-regulated, and resulting in dangerous and toxic conditions.

Key centers of disassembly are in Guiyu, China; Agbogbloshie near Accra, Ghana; and Shershah in Karachi, Pakistan, receive and recover the largest quantities of e-waste. Within these informal centers, there are sites dedicated to burning, smelting, breaking, smashing, and other actions. The activities necessary to disassemble and separate materials generate chemical ecologies of toxic water, land, and air radiating outward from these sites. A workforce of e-waste specialists are instrumental to the disassembly and chemical processes.

12. Despite nearly all e-waste being recyclable, only 16% of total global e-waste generation in 2014 was recycled by government agencies and approved companies, according to United Nations reports. (Baldé, C.P., Wang, F., Kuehr, R., Huisman, J., "The Global E-Waste Monitor 2014: Quantities, flows and resources," United Nations University, Institute for the Advanced Study of Sustainability, Bonn, Germany, 2015.)

Toxic Colonialism

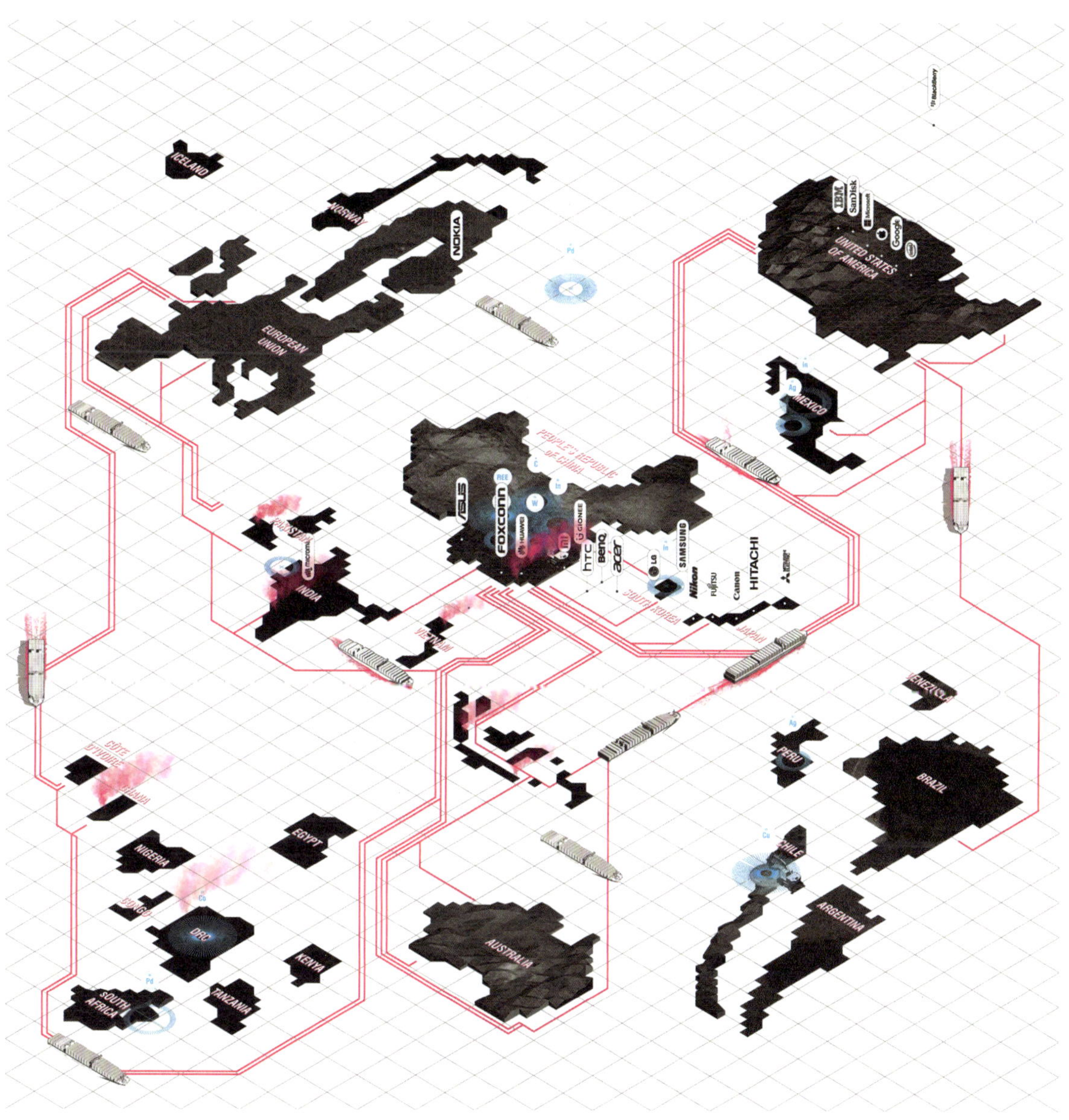

From Product to Material

This precarious labour force, as well as its local residents, are exposed to considerable health hazards yielding a contemporary form of colonialism from toxicity. These management sites produce three primary outcomes for materials: toxic waste, scrap recovery, or landfill.

Commons III: From Product to Material

The products of e-waste are an array of devices and products fully entangled within our contemporary social and work culture. These products change and evolve in a manner that demands a frequent cycle of disposal and upgrade. Two factors contribute to this dependence on newness. First, there is the issue of planned obsolescence, and second there is the issue of inaccessible repair. Products were previously subjected to Moore's Law, but there is also the diminishing convenience for user's to physically repair and renew products. And this manufacturing cycle makes it cheaper to buy it again new than repair the old. Products—from laptops to cell phones—have become more compact, with components physically integrated, which makes repair complex and partial replacement expensive. But the preciousness and value of finite raw materials is great enough that recovery is not only necessary but also valuable.

Un-Commons: Collections and Collectives

The Basel convention prohibits the transfer of hazardous waste without the explicit and informed consent of all parties and nations involved. The Convention also created regional and coordinating centers for training and technology transfer (BCRCs) to educate governments and regions regarding the management of hazardous wastes. The centres support developing countries and countries with economies in transition in the implementation of the Convention, offering training and education on the reporting, monitoring and management of waste. What is lacking within this global network of landscapes and spaces of e-waste, however, are centres within economically developed nations (also the largest producers of e-waste), which might manage e-waste at its origin before it is shipped to other nations. Increased environmental awareness in the last four decades created a multitude of new program types and economies—from eco-tourism, to organic food production, to the promotion of local food cultures, to new construction methods, among others. The emerging awareness of e-waste issues, paired with a growing hacker and DIY culture, and the desire for greater participation in product technology, promises potential new building types, and new forms of commons emerging from our global e-waste economies.

States of Disassembly observes the possibility of a series of building and landscape types that recognize an emergent e-waste commons—leveraging trends in reuse, repair, education, and entertainment. The proposed types are situated in city centers, on the peri-urban edge, and in urban hinterlands. The seven types test new programmatic pairings and new forms of commons that might be fostered if we design for the e-waste stream. These e-waste commons, under-pinned by a desire to make our collective footprint on the globe more legible and tangible might incite new actions.

Author biographies

Alejandro Zaera-Polo is an accomplished contemporary architect. His work has consistently merged the practice of architecture with theoretical practice, deftly integrating architecture, urban design and landscape architecture in his projects. He trained at the Escuela Técnica Superior de Arquitectura de Madrid, graduating with Honors, and went on to do a Master in Architecture (MARCH II) at the Graduate School of Design, Harvard University, USA, where he graduated with Distinction. He worked at OMA in Rotterdam between 1991 and 1993, prior to establishing Foreign Office Architects in 1993, and AZPML in 2011. He was the Dean of Princeton SoA 2012-2014 and of the Berlage Institute in Rotterdam from 2000-2005 where he held the Berlage Chair at the Technical University in Delft, the Netherlands. He was the inaugural recipient of the Norman Foster professorship at Yale University School of Architecture between 2010 and 2011, and has been a Visiting Critic at Columbia GSAPP and UCLA School of Architecture. He led a Diploma Unit between 1993 and 1999 years at the Architectural Association in London. He is a tenured professor at Princeton SoA.

Jeffrey S. Anderson is an architectural designer and researcher. He has worked with renowned architects, theorists, and designers including Alejandro Zaera-Polo, DS+R, Jimenez Lai, Jeffrey Kipnis, and Cesar Pelli and his work has been exhibited at Princeton University (2016), the Gwangju Asia Culture Center (2015), the Venice Architecture Biennale (2014, 2012), the Southern California Institute of Architecture (2014), and Ohio State University (2013). He holds a Master of Architecture II from Princeton University, and a Bachelor of Science in Architecture from the Knowlton School of Architecture at OSU. He was recently a recipient of Princeton University's Suzanne Kolarik Underwood Prize (2016) for his design thesis.

Liam Young is an Australian born architect who operates in the spaces between design, fiction and futures. He is founder of the think tank Tomorrows Thoughts Today, a group whose work explores the possibilities of fantastic, speculative and imaginary urbanisms. Building his design fictions from the realities of present, Young also co-runs the Unknown Fields Division, a nomadic research studio that travels on location shoots and expeditions to the ends of the earth to document emerging trends and uncover the weak signals of possible futures.

Tomás Saraceno is known for his sculptural work and installations that merge art, architecture, and science. Saraceno's practice is concerned with our living environments, their conceptual design, and speculative futures. His experimental, engaging, and compelling works seek an alternative artistic imaginary to re-frame our awareness of the world. Saraceno is the winner of the Calder Prize and was artist-in-residence at the International Space Studies Program of NASA in summer 2009.

Maider Llaguno-Munitxa is an Adjunct Assistant Professor at Columbia GSAPP and co-founded the London and New York based architecture office AZPML in 2011. In 2016 Maider Llaguno- Munitxa completed her Ph.D. from the Institute of Technology in Architecture at the ETH in Zurich. Her Ph.D. topic focused on the study of the interaction of architecture, urban microclimate and its dynamics of flow and transport. Before initiating her Ph.D. studies, Maider graduated from ETSASS/ETSAB with Honors in 2006 and from Columbia GSAPP Columbia with Excellence in Design in 2010. Maider is currently a scientific researcher at the department of Civil and Environmental Engineering at Princeton University.

Biayna Bogosian is an architect and interactive media designer researching perceptual and cognitive interaction design that highlight the relationship between urban and environmental data patterns. Biayna is pursuing a Ph.D. in Media Arts & Practice in the School of Cinematic Arts at the University of Southern California. She holds a Master of Science in Advanced Architectural Design from Columbia University, and a Bachelors of Architecture from Woodbury University.

Nerea Calvillo is an architect and researcher who studied at the Escuela Tecnica Superior de Arquitectura de Madrid (ETSAM). She was awarded the Fulbright grant to pursue studies at Columbia University (MsAAD), and she received her doctorate in 2014. She has worked at NO.MAD and Foreign Office Architects (FOA) before funding her own office C+ (2004), winning several national and international competitions. Her work and articles have been published in architecture magazines, academic journals and general media.

MAP Office is a multidisciplinary platform devised by Laurent Gutierrez (1966, Casablanca, Morocco) and Valérie Portefaix (1969, Saint-Étienne, France). This duo of artists has been based in Hong Kong since 1996, working on physical and imaginary territories using varied means of expression.

Carlo Ratti An architect and engineer by training, Carlo Ratti practices in Italy and teaches at the Massachusetts Institute of Technology, where he directs the Senseable City Lab. He graduated from the Politecnico di Torino and the École Nationale des Ponts et Chaussées in Paris, and later earned his MPhil and PhD at the University of Cambridge, UK.

RAAD Studio is an award-winning Manhattan-based design firm with a portfolio of over 100 completed projects. Founded by designer James Ramsey in 2004, the firm specializes in the exploration of materiality, form and scale in a way that reveals the limitless potential of design, and that marries innovative thinking about function with a deep respect for the traditions of everyday living. Raad specializes in objects and spaces that emphasize the process of construction, an expertise gleaned from close and continued collaboration with builders.

Andrew Cruse is an Assistant Professor of Architecture at the Knowlton School of Architecture as well as a practicing architect. He is a member of the AIA, NCARB and is a LEED Accredited Professional. Cruse's research focuses on architecture and energy. Cruse was an Assistant Professor of Architecture at Washington University in St Louis (2010-2013), and an Associate at Machado and Silvetti Associates in Boston (2000-2010). Cruse earned his BA in Art History from Columbia University and his M.Arch from Rice University. While at Rice, he spent a year on a Fulbright Fellowship in Barcelona, Spain.

Nikolaus Hirsch/Michel Müller is a Frankfurt-based office for architecture. Their work on institutional models resulted in realized projects such as the Bockenheimer Depot Theater (with William Forsythe), Unitednationsplaza in Berlin (with Anton Vidokle), Cybermohalla Hub in Delhi, and Do We Dream Under The Same Sky at Art Basel (2015) and Aarhus (2017). They designed several exhibitions, including "Making Things Public" at ZKM (curated by Bruno Latour and Peter Weibel, 2005) and 'Indian Highway' (Serpentine Gallery, 2008). Nikolaus Hirsch is the founder and editor of e-flux architecture. Between 2010 and 2013, he was the dean of Städelschule and Portikus in Frankfurt. Michel Müller is a professor at the University of Sciences in Cologne, Germany.

Philippe Rahm is a Swiss architect, principal in the office of Philippe Rahm architectes, based in Paris, France. His work, which extends the field of architecture from the physiological to the meteorological, has received an international audience in the context of sustainability. He starts to teach architecture design at the GSD, Harvard University, USA, in Fall 2014.

Stoss is a cutting-edge design firm that believes in the productive role of landscape in the making and re-making of cities and social spaces.

Dirk Hebel is Assistant Professor of Architecture and Construction at the Future Cities Laboratory in Singapore. Prior to that, he was the founding Scientific Director of the Ethiopian Institute of Architecture, Building Construction and City Development in Addis Ababa, Ethiopia. Between 2002 and 2009 he taught at the Department of Architecture, ETH Zurich as the coordinator for the first year architectural design program and the director of the Master of Advanced Studies programme in Urban Design with Prof Dr Marc Angélil.

Turenscape was founded by Doctor and Professor Kongjian Yu (Doctor of Design, GSD, Harvard University) in 1998 and the company is a certificated first-level design institute by the Chinese government. With over 500 professionals, Turenscape is a multi- disciplinary design team that provides quality and holistic services in Architectural Design, Landscape Design, Urban Design, Environmental Design, and Engineering.

Terreform ONE [Open Network Ecology] is a non-profit architecture group that promotes smart design in cities. Through our creative projects and outreach efforts, we aim to illuminate the environmental possibilities of New York City and inspire solutions in areas like it around the world.

Philippe Block is Associate Professor at the Institute of Technology in Architecture at ETH Zurich, where he co-directs the Block Research Group (BRG) together with Dr. Tom Van Mele. He is director of the Swiss National Centre of Competence in Research (NCCR) in Digital Fabrication, and founding partner of Ochsendorf DeJong & Block (ODB Engineering).

Axel Kilian is an Assistant Professor at the Princeton University School of Architecture. He previously taught Computational Design at the Department of Architecture at MIT and at TU Delft. In 2006 he completed a PhD in Design and Computation at MIT on design exploration. In addition he holds a Master of Science from MIT and a professional degree in architecture from the University of the Arts Berlin.

David Benjamin is Founding Principal of The Living and Assistant Professor at Columbia GSAPP. He also directs the GSAPP Incubator at the New Museum's NEW INC. Benjamin's work combines research and practice, and it involves exploring new ideas through prototyping. Focusing on the intersection of biology, computation, and design, Benjamin has articulated three frameworks for harnessing living organisms for architecture: bio-processing, bio-sensing, and bio-manufacturing.

The Living has won many design prizes, including the Emerging Voices Award from the Architectural League, the New Practices Award from the American Institute of Architects New York Chapter, the Young Architects Program Award from the Museum of Modern Art and MoMA PS1, and a Holcim Sustainability Award. Recent projects include the Princeton Architecture Laboratory (a new building for research on next-generation design and construction technologies), Pier 35 EcoPark (a 200-foot-long floating pier in the East River that changes color according to water quality), and Hy-Fi (a branching tower for the Museum of Modern Art and MoMA PS1 made of a new type of biodegradable brick).

Mark Wasiuta is an Adjunct Assistant Professor at Columbia GSAPP and Co-Director of the Critical, Curatorial and Conceptual Practices in Architecture program.

Farzin Farzin (Farzin Lotfi-Jam) investigates the means by which objects, sites and systems acquire cultural value and examines the representation of value in architectural form. Farzin Farzin was founded in 2008 by Farzin Lotfi-Jam. Lotfi-Jam is an adjunct professor in architecture at Columbia University, and holds advanced degrees from Columbia University and RMIT University in Melbourne Australia. He is a 2015-2017 Fellow of the Akademie Schloss Solitude in Stuttgart and was a 2013-2014 Sanders Fellow at the University of Michigan.

Future Cities Lab is a design studio, workshop and urban design think tank operating globally out of San Francisco, California. Since 2005, founders Jason Kelly Johnson and Nataly Gattegno have collaborated on a range of cutting-edge projects exploring the intersections of art and design with public space, performance, advanced fabrication technologies, robotics, and responsive building systems.

Sissel Tolaas is a smell designer, artist, chemist, researcher, odor theorist—a "professional in-betweener" as she calls it, working amid research, commercial, and creative innovation. Smell is Tolaas's medium, but her interest is not a conventional approach to scent, which is characterized by perfumes that camouflage, deodorize, and sanitize reality. For Tolaas, smell is information.

Andrés Jaque is the founder of the Office for Political Innovation. He is Advanced Design Professor at Graduate School of Architecture, Planning and Preservation GSAPP Columbia University and Visiting Professor at Princeton University SoA. He has been Tessenow Stipendiat 1998 by the Alfred Toepfer Stiftung FVS, in Hamburg, and visiting professor in a number of international universities. He has lectured extensively throughout the world including Eidgenössische Technische Hochschule in Zurich, MIT (Boston), Instituto Politecnico di Milano, Centre International pour la Ville de Paris, Centre pour l'Architecture et le Paysage (Brussels), Sociedad Central (Buenos Aires), Berlage Institut (Rotterdam) or Museo Nacional (Bogotá).

Pablo Garcia is Associate Professor in the Department of Contemporary Practices at the School of the Art Institute of Chicago. Trained as an architect, Pablo's recent work has evolved from design-for-hire to internationally exhibited artworks, provocations and research studies. Previously, Pablo has taught at Carnegie Mellon University, Parsons School of Design, and The University of Michigan. From 2004-2007, he also worked as an architect and designer for Diller Scofidio + Renfro. He holds architecture degrees from Cornell and Princeton Universities.

Beatriz Colomina is an internationally renowned architectural historian and theorist who has written extensively on questions of architecture and media. Ms. Colomina has taught in the School since 1988, and is the Founding Director of the Program in Media and Modernity at Princeton University, a graduate program that promotes the interdisciplinary study of forms of culture that came to prominence during the last century and looks at the interplay between culture and technology.

Dark Matter labs aims to apply complex systems science to Urban & Regional Renewal; turning what is generally perceived as a threat of our time – spill-over effects across borders, boundaries and silos – into a resource to solve the wicked challenges society faces in the 21st century. Dark Matter Laboratories utilises an experimentation method typical of a fieldwork scientific laboratory, we undertake real-world research and prototyping inorder to seed the next generation of 21st Century institutional infrastructure.

Indy Johar is an architect, co-founder of 00 (project00.cc) and a Senior Innovation Associate with the Young Foundation and Visiting Professor at the University of Sheffield. Indy, on behalf of 00, has co-founded multiple social ventures from Impact Hub Westminster to Impact Hub Birmingham and the HubLaunchpad Accelerator, along with working with large global multinationals & institutions to support their transition to a positive Systems Economy. Indy is a Fellow of the RSA, Respublica Fellow, JRF Anti-Poverty Strategy Programme Advisory Group member and a member of the Mayor of London's SME Working Group and most recently a member of the RSA Inclusive Growth Commission.

Clare Lyster is an architect, educator and writer. A native of Ireland she is now based in Chicago, where she is an Associate Professor at the UIC School of Architecture. Her work explores a+u from the perspective of contemporary theories in landscape, infrastructure and globalization. Clare is a registered architect in New York and Illinois and holds a BArch from University College Dublin (Ireland) and a MArch from Yale University. She has also taught at Syracuse University, University of Toronto, and Harvard University and is the Gillmor Lecturer at the University of Calgary in fall 2017.

Jesse LeCavalier is an award-winning designer, writer, and educator whose work explores the architectural and urban implications of contemporary logistics. He is the author of The Rule of Logistics: Walmart and the Architecture of Fulfillment (University of Minnesota Press). LeCavalier is an assistant professor of architecture at the New Jersey Institute of Technology where he coordinates the Special Topics and Integrated Studio sequence.

Philipp Rode is Executive Director of LSE Cities and Associate Professorial Research Fellow at the London School of Economics and Political Science. He is co-director of the LSE Executive MSc in Cities and co-convenes the LSE Sociology Course on 'City Making: The Politics of Urban Form'. He holds a PhD from the Department of Sociology at the LSE that focused on urban governance and integrated policy making. As researcher, consultant and advisor he has been directing interdisciplinary projects comprising urban governance, transport, city planning and urban design at the LSE since 2003.

Rahul Mehrotra is an architect, urbanist and educator who is the Founder Principal of RMA Architects and is Professor of Urban Design and Planning and Chair of the Department of Urban Planning and Design at Harvard University's Graduate School of Design. He studied at the School of Architecture, Ahmedabad graduated with a Master's Degree in Urban Design with distinction from the Graduate School of Design at Harvard (1987). Apart from his engagement with the design of buildings, Mehrotra has been actively involved in civic and urban affairs in Mumbai, having served on commissions for historic preservation and environmental issues. He was the Executive Director (1994–2004) of the Urban Design Research Institute (UDRI), where he is now a Trustee and has taught at the University of Michigan (2003–2007) and at the School of Architecture and Urban Planning at MIT (2007–2010).

Urtzi Grau is principal of Fake Industries Architectural Agonism. He graduated from the School of Architecture of Barcelona in 2000, was awarded Master of Science in Advanced Architectural Design by the Graduate School of Architecture Planning and Preservation, Columbia University in 2004, and is currently completing his Ph.D. at Princeton University School of Architecture on the 1970's urban renewal of Barcelona. He teaches at the Princeton School of Architecture and Cooper Union and his work and writings have been published in different international journals such as 306090, Architect's Newspaper, Domus, Pasajes de Arquitectura y Critica, Pidgin, Volume, Via Arquitectura and Visions.

Matter Design is an interdisciplinary design practice founded in 2008 by Brandon Clifford and Wes McGee. This pairing centers the practice on the continual interrogation of the reciprocity between drawing and making. Their shared interests in design coupled with proficiency in the means and methods of production have led Clifford and McGee to collaborate on a range of experimental projects which break conventional disciplinary notions of scale.

Mariana Ibanez is an architect in Argentina, and a newly appointed tenure-track faculty at the MIT School of Architecture and Planning, after 11 years at Harvard University. Mariana is also Adjunct Associate Professor at Columbia University Graduate School of Architecture, Planning, and Preservation for 2017.

Simon Kim, AIA, is a registered architect, Associate Professor at the University of Pennsylvania's School of Design, and Director of the Immersive Kinematics Research Group. As principal of Ibañez Kim, he is interested in the integration of architecture and urbanism with active and emotive behaviors in new media. In particular, Simon works to bring agency into architecture and design with meaningful and sensate technologies for our homes and cities.

Ryan Luke Johns is a visiting lecturer at the Princeton University School of Architecture. He holds a Bachelor of Arts in Architecture with a concentration in Mathematics from Columbia University and a Master of Architecture from Princeton University.

Husum & Lindholm Architects was established by Sine Lindholm (Architect MAA) and Mads-Ulrik Husum (Architect MAA). Husum & Lindholm develop ideas from the ideology of sharing culture and thereby working with the concept of open-source design. They want to create Architecture that is available, accessible and understandable for everyone.

Sine Lindholm is an Architect MAA from Denmark. She holds a Master of Architecture from Aarhus School of Architecture in 2014. In addition to Architecture she also studied Psychology. This shows in her projects where she is uniting the two subjects with a phenomenological approach to architecture. In 2015 she did a funded study in Bermuda of the Architecture and unique rainwater harvesting systems. Together with Architect Mads-Ulrik Husum she established the company Husum & Lindholm Architecture in 2016.

Mads-Ulrik Husum is an Architect MAA from Denmark. He holds a Master of Architecture from Aarhus School of Architecture. After his studies he did an apprenticeship as a cabinetmaker, where he further developed his skills and knowledge on construction in Architecture and Design. He works from a hands on approach and likes to examine and develop structures and assemblies that is incorporated as a part of the design aesthetic. He established the company Husum & Lindholm Architecture in 2016 together with Architect Sine Lindholm

Design Earth is a collaborative practice led by El Hadi Jazairy and Rania Ghosn. The office's work engages the geographic to open up a range of aesthetic and political concerns for architecture and urbanism.

Rania Ghosn is an architect, geographer and partner of Design Earth. She is currently assistant professor at Massachusetts Institute of Technology School of Architecture + Planning. Rania holds a Doctor of

Design from Harvard University Graduate School of Design, a Master in Geography from University College London, and a Bachelor of Architecture from American University of Beirut. Prior to joining MIT, she was an Assistant Professor at University of Michigan and a Mellon Postdoctoral Fellow at Boston University. Rania is founding editor of the journal New Geographies and editor-in-chief of NG2: Landscapes of Energy.

El Hadi Jazairy is a licensed architect and a founding partner of Design Earth. He is currently assistant professor of architecture at the University of Michigan. El Hadi holds a Doctorate of Design from Harvard, a Master of Architecture from Cornell, and a Bachelor of Architecture from La Cambre in Brussels. Prior to his appointment at the University of Michigan, El Hadi was Lecturer at MIT, and a Postdoctoral Fellow at Harvard. El Hadi is founding editor of the journal New Geographies and editor-in-chief of NG4: Scales of the Earth.

Common Accounts Igor Bragado and Miles Gertler founded Common Accounts at Princeton University in 2015. Equipped with excellent data plans, the office operates over satellite, server and fibre cable.

Jihoi Lee is an Architecture Curator at the Museum of Modern and Contemporary Art, Korea. She was the Curator of Imagining New Eurasia Project at the Asia Culture Center, Gwangju, Deputy Curator and Managing Director for Crow's Eye View: The Korean Peninsula, and exhibition for the Korean Pavilion at the 2014 Venice Biennale, which received the Golden Lion. Lee was also the Associate Curator for Before/After: Mass Studies Does Architecture at the PLATEAU, Samsung Museum of Art in Seoul. She is a graduate from Columbia University GSAPP.

Yusuke Obuchi is an Associate Professor in Architecture at the University of Tokyo, where he has directed Obuchi Laboratory at the Department of Architecture since 2010. He is also a founding Co-director of the Advanced Design Studies Program, which consists of Digital Fabrication Lab, Sustainable Prototyping Lab, Media Initiative Lab, Design Think Tank, Design Practice Lab, Social Design Lab, and Computational Unit. He studied architecture at Princeton University, Southern California Institute of

Architecture, the University of Toronto, and received his Ph.D from the University of Tokyo. He has previously taught at Princeton University, Harvard University's Graduate School of Design, University of Kentucky, and New Jersey Institute of Technology.

Sarah Mineko Ichioka is an experienced leader, influencer, and innovator whose diverse portfolio includes high-profile management, curatorial, and editorial work with some of the world's most respected institutions of culture, policy, and research. Unifying her work is a passion for cities and their potential. From 2008 to 2014 Ichioka was director of The Architecture Foundation, the UK's leading independent center for architecture and urbanism.

Lateral Office founded in 2003 by Mason White and Lola Sheppard, is an experimental design practice that operates at the intersection of architecture, landscape, and urbanism. The studio describes its practice process as a commitment to "design as a research vehicle to pose and respond to complex, urgent questions in the built environment," engaging in the "wider context and climate of a project– social, ecological, or political." Lateral Office is committed to an architecture that responds directly to the demands of the 21st century— and the subsequent new typologies made possible by an architecture that brazenly confronts today.

SEOUL BIENNALE OF ARCHITECTURE AND URBANISM 2017: IMMINENT COMMONS

HOSTED BY
Seoul Metropolitan Government
Seoul Design Foundation

DIRECTORS
Hyungmin Pai
Alejandro Zaera-Polo

GENERAL MANAGER
Soik Jung

CURATORS THEMATIC EXHIBITION
Jeffrey S. Anderson
Youngseok Lee

PROJECT MANAGERS THEMATIC EXHIBITION
Jina Lee
May Jeong

PROJECT MANAGERS BIENNALE
Nayeon Kim
Hye Seong Park
Myungcheol Shin
Myeongju Deum
Suna Lee
Green Kim
Ri Jin Yoo
Jina Lee
Sunjae Kim
Sobaek Oh

BOOK 2
IMMINENT COMMONS: THE EXPANDED CITY

PUBLISHED BY
Actar Publishers and the Seoul Biennale of Architecture and Urbanism

EDITED BY
Alejandro Zaera-Polo
Jeffrey S. Anderson

COPY-EDITING
Paula Woolley

GRAPHIC DESIGN OF THE BOOK
Ramon Prat Homs

WITH THE COLLABORATION OF
Ricardo Devesa
Mahgol Motalebi

GRAPHIC IDENTITY OF THE SEOULBIENNALE
Sulki and Min

DISTRIBUTED BY
Actar Publishers
440 Park Avenue South, 17th Floor
New York, NY 10016
T +1 212 966 2207
F +1 212 966 2214
salesnewyork@actar-d.com

Barcelona
Roca i Batlle 2-4
08023 Barcelona
T +34 933 282 183
salesbarcelona@actar-d.com
eurosales@actar-d.com

COPYRIGHT
© 2017 Actar Publishers and the Seoul Biennale of Architecture and Urbanism
© Text and images by the authors

All rights reserved. No part of this publication may be reproduced, stored in a retrieval system, or transmitted in any form or by any means, electronic, mechanical, photocopyng, recording, or otherwise, without prior written consent of the publishers, except in the context of reviews.

The editors have made every effort to contact and acknowledge copyright owners. If there are instances where proper credit is not given, the publisher will make necessary changes in subsequent editions.

ISBN 978-1-945150-64-7
Library of Congress Control Number: 2017952344
A CIP catalogue record for this book is available from the Library of Congress, Washington D.C., USA.

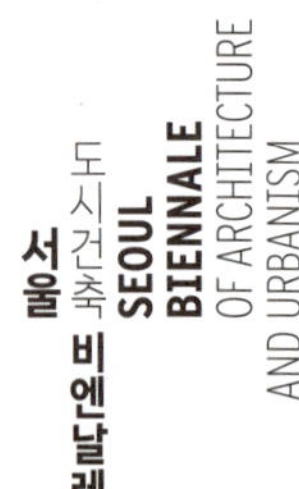